PEARSON

ALWAYS LEARNING

Muhammad A. Mazidi • Rolin D. McKinlay • Janice G. Mazidi

8051 Microprocessors and Embedded Systems with Lab Manual

Custom Edition

Taken from:
The 8051 Microcontroller: A Systems Approach
By Muhammad Ali Mazidi, Janice Gillispie Mazidi, and Rolin D. McKinlay

Lab Manual for The 8051 Microcontroller: A Systems Approach
By Muhammad Ali Mazidi, Janice Gillispie Mazidi, and Rolin D. McKinlay

Cover Art: Courtesy of Photodisc/Getty Images

Taken from:

The 8051 Microcontroller: A Systems Approach
By Muhammad Ali Mazidi, Janice Gillispie Mazidi, and Rolin D. McKinlay
Copyright © 2013 by Pearson Education, Inc.
Published by Pearson Education, Inc.
Upper Saddle River, New Jersey 07458

Lab Manual for The 8051 Microcontroller: A Systems Approach
By Muhammad Ali Mazidi, Janice Gillispie Mazidi, and Rolin D. McKinlay
Copyright © 2013 by Pearson Education, Inc.

This special edition published in cooperation with Pearson Learning Solutions.

All trademarks, service marks, registered trademarks, and registered service marks are the property of their respective owners and are used herein for identification purposes only.

Pearson Learning Solutions, 501 Boylston Street, Suite 900, Boston, MA 02116
A Pearson Education Company
www.pearsoned.com

Printed in the United States of America

2 3 4 5 6 7 8 9 10 V031 17 16 15 14 13

000200010271693427

AN

 ISBN 10: 1-256-86627-X
ISBN 13: 978-1-256-86627-5

*This volume is dedicated to the memory of Dr. A. Davoodi, Professor
of Tehran University, who in the tumultuous years of my youth taught me
the importance of an independent search for truth.*

—Muhammad Ali Mazidi

To Betsy, for all the love, encouragement, and sacrifice she has made for me.

—Rolin D. McKinlay

Regard man as a mine rich in gems of inestimable value. Education can, alone, cause it to reveal its treasures, and enable mankind to benefit therefrom.

—Baha'u'llah

BRIEF CONTENTS

CONTENTS

CONTENTS

PREFACE

The 8051 is a widely used microprocessor. There are many reasons for this, including the existence of multiple producers and its simple architecture. This book is intended for use in college-level courses teaching microprocessors and embedded systems. It not only establishes a foundation of Assembly language programming, but also provides a comprehensive treatment of 8051 interfacing for engineering students. From this background, the design and interfacing of micro controller-based embedded systems can be explored. This book can be also used by practicing technicians, hardware engineers, computer scientists, and hobbyists. It is an ideal source for those building stand-alone projects, or projects in which data is collected and fed into a PC for distribution on a network.

PREREQUISITES

Readers should have had an introductory digital course. Knowledge of Assembly language would be helpful but is not necessary. Although the book is written for those with no background in Assembly language programming, students with prior Assembly language experience will be able to gain a mastery of 8051 architecture very rapidly and start on their projects right away. For the 8051 C programming sections of the book, a basic knowledge of C programming is required.

ORGANIZATION OF THE BOOK

A systematic, step-by-step approach is used to cover various aspects of 8051 C and Assembly language programming and interfacing. Many examples and sample programs are given to clarify the concepts and provide students with an opportunity to learn by doing. Review questions are provided at the end of each section to reinforce the main points of the section.

Chapter 0 covers number systems (binary, decimal, and hex) and provides an introduction to basic logic gates and memory terminology. It also examines the concepts of memory and I/O address decoding.

Chapter 1 discusses the history of the 8051 and features of other 8051 family members such as the 8031, 8751, 89C51, DS5000, and DS89C4x0. It also provides a list of various producers of 8051 chips.

Chapter 2 discusses the internal architecture of the 8051 and explains the use of an 8051 assembler to create ready-to-run programs. It also explores the stack and the flag register. The concepts of RISC and CISC architectures are also examined.

In Chapter 3, the topics of loop, jump, and call instructions are discussed, with many programming examples.

Chapter 4 is dedicated to the discussion of I/O ports. This allows students who are working on a project to start experimenting with 8051 I/O interfacing and start the project as soon as possible.

Chapter 5 covers the 8051 addressing modes and explains how to use the code space of the 8051 to store data, as well as how to access data.

Chapter 6 is dedicated to arithmetic, logic instructions, and programs.

The C programming of the 8051 is covered in Chapter 7.

In Chapter 8, we discuss the hardware connection of the 8051 chip.

Chapter 9 describes the 8051 timers and how to use them as event counters.

Chapter 10 is dedicated to serial data communication of the 8051 and its interfacing to the RS232. It also shows 8051 communication with COM ports of the x86 PCs. In addition, the second serial port of the DS89C4x0 is also covered.

Chapter 11 provides a detailed discussion of 8051 interrupts with many examples on how to write interrupt handler programs.

Chapter 12 shows 8051 interfacing with real-world devices such as LCDs and keyboards.

Chapter 13 shows 8051 interfacing with real-world devices such as DAC chips, ADC chips, and sensors.

In Chapter 14, we cover 8031/51 interfacing with external memories, both ROM and RAM.

Chapter 15 examines the topics of optoisolator, relay, and stepper motor.

Chapter 16 shows how to connect and program the DS12887 real-time clock chip.

Chapter 17 shows basic interfacing of DC motor and using PWM.

Finally, Chapter 18 shows basic concepts of I2C and SPI protocols.

The appendices have been designed to provide all reference material required for the topics covered in the book. Appendix A describes each 8051 instruction in detail, with examples. It also provides the clock count for instructions, 8051 register diagrams, and RAM memory maps. Appendix B describes basics of wire wrapping. Appendix C covers IC technology and logic families, as well as 8051 I/O port interfacing and fan-out. Make sure you study this before connecting the 8051 to an external device. In Appendix D, the use of flowcharts and psuedocode is explored. Appendix E is for students familiar with x86 architecture who need to make a rapid transition to 8051 architecture. Appendix F provides the table of ASCII characters. Appendix G lists resources for assembler shareware and electronics parts.

Assemblers

The following websites provide information on assemblers:

www.MicroDigitalEd.com
www.keil.com   for Keil Corporation

The authors can be contacted at the following e-mail address if you have any comments or suggestions, or if you find any errors. Please mention 8051 in subject line.

mdebooks@yahoo.com

SUPPLEMENTS

Instructor Resources

* 0135084431 / 9780135084434 Instructor's Resource Manual (Download only)

* 0132622807 / 9780132622806 PowerPoint Presentation (Download only)

* 0132989891 / 9780132989893 TestGen® Computerized Test Bank (All supplements can be downloaded from the Pearson Instructor's Resource Site: www.pearsonhighered.com/irc <http://www.pearsonhighered.com/irc>)

Student Resources

* 0132989646 / 9780132989640 Student Lab Manual to accompany The 8051 Microprocessor: A Systems Approach

Datasheet, Sample Programs, Tutorials, and Trainer

The following website provides details on data sheet, sample programs, tutorial, and trainer information:

www.MicroDigitalEd.com

ABOUT THE AUTHORS

Muhammad Ali Mazidi graduated from Tabriz University and holds master's degrees from both Southern Methodist University and the University of Texas at Dallas. He worked on his Ph.D. in the Electrical Engineering Department of Southern Methodist University. He is the co-author of some widely used textbooks including *The x86 IBM PC, PIC Microprocessor and Embedded Systems, HCS12 Microprocessor and Embedded Systems*, and *AVR Microprocessor and Embedded Systems*, available from Prentice Hall. He teaches microprocessor-based system design at DeVry University in Dallas, Texas. He is the founder of the website www.MicroDigitalEd.com.

Janice Gillispie Mazidi has a master's degree in Computer Science from the University of North Texas. She has several years of experience as a software engineer in Dallas. She is the co-author of some widely used textbooks including *The x86 PC*, available from Prentice Hall. She teaches programming in colleges in the Dallas area.

Rolin D. McKinlay has a bachelor's degree in Electronics Engineering Technology from DeVry University. He works as embedded system engineer and FPGA design consultant in the Dallas area. The authors can be contacted at the following e-mail address if you have any comments or suggestions, or if you find any errors: mdebooks@yahoo.com

CHAPTER 0

INTRODUCTION TO COMPUTING

OBJECTIVES

Upon completion of this chapter, you will be able to:

>> Convert any number from base 2, base 10, or base 16 to any of the other two bases.
>> Describe the logical operations AND, OR, NOT, XOR, NAND, and NOR.
>> Use logic gates to diagram simple circuits.
>> Explain the difference between a bit, a nibble, a byte, and a word.
>> Give precise mathematical definitions of the terms *kilobyte*, *megabyte*, *gigabyte*, and *terabyte*.
>> Describe the purpose of the major components of a computer system.
>> Describe the role of the CPU in computer systems.
>> Contrast and compare various types of semiconductor memories in terms of their capacity, organization, and access time.
>> Describe the relationship between the number of memory locations on a chip, the number of data pins, and the chip's memory capacity.
>> Contrast and compare PROM, EPROM, UV-EPROM, EEPROM, Flash memory EPROM, and mask ROM memories.
>> Contrast and compare SRAM, NV-RAM, and DRAM memories.
>> List the steps a CPU follows in memory address decoding.
>> List the three types of buses found in computers and describe the purpose of each type of bus.
>> Describe the peripheral and memory-mapped I/O buses.
>> Design decoders for memory and I/O.
>> List the major components of the CPU and describe the purpose of each.
>> Understand the Harvard architecture.

1

To understand the software and hardware of a microprocessor-based system, one must first master some very basic concepts underlying computer architecture. In this chapter (which in the tradition of digital computers is called Chapter 0), the fundamentals of numbering and coding systems are presented in Section 0.1. An overview of logic gates is provided in Section 0.2. The semiconductor memory is discussed in Section 0.3. In Section 0.4, we examine the bus connection to memory and address decoding. In Section 0.5, we explore the I/O (input/output) address decoding. Finally, in the last section, Harvard and von Neumann CPU architectures are discussed. Although some readers may have an adequate background in many of the topics of this chapter, it is recommended that the material be reviewed, however briefly.

0.1: NUMBERING AND CODING SYSTEMS

Whereas human beings use the base 10 (*decimal*) arithmetic, computers use the base 2 (*binary*) system. In this section, we explain how to convert from the decimal system to the binary system, and vice versa. The convenient representation of binary numbers, called *hexadecimal,* also is covered. Finally, the binary format of the alphanumeric code, called *ASCII,* is explored.

Decimal and binary number systems

Although there has been speculation that the origin of the base 10 system is the fact that human beings have 10 fingers, there is absolutely no speculation about the reason behind the use of the binary system in computers. The binary system is used in computers because 1 and 0 represent the two voltage levels of on and off. Whereas in base 10 there are 10 distinct symbols or digits, 0, 1, 2, ..., 9, in base 2 there are only two, 0 and 1, with which to generate numbers. These two binary digits, 0 and 1, are commonly referred to as *bits*.

Converting from decimal to binary

One method of converting from decimal to binary is to divide the decimal number by 2 repeatedly, keeping track of the remainders. This process continues until the quotient becomes zero. The remainders are then written in reverse order to obtain the binary number. This is demonstrated in Example 0-1.

Converting from binary to decimal

To convert from binary to decimal, it is important to understand the concept of weight associated with each digit position. First, as an analogy, recall the weight of numbers in the base 10 system, as shown in the display.

$$
\begin{array}{lll}
740683_{10} & = & \\
\\
3 \leftrightarrow 10^0 & = & 3 \\
8 \leftrightarrow 10^1 & = & 80 \\
6 \leftrightarrow 10^2 & = & 600 \\
0 \leftrightarrow 10^3 & = & 0000 \\
4 \leftrightarrow 10^4 & . = & 40000 \\
7 \leftrightarrow 10^5 & = & \underline{700000} \\
& & 740683
\end{array}
$$

Example 0-1

Convert 25_{10} to binary.

Solution:

```
        Quotient   Remainder
25/2   = 12        1  LSB (least significant bit)
12/2  =  6         0
6/2   =  3         0
3/2   =  1         1
1/2   =  0         1  MSB (most significant bit)
```

Therefore, $25_{10} = 11001_2$.

By the same token, each digit position of a number in base 2 has a weight associated with it:

```
110101₂ =                          Decimal      Binary
1 × 2⁰   =    1 × 1   =     1                         1
0 × 2¹   =    0 × 2   =     0                        00
1 × 2²   =    1 × 4   =     4                       100
0 × 2³   =    0 × 8   =     0                      0000
1 × 2⁴   =    1 × 16  =    16                     10000
1 × 2⁵   =    1 × 32  =    32                    100000
                          53                    110101
```

Knowing the weight of each bit in a binary number makes it simple to add them together to get its decimal equivalent, as shown in Example 0-2.

Knowing the weight associated with each binary bit position allows one to convert a decimal number to binary directly instead of going through the process of repeated division. This is shown in Example 0-3.

Example 0-2

Convert 11001_2 to decimal.

Solution:

Weight:	16	8	4	2	1
Digits:	1	1	0	0	1
Sum:	16 +	8 +	0 +	0 +	1 = 25_{10}

Example 0-3

Use the concept of weight to convert 39_{10} to binary.

Solution:

Weight:	32	16	8	4	2	1
	1	0	0	1	1	1
	32 +	0 +	0 +	4 +	2 +	1 = 39

Therefore, $39_{10} = 100111_2$.

Hexadecimal system

Base 16, or the *hexadecimal* system as it is called in computer literature, is used as a convenient representation of binary numbers. For example, it is much easier for a human being to represent a string of 0s and 1s such as 100010010110 as its hexadecimal equivalent of 896H. The binary system has 2 digits, 0 and 1. The base 10 system has 10 digits, 0 through 9. The hexadecimal (base 16) system has 16 digits. In base 16, the first 10 digits, 0 to 9, are the same as in decimal, and for the remaining six digits, the letters A, B, C, D, E, and F are used. Table 0-1 shows the equivalent binary, decimal, and hexadecimal representations for 0 to 15.

Converting between binary and hex

To represent a binary number as its equivalent hexadecimal number, start from the right and group 4 bits at a time, replacing each 4-bit binary number with its hex equivalent shown in Table 0-1. To convert from hex to binary, each hex digit is replaced with its 4-bit binary equivalent. See Examples 0-4 and 0-5.

Converting from decimal to hex

Converting from decimal to hex could be approached in two ways:

1. Convert to binary first and then convert to hex. Example 0-6 shows this method of converting decimal to hex.
2. Convert directly from decimal to hex by repeated division, keeping track of the remainders. Experimenting with this method is left to the reader.

Table 0-1. Base 16 Number System

Decimal	Binary	Hex
0	0000	0
1	0001	1
2	0010	2
3	0011	3
4	0100	4
5	0101	5
6	0110	6
7	0111	7
8	1000	8
9	1001	9
10	1010	A
11	1011	B
12	1100	C
13	1101	D
14	1110	E
15	1111	F

Example 0-4

Represent binary 100111110101 in hex.

Solution:

First, the number is grouped into sets of 4 bits: 1001 1111 0101.
Then, each group of 4 bits is replaced with its hex equivalent:

        1001   1111   0101
          9   F   5

Therefore, 100111110101_2 = 9F5 hexadecimal.

Example 0-5

Convert hex 29B to binary.

Solution:

               2   9   B
29B   =   0010 1001 1011

Dropping the leading zeros gives 1010011011.

Example 0-6

(a) Convert 45_{10} to hex.

32	16	8	4	2	1
1	0	1	1	0	1

First, convert to binary.
$32 + 8 + 4 + 1 = 45$

$45_{10} = 0010\ 1101_2 = $ 2D hex

(b) Convert 629_{10} to hex.

512	256	128	64	32	16	8	4	2	1
1	0	0	1	1	1	0	1	0	1

$629_{10} = (512 + 64 + 32 + 16 + 4 + 1) = 0010\ 0111\ 0101_2 = $ 275 hex

(c) Convert 1714_{10} to hex.

1024	512	256	128	64	32	16	8	4	2	1
1	1	0	1	0	1	1	0	0	1	0

$1714_{10} = (1024 + 512 + 128 + 32 + 16 + 2) = 0110\ 1011\ 0010_2 = $ 6B2 hex

Converting from hex to decimal

Conversion from hex to decimal can also be approached in two ways:

1. Convert from hex to binary and then to decimal. Example 0-7 demonstrates this method of converting from hex to decimal.
2. Convert directly from hex to decimal by summing the weight of all digits.

Example 0-7

Convert the following hexadecimal numbers to decimal.

(a) $6B2_{16} = 0110\ 1011\ 0010_2$

1024	512	256	128	64	32	16	8	4	2	1
1	1	0	1	0	1	1	0	0	1	0

$1024 + 512 + 128 + 32 + 16 + 2 = 1714_{10}$

(b) $9F2D_{16} = 1001\ 1111\ 0010\ 1101_2$

32768	16384	8192	4096	2048	1024	512	256	128	64	32	16	8	4	2	1
1	0	0	1	1	1	1	1	0	0	1	0	1	1	0	1

$32768 + 4096 + 2048 + 1024 + 512 + 256 + 32 + 8 + 4 + 1 = 40,749_{10}$

Counting in bases 10, 2, and 16

To show the relationship between all three bases, in Table 0-2 we show the sequence of numbers from 0 to 31 in decimal, along with the equivalent binary and hex numbers. Notice in each base that when one more is added to the highest digit, that digit becomes zero and a 1 is carried to the next-highest digit position. For example, in decimal, $9 + 1 = 0$ with a carry to the next-highest position. In binary, $1 + 1 = 0$ with a carry; similarly, in hex, $F + 1 = 0$ with a carry.

Addition of binary and hex numbers

The addition of binary numbers is a very straightforward process. Table 0-3 shows the addition of two bits. The discussion of subtraction of binary numbers is bypassed since all computers use the addition process to implement subtraction. Although computers have adder circuitry, there is no separate circuitry for subtractors. Instead, adders are used in conjunction with *2's complement* circuitry to perform subtraction. In other words, to implement $x - y$, the computer takes the 2's complement of y and adds it to x. The concept of 2's complement is reviewed next. Example 0-8 shows the addition of binary numbers.

2's complement

To get the 2's complement of a binary number, invert all the bits and then add 1 to the result. Inverting the bits is simply a matter of changing all 0s to 1s and 1s to 0s. This is called the *1's complement*. See Example 0-9.

Addition and subtraction of hex numbers

In studying issues related to software and hardware of computers, it is often necessary to add or

Table 0-2. Counting in Bases

Decimal	Binary	Hex
0	00000	0
1	00001	1
2	00010	2
3	00011	3
4	00100	4
5	00101	5
6	00110	6
7	00111	7
8	01000	8
9	01001	9
10	01010	A
11	01011	B
12	01100	C
13	01101	D
14	01110	E
15	01111	F
16	10000	10
17	10001	11
18	10010	12
19	10011	13
20	10100	14
21	10101	15
22	10110	16
23	10111	17
24	11000	18
25	11001	19
26	11010	1A
27	11011	1B
28	11100	1C
29	11101	1D
30	11110	1E
31	11111	1F

Table 0-3. Binary Addition

A + B	Carry	Sum
0 + 0	0	0
0 + 1	0	1
1 + 0	0	1
1 + 1	1	0

Example 0-8

Add the following binary numbers. Check against their decimal equivalents.

Solution:

Binary	Decimal
1101	13
+ 1001	9
10110	22

Example 0-9

Take the 2's complement of 10011101.

Solution:

10011101	binary number
01100010	1's complement
+ 1	
01100011	2's complement

subtract hex numbers. Mastery of these techniques is essential. Hex addition and subtraction are discussed subsequently.

Addition of hex numbers

This section describes the process of adding hex numbers. Starting with the least significant digits, the digits are added together. If the result is less than 16, write that digit as the sum for that position. If it is greater than 16, subtract 16 from it to get the digit and carry 1 to the next digit. The best way to explain this is by example, as shown in Example 0-10.

Subtraction of hex numbers

In subtracting two hex numbers, if the second digit is greater than the first, borrow 16 from the preceding digit. See Example 0-11.

ASCII code

The discussion so far has revolved around the representation of number systems. Because all information in the computer must be represented by

Example 0-10

Perform hex addition: 23D9 + 94BE.

Solution:

23D9	LSD: $9 + 14 = 23$	$23 - 16 = 7$ with a carry
+ 94BE	$1 + 13 + 11 = 25$	$25 - 16 = 9$ with a carry
B897	$1 + 3 + 4 = 8$	
	MSD: $2 + 9 = B$	

Example 0-11

Perform hex subtraction: 59F–2B8.

Solution:

$$
\begin{array}{r}
59F \\
-\ 2B8 \\
\hline
2E7
\end{array}
$$

LSD: 8 from 15 = 7

11 from 25 (9 + 16) = 14 (E)

2 from 4 (5 – 1) = 2

0s and 1s, binary patterns must be assigned to letters and other characters. In the 1960s, a standard representation called *ASCII* (American Standard Code for Information Interchange) was established. The ASCII (pronounced "ask-E") code assigns binary patterns for numbers 0 to 9, all the letters of the English alphabet, both uppercase (capital) and lowercase, and many control codes and punctuation marks. The great advantage of this system is that it is used by most computers, so that information can be shared among computers. The ASCII system uses a total of 7 bits to represent each code. For example, 100 0001 is assigned to the uppercase letter "A" and 110 0001 is for the lowercase "a". Often, a zero is placed in the most-significant bit position to make it an 8-bit code. Figure 0-1 shows selected ASCII codes. A complete list of ASCII codes is given in Appendix F. The use of ASCII is a standard not only for keyboards used in the United States and many other countries but also for printing and displaying characters by output devices such as printers and monitors.

Hex	Symbol	Hex	Symbol
41	A	61	a
42	B	62	b
43	C	63	c
44	D	64	d
...	...	...	...
59	Y	79	y
5A	Z	7A	z

Figure 0-1. Selected ASCII Codes

Notice that the pattern of ASCII codes was designed to allow for easy manipulation of ASCII data. For example, digits 0 through 9 are represented by ASCII codes 30 through 39. This enables a program to easily convert ASCII to decimal by masking off the "3" in the upper nibble. Also notice that there is a relationship between the uppercase and lowercase letters. The uppercase letters are represented by ASCII codes 41 through 5A, while lowercase letters are represented by codes 61 through 7A. Looking at the binary code, the only bit that is different between the uppercase "A" and lowercase "a" is bit 5. Therefore, conversion between uppercase and lowercase is as simple as changing bit 5 of the ASCII code.

REVIEW QUESTIONS

1. Why do computers use the binary number system instead of the decimal system?
2. Convert 34_{10} to binary and hex.
3. Convert 110101_2 to hex and decimal.
4. Perform binary addition: 101100 + 101.
5. Convert 101100_2 to its 2's complement representation.
6. Add 36BH + F6H.

7. Subtract 36BH – F6H.
8. Write "80x86 CPUs" in its ASCII code (in hex form).

0.2: DIGITAL PRIMER

This section gives an overview of digital logic and design. First, we cover binary logic operations, then we show gates that perform these functions. Next, logic gates are put together to form simple digital circuits. Finally, we cover some logic devices commonly found in microprocessor interfacing.

Binary logic

As mentioned earlier, computers use the binary number system because the two voltage levels can be represented as the two digits 0 and 1. Signals in digital electronics have two distinct voltage levels. For example, a system may define 0 V as logic 0 and +5 V as logic 1. Figure 0-2 shows this system with the built-in tolerances for variations in the voltage. A valid digital signal in this example should be within either of the two shaded areas.

Logic gates

Binary logic gates are simple circuits that take one or more input signals and send out one output signal. Several of these gates are defined below.

AND gate

The AND gate takes two or more inputs and performs a logic AND on them. See the truth table and diagram of the AND gate. Notice that if both inputs to the AND gate are 1, the output will be 1. Any other combination of inputs will give a 0 output. The example shows two inputs, x and y. Multiple outputs are also possible for logic gates. In the case of AND, if all inputs are 1, the output is 1. If any input is 0, the output is 0.

OR gate

The OR logic function will output a 1 if one or more inputs is 1. If all inputs are 0, then and only then will the output be 0.

Tri-state buffer

A buffer gate does not change the logic level of the input. It is used to isolate or amplify the signal.

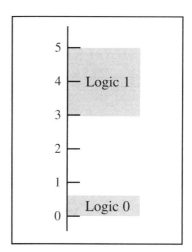

Figure 0-2. Binary Signals

Logical AND Function

Inputs		Output
X	Y	X AND Y
0	0	0
0	1	0
1	0	0
1	1	1

Logical OR Function

Inputs		Output
X	Y	X OR Y
0	0	0
0	1	1
1	0	1
1	1	1

Buffer

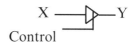

Inverter

The inverter, also called NOT, outputs the value opposite to that input to the gate. That is, a 1 input will give a 0 output, while a 0 input will give a 1 output.

XOR gate

The XOR gate performs an exclusive-OR operation on the inputs. Exclusive-OR produces a 1 output if one (but only one) input is 1. If both operands are 0, the output is 0. Likewise, if both operands are 1, the output is 0. Notice from the XOR truth table that whenever the two inputs are the same, the output is 0. This function can be used to compare two bits to see if they are the same.

NAND and NOR gates

The NAND gate functions like an AND gate with an inverter on the output. It produces a 0 output when all inputs are 1; otherwise, it produces a 1 output. The NOR gate functions like an OR gate with an inverter on the output. It produces a 1 if all inputs are 0; otherwise, it produces a 0. NAND and NOR gates are used extensively in digital design because they are easy and inexpensive to fabricate. Any circuit that can be designed with AND, OR, XOR, and Inverter gates can be implemented using only NAND and NOR gates.

Notice in NAND that if any input is 0, the output is 1. Notice in NOR that if any input is 1, the output is 0.

Logic design using gates

Next, we will show a simple logic design to add two binary digits. If we add two binary digits there are four possible outcomes:

	Carry	Sum
0 + 0 =	0	0
0 + 1 =	0	1
1 + 0 =	0	1
1 + 1 =	1	0

Notice that when we add 1 + 1 we get 0 with a carry to the next higher place. We will need to determine the sum and the carry for this design. Notice that the sum column matches the output for the XOR function and that the carry column matches the output for the AND function.

Logical Inverter

Input	Output
X	NOT X
0	1
1	0

X ———▷o— NOT X

Logical XOR Function

Inputs		Output
X	Y	X XOR Y
0	0	0
0	1	1
1	0	1
1	1	0

X, Y ——⊅— X XOR Y

Logical NAND Function

Inputs		Output
X	Y	X NAND Y
0	0	1
0	1	1
1	0	1
1	1	0

X, Y ——Do— X NAND Y

Logical NOR Function

Inputs		Output
X	Y	X NOR Y
0	0	1
0	1	0
1	0	0
1	1	0

X, Y ——⊅o— X NOR Y

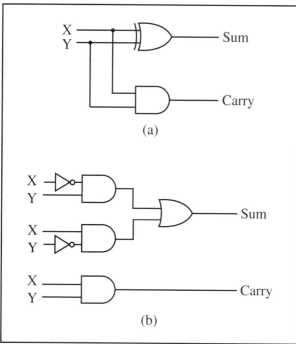

Figure 0-3. Two Implementations of a Half-Adder: (a) Half-Adder using XOR and AND; (b) Half-Adder Using AND, OR, Inverters

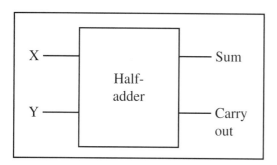

Figure 0-4. Block Diagram of a Half-Adder

Figure 0-3(a) shows a simple adder implemented with XOR and AND gates. Figure 0-3(b) shows the same logic circuit implemented with AND and OR gates and inverters.

Figure 0-4 shows a block diagram of a half-adder. Two half-adders can be combined to form an adder that can add three input digits. This is called a full-adder. Figure 0-5 shows the logic diagram of a full-adder, along with a block diagram that masks the details of the circuit. Figure 0-6 shows a 3-bit adder using three full-adders.

Flip-flops

A widely used component in digital systems is the flip-flop. Frequently, flip-flops are used to store data. Figure 0-7 shows the logic diagram, block diagram, and truth table for a flip-flop.

The D flip-flop is widely used to latch data. Notice from the truth table that a D-FF grabs the data at the input as the clock is activated. A D-FF holds the data as long as the power is on.

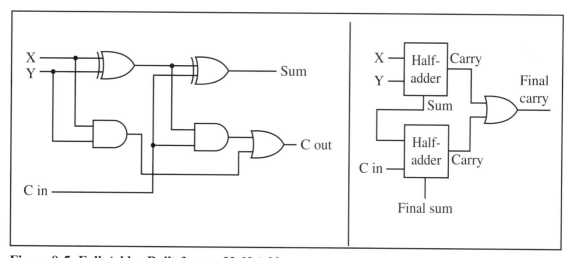

Figure 0-5. Full-Adder Built from a Half-Adder

REVIEW QUESTIONS

1. The logical operation _____ gives a 1 output when all inputs are 1.
2. The logical operation _____ gives a 1 output when one or more of its inputs is 1.
3. The logical operation _____ is often used to compare two inputs to determine whether they have the same value.
4. A _____ gate does not change the logic level of the input.
5. Name a common use for flip-flops.
6. An address _____ is used to identify a predetermined binary address.

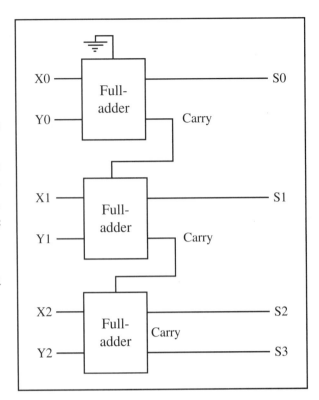

Figure 0-6. 3-Bit Adder Using Three Full-Adders

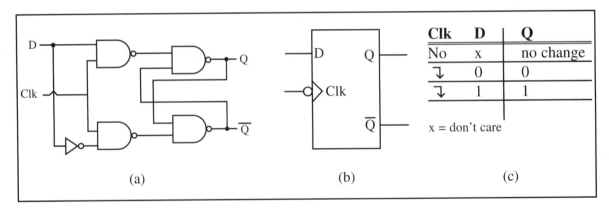

Figure 0-7. D Flip-Flops: (a) Circuit Diagram; (b) Block Diagram; (c) Truth Table

0.3: SEMICONDUCTOR MEMORY

In this section, we discuss various types of semiconductor memories and their characteristics such as capacity, organization, and access time. Before we embark on the subject of memory, it will be helpful to give an overview of computer organization and review some widely used terminology in computer literature.

Some important terminology

Recall from the discussion earlier that a *bit* is a binary digit that can have the value 0 or 1. A *byte* is defined as 8 bits. A *nibble* is half a byte, or 4 bits. A *word* is two bytes, or 16 bits. The display is intended

```
Bit                            0
Nibble                      0000
Byte                  0000 0000
Word  0000 0000 0000 0000
```

to show the relative size of these units. Of course, they could all be composed of any combination of zeros and ones.

A *kilobyte* is 2^{10} bytes, which is 1024 bytes. The abbreviation K is often used to represent kilobytes. A *megabyte*, or *meg* as some call it, is 2^{20} bytes. That is a little over 1 million bytes; it is exactly 1,048,576 bytes. Moving rapidly up the scale in size, a *gigabyte* is 2^{30} bytes (over 1 billion), and a *terabyte* is 2^{40} bytes (over 1 trillion). As an example of how some of these terms are used, suppose that a given computer has 16 megabytes of memory. That would be 16×2^{20}, or $2^4 \times 2^{20}$, which is 2^{24}. Therefore, 16 megabytes is 2^{24} bytes.

Two types of memory commonly used in microcomputers are *RAM*, which stands for "random access memory" (sometimes called *read/write memory*), and *ROM*, which stands for "read-only memory." RAM is used by the computer for temporary storage of programs that it is running. That data is lost when the computer is turned off. For this reason, RAM is sometimes called *volatile memory*. ROM contains programs and information essential to operation of the computer. The information in ROM is permanent, cannot be changed by the user, and is not lost when the power is turned off. Therefore, it is called *nonvolatile memory*.

Internal organization of computers

The internal working of every computer can be broken down into three parts: CPU (central processing unit), memory, and I/O (input/output) devices. Figure 0-8 shows a block diagram of the internal organization of a computer. The function of the CPU is to execute (process) information stored in memory. The function of I/O devices such as the keyboard and video monitor is to provide a means of communicating with the CPU. As you will see in the next section, CPU is connected to memory and I/O through strips of wire called a *bus*.

Next, we discuss various types of semiconductor memories and their characteristics such as capacity, organization, and access time.

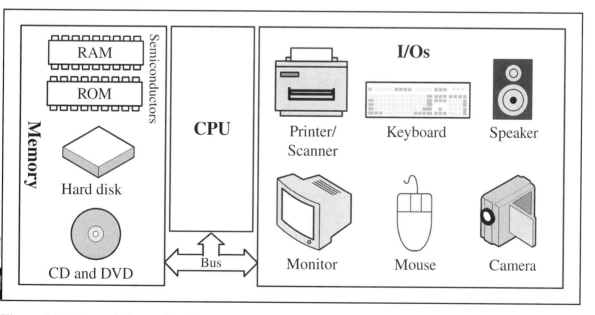

Figure 0-8. Internal Parts of a Computer

Memory characteristics

Memory capacity

The number of bits that a semiconductor memory chip can store is called chip *capacity*. It can be in units of Kbits (kilobits), Mbits (megabits), and so on. This must be distinguished from the storage capacity of computer systems. While the memory capacity of a memory IC chip is always given in bits, the memory capacity of a computer system is given in bytes. For example, an article in a technical journal may state that the 128M chip has become popular. In that case, it is understood, although it is not mentioned, that 128M means 128 megabits since the article is referring to an IC memory chip. However, if an advertisement states that a computer comes with 128M memory, it is understood that 128M means 128 megabytes since it is referring to a computer system.

Memory organization

Memory chips are organized into a number of locations within the IC. Each location can hold 1 bit, 4 bits, 8 bits, or even 16 bits, depending on how it is designed internally. The number of bits that each location within the memory chip can hold is always equal to the number of data pins on the chip. How many locations exist inside a memory chip? That depends on the number of address pins. The number of locations within a memory IC always equals 2 to the power of the number of address pins. Therefore, the total number of bits that a memory chip can store is equal to the number of locations times the number of data bits per location. To summarize,

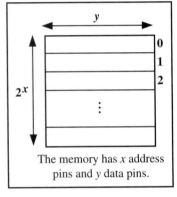

The memory has x address pins and y data pins.

Figure 0-9. $2^x \times y$

1. A memory chip contains 2^x locations, where x is the number of address pins.
2. Each location contains y bits, where y is the number of data pins on the chip.
3. The entire chip will contain $2^x \times y$ bits, where x is the number of address pins and y is the number of data pins on the chip. See Figure 0-9.

Speed

One of the most important characteristics of a memory chip is the speed at which its data can be accessed. To access the data, the address is presented to the address pins, the READ (OE) pin is activated, and after a certain amount of time has elapsed, the data shows up at the data pins. The shorter is the elapsed time, the better, and consequently, the more expensive is the memory chip. The speed of the memory chip is commonly referred to as its *access time*. The access time of memory chips varies from a few nanoseconds to hundreds of nanoseconds, depending on the IC technology used in the design and fabrication process.

Table 0-4. Powers of 2

x	2^x
10	1K
11	2K
12	4K
13	8K
14	16K
15	32K
16	64K
17	128K
18	256K
19	512K
20	1M
21	2M
22	4M
23	8M
24	16M
25	32M
26	64M

The three important memory characteristics of capacity, organization, and access time will be explored extensively in this chapter. Table 0-4 serves as a reference for the calculation of memory organization. Examples 0-12 and 0-13 demonstrate these concepts.

ROM (read-only memory)

ROM is a type of memory that does not lose its contents when the power is turned off. For this reason, ROM is also called *nonvolatile* memory. There are different types of read-only memory, such as PROM, EPROM, EEPROM, Flash EPROM, and mask ROM. Each is explained next.

PROM (programmable ROM) and OTP

PROM refers to the kind of ROM that the user can burn information into. In other words, PROM is a user-programmable memory. For every bit of the PROM, there exists a fuse. PROM is programmed by blowing the fuses. If the information burned into PROM is wrong, that PROM must be discarded since its internal fuses are blown permanently. For this reason, PROM is also referred to as OTP (one-time programmable). Programming ROM, also called *burning* ROM, requires special equipment called a ROM burner or ROM programmer.

Example 0-12

A given memory chip has 12 address pins and 4 data pins. Find:
(a) the organization and (b) the capacity.

Solution:

(a) This memory chip has 4,096 locations (2^{12} = 4,096), and each location can hold 4 bits of data. This gives an organization of 4,096 × 4, often represented as 4K × 4.

(b) The capacity is equal to 16K bits since there is a total of 4K locations and each location can hold 4 bits of data.

Example 0-13

A 512K memory chip has 8 pins for data. Find:
(a) the organization and (b) the number of address pins for this memory chip.

Solution:

(a) A memory chip with 8 data pins means that each location within the chip can hold 8 bits of data. To find the number of locations within this memory chip, divide the capacity by the number of data pins. 512K/8 = 64K; therefore, the organization for this memory chip is 64K × 8.

(b) The chip has 16 address lines since 2^{16} = 64K.

27256	27128	2732A	2716	2764 (pins 1–14)		2764 (pins 15–28)	2716	2732A	27128	27256
V_{pp}	V_{pp}			V_{pp} — 1	28 — V_{cc}				V_{cc} / $\overline{PGM}$	V_{cc} / A14
A12	A12			A12 — 2	27 — $\overline{PGM}$				A13	A13
A7	A7	A7	A7	A7 — 3	26 — N.C.		V_{cc}	V_{cc}	A8	A8
A6	A6	A6	A6	A6 — 4	25 — A8		A8	A8	A9	A9
A5	A5	A5	A5	A5 — 5	24 — A9		A9	A9	V_{pp}	V_{pp}
A4	A4	A4	A4	A4 — 6	23 — A11		V_{pp}	A11	$\overline{OE}$	$\overline{OE}$
A3	A3	A3	A3	A3 — 7	22 — $\overline{OE}$		$\overline{OE}$	$\overline{OE}/V_{pp}$	A10	A10
A2	A2	A2	A2	A2 — 8	21 — A10		A10	A10	$\overline{CE}$	$\overline{CE}$
A1	A1	A1	A1	A1 — 9	20 — $\overline{CE}$		$\overline{CE}$	$\overline{CE}$	O7	O7
A0	A0	A0	A0	A0 — 10	19 — O7		O7	O7	O6	O6
O0	O0	O0	O0	O0 — 11	18 — O6		O6	O6	O5	O5
O1	O1	O1	O1	O1 — 12	17 — O5		O5	O5	O4	O4
O2	O2	O2	O2	O2 — 13	16 — O4		O4	O4	O3	O3
GND	GND	GND	GND	GND — 14	15 — O3		O3	O3		

Figure 0-10. Pin Configurations for 27xx ROM Family

EPROM (erasable programmable ROM) and UV-EPROM

EPROM was invented to allow making changes in the contents of PROM after it is burned. In EPROM, one can program the memory chip and erase it thousands of times. This is especially necessary during development of the prototype of a microprocessor-based project. A widely used EPROM is called UV-EPROM, where UV stands for ultraviolet. The only problem with UV-EPROM is that erasing its contents can take up to 20 minutes. All UV-EPROM chips have a window through which the programmer can shine ultraviolet (UV) radiation to erase the chip's contents. For this reason, EPROM is also referred to as UV-erasable EPROM or simply UV-EPROM. Figure 0-10 shows the pins for UV-EPROM chips.

To program a UV-EPROM chip, the following steps must be taken:

1. Its contents must be erased. To erase a chip, remove it from its socket on the system board and place it in EPROM erasure equipment to expose it to UV radiation for 15–20 minutes.
2. Program the chip. To program a UV-EPROM chip, place it in the ROM burner (programmer). To burn code or data into EPROM, the ROM burner uses 12.5 V or higher, depending on the EPROM type. This voltage is referred to as V_{pp} in the UV-EPROM data sheet.
3. Place the chip back into its socket on the system board.

As can be seen from the above steps, not only is there an EPROM programmer (burner), but there is also separate EPROM erasure equipment. The main problem, and indeed the major disadvantage of UV-EPROM, is that it cannot be erased and programmed while it is in the system board. To provide a solution to this problem, EEPROM was invented.

Notice the patterns of the IC numbers in Table 0-5. For example, part number 27128-25 refers to UV-EPROM that has a capacity of 128K bits

Table 0-5. Some UV-EPROM Chips

Part No.	Capacity	Org.	Access	Pins	V_{pp}
2716	16K	2K × 8	450 ns	24	25 V
2732	32K	4K × 8	450 ns	24	25 V
2732A-20	32K	4K × 8	200 ns	24	21 V
27C32-1	32K	4K × 8	450 ns	24	12.5 V CMOS
2764-20	64K	8K × 8	200 ns	28	21 V
2764A-20	64K	8K × 8	200 ns	28	12.5 V
27C64-12	64K	8K × 8	120 ns	28	12.5 V CMOS
27128-25	128K	16K × 8	250 ns	28	21 V
27C128-12	128K	16K × 8	120 ns	28	12.5 V CMOS
27256-25	256K	32K × 8	250 ns	28	12.5 V
27C256-15	256K	32K × 8	150 ns	28	12.5 V CMOS
27512-25	512K	64K × 8	250 ns	28	12.5 V
27C512-15	512K	64K × 8	150 ns	28	12.5 V CMOS
27C010-15	1024K	128K × 8	150 ns	32	12.5 V CMOS
27C020-15	2048K	256K × 8	150 ns	32	12.5 V CMOS
27C040-15	4096K	512K × 8	150 ns	32	12.5 V CMOS

and access time of 250 ns. The capacity of the memory chip is indicated in the part number and the access time is given with a zero dropped. See Example 0-14.

In part numbers, C refers to CMOS technology. Notice that 27XX always refers to UV-EPROM chips. For a comprehensive list of available memory chips, see the JAMECO (jameco.com) or JDR (jdr.com) catalogs.

EEPROM (electrically erasable programmable ROM)

EEPROM has several advantages over EPROM, such as the fact that its method of erasure is electrical and therefore instant, as opposed to the 20-minute erasure time required for UV-EPROM. In addition, in EEPROM one can select which byte to be erased, in contrast to UV-EPROM, in which the entire contents of ROM are erased. However, the main advantage of EEPROM is that one can program and erase its contents while it is still in the system board. It does not require physical removal of the memory chip from its socket. In other

---

Example 0-14

For ROM chip 27128, find the number of data and address pins.

Solution:

The 27128 has a capacity of 128K bits. It has 16K × 8 organization (all ROMs have 8 data pins), which indicates that there are 8 pins for data and 14 pins for address (2^{14} = 16K).

---

words, unlike UV-EPROM, EEPROM does not require an external erasure and programming device. To utilize EEPROM fully, the designer must incorporate the circuitry to program the EEPROM into the system board. In general, the cost per bit for EEPROM is much higher than for UV-EPROM.

Flash memory EPROM

Since the early 1990s, Flash EPROM has become a popular user-programmable memory chip, and for good reasons. First, the erasure of the entire contents takes less than a second, or one might say in a flash, hence its name, Flash memory. In addition, the erasure method is electrical, and for this reason it is sometimes referred to as Flash EEPROM. To avoid confusion, it is commonly called Flash memory. The major difference between EEPROM and Flash memory is that when Flash memory's contents are erased, the entire device is erased, in contrast to EEPROM, where one can erase a desired byte. Although in many Flash memories recently made available the contents are divided into blocks and the erasure can be done block by block, unlike EEPROM, Flash memory has no byte erasure option. Because Flash memory can be programmed while it is in its socket on the system board, it is widely used to upgrade the BIOS ROM of the PC. Some designers believe that Flash memory will replace the hard disk as a mass storage medium. This would increase the performance of the computer tremendously, since Flash memory is semiconductor memory with access time in the range of 100 ns compared with disk access time in the range of tens of milliseconds. For this to happen, Flash memory's program/erase cycles must become infinite, just like hard disks. Program/erase cycle refers to the number of times that a chip can be erased and reprogrammed before it becomes unusable. At this time, the program/erase cycle is 100,000 for Flash and EEPROM, 1000 for UV-EPROM, and infinite for RAM and disks. See Table 0-6 for some sample chips.

Table 0-6. Some EEPROM and Flash Chips

EEPROMs

Part No.	Capacity	Org.	Speed	Pins	V_{pp}
2816A-25	16K	2K × 8	250 ns	24	5 V
2864A	64K	8K × 8	250 ns	28	5 V
28C64A-25	64K	8K × 8	250 ns	28	5 V CMOS
28C256-15	256K	32K × 8	150 ns	28	5 V
28C256-25	256K	32K × 8	250 ns	28	5 V CMOS

Flash

Part No.	Capacity	Org.	Speed	Pins	V_{pp}
28F256-20	256K	32K × 8	200 ns	32	12 V CMOS
28F010-15	1024K	128K × 8	150 ns	32	12 V CMOS
28F020-15	2048K	256K × 8	150 ns	32	12 V CMOS

Mask ROM

Mask ROM refers to a kind of ROM in which the contents are programmed by the IC manufacturer. In other words, it is not a user-programmable ROM. The term *mask* is used in IC fabrication. Since the process is costly, mask ROM is used when the needed volume is high (hundreds of thousands), and it is absolutely certain that the contents will not change. It is common practice to use UV-EPROM or Flash for the development phase of a project, and only after the code/data have been finalized is the mask version of the product ordered. The main advantage of mask ROM is its cost, since it is significantly cheaper than other kinds of ROM, but if an error is found in the data/code, the entire batch must be thrown away. It must be noted that all ROM memories have 8 bits for data pins; therefore, the organization is × 8.

RAM (random access memory)

RAM memory is called *volatile* memory since cutting off the power to the IC results in the loss of data. Sometimes RAM is also referred to as RAWM (read and write memory), in contrast to ROM, which cannot be written to.

There are three types of RAM: static RAM (SRAM), NV-RAM (nonvolatile RAM), and dynamic RAM (DRAM). Each is explained separately.

SRAM (static RAM)

Storage cells in static RAM memory are made of flip-flops and therefore do not require refreshing in order to keep their data. This is in contrast to DRAM, discussed below. The problem with the use of flip-flops for storage cells is that each cell requires at least six transistors to build, and the cell holds only 1 bit of data. In recent years, the cells have been made of four transistors, which still is too many. The use of four-transistor cells and the use of CMOS technology have given birth to a high-capacity SRAM, but its capacity is far below DRAM. Figure 0-11 shows the pin diagram for an SRAM chip. The following is a description of the 6116 SRAM pins:

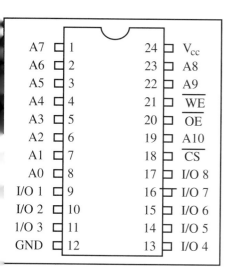

Figure 0-11. 2K × 8 SRAM Pins

A0–A10 are for address inputs, where 11 address lines give $2^{11} = 2K$.

WE (write enable) is for writing data into SRAM (active low).

OE (output enable) is for reading data out of SRAM (active low).

CS (chip select) is used to select the memory chip.

I/O0–I/O7 are for data I/O, where 8-bit data lines give an organization of 2K ↔ 8.

The functional diagram for the 6116 SRAM is given in Figure 0-12.

Figure 0-13 shows the following steps to write data into SRAM.

1. Provide the addresses to pins A0–A10.

2. Activate the CS pin.

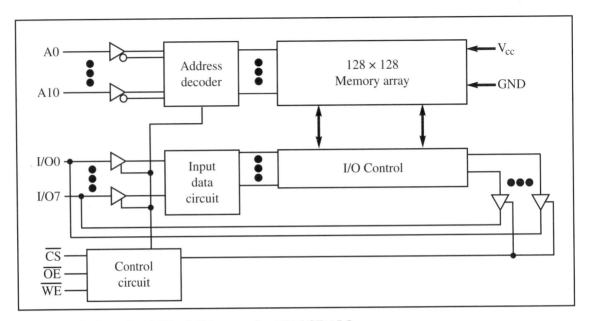

Figure 0-12. Functional Block Diagram for 6116 SRAM

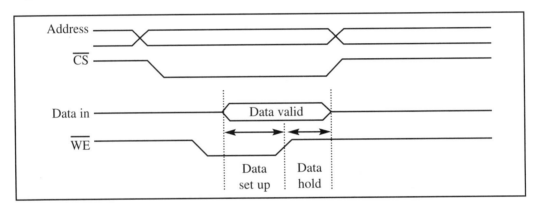

Figure 0-13. Memory Write Timing for SRAM

3. Make WE = 0 while OE = 1.

4. Provide the data to pins I/O0–I/O7.

5. Make WE = 1 and data will be written into SRAM on the positive edge of the WE signal.

The following are steps to read data from SRAM. See Figure 0-14.

1. Provide the addresses to pins A0–A10. This is the start of the access time (t_{AA}).

2. Activate the CS pin.

3. While WE = 1, a high-to-low pulse on the OE pin will read the data out of the chip.

NV-RAM (nonvolatile RAM)

Whereas SRAM is volatile, there is a new type of nonvolatile RAM called NV-RAM. Like other RAMs, it allows the CPU to read and write to it, but when the power is turned off the contents are not lost. NV-RAM combines the

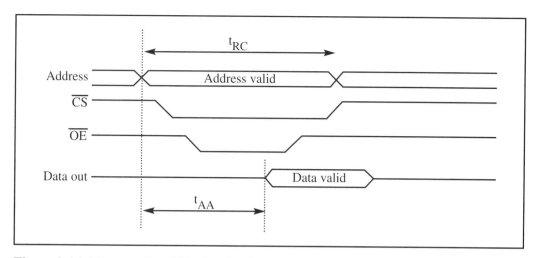

Figure 0-14. Memory Read Timing for SRAM

best of RAM and ROM: the read and write ability of RAM, plus the nonvolatility of ROM. To retain its contents, every NV-RAM chip internally is made of the following components:

1. It uses extremely power-efficient (very low-power consumption) SRAM cells built out of CMOS.

2. It uses an internal lithium battery as a backup energy source.

3. It uses an intelligent control circuitry. The main job of this control circuitry is to monitor the V_{cc} pin constantly to detect loss of the external power supply. If the power to the V_{cc} pin falls below out-of-tolerance conditions, the control circuitry switches automatically to its internal power source, the lithium battery. The internal lithium power source is used to retain the NV-RAM contents only when the external power source is off.

It must be emphasized that all three of the components are incorporated into a single IC chip, and for this reason nonvolatile RAM is a very expensive type of RAM as far as cost per bit is concerned. Offsetting the cost, however, is the fact that it can retain its contents up to ten years after the power has been turned off and allows one to read and write in exactly the same way as SRAM. Table 0-7 shows some examples of SRAM and NV-RAM parts.

DRAM (dynamic RAM)

Since the early days of the computer, the need for huge, inexpensive read/write memory has been a major preoccupation of computer designers. In 1970, Intel Corporation introduced the first dynamic RAM (random access memory). Its density (capacity) was 1024 bits and it used a capacitor to store each bit. Using a capacitor to store data cuts down the number of transistors needed to build the cell; however, it requires constant refreshing due to leakage. This is in contrast to SRAM (static RAM), whose individual cells are made of flip-flops. Since each bit in SRAM uses a single flip-flop, and each flip-flop requires six transistors, SRAM has much larger memory cells and consequently lower density. The use of capacitors as storage cells in DRAM results in much smaller net memory cell size.

Table 0-7. Some SRAM and NV-RAM Chips

SRAM

Part No.	Capacity	Org.	Speed	Pins	V_{pp}
6116P-1	16K	2K × 8	100 ns	24	CMOS
6116P-2	16K	2K × 8	120 ns	24	CMOS
6116P-3	16K	2K × 8	150 ns	24	CMOS
6116LP-1	16K	2K × 8	100 ns	24	Low-power CMOS
6116LP-2	16K	2K × 8	120 ns	24	Low-power CMOS
6116LP-3	16K	2K × 8	150 ns	24	Low-power CMOS
6264P-10	64K	8K × 8	100 ns	28	CMOS
6264LP-70	64K	8K × 8	70 ns	28	Low-power CMOS
6264LP-12	64K	8K × 8	120 ns	28	Low-power CMOS
62256LP-10	256K	32K × 8	100 ns	28	Low-power CMOS
62256LP-12	256K	32K × 8	120 ns	28	Low-power CMOS

NV-RAM from Dallas Semiconductor (Maxim)

Part No.	Capacity	Org.	Speed	Pins	V_{pp}
DS1220Y-150	16K	2K × 8	150 ns	24	12 V CMOS
DS1225AB-150	64K	8K × 8	150 ns	28	12 V CMOS
DS1230Y-85	256K	32K × 8	85 ns	28	12 V CMOS

The advantages and disadvantages of DRAM memory can be summarized as follows. The major advantages are high density (capacity), cheaper cost per bit, and lower power consumption per bit. The disadvantage is that it must be refreshed periodically because the capacitor cell loses its charge; furthermore, while DRAM is being refreshed, the data cannot be accessed. This is in contrast to SRAM's flip-flops, which retain data as long as the power is on, do not need to be refreshed, and whose contents can be accessed at any time. Since 1970, the capacity of DRAM has exploded. After the 1K-bit (1024) chip came the 4K-bit in 1973, and then the 16K chip in 1976. The 1980s saw the introduction of 64K, 256K, and finally 1M and 4M memory chips. The 1990s saw 16M, 64M, 256M, and the beginning of 1G-bit DRAM chips. In the 2000s, 2G-bit chips were standard, and as the fabrication process gets smaller, larger memory chips will be rolling off the manufacturing line. Keep in mind that when talking about IC memory chips, the capacity is always assumed to be in bits. Therefore, a 1M chip means a 1-megabit chip and a 256K chip means a 256K-bit memory chip. However, when talking about the memory of a computer system, it is always assumed to be in bytes.

Packaging issue in DRAM

In DRAM, there is a problem of packing a large number of cells into a single chip with the normal number of pins assigned to addresses. For example,

CHAPTER 0: INTRODUCTION TO COMPUTING

a 64K-bit chip (64K × 1) must have 16 address lines and 1 data line, requiring 16 pins to send in the address if the conventional method is used. This is in addition to V_{cc} power, ground, and read/write control pins. Using the conventional method of data access, the large number of pins defeats the purpose of high density and small packaging, so dearly cherished by IC designers. Therefore, to reduce the number of pins needed for addresses, multiplexing or demultiplexing is used. The method used is to split the address in half and send in each half of the address through the same pins, thereby requiring fewer address pins. Internally, the DRAM structure is divided into a square of rows and columns the first half of the address is called the row and the second half is called the column. For example, in the case of DRAM of 64K × 1 organization, the first half of the address is sent in through the 8 pins A0–A7, and by activating RAS (row address strobe), the internal latches inside DRAM grab the first half of the address. After that, the second half of the address is sent in through the same pins, and by activating CAS (column address strobe), the internal latches inside DRAM latch the second half of the address. This results in using 8 pins for addresses plus RAS and CAS, for a total of 10 pins, instead of the 16 pins that would be required without multiplexing. To access a bit of data from DRAM, both row and column addresses must be provided. For this concept to work, there must be a 2-by-1 multiplexer outside the DRAM circuitry and a demultiplexer inside every DRAM chip. Due to the complexities associated with DRAM interfacing (RAS, CAS, the need for multiplexer and refreshing circuitry), some DRAM controllers are designed to make DRAM interfacing much easier. However, many small microprocessor-based projects that do not require much RAM (usually less than 64K bytes) use SRAM of types EEPROM and NV-RAM, instead of DRAM.

DRAM organization

In the discussion of ROM, we noted that all of these chips have 8 pins for data. This is not the case for DRAM memory chips, which can have × 1, × 4, × 8, or × 16 organizations. See Example 0-15 and Table 0-8.

In memory chips, the data pins are also called I/O. In some DRAMs there are separate D_{in} and D_{out} pins. Figure 0-15 shows a 256K × 1 DRAM chip with pins A0–A8 for address, RAS and CAS, WE (write enable), and data in and data out, as well as power and ground.

Example 0-15

Discuss the number of pins set aside for addresses in each of the following memory chips:　　　(a) 16K × 4 DRAM　　　(b) 16K × 4 SRAM.

Solution:

Since $2^{14} = 16$K:
(a) For DRAM, we have 7 pins (A0–A6) for the address pins and 2 pins for RAS and CAS.
(b) For SRAM, we have 14 pins for address and no pins for RAS and CAS since they are associated only with DRAM. In both cases, we have 4 pins for the data bus.

Table 0-8. Some DRAMs

Part No.	Speed	Capacity	Org.	Pins
4164-15	150 ns	64K	64K × 1	16
41464-8	80 ns	256K	64K × 4	18
41256-15	150 ns	256K	256K × 1	16
41256-6	60 ns	256K	256K × 1	16
414256-10	100 ns	1M	256K × 4	20
511000P-8	80 ns	1M	1M × 1	18
514100-7	70 ns	4M	4M × 1	20

REVIEW QUESTIONS

Figure 0-15. 256K × 1 DRAM

1. How many bytes is 24 kilobytes?
2. What does "RAM" stand for? How is it used in computer systems?
3. What does "ROM" stand for? How is it used in computer systems?
4. Why is RAM called volatile memory?
5. List the three major components of a computer system.
6. What does "CPU" stand for? Explain its function in a computer.
7. The speed of semiconductor memory is in the range of
   (a) microseconds (b) milliseconds
   (c) nanoseconds (d) picoseconds
8. Find the organization and chip capacity for each ROM with the indicated number of address and data pins.
   (a) 14 address, 8 data (b) 16 address, 8 data (c) 12 address, 8 data
9. Find the organization and chip capacity for each RAM with the indicated number of address and data pins.
   (a) 11 address, 1 data SRAM (b) 13 address, 4 data SRAM
   (c) 17 address, 8 data SRAM (d) 8 address, 4 data DRAM
   (e) 9 address, 1 data DRAM (f) 9 address, 4 data DRAM
10. Find the capacity and number of pins set aside for address and data for memory chips with the following organizations.
    (a) 16K × 4 SRAM   (b) 32K × 8 EPROM   (c) 1M × 1 DRAM
    (d) 256K × 4 SRAM   (e) 64K × 8 EEPROM   (f) 1M × 4 DRAM
11. Which of the following is (are) volatile memory?
    (a) EEPROM   (b) SRAM   (c) DRAM   (d) NV-RAM

0.4: BUS DESIGNING AND ADDRESS DECODING

In this section, we show how the CPU accesses different parts of the computer using the bus. Then, we demonstrate how to connect I/O and memory to computer.

CHAPTER 0: INTRODUCTION TO COMPUTING

Bus designing

In computers, the CPU needs to send/receive data to/from memory and I/O. Connecting the devices (memory or I/O) to the CPU with unique wires considerably increases the number of CPU pins; therefore, the CPU is connected to memory and I/O through shared strips of wire called the *bus*. A computer bus allows information to be carried from place to place just as a street allows cars to carry people from place to place, as shown in Figure 0-16. In every computer there are three types of buses: address bus, data bus, and control bus.

Consider a conference room: each chair has a unique number; when the chairman wants to speak to a specific person, the chairman can address him using his chair number. Similarly, in a computer a unique address is assigned to each device (memory or I/O); no two devices are allowed to have the same address. The CPU puts the address (in binary, of course) on the address bus. Then the CPU uses the data bus either to get data from that device or to send data to it. The control bus is used to provide read or write signals to the device to indicate if the CPU is asking for information or sending information.

Of the three buses, the address bus and data bus determine the capability of a given CPU.

More about the data bus

Because data buses are used to carry information in and out of a CPU, the more data buses are available, the better is the CPU. If one thinks of data buses as highway lanes, it is clear that more lanes provide a better pathway between the CPU and its external devices (printers, RAM, ROM, etc.; see Figure 0-17). By the same token, that increase in the number of lanes increases the cost of construction. More data buses mean a more expensive CPU and computer. The average size of data buses in CPUs varies between 8 and 64 bits. Early personal computers such as Apple 2 used an 8-bit data bus, while supercomputers such as Cray used a 64-bit data bus. Data buses are bidirectional because the CPU must use them either to receive or to send data. The processing power of a computer is related to the size of its buses in that an 8-bit bus can send out one byte at a time, but a 16-bit bus can send out two bytes at a time, which is twice as fast.

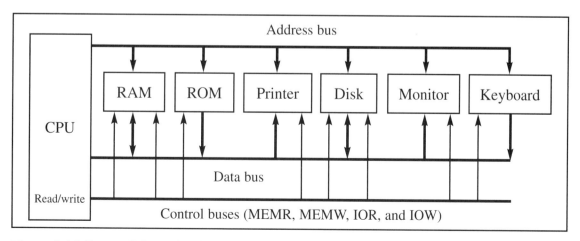

Figure 0-16. Internal Organization of a Computer

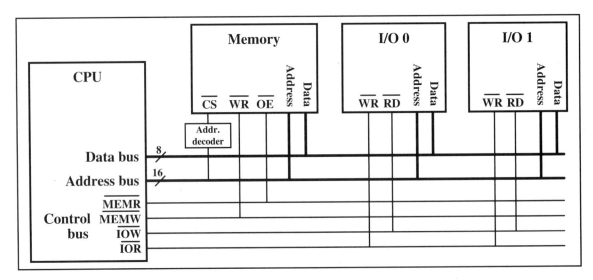

Figure 0-17. A Simple System Using Peripheral I/O

The address bus

Because the address bus is used to identify the devices and memory connected to the CPU, the more address buses are available, the larger the number of devices that can be addressed. In other words, the number of address buses for a CPU determines the number of locations with which it can communicate. The number of locations is always equal to 2^x, where x is the number of address lines, regardless of the size of the data bus. For example, a CPU with 16 address lines can provide a total of 65,536 (2^{16}) or 64K of addressable memory. Each location can have a maximum of 1 byte of data. This is because all general-purpose microprocessor CPUs are what is called *byte addressable*. As another example, the IBM PC AT uses a CPU with 24 address lines and 16 data lines. Thus, the total accessible memory is 16 megabytes (2^{24} = 16 megabytes). In this example there would be 2^{24} locations, and because each location is 1 byte, there would be 16 megabytes of memory. The address bus is a *unidirectional* bus, which means that the CPU uses the address bus only to send out addresses. To summarize, the total number of memory locations addressable by a given CPU is always equal to 2^x, where x is the number of address bits, regardless of the size of the data bus.

More about the address bus

In some computers, there are separate control signals for I/O and memory. For example, in x86 PCs, the control bus has the following signals: MEMR (memory read), MEMW (memory write), IOR (IO read), and IOW (IO write). To read from memory, the CPU enables MEMR; in order to read from I/O, CPU activates the IOR; and so on. In these computers the CPU has separate instructions for accessing I/O and memory. In Figure 0-17, you see a sample system with its control signals.

In this system, for example, when the CPU wants to store 50 into address 15 of memory, it passes through the following steps:

1. The CPU puts 15 on the address bus and 50 on the data bus.

2. The CPU activates MEMW. This indicates that the CPU wants to write to memory; as a result, data is stored in memory.

To look at another example, when the CPU wants to get data from an I/O device whose address is 40, the following takes place:

1. The CPU puts 40 on the address bus.

2. The CPU activates the IOR. This indicates that the CPU wants to get data from I/O with address 40. In response, the device whose address is 40 puts data on the data bus.

CPU and its relation to RAM and ROM

For the CPU to process information, the data must be stored in RAM or ROM. The function of ROM in computers is to provide information that is fixed and permanent. This is information such as tables for character patterns to be displayed on the video monitor, or programs that are essential to the working of the computer—such as programs for testing and finding the total amount of RAM installed on the system—or for displaying information on the video monitor. By contrast, RAM stores temporary information that can change with time, such as various versions of the operating system and application packages such as word processing or tax calculation packages. These programs are loaded from the hard drive into RAM to be processed by the CPU. The CPU cannot get the information from the disk directly because the disk is too slow. In other words, the CPU first seeks the information to be processed from RAM (or ROM). Only if the data is not there does the CPU seek it from a mass storage device such as a disk, and then it transfers the information to RAM. For this reason, RAM and ROM are sometimes referred to as *primary memory* and disks are called *secondary memory*.

Memory address decoding

Next we discuss address decoding. The CPU provides the address of the data desired, but it is the job of the decoding circuitry to locate the selected memory block. To explore the concept of decoding circuitry, we look at various methods used in decoding the addresses. In this discussion, we use SRAM or ROM for the sake of simplicity.

Memory chips have one or more pins called CS (chip select), which must be activated for the memory's contents to be accessed. Sometimes the chip select is also referred to as chip enable (CE). In connecting a memory chip to the CPU, note the following points.

1. The data bus of the CPU is connected directly to the data pins of the memory chip.

2. Control signals MEMR (memory read) and MEMW (memory write) from the CPU are connected to the OE (output enable) and WE (write enable) pins of the memory chip, respectively.

3. In the case of the address buses, while the lower bits of the addresses from the CPU go directly to the memory chip address pins, the upper ones are

used to activate the CS pin of the memory chip. It is the CS pin that along with RD/WR allows the flow of data in or out of the memory chip. No data can be written into or read from the memory chip unless CS is activated.

As can be seen from the data sheets of SRAM and ROM, the CS input of a memory chip is normally active low and is activated by the output of the memory decoder. Normally memories are divided into blocks, and the output of the decoder selects a given memory block. There are three ways to generate a memory block selector: (a) using simple logic gates, (b) using the 74LS138, or (c) using programmable logics such as CPLD and FPGA. Each method is described below.

Simple logic gate address decoder

The simplest method of constructing decoding circuitry is the use of a NAND gate. The output of a NAND gate is active low, and the CS pin is also active low, which makes them a perfect match. In cases where the CS input is active high, an AND gate must be used. Using a combination of NAND gates and inverters, one can decode any address range. An example of this is given in Figure 0-18, which shows that A15–A12 must be 0011 in order to select the chip. This results in the assignment of addresses 3000H to 3FFFH to this memory chip. When the address is in the range, the output of the NAND gate is low, and the CS pin is also low; this makes the memory active.

In this example, we can omit the NAND gate and connect the CS chip directly to the ground, as shown in Figure 0-19. Memory is connected to the system without using any logic gates which creates what are called *aliases*: the same device with multiple addresses. For example, in this system, the first location of memory has 16 different addresses: 0000H, 1000H, 2000H, ..., F00H. All of the above addresses refer to the same location of memory since some bits of address bus (A12 to A15) are not considered in address decoding.

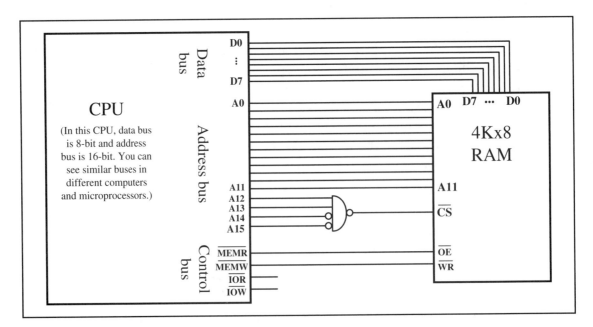

Figure 0-18. Logic Gate as Decoder

CHAPTER 0: INTRODUCTION TO COMPUTINC

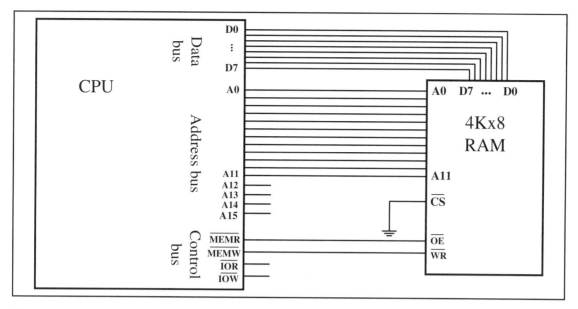

Figure 0-19. Connecting Memory Directly to the CPU

In some cases, we cannot omit the logic gates (e.g., whenever there is more than one memory chip). See Figure 0-20. In this system, four 8K × 8 memories are used together to provide a 32K × 8 memory. The data pins of memories are connected to the data bus. The lower bits of the addresses from the CPU go directly to the memory chip address pins while the upper ones are used to activate the CS pin of the proper memory chip.

Table 0-9 shows the address range assigned to each memory chip in Figure 0-20.

In this example, the memories are distincted from each other by A13 and A14, while decoding A15 prevents aliasing. In other words, the above circuit can be simplified by omitting A15 and using a two-input ANDs to decode A13 and A14, but this creates aliases.

Generally speaking, we can design simpler circuits by using partial decoding; however, in systems which need to be expandable, we should prevent aliasing by using all address pins; otherwise, we will not be able to add extra memories in the future.

Next, we learn to use a decoder instead of logic gates.

Using the 74LS138 3-8 decoder

This used to be one of the most widely used address decoders. The three inputs A, B, and C generate eight active-low outputs Y0–Y7. See Figure 0-21. Each Y output is connected to CS of a memory chip, allowing control of eight memory blocks by a single 74LS138. In the 74LS138 decoder, where A, B, and C select which output is activated, there are three additional inputs, G2A, G2B, and G1. G2A and G2B are both active low, and G1 is active high. If any one of the inputs

Table 0-9. Memory Map of System

Address Range	
0000H–1FFFH	RAM 0
2000H–3FFFH	RAM 1
4000H–5FFFH	RAM 2
6000H–7FFFH	RAM 3
8000H–FFFFH	Not used

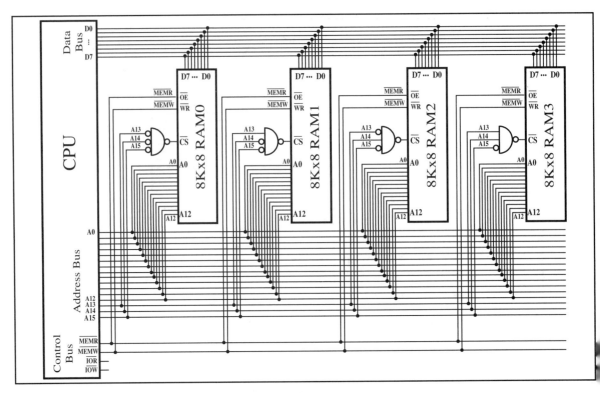

Figure 0-20. Connecting Four Memory Chips to the CPU

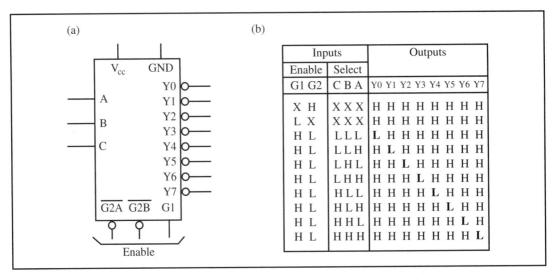

Inputs		Outputs	
Enable	Select		
G1 G2	C B A	Y0 Y1 Y2 Y3 Y4 Y5 Y6 Y7	
X H	X X X	H H H H H H H H	
L X	X X X	H H H H H H H H	
H L	L L L	L H H H H H H H	
H L	L L H	H L H H H H H H	
H L	L H L	H H L H H H H H	
H L	L H H	H H H L H H H H	
H L	H L L	H H H H L H H H	
H L	H L H	H H H H H L H H	
H L	H H L	H H H H H H L H	
H L	H H H	H H H H H H H L	

Figure 0-21. 74LS138 Decoder: (a) Block diagram; (b) Function table

G1, G2A, or G2B is not connected to an address signal (sometimes they are connected to a control signal), they must be activated permanently by either V_{cc} or ground, depending on the activation level.

Example 0-16 shows the design and the address range calculation for the 74LS138 decoder.

Example 0-17 shows how to decode an address using the 74LS138.

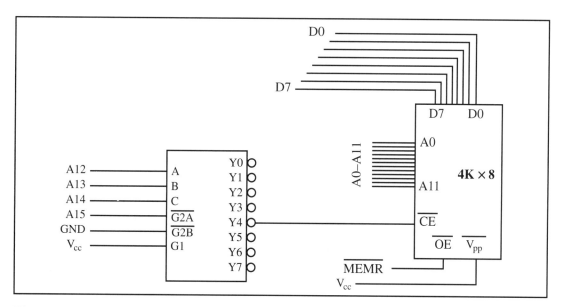

Figure 0-22. Using 74LS138 as Decoder

Example 0-16

Looking at the design in Figure 0-22, find the address range for the following:
(a) Y4, (b) Y2, and (c) Y7.

Solution:

(a) The address range for Y4 is calculated as follows.

A15	A14	A13	A12	A11	A10	A9	A8	A7	A6	A5	A4	A3	A2	A1	A0
0	1	0	0	0	0	0	0	0	0	0	0	0	0	0	0
0	1	0	0	1	1	1	1	1	1	1	1	1	1	1	1

This shows that the range for Y4 is 4000H to 4FFFH. In Figure 0-22, notice that A15 must be 0 for the decoder to be activated. Y4 will be selected when A14 A13 A12 = 100 (4 in binary). The remaining A11–A0 will be 0 for the lowest address and 1 for the highest address.

(b) The address range for Y2 is 2000H to 2FFFH.

A15	A14	A13	A12	A11	A10	A9	A8	A7	A6	A5	A4	A3	A2	A1	A0
0	0	1	0	0	0	0	0	0	0	0	0	0	0	0	0
0	0	1	0	1	1	1	1	1	1	1	1	1	1	1	1

(c) The address range for Y7 is 7000H to 7FFFH.

A15	A14	A13	A12	A11	A10	A9	A8	A7	A6	A5	A4	A3	A2	A1	A0
0	1	1	1	0	0	0	0	0	0	0	0	0	0	0	0
0	1	1	1	1	1	1	1	1	1	1	1	1	1	1	1

Example 0-17

Redesign the system drawn in Figure 0-20 using 74LS138.

Solution:

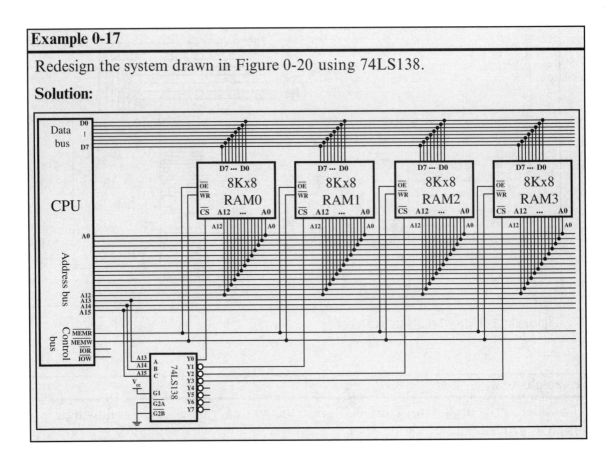

Using programmable logic as an address decoder

Other widely used decoders are programmable logic chips such as PAL, GAL, and FPGA chips. One disadvantage of these chips is that they require PAL/GAL/FPGA software and a burner (programmer), whereas the 74LS138 needs neither of these. The advantage of these chips is that they can be programmed for any combination of address ranges, and so are much more versatile. The fact that PAL/GAL/FPGA chips have 10 or more inputs (in contrast to six in the 74138) means that they can accommodate more address inputs.

REVIEW QUESTIONS

1. List the three types of buses found in computer systems and state briefly the purpose of each type of bus.
2. State which of the following is unidirectional and which is bidirectional: (a) data bus (b) address bus.
3. If an address bus for a given computer has 16 lines, what is the maximum amount of memory it can access (Each memory location is 8-bit).?
4. A given memory block uses addresses 4000H–7FFFH. How many kilobytes is this memory block?
5. The 74138 is a(n) _____ by _____ decoder.
6. In the 74138, give the status of G2A and G2B for the chip to be enabled.
7. In the 74138, give the status of G1 for the chip to be enabled.
8. In Figure 0-22, what is the range of addresses assigned to Y5?

0.5: I/O ADDRESS DECODING AND DESIGN

In this section, we show the design of simple I/O ports using TTL logic gates 74LS373 and 74LS244. For the purpose of clarity, we use simple logic gates such as AND and inverter gates for decoders. The concept of address bus decoding for I/O instructions is exactly the same as for memory. The following are the steps:

1. The control signals IOR and IOW are used along with the decoder. (In memory mapped I/O, RD and WR signals are used.)
2. The address bus is decoded.

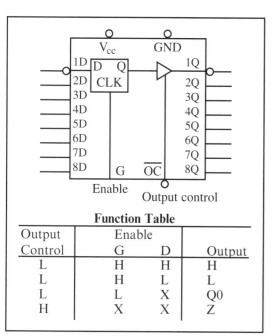

Function Table

Output Control	Enable		Output
	G	D	
L	H	H	H
L	H	L	L
L	L	X	Q0
H	X	X	Z

Figure 0-23. 74LS373 D Latch

Using the 74LS373 in an output port design

In every computer, whenever data is sent out by the CPU via the data bus, the data must be latched by the receiving device. While memories have an internal latch to grab the data, a latching system must be designed for simple I/O ports. The 74LS373 can be used for this purpose. Notice in Figure 0-23 that in order to make the 74LS373 work as a latch, the OC pin must be grounded. For an output latch, it is common to AND the output of the address decoder with the control signal IOW to provide the latching action, as shown in Figures 0-24 and 0-25.

Input port design using the 74LS244

Likewise, when data is coming in by way of a data bus, it must come in through a three-state buffer. This is referred to as *tristated*, which comes from the term *tri-state buffer*.

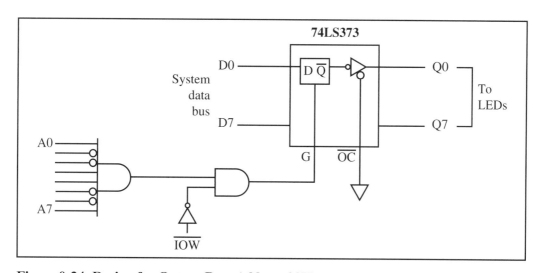

Figure 0-24. Design for Output Port Address 99H.

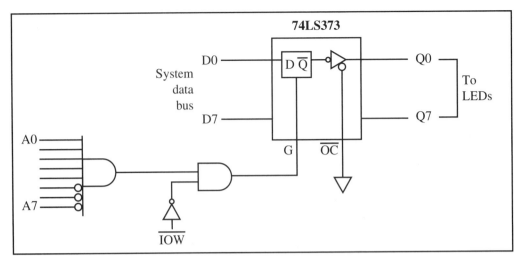

Figure 0-25. Design for Output Port Address 1FH.

As was the case for memory chips, such a tri-state buffer is internal and therefore invisible. For the simple input ports we use the 74LS244 chip. See Figure 0-26 for the internal circuitry of the 74LS244. Notice that since 1G and 2G each control only 4 bits of the 74LS244, they both must be activated for the 8-bit input.

Examine Figure 0-27 to see the use of the 74LS244 as an entry port to the system data bus. Notice in Figures 0-27 and 0-28 how the address decoder and the IOR control signal together activate the tri-state input.

The 74LS244 not only plays the role of buffer but also provides the incoming data with sufficient driving capability to travel all the way to the CPU. Indeed, the 74LS244 chip is widely used for buffering and providing high driving capability for unidirectional buses. In bidirectional buses, the 74LS245 can be used.

In Examples 0-18 and 0-19, you see I/Os that are connected to a system.

Absolute versus linear select address decoding

In decoding addresses, either all of them or a selected number of them are decoded. If all the address lines are decoded, it is called *absolute decoding*. If only selected address pins are used for decoding, it is called *linear select decoding*. Linear select is cheaper, since the less input there is, the fewer the gates needed for decoding. The disadvantage is that it creates what are called *aliases*, the same port with multiple addresses. In cases where linear select is used, we must document all devices addresses in the system map (memory and I/O map) thoroughly.

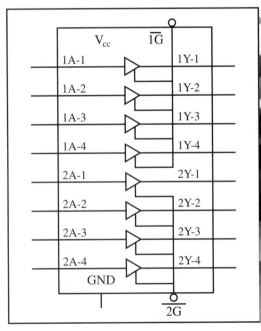

Figure 0-26. 74LS244 Octal Buffer

CHAPTER 0: INTRODUCTION TO COMPUTING

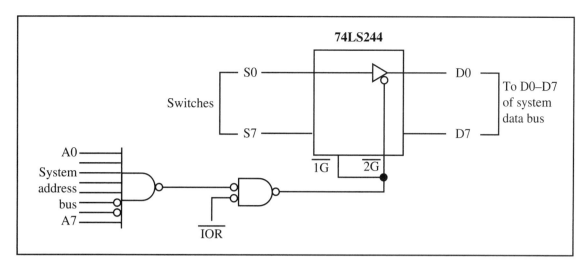

Figure 0-27. Design for Input Port Address 9FH

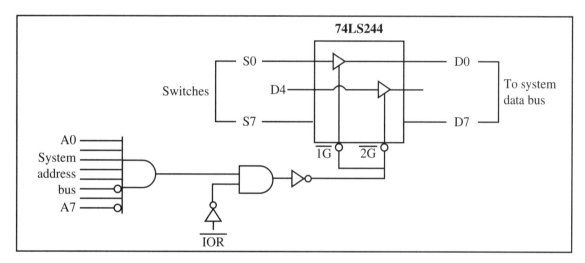

Figure 0-28. Design for Input Port Address 5FH

Figure 0-29 shows an output circuit which is similar to Example 0-18 but decodes just A0–A10. This output circuit has 32 aliases including 029EH, 069EH, ..., FE9EH. As you can see, using linear decoding results in simpler circuits but makes aliases and wastes the address space.

Peripheral I/O versus memory-mapped I/O

Communicating with I/O devices using separate control signals for memory and I/O is referred to as *peripheral I/O*. Some designers also refer to it as *isolated I/O*. However, in many computers and microprocessors there are not separate control signals to distinguish I/O from memory. The addresses of I/Os and memory are assigned so that they do not overlap with each other. In these computers, I/Os are accessed as if they are parts of memory. This kind of bus is called *memory-mapped I/O*. Figure 0-30 shows a simple system designed by memory-mapped I/O.

Example 0-18

Using the 74LS373, provide an output port for the system shown in Figure 0-17. Assign address 029EH to the device.

Solution:

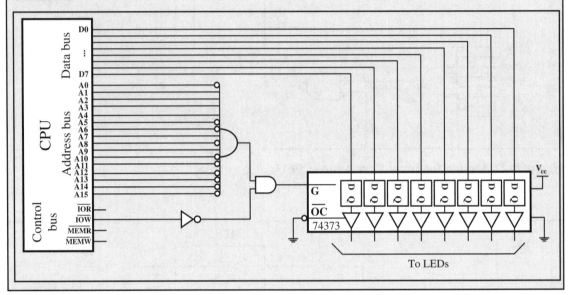

Example 0-19

Using a 74LS244 connect 8 switches to the bus of a system. Assign address 0401H to the input device.

Solution:

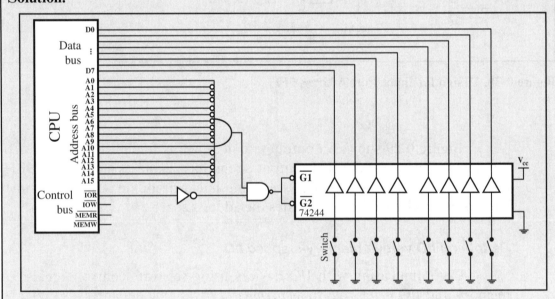

The following are the differences between peripheral I/O and memory-mapped I/O for a system with 16 address (A0-A15) pins:

1. In peripheral I/O, special I/O instructions are used to access I/O devices. However, in memory-mapped I/O, we must use instructions that access

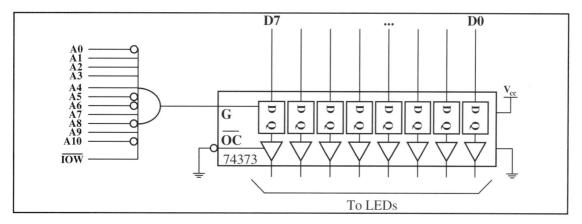

Figure 0-29. Linear Address Decoding

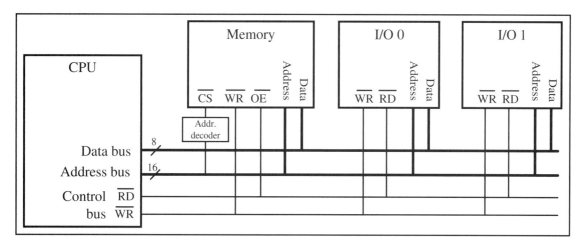

Figure 0-30. A Simple System Using Memory-Mapped I/O

memory locations to access the I/O ports instead of Input and Output instructions. In that way, there is no difference between memory locations and I/O ports.

2. In memory-mapped I/O circuit interfacing, control signals RD and WR are used to access both I/O and memory devices. This is in contrast to peripheral I/O, in which IOR and IOW are used.

3. One major and severe disadvantage of memory-mapped I/O is that it uses memory address space, which could lead to memory space fragmentation.

4. In memory-mapped I/O, the entire address must be decoded. Otherwise, the I/O aliases overlap the memory space. This is in contrast to peripheral I/O, in which linear decoding can be used. This makes decoding circuitry for memory-mapped I/O more expensive.

In Examples 0-20 and 0-21 you see input and output circuits for a memory-mapped I/O system.

Example 0-20

Using a 74LS373, design an output port for a memory-mapped I/O system. Assign address 029EH to the device.

Solution:

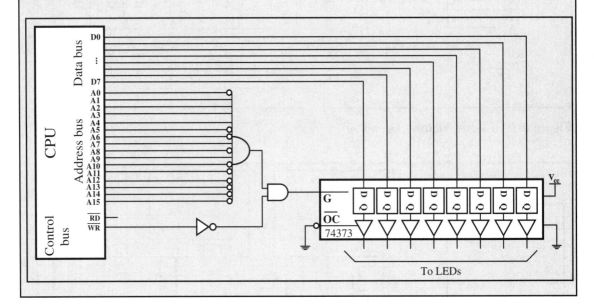

Example 0-21

Using a 74LS244, connect an 8-bit switch to a memory-mapped I/O system. Assign address 0401H to the device.

Solution:

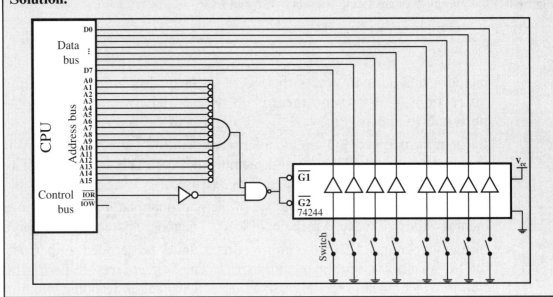

REVIEW QUESTIONS

1. Designers use a _____ (latch, tri-state buffer) for output and a _____ (latch, tri-state buffer) for input.
2. Why do we use latches in I/O design?

3. To use the 74LS373 as a latch, OC must be set to _____ permanently.
4. In memory-mapped I/O, which signal is used to select the (a) output, and (b) input devices?

0.6: CPU ARCHITECTURE

In this section, we will examine the internals of a CPU. Then, we will compare the Harvard and von Neumann architectures.

Inside CPU

A program stored in memory provides instructions to the CPU to perform an action. The action can simply be adding data such as payroll data or controlling a machine such as a robot. The function of the CPU is to fetch these instructions from memory and execute them. See Figure 0-31. To perform the actions of fetch and execute, all CPUs are equipped with resources such as the following:

1. Foremost among the resources at the disposal of the CPU are a number of *registers*. The CPU uses registers to store information temporarily. The information could be two values to be processed, or the address of the value needed to be fetched from memory. Registers inside the CPU can be 8-bit, 16-bit, 32-bit, or even 64-bit, depending on the CPU. In general, the more and bigger are the registers, the better is the CPU. The disadvantage of more and bigger registers is the increased cost of such a CPU.

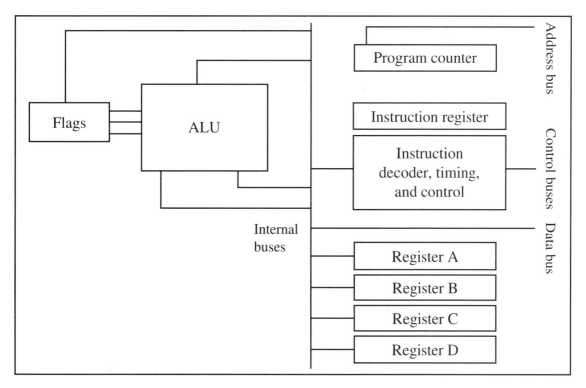

Figure 0-31. Internal Block Diagram of a CPU.

2. The CPU also has what is called the *ALU* (arithmetic/logic unit). The ALU section of the CPU is responsible for performing arithmetic functions such as add, subtract, multiply, and divide, and logic functions such as AND, OR, and NOT.

3. Every CPU has what is called a *program counter*. The function of the program counter is to point to the address of the next instruction to be executed. As each instruction is executed, the program counter is incremented to point to the address of the next instruction to be executed. The contents of the program counter are placed on the address bus to find and fetch the desired instruction. In the IBM PC, the program counter is a register called IP, or the instruction pointer.

4. The function of the *instruction decoder* is to interpret the instruction fetched into the CPU. One can think of the instruction decoder as a kind of dictionary, storing the meaning of each instruction and what steps the CPU should take upon receiving a given instruction. Just as a dictionary requires more pages the more words it defines, a CPU capable of understanding more instructions requires more transistors to design.

Internal working of CPUs

Figure 0-32 shows the steps that the CPU goes through to execute an instruction.

To demonstrate some of the concepts discussed earlier, a step-by-step analysis of the process a CPU goes through to add three numbers is given next. Assume that an imaginary CPU has registers called A, B, C, and D. It has an 8-bit data bus and a 16-bit address bus. Therefore, the CPU can access memory from addresses 0000 to FFFFH (for a total of 10000H locations).

The action to be performed by the CPU is to put hexadecimal value 21 into register A, and then add to register A the values 42H and 12H. Assume that the code for the CPU to move a value to register A is 1011 0000 (B0H) and the code for adding a value to register A is 0000 0100 (04H). The necessary steps and code to perform these operations are as follows.

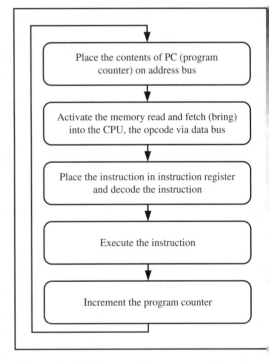

Figure 0-32. Steps of Instruction Process

Action	Code	Data
Move value 21H into register A	B0H	21H
Add value 42H to register A	04H	42H
Add value 12H to register A	04H	12H

If the program to perform the actions listed above is stored in memory locations starting at 1400H, the following would represent the contents for each memory address location:

```
Memory address   Contents of memory address
1400             (B0) code for moving a value to register A
1401             (21) value to be moved
1402             (04) code for adding a value to register A
1403             (42) value to be added
1404             (04) code for adding a value to register A
1405             (12) value to be added
1406             (F4) code for halt
```

The actions performed by the CPU to run the program above would be as follows:

1. The CPU's program counter can have a value between 0000 and FFFFH. The program counter must be set to the value 1400H, indicating the address of the first instruction code to be executed. After the program counter has been loaded with the address of the first instruction, the CPU is ready to execute.

2. The CPU puts 1400H on the address bus and sends it out. The memory circuitry finds the location while the CPU activates the READ signal, indicating to memory that it wants the byte at location 1400H. This causes the contents of memory location 1400H, which is B0, to be put on the data bus and brought into the CPU.

3. The CPU decodes the instruction B0 with the help of its instruction decoder dictionary. When it finds the definition for that instruction it knows it must bring the byte in the next memory location into register A of the CPU. Therefore, it commands its controller circuitry to do exactly that. When it brings in value 21H from memory location 1401, it makes sure that the doors of all registers are closed except register A. Therefore, when value 21H comes into the CPU it will go directly into register A. After completing one instruction, the program counter points to the address of the next instruction to be executed, which in this case is 1402H. Address 1402 is sent out on the address bus to fetch the next instruction.

4. From memory location 1402H the CPU fetches code 04H. After decoding, the CPU knows that it must add the byte sitting at the next address (1403) to the contents of register A. After the CPU brings the value (in this case, 42H) into register A, it provides the contents of register A along with this value to the ALU to perform the addition. It then takes the result of the addition from the ALU's output and puts it into register A. Meanwhile, the program counter becomes 1404, which is the address of the next instruction.

5. Address 1404H is put on the address bus and the code is fetched into the CPU, decoded, and executed. This code again is adding a value to register A. The program counter is updated to 1406H.

6. Finally, the contents of address 1406 are fetched in and executed. This HALT instruction tells the CPU to stop incrementing the program counter and asking for the next instruction. Without the HALT, the CPU would continue updating the program counter and fetching instructions.

Now suppose that address 1403H contained value 04 instead of 42H. How would the CPU distinguish between data 04 to be added and code 04? Remember that code 04 for this CPU means "move the next value into register A." Therefore, the CPU will not try to decode the next value. It simply moves the contents of the following memory location into register A, regardless of its value.

Harvard and von Neumann architectures

Every microprocessor must have memory space to store program (code) and data. While code provides instructions to the CPU, the data provides the information to be processed. The CPU uses buses (wire traces) to access the code ROM and data RAM memory spaces. The early computers used the same bus for accessing both the code and data. Such an architecture is commonly referred to as *von Neumann (Princeton) architecture*. That means for von Neumann computers, the process of accessing the code or data could cause them to get in each other's way and slow down the processing speed of the CPU, because each had to wait for the other to finish fetching. To speed up the process of program execution, some CPUs use what is called *Harvard architecture*. In Harvard architecture, we have separate buses for the code and data memory. See Figure 0-33. That means that we need four sets of buses: (1) a set of data buses for carrying data into and out of the CPU, (2) a set of address

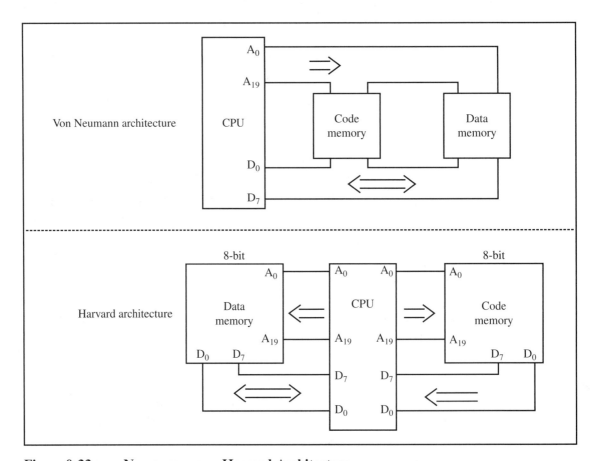

Figure 0-33. von Neumann versus Harvard Architecture.

buses for accessing the data, (3) a set of data buses for carrying code into the CPU, and (4) an address bus for accessing the code. This is easy to implement inside an IC chip such as a microprocessor where both ROM code and data RAM are internal (on-chip) and distances are on the micron and millimeter scale. But implementing Harvard architecture for systems such as x86 IBM PC-type computers is very expensive because the RAM and ROM that hold code and data are external to the CPU. Separate wire traces for data and code on the motherboard will make the board large and expensive. For example, for a Pentium microprocessor with a 64-bit data bus and a 32-bit address bus, we will need about 100 wire traces on the motherboard if it is von Neumann architecture (96 for address and data, plus a few others for control signals of read and write and, etc.). But the number of wire traces will double to 200 if we use Harvard architecture. Harvard architecture will also necessitate a large number of pins coming out of the microprocessor itself. For this reason, you do not see Harvard architecture implemented in the world of PCs and workstations. This is also the reason that microprocessors such as AVR use Harvard architecture internally, but they still use von Neumann architecture if they need external memory for code and data space. The von Neumann architecture was developed at Princeton University, while the Harvard architecture was the work of Harvard University.

REVIEW QUESTIONS

1. What does "ALU" stand for? What is its purpose?
2. How are registers used in computer systems?
3. What is the purpose of the program counter?
4. What is the purpose of the instruction decoder?
5. True or false. Harvard architecture uses the same address and data buses to fetch both code and data.

SUMMARY

The binary number system represents all numbers with a combination of the two binary digits, 0 and 1. The use of binary systems is necessary in digital computers because only two states can be represented: on or off. Any binary number can be coded directly into its hexadecimal equivalent for the convenience of humans. Converting from binary/hex to decimal, and vice versa, is a straightforward process that becomes easy with practice. ASCII code is a binary code used to represent alphanumeric data internally in the computer. It is frequently used in peripheral devices for input and/or output.

The AND, OR, and inverter logic gates are the basic building blocks of simple circuits. NAND, NOR, and XOR gates are also used to implement circuit design. Diagrams of half-adders and full-adders were given as examples of the use of logic gates for circuit design. Decoders are used to detect certain addresses. Flip-flops are used to latch in data until other circuits are ready for it.

The major components of any computer system are the CPU, memory, and I/O devices. "Memory" refers to temporary or permanent storage of data. In most systems, memory can be accessed as bytes or words. The terms *kilobyte, megabyte, gigabyte,* and *terabyte* are used to refer to large numbers of bytes. There are two main types of memory in computer systems: RAM and ROM. RAM (random access memory) is used for temporary storage of programs and data. ROM (read-only memory) is used for permanent storage of programs and data that the computer system must have in order to function. All components of the computer system are under the control of the CPU. Peripheral devices such as I/O (input/output) devices allow the CPU to communicate with humans or other computer systems. There are three types of buses in computers: address, control, and data. Control buses are used by the CPU to direct other devices. The address bus is used by the CPU to locate a device or a memory location. Data buses are used to send information back and forth between the CPU and other devices.

This chapter provided an overview of semiconductor memories. Types of memories were compared in terms of their capacity, organization, and access time. ROM is nonvolatile memory typically used to store programs in embedded systems. The relative advantages of various types of ROM were described, including PROM, EPROM, UV-EPROM, EEPROM, Flash memory EPROM, and mask ROM.

Address decoding techniques using simple logic gates, decoders, and programmable logic were covered.

The computer organization and the internals of the CPU were also covered.

PROBLEMS

0.1: NUMBERING AND CODING SYSTEMS

1. Convert the following decimal numbers to binary:
   (a) 12   (b) 123   (c) 63   (d) 128   (e) 1000
2. Convert the following binary numbers to decimal:
   (a) 100100   (b) 1000001   (c) 11101   (d) 1010   (e) 00100010
3. Convert the values in Problem 2 to hexadecimal.
4. Convert the following hex numbers to binary and decimal:
   (a) 2B9H   (b) F44H   (c) 912H   (d) 2BH   (e) FFFFH
5. Convert the values in Problem 1 to hex.
6. Find the 2's complement of the following binary numbers:
   (a) 1001010   (b) 111001   (c) 10000010   (d) 111110001
7. Add the following hex values:
   (a) 2CH + 3FH   (b) F34H + 5D6H   (c) 20000H + 12FFH
   (d) FFFFH + 2222H
8. Perform hex subtraction for the following:
   (a) 24FH–129H   (b) FE9H–5CCH   (c) 2FFFFH–FFFFFH
   (d) 9FF25H–4DD99H
9. Show the ASCII codes for numbers 0, 1, 2, 3, ..., 9 in both hex and binary.

CHAPTER 0: INTRODUCTION TO COMPUTING

10. Show the ASCII code (in hex) for the following strings:
    "U.S.A. is a country" CR,LF
    "in North America" CR,LF
    (CR is carriage return, LF is line feed)

0.2: DIGITAL PRIMER

11. Draw a three-input OR gate using a two-input OR gate.
12. Show the truth table for a three-input OR gate.
13. Draw a three-input AND gate using a two-input AND gate.
14. Show the truth table for a three-input AND gate.
15. Design a three-input XOR gate with a two-input XOR gate. Show the truth table for a three-input XOR.
16. List the truth table for a three-input NAND.
17. List the truth table for a three-input NOR.
18. Show the decoder for binary 1100.
19. Show the decoder for binary 11011.
20. List the truth table for a D-FF.

0.3: SEMICONDUCTOR MEMORY

21. Answer the following:
    (a) How many nibbles are 16 bits?
    (b) How many bytes are 32 bits?
    (c) If a word is defined as 16 bits, how many words is a 64-bit data item?
    (d) What is the exact value (in decimal) of 1 meg?
    (e) How many kilobytes is 1 meg?
    (f) What is the exact value (in decimal) of 1 gigabyte?
    (g) How many kilobytes is 1 gigabyte?
    (h) How many megs is 1 gigabyte?
    (i) If a given computer has a total of 8 megabytes of memory, how many bytes (in decimal) is this? How many kilobytes is this?
22. A given mass storage device such as a hard disk can store 2 gigabytes of information. Assuming that each page of text has 25 rows and each row has 80 columns of ASCII characters (each character = 1 byte), approximately how many pages of information can this disk store?
23. What is the difference in capacity between a 4M memory chip and 4M of computer memory?
24. True or false. The more address pins, the more memory locations are inside the chip. (Assume that the number of data pins is fixed.)
25. True or false. The more data pins, the more each location inside the chip will hold.
26. True or false. The more data pins, the higher the capacity of the memory chip.
27. True or false. The more data pins and address pins, the greater the capacity of the memory chip.
28. The speed of a memory chip is referred to as its _____.
29. True or false. The price of memory chips varies according to capacity and speed.

30. The main advantage of EEPROM over UV-EPROM is _____.
31. True or false. SRAM has a larger cell size than DRAM.
32. Which of the following must be refreshed periodically?
    (a) EPROM (b) DRAM (c) SRAM
33. Which memory is used for PC cache?
34. Which of the following is volatile memory?
    (a) SRAM (b) UV-EPROM (c) NV-RAM (d) DRAM
35. RAS and CAS are associated with which type of memory?
    (a) EPROM (b) SRAM (c) DRAM (d) all of the above
36. Which type of memory needs an external multiplexer?
    (a) EPROM (b) SRAM (c) DRAM (d) all of the above
37. Find the organization and capacity of memory chips with the following pins.
    (a) EEPROM A0–A14, D0–D7   (b) UV-EPROM A0–A12, D0–D7
    (c) SRAM A0–A11, D0–D7   (d) SRAM A0–A12, D0–D7
    (e) DRAM A0–A10, D0   (f) SRAM A0–A12, D0
    (g) EEPROM A0–A11, D0–D7   (h) UV-EPROM A0–A10, D0–D7
    (i) DRAM A0–A8, D0–D3   (j) DRAM A0–A7, D0–D7
38. Find the capacity, address, and data pins for the following memory organizations.
    (a) 16K × 8 ROM   (b) 32K × 8 ROM
    (c) 64K × 8 SRAM   (d) 256K × 8 EEPROM
    (e) 64K × 8 ROM   (f) 64K × 4 DRAM
    (g) 1M × 8 SRAM   (h) 4M × 4 DRAM
    (i) 64K × 8 NV-RAM

0.4: BUS DESIGNING AND ADDRESS DECODING

39. In a given byte-addressable computer, memory locations 10000H to 9FFFFH are available for user programs. The first location is 10000H and the last location is 9FFFFH. Calculate the following:
    (a) The total number of bytes available (in decimal)
    (b) The total number of kilobytes (in decimal)
40. A given computer has a 32-bit data bus. What is the largest number that can be carried into the CPU at a time?
41. Below are listed several computers with their data bus widths. For each computer, list the maximum value that can be brought into the CPU at a time (in both hex and decimal).
    (a) Apple 2 with an 8-bit data bus
    (b) x86 PC with a 16-bit data bus
    (c) x86 PC with a 32-bit data bus
    (d) Cray supercomputer with a 64-bit data bus
42. Find the total amount of memory, in the units requested, for each of the following CPUs, given the size of the address buses (Each memory location is 8-bit.):
    (a) 16-bit address bus (in K)
    (b) 24-bit address bus (in megs)

(c) 32-bit address bus (in megabytes and gigabytes)

(d) 48-bit address bus (in megabytes, gigabytes, and terabytes)

43. Of the data bus and address bus, which is unidirectional and which is bidirectional?

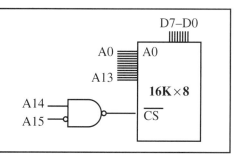

Diagram for Problem 44

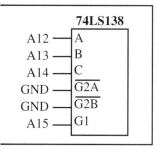

Diagram for Problem 46

44. Find the address range of the memory design in the diagram.

45. Using NAND gates and inverters, design decoding circuitry for the address range 2000H–2FFFH.

46. Find the address range for Y0, Y3, and Y6 of the 74LS138 for the diagrammed design.

47. Using the 74138, design the memory decoding circuitry in which the memory block controlled by Y0 is in the range 0000H to 1FFFH. Indicate the size of the memory block controlled by each Y.

48. Find the address range for Y3, Y6, and Y7 in Problem 47.

49. Using the 74138, design memory decoding circuitry in which the memory block controlled by Y0 is in the 0000H to 3FFFH space. Indicate the size of the memory block controlled by each Y.

50. Find the address range for Y1, Y2, and Y3 in Problem 49.

0.5: I/O ADDRESS DECODING AND DESIGN

51. A _____ (latch, tri-state buffer) is used in the design of input ports.

52. A _____ (latch, tri-state buffer) is used in the design of output ports.

53. Which one is more economical, the linear address select or absolute address decoding?

54. Explain address aliasing.

55. Which one creates aliases, the linear address select or absolute address decoding?

56. Explain memory-mapped I/O.

57. True or false. In peripheral I/O, an input port is distinguished from an output port by the IOR and IOW control signals.

58. _____ (IOR, IOW) is used in the design of input ports.

59. _____ (IOR, IOW) is used in the design of output ports.

60. Design an output port using NAND and inverter gates in addition to a 74LS373. Assign address 16H to it and use IOW control signal.

61. Design an input port using NAND and inverter gates in addition to a 74LS244. Assign address 81H to it and use IOR control signal.

62. Design an output port using NAND and inverter gates in addition to a 74LS373. Assign address 0924H to it and use memory mapped I/O.

63. Design an input port using NAND and inverter gates in addition to a 74LS244. Assign address 09090H to it and use memory mapped I/O.

0.6: CPU AND HARVARD ARCHITECTURE

64. Which register of the CPU holds the address of the instruction to be fetched?

65. Which section of the CPU is responsible for performing addition?

66. List the three bus types present in every CPU.

ANSWERS TO REVIEW QUESTIONS

0.1: NUMBERING AND CODING SYSTEMS

1. Computers use the binary system because each bit can have one of two voltage levels: on and off.
2. $34_{10} = 100010_2 = 22_{16}$
3. $110101_2 = 35_{16} = 53_{10}$
4. 1110001
5. 010100
6. 461
7. 275
8. 38 30 78 38 36 20 43 50 55 73

0.2: DIGITAL PRIMER

1. AND
2. OR
3. XOR
4. Buffer
5. Storing data
6. Decoder

0.3: SEMICONDUCTOR MEMORY

1. 24,576
2. Random access memory; it is used for temporary storage of programs that the CPU is running, such as the operating system or word processing programs.
3. Read-only memory; it is used for permanent programs such as those that control the keyboard.
4. The contents of RAM are lost when the computer is powered off.
5. The CPU, memory, and I/O devices
6. Central processing unit; it can be considered the "brain" of the computer; it executes the programs and controls all other devices in the computer.
7. c
8. (a) $16K \times 8$, 128K bits   (b) $64K \times 8$, 512K   (c) $4K \times 8$, 32K
9. (a) $2K \times 1$, 2K bits   (b) $8K \times 4$, 32K   (c) $128K \times 8$, 1M
   (d) $64K \times 4$, 256K   (e) $256K \times 1$, 256K   (f) $256K \times 4$, 1M
10. (a) 64K bits, 14 address, and 4 data   (b) 256K, 15 address, and 8 data
    (c) 1M, 10 address, and 1 data   (d) 1M, 18 address, and 4 data
    (e) 512K, 16 address, and 8 data   (f) 4M, 10 address, and 4 data
11. b, c

0.4: BUS DESIGNING AND ADDRESS DECODING

1. The address bus carries the location (address) needed by the CPU; the data bus carries information in and out of the CPU; the control bus is used by the CPU to send signals controlling I/O devices.

2. (a) bidirectional (b) unidirectional
3. 64K, or 65,536 bytes
4. 16K bytes
5. 3, 8
6. Both must be low.
7. G1 must be high.
8. 5000H–5FFFH

0.5: I/O ADDRESS DECODING AND DESIGN

1. Latch, tri-state buffer
2. The CPU provides the data on the data bus only for a short amount of time. Therefore, it must be latched before it is lost.
3. Low
4. (a) WR (b) RD

0.6: CPU ARCHITECTURE

1. Arithmetic/logic unit; it performs all arithmetic and logic operations.
2. They are used for temporary storage of information.
3. It holds the address of the next instruction to be executed.
4. It tells the CPU what actions to perform for each instruction.
5. False

CHAPTER 1

THE 8051 MICROPROCESSORS

OBJECTIVES

Upon completion of this chapter, you will be able to:

- >> Compare and contrast microprocessors and microprocessors.
- >> Describe the advantages of microprocessors for some applications.
- >> Explain the concept of embedded systems.
- >> Discuss criteria for considering a microprocessor.
- >> Explain the variations of speed, packaging, memory, and cost per unit and how these affect choosing a microprocessor.
- >> Compare and contrast the various members of the 8051 family.
- >> Compare 8051 microprocessors offered by various manufacturers.

This chapter begins with a discussion of the role and importance of microprocessors in everyday life. In Section 1.1, we discuss criteria to consider in choosing a microprocessor, as well as the use of microprocessors in the embedded market. Section 1.2 covers various members of the 8051 family, such as the 8052 and 8031, and their features. In addition, we discuss various versions of the 8051 such as the 8751, AT89C51, and DS5000.

1.1: MICROPROCESSORS AND EMBEDDED PROCESSORS

In this section, we discuss the need for microprocessors and contrast them with general-purpose microprocessors such as the Pentium and other x86 microprocessors. We also look at the role of microprocessors in the embedded market. In addition, we provide some criteria on how to choose a microprocessor.

Microprocessor versus general-purpose microprocessor

What is the difference between a microprocessor and microprocessor? By microprocessor is meant the general-purpose microprocessors such as Intel's x86 family (8086, 80286, 80386, 80486, and the Pentium) or Motorola's 680x0 family (68000, 68010, 68020, 68030, 68040, etc.). These microprocessors contain no RAM, no ROM, and no I/O ports on the chip itself. For this reason, they are commonly referred to as *general-purpose microprocessors*. See Figure1-1.

A system designer using a general-purpose microprocessor such as the Pentium or the 68040 must add RAM, ROM, I/O ports, and timers externally to make them functional. Although the addition of external RAM, ROM, and I/O ports makes these systems bulkier and much more expensive, they have the advantage of versatility such that the designer can decide on the amount of RAM, ROM, and I/O ports needed to fit the task at hand. This is not the case with microprocessors. A microprocessor has a CPU (a microprocessor) in addition to a fixed amount of RAM, ROM, I/O ports, and a timer all on a single chip. In other words, the processor, RAM, ROM, I/O ports, and timer are all embedded together on one chip; therefore, the designer cannot add any

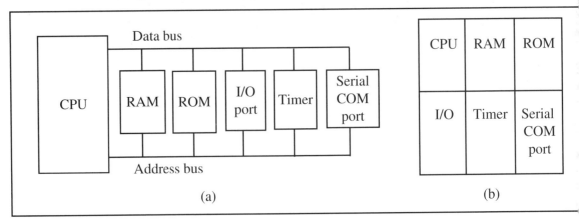

Figure 1-1. General-Purpose Microprocessor (a) System Contrasted With Microprocessor (b) Syste

Table 1-1. Some Embedded Products Using Microprocessors

external memory, I/O, or timer to it. The fixed amount of on-chip ROM, RAM, and number of I/O ports in microprocessors makes them ideal for many applications in which cost and space are critical. In many applications, for example a TV remote control, there is no need for the computing power of a 486 or even an 8086 microprocessor because the space it takes, the power it consumes, and the price per unit are much more critical considerations than the computing power. These applications most often require some I/O operations to read signals and turn on and off certain bits. For this reason some call these processors IBP, "itty-bitty processors" (see "Good Things in Small Packages Are Generating Big Product Opportunities," by Rick Grehan, BYTE magazine, September 1994; www.byte.com, for an excellent discussion of microprocessors).

It is interesting to note that some microprocessor manufacturers have gone as far as integrating an ADC (analog-to-digital converter) and other peripherals into the microprocessor.

Microprocessors for embedded systems

In the literature discussing microprocessors, we often see the term *embedded system*. Microprocessors and microprocessors are widely used in embedded system products. An embedded product uses a microprocessor (or microprocessor) to do one task and one task only. A printer is an example of embedded system since the processor inside it performs only one task—namely, getting the data and printing it. Contrast this with a Pentium-based PC (or any x86 IBM-compatible PC). A PC can be used for any number of applications such as word processor, print server, bank teller terminal, video game player, network server, or internet terminal. Software for a variety of applications can be loaded and run. Of course the reason a PC can perform myriad tasks is that it has RAM memory and an operating system that loads the application software into RAM and lets the CPU run it. In an embedded system, there is only one application software that is typically burned into ROM. The x86 PC contains or is connected to various embedded products such as the keyboard, printer, modem, disk controller, sound card, CD-ROM driver, or mouse. Each one of these peripherals has a microprocessor inside it that performs only one task. For example, inside every mouse there is a microprocessor that performs the task of finding the mouse position and sending it to the PC. Table 1-1 lists some embedded products.

x86 PC embedded applications

Although microprocessors are the preferred choice for many embedded systems, there are times that a microprocessor is inadequate for the task. For this reason, in recent years many manufacturers of general-purpose microprocessors such as Intel, Freescale Semiconductor Inc. (formerly Motorola), and AMD (Advanced Micro Devices, Inc.) have targeted their microprocessor for the high end of the embedded market. While Intel and AMD push their x86 processors for both the embedded and desktop PC markets, Freescale has updated the 68000 family in the form of Coldfire to be used mainly for the high end of embedded systems now that Apple no longer uses the 680x0 in their Macintosh. Since the early 1990s, a new processor called ARM has been used in many embedded systems. Currently the ARM is the most widely used microprocessor in the world and is targeted for the high end of the embedded market as well as the PC and tablet market. It must be noted that when a company targets a general-purpose microprocessor for the embedded market, it optimizes the processor used for embedded systems. For this reason, these processors are often called *high-end embedded processors*. Very often the terms *embedded processor* and *microprocessor* are used interchangeably.

One of the most critical needs of an embedded system is to decrease power consumption and space. This can be achieved by integrating more functions into the CPU chip. All the embedded processors based on the x86 and 680x0 have low power consumption in addition to some forms of I/O, COM port, and ROM all on a single chip. In high-performance embedded processors, the trend is to integrate more and more functions on the CPU chip and let the designer decide which features he or she wants to use. This trend is invading PC system design as well. Normally, in designing the PC motherboard we need a CPU plus a chip-set containing I/O, a cache controller, a flash ROM containing BIOS, and finally a secondary cache memory. New designs are emerging in industry. For example, Cyrix has announced that it is working on a chip that contains the entire PC, except for DRAM. In other words, we are about to see an entire computer on a chip.

Currently, because of MS-DOS and Windows standardization many embedded systems are using x86 PCs. In many cases, using the x86 PCs for the high-end embedded applications not only saves money but also shortens development time since there is a vast library of software already written for the DOS and Windows platforms. The fact that Windows is a widely used and well understood platform means that developing a Windows-based embedded product reduces the cost and shortens the development time considerably.

Choosing a microprocessor

There are four major 8-bit microprocessors. They are: Freescale's 6811, Intel's 8051, Zilog's Z8, and PIC 16X from Microchip Technology. Each of these microprocessors has a unique instruction set and register set; therefore, they are not compatible with each other. Programs written for one will not run on the others. There are also 16-bit and 32-bit microprocessors made by various chip makers. With all these different microprocessors, what criteria do designers consider in choosing one? Three criteria in choosing microprocessors are as follows: (1) meeting the computing needs of the task at hand efficiently and cost-effectively, (2) availability of software development tools such as compilers, assemblers, and debuggers, and (3) wide availability and reliable sources of the microprocessor. Next, we elaborate further on each of the above criteria.

Criteria for choosing a microprocessor

1. The first and foremost criterion in choosing a microprocessor is that it must meet the task at hand efficiently and cost-effectively. In analyzing the needs of a microprocessor-based project, we must first see whether an 8-bit, 16-bit, or 32-bit microprocessor can best handle the computing needs of the task most effectively. Among other considerations in this category are:
   (a) Speed. What is the highest speed that the microprocessor supports?
   (b) Packaging. Does it come in a 40-pin DIP (dual inline package) or a QFP (quad flat package), or some other packaging format? This is important in terms of space, assembling, and prototyping the end product.
   (c) Power consumption. This is especially critical for battery-powered products.
   (d) The amount of RAM and ROM on chip.
   (e) The number of I/O pins and the timer on the chip.
   (f) How easy it is to upgrade to higher-performance or lower power-consumption versions.
   (g) Cost per unit. This is important in terms of the final cost of the product in which a microprocessor is used. For example, there are microprocessors that cost 50 cents per unit when purchased 100,000 units at a time.

2. The second criterion in choosing a microprocessor is how easy it is to develop products around it. Key considerations include the availability of an assembler, debugger, a code-efficient C language compiler, emulator, technical support, and both in-house and outside expertise. In many cases, third-party vendor (i.e., a supplier other than the chip manufacturer) support for the chip is as good as, if not better than, support from the chip manufacturer.

3. The third criterion in choosing a microprocessor is its ready availability in needed quantities both now and in the future. For some designers, this is even more important than the first two criteria. Currently, of the leading 8-bit microprocessors, the 8051 family has the largest number of diversified (multiple source) suppliers. By supplier is meant a producer besides the originator of the microprocessor. In the case of the 8051, which was originated by Intel, several companies also currently produce (or have produced in the past) the 8051. These companies include Intel, Atmel, Philips/Signetics, SiLab, Infineon (formerly Siemens), Matra, and Dallas Semiconductor. See Table 1-2.

It should be noted that Freescale, Zilog, and

Table 1-2. Some of the Companies Producing a Member of the 8051 Family

Company	Website
Intel	www.intel.com/design/mcs51
Atmel	www.atmel.com
Philips/Signetics	www.semiconductors.philips.com
Infineon	www.infineon.com
Dallas Semi/Maxim	www.maxim-ic.com
Silicon Labs	www.silabs.com

Microchip Technology have all dedicated massive resources to ensure wide and timely availability of their product since their product is stable, mature, and single sourced. In recent years, they also have begun to sell the ASIC (application-specific integrated circuit) library cell of the microprocessor.

REVIEW QUESTIONS

1. True or false. Microprocessors are normally less expensive than microprocessors.
2. When comparing a system board based on a microprocessor and a general-purpose microprocessor, which one is cheaper?
3. A microprocessor normally has which of the following devices on-chip?
   (a) RAM   (b) ROM   (c) I/O   (d) all of the above
4. A general-purpose microprocessor normally needs which of the following devices to be attached to it?
   (a) RAM   (b) ROM   (c) I/O   (d) all of the above
5. An embedded system is also called a dedicated system. Why?
6. What does the term *embedded system* mean?
7. Why does having multiple sources of a given product matter?

1.2: OVERVIEW OF THE 8051 FAMILY

In this section, we first look at the various members of the 8051 family of microprocessors and their internal features. In addition, we see who are the different manufacturers of the 8051 and what kind of products they offer.

A brief history of the 8051

In 1981, Intel Corporation introduced an 8-bit microprocessor called the 8051. This microprocessor had 128 bytes of RAM, 4K bytes of on-chip ROM, two timers, one serial port, and four ports (each 8-bits wide) all on a single chip. At the time, it was also referred to as a "system on a chip." The 8051 is an 8-bit processor, meaning that the CPU can work on only 8 bits of data at a time. Data larger than 8 bits has to be broken into 8-bit pieces to be processed by the CPU. The 8051 has a total of four I/O ports, each 8-bits wide. See Figure 1-2. Although the 8051 can have a maximum of 64K bytes of on-chip ROM, many manufacturers have put only 4K bytes on the chip. This will be discussed in more detail later.

The 8051 became widely popular after Intel allowed other manufacturers to make and market any flavors of the 8051 they please with the condition that they remain code-compatible with the 8051. This has led to many versions of the 8051 with different speeds and amounts of on-chip ROM marketed by more than half a dozen manufacturers. Next, we review some of them. It is important to note that although there are different flavors of the 8051 in terms of speed and amount of on-chip ROM, they are all compatible with the original 8051 as far as the instructions are concerned. This means that if you write your program for one, it will run on any of them regardless of the manufacturer.

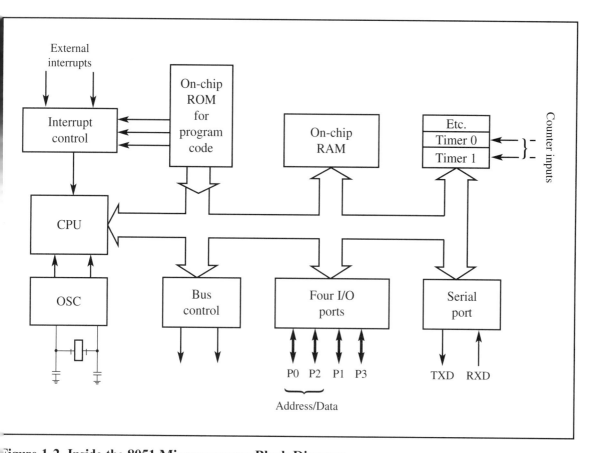

Figure 1-2. Inside the 8051 Microprocessor Block Diagram

8051 microprocessor

The 8051 is the original member of the 8051 family. Intel refers to it as MCS-51. Table 1-3 shows the main features of the 8051.

Other members of the 8051 family

There are two other members in the 8051 family of microprocessors. They are the 8052 and the 8031.

Table 1-3. Features of the 8051

Feature	Quantity
ROM	4K bytes
RAM	128 bytes
Timer	2
I/O pins	32
Serial port	1
Interrupt sources	6

Note: ROM amount indicates on-chip program space.

8052 microprocessor

The 8052 is another member of the 8051 family. The 8052 has all the standard features of the 8051 as well as an extra 128 bytes of RAM and an extra timer. In other words, the 8052 has 256 bytes of RAM and three timers. It also has 8K bytes of on-chip program ROM instead of 4K bytes.

As can be seen from Table 1-4, the 8051 is a subset of the 8052; therefore, all programs written for the 8051 will run on the 8052, but the reverse is not true.

Table 1-4. Comparison of 8051 Family Members

Feature	8051	8052	8031
ROM (on-chip program space in bytes)	4K	8K	0K
RAM (bytes)	128	256	128
Timers	2	3	2
I/O pins	32	32	32
Serial port	1	1	1
Interrupt sources	6	8	6

8031 microprocessor

Another member of the 8051 family is the 8031 chip. This chip is often referred to as a ROM-less 8051 since it has 0K bytes of on-chip ROM. To use this chip, you must add external ROM to it. This external ROM must contain the program that the 8031 will fetch and execute. Contrast that to the 8051 in which the on-chip ROM contains the program to be fetched and executed but is limited to only 4K bytes of code. The ROM containing the program attached to the 8031 can be as large as 64K bytes. In the process of adding external ROM to the 8031, you lose two ports. That leaves only two ports (of the four ports) for I/O operations. To solve this problem, you can add external I/O to the 8031. Interfacing the 8031 with memory is discussed in Chapter 14. There are also various speed versions of the 8031 available from different companies.

Various 8051 microprocessors

Although the 8051 is the most popular member of the 8051 family, you will not see "8051" in the part number. This is because the 8051 is available in different memory types, such as UV-EPROM, Flash, and NV-RAM, all of which have different part numbers. A discussion of the various types of ROM will be given in Chapter 14. The UV-EPROM version of the 8051 is the 8751. The flash ROM version is marketed by many companies including Atmel Corp. and Dallas Semiconductor. The Atmel Flash 8051 is called AT89C51, while Dallas Semiconductor calls theirs DS89C4x0 (DS89C430/440/450). The NV-RAM version of the 8051 made by Dallas Semiconductor is called DS5000. There is also an OTP (one-time programmable) version of the 8051 made by various manufacturers. Next, we discuss briefly each of these chips and their applications.

8751 microprocessor

This 8751 chip has only 4K bytes of on-chip UV-EPROM. Using this chip for development requires access to a PROM burner, as well as a UV-EPROM eraser to erase the contents of UV-EPROM inside the 8751 chip before you can program it again. Because the on-chip ROM for the 8751 is UV-EPROM, it takes around 20 minutes to erase the 8751 before it can be programmed again. This has led many manufacturers to introduce flash and NV-RAM versions of the 8051, as we will discuss next. There are also various speed versions of the 8751 available from different companies.

DS89C4x0 from Dallas Semiconductor (Maxim)

Many popular 8051 chips have on-chip ROM in the form of flash memory. The AT89C51 from Atmel Corp. is one example of an 8051 with flash ROM. This is ideal for fast development since flash memory can be erased in seconds compared to the 20 minutes or more needed for the 8751. For this reason, the AT89C51 is used in place of the 8751 to eliminate the waiting time needed to erase the chip and thereby speed up the development time. Using the AT89C51 to develop a microprocessor-based system requires a ROM burner that supports flash memory; however, a ROM eraser is not needed. Notice that in flash memory you must erase the entire contents of ROM in order to program it again. This erasing of flash is done by the PROM burner itself, which is why a separate eraser is not needed. To eliminate the need for a PROM burner, Dallas Semiconductor, now part of the Maxim Corp., has a version of the 8051/52 called DS89C4x0 (DS89C430/...) that can be programmed via the serial COM port of the x86 PC.

Notice that the on-chip ROM for the DS89C4x0 is in the form of flash. The DS89C4x0 (430/440/450) comes with an on-chip loader, which allows the program to be loaded into the on-chip flash ROM while it is in the system. This can be done via the serial COM port of the x86 PC. This in-system program loading of the DS89C4x0 via a PC serial COM port makes it an ideal home development system. Dallas Semiconductor also has an NV-RAM version of the 8051 called DS5000. The advantage of NV-RAM is the ability to change the ROM contents one byte at a time. The DS5000 also comes with a loader, allowing it to be programmed via the PC's COM port. From Table 1-5, notice that the DS89C4x0 is really an 8052 chip since it has 256 bytes of RAM and three timers. More details of this chip are given throughout the book.

DS89C4x0 Trainer

In Chapter 8, we discuss the design of DS89C4x0 Trainer extensively. The MDE8051 Trainer is available from www.MicroDigitalEd.com. This

Table 1-5: Versions of 8051/52 Microprocessor From Dallas Semiconductor (Maxim)

Part No.	ROM	RAM	I/O pins	Timers	Interrupts	V_{cc}
DS89C30	16K (Flash)	256	32	3	6	5 V
DS89C440	32K (Flash)	256	32	3	6	5 V
DS89C450	64K (Flash)	256	32	3	6	5 V
DS5000	8K (NV-RAM)	128	32	2	6	5 V
DS80C320	0K	256	32	3	6	5 V
DS87520	16K (UVROM)	256	32	3	6	5 V

Source: www.maxim-ic.com/products/microprocessors/8051_drop_in.cfm

Table 1-6. Versions of 8051 From Atmel (All ROM Flash)

Part No.	ROM	RAM	I/O Pins	Timer	Interrupt	V_{cc}	Packaging
AT89C51	4K	128	32	2	6	5V	40
AT89LV51	4K	128	32	2	6	3V	40
AT89C1051	1K	64	15	1	3	3V	20
AT89C2051	2K	128	15	2	6	3V	20
AT89C52	8K	128	32	3	8	5V	40
AT89LV52	8K	128	32	3	8	3V	40

Note: "C" in the part number indicates CMOS.

Table 1-7. Various Speeds of 8051 From Atmel

Part No.	Speed	Pins	Packaging	Use
AT89C51-12PC	12 MHz	40	DIP plastic	Commercial
AT89C51-16PC	16 MHz	40	DIP plastic	Commercial
AT89C51-20PC	20 MHz	40	DIP plastic	Commercial

Trainer allows you to program the DS89C4x0 chip from the COM port of the x86 PC, with no need for a ROM burner.

AT89C51 from Atmel Corporation

The Atmel Corp. has a wide selection of 8051 chips, as shown in Tables 1-6 and 1-7. For example, the AT89C51 is a popular and inexpensive chip used in many small projects. It has 4K bytes of flash ROM. Notice the AT89C51-12PC, where "C" before the 51 stands for CMOS, which has a low power consumption, "12" indicates 12 MHz, "P" is for plastic DIP package, and "C" is for commercial.

OTP version of the 8051

There are also OTP (one-time programmable) versions of the 8051 available from different sources. Flash and NV-RAM versions are typically used for product development. When a product is designed and absolutely finalized, the OTP version of the 8051 is used for mass production since it is much cheaper in terms of price per unit.

8051 family from Philips

Another major producer of the 8051 family is Philips Corporation. Indeed, it has one of the largest selections of 8051 microprocessors. Many of its products include features such as A-to-D converters, D-to-A converters, extended I/O, and both OTP and flash.

Table 1-8. The 8051 Chips From Silicon Labs

Part No.	Flash	RAM	Pins	Packaging
C8051F000	32K	256	64	TQFP
C8051F020	64K	4352	100	TQFP
C8051F350	8K	768	32	TQFP

Source: www.SiLabs.com

8051 family from SiLabs

Another major producer of the 8051 family is Silicon Labs Corporation. Indeed, it has become one of the largest producers of 8051 microprocessors. Many of its products include features such as A-to-D converters, D-to-A converters, extended I/O, PWM, I2C, and SPI. See Table 1-8.

REVIEW QUESTIONS

1. Name three features of the 8051.
2. What is the major difference between the 8051 and 8052 microprocessors?
3. Give the size of RAM in each of the following.
   (a) 8051   (b) 8052   (c) 8031
4. Give the size of the on-chip ROM in each of the following.
   (a) 8051   (b) 8052   (c) 8031
5. The 8051 is a(n) _____-bit microprocessor.
6. State a major difference between the 8751, the AT89C51, and the DS89C430.
7. True or false. The DS89C430 is really an 8052 chip.
8. True or false. The DS89C430 has a loader embedded to the chip, eliminating the need for ROM burner.
9. The DS89C430 chip has _____ bytes of on-chip ROM.
10. The DS89C430 chip has _____ bytes of RAM.

SUMMARY

This chapter discussed the role and importance of microprocessors in everyday life. Microprocessors and microprocessors were contrasted and compared. We discussed the use of microprocessors in the embedded market. We also discussed criteria to consider in choosing a microprocessor such as speed, memory, I/O, packaging, and cost per unit. It also provided an overview of the various members of the 8051 family of microprocessors, such as the 8052 and 8031, and their features. In addition, we discussed various versions of the 8051, such as the AT89C51 and DS89C4x0, which are marketed by suppliers other than Intel.

RECOMMENDED WEB LINKS

For a DS89C4x0-based Trainer, see www.MicroDigitalEd.com. For a SiLabs trainer tutorial, see www.MicroDigitalEd.com.

See the following websites for 8051 products and their features from various companies:

- www.8052.com/chips.phtml
- www.MicroDigitalEd.com

PROBLEMS

1.1: MICROPROCESSORS AND EMBEDDED PROCESSORS

1. True or False. A general-purpose microprocessor has on-chip ROM.
2. True or False. A microprocessor has on-chip ROM.
3. True or False. A microprocessor has on-chip I/O ports.
4. True or False. A microprocessor has a fixed amount of RAM on the chip.
5. What components are normally put together with the microprocessor into a single chip?
6. Intel's Pentium chips used in Windows PCs need external _____ and _____ chips to store data and code.
7. List three embedded products attached to a PC.
8. Why would someone want to use an x86 as an embedded processor?
9. Give the name and the manufacturer of some of the most widely used 8-bit microprocessors.
10. In Question 9, which microprocessor has the most manufacture sources?
11. In a battery-based embedded product, what is the most important factor in choosing a microprocessor?
12. In an embedded controller with on-chip ROM, why does the size of the ROM matter?
13. In choosing a microprocessor, how important is it to have multiple sources for that chip?
14. What does the term *third-party support* mean?
15. If a microprocessor architecture has both 8-bit and 16-bit versions, which of the following statements is true?
    (a) The 8-bit software will run on the 16-bit system.
    (b) The 16-bit software will run on the 8-bit system.

1.2: OVERVIEW OF THE 8051 FAMILY

16. The 8751 has _____ bytes of on-chip ROM.
17. The AT89C51 has _____ bytes of on-chip RAM.
18. The 8051 has ___ on-chip timer(s).
19. The 8052 has ____ bytes of on-chip RAM.

20. The ROM-less version of the 8051 uses _____ as the part number.
21. The 8051 family has ____ pins for I/O.
22. The 8051 family has circuitry to support _____ serial ports.
23. The 8751 on-chip ROM is of type _____.
24. The AT89C51 on-chip ROM is of type _____.
25. The DS5000 on-chip ROM is of type _____.
26. The DS89C430 on-chip ROM is of type _____.
27. Give the amount of ROM and RAM for the following chips.
    (a) AT89C51   (b) DS89C430   (c) DS89C440
28. Of the 8051 family, which memory type is the most cost-effective if you are using a million of them in an embedded product?
29. What is the difference between the 8031 and 8051?
30. Of the 8051 microprocessors, which one is the best for a home development environment? (You do not have access to a ROM burner.)

ANSWERS TO REVIEW QUESTIONS

1.1: MICROPROCESSORS AND EMBEDDED PROCESSORS

1. True
2. A microprocessor-based system
3. (d)
4. (d)
5. It is dedicated to doing one type of job.
6. Embedded system means that the application and processor are combined into a single system.
7. Having multiple sources for a given part means you are not hostage to one supplier. More importantly, competition among suppliers brings about lower cost for that product.

1.2: OVERVIEW OF THE 8051 FAMILY

1. 128 bytes of RAM, 4K bytes of on-chip ROM, four 8-bit I/O ports.
2. The 8052 has everything that the 8051 has, plus an extra timer, and the on-chip ROM is 8K bytes instead of 4K bytes. The RAM in the 8052 is 256 bytes instead of 128 bytes.
3. Both the 8051 and the 8031 have 128 bytes of RAM and the 8052 has 256 bytes.
4. (a) 4K bytes   (b) 8K bytes   (c) 0K bytes
5. 8
6. The main difference is the type of on-chip ROM. In the 8751, it is UV-EPROM; in the AT89C51, it is flash; and in the DS89C430, it is flash with a loader on the chip.
7. True
8. True
9. 16K
10. 256

CHAPTER 2

8051 ASSEMBLY LANGUAGE PROGRAMMING

OBJECTIVES

Upon completion of this chapter, you will be able to:

>> List the registers of the 8051 microprocessor.
>> Manipulate data using the registers and MOV instructions.
>> Code simple 8051 Assembly language instructions.
>> Assemble and run an 8051 program.
>> Describe the sequence of events that occur upon 8051 power-up.
>> Examine programs in ROM code of the 8051.
>> Explain the ROM memory map of the 8051.
>> Detail the execution of 8051 Assembly language instructions.
>> Describe 8051 data types.
>> Explain the purpose of the PSW (program status word) register.
>> Discuss RAM memory space allocation in the 8051.
>> Diagram the use of the stack in the 8051.
>> Manipulate the register banks of the 8051.
>> Understand the RISC and CISC architectures.

In Section 2.1, we look at the inside of the 8051. We demonstrate some of the widely used registers of the 8051 with simple instructions such as MOV and ADD. In Section 2.2, we examine Assembly language and machine language programming and define terms such as *mnemonics, opcode, and operand.* The process of assembling and creating a ready-to-run program for the 8051 is discussed in Section 2.3. Step-by-step execution of an 8051 program and the role of the program counter are examined in Section 2.4. In Section 2.5, we look at some widely used Assembly language directives, pseudocode, and data types related to the 8051. In Section 2.6, we discuss the flag bits and how they are affected by arithmetic instructions. Allocation of RAM memory inside the 8051 plus the stack and register banks of the 8051 are discussed in Section 2.7. Section 2.8 examines the concepts of RISC and CISC architectures.

2.1: INSIDE THE 8051

In this section, we examine the major registers of the 8051 and show their use with the simple instructions MOV and ADD.

Registers

D7	D6	D5	D4	D3	D2	D1	D0

In the CPU, registers are used to store information temporarily. That information could be a byte of data to be processed, or an address pointing to the data to be fetched. The vast majority of 8051 registers are 8-bit registers. In the 8051, there is only one data type: 8 bits. The 8 bits of a register are shown in the diagram from the MSB (most significant bit) D7 to the LSB (least significant bit) D0. With an 8-bit data type, any data larger than 8 bits must be broken into 8-bit chunks before it is processed. Since there are a large number of registers in the 8051, we will concentrate on some of the widely used general-purpose registers and cover special registers in future chapters. See Appendix A.2 for a complete list of 8051 registers.

The most widely used registers of the 8051 are A (accumulator), B, R0, R1, R2, R3, R4, R5, R6, R7, DPTR (data pointer), and PC (program counter). All of the above registers are 8 bits, except DPTR and the program counter. See Figure 2-1(a) and (b).

A
B
R0
R1
R2
R3
R4
R5
R6
R7

Figure 2-1(a). Some 8-bit Registers of the 8051

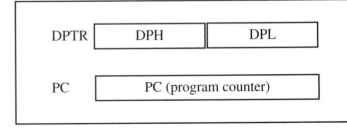

Figure 2-1(b). Some 8051 16-bit Registers

CHAPTER 2: 8051 ASSEMBLY LANGUAGE PROGRAMMING

The accumulator, register A, is used for all arithmetic and logic instructions. To understand the use of these registers, we will show them in the context of two simple instructions, MOV and ADD.

MOV instruction

Simply stated, the MOV instruction copies data from one location to another. It has the following format:

```
MOV destination,source ;copy source to dest.
```

This instruction tells the CPU to move (in reality, copy) the source operand to the destination operand. For example, the instruction "MOV A,R0" copies the contents of register R0 to register A. After this instruction is executed, register A will have the same value as register R0. The MOV instruction does not affect the source operand. The following program first loads register A with value 55H (that is 55 in hex), then moves this value around to various registers inside the CPU. Notice the "#" in the instruction. This signifies that it is a value. The importance of this will be discussed soon.

```
MOV A,#55H      ;load value 55H into reg. A
MOV R0,A        ;copy contents of A into R0
                ;(now A=R0=55H)
MOV R1,A        ;copy contents of A into R1
                ;(now A=R0=R1=55H)
MOV R2,A        ;copy contents of A into R2
                ;now A=R0=R1=R2=55H)
MOV R3,#95H     ;load value 95H into R3
                ;(now R3=95H)
MOV A,R3        ;copy contents of R3 into A
                ;now A=R3=95H)
```

When programming the 8051 microprocessor, the following points should be noted:

1. Values can be loaded directly into any of registers A, B, or R0–R7. However, to indicate that it is an immediate value it must be preceded with a pound sign (#). This is shown next.

```
MOV A,#23H      ;load 23H into A (A=23H)
MOV R0,#12H     ;load 12H into R0 (R0=12H)
MOV R1,#1FH     ;load 1FH into R1 (R1=1FH)
MOV R2,#2BH     ;load 2BH into R2 (R2=2BH)
MOV B,#3CH      ;load 3CH into B (B=3CH)
MOV R7,#9DH     ;load 9DH into R7 (R7=9DH)
MOV R5,#0F9H    ;load F9H into R5 (R5=F9H)
MOV R6,#12      ;load 12 decimal (0CH)
                ;into reg. R6 (R6=0CH)
```

Notice in instruction "MOV R5,#0F9H" a 0 is used between the # and F to indicate that F is a hex number and not a letter. In other words, "MOV R5,#F9H" will cause an error.

2. If values 0 to F are moved into an 8-bit register, the rest of the bits are assumed to be all zeros. For example, in "MOV A,#5" the result will be A = 05: that is, A = 00000101 in binary.

3. Moving a value that is too large into a register will cause an error.

```
MOV A,#7F2H ;ILLEGAL: 7F2H > 8 bits (FFH)
MOV R2,#456 ;ILLEGAL: 456 > 255 decimal (FFH)
```

4. A value to be loaded into a register must be preceded with a pound sign (#). Otherwise it means to load from a memory location. For example, "MOV A,17H" means to move into A the value held in memory location 17H, which could have any value. In order to load the value 17H into the accumulator, we must write "MOV A,#17H" with the # preceding the number. Notice that the absence of the pound sign will not cause an error by the assembler since it is a valid instruction. However, the result would not be what the programmer intended. This is a common error for beginning programmers in the 8051.

ADD instruction

The ADD instruction has the following format:

```
ADD A,source    ;ADD the source operand
                ;to the accumulator
```

The ADD instruction tells the CPU to add the source byte to register A and put the result in register A. To add two numbers such as 25H and 34H, each can be moved to a register and then added together:

```
MOV A,#25H    ;load 25H into A
MOV R2,#34H   ;load 34H into R2
ADD A,R2      ;add R2 to accumulator
              ;(A = A + R2)
```

Executing the program above results in A = 59H (25H + 34H = 59H) and R2 = 34H. Notice that the content of R2 does not change. The program above can be written in many ways, depending on the registers used. Another way might be:

```
MOV R5,#25H    ;load 25H into R5 (R5=25H)
MOV R7,#34H    ;load 34H into R7  (R7=34H)
MOV A,#0       ;load 0 into A (A=0,clear A)
ADD A,R5       ;add to A content of R5
               ;where A = A + R5
ADD A,R7       ;add to A content of R7
               ;where A = A + R7
```

The program above results in A = 59H. There are always many ways to write the same program. One question that might come to mind after looking at the program is whether it is necessary to move both data items into registers before adding them together. The answer is no, it is not necessary. Look at the following variation of the same program:

```
MOV A,#25H ;load one operand into A (A=25H)
ADD A,#34H ;add the second operand 34H to A
```

In the above case, while one register contained one value, the second value followed the instruction as an operand. This is called an *immediate* operand. The examples shown so far for the ADD instruction indicate that the source operand can be either a register or immediate data, but the destination must always be register A, the accumulator. In other words, an instruction such as "ADD R2,#12H" is invalid since register A (accumulator) must be involved in any arithmetic operation. Notice that "ADD R4,A" is also invalid for the reason that A must be the destination of any arithmetic operation. To put it simply: In the 8051, register A must be involved and be the destination for all arithmetic operations. The foregoing discussion explains why register A is referred to as the accumulator. The format for Assembly language instructions, descriptions of their use, and a listing of legal operand types are provided in Appendix A.1.

There are two 16-bit registers in the 8051: program counter and data pointer. The importance and use of the program counter are covered in Section 2.3. The DPTR register is used in accessing data and is discussed in Chapter 5 where addressing modes are covered.

REVIEW QUESTIONS

1. Write the instructions to move value 34H into register A and value 3FH into register B, then add them together.
2. Write the instructions to add the values 16H and CDH. Place the result in register R2.
3. True or false. No value can be moved directly into registers R0–R7.
4. What is the largest hex value that can be moved into an 8-bit register? What is the decimal equivalent of the hex value?
5. The vast majority of registers in 8051 are _____ bits.

2.2: INTRODUCTION TO 8051 ASSEMBLY PROGRAMMING

In this section, we discuss Assembly language format and define some widely used terminology associated with Assembly language programming.

While the CPU can work only in binary, it can do so at a very high speed. For humans, however, it is quite tedious and slow to deal with 0s and 1s in order to program the computer. A program that consists of 0s and 1s is called *machine language*. In the early days of the computer, programmers coded programs in machine language. Although the hexadecimal system was used as a more efficient way to represent binary numbers, the process of working in machine code was still cumbersome for humans. Eventually, Assembly languages were developed that provided mnemonics for the machine code instructions, plus other features that made programming faster and less prone to error. The term *mnemonic* is frequently used in computer science and engineering literature to refer to codes and abbreviations that are relatively easy to remember. Assembly language programs must be translated into machine code by a program called an *assembler*. Assembly language is referred to as a *low-level language* because it deals directly with the internal structure of the CPU. To program in Assembly language, the programmer must know all the registers of the CPU and the size of each, as well as other details.

Today, one can use many different programming languages, such as BASIC, Pascal, C, C++, Java, and numerous others. These languages are called *high-level languages* because the programmer does not have to be concerned with the internal details of the CPU. Whereas an *assembler* is used to translate an Assembly language program into machine code (sometimes also called *object code* or opcode for operation code), high-level languages are translated into machine code by a program called a *compiler*. For instance, to write a program in C, one must use a C compiler to translate the program into machine language. Now we look at 8051 Assembly language format and use an 8051 assembler to create a ready-to-run program.

Structure of Assembly language

An Assembly language program consists of, among other things, a series of lines of Assembly language instructions. An Assembly language instruction consists of a mnemonic, optionally followed by one or two operands. The operands are the data items being manipulated, and the mnemonics are the commands to the CPU, telling it what to do with those items.

A given Assembly language program (see Program 2-1) is a series of statements, or lines, which are either Assembly language instructions such as

```
        ORG  0H          ;start (origin) at location 0
        MOV  R5,#25H     ;load 25H into R5
        MOV  R7,#34H     ;load 34H into R7
        MOV  A,#0        ;load 0 into A
        ADD  A,R5        ;add contents of R5 to A
                         ;now A = A + R5
        ADD  A,R7        ;add contents of R7 to A
                         ;now A = A + R7
        ADD  A,#12H      ;add to A value 12H
                         ;now A = A + 12H
HERE:SJMP HERE           ;stay in this loop
        END              ;end of asm source file
```

Program 2-1. Sample of an Assembly Language Program

ADD and MOV, or statements called directives. While instructions tell the CPU what to do, directives (also called pseudo-instructions) give directions to the assembler. For example, in the above program while the MOV and ADD instructions are commands to the CPU, ORG and END are directives to the assembler. ORG tells the assembler to place the opcode at memory location 0, while END indicates to the assembler the end of the source code. In other words, one is for the start of the program and the other one for the end of the program.

An Assembly language instruction consists of four fields:

```
[label:]    mnemonic    [operands]    [;comment]
```

Brackets indicate that a field is optional, and not all lines have them. Brackets should not be typed in. Regarding the above format, the following points should be noted.

1. The label field allows the program to refer to a line of code by name. The label field cannot exceed a certain number of characters. Check your assembler for the rule.

2. The Assembly language mnemonic (instruction) and operand(s) fields together perform the real work of the program and accomplish the tasks for which the program was written. In Assembly language statements such as

```
ADD A,B
MOV A,#67
```

ADD and MOV are the mnemonics, which produce opcodes; and "A, B" and "A, #67" are the operands. Instead of a mnemonic and an operand, these two fields could contain assembler pseudo-instructions, or directives. Remember that directives do not generate any machine code (opcode) and are used only by the assembler, as opposed to instructions that are translated into machine code (opcode) for the CPU to execute. In Program 2-1, the commands ORG (origin) and END are examples of directives (some 8051 assemblers use .ORG and .END). Check your assembler for the rules. More of these pseudo-instructions are discussed in detail in Section 2.5.

3. The comment field begins with a semicolon comment indicator ";". Comments may be at the end of a line or on a line by themselves. The assembler ignores comments, but they are indispensable to programmers. Although comments are optional, it is recommended that they be used to describe the program and make it easier for someone else to read and understand, or for the programmer to remember what they wrote.

4. Notice the label "HERE" in the label field in Program 2-1. Any label referring to an instruction must be followed by a colon, ":". In the SJMP (short jump instruction), the 8051 is told to stay in this loop indefinitely. If your system has a monitor program you do not need this line and it should be deleted from your program. In the next section, we will see how to create a ready-to-run program.

REVIEW QUESTIONS

1. What is the purpose of pseudo-instructions?
2. _____ are translated by the assembler into machine code, whereas _____ are not.
3. True or false. Assembly language is a high-level language.
4. Which of the following produces opcode?
   (a) ADD A,R2   (b) MOV A,#12   (c) ORG 2000H   (d) SJMP HERE
5. Pseudo-instructions are also called _____.
6. True or false. Assembler directives are not used by the CPU itself. They are simply a guide to the assembler.
7. In Question 4, which one is an assembler directive?

2.3: ASSEMBLING AND RUNNING AN 8051 PROGRAM

Now that the basic form of an Assembly language program has been given, the next question is this: How it is created, assembled, and made ready to run? The steps to create an executable Assembly language program are outlined as follows. See Figure 2-2.

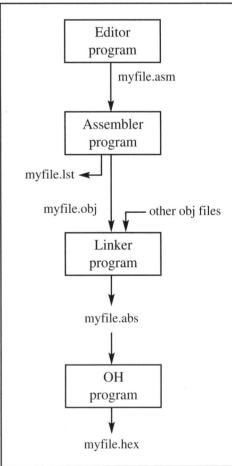

1. First we use an editor to type in a program similar to Program 2-1. Many excellent editors or word processors are available that can be used to create and/or edit the program. A widely used editor is the MS-DOS EDIT program (or Notepad in Windows), which comes with all Microsoft operating systems. Notice that the editor must be able to produce an ASCII file. For many assemblers, the file names follow the usual DOS conventions, but the source file has the extension "asm" or "src", depending on which assembler you are using. Check your assembler for the convention. The "asm" extension for the source file is used by an assembler in the next step.

2. The "asm" source file containing the program code created in step 1 is fed to an 8051 assembler. The assembler converts the instructions into machine code. The assembler will produce an object file and a list file. The extension for the object file is "obj" while the extension for the list file is "lst".

Figure 2-2. Steps to Create a Program

```
1  0000                    ORG 0H              ;start (origin) at 0
2  0000 7D25               MOV R5,#25H         ;load 25H into R5
3  0002 7F34               MOV R7,#34H         ;load 34H into R7
4  0004 7400               MOV A,#0            ;load 0 into A
5  0006 2D                 ADD A,R5            ;add contents of R5 to A
                                               ;now A = A + R5
6  0007 2F                 ADD A,R7            ;add contents of R7 to A
                                               ;now A = A + R7
7  0008 2412               ADD A,#12H          ;add to A value 12H
                                               ;now A = A + 12H
8  000A 80FE HERE:         SJMP HERE           ;stay in this loop
9  000C                    END                 ;end of asm source file
```

Program 2-2. List File for Program 2-1

3. Assemblers require a third step called *linking*. The link program takes one or more object files and produces an absolute object file with the extension "abs". This abs file is used by 8051 trainers that have a monitor program.

4. Next, the "abs" file is fed into a program called "OH" (object to hex converter), which creates a file with extension "hex" that is ready to burn into ROM. This program comes with all 8051 assemblers. Recent Windows-based assemblers combine steps 2 through 4 into one step.

More about "asm" and "obj" files

The "asm" file is also called the *source* file and for this reason some assemblers require that this file have the "src" extension. Check your 8051 assembler to see which extension it requires. As mentioned earlier, this file is created with an editor such as DOS EDIT or Windows Notepad. The 8051 assembler converts the asm file's Assembly language instructions into machine language and provides the obj (object) file. In addition to creating the object file, the assembler also produces the lst file (list file).

lst file

The lst (list) file, which is optional, is very useful to the programmer because it lists all the opcodes and addresses, as well as errors that the assembler detected. See Program 2-2. Many assemblers assume that the list file is not wanted unless you indicate that you want to produce it. This file can be accessed by an editor such as DOS EDIT and displayed on the monitor or sent to the printer to produce a hard copy. The programmer uses the list file to find syntax errors. It is only after fixing all the errors indicated in the lst file that the obj file is ready to be input to the linker program.

REVIEW QUESTIONS

1. True or false. The DOS program EDIT produces an ASCII file.
2. True or false. Generally, the extension of the source file is "asm" or "src".
3. Which of the following files can be produced by the DOS EDIT program?
   (a) myprog.asm (b) myprog.obj (c) myprog.exe (d) myprog.lst
4. Which of the following files is produced by an 8051 assembler?
   (a) myprog.asm (b) myprog.obj (c) myprog.hex (d) myprog.lst
5. Which of the following files lists syntax errors?
   (a) myprog.asm (b) myprog.obj (c) myprog.hex (d) myprog.lst

2.4: THE PROGRAM COUNTER AND ROM SPACE IN THE 8051

In this section, we examine the role of the program counter (PC) register in executing an 8051 program. We also discuss ROM memory space for various 8051 family members.

Program counter in the 8051

Another important register in the 8051 is the program counter. The program counter points to the address of the next instruction to be executed. As the CPU fetches the opcode from the program ROM, the program counter is incremented to point to the next instruction. The program counter in the 8051 is 16-bits wide. This means that the 8051 can access program addresses 0000 to FFFFH, a total of 64K bytes of code. However, not all members of the 8051 have the entire 64K bytes of on-chip ROM installed, as we will see soon. Where does the 8051 wake up when it is powered? We will discuss this important topic next.

Where the 8051 wakes up when it is powered up

One question that we must ask about any microprocessor (or microprocessor) is, At what address does the CPU wake up upon applying power to it? Each microprocessor is different. In the case of the 8051 family (i.e., all members regardless of the maker and variation), the microprocessor wakes up at memory address 0000 when it is powered up. By powering up, we mean applying V_{cc} to the RESET pin, as discussed in Chapter 4. In other words, when the 8051 is powered up, the program counter has the value of 0000 in it. This means that it expects the first opcode to be stored at ROM address 0000H. For this reason, in the 8051 system, the first opcode must be burned into memory location 0000H of program ROM since this is where it looks for the first instruction when it is booted. We achieve this by the ORG statement in the source program as shown earlier. Next, we discuss the step-by-step action of the program counter in fetching and executing a sample program.

Placing code in program ROM

To get a better understanding of the role of the program counter in fetching and executing a program, we examine the action of the program counter as each instruction is fetched and executed. For example, consider the list file of Program 2-2 and how the code is placed in the ROM of an 8051 chip. As we can see, the opcode and operand for each instruction are listed on the left side of the list file.

After the program is burned into ROM of an 8051 family member, such as 8751 or AT8951 or DS5000, the opcode and operand are placed in ROM memory locations starting at 0000 as shown in the table below.

ROM Address	Machine Language	Assembly Language
0000	7D25	MOV R5,#25H
0002	7F34	MOV R7,#34H
0004	7400	MOV A,#0
0006	2D	ADD A,R5
0007	2F	ADD A,R7
0008	2412	ADD A,#12H
000A	80FE	HERE: SJMP HERE

The table shows that address 0000 contains 7D, which is the opcode for moving a value into register R5, and address 0001 contains the operand (in this case 25H) to be moved to R5. Therefore, the instruction "MOV R5,#25H" has a machine code of "7D25", where 7D is the opcode and 25 is the operand. Similarly, the machine code "7F34" is located in memory locations 0002 and 0003 and represents the opcode and the operand for the instruction "MOV R7,#34H". In the same way, machine code "7400" is located in memory locations 0004 and 0005 and represents the opcode and the operand for the instruction "MOV A,#0". The memory location 0006 has the opcode of 2D, which is the opcode for the instruction "ADD A,R5" and memory location 0007 has the content 2F, which is the opcode for the "ADD A,R7" instruction. The opcode for the instruction "ADD A,#12H" is located at address 0008 and the operand 12H at address 0009. The memory location 000A has the opcode for the SJMP instruction and its target address is located in location 000B. The reason the target address is FE is explained in the next chapter. Table 2-1 shows the ROM contents.

Table 2-1: ROM Contents

Address	Code
000	7D
001	25
002	7F
003	34
004	74
005	00
006	2D
007	2F
008	24
009	12
00A	80
00B	FE

Executing a program byte by byte

Assuming that the above program is burned into the ROM of an 8051 chip (8751, AT8951, or DS5000), the following is a step-by-step description of the action of the 8051 upon applying power to it.

1. When the 8051 is powered up, the program counter has 0000 and starts to fetch the first opcode from location 0000 of the program ROM. In the case of the above program the first opcode is 7D, which is the code for moving an operand to R5. Upon executing the opcode, the CPU fetches the value 25 and places it in R5. Now one instruction is finished. Then the program counter is incremented to point to 0002 (PC = 0002), which contains opcode 7F, the opcode for the instruction "MOV R7,...".

2. Upon executing the opcode 7F, the value 34H is moved into R7. Then the program counter is incremented to 0004.

3. ROM location 0004 has the opcode for the instruction "MOV A,#0". This instruction is executed and now PC = 0006. Notice that all the above instructions are 2-byte instructions; that is, each one takes two memory locations.

4. Now PC = 0006 points to the next instruction, which is "ADD A,R5". This is a 1-byte instruction. After the execution of this instruction, PC = 0007.

5. The location 0007 has the opcode 2F, which belongs to the instruction "ADD A,R7". This also is a 1-byte instruction. Upon execution of this instruction, PC is incremented to 0008. This process goes on until all the instructions are fetched and executed. The fact that the program counter points at the next instruction to be executed explains why some microprocessors (notably the x86) call the program counter the *instruction pointer*.

ROM memory map in the 8051 family

As we saw in the last chapter, some family members have only 4K bytes of on-chip ROM (e.g., 8751, AT8951) and some, such as the AT89C52, have 8K bytes of ROM. Dallas Semiconductor's DS5000-32 has 32K bytes of on-chip ROM. Dallas Semiconductor also has an 8051 with 64K bytes of on-chip ROM. See Figure 2-3. The point to remember is that no member of the 8051 family can access more than 64K bytes of opcode since the program counter in the 8051 is a 16-bit register (0000 to FFFF address range). It must be noted that while the first location of program ROM inside the

---

Example 2-1

Find the ROM memory address of each of the following 8051 chips:
(a) AT89C51 with 4KB (b) DS89C420 with 16KB (c) DS5000-32 with 32KB.

Solution:

(a) With 4K bytes of on-chip ROM memory space, we have 4096 bytes (4 × 1024 = 4096). This maps to address locations of 0000 to 0FFFH. Notice that 0 is always the first location. (b) With 16K bytes of on-chip ROM memory space, we have 16,384 bytes (16 × 1024 = 16,384), which gives 0000–3FFFH. (c) With 32K bytes we have 32,768 bytes (32 × 1024 = 32,768). Converting 32,768 to hex, we get 8000H; therefore, the memory space is 0000 to 7FFFH.

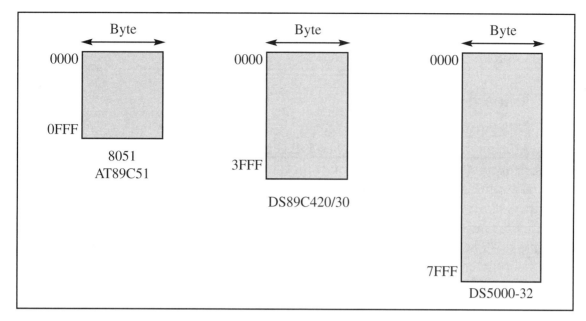

Figure 2-3. 8051 On-Chip ROM Address Range

8051 has the address of 0000, the last location can be different depending on the size of the ROM on the chip. Among the 8051 family members, the 8751 and AT8951 have 4K bytes of on-chip ROM. This 4K bytes of ROM memory has memory addresses of 0000 to 0FFFH. Therefore, the first location of on-chip ROM of this 8051 has an address of 0000 and the last location has the address of 0FFFH. Look at Example 2-1 to see how this is computed.

REVIEW QUESTIONS

1. In the 8051, the program counter is _____ bits wide.
2. True or false. Every member of the 8051 family, regardless of the maker, wakes up at memory 0000H when it is powered up.
3. At what ROM location do we store the first opcode of an 8051 program?
4. The instruction "MOV A,#44H" is a ____-byte instruction.
5. What is the ROM address space for the 8052 chip?

2.5: 8051 DATA TYPES AND DIRECTIVES

In this section, we look at some widely used data types and directives supported by the 8051 assembler.

8051 data type and directives

The 8051 microprocessor has only one data type. It is 8 bits, and the size of each register is also 8 bits. It is the job of the programmer to break down data larger than 8 bits (00 to FFH, or 0 to 255 in decimal) to be processed by the CPU. For examples of how to process data larger than 8 bits, see Chapter 6. The data types used by the 8051 can be positive or negative. A discussion of signed numbers is given in Chapter 6.

DB (define byte)

The DB directive is the most widely used data directive in the assembler. It is used to define the 8-bit data. When DB is used to define data, the numbers can be in decimal, binary, hex, or ASCII formats. For decimal, the "D" after the decimal number is optional, but using "B" (binary) and "H" (hexadecimal) for the others is required. Regardless of which is used, the assembler will convert the numbers into hex. To indicate ASCII, simply place the characters in quotation marks ("like this"). The assembler will assign the ASCII code for the numbers or characters automatically. The DB directive is the only directive that can be used to define ASCII strings larger than two characters; therefore, it should be used for all ASCII data definitions. Following are some DB examples:

```
        ORG   500H
DATA1:  DB    28                      ;DECIMAL(1C in hex)
DATA2:  DB    00110101B               ;BINARY (35 in hex)
DATA3:  DB    39H                     ;HEX
        ORG   510H
DATA4:  DB    "2591"                  ;ASCII NUMBERS
        ORG   518H
DATA6:  DB    "My name is Joe"        ;ASCII CHARACTERS
```

Either single or double quotes can be used around ASCII strings. This can be useful for strings, which contain a single quote such as "O'Leary". DB is also used to allocate memory in byte-sized chunks.

Assembler directives

The following are some more widely used directives of the 8051.

ORG (origin)

The ORG directive is used to indicate the beginning of the address. The number that comes after ORG can be either in hex or in decimal. If the number is not followed by H, it is decimal and the assembler will convert it to hex. Some assemblers use ".ORG" (notice the dot) instead of "ORG" for the origin directive. Check your assembler.

EQU (equate)

This is used to define a constant without occupying a memory location. The EQU directive does not set aside storage for a data item but associates a constant value with a data label so that when the label appears in the program, its constant value will be substituted for the label. The following uses EQU for the counter constant and then the constant is used to load the R3 register.

```
COUNT      EQU   25
...        ....
MOV        R3,#COUNT
```

When executing the instruction "MOV R3,#COUNT", the register R3 will be loaded with the value 25 (notice the # sign). What is the advantage of using EQU? Assume that there is a constant (a fixed value) used in many different places in the program, and the programmer wants to change its value throughout. By the use of EQU, the programmer can change it once and the assembler will change all of its occurrences, rather than search the entire program trying to find every occurrence.

END directive

Another important pseudocode is the END directive. This indicates to the assembler the end of the source (asm) file. The END directive is the last line of an 8051 program, meaning that in the source code anything after the END directive is ignored by the assembler. Some assemblers use ".END" (notice the dot) instead of "END".

Rules for labels in Assembly language

By choosing label names that are meaningful, a programmer can make a program much easier to read and maintain. There are several rules that names must follow. First, each label name must be unique. The names used for labels in Assembly language programming consist of alphabetic letters in both uppercase and lowercase, the digits 0 through 9, and the special characters question mark (?), period (.), at (@), underline (_), and dollar sign ($). The first character of the label must be an alphabetic character. In other words it cannot be a number. Every assembler has some reserved words that must not be used as labels in the program. Foremost among the reserved words are the mnemonics for the instructions. For example, MOV and ADD are reserved since they are instruction mnemonics. In addition to the mnemonics there are some other reserved words. Check your assembler for the list of reserved words.

REVIEW QUESTIONS

1. The _____ directive is always used for ASCII strings.
2. How many bytes are used by the following?
   DATA_1: DB "AMERICA"
3. What is the advantage in using the EQU directive to define a constant value?
4. How many bytes are set aside by each of the following directives?
   (a) ASC_DATA: DB "1234" (b) MY_DATA: DB "ABC1234"
5. State the contents of memory locations 200H–205H for the following:
   ```
            ORG   200H
   MYDATA:   DB    "ABC123"
   ```

2.6: 8051 FLAG BITS AND THE PSW REGISTER

Like any other microprocessor, the 8051 has a flag register to indicate arithmetic conditions such as the carry bit. The flag register in the 8051 is called the *program status word* (PSW) register. In this section, we discuss various bits of this register and provide some examples of how it is altered.

PSW (program status word) register

The PSW register is an 8-bit register. It is also referred to as the *flag register*. Although the PSW register is 8 bits wide, only 6 bits of it are used by the 8051. The two unused bits are user-definable flags. Four of the flags are called *conditional flags*, meaning that they indicate some conditions that result after an instruction is executed. These four are CY (carry), AC (auxiliary carry), P (parity), and OV (overflow).

As seen from Figure 2-4, the bits PSW.3 and PSW.4 are designated as RS0 and RS1, respectively, and are used to change the bank registers. They are explained in the next section. The PSW.5 and PSW.1 bits are general-purpose status flag bits and can be used by the programmer for any purpose. In other words, they are user definable.

The following is a brief explanation of four of the flag bits of the PSW register. The impact of instructions on these registers is then discussed.

CY	AC	F0	RS1	RS0	OV	--	P

CY	PSW.7	Carry flag
AC	PSW.6	Auxiliary carry flag
F0	PSW.5	Available to the user for general purpose
RS1	PSW.4	Register bank selector bit 1
RS0	PSW.3	Register bank selector bit 0
OV	PSW.2	Overflow flag
--	PSW.1	User-definable bit
P	PSW.0	Parity flag. Set/cleared by hardware each instruction cycle to indicate an odd/even number of 1 bits in the accumulator.

RS1	RS0	Register Bank	Address
0	0	0	00H–07H
0	1	1	08H–0FH
1	0	2	10H–17H
1	1	3	18H–1FH

Figure 2-4. Bits of the PSW Register

Table 2-2. Instructions That Affect Flag Bits

Instruction	CY	OV	AC
ADD	X	X	X
ADDC	X	X	X
SUBB	X	X	X
MUL	0	X	
DIV	0	X	
DA	X		
RRC	X		
RLC	X		
SETB C	1		
CLR C	0		
CPL C	X		
ANL C, bit	X		
ANL C, /bit	X		
ORL C, bit	X		
ORL C, /bit	X		
MOV C, bit	X		
CJNE	X		

Note: X can be 0 or 1.

CY, the carry flag

This flag is set whenever there is a carry out from the D7 bit. This flag bit is affected after an 8-bit addition or subtraction. It can also be set to 1 or 0 directly by an instruction such as "SETB C" or "CLR C", where "SETB C" stands for "set bit carry" and "CLR C" for "clear carry". More about these and other bit-addressable instructions will be given in Chapter 8.

AC, the auxiliary carry flag

If there is a carry from D3 to D4 during an ADD or SUB operation, this bit is set; otherwise, it is cleared. This flag is used by instructions that perform BCD (binary coded decimal) arithmetic. See Chapter 6 for more information.

P, the parity flag

The parity flag reflects the number of 1s in the A (accumulator) register only. If the A register contains an odd number of 1s, then P = 1. Therefore, P = 0 if A has an even number of 1s.

OV, the overflow flag

This flag is set whenever the result of a signed number operation is too large, causing the high-order bit to overflow into the sign bit. In general, the carry flag is used to detect errors in unsigned arithmetic operations. The overflow flag is only used to detect errors in signed arithmetic operations and is discussed in detail in Chapter 6. Table 2-2 lists the instructions that affect flag bits.

ADD instruction and PSW

Next, we examine the impact of the ADD instruction on the flag bits CY, AC, and P of the PSW register. Some examples should clarify their status. Although the flag bits affected by the ADD instruction are CY (carry flag), P (parity flag), AC (auxiliary carry flag), and OV (overflow flag), we will focus on flags CY, AC, and P for now. A discussion of the overflow flag is given in Chapter 6, since it relates only to signed number arithmetic. How the various flag bits are used in programming is discussed in future chapters in the context of many applications.

See Examples 2-2 through 2-4 for the impact on selected flag bits as a result of the ADD instruction.

Example 2-2

Show the status of the CY, AC, and P flags after the addition of 38H and 2FH in the following instructions.

```
MOV A,#38H
ADD A,#2FH        ;after the addition A=67H, CY=0
```

Solution:

```
      38          00111000
    + 2F          00101111
      67          01100111
```

CY = 0 since there is no carry beyond the D7 bit.

AC = 1 since there is a carry from the D3 to the D4 bit.

P = 1 since the accumulator has an odd number of 1s (it has five 1s).

Example 2-3

Show the status of the CY, AC, and P flags after the addition of 9CH and 64H in the following instructions.

```
MOV A,#9CH
ADD A,#64H        ;after addition A=00 and CY=1
```

Solution:

```
      9C          10011100
    + 64          01100100
     100          00000000
```

CY = 1 since there is a carry beyond the D7 bit.

AC = 1 since there is a carry from the D3 to the D4 bit.

P = 0 since the accumulator has an even number of 1s (it has zero 1s).

Example 2-4

Show the status of the CY, AC, and P flags after the addition of 88H and 93H in the following instructions.

```
MOV A,#88H
ADD A,#93H        ;after the addition A=1BH,CY=1
```

Solution:

```
      88          10001000
    + 93          10010011
     11B          00011011
```

CY = 1 since there is a carry beyond the D7 bit.

AC = 0 since there is no carry from the D3 to the D4 bit.

P = 0 since the accumulator has an even number of 1s (it has four 1s).

REVIEW QUESTIONS

1. The flag register in the 8051 is called _____.
2. What is the size of the flag register in the 8051?
3. Which bits of the PSW register are user-definable?
4. Find the CY and AC flag bits for the following code.
   ```
   MOV   A,#0FFH
   ADD   A,#01
   ```
5. Find the CY and AC flag bits for the following code.
   ```
   MOV   A,#0C2H
   ADD   A,#3DH
   ```

2.7: 8051 REGISTER BANKS AND STACK

The 8051 microprocessor has a total of 128 bytes of RAM. In this section, we discuss the allocation of these 128 bytes of RAM and examine their usage as registers and stack.

RAM memory space allocation in the 8051

There are 128 bytes of RAM in the 8051 (some members, notably the 8052, have 256 bytes of RAM). The 128 bytes of RAM inside the 8051 are assigned addresses 00 to 7FH. As we will see in Chapter 5, they can be accessed directly as memory locations. These 128 bytes are divided into three different groups as follows.

1. A total of 32 bytes from locations 00 to 1F hex are set aside for register banks and the stack.
2. A total of 16 bytes from locations 20H to 2FH are set aside for bit-addressable read/write memory. A detailed discussion of bit-addressable memory and instructions is given in Chapter 8.
3. A total of 80 bytes from locations 30H to 7FH are used for read and write storage, or what is normally called a *scratch pad*. These 80 locations of RAM are widely used for the purpose of storing data and parameters by 8051 programmers. We will use them in future chapters to store data brought into the CPU via I/O ports. See Figure 2-5.

Register banks in the 8051

As mentioned earlier, a total of 32 bytes of RAM are set aside for the register banks and stack. These 32 bytes are divided into four banks of registers in which each bank has eight registers, R0–R7. RAM locations from 0 to 7 are set aside for bank 0 of R0–R7 where R0 is RAM location 0, R1 is RAM location 1, R2 is location 2, and so on, until memory location 7, which belongs to R7 of bank 0. The second bank of registers R0–R7 starts at RAM location 08 and goes to location 0FH. The third bank of R0–R7 starts at memory location 10H and goes to location 17H. Finally, RAM locations 18H to 1FH are set aside for the fourth bank of R0–R7. Figure 2-6 shows how the 32 bytes are allocated into four banks:

As we can see from Figure 2-6, bank 1 uses the same RAM space as the stack. This is a major problem in programming the 8051. We must either not use register bank 1 or allocate another area of RAM for the stack. This will be discussed below.

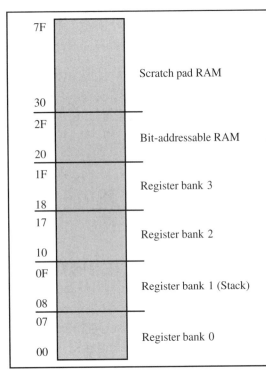

Figure 2-5. RAM Allocation in the 8051

Default register bank

If RAM locations 00–1F are set aside for the four register banks, which register bank of R0–R7 do we have access to when the 8051 is powered up? The answer is register bank 0; that is, RAM locations 0, 1, 2, 3, 4, 5, 6, and 7 are accessed with the names R0, R1, R2, R3, R4, R5, R6, and R7 when programming the 8051. It is much easier to refer to these RAM locations with names R0, R1, and so on, than by their memory locations. Examples 2-5 and 2-6 clarify this concept.

How to switch register banks

As stated above, register bank 0 is the default when the 8051 is powered up. We can switch to other banks by use of the PSW register. Bits D4 and D3 of the PSW are used to select the desired register bank, as shown in Table 2-3.

Bank 0		Bank 1		Bank 2		Bank 3	
7	R7	F	R7	17	R7	1F	R7
6	R6	E	R6	16	R6	1E	R6
5	R5	D	R5	15	R5	1D	R5
4	R4	C	R4	14	R4	1C	R4
3	R3	B	R3	13	R3	1B	R3
2	R2	A	R2	12	R2	1A	R2
1	R1	9	R1	11	R1	19	R1
0	R0	8	R0	10	R0	18	R0

Figure 2-6. 8051 Register Banks and Their RAM Addresses

CHAPTER 2: 8051 ASSEMBLY LANGUAGE PROGRAMMIN

Example 2-5

State the contents of the RAM locations after the following program:

```
MOV R0,#99H    ;load R0 with value 99H
MOV R1,#85H    ;load R1 with value 85H
MOV R2,#3FH    ;load R2 with value 3FH
MOV R7,#63H    ;load R7 with value 63H
MOV R5,#12H    ;load R5 with value 12H
```

Solution:

After the execution of the above program, we have the following:
RAM location 0 has value 99H   RAM location 1 has value 85H
RAM location 2 has value 3FH   RAM location 7 has value 63H
RAM location 5 has value 12H

Example 2-6

Repeat Example 2-5 using RAM addresses instead of register names.

Solution:

This is called direct addressing mode and uses the RAM address location for the destination address. See Chapter 5 for a more detailed discussion of addressing modes.

```
MOV 00,#99H    ;load R0 with value 99H
MOV 01,#85H    ;load R1 with value 85H
MOV 02,#3FH    ;load R2 with value 3FH
MOV 07,#63H    ;load R7 with value 63H
MOV 05,#12H    ;load R5 with value 12H
```

Table 2-3. PSW Bits Bank Selection

	RS1 (PSW.4)	RS0 (PSW.3)
Bank 0	0	0
Bank 1	0	1
Bank 2	1	0
Bank 3	1	1

The D3 and D4 bits of register PSW are often referred to as PSW.4 and PSW.3 since they can be accessed by the bit-addressable instructions SETB and CLR. For example, "SETB PSW.3" will make PSW.3 = 1 and select bank register 1. See Example 2-7.

Stack in the 8051

The stack is a section of RAM used by the CPU to store information temporarily. This information could be data or an address. The CPU needs this storage area since there are only a limited number of registers.

How stacks are accessed in the 8051

If the stack is a section of RAM, there must be registers inside the CPU to point to it. The register used to access the stack is called the SP (stack pointer) register. The stack pointer in the 8051 is only 8 bits wide, which means that it

---

Example 2-7

State the contents of the RAM locations after the following program:

```
        SETB PSW.4      ;select bank 2
        MOV R0,#99H     ;load R0 with value 99H
        MOV R1,#85H     ;load R1 with value 85H
        MOV R2,#3FH     ;load R2 with value 3FH
        MOV R7,#63H     ;load R7 with value 63H
        MOV R5,#12H     ;load R5 with value 12H
```

Solution:

By default, PSW.3=0 and PSW.4=0; therefore, the instruction "SETB PSW.4" sets RS1=1 and RS0=0, thereby selecting register bank 2. Register bank 2 uses RAM locations 10H–17H. After the execution of the above program, we have the following:

RAM location 10H has value 99H   RAM location 11H has value 85H
RAM location 12H has value 3FH   RAM location 17H has value 63H
RAM location 15H has value 12H

---

can take values of 00 to FFH. When the 8051 is powered up, the SP register contains value 07. This means that RAM location 08 is the first location used for the stack by the 8051. The storing of a CPU register in the stack is called a PUSH, and pulling the contents off the stack back into a CPU register is called a POP. In other words, a register is pushed onto the stack to save it and popped off the stack to retrieve it. The job of the SP is very critical when push and pop actions are performed. To see how the stack works, let's look at the PUSH and POP instructions.

Pushing onto the stack

In the 8051, the stack pointer points to the last used location of the stack. As we push data onto the stack, the stack pointer is incremented by one. Notice that this is different from many microprocessors, notably x86 processors in which the SP is decremented when data is pushed onto the stack. Examining Example 2-8, we see that as each PUSH is executed, the contents of the register are saved on the stack and SP is incremented by 1. Notice that for every byte of data saved on the stack, SP is incremented only once. Notice also that to push the registers onto the stack we must use their RAM addresses. For example, the instruction "PUSH 1" pushes register R1 onto the stack.

Popping from the stack

Popping the contents of the stack back into a given register is the opposite process of pushing. With every pop, the top byte of the stack is copied to the register specified by the instruction and the stack pointer is decremented once. Example 2-9 demonstrates the POP instruction.

Example 2-8

Show the stack and stack pointer for the following. Assume the default stack area and register 0 is selected.

```
MOV   R6,#25H
MOV   R1,#12H
MOV   R4,#0F3H
PUSH  6
PUSH  1
PUSH  4
```

Solution:

		After PUSH 6		After PUSH 1		After PUSH 4	
0B		0B		0B		0B	
0A		0A		0A		0A	F3
09		09		09	12	09	12
08		08	25	08	25	08	25
Start SP = 07		SP = 08		SP = 09		SP = 0A	

Example 2-9

Examining the stack, show the contents of the registers and SP after execution of the following instructions. All values are in hex.

```
POP   3      ;POP stack into R3
POP   5      ;POP stack into R5
POP   2      ;POP stack into R2
```

Solution:

		After POP 3		After POP 5		After POP 2	
0B	54	0B		0B		0B	
0A	F9	0A	F9	0A		0A	
09	76	09	76	09	76	09	
08	6C	08	6C	08	6C	08	6C
Start SP = 0B		SP = 0A		SP = 09		SP = 08	

The upper limit of the stack

As mentioned earlier, locations 08 to 1F in the 8051 RAM can be used for the stack. This is because locations 20–2FH of RAM are reserved for bit-addressable memory and must not be used by the stack. If in a given program we need more than 24 bytes (08 to 1FH = 24 bytes) of stack, we can change the SP to point to RAM locations 30–7FH. This is done with the instruction "MOV SP,#xx".

CALL instruction and the stack

In addition to using the stack to save registers, the CPU also uses the stack to save the address of the instruction just below the CALL instruction. This is how the CPU knows where to resume when it returns from the called subroutine. More information on this will be given in Chapter 3 when we discuss the CALL instruction.

Stack and bank 1 conflict

Recall from our earlier discussion that the stack pointer register points to the current RAM location available for the stack. As data is pushed onto the stack, SP is incremented. Conversely, it is decremented as data is popped off the stack into the registers. The reason that the SP is incremented after the push is to make sure that the stack is growing toward RAM location 7FH, from lower addresses to upper addresses. If the stack pointer were decremented after push instructions, we would be using RAM locations 7, 6, 5, and so on, which belong to R7 to R0 of bank 0, the default register bank. This incrementing of the stack pointer for push instructions also ensures that the stack will not reach location 0 at the bottom of RAM, and consequently run out of space for the stack. However, there is a problem with the default setting of the stack. Since SP = 07 when the 8051 is powered up, the first location of the stack is RAM location 08, which also belongs to register R0 of register bank 1. In other words, register bank 1 and the stack are using the same memory space. If in a given program we need to use register banks 1 and 2, we can reallocate another section of RAM to the stack. For example, we can allocate RAM locations 60H and higher to the stack, as shown in Example 2-10.

Viewing registers and memory with a simulator

Many assemblers and C compilers come with a simulator. Simulators allow us to view the contents of registers and memory after executing each instruction (single-stepping). We strongly recommend that you use a simulator to single-step some of the programs in this chapter and future chapters. Single-stepping a program with a simulator gives us a deeper understanding

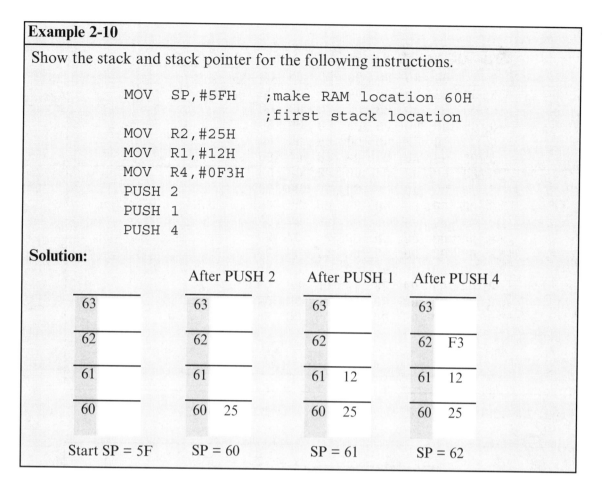

Example 2-10

Show the stack and stack pointer for the following instructions.

```
        MOV   SP,#5FH    ;make RAM location 60H
                         ;first stack location
        MOV   R2,#25H
        MOV   R1,#12H
        MOV   R4,#0F3H
        PUSH  2
        PUSH  1
        PUSH  4
```

Solution:

		After PUSH 2		After PUSH 1		After PUSH 4	
63		63		63		63	
62		62		62		62	F3
61		61		61	12	61	12
60		60	25	60	25	60	25
Start SP = 5F		SP = 60		SP = 61		SP = 62	

of microprocessor architecture, in addition to the fact that we can use it to find errors in our programs. Figures 2-7 through 2-10 show screenshots for 8051 simulators from ProView 32 and Keil. See www.MicroDigitalEd.com for tutorials on how to use the simulators.

Figure 2-7. Register's Screen from ProView 32 Simulator

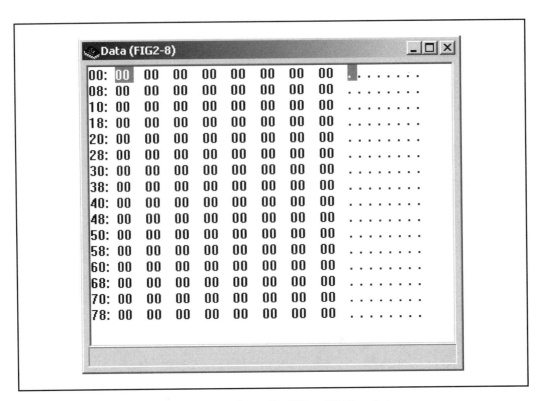

Figure 2-8. 128-Byte Memory Space from ProView 32 Simulator

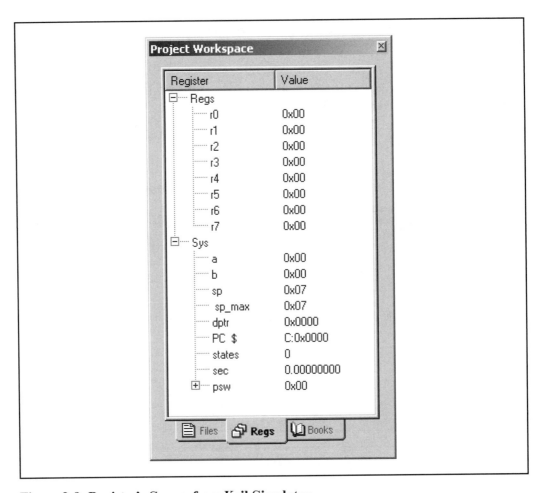

Figure 2-9. Register's Screen from Keil Simulator

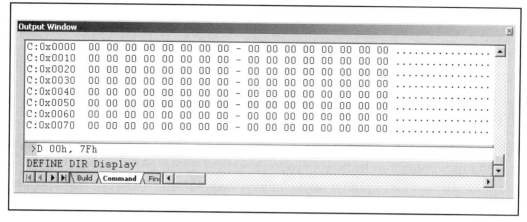

Figure 2-10. 128-Byte Memory Space from Keil Simulator

Ways to increase the CPU power

There are three ways available to microprocessor designers to increase the processing power of the CPU:

1. Increase the clock frequency of the chip. One drawback of this method is that the higher is the frequency, the more is the power and heat dissipation. Power and heat dissipation is especially a problem for handheld devices.

2. Use Harvard architecture by increasing the number of buses to bring more information (code and data) into the CPU to be processed. While in the case of x86 and other general-purpose microprocessors this architecture is very expensive and unrealistic, in today's single-chip computers (microprocessors) this is not a problem.

3. Change the internal architecture of the CPU and use what is called RISC architecture.

REVIEW QUESTIONS

1. What is the size of the SP register?
2. With each PUSH instruction, the stack pointer register, SP, is _____ (incremented, decremented) by 1.
3. With each POP instruction, the SP is _____ (incremented, decremented) by 1.
4. On power-up, the 8051 uses RAM location _____ as the first location of the stack.
5. On power-up, the 8051 uses bank ____ for registers R0–R7.
6. On power-up, the 8051 uses RAM locations _____ to _____ for registers R0–R7 (register bank 0).
7. Which register bank is used if we alter RS0 and RS1 of the PSW by the following two instructions?
   ```
   SETB PSW.3
   SETB PSW.4
   ```
8. In Question 7, what RAM locations are used for registers R0–R7?

2.8: RISC ARCHITECTURE

In this section, we will examine the merits of the RISC architecture. You can skip this and come back to it after you have studied chapters 3 through 6.

What is RISC

In the early 1980s, a controversy broke out in the computer design community, but unlike most controversies, it did not go away. Since the 1960s, in all mainframes and minicomputers, designers put as many instructions as they could think of into the CPU. Some of these instructions performed complex tasks. An example is adding data memory locations and storing the sum into memory. Naturally, microprocessor designers followed the lead of minicomputer and mainframe designers. Because these microprocessors used such a large number of instructions and many of them performed highly complex activities, they came to be known as CISC (complex instruction set computer). According to several studies in the 1970s, many of these complex instructions etched into the brain of the CPU were never used by programmers and compilers. The huge cost of implementing a large number of instructions (some of them complex) into the microprocessor, plus the fact that a good portion of the transistors on the chip are used by the instruction decoder, made some designers think of simplifying and reducing the number of instructions. As this concept developed, the resulting processors came to be known as RISC (reduced instruction set computer).

Features of RISC

The following are some of the features of RISC.

Feature 1

RISC processors have a fixed instruction size. In a CISC microprocessor such as the 8051, instructions can be 1, 2, or even 3 bytes. For example, look at the following instructions in the 8051:

```
CLR A                 ;Clear Accumulator, a 1-byte
                      instruction
ADD A, #mybyte        ;Add mybyte to Accumulator, a
                      2-byte instruction
LJMP target_address   ;Long Jump, a 3-byte instruc-
                      tion
```

This variable instruction size makes the task of the instruction decoder very difficult because the size of the incoming instruction is never known. In a RISC architecture, the size of all instructions is fixed. Therefore, the CPU can decode the instructions quickly. This is like a bricklayer working with bricks of the same size as opposed to using bricks of variable sizes. Of course, it is much more efficient to use bricks of the same size.

Feature 2

One of the major characteristics of RISC architecture is a large number of registers. All RISC architectures have at least 16 registers. Of these 16 registers, only a few are assigned to a dedicated function. One advantage of a large number of registers is that it avoids the need for a large stack to store parameters. Although a stack can be implemented on a RISC processor, it is not as essential as in CISC because so many registers are available.

Feature 3

RISC processors have a small instruction set. RISC processors have only the basic instructions such as ADD, SUB, MUL, LOAD, STORE, AND, OR, EXOR, CALL, and JUMP. The limited number of instructions is one of the criticisms leveled at the RISC processor because it makes the job of Assembly language programmers much more tedious and difficult compared to CISC Assembly language programming. This is one reason that RISC is used more commonly in high-level language environments such as the C programming language rather than Assembly language environments. It is interesting to note that some defenders of CISC have called it "complete instruction set computer" instead of "complex instruction set computer" because it has a complete set of every kind of instruction. How many of these instructions are used and how often is another matter. The limited number of instructions in RISC leads to programs that are large. Although these programs can use more memory, this is not a problem because memory is cheap. Before the advent of semiconductor memory in the 1960s, however, CISC designers had to pack as much action as possible into a single instruction to get the maximum bang for their buck.

Feature 4

At this point, one might ask, with all the difficulties associated with RISC programming, what is the gain? The most important characteristic of the RISC processor is that more than 95% of instructions are executed with only one clock cycle, in contrast to CISC instructions. Even some of the 5% of the RISC instructions that are executed with two clock cycles can be executed with one clock cycle by juggling instructions around (code scheduling). Code scheduling is most often the job of the compiler.

Feature 5

Because CISC has such a large number of instructions, each with so many different addressing modes, microinstructions (microcode) are used to implement them. The implementation of microinstructions inside the CPU takes more than 40–60% of transistors in many CISC processors. In the case of RISC, however, due to the small set of instructions, they are implemented using the hardwire method. Hardwiring of RISC instructions takes no more than 10% of the transistors.

RISC uses load/store architecture. In CISC microprocessors, data can be manipulated while it is still in memory. For example, in instructions such as "ADD Reg, Memory", the microprocessor must bring the contents of the external memory location into the CPU, add it to the contents of the register, then move the result back to the external memory location. The problem is there might be a delay in accessing the data from external memory. Then the whole process would be stalled, preventing other instructions from proceeding in the pipeline. In RISC, designers did away with these kinds of instructions. In RISC, instructions can only load from external memory into registers or store registers into external memory locations. There is no direct way of doing arithmetic and logic operations between a register and the contents of external memory locations. All these instructions must be performed by first bringing both operands into the registers inside the CPU, then performing the arithmetic or logic operation, and then sending the result back to memory. This idea was first implemented by the Cray 1 supercomputer in 1976 and is commonly referred to as load/store architecture.

In concluding this discussion of RISC processors, it is interesting to note that RISC technology was explored by the scientists in IBM in the mid-1970s, but it was David Patterson of the University of California at Berkeley who in 1980 brought the merits of RISC concepts to the attention of computer scientists. It must also be noted that in recent years, CISC processors such as the Pentium have used some of the RISC features in their design. This was the only way they could enhance the processing power of the x86 processors and stay competitive. Of course, they had to use lots of gates to do the job, because they had to deal with all the CISC instructions of the 8086/286/386/486 processors and the legacy software of DOS.

REVIEW QUESTIONS

1. What do RISC and CISC stand for?
2. True or false. Instructions such as "ADD memory, memory" do not exist in RISC CPU.
3. True or false. While CISC instructions are of variable sizes, RISC instructions are all the same size.
4. Which of the following operations do not exist for the ADD instruction in RISC?
   (a) register to register (b) immediate to register (c) memory to memory

SUMMARY

This chapter began with an exploration of the major registers of the 8051, including A, B, R0, R1, R2, R3, R4, R5, R6, R7, DPTR, and PC. The use of these registers was demonstrated in the context of programming examples. The process of creating an Assembly language program was described from writing the source file, to assembling it, linking, and executing the program. The PC (program counter) register always points to the next instruction to be executed. The way the 8051 uses program ROM space was explored because 8051 Assembly language programmers must be aware of where programs are placed in ROM, and how much memory is available.

An Assembly language program is composed of a series of statements that are either instructions or pseudo-instructions, also called *directives*. Instructions are translated by the assembler into machine code. Pseudo-instructions are not translated into machine code: They direct the assembler in how to translate instructions into machine code. Some pseudo-instructions, called *data directives*, are used to define data. Data is allocated in byte-size increments. The data can be in binary, hex, decimal, or ASCII formats.

Flags are useful to programmers since they indicate certain conditions, such as carry or overflow, that result from execution of instructions. The stack is used to store data temporarily during execution of a program. The stack resides in the RAM space of the 8051, which was diagrammed and explained. Manipulation of the stack via POP and PUSH instructions was also explored. We also examined the concepts of RISC and CISC architectures.

PROBLEMS

2.1: INSIDE THE 8051

1. Most registers in the 8051 are _____ bits wide.
2. Registers R0–R7 are all _____ bits wide
3. Registers ACC and B are _____ bits wide.
4. Name a 16-bit register in the 8051.
5. To load R4 with the value 65H, the pound sign is _____ (necessary, optional) in the instruction "MOV R4,#65H".
6. What is the result of the following code and where is it kept?
   ```
   MOV   A,#15H
   MOV   R2,#13H
   ADD   A,R2
   ```
7. Which of the following is (are) illegal?
   (a) MOV R3,#500   (b) MOV R1,#50   (c) MOV R7,#00
   (d) MOV A,#255H   (e) MOV A,#50H   (f) MOV A,#F5H
   (g) MOV R9,#50H
8. Which of the following is (are) illegal?
   (a) ADD R3,#50H   (b) ADD A,#50H   (c) ADD R7,R4
   (d) ADD A,#255H   (e) ADD A,R5   (f) ADD A,#F5H
   (g) ADD R3,A
9. What is the result of the following code and where is it kept?
   ```
   MOV   R4,#25H
   MOV   A,#1FH
   ADD   A,R4
   ```
10. What is the result of the following code and where is it kept?
   ```
   MOV   A,#15
   MOV   R5,#15
   ADD   A,R5
   ```

2.2: INTRODUCTION TO 8051 ASSEMBLY PROGRAMMING AND
2.3: ASSEMBLING AND RUNNING AN 8051 PROGRAM

11. Assembly language is a_____ (low, high) -level language while C is a _____ (low, high) -level language.
12. Of C and Assembly language, which is more efficient in terms of code generation (i.e., the amount of ROM space it uses)?
13. Which program produces the "obj" file?
14. True or false. The source file has the extension "src" or "asm".
15. Which file provides the listing of error messages?
16. True or false. The source code file can be a non-ASCII file.
17. True or false. Every source file must have ORG and END directives.
18. Do the ORG and END directives produce opcodes?
19. Why are the ORG and END directives also called pseudocode?
20. True or false. The ORG and END directives appear in the ".lst" file.

2.4: THE PROGRAM COUNTER AND ROM SPACE IN THE 8051

21. Every 8051 family member wakes up at address _____ when it is powered up.
22. A programmer puts the first opcode at address 100H. What happens when the microprocessor is powered up?
23. Find the number of bytes each of the following instruction can take.
    (a) MOV A,#55H   (b) MOV R3,#3   (c) INC R2
    (d) ADD A,#0   (e) MOV A,R1   (f) MOV R3,A
    (g) ADD A,R2
24. Pick up a program listing of your choice, and show the ROM memory addresses and their contents.
25. Find the address of the last location of on-chip ROM for each of the following.
    (a) DS5000-16   (b) DS5000-8   (c) DS5000-32
    (d) AT89C52   (e) 8751   (f) AT89C51
    (g) DS5000-64
26. Show the lowest and highest values (in hex) that the 8051 program counter can take.
27. A given 8051 has 7FFFH as the address of its last location of on-chip ROM. What is the size of on-chip ROM for this 8051?
28. Repeat Question 27 for 3FFH.

2.5: 8051 DATA TYPES AND DIRECTIVES

29. Compile and state the contents of each ROM location for the following data.

```
          ORG   200H
MYDAT_1:  DB    "Earth"
MYDAT_2:  DB    "987-65"
MYDAT_3:  DB    "GABEH 98"
```

30. Compile and state the contents of each ROM location for the following data.

```
            ORG   340H
DAT_1:      DB    22,56H,10011001B,32,0F6H,11111011B
```

2.6: 8051 FLAG BITS AND THE PSW REGISTER

31. The PSW is a(n) _____ -bit register.
32. Which bits of PSW are used for the CY and AC flag bits, respectively?
33. Which bits of PSW are used for the OV and P flag bits, respectively?
34. In the ADD instruction, when is CY raised?
35. In the ADD instruction, when is AC raised?
36. What is the value of the CY flag after the following code?

```
    CLR   C             ;CY = 0
    CPL   C             ;complement carry
```

37. Find the CY flag value after each of the following codes.

```
    (a) MOV A,#54H      (b) MOV A,#00      (c) MOV A,#250
        ADD A,#0C4H         ADD A,#0FFH        ADD A,#05
```

38. Write a simple program in which the value 55H is added 5 times.

2.7: 8051 REGISTER BANKS AND STACK

39. Which bits of the PSW are responsible for selection of the register banks?
40. On power-up, what is the location of the first stack?
41. In the 8051, which register bank conflicts with the stack?
42. In the 8051, what is the size of the stack pointer (SP) register?
43. On power-up, which of the register banks is used?
44. Give the address locations of RAM assigned to various banks.
45. Assuming the use of bank 0, find at what RAM location each of the following lines stored the data.

```
    (a) MOV R4,#32H     (b) MOV R0,#12H
    (c) MOV R7,#3FH     (d) MOV R5,#55H
```

46. Repeat Problem 45 for bank 2.
47. After power-up, show how to select bank 2 with a single instruction.
48. Show the stack and stack pointer for each line of the following program.

```
        ORG   0
    MOV   R0,#66H
    MOV   R3,#7FH
    MOV   R7,#5DH
    PUSH  0
    PUSH  3
    PUSH  7
    CLR   A
    MOV   R3,A
    MOV   R7,A
    POP   3
    POP   7
    POP   0
```

49. In Problem 48, does the sequence of POP instructions restore the original values of registers R0, R3, and R7? If not, show the correct sequence of instructions.

50. Show the stack and stack pointer for each line of the following program.

```
        ORG   0
   MOV  SP,#70H
   MOV  R5,#66H
   MOV  R2,#7FH
   MOV  R7,#5DH
   PUSH 5
   PUSH 2
   PUSH 7
   CLR  A
   MOV  R2,A
   MOV  R7,A
   POP  7
   POP  2
   POP  5
```

2.8: RISC ARCHITECTURE

51. What do RISC and CISC stand for?
52. In _____ (RISC, CISC) architecture, we can have 1-, 2-, 3-, or 4-byte instructions.
53. In _____ (RISC, CISC) architecture, instructions are fixed in size.
54. In _____ (RISC, CISC) architecture, instructions are mostly executed in one or two cycles.
55. In _____ (RISC, CISC) architecture, we can have an instruction to ADD a register to external memory.

ANSWERS TO REVIEW QUESTIONS

2.1: INSIDE THE 8051

1. MOV A,#34H
    MOV B,#3FH
    ADD A,B
2. MOV A,#16H
    ADD A,#0CDH
    MOV R2,A
3. False
4. FF hex and 255 in decimal
5. 8

2.2: INTRODUCTION TO 8051 ASSEMBLY PROGRAMMING

1. The real work is performed by instructions such as MOV and ADD. Pseudo-instructions, also called assembler directives, instruct the assembler in doing its job.
2. The instruction mnemonics, pseudo-instructions
3. False

4. All except (c)
5. Assembler directives
6. True
7. (c)

2.3: ASSEMBLING AND RUNNING AN 8051 PROGRAM

1. True
2. True
3. (a)
4. (b) and (d)
5. (d)

2.4: THE PROGRAM COUNTER AND ROM SPACE IN THE 8051

1. 16
2. True
3. 0000H
4. 2
5. With 8K bytes, we have 8192 (8 × 1024 = 8192) bytes, and the ROM space is 0000 to 1FFFH.

2.5: 8051 DATA TYPES AND DIRECTIVES

1. DB
2. 7
3. If the value is to be changed later, it can be done once in one place instead of at every occurrence.
4. (a) 4 bytes   (b) 7 bytes
5. This places the ASCII values for each character in memory locations starting at 200H. Notice that all values are in hex.

   200 = (41)
   201 = (42)
   202 = (43)
   203 = (31)
   204 = (32)
   205 = (33)

2.6: 8051 FLAG BITS AND THE PSW REGISTER

1. PSW (program status register)
2. 8 bits
3. D1 and D5, which are referred to as PSW.1 and PSW.5, respectively.
4.

```
    Hex           binary
     FF         1111 1111
 +    1       +          1
    100         10000 0000
```

This leads to CY=1 and AC=1.

5.

```
   Hex        binary
   C2         1100 0010
+  3D       + 0011 1101
   FF         1111 1111
```

This leads to CY = 0 and AC = 0.

2.7: 8051 REGISTER BANKS AND STACK

1. 8-bit
2. Incremented
3. Decremented
4. 08
5. 0
6. 0, 7
7. Register bank 3
8. RAM locations 18H to 1FH

2.8: RISC ARCHITECTURE

1. CISC stands for complex instruction set computer; RISC is reduced instruction set computer.
2. True
3. True
4. (c)

CHAPTER 3

JUMP, LOOP, AND CALL INSTRUCTIONS

OBJECTIVES

Upon completion of this chapter, you will be able to:

>> Code 8051 Assembly language instructions using loops.
>> Code 8051 Assembly language conditional jump instructions.
>> Explain conditions that determine each conditional jump instruction.
>> Code long jump instructions for unconditional jumps.
>> Code short jump instructions for unconditional short jumps.
>> Calculate target addresses for jump instructions.
>> Code 8051 subroutines.
>> Describe precautions in using the stack in subroutines.
>> Discuss crystal frequency versus machine cycle.
>> Code 8051 programs to generate a time delay.

In the sequence of instructions to be executed, it is often necessary to transfer program control to a different location. There are many instructions in the 8051 to achieve this. This chapter covers the control transfer instructions available in 8051 Assembly language. In the first section, we discuss instructions used for looping, as well as instructions for conditional and unconditional jumps. In the second section, we examine CALL instructions and their uses. In the third section, time delay subroutines are described for both the traditional 8051 and its newer generation.

3.1: LOOP AND JUMP INSTRUCTIONS

In this section, we first discuss how to perform a looping action in the 8051 and then talk about jump instructions, both conditional and unconditional.

Looping in the 8051

Repeating a sequence of instructions a certain number of times is called a *loop*. The loop is one of the most widely used actions that any microprocessor performs. In the 8051, the loop action is performed by the instruction "DJNZ reg, label". In this instruction, the register is decremented; if it is not zero, it jumps to the target address referred to by the label. Prior to the start of the loop, the register is loaded with the counter for the number of repetitions. Notice that in this instruction both the register decrement and the decision to jump are combined into a single instruction.

In the program in Example 3-1, the R2 register is used as a counter. The counter is first set to 10. In each iteration the instruction DJNZ decrements R2 and checks its value. If R2 is not zero, it jumps to the target address associated with the label "AGAIN". This looping action continues until R2 becomes zero. After R2 becomes zero, it falls through the loop and executes the instruction immediately below it, in this case the "MOV R5, A" instruction.

Notice in the DJNZ instruction that the registers can be any of R0–R7. The counter can also be a RAM location, as we will see in Chapter 5.

Example 3-1

Write a program to
(a) clear accumulator, then
(b) add 3 to the accumulator 10 times.

Solution:

```
;This program adds value 3 to the ACC ten times

        MOV   A,#0        ;A=0, clear ACC
        MOV   R2,#10      ;load counter R2=10
AGAIN:  ADD   A,#03       ;add 03 to ACC
        DJNZ  R2,AGAIN    ;repeat until R2=0(10 times)
        MOV   R5,A        ;save A in R5
```

Example 3-2

What is the maximum number of times that the loop in Example 3-1 can be repeated?

Solution:

Since R2 holds the count and R2 is an 8-bit register, it can hold a maximum of FFH (255 decimal); therefore, the loop can be repeated a maximum of 256 times.

Loop inside a loop

As shown in Example 3-2, the maximum count is 256. What happens if we want to repeat an action more times than 256? To do that, we use a loop inside a loop, which is called a *nested loop*. In a nested loop, we use two registers to hold the count. See Example 3-3.

Other conditional jumps

Conditional jumps for the 8051 are summarized in Table 3-1. More details of each instruction are provided in Appendix A. In Table 3-1, notice that some of the instructions, such as JZ (jump if A = zero) and JC (jump if carry), jump only if a certain condition is met. Next, we examine some conditional jump instructions with examples.

Example 3-3

Write a program to (a) load the accumulator with the value 55H, and (b) complement the ACC 700 times.

Solution:

Since 700 is larger than 255 (the maximum capacity of any register), we use two registers to hold the count. The following code shows how to use R2 and R3 for the count.

```
        MOV   A,#55H     ;A=55H
        MOV   R3,#10     ;R3=10, the outer loop count
NEXT:   MOV   R2,#70     ;R2=70, the inner loop count
AGAIN:  CPL   A          ;complement A register
        DJNZ  R2,AGAIN   ;repeat it 70 times (inner loop)
        DJNZ  R3,NEXT
```

In this program, R2 is used to keep the inner loop count. In the instruction "DJNZ R2,AGAIN", whenever R2 becomes 0 it falls through and "DJNZ R3,NEXT" is executed. This instruction forces the CPU to load R2 with the count 70 and the inner loop starts again. This process will continue until R3 becomes zero and the outer loop is finished.

CHAPTER 3: JUMP, LOOP, AND CALL INSTRUCTIONS

Table 3-1. 8051 Conditional Jump Instructions

Instruction	Action
JZ	Jump if A = 0
JNZ	Jump if A ≠ 0
DJNZ	Decrement and jump if register ≠ 0
CJNE A, data	Jump if A ≠ data
CJNE reg, #data	Jump if byte ≠ #data
JC	Jump if CY = 1
JNC	Jump if CY = 0
JB	Jump if bit = 1
JNB	Jump if bit = 0
JBC	Jump if bit = 1 and clear bit

JZ (jump if A = 0)

In this instruction the content of register A is checked. If it is zero, it jumps to the target address. For example, look at the following code.

```
        MOV   A,R0          ;A=R0
        JZ    OVER          ;jump if A = 0
        MOV   A,R1          ;A=R1
        JZ    OVER          ;jump if A = 0
        . . .
OVER:
```

In this program, if either R0 or R1 is zero, it jumps to the label OVER. Notice that the JZ instruction can be used only for register A. It can only check to see whether the accumulator is zero, and it does not apply to any other register. More importantly, you don't have to perform an arithmetic instruction such as decrement to use the JNZ instruction. See Example 3-4.

JNC (jump if no carry, jumps if CY = 0)

In this instruction, the carry flag bit in the flag (PSW) register is used to make the decision whether to jump. In executing "JNC label", the processor looks at the carry flag to see if it is raised (CY = 1). If it is not, the CPU starts

---

Example 3-4

Write a program to determine if R5 contains the value 0. If so, put 55H in it.

Solution:

```
        MOV   A,R5          ;copy R5 to A
        JNZ   NEXT          ;jump if A is not zero
        MOV   R5,#55H
NEXT:         . . .
```

Example 3-5

Find the sum of the values 79H, F5H, and E2H. Put the sum in registers R0 (low byte) and R5 (high byte).

Solution:

```
        MOV   A,#0        ;clear A(A=0)
        MOV   R5,A        ;clear R5
        ADD   A,#79H      ;A=0+79H=79H
        JNC   N_1         ;if no carry, add next number
        INC   R5          ;if CY=1, increment R5
N_1:    ADD   A,#0F5H     ;A=79+F5=6E and CY=1
        JNC   N_2         ;jump if CY=0
        INC   R5          ;If CY=1 then increment R5(R5=1)
N_2:    ADD   A,#0E2H     ;A=6E+E2=50 and CY=1
        JNC   OVER        ;jump if CY=0
        INC   R5          ;if CY=1, increment 5
OVER:   MOV   R0,A        ;Now R0=50H, and R5=02
```

to fetch and execute instructions from the address of the label. If CY = 1, it will not jump but will execute the next instruction below JNC. See Example 3-5.

Note that there is also a "JC label" instruction. In the JC instruction, if CY = 1 it jumps to the target address. We will give more examples of these instructions in the context of applications in future chapters.

There are also JB (jump if bit is high) and JNB (jump if bit is low) instructions. These are discussed in Chapters 4 and 8 when bit manipulation instructions are discussed.

All conditional jumps are short jumps

It must be noted that all conditional jumps are short jumps, meaning that the address of the target must be within −128 to +127 bytes of the contents of the program counter (PC). This very important concept is discussed at the end of this section.

Unconditional jump instructions

The unconditional jump is a jump in which control is transferred unconditionally to the target location. In the 8051 there are two unconditional jumps: LJMP (long jump) and SJMP (short jump). Each is discussed below.

LJMP (long jump)

LJMP is an unconditional long jump. It is a 3-byte instruction in which the first byte is the opcode and the second and third bytes represent the 16-bit address of the target location. The 2-byte target address allows a jump to any memory location from 0000 to FFFFH.

Remember that although the program counter in the 8051 is 16-bit, thereby giving a ROM address space of 64K bytes, not all 8051 family members have that much on-chip program ROM. The original 8051 had only 4K bytes of on-chip ROM for program space; consequently, every byte was precious. For this reason there is also an SJMP (short jump) instruction, which is a 2-byte instruction as opposed to the 3-byte LJMP instruction. This can save some bytes of memory in many applications where memory space is in short supply.

SJMP (short jump)

In this 2-byte instruction, the first byte is the opcode and the second byte is the relative address of the target location. The relative address range of 00–FFH is divided into forward and backward jumps: that is, within –128 to +127 bytes of memory relative to the address of the current PC (program counter). If the jump is forward, the target address can be within a space of 127 bytes from the current PC. If the target address is backward, it can be within –128 bytes from the current PC. This is explained in detail next.

Calculating the short jump address

In addition to the SJMP instruction, all conditional jumps such as JNC, JZ, and DJNZ are also short jumps due to the fact that they are all 2-byte instructions. In these instructions, the first byte is the opcode and the second byte is the relative address. The target address is relative to the value of the program counter. To calculate the target address, the second byte is added to the PC of the instruction immediately below the jump. To understand this, look at Example 3-6.

Jump backward target address calculation

While in the case of a forward jump, the displacement value is a positive number between 0 to 127 (00 to 7F in hex), for the backward jump the displacement is a negative value of 0 to –128, as explained in Example 3-7.

It must be emphasized that regardless of whether the SJMP is a forward or backward jump, for any short jump the target address can never be more than –128 to +127 bytes from the address associated with the instruction below the SJMP. If any attempt is made to violate this rule, the assembler will generate an error stating the jump is out of range.

REVIEW QUESTIONS

1. The mnemonic DJNZ stands for _____.
2. True or false. "DJNZ R5, BACK" combines a decrement and a jump in a single instruction.
3. "JNC HERE" is a ___-byte instruction.
4. In "JZ NEXT", which register's content is checked to see if it is zero?
5. LJMP is a ___-byte instruction.

Example 3-6

Using the following list file, verify the jump forward address calculation.

```
Line  PC        Opcode              Mnemonic Operand
01    0000                          ORG   0000
02    0000      7800                MOV   R0,#0
03    0002      7455                MOV   A,#55H
04    0004      6003                JZ    NEXT
05    0006      08                  INC   R0
06    0007      04        AGAIN:    INC   A
07    0008      04                  INC   A
08    0009      2477      NEXT:     ADD   A,#77h
09    000B      5005                JNC   OVER
10    000D      E4                  CLR   A
11    000E      F8                  MOV   R0,A
12    000F      F9                  MOV   R1,A
13    0010      FA                  MOV   R2,A
14    0011      FB                  MOV   R3,A
15    0012      2B        OVER:     ADD   A,R3
16    0013      50F2                JNC   AGAIN
17    0015      80FE      HERE:     SJMP  HERE
18    0017                          END
```

Solution:

First notice that the JZ and JNC instructions both jump forward. The target address for a forward jump is calculated by adding the PC of the following instruction to the second byte of the short jump instruction, which is called the relative address. In line 4, the instruction "JZ NEXT" has opcode of 60 and operand of 03 at the addresses of 0004 and 0005. The 03 is the relative address, relative to the address of the next instruction INC R0, which is 0006. By adding 0006 to 3, the target address of the label NEXT, which is 0009, is generated. In the same way for line 9, the "JNC OVER" instruction has opcode and operand of 50 and 05 where 50 is the opcode and 05 the relative address. Therefore, 05 is added to 000D, the address of instruction "CLR A", giving 12H, the address of label OVER.

Example 3-7

Verify the calculation of backward jumps in Example 3-6.

Solution:

In that program list, "JNC AGAIN" has opcode 50 and relative address F2H. When the relative address of F2H is added to 15H, the address of the instruction below the jump, we have 15H + F2H = 07 (the carry is dropped). Notice that 07 is the address of label AGAIN. Look also at "SJMP HERE", which has 80 and FE for the opcode and relative address, respectively. The PC of the following instruction 0017H is added to FEH, the relative address, to get 0015H, address of the HERE label (17H + FEH = 15H). Notice that FEH is -2 and 17H + (-2) = 15H. For further discussion of the addition of negative numbers, see Chapter 6.

3.2: CALL INSTRUCTIONS

Another control transfer instruction is the CALL instruction, which is used to call a subroutine. Subroutines are often used to perform tasks that need to be performed frequently. This makes a program more structured in addition to saving memory space. In the 8051 there are two instructions for call: LCALL (long call) and ACALL (absolute call). Deciding which one to use depends on the target address. Each instruction is explained next.

LCALL (long call)

In this 3-byte instruction, the first byte is the opcode and the second and third bytes are used for the address of the target subroutine. Therefore, LCALL can be used to call subroutines located anywhere within the 64K-byte address space of the 8051. To make sure that after execution of the called subroutine the 8051 knows where to come back to, the processor automatically saves on the stack the address of the instruction immediately below the LCALL. When a subroutine is called, control is transferred to that subroutine, and the processor saves the program counter on the stack and begins to fetch instructions from the new location. After finishing execution of the subroutine, the instruction RET (return) transfers control back to the caller. Every subroutine needs RET as the last instruction. See Example 3-8.

The following points should be noted for the program in Example 3-8.

1. Notice the DELAY subroutine. Upon executing the first "LCALL DELAY", the address of the instruction right below it, "MOV A, #0AAH", is pushed onto the stack, and the 8051 starts to execute instructions at address 300H.

Example 3-8

Write a program to toggle all the bits of port 1 by sending to it the values 55H and AAH continuously. Put a time delay in between each issuing of data to port 1. This program will be used to test the ports of the 8051 in the next chapter.

Solution:

```
        ORG     0
BACK:   MOV     A,#55H      ;load A with 55H
        MOV     P1,A        ;send 55H to port 1
        LCALL   DELAY       ;time delay
        MOV     A,#0AAH     ;load A with AA (in hex)
        MOV     P1,A        ;send AAH to port 1
        LCALL   DELAY
        SJMP    BACK        ;keep doing this indefinitely
;------ this is the delay subroutine
        ORG     300H        ;put time delay at address 300H
DELAY:  MOV     R5,#0FFH    ;R5 = 255(FF in hex),the counter
AGAIN:  DJNZ    R5,AGAIN    ;stay here until R5 becomes 0
        RET                 ;return to caller (when R5 = 0)
        END                 ;end of asm file
```

---

2. In the DELAY subroutine, first the counter R5 is set to 255 (R5 = FFH); therefore, the loop is repeated 256 times. When R5 becomes 0, control falls to the RET instruction, which pops the address from the stack into the program counter and resumes executing the instructions after the CALL.

The amount of time delay in Example 3-8 depends on the frequency of the 8051. How to calculate the exact time will be explained in detail in Chapter 4. However, you can increase the time delay by using a nested loop as shown below.

```
DELAY:                        ;nested loop delay
        MOV   R4,#255         ;R4 = 255(FF in hex)
NEXT:   MOV   R5,#255         ;R5 = 255(FF in hex)
AGAIN:  DJNZ  R5,AGAIN        ;stay here until R5 becomes 0
        DJNZ  R4,NEXT         ;decrement R4
                              ;keep loading R5 until R4 = 0
        RET                   ;return (when R4 = 0)
```

CALL instruction and the role of the stack

The stack and stack pointer were covered in the last chapter. To understand the importance of the stack in microprocessors, we now examine the contents of the stack and stack pointer for Example 3-8. This is shown in Example 3-9.

Example 3-9

Analyze the stack contents after the execution of the first LCALL in the following.

Solution:
```
001  0000                   ORG   0
002  0000 7455   BACK:      MOV   A,#55H  ;load A with 55H
003  0002 F590              MOV   P1,A    ;send 55H to port 1
004  0004 120300            LCALL DELAY   ;time delay
005  0007 74AA              MOV   A,#0AAH ;load A with AAH
006  0009 F590              MOV   P1,A    ;send AAH to port 1
007  000B 120300            LCALL DELAY
008  000E 80F0              SJMP  BACK    ;keep doing this
009  0010
010  0010 ;--------this is the delay subroutine
011  0300                   ORG 300H
012  0300         DELAY:
013  0300 7DFF              MOV   R5,#0FFH ;R5=255
014  0302 DDFE   AGAIN:     DJNZ  R5,AGAIN ;stay here
015  0304 22                RET            ;return to caller
016  0305                   END            ;end of asm file
```

When the first LCALL is executed, the address of the instruction "MOV A,#0AAH" is saved on the stack. Notice that the low byte goes first and the high byte is last. The last instruction of the called subroutine must be a RET instruction, which directs the CPU to POP the top bytes of the stack into the PC and resume executing at address 07. The diagram shows the stack frame after the first LCALL.

	0A	
09	00	
08	07	

SP = 09

Use of PUSH and POP instructions in subroutines

Upon calling a subroutine, the stack keeps track of where the CPU should return after completing the subroutine. For this reason, we must be very careful in any manipulation of stack contents. The rule is that the number of PUSH and POP instructions must always match in any called subroutine. In other words, for every PUSH there must be a POP. See Example 3-10.

Example 3-10

Analyze the stack for the first LCALL instruction in the following program.

```
01 0000                    ORG   0
02 0000 7455 BACK:  MOV   A,#55H      ;load A with 55H
03 0002 F590        MOV   P1,A        ;send 55H to port 1
04 0004 7C99        MOV   R4,#99H
05 0006 7D67        MOV   R5,#67H
06 0008 120300      LCALL DELAY       ;time delay
07 000B 74AA        MOV   A,#0AAH     ;load A with AA
08 000D F590        MOV   P1,A        ;send AAH to port 1
09 000F 120300      LCALL DELAY
10 0012 80EC        SJMP  BACK        ;keep doing this
11 0014        ;————this is the delay subroutine
12 0300                    ORG   300H
13 0300 C004 DELAY: PUSH  4           ;PUSH R4
14 0302 C005        PUSH  5           ;PUSH R5
15 0304 7CFF        MOV   R4,#0FFH    ;R4=FFH
16 0306 7DFF NEXT:  MOV   R5,#0FFH    ;R5=255
17 0308 DDFE AGAIN: DJNZ  R5,AGAIN
18 030A DCFA        DJNZ  R4,NEXT
19 030C D005        POP   5           ;POP into R5
20 030E D004        POP   4           ;POP into R4
21 0310 22          RET               ;return to caller
22 0311             END               ;end of asm file
```

Solution:

First notice that for the PUSH and POP instructions, we must specify the direct address of the register being pushed or popped. Here is the stack frame.

After the first LCALL			After PUSH 4			After PUSH 5		
0B			0B			0B	67	R5
0A			0A	99	R4	0A	99	R4
09	00	PCH	09	00	PCH	09	00	PCH
08	0B	PCL	08	0B	PCL	08	0B	PCL

Calling subroutines

In Assembly language programming, it is common to have one main program and many subroutines that are called from the main program. See Figure 3-1. This allows you to make each subroutine into a separate module. Each module can be tested separately and then brought together with the main program. More importantly, in a large program the modules can be assigned to different programmers in order to shorten development time.

It needs to be emphasized that in using LCALL, the target address of the subroutine can be anywhere within the 64K-byte memory space of the 8051. This is not the case for the other call instruction, ACALL, which is explained next.

ACALL (absolute call)

ACALL is a 2-byte instruction in contrast to LCALL, which has 3 bytes. Since ACALL is a 2-byte instruction, the target address of the subroutine must be within 2K bytes because only 11 bits of the 2 bytes are used for the address. There is no difference between ACALL and LCALL in terms of saving the program counter on the stack or the function of the RET instruction. The only difference is that the target address for LCALL can be anywhere within the 64K-byte

```
;MAIN program calling subroutines
          ORG   0
MAIN:     LCALL     SUBR_1
          LCALL     SUBR_2
          LCALL     SUBR_3

HERE:     SJMP      HERE
;————————end of MAIN
;
SUBR_1:   ....
          ....
          RET
;————————end of subroutine 1
;
SUBR_2:   ....
          ....
          RET
;————————end of subroutine 2

SUBR_3:   ....
          ....
          RET
;————————end of subroutine 3
          END         ;end of the asm file
```

Figure 3-1. 8051 Assembly Main Program That Calls Subroutines

Example 3-11

A developer is using the Atmel AT89C1051 microprocessor chip for a product. This chip has only 1K byte of on-chip flash ROM. Which instruction, LCALL or ACALL, is more useful in programming this chip?

Solution:

The ACALL instruction is more useful since it is a 2-byte instruction. It saves one byte each time the call instruction is used.

---

address space of the 8051, while the target address of ACALL must be within a 2K-byte range. In many variations of the 8051 marketed by different companies, on-chip ROM is as low as 1K byte. In such cases, the use of ACALL instead of LCALL can save a number of bytes of program ROM space. See Example 3-11.

Of course, in addition to using compact instructions, we can program efficiently by having a detailed knowledge of all the instructions supported by a given microprocessor, and using them wisely. Look at Example 3-12.

REVIEW QUESTIONS

1. What do the mnemonics "LCALL" and "ACALL" stand for?
2. True or false. In the 8051, control can be transferred anywhere within the 64K bytes of code space if using the LCALL instruction.
3. How does the CPU know where to return to after executing the RET instruction?

Example 3-12

Rewrite Example 3-8 as efficiently as you can.

Solution:

```
        ORG   0
        MOV   A,#55H    ;load A with 55H
BACK:   MOV   P1,A      ;issue value in reg A to port 1
        ACALL DELAY     ;time delay
        CPL   A         ;complement reg A
        SJMP  BACK      ;keep doing this indefinitely

;————————this is the delay subroutine
DELAY:
        MOV   R5,#0FFH  ;R5=255(FF in hex), the counter
AGAIN:  DJNZ  R5,AGAIN ;stay here until R5 becomes 0
        RET             ;return to caller
        END             ;end of asm file
```

Notice in this program that register A is set to 55H. By complementing 55H, we have AAH, and by complementing AAH we have 55H. Why? "01010101" in binary (55H) becomes "10101010" in binary (AAH) when it is complemented, and "10101010" becomes "01010101" if it is complemented.

---

4. Describe briefly the function of the RET instruction.
5. The LCALL instruction is a ___-byte instruction.

3.3: TIME DELAY FOR VARIOUS 8051 CHIPS

In the last section, we used the DELAY subroutine. In this section, we discuss how to generate various time delays and calculate exact delays for the 8051 and DS89C4x0.

Machine cycle for the 8051

The CPU takes a certain number of clock cycles to execute an instruction. In the 8051 family, these clock cycles are referred to as *machine cycles* (*MC*). While the original 8051 design used 12 clock periods per machine cycle, many of the newer generations of the 8051 use much fewer clocks per machine cycle. For example, the DS5000 uses 4 clock periods per machine cycle, while the DS89C4x0 uses only 1 clock per machine cycle. See Table 3-2. Table A-1 in Appendix A provides the list of 8051 instructions and their machine cycles. To calculate a time delay, we use this list. In the 8051 family, the length of the machine cycle depends on the frequency of the crystal oscillator connected to the 8051 system. The crystal oscillator, along with on-chip circuitry, provides the clock source for the 8051 CPU (see Chapter 8). The frequency of the crystal connected to the 8051 family can vary from 4 MHz to 30 MHz, depending on the chip rating and manufacturer. Very often the 11.0592 MHz crystal oscillator is used to make the 8051-based system compatible with the serial port of the x86 PC (see Chapter 10). In the original 8051, 1 machine cycle lasts 12 oscillator periods. Therefore, to calculate the machine cycle for the 8051, we take 1/12 of the crystal frequency, then take its inverse, as shown in Examples 3-13 and 3-14.

Table 3-2. Clocks per Machine Cycle for Various 8051 Versions

Chip/Maker	Clocks per Machine Cycle
AT89C51 Atmel	12
P89C54X2 Philips	6
DS5000 Dallas Semi	4
DS89C430/40/50 Dallas Semi	1

Example 3-13

The following shows crystal frequency for three different 8051-based systems. Find the period of the machine cycle in each case.
(a) 11.0592 MHz   (b) 16 MHz   (c) 20 MHz

Solution:

(a) 11.0592 MHz/12 = 921.6 kHz; machine cycle is 1/921.6 kHz = 1.085 μs (microsecond)
(b) 16 MHz/12 = 1.333 MHz; machine cycle = 1/1.333 MHz = 0.75 μs
(c) 20 MHz/12 = 1.66 MHz; machine cycle = 1/1.66 MHz = 0.60 μs

---

Example 3-14

For an 8051 system of 11.0592 MHz, find how long it takes to execute each of the following instructions.

(a) MOV R3,#55 (b) DEC R3   (c) DJNZ R2,target
(d) LJMP   (e) SJMP   (f) NOP (no operation)
(g) MUL AB

Solution:

The machine cycle for a system of 11.0592 MHz is 1.085 µs, as shown in Example 3-13. Table A-1 in Appendix A shows machine cycles for each of the above instructions. Therefore, we have:

Instruction	Machine Cycles	Time to Execute
(a) MOV R3,#55	1	1×1.085 µs = 1.085 µs
(b) DEC R3	1	1×1.085 µs = 1.085 µs
(c) DJNZ R2,target	2	2×1.085 µs = 2.17 µs
(d) LJMP	2	2×1.085 µs = 2.17 µs
(e) SJMP	2	2×1.085 µs = 2.17 µs
(f) NOP	1	1×1.085 µs = 1.085 µs
(g) MUL AB	4	4×1.085 µs = 4.34 µs

Delay calculation for 8051

As seen in the last section, a DELAY subroutine consists of two parts: (1) setting a counter and (2) a loop. Most of the time delay is performed by the body of the loop, as shown in Example 3-15.

Very often, we calculate the time delay based on the instructions inside the loop and ignore the clock cycles associated with the instructions outside the loop.

In Example 3-15, the largest value the R3 register can take is 255; therefore, one way to increase the delay is to use NOP instructions in the loop. NOP, which stands for "no operation," simply wastes time. This is shown in Example 3-16.

Loop inside loop delay

Another way to get a large delay is to use a loop inside a loop, which is also called a *nested loop*. See Example 3-17.

Example 3-15

Find the size of the delay in the following program, if the crystal frequency is 11.0592 MHz.

```
             MOV  A,#55H       ;load A with 55H
AGAIN:       MOV  P1,A         ;issue value in reg A to port 1
             ACALL DELAY       ;time delay
             CPL  A            ;complement reg A
             SJMP AGAIN        ;keep doing this indefinitely
; ——Time delay
DELAY:       MOV  R3,#200      ;load R3 with 200
HERE:        DJNZ R3,HERE      ;stay here until R3 become 0
             RET               ;return to caller
```

Solution:

From Table A-1 in Appendix A, we have the following machine cycles for each instruction of the DELAY subroutine.

		Machine Cycle
DELAY:	MOV R3,#200	1
HERE:	DJNZ R3,HERE	2
	RET	2

Therefore, we have a time delay of $[(200 \times 2) + 1 + 2] \times 1.085$ µs = 436.255 µs.

Example 3-16

For an 8051 system of 11.0592 MHz, find the time delay for the following subroutine:

		Machine Cycle
DELAY:	MOV R3,#250	1
HERE:	NOP	1
	NOP	1
	NOP	1
	NOP	1
	DJNZ R3,HERE	2
	RET	2

Solution:

The time delay inside the HERE loop is $[250(1 + 1 + 1 + 1 + 2)] \times 1.085$ µs = 1500 × 1.085 µs = 1627.5 µs. Adding the two instructions outside the loop, we have 1627.5 µs + 3 × 1.085 µs = 1630.755 µs.

If machine cycle timing is critical to your system design, make sure that you check the manufacture's data sheets for the device specification. For example, the DS89C430 has 3 machine cycles instead of 2 machine cycles for the RET instruction.

CHAPTER 3: JUMP, LOOP, AND CALL INSTRUCTIONS

Example 3-17

For a machine cycle of 1.085 μs, find the time delay in the following subroutine.

```
DELAY:                        Machine Cycle
        MOV   R2,#200           1
AGAIN:  MOV   R3,#250           1
HERE:   NOP                     1
        NOP                     1
        DJNZ  R3,HERE           2
        DJNZ  R2,AGAIN          2
        RET                     2
```

Solution:

For the HERE loop, we have (4 × 250) ×1.085 μs = 1085 μs. The AGAIN loop repeats the HERE loop 200 times; therefore, we have 200 × 1085 μs = 217000, if we do not include the overhead. However, the instructions "MOV R3, #250" and "DJNZ R2, AGAIN" at the beginning and end of the AGAIN loop add (3 × 200 × 1.085 μs) = 651 μs to the time delay. As a result, we have 217000 + 651 = 217651 μs = 217.651 milliseconds for total time delay associated with the above DELAY subroutine. Notice that in the case of a nested loop, as in all other time delay loops, the time is approximate since we have ignored the first and last instructions in the subroutine.

Delay calculation for other versions of 8051

In creating a time delay using Assembly language instructions, one must be mindful of two factors that can affect the accuracy of the delay.

1. **The crystal frequency:** The frequency of the crystal oscillator connected to the X1–X2 input pins is one factor in the time delay calculation. The duration of the clock period for the machine cycle is a function of this crystal frequency.

2. **The 8051 design:** Since the original 8051 was designed in 1980, both the field of IC technology and the architectural design of microprocessors have seen great advancements. Due to the limitations of IC technology and limited CPU design experience at that time, the machine cycle duration was set at 12 clocks. Advances in both IC technology and CPU design in recent years have made the 1-clock machine cycle a common feature of many new 8051 chips. Indeed, one way to increase the 8051 performance without losing code compatibility with the original 8051 is to reduce the number of clock cycles it takes to execute an instruction. For these reasons, the number of machine cycles and the number of clock periods per machine cycle varies among the different versions of the 8051 microprocessors. While the original 8051 design used 12 clock periods per machine cycle, many of the newer generations of the 8051 use much fewer clocks per machine cycle. For example, the DS5000 uses 4 clock periods per machine cycle, while the

Example 3-18

From Table 3-2, find the period of the machine cycle in each case if XTAL = 11.0592 MHz, and discuss the impact on performance:
(a) AT89C51   (b) P89C54X2   (c) DS5000   (d) DS89C4x0.

Solution:

(a) 11.0592 MHz/12 = 921.6 kHz; MC is 1/921.6 kHz = 1.085 μs (microsecond) = 1085 ns
(b) 11.0592 MHz/6 = 1.8432 MHz; MC is 1/1.8432 MHz = 0.5425 μs = 542 ns
(c) 11.0592 MHz/4 = 2.7648 MHz; MC is 1/2.7648 MHz = 0.36 μs = 360 ns
(d) 11.0592 MHz/1 = 11.0592 MHz; MC is 1/11.0592 MHz = 0.0904 μs = 90 ns

This means that if we connect an AT89C51 and a DS89C4x0 to a crystal of the same frequency, we get approximately 9 to 10 times performance boost for the DS89C4x0 chip over the AT89C51. See Example 3-20.

DS89C4x0 uses only 1 clock per machine cycle. The 8051 products from Philips Semiconductors have the option of using either 6 or 12 clocks per machine cycle. Table 3-2 shows some of the 8051 versions with their machine cycles.

Delay calculation for DS89C4x0

In the case of the DS89C4x0, since the number of clocks per machine cycle was reduced from 12 to 1, the number of machine cycles used to execute an instruction had to be changed to reflect this reality. Table 3-3 compares the machine cycles for the DS89C4x0 and 8051 for some instructions. See Examples 3-18 through 3-22.

From the above discussion, we conclude that use of the instruction in generating time delay is not the most reliable method. To get more accurate time delay we use timers, as described in Chapter 9. Meanwhile, to get an accurate time delay for a given 8051 microprocessor, we must use an oscilloscope to measure the exact time delay.

Table 3-3. Comparison of 8051 and DS89C4x0 Machine Cycles

Instruction	8051	DS89C4x0
MOV R3,#value	1	2
DEC Rx	1	1
DJNZ	2	4
LJMP	2	3
SJMP	2	3
NOP	1	1
MUL AB	4	9

Example 3-19

For an AT8051 and DS89C430/40/50 system of 11.0592 MHz, find how long it takes to execute each of the following instructions.

(a) MOV R3,#55 (b) DEC R3   (c) DJNZ R2,target
(d) LJMP   (e) SJMP   (f) NOP (no operation)
(g) MUL AB

Solution:

The machine cycle time for the AT8951 and DS89C430 was shown in Example 3-18. Table 3-3 shows machine cycles for each of the above instructions. Therefore, we have:

Instruction	*AT8051*	*DS89C430/40/50*
(a) MOV R3,#55	1×1085 ns = 1085 ns	2×90 ns = 180 ns
(b) DEC R3	1×1085 ns = 1085 ns	1×90 ns = 90 ns
(c) DJNZ R2,..	2×1085 ns = 2170 ns	4×90 ns = 360 ns
(d) LJMP	2×1085 ns = 2170 ns	3×90 ns = 270 ns
(e) SJMP	2×1085 ns = 2170 ns	3×90 ns = 270 ns
(f) NOP	1×1085 ns = 1085 ns	1×90 ns = 90 ns
(g) MUL AB	4×1085 ns = 4340 ns	9×90 ns = 810 ns

Example 3-20

Find the time delay for the loop section of the following subroutine if it is run on a DS89C430 chip, assuming a crystal frequency of 11.0592 MHz.

```
                            DS89C430 Machine Cycle
DELAY:      MOV   R3,#250

HERE:       NOP                         1
            NOP                         1
            NOP                         1
            NOP                         1
            DJNZ R3,HERE                4

            RET
```

Solution:

The time delay inside the HERE loop is [250(1 + 1 + 1 + 1 + 4)] × 90 ns = 2000 × 90 ns = 180 µs. Comparing this with Example 3-16, we see DS89C4x0 is about 9 times faster (1627 µs / 180 µs = 9).

Example 3-21

Write a program to toggle all the bits of P1 every 200 ms. Assume that the crystal frequency is 11.0592 MHz and that the system is using the AT89C51.

Solution:

```
;Tested for AT89C51 of 11.0592 MHz.

            MOV    A,#55H
AGAIN:      MOV    P1,A
            ACALL  DELAY
            CPL    A
            SJMP   AGAIN

; ——Time delay
DELAY:      MOV    R5,#2
HERE1:      MOV    R4,#180
HERE2:      MOV    R3,#255
HERE3:      DJNZ   R3,HERE3
            DJNZ   R4,HERE2
            DJNZ   R5,HERE1
            RET
```

$2 \times 180 \times 255 \times 2$ MC $\times 1.085$ μs $= 199,206$ μs

---

Example 3-22

Write a program to toggle all the bits of P1 every 200 ms. Assume the crystal frequency is 11.0592 MHz and the system is using DS89C430/40/50.

Solution:

```
;Tested for DS89C430 of 11.0592 MHz.
            MOV    A,#55H
AGAIN:      MOV    P1,A
            ACALL  DELAY_200m
            CPL    A
            SJMP   AGAIN

; ——Time delay
DELAY_200m:
            MOV    R5,#9
HERE1:      MOV    R4,#242
HERE2:      MOV    R3,#255
HERE3:      DJNZ   R3,HERE3
            DJNZ   R4,HERE2
            DJNZ   R5,HERE1
            RET
```

Delay $9 \times 242 \times 255 \times 4$ MC $\times 90$ ns $= 199,940$ μs

Use an oscilloscope to measure the system square wave period to verify delay.

SJMP to itself using $ sign

In cases where there is no monitor program, we need to short jump to itself in order to keep the microprocessor busy. A simple way of doing that is to use the $ sign. That means in place of this

```
HERE:      SJMP HERE
```

we can use the following:

```
SJMP $
```

REVIEW QUESTIONS

1. True or false. In the 8051, the machine cycle lasts 12 clock cycles of the crystal frequency.
2. The minimum number of machine cycles needed to execute an 8051 instruction is _____.
3. For Question 2, what is the maximum number of cycles needed, and for which instructions?
4. Find the machine cycle for a crystal frequency of 12 MHz.
5. Assuming a crystal frequency of 12 MHz, find the time delay associated with the loop section of the following DELAY subroutine.

```
DELAY:     MOV   R3,#100
HERE:      NOP
           NOP
           NOP
           DJNZ  R3,HERE
           RET
```

6. True or false. In the DS89C430, the machine cycle lasts 12 clock cycles of the crystal frequency.
7. Find the machine cycle for a DS89C430 if the crystal frequency is 11.0592 MHz.

SUMMARY

The flow of a program proceeds sequentially, from instruction to instruction, unless a control transfer instruction is executed. The various types of control transfer instructions in Assembly language include conditional and unconditional jumps, and call instructions.

The looping action in 8051 Assembly language is performed using a special instruction, which decrements a counter and jumps to the top of the loop if the counter is not zero. Other jump instructions jump conditionally, based on the value of the carry flag, the accumulator, or bits of the I/O port. Unconditional jumps can be long or short, depending on the relative value of the target address. Special attention must be given to the effect of LCALL and ACALL instructions on the stack.

RECOMMENDED WEB LINKS

See the following websites for DS89C430/40/50 instructions and timing:

- www.maxim-ic.com
- www.MicroDigitalEd.com

See the following websites for 8051 products and their features from various companies:

- www.8052.com
- www.MicroDigitalEd.com

PROBLEMS

3.1: LOOP AND JUMP INSTRUCTIONS

1. In the 8051, looping action with the instruction "DJNZ   Rx,rel address" is limited to ____ iterations.
2. If a conditional jump is not taken, what is the next instruction to be executed?
3. In calculating the target address for a jump, a displacement is added to the contents of register _____.
4. The mnemonic SJMP stands for _____ and it is a ___-byte instruction.
5. The mnemonic LJMP stands for _____ and it is a ___-byte instruction.
6. What is the advantage of using SJMP over LJMP?
7. True or false. The target of a short jump is within –128 to +127 bytes of the current PC.
8. True or false. All 8051 jumps are short jumps.
9. Which of the following instructions is (are) not a short jump?
   (a) JZ   (b) JNC   (c) LJMP   (d) DJNZ
10. A short jump is a ___-byte instruction. Why?
11. True or false. All conditional jumps are short jumps.
12. Show code for a nested loop to perform an action 1000 times.
13. Show code for a nested loop to perform an action 100,000 times.
14. Find the number of times the following loop is performed.

```
        MOV   R6,#200
BACK:   MOV   R5,#100
HERE:   DJNZ R5,HERE
        DJNZ R6,BACK
```

15. The target address of a jump backward is a maximum of _____ bytes from the current PC.
16. The target address of a jump forward is a maximum of _____ bytes from the current PC.

3.2: CALL INSTRUCTIONS

17. LCALL is a ___-byte instruction.
18. ACALL is a ___-byte instruction.
19. The ACALL target address is limited to ____ bytes from the present PC.
20. The LCALL target address is limited to ____ bytes from the present PC.
21. When LCALL is executed, how many bytes of the stack are used?
22. When ACALL is executed, how many bytes of the stack are used?
23. Why do the PUSH and POP instructions in a subroutine need to be equal in number?
24. Describe the action associated with the POP instruction.
25. Show the stack for the following code.

```
000B  120300              LCALL DELAY
000E  80F0                SJMP BACK      ;keep doing this
0010
0010  ;--------this is the delay subroutine
0300                      ORG 300H
0300          DELAY:
0300  7DFF                MOV  R5,#0FFH  ;R5=255
0302  DDFE  AGAIN:        DJNZ R5,AGAIN  ;stay here
0304  22                  RET            ;return
```

26. Reassemble Example 3-10 at ORG 200 (instead of ORG 0) and show the stack frame for the first LCALL instruction.

3.3: TIME DELAY FOR VARIOUS 8051 CHIPS

27. Find the system frequency if the machine cycle = 1.2 μs.
28. Find the machine cycle if the crystal frequency is 18 MHz.
29. Find the machine cycle if the crystal frequency is 12 MHz.
30. Find the machine cycle if the crystal frequency is 25 MHz.
31. True or false. LJMP and SJMP instructions take the same amount of time to execute even though one is a 3-byte instruction and the other is a 2-byte instruction.
32. Find the time delay for the delay subroutine shown to the right, if the system has an 8051 with frequency of 11.0592 MHz.`

```
DELAY:       MOV   R3,#150
HERE:        NOP
             NOP
             NOP
             DJNZ  R3,HERE
             RET
```

33. Find the time delay for the delay subroutine shown to the right, if the system has an 8051 with frequency of 16 MHz.

```
DELAY:       MOV   R3,#200
HERE:        NOP
             NOP
             NOP
             DJNZ  R3,HERE
             RET
```

```
DELAY:    MOV   R5,#100
BACK:     MOV   R2,#200
AGAIN:    MOV   R3,#250
HERE:     NOP
          NOP
          DJNZ  R3,HERE
          DJNZ  R2,AGAIN
          DJNZ  R5,BACK
          RET
```

34. Find the time delay for the delay subroutine shown to the left, if the system has an 8051 with frequency of 11.0592 MHz.

```
DELAY:    MOV   R2,#150
AGAIN:    MOV   R3,#250
HERE:     NOP
          NOP
          NOP
          DJNZ  R3,HERE
          DJNZ  R2,AGAIN
          RET
```

35. Find the time delay for the delay subroutine shown to the left, if the system has an 8051 with frequency of 16 MHz.

36. Repeat Problem 32 for DS89C430.
37. Repeat Problem 33 for DS89C430.
38. Repeat Problem 34 for DS89C430.
39. Repeat Problem 35 for DS89C430.
40. In an AT89C51-based system, explain performance improvement if we replace the AT89C51 chip with a DS89C430. Is it 12 times faster?

ANSWERS TO REVIEW QUESTIONS

3.1: LOOP AND JUMP INSTRUCTIONS

1. Decrement and jump if not zero
2. True
3. 2
4. A
5. 3

3.2: CALL INSTRUCTIONS

1. Long CALL and absolute CALL
2. True
3. The address of where to return is in the stack.
4. Upon executing the RET instruction, the CPU pops off the top 2 bytes of the stack into the PC register and starts to execute from this new location.
5. 3

3.3: TIME DELAY FOR VARIOUS 8051 CHIPS

1. True
2. 1
3. MUL and DIV each take 4 machine cycles.
4. 12 MHz / 12 = 1 MHz, and MC = 1/1 MHz = 1 μs.
5. $[100(1 + 1 + 1 + 2)] \times 1$ μs = 500 μs = 0.5 milliseconds.
6. False. It takes 1 clock.
7. 11.0592 MHz/1 = 11.0592 MHz; machine cycle is 1/11.0592 MHz = 0.0904 μs = 90.4 ns

CHAPTER 4

I/O PORT PROGRAMMING

OBJECTIVES

Upon completion of this chapter, you will be able to:

>> List the four ports of the 8051.
>> Describe the dual role of port 0 in providing both data and addresses.
>> Code Assembly language to use the ports for input or output.
>> Explain the dual role of port 0 and port 2.
>> Code 8051 instructions for I/O handling.
>> Code I/O bit-manipulation programs for the 8051.

This chapter describes the I/O port programming of the 8051 with many examples. In Section 4.1, we describe I/O access using byte-size data, and in Section 4.2, bit manipulation of the I/O ports is discussed in detail.

4.1: 8051 I/O PROGRAMMING

In the 8051, there are a total of four ports for I/O operations. Examining Figure 4-1, note that of the 40 pins, a total of 32 pins are set aside for the four ports P0, P1, P2, and P3, where each port takes 8 pins. The rest of the pins are designated as V_{cc}, GND, XTAL1, XTAL2, RST, $\overline{EA}$, ALE/$\overline{PROG}$, and $\overline{PSEN}$ and are discussed in Chapter 8.

I/O port pins and their functions

The four ports P0, P1, P2, and P3 each use 8 pins, making them 8-bit ports. All the ports upon RESET are configured as inputs, ready to be used as input ports. When the first 0 is written to a port, it becomes an output. To reconfigure it as an input, a 1 must be sent to the port. To use any of these ports as an input port, it must be programmed, as we will explain throughout this section. First, we describe each port.

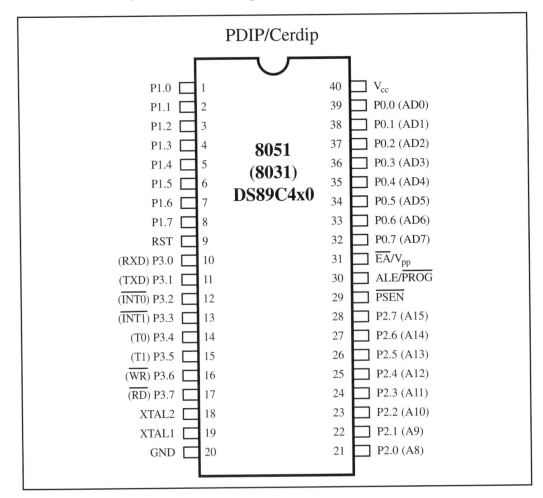

Figure 4-1. 8051 Pin Diagram

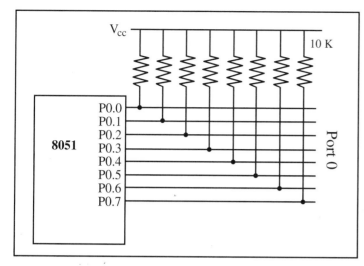

Figure 4-2. Port 0 with Pull-Up Resistors

Port 0

Port 0 occupies a total of 8 pins (pins 32–39). It can be used for input or output. To use the pins of port 0 as both input and output ports, each pin must be connected externally to a 10K-ohm pull-up resistor. This is due to the fact that P0 is an open drain, unlike P1, P2, and P3, as we will soon see. *Open drain* is a term used for MOS chips in the same way that *open collector* is used for TTL chips. In any system using the 8051/52 chip, we normally connect P0 to pull-up resistors. See Figure 4-2. In this way we take advantage of port 0 for both input and output. For example, the following code will continuously send out to port 0 the alternating values of 55H and AAH.

```
;Toggle all bits of P0
BACK:      MOV   A,#55H
           MOV   P0,A
           ACALL DELAY
           MOV   A,#0AAH
           MOV   P0,A
           ACALL DELAY
           SJMP  BACK
```

It must be noted that complementing 55H (01010101) turns it into AAH (10101010). By sending 55H and AAH to a given port continuously, we toggle all the bits of that port.

Port 0 as input

With resistors connected to port 0, in order to make it an input, the port must be programmed by writing 1 to all the bits. In the following code, port 0 is configured first as an input port by writing 1s to it, and then data is received from that port and sent to P1.

```
;Get a byte from P0 and send it to P1
           MOV   A,#0FFH   ;A = FF hex
           MOV   P0,A      ;make P0 an input port
                           ;by writing all 1s to it
BACK:      MOV   A,P0      ;get data from P0
           MOV   P1,A      ;send it to port 1
           SJMP  BACK      ;keep doing it
```

Dual role of port 0

As shown in Figure 4-1, port 0 is also designated as AD0–AD7, allowing it to be used for both address and data. When connecting an 8051/31 to an external memory, port 0 provides both address and data. The 8051 multiplexes address and data through port 0 to save pins. We discuss that in Chapter 14.

Port 1

Port 1 occupies a total of 8 pins (pins 1 through 8). It can be used as input or output. In contrast to port 0, this port does not need any pull-up resistors since it already has pull-up resistors internally. Upon reset, port 1 is configured as an input port. The following code will continuously send out to port 1 the alternating values 55H and AAH.

```
;Toggle all bits of P1 continuously
        MOV    A,#55H
BACK:   MOV    P1,A
        ACALL  DELAY
        CPL    A          ;complement(Invert) reg. A
        SJMP   BACK
```

Port 1 as input

If port 1 has been configured as an output port, to make it an input port again, it must be programmed as such by writing 1 to all its bits. The reason for this is discussed in Appendix C.2. In the following code, port 1 is configured first as an input port by writing 1s to it, then data is received from that port and saved in R7, R6, and R5.

```
        MOV    A,#0FFH    ;A=FF hex
        MOV    P1,A       ;make P1 an input port
                          ;by writing all 1s to it
        MOV    A,P1       ;get data from P1
        MOV    R7,A       ;save it in reg R7
        ACALL  DELAY      ;wait
        MOV    A,P1       ;get another data from P1
        MOV    R6,A       ;save it in reg R6
        ACALL  DELAY      ;wait
        MOV    A,P1       ;get another data from P1
        MOV    R5,A       ;save it in reg R5
```

Port 2

Port 2 occupies a total of 8 pins (pins 21 through 28). It can be used as input or output. Just like P1, port 2 does not need any pull-up resistors since it already has pull-up resistors internally. Upon reset, port 2 is configured as an input port. The following code will continuously send out to port 2 the alternating values 55H and AAH. That is, all the bits of P2 toggle continuously.

```
              MOV    A,#55H
BACK:         MOV    P2,A
              ACALL  DELAY
              CPL    A          ;complement reg. A
              SJMP   BACK
```

Port 2 as input

To make port 2 an input, it must programmed as such by writing 1 to all its bits. In the following code, port 2 is configured first as an input port by writing 1s to it. Then data is received from that port and is sent to P1 continuously.

```
;Get a byte from P2 and send it to P1
              MOV    A,#0FFH    ;A=FF hex
              MOV    P2,A       ;make P2 an input port by
                               ;writing all 1s to it
BACK:         MOV    A,P2       ;get data from P2
              MOV    P1,A       ;send it to Port 1
              SJMP   BACK       ;keep doing that
```

Dual role of port 2

In many systems based on the 8051, P2 is used as simple I/O. However, in 8031-based systems, port 2 must be used along with P0 to provide the 16-bit address for external memory. As shown in Figure 4-1, port 2 is also designated as A8–A15, indicating its dual function. Since an 8051/31 is capable of accessing 64K bytes of external memory, it needs a path for the 16 bits of the address. While P0 provides the lower 8 bits via A0–A7, it is the job of P2 to provide bits A8–A15 of the address. In other words, when the 8051/31 is connected to external memory, P2 is used for the upper 8 bits of the 16-bit address, and it cannot be used for I/O. This is discussed in detail in Chapter 14.

From the discussion so far, we conclude that in systems based on 8751, 89C51, or DS589C4x0 microprocessors, we have three ports, P0, P1, and P2, for I/O operations. This should be enough for most micro-processor applications. That leaves port 3 for interrupts as well as other signals, as we will see next.

Table 4-1. Port 3 Alternate Functions

P3 Bit	Function	Pin
3.0	RxD	10
3.1	TxD	11
3.2	INT0	12
3.3	INT1	13
3.4	T0	14
3.5	T1	15
3.6	WR	16
3.7	RD	17

Port 3

Port 3 occupies a total of 8 pins, pins 10 through 17. It can be used as input or output. P3 does not need any pull-up resistors, just as P1 and P2 did not. Although port 3 is configured as an input port upon reset, this is not the way it is most commonly used. Port 3 has the additional function of providing some extremely important signals such as interrupts. Table 4-1 provides these alternate functions of P3. This information applies to both 8051 and 8031 chips.

P3.0 and P3.1 are used for the RxD and TxD serial communication signals. See Chapter 10 to see how they are connected. Bits P3.2 and P3.3 are set aside for external interrupts, and are discussed in Chapter 11. Bits P3.4 and P3.5 are used for timers 0 and 1, and are discussed in Chapter 9 where timers are discussed. Finally, P3.6 and P3.7 are used to provide the $\overline{WR}$ and $\overline{RD}$ signals of external memories connected in 8031-based systems. Chapter 14 discusses how they are used in 8031-based systems. In systems based on the 8751, 89C51, or DS89C4x0, pins 3.6 and 3.7 are used for I/O while the rest of the pins in port 3 are normally used in the alternate function role. See Example 4-1.

Example 4-1

Write a test program for the DS89C4x0 chip to toggle all the bits of P0, P1, and P2 every 1/4 of a second. Assume a crystal frequency of 11.0592 MHz.

Solution:

```
;Tested for the DS89C4x with XTAL = 11.0592 MHz.

            ORG    0
BACK:       MOV    A,#55H
            MOV    P0,A
            MOV    P1,A
            MOV    P2,A
            ACALL  QSDELAY          ;Quarter of a second delay
            MOV    A,#0AAH
            MOV    P0,A
            MOV    P1,A
            MOV    P2,A
            ACALL  QSDELAY
            SJMP   BACK
;-----------1/4 SECOND DELAY
QSDELAY:
            MOV    R5, #11
H3:         MOV    R4, #248
H2:         MOV    R3, #255
H1:         DJNZ   R3, H1           ;4 MC for DS89C4x0
            DJNZ   R4, H2
            DJNZ   R5, H3
            RET
            END
```

Delay = $11 \times 248 \times 255 \times 4$ MC $\times 90$ ns $= 250,430$ μs

Use an oscilloscope to verify the delay size.

Different ways of accessing the entire 8 bits

In the following code, as in many previous I/O examples, the entire 8 bits of port 1 are accessed.

```
BACK:     MOV    A,#55H
          MOV    P1,A
          ACALL  DELAY
          MOV    A,#0AAH
          MOV    P1,A
          ACALL  DELAY
          SJMP   BACK
```

The above code toggles every bit of P1 continuously. We have seen a variation of the above program earlier. Now we can rewrite the code in a more efficient manner by accessing the port directly without going through the accumulator. This is shown next.

```
BACK:     MOV    P1,#55H
          ACALL  DELAY
          MOV    P1,#0AAH
          ACALL  DELAY
          SJMP   BACK
```

The following is another way of doing the same thing.

```
          MOV    A,#55H      ;A=55 HEX
BACK:     MOV    P1,A
          ACALL  DELAY
          CPL    A           ;complement reg. A
          SJMP   BACK
```

We can write another variation of the above code by using a technique called *read–modify–write*. This is shown at the end of this chapter.

Ports status upon reset

Upon reset, all ports have value FFH on them as shown in Table 4-2. This makes them input ports upon reset.

Table 4-2. Reset Value of Some 8051 Ports

Register	Reset Value (Binary)
P0	11111111
P1	11111111
P2	11111111
P3	11111111

REVIEW QUESTIONS

1. There are a total of _____ ports in the 8051 and each has _____ bits.
2. True or false. All of the 8051 ports can be used for both input and output.
3. Which 8051 ports need pull-up resistors to function as an I/O port?

4. True or false. Upon power-up, the I/O pins are configured as output ports.
5. Show simple statements to send 99H to ports P1 and P2.

4.2: I/O BIT-MANIPULATION PROGRAMMING

In this section, we further examine 8051 I/O instructions. We pay special attention to I/O bit manipulation since it is a powerful and widely used feature of the 8051 family.

I/O ports and bit-addressability

Sometimes we need to access only 1 or 2 bits of the port instead of the entire 8 bits. A powerful feature of 8051 I/O ports is their capability to access individual bits of the port without altering the rest of the bits in that port. Of the four 8051 ports, we can access either the entire 8 bits or any single bit without altering the rest. When accessing a port in single-bit manner, we use the syntax "SETB Px.y" where x is the port number 0, 1, 2, or 3, and y is the desired bit number from 0 to 7 for data bits D0 to D7. For example, "SETB P1.5" sets high bit 5 of port 1. Remember that D0 is the LSB and D7 is the MSB. For example, the following code toggles bit P1.2 continuously.

```
BACK:      CPL    P1.2      ;complement P1.2 only
           ACALL  DELAY
           SJMP   BACK

;another variation of the above program follows
AGAIN:     SETB   P1.2      ;change only P1.2=high
           ACALL  DELAY
           CLR    P1.2      ;change only P1.2=low
           ACALL  DELAY
           SJMP   AGAIN
```

Notice that P1.2 is the third bit of P1, since the first bit is P1.0, the second bit is P1.1, and so on. Table 4-3 shows the bits of the 8051 I/O ports. See Example 4-2 for bit manipulation of I/O ports. Notice in Example 4-2

Table 4-3. Single-Bit Addressability of Ports

P0	P1	P2	P3	Port Bit
P0.0	P1.0	P2.0	P3.0	D0
P0.1	P1.1	P2.1	P3.1	D1
P0.2	P1.2	P2.2	P3.2	D2
P0.3	P1.3	P2.3	P3.3	D3
P0.4	P1.4	P2.4	P3.4	D4
P0.5	P1.5	P2.5	P3.5	D5
P0.6	P1.6	P2.6	P3.6	D6
P0.7	P1.7	P2.7	P3.7	D7

Example 4-2

Write the following programs.

(a) Create a square wave of 50% duty cycle on bit 0 of port 1.

(b) Create a square wave of 66% duty cycle on bit 3 of port 1.

Solution:

(a) The 50% duty cycle means that the "on" and "off" states (or the high and low portions of the pulse) have the same length. Therefore, we toggle P1.0 with a time delay in between each state.

```
HERE:       SETB   P1.0      ;set to high bit 0 of port 1
            LCALL  DELAY     ;call the delay subroutine
            CLR    P1.0      ;P1.0=0
            LCALL  DELAY
            SJMP   HERE      ;keep doing it
```

Another way to write the above program is:

```
HERE:       CPL    P1.0      ;complement bit 0 of port 1
            LCALL  DELAY     ;call the delay subroutine
            SJMP   HERE      ;keep doing it
```

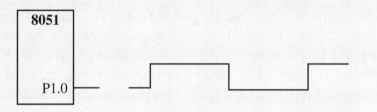

(b)   The 66% duty cycle means the "on" state is twice the "off" state.

```
BACK:       SETB   P1.3      ;set port 1 bit 3 high
            LCALL  DELAY     ;call the delay subroutine
            LCALL  DELAY     ;call the delay subroutine again
            CLR    P1.3      ;clear bit 2 of port 1(P1.3=low)
            LCALL  DELAY     ;call the delay subroutine
            SJMP   BACK      ;keep doing it
```

Table 4-4. Single-Bit Instructions

Instruction	Function
SETB bit	Set the bit (bit = 1)
CLR bit	Clear the bit (bit = 0)
CPL bit	Complement the bit (bit = NOT bit)
JB bit,target	Jump to target if bit = 1 (jump if bit)
JNB bit,target	Jump to target if bit = 0 (jump if no bit)
JBC bit,target	Jump to target if bit = 1, clear bit (jump if bit, then clear)

that unused portions of ports 1 and 2 are undisturbed. This single-bit address-ability of I/O ports is one of most powerful features of the 8051 microprocessor and is among the reasons that many designers choose the 8051 over other microprocessors. We will see the use of the bit-addressability of I/O ports in future chapters.

Table 4-4 lists the single-bit instructions for the 8051. We will see the use of these instructions in future chapters.

Checking an input bit

The JNB (jump if no bit) and JB (jump if bit = 1) instructions are also widely used single-bit operations. They allow you to monitor a bit and make a decision depending on whether it is 0 or 1. Instructions JNB and JB can be used for any bits of I/O ports 0, 1, 2, and 3, since all ports are bit-addressable. However, most of port 3 is used for interrupts and serial communication

---

Example 4-3

Write a program to perform the following:
(a) keep monitoring the P1.2 bit until it becomes high
(b) when P1.2 becomes high, write value 45H to port 0
(c) send a high-to-low (H-to-L) pulse to P2.3

Solution:

```
        SETB P1.2           ;make P1.2 an input
        MOV  A,#45H         ;A=45H
AGAIN:  JNB  P1.2,AGAIN     ;get out when P1.2=1
        MOV  P0,A           ;issue A to P0
        SETB P2.3           ;make P2.3 high
        CLR  P2.3           ;make P2.3 low for H-to-L
```

In this program, instruction "JNB P1.2,AGAIN" (JNB means jump if no bit) stays in the loop as long as P1.2 is low. When P1.2 becomes high, it gets out of the loop, writes the value 45H to port 0, and creates an H-to-L pulse by the sequence of instructions SETB and CLR.

CHAPTER 4: I/O PORT PROGRAMMIN

Table 4-5. Instructions For Reading the Status of an Input Port

Mnemonic	Example	Description
MOV A, PX	MOV A, P2	Bring into A the data at P2 pins
JNB PX.Y,..	JNB P2.1, TARGET	Jump if pin P2.1 is low
JB PX.Y,..	JB P1.3, TARGET	Jump if pin P1.2 is high
MOV C, PX.Y	MOV C, P2.4	Copy status of pin P2.4 to CY
CJNE A, PX,..	CJNE A, P1,TARGET	Compare A with P1and jump if not equal

signals, and typically is not used for any I/O, either single-bit or byte-wise. This is discussed in Chapters 10 and 11. Table 4-5 shows a list of instructions for reading the ports. See Examples 4-4 through 4-5.

Reading a single bit into the carry flag

We can also use the carry flag to save or examine the status of a single bit of the port. To do that, we use the instruction "MOV C, Px.y" as shown in the next two examples.

Notice in Examples 4-6 and 4-7 how the carry flag is used to get a bit of data from the port.

Example 4-4

Assume that bit P2.3 is an input and represents the condition of an oven. If it goes high, it means that the oven is hot. Monitor the bit continuously. Whenever it goes high, send a high-to-low pulse to port P1.5 to turn on a buzzer.

Solution:

```
      HERE:JNB  P2.3,HERE      ;keep monitoring for high
           SETB P1.5           ;set bit P1.5=1
           CLR  P1.5           ;make high-to-low
           SJMP HERE           ;keep repeating
```

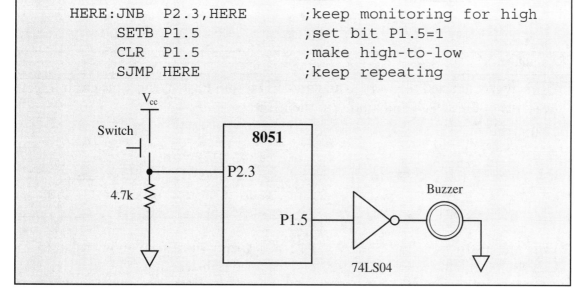

Example 4-5

A switch is connected to pin P1.7. Write a program to check the status of the switch (sw) and perform the following:
(a) If sw=0, send letter "N" to P2.
(b) If sw=1, send letter "Y" to P2.

Solution:

```
          SETB P1.7              ;make P1.7 an input
AGAIN:    JB   P1.2,OVER         ;jump if P1.7=1
          MOV  P2,#'N'           ;SW=0, issue 'N' to P2
          SJMP AGAIN             ;keep monitoring
OVER:     MOV  P2,#'Y'           ;SW=1, issue 'Y' to P2
          SJMP AGAIN             ;keep monitoring
```

Example 4-6

A switch is connected to pin P1.7. Write a program to check the status of the switch and perform the following:
(a) If sw = 0, send letter "N" to P2.
(b) If sw = 1, send letter "Y" to P2.

Use the carry flag to check the switch status. This is a repeat of the last example.

Solution:

```
          SETB P1.7              ;make P1.7 an input
AGAIN:    MOV  C,P1.2            ;read the SW status into CF
          JC   OVER             ;jump if SW = 1
          MOV  P2,#'N'           ;SW = 0, issue 'N' to P2
          SJMP AGAIN             ;keep monitoring
OVER:     MOV  P2,#'Y'           ;SW = 1, issue 'Y' to P2
          SJMP AGAIN             ;keep monitoring
```

Example 4-7

A switch is connected to pin P1.0 and an LED to pin P2.7. Write a program to get the status of the switch and send it to the LED.

Solution:

```
          SETB P1.7              ;make P1.7 an input
AGAIN:    MOV  C,P1.0            ;read the SW status into CF
          MOV  P2.7,C            ;send the SW status to LED
          SJMP AGAIN             ;keep repeating
```

Note: The instruction "MOV P2.7, P1.0" is wrong since such an instruction does not exist. However, "MOV P2, P1" is a valid instruction.

Reading Input Pins versus Port Latch

In reading a port, some instructions read the status of port pins while others read the status of an internal port latch. Therefore, when reading ports there are two possibilities:

1. Read the status of the input pin.
2. Read the internal latch of the output port.

We must make a distinction between these two categories of instructions since confusion between them is a major source of errors in 8051 programming, especially where external hardware is concerned. We discuss these instructions briefly. However, readers must study and understand the material on this topic and on the internal working of ports that is given in Appendix C.2.

Instructions for reading input ports

As stated earlier, to make any bit of any 8051 port an input port, we must write 1 (logic high) to that bit. After we configure the port bits as input, we can use only certain instructions in order to get the external data present at the pins into the CPU. Table 4-5 shows the list of such instructions.

Reading latch for output port

Some instructions read the contents of an internal port latch instead of reading the status of an external pin. Table 4-6 provides a list of these instructions. For example, look at the "ANL P1, A" instruction. The sequence of actions taken when such an instruction is executed is as follows.

1. The instruction reads the internal latch of the port and brings that data into the CPU.
2. This data is ANDed with the contents of register A.
3. The result is rewritten back to the port latch.
4. The port pin data is changed and now has the same value as the port latch.

From the above discussion, we conclude that the instructions that read the port latch normally read a value, perform an operation (and possibly change it), and then rewrite it back to the port latch. This is often called *"read–modify–write"*.

Read–modify–write feature

The ports in the 8051 can be accessed by the read–modify–write technique. This feature saves many lines of code by combining in a single instruction all three actions of (1) reading the port, (2) modifying its value, and (3) writing to the port. The following code first places 01010101 (binary) into

Table 4-6. Instructions for Reading a Latch (Read–Modify–Write)

Mnemonic	Example
ANL Px	ANL P1,A
ORL Px	ORL P2,A
XRL Px	XRL P0,A
JBC PX.Y,TARGET	JBC P1.1,TARGET
CPL PX.Y	CPL P1.2
INC Px	INC P1
DEC Px	DEC P2
DJNZ PX.Y,TARGET	DJNZ P1,TARGET
MOV PX.Y,C	MOV P1.2,C
CLR PX.Y	CLR P2.3
SETB PX.Y	SETB P2.3

Note: x is 0, 1, 2, or 3 for P0–P3.

port 1. Next, the instruction "XLR P1,#0FFH" performs an XOR logic operation on P1 with 1111 1111 (binary), and then writes the result back into P1.

```
            MOV    P1,#55H      ;P1 = 01010101
AGAIN:      XLR    P1,#0FFH     ;EX-OR P1 with 11111111
            ACALL  DELAY
            SJMP   AGAIN
```

Notice that the XOR of 55H and FFH gives AAH. Likewise, the XOR of AAH and FFH gives 55H. Logic instructions are discussed in Chapter 6.

REVIEW QUESTIONS

1. True or false. The instruction "SETB P2.1" makes pin P2.1 high while leaving other bits of P2 unchanged.
2. Show one way to toggle the pin P1.7 continuously using 8051 instructions.

NOTE

Intel's Datasheet on I/O ports of 8051 upon Reset mentions the following: **"All the port latches in the 8051 have 1s written to them by the reset function. If a 0 subsequently written to a port latch, it can be reconfigured as an input by writing a 1 to it."** The only reason we write 1s to the port upon Reset is to emphasize the above point. We write 0 to a given port to make it an output and 1 to make it an input.

---

3. Using the instruction "JNB   P2.5,HERE" assume that bit P2.5 is an _____ (input, output).
4. Write instructions to get the status of P2.7 and put it on P2.0.
5. Write instructions to toggle both bits of P1.7 and P1.0 continuously.

SUMMARY

This chapter focused on the I/O ports of the 8051. The four ports of the 8051, P0, P1, P2, and P3, each use 8 pins, making them 8-bit ports. These ports can be used for input or output. Port 0 can be used for both address and data. Port 3 can be used to provide interrupt and serial communication signals. Then I/O instructions of the 8051 were explained, and numerous examples were given. We also discussed the bit-addressability of the 8051 ports.

PROBLEMS

4.1: 8051 I/O PROGRAMMING

1. The 8051 DIP (dual in-line) package is a ____-pin package.
2. Which pins are assigned to V_{cc} and GND?
3. In the 8051, how many pins are designated as I/O port pins?
4. How many pins are designated as P0 and which number are they in the DIP package?
5. How many pins are designated as P1 and which number are they in the DIP package?
6. How many pins are designated as P2 and which number are they in the DIP package?
7. How many pins are designated as P3 and which number are they in the DIP package?
8. Upon RESET, all the bits of ports are configured as _input_ (input, output).
9. In the 8051, which port needs a pull-up resistor in order to be used as I/O?
10. Which port of the 8051 does not have any alternate function and can be used solely for I/O?
11. Write a program to get 8-bit data from P1 and send it to ports P0, P2, and P3.
12. Write a program to get 8-bit data from P2 and send it to ports P0 and P1.
13. In P3, which pins are for RxD and TxD?

14. At what memory location does the 8051 wake up upon RESET? What is the implication of that?
15. Write a program to toggle all the bits of P1 and P2 continuously
    (a) using AAH and 55H (b) using the CPL instruction.

4.2: I/O BIT-MANIPULATION PROGRAMMING

16. Which ports of the 8051 are bit-addressable?
17. What is the advantage of bit-addressability for 8051 ports?
18. When P1 is accessed as a single-bit port, it is designated as _____.
19. Is the instruction "CPL P1" a valid instruction?
20. Write a program to toggle P1.2 and P1.5 continuously without disturbing the rest of the bits.
21. Write a program to toggle P1.3, P1.7, and P2.5 continuously without disturbing the rest of the bits.
22. Write a program to monitor bit P1.3. When it is high, send 55H to P2.
23. Write a program to monitor the P2.7 bit. When it is low, send 55H and AAH to P0 continuously.
24. Write a program to monitor the P2.0 bit. When it is high, send 99H to P1. If it is low, send 66H to P1.
25. Write a program to monitor the P1.5 bit. When it is high, make a low-to-high-to-low pulse on P1.3.
26. Write a program to get the status of P1.3 and put it on P1.4.
27. The P1.4 refers to which bit of P1?
28. Write a program to get the status of P1.7 and P1.6 and put them on P1.0 and P1.7, respectively.

ANSWERS TO REVIEW QUESTIONS

4.1: 8051 I/O PROGRAMMING

1. 4, 8.
2. True
3. P0
4. False
5.  ```
    MOV P1,#99H
    MOV P2,#99H
    ```

4.2: I/O BIT-MANIPULATION PROGRAMMING

1. True
2.  ```
    H1: CPL P1.7
        SJMP H1
    ```
3. Input
4.  ```
    MOV C,P2.7
    MOV P2.0,C
    ```
5.  ```
    H1: CPL P1.7
        CPL P1.0
        SJMP H1
    ```

CHAPTER 5

8051 ADDRESSING MODES

OBJECTIVES

Upon completion of this chapter, you will be able to:

>>   List the five addressing modes of the 8051 microprocessor.
>>   Contrast and compare the addressing modes.
>>   Code 8051 Assembly language instructions using each addressing mode.
>>   Access RAM using various addressing modes.
>>   List the SFR (special function registers) addresses.
>>   Discuss how to access the SFR.
>>   Manipulate the stack using direct addressing mode.
>>   Code 8051 instructions to manipulate a look-up table.
>>   Access RAM, I/O, and ports using bit addresses.
>>   Discuss how to access the extra 128 bytes of RAM space in the 8052.

The CPU can access data in various ways. The data could be in a register, or in memory, or be provided as an immediate value. These various ways of accessing data are called *addressing modes*. In this chapter, we discuss 8051/52 addressing modes in the context of some examples.

The various addressing modes of a microprocessor are determined when it is designed, and therefore cannot be changed by the programmer. The 8051 provides a total of five distinct addressing modes. They are as follows:

1. immediate
2. register
3. direct
4. register indirect
5. indexed

In Section 5.1, we look at immediate and register addressing modes. In Section 5.2, we cover accessing memory using the direct, register indirect, and indexed addressing modes. Section 5.3 discusses the bit-addressability of RAM, registers, and I/O ports. In Section 5.4, we show how to access the extra 128 bytes of RAM in the 8052.

5.1: IMMEDIATE AND REGISTER ADDRESSING MODES

In this section, we first examine immediate addressing mode and then register addressing mode.

Immediate addressing mode

In this addressing mode, the source operand is a constant. In immediate addressing mode, as the name implies, when the instruction is assembled, the operand comes immediately after the opcode. Notice that the immediate data must be preceded by the pound sign, "#". This addressing mode can be used to load information into any of the registers, including the DPTR register. Examples follow.

```
MOV A,#25H          ;load 25H into A
MOV R4,#62          ;load the decimal value 62 into R4
MOV B,#40H          ;load 40H into B
MOV DPTR,#4521H     ;DPTR=4512H
```

Although the DPTR register is 16-bit, it can also be accessed as two 8-bit registers, DPH and DPL, where DPH is the high byte and DPL is the low byte. Look at the following code.

```
MOV DPTR,#2550H
        is the same as:
MOV DPL,#50H
MOV DPH,#25H
```

Also notice that the following code would produce an error since the value is larger than 16 bits.

```
MOV DPTR,#68975 ;illegal!! value > 65535 (FFFFFH)
```

We can use the EQU directive to access immediate data as shown below.

```
        COUNT       EQU   30
        . . .       . .
        MOV         R4,#COUNT       ;R4=1E(30=1EH)
        MOV         DPTR,#MYDATA    ;DPTR=200H


        ORG   200H
MYDATA: DB    "America"
```

Notice that we can also use immediate addressing mode to send data to 8051 ports. For example, "MOV P1,#55H" is a valid instruction.

Register addressing mode

Register addressing mode involves the use of registers to hold the data to be manipulated. Examples of register addressing mode follow.

```
MOV A,R0  ;copy the contents of R0 into A
MOV R2,A  ;copy the contents of A into R2
ADD A,R5  ;add the contents of R5 to contents of A
ADD A,R7  ;add the contents of R7 to contents of A
MOV R6,A  ;save accumulator in R6
```

It should be noted that the source and destination registers must match in size. In other words, coding "MOV DPTR,A" will give an error, since the source is an 8-bit register and the destination is a 16-bit register. See the following.

```
        MOV DPTR,#25F5H
        MOV R7,DPL
        MOV R6,DPH
```

Notice that we can move data between the accumulator and Rn (for $n = 0$ to 7) but movement of data between Rn registers is not allowed. For example, the instruction "MOV R4,R7" is invalid.

In the first two addressing modes, the operands are either inside one of the registers or tagged along with the instruction itself. In most programs, the data to be processed is often in some memory location of RAM or in the code space of ROM. There are many ways to access this data. The next section describes these different methods.

CHAPTER 5: 8051 ADDRESSING MODES   143

REVIEW QUESTIONS

1. Can the programmer of a microprocessor make up new addressing modes?
2. Show the instruction to load 1000 0000 (binary) into R3.
3. Why is the following invalid?
   "MOV R2,DPTR"
4. True or false. DPTR is a 16-bit register that is also accessible in low-byte and high-byte formats.
5. Is the PC (program counter) also available in low-byte and high-byte formats?

5.2: ACCESSING MEMORY USING VARIOUS ADDRESSING MODES

We can use direct or register indirect addressing modes to access data stored either in RAM or in registers of the 8051. This topic will be discussed thoroughly in this section. We will also show how to access on-chip ROM containing data using indexed addressing mode.

Direct addressing mode

As mentioned in Chapter 2, there are 128 bytes of RAM in the 8051. The RAM has been assigned addresses 00 to 7FH. The following is a summary of the allocation of these 128 bytes.

1. RAM locations 00–1FH are assigned to the register banks and stack.
2. RAM locations 20–2FH are set aside as bit-addressable space to save single-bit data. This is discussed in Section 5.3.
3. RAM locations 30–7FH are available as a place to save byte-sized data.

Although the entire 128 bytes of RAM can be accessed using direct addressing mode, it is most often used to access RAM locations 30–7FH. This is due to the fact that register bank locations are accessed by the register names of R0–R7, but there is no such name for other RAM locations. In the direct addressing mode, the data is in a RAM memory location whose address is known, and this address is given as a part of the instruction. Contrast this with immediate addressing mode, in which the operand itself is provided with the instruction. The "#" sign distinguishes between the two modes. See the examples below, and note the absence of the "#" sign.

```
MOV R0,40H     ;save content of RAM location 40H in R0
MOV 56H,A      ;save content of A in RAM location 56H
MOV R4,7FH     ;move contents of RAM location 7FH to R4
```

As discussed earlier, RAM locations 0 to 7 are allocated to bank 0 registers R0–R7. These registers can be accessed in two ways, as shown below.

```
MOV A,4        ;is the same as
MOV A,R4       ;which means copy R4 into A

MOV A,7        ;is the same as
MOV A,R7       ;which means copy R7 into A
```

```
MOV A,2        ;is the same as
MOV A,R2       ;which means copy R2 into A

MOV A,0        ;is the same as
MOV A,R0       ;which means copy R0 into A
```

The above examples should reinforce the importance of the "#" sign in 8051 instructions. See the following code.

```
MOV R2,#5  ;R2 with value 5
MOV A,2    ;copy R2 to A (A=R2=05)
MOV B,2    ;copy R2 to B (B=R2=05)
MOV 7,2    ;copy R2 to R7
           ;since "MOV R7,R2" is invalid
```

Although it is easier to use the names R0–R7 than their memory addresses, RAM locations 30H to 7FH cannot be accessed in any way other than by their addresses since they have no names.

SFR registers and their addresses

Among the registers we have discussed so far, we have seen that R0–R7 are part of the 128 bytes of RAM memory. What about registers A, B, PSW, and DPTR? Do they also have addresses? The answer is yes. In the 8051, registers A, B, PSW, and DPTR are part of the group of registers commonly referred to as SFRs (special function registers). There are many special function registers and they are widely used, as we will discuss in future chapters. The SFR can be accessed by their names (which is much easier) or by their addresses. For example, register A has address E0H, and register B has been designated the address F0H, as shown in Table 5-1. Notice how the following pairs of instructions mean the same thing.

```
MOV 0E0H,#55H  ;is the same as
MOV A,#55H     ;which means load 55H into A (A=55H)

MOV 0F0H,#25H  ;is the same as
MOV B,#25H     ;which means load 25H into B (B=25H)

MOV 0E0H,R2    ;is the same as
MOV A,R2       ;which means copy R2 into A

MOV 0F0H,R0    ;is the same as
MOV B,R0       ;which means copy R0 into B

MOV P1, A      ;is the same as
MOV 90H,A      ;which means copy reg A to P1
```

Table 5-1 lists the 8051 special function registers and their addresses.

Table 5-1. 8051 Special Function Register Addresses

Symbol	Name	Address
ACC*	Accumulator	0E0H
B*	B register	0F0H
PSW*	Program status word	0D0H
SP	Stack pointer	81H
DPTR	Data pointer 2 bytes	
DPL	Low byte	82H
DPH	High byte	83H
P0*	Port 0	80H
P1*	Port 1	90H
P2*	Port 2	0A0H
P3*	Port 3	0B0H
IP*	Interrupt priority control	0B8H
IE*	Interrupt enable control	0A8H
TMOD	Timer/counter mode control	89H
TCON*	Timer/counter control	88H
T2CON*	Timer/counter 2 control	0C8H
T2MOD	Timer/counter mode control	0C9H
TH0	Timer/counter 0 high byte	8CH
TL0	Timer/counter 0 low byte	8AH
TH1	Timer/counter 1 high byte	8DH
TL1	Timer/counter 1 low byte	8BH
TH2	Timer/counter 2 high byte	0CDH
TL2	Timer/counter 2 low byte	0CCH
RCAP2H	T/C 2 capture register high byte	0CBH
RCAP2L	T/C 2 capture register low byte	0CAH
SCON*	Serial control	98H
SBUF	Serial data buffer	99H
PCON	Power control	87H

* Bit-addressable

The following two points should be noted about the SFR addresses.

1. The special function registers have addresses between 80H and FFH. These addresses are above 80H, since the addresses 00 to 7FH are addresses of RAM memory inside the 8051.

2. Not all the address space of 80 to FF is used by the SFR. The unused locations 80H to FFH are reserved and must not be used by the 8051 programmer.

Regarding direct addressing mode, notice the following two points: (a) the address value is limited to one byte, 00–FFH, which means this addressing mode is limited to accessing RAM locations and registers located inside the

```
Example 5-1
```

Write a code to send 55H to ports P1 and P2, using (a) their names, (b) their addresses.

Solution:

(a)
```
     MOV A,#55H      ;A=55H
     MOV P1,A        ;P1=55H
     MOV P2,A        ;P2=55H
```

(b)   From Table 5-1, P1 address = 90H; P2 address = A0H
```
     MOV A,#55H      ;A=55H
     MOV 90H,A       ;P1=55H
     MOV 0A0H,A      ;P2=55H
```

8051; (b) if you examine the lst file for an Assembly language program, you will see that the SFR registers' names are replaced with their addresses as listed in Table 5-1. See Example 5-1.

Stack and direct addressing mode

Another major use of direct addressing mode is the stack. In the 8051 family, only direct addressing mode is allowed for pushing onto the stack. Therefore, an instruction such as "PUSH A" is invalid. Pushing the accumulator onto the stack must be coded as "PUSH 0E0H" where 0E0H is the address of register A. Similarly, pushing R3 of bank 0 is coded as "PUSH 03". Direct addressing mode must be used for the POP instruction as well. For example, "POP 04" will pop the top of the stack into R4 of bank 0.

Register indirect addressing mode

In the register indirect addressing mode, a register is used as a pointer to the data. If the data is inside the CPU, only registers R0 and R1 are used for this purpose. See Example 5-2. In other words, R2–R7 cannot be used to hold

```
Example 5-2
```

Show the code to push R5, R6, and A onto the stack and then pop them back into R2, R3, and B, where register B = register A, R2 = R6, and R3 = R5.

Solution:
```
     PUSH 05        ;push R5 onto stack
     PUSH 06        ;push R6 onto stack
     PUSH 0E0H      ;push register A onto stack
     POP  0F0H      ;pop top of stack into register B
                    ;now register B = register A
     POP  02        ;pop top of stack into R2
                    ;now R2 = R6
     POP  03        ;pop top of stack into R3
                    ;now R3 = R5
```

the address of an operand located in RAM when using this addressing mode. When R0 and R1 are used as pointers, that is, when they hold the addresses of RAM locations, they must be preceded by the "@" sign, as shown below.

```
MOV A,@R0 ;move contents of RAM location whose
          ;address is held by R0 into A
MOV @R1,B ;move contents of B into RAM location
          ;whose address is held by R1
```

Notice that R0 (as well as R1) is preceded by the "@" sign. In the absence of the "@" sign, MOV will be interpreted as an instruction moving the contents of register R0 to A, instead of the contents of the memory location pointed to by R0.

Advantage of register indirect addressing mode

One of the advantages of register indirect addressing mode is that it makes accessing data dynamic rather than static as in the case of direct addressing mode. Example 5-3 shows two cases of copying 55H into RAM locations 40H to 45H and Example 5-4 shows how to clear contents of RAM location. Notice in solution (b) that there are two instructions that are repeated numerous times. We can create a loop with those two instructions as shown in solution (c). Solution (c) is the most efficient and is possible only because of register indirect addressing mode. Looping is not possible in direct addressing mode. This is the main difference between the direct and register indirect addressing modes.

An example of how to use both R0 and R1 in the register indirect addressing mode in a block transfer is given in Example 5-5.

Limitation of register indirect addressing mode in the 8051

As stated earlier, R0 and R1 are the only registers that can be used for pointers in register indirect addressing mode. Since R0 and R1 are 8 bits wide, their use is limited to accessing any information in the internal RAM (scratch pad memory of 30H–7FH, or SFR). However, there are times when we need to access data stored in external RAM or in the code space of on-chip ROM. Whether accessing externally connected RAM or on-chip ROM, we need a 16-bit pointer. In such cases, the DPTR register is used, as shown next.

Indexed addressing mode and on-chip ROM access

Indexed addressing mode is widely used in accessing data elements of look-up table entries located in the program ROM space of the 8051. The instruction used for this purpose is "MOVC A,@A+DPTR". The 16-bit register DPTR and register A are used to form the address of the data element stored in on-chip ROM. Because the data elements are stored in the program (code) space ROM of the 8051, the instruction MOVC is used instead of MOV. The "C" means code. In this instruction the contents of A are added to the 16-bit register DPTR to form the 16-bit address of the needed data. See Examples 5-6 and 5-7.

Example 5-3

Write a program to copy the value 55H into RAM memory locations 40H to 45H using
(a) direct addressing mode,
(b) register indirect addressing mode without a loop, and
(c) with a loop.

Solution:

(a)

```
MOV A,#55H      ;load A with value 55H
MOV 40H,A       ;copy A to RAM location 40H
MOV 41H,A       ;copy A to RAM location 41H
MOV 42H,A       ;copy A to RAM location 42H
MOV 43H,A       ;copy A to RAM location 43H
MOV 44H,A       ;copy A to RAM location 44H
```

(b)

```
MOV A,#55H      ;load A with value 55H
MOV R0,#40H     ;load the pointer. R0=40H
MOV @R0,A       ;copy A to RAM location R0 points to
INC R0          ;increment pointer. Now R0=41H
MOV @R0,A       ;copy A to RAM location R0 points to
INC R0          ;increment pointer. Now R0=42H
MOV @R0,A       ;copy A to RAM location R0 points to
INC R0          ;increment pointer. Now R0=43H
MOV @R0,A       ;copy A to RAM location R0 points to
INC R0          ;increment pointer. Now R0=44H
MOV @R0,A
```

(c)

```
        MOV  A,#55H   ;A=55H
        MOV  R0,#40H  ;load pointer. R0=40H, RAM address
        MOV  R2,#05   ;load counter, R2=5
AGAIN:  MOV  @R0,A    ;copy 55H to RAM location R0 points to
        INC  R0       ;increment R0 pointer
        DJNZ R2,AGAIN ;loop until counter = zero
```

Example 5-4

Write a program to clear 16 RAM locations starting at RAM address 60H.

Solution:

```
        CLR   A          ;A=0
        MOV   R1,#60H    ;load pointer. R1=60H
        MOV   R7,#16     ;load counter, R7=16 (10 in hex)
AGAIN:  MOV   @R1,A      ;clear RAM location R1 points to
        INC   R1         ;increment R1 pointer
        DJNZ  R7,AGAIN   ;loop until counter = zero
```

Example 5-5

Write a program to copy a block of 10 bytes of data from RAM locations starting at 35H to RAM locations starting at 60H.

Solution:

```
        MOV  R0,#35H    ;source pointer
        MOV  R1,#60H    ;destination pointer
        MOV  R3,#10     ;counter
BACK:   MOV  A,@R0      ;get a byte from source
        MOV  @R1,A      ;copy it to destination
        INC  R0         ;increment source pointer
        INC  R1         ;increment destination pointer
        DJNZ R3,BACK    ;keep doing it for all ten bytes
```

Example 5-6

In this program, assume that the word "USA" is burned into ROM locations starting at 200H, and that the program is burned into ROM locations starting at 0. Analyze how the program works and state where "USA" is stored after this program is run.

Solution:

```
        ORG  0000H          ;burn into ROM starting at 0
        MOV  DPTR,#200H     ;DPTR=200H look-up table address
        CLR  A              ;clear A(A=0)
        MOVC A,@A+DPTR      ;get the char from code space
        MOV  R0,A           ;save it in R0
        INC  DPTR           ;DPTR=201 pointing to next char
        CLR  A              ;clear A(A=0)
        MOVC A,@A+DPTR      ;get the next char
        MOV  R1,A           ;save it in R1
        INC  DPTR           ;DPTR=202 pointing to next char
        CLR  A              ;clear A(A=0)
        MOVC A,@A+DPTR      ;get the next char
        MOV  R2,A           ;save it in R2
HERE:SJMP HERE             ;stay here
;Data is burned into code space starting at 200H
        ORG 200H
MYDATA:   DB "USA"
        END                ;end of program
```

In the above program, ROM locations 200H–202H have the following contents.
200=('U') 201=('S') 202=('A')
We start with DPTR = 200H and A = 0. The instruction "MOVC A, @A+DPTR" moves the contents of ROM location 200H (200H + 0 = 200H) to register A. Register A contains 55H, the ASCII value for "U." This is moved to R0. Next, DPTR is incremented to make DPTR = 201H. A is set to 0 again to get the contents of the next ROM location 201H, which holds character "S." After this program is run, we have R0 = 55H, R1 = 53H, and R2 = 41H, the ASCII values for the characters "U," "S," and "A."

Example 5-7

Assuming that ROM space starting at 250H contains "America," write a program to transfer the bytes into RAM locations starting at 40H.

Solution:

```
;(a) This method uses a counter
          ORG   0000
          MOV   DPTR,#MYDATA      ;load ROM pointer
          MOV   R0,#40H           ;load RAM pointer
          MOV   R2,#7             ;load counter
  BACK:   CLR   A                 ;A = 0
          MOVC  A,@A+DPTR         ;move data from code space
          MOV   @R0,A             ;save it in RAM
          INC   DPTR              ;increment ROM pointer
          INC   R0                ;increment RAM pointer
          DJNZ  R2,BACK           ;loop until counter=0
  HERE:   SJMP  HERE


;----------On-chip code space used for storing data
          ORG   250H
  MYDATA: DB    "AMERICA"
          END


;(b) This method uses null char for end of string
          ORG   0000
          MOV   DPTR,#MYDATA      ;load ROM pointer
          MOV   R0,#40H           ;load RAM pointer
  BACK:   CLR   A                 ;A=0
          MOVC  A,@A+DPTR         ;move data from code space
          JZ    HERE              ;exit if null character
          MOV   @R0,A             ;save it in RAM
          INC   DPTR              ;increment ROM pointer
          INC   R0                ;increment RAM pointer
          SJMP  BACK              ;loop
  HERE:   SJMP  HERE


;----------On-chip code space used for storing data
          ORG   250H
  MYDATA: DB    "AMERICA",0       ;notice null char for
                                  ;end of string
          END
```

Notice the null character, 0, indicating the end of the string, and how we use the JZ instruction to detect that.

Look-up table and the MOVC instruction

The look-up table is a widely used concept in microprocessor programming. It allows access to elements of a frequently used table with minimum operations. As an example, assume that for a certain application we need x^2 values in the range of 0 to 9. We can use a look-up table instead of calculating it. See Examples 5-8 and 5-9.

Example 5-8

Write a program to get the x value from P1 and send x^2 to P2, continuously.

Solution:

```
            ORG  0
            MOV  DPTR,#300H    ;load look-up table address
            MOV  A,#0FFH       ;A=FF
            MOV  P1,A          ;configure P1 as input port
BACK:       MOV  A,P1          ;get X
            MOVC A,@A+DPTR     ;get X squared from table
            MOV  P2,A          ;issue it to P2
            SJMP BACK          ;keep doing it


            ORG  300H
XSQR_TABLE:
            DB   0,1,4,9,16,25,36,49,64,81
            END
```

Notice that the first instruction could be replaced with "MOV DPTR,#XSQR_TABLE".

Example 5-9

Answer the following questions for Example 5-8.
(a) Indicate the content of ROM locations 300–309H.
(b) At what ROM location is the square of 6, and what value should be there?
(c) Assume that P1 has a value of 9. What value is at P2 (in binary)?

Solution:

(a) All values are in hex.

```
    300 = (00)     301 = (01)   302 = (04)   303 = (09)
    304 = (10)     4 × 4 = 16 = 10 in hex
    305 = (19)     5 × 5 = 25 = 19 in hex
    306 = (24)     6 × 6 = 36 = 24H
    307 = (31)     308 = (40)   309 = (51)
```

(b) 306H; it is 24H

(c) 01010001B, which is 51H and 81 in decimal ($9^2 = 81$).

In addition to being used to access program ROM, DPTR can be used to access memory externally connected to the 8051. This is discussed in Chapter 14.

Another register used in indexed addressing mode is the program counter. This is discussed in Appendix A.

In many of the examples above, the MOV instruction was used for the sake of clarity, even though one can use any instruction as long as that instruction supports the addressing mode. For example, the instruction "ADD A,@ R0" would add the contents of the memory location pointed to by R0 to the contents of register A. We will see more examples of using addressing modes with various instructions in the next few chapters.

Indexed addressing mode and MOVX instruction

As we have stated earlier, the 8051 has 64K bytes of code space under the direct control of the PC register. We just showed how to use the MOVC instruction to access a portion of this 64K-byte code space as data memory space. In many applications, the size of program code does not leave any room to share the 64K-byte code space with data. For this reason, the 8051 has another 64K bytes of memory space set aside exclusively for data storage. This data memory space is referred to as *external memory* and it is accessed only by the MOVX instruction. In other words, the 8051 has a total of 128K bytes of memory space since 64K bytes of code added to 64K bytes of data space gives us 128K bytes. One major difference between the code space and data space is that, unlike code space, the data space cannot be shared between code and data. This is such an important topic that we have dedicated an entire chapter to it: Chapter 14.

Accessing RAM Locations 30–7FH as scratch pad

As we have seen so far, in accessing registers R0–R7 of various banks, it is much easier to refer them by their R0–R7 names than by their RAM locations. The only problem is that we have only four banks and very often the task of bank switching and keeping track of register bank usage is tedious and prone to errors. For this reason, in many applications we use RAM locations 30–7FH as scratch pad and leave addresses 8–1FH for stack usage. That means that we use R0–R7 of bank 0, and if we need more registers we simply use RAM locations 30–7FH. Look at Example 5-10.

Example 5-10

Write a program to toggle P1 a total of 200 times. Use RAM location 32H to hold your counter value instead of registers R0–R7.

Solution:

```
        MOV    P1,#55H   ;P1=55H
        MOV    32H,#200  ;load counter value into RAM loc 32h
LOP1:CPL    P1           ;toggle P1
        ACALL  DELAY
        DJNZ   32H,LOP1  ;repeat 200 times
```

REVIEW QUESTIONS

1. The instruction "MOV A,40H" uses _____ addressing mode. Why?
2. What address is assigned to register R2 of bank 0?
3. What address is assigned to register R2 of bank 2?
4. What address is assigned to register A?
5. Which registers are allowed to be used for register indirect addressing mode if the data is in on-chip RAM?

5.3: BIT ADDRESSES FOR I/O AND RAM

Many microprocessors such as the 386 or Pentium allow programs to access registers and I/O ports in byte size only. In other words, if you need to check a single bit of an I/O port, you must read the entire byte first and then manipulate the whole byte with some logic instructions to get hold of the desired single bit. This is not the case with the 8051. Indeed, one of the most important features of the 8051 is the ability to access the registers, RAM, and I/O ports in bits instead of bytes. This is a very unique and powerful feature for a microprocessor made in the early 1980s. In this section, we show address assignment of bits of I/O, register, and memory, in addition to ways of programming them.

Bit-addressable RAM

Of the 128-byte internal RAM of the 8051, only 16 bytes are bit-addressable. The rest must be accessed in byte format. The bit-addressable RAM locations are 20H to 2FH. These 16 bytes provide 128 bits of RAM bit-addressability since $16 \times 8 = 128$. They are addressed as 0 to 127 (in decimal) or 00 to 7FH. Therefore, the bit addresses 0 to 7 are for the first byte of internal RAM location 20H, and 8 to 0FH are the bit addresses of the second byte of RAM location 21H, and so on. The last byte of 2FH has bit addresses of 78H to 7FH. See Figure 5-1 and Example 5-11. Note that internal RAM locations

---

Example 5-11

Find out to which byte each of the following bits belongs. Give the address of the RAM byte in hex.

(a) SETB 42H ;set bit 42H to 1 (d) SETB 28H ;set bit 28H to 1
(b) CLR 67H ;clear bit 67   (e) CLR 12 ;clear bit 12 (decimal)
(c) CLR 0FH ;clear bit 0FH   (f) SETB 05

Solution:

(a) RAM bit address of 42H belongs to D2 of RAM location 28H.
(b) RAM bit address of 67H belongs to D7 of RAM location 2CH.
(c) RAM bit address of 0FH belongs to D7 of RAM location 21H.
(d) RAM bit address of 28H belongs to D0 of RAM location 25H.
(e) RAM bit address of 12 belongs to D4 of RAM location 21H.
(f) RAM bit address of 05 belongs to D5 of RAM location 20H.

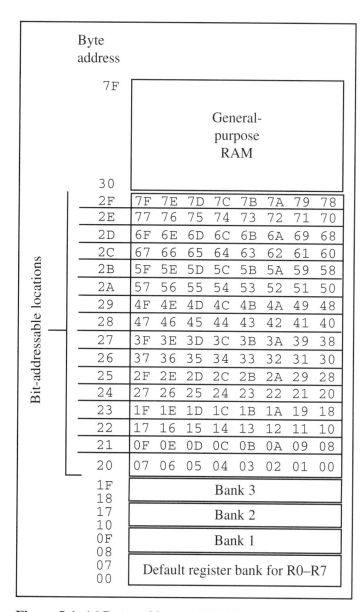

Figure 5-1. 16 Bytes of Internal RAM
Note: They are both bit- and byte-accessible.

20–2FH are both byte-addressable and bit-addressable.

In order to avoid confusion regarding the addresses 00–7FH, the following two points must be noted.

1. The 128 bytes of RAM have the byte addresses of 00–7FH and can be accessed in byte size using various addressing modes such as direct and register indirect, as we have seen in this chapter and previous chapters. These 128 bytes are accessed using byte-type instructions.

2. The 16 bytes of RAM locations 20–2FH also have bit addresses of 00–7FH since $16 \times 8 = 128$. In order to access these 128 bits of RAM locations and other bit-addressable space of 8051 individually, we can use only the single-bit instructions such as SETB. Table 5-2 provides a list of single-bit instructions. Notice that the single-bit instructions use only one addressing mode and that is direct addressing mode. The first two sections of this chapter showed various addressing modes of byte-addressable space of the 8051, including indirect addressing mode. It must be noted that there is no indirect addressing mode for single-bit instructions.

Table 5-2. Single-Bit Instructions

Instruction		Function
SETB	bit	Set the bit (bit = 1)
CLR	bit	Clear the bit (bit = 0)
CPL	bit	Complement the bit (bit = NOT bit)
JB	bit,target	Jump to target if bit = 1 (jump if bit)
JNB	bit,target	Jump to target if bit = 0 (jump if no bit)
JBC	bit,target	Jump to target if bit = 1, clear bit (jump if bit, then clear)

I/O port bit addresses

As we discussed in Chapter 4, the 8051 has four 8-bit I/O ports: P0, P1, P2, and P3. We can access either the entire 8 bits or any single bit without altering the rest. When accessing a port in a single-bit manner, we use the syntax "SETB X.Y" where X is the port number 0, 1, 2, or 3, and Y is the desired bit number from 0 to 7 for data bits D0 to D7. See Figure 5-2. For example, "SETB P1.5" sets high bit 5 of port 1. Remember that D0 is the LSB and D7 is the MSB.

As mentioned earlier in this chapter, every SFR register is assigned a byte address and ports P0–P3 are part of the SFR. For example, P0 is assigned byte address 80H, and P1 has address of 90H as shown in Figure 5-2. While all of the SFR registers are byte-addressable some of them are also bit-addressable. The P0–P3 are among this category of SFR registers. From Figure 5-2, we see that the bit addresses for P0 are 80H to 87H, and for P1 are 90H to 97H, and so on.

Notice that when code such as "SETB P1.0" is assembled, it becomes "SETB 90H" since P1.0 has the RAM address of 90H. Also notice from Figures 5-1 and 5-2 that bit addresses 00–7FH belong to RAM byte addresses 20–2FH, and bit addresses 80–F7H belong to SFR of P0, TCON, P1, SCON, P2 and so on. The bit addresses for P0–P3 are shown in Table 5-3 and discussed next.

Bit memory map

From Figures 5-1 and 5-2 and Table 5-3, once again notice the following facts.

1. The bit addresses 00–7FH are assigned to RAM locations of 20–2FH.

Byte address	Bit address								
FF									
F0	F7	F6	F5	F4	F3	F2	F1	F0	B
E0	E7	E6	E5	E4	E3	E2	E1	E0	ACC
D0	D7	D6	D5	D4	D3	D2	D1	D0	PSW
B8	--	--	--	BC	BB	BA	B9	B8	IP
B0	B7	B6	B5	B4	B3	B2	B1	B0	P3
A8	AF	--	--	AC	AB	AA	A9	A8	IE
A0	A7	A6	A5	A4	A3	A2	A1	A0	P2
99	Not bit-addressable								SBUF
98	9F	9E	9D	9C	9B	9A	99	98	SCON
90	97	96	95	94	93	92	91	90	P1
8D	Not bit-addressable								TH1
8C	Not bit-addressable								TH0
8B	Not bit-addressable								TL1
8A	Not bit-addressable								TL0
89	Not bit-addressable								TMOD
88	8F	8E	8D	8C	8B	8A	89	88	TCON
87	Not bit-addressable								PCON
83	Not bit-addressable								DPH
82	Not bit-addressable								DPL
81	Not bit-addressable								SP
80	87	86	85	84	83	82	81	80	P0

Special function registers

Figure 5-2. SFR RAM Address (Byte and Bit)

Table 5-3. Bit Addresses for All Ports

P0	Address	P1	Address	P2	Address	P3	Address	Port's Bit
P0.0	80	P1.0	90	P2.0	A0	P3.0	B0	D0
P0.1	81	P1.1	91	P2.1	A1	P3.1	B1	D1
P0.2	82	P1.2	92	P2.2	A2	P3.2	B2	D2
P0.3	83	P1.3	93	P2.3	A3	P3.3	B3	D3
P0.4	84	P1.4	94	P2.4	A4	P3.4	B4	D4
P0.5	85	P1.5	95	P2.5	A5	P3.5	B5	D5
P0.6	86	P1.6	96	P2.6	A6	P3.6	B6	D6
P0.7	87	P1.7	97	P2.7	A7	P3.7	B7	D7

2. The bit addresses 80–87H are assigned to the P0 port.
3. The bit addresses 88–8FH are assigned to the TCON register.
4. The bit addresses 90–97H are assigned to the P1 port.
5. The bit addresses 98–9FH are assigned to the SCON register.
6. The bit addresses A0–A7H are assigned to the P2 port.
7. The bit addresses A8–AFH are assigned to the IE register.
8. The bit addresses B0–B7H are assigned to the P3 port.
9. The bit addresses B8–BFH are assigned to IP.
10. The bit addresses C0–CFH are not assigned.
11. The bit addresses D0–D7H are assigned to the PSW register.
12. The bit addresses D8–DFH are not assigned.
13. The bit addresses E0–E7H are assigned to the accumulator register.
14. The bit addresses E8–EFH are not assigned.
15. The bit addresses F0–F7H are assigned to the B register. See Example 5-12.

Example 5-12

For each of the following instructions, state to which port the bit belongs. Use Table 5-3.

(a) SETB 86H   (b) CLR 87H   (c) SETB 92H   (d) SETB 0A7H

Solution:

(a) SETB 86H is for SETB P0.6.
(b) CLR 87H is for CLR P0.7.
(c) SETB 92H is for SETB P1.2.
(d) SETB 0A7H is for SETB P2.7.

Registers bit-addressability

While all I/O ports are bit-addressable, that is not the case with registers, as seen from Figure 5-1. Only registers A, B, PSW, IP, IE, ACC, SCON, and TCON are bit-addressable. Of the bit-addressable registers, we will concentrate on the familiar registers A, B, and PSW. The rest will be discussed in future chapters.

Now let's see how we can use bit-addressability of registers A and PSW. As we discussed in Chapter 2, in the PSW register, two bits are set aside for the selection of the register banks. See Figure 5-3. Upon RESET, bank 0 is selected. We can select any other banks using the bit-addressability of the PSW, as was shown in Chapter 2. The bit addressability of PSW also eliminates the need for instructions such as JOV (Jump if OV=1). See Examples 5-13 and 5-14.

Examples 5-15 through 5-19 provide a better understanding of the bit-addressability of the 8051.

CY	AC	F0	RS1	RS0	OV	--	P

RS1	RS0	Register Bank	Address
0	0	0	00H–07H
0	1	1	08H–0FH
1	0	2	10H–17H
1	1	3	18H–1FH

Figure 5-3. Bits of the PSW Register

Example 5-13

Write a program to save the accumulator in R7 of bank 2.

Solution:

```
        CLR   PSW.3
        SETB  PSW.4
        MOV   R7,A
```

Example 5-14

While there are instructions such as JNC and JC to check the carry flag bit (CY), there are no such instructions for the overflow flag bit (OV). How would you write code to check OV?

Solution:

The OV flag is PSW.2 of the PSW register. PSW is a bit-addressable register; therefore, we can use the following instruction to check the OV flag.

```
        JB    PSW.2,TARGET   ;jump if OV=1
```

Example 5-15

Write a program to see if the RAM location 37H contains an even value. If so, send it to P2. If not, make it even and then send it to P2.

Solution:

```
     MOV  A,37H      ;load RAM location 37H into accumulator
     JNB  ACC.0,YES  ;is D0 of reg A 0? if so jump
     INC  A          ;it is odd, make it even
YES: MOV  P2,A       ;send it to P2
```

Example 5-16

Assume that bit P2.3 is an input and represents the condition of a door. If it goes high, it means that the door is open. Monitor the bit continuously. Whenever it goes high, send a low-to-high pulse to port P1.5 to turn on a buzzer.

Solution:

```
     HERE:JNB    P2.3,HERE    ;keep monitoring for high
          CLR    P1.5         ;Clear bit (P1.5 = 0)
          ACALL  DELAY
          SETB   P1.5         ;P1.5=1 (low-to-high pulse)
          ACALL  DELAY
          SJMP   HERE
```

Example 5-17

The status of bits P1.2 and P1.3 of I/O port P1 must be saved before they are changed. Write a program to save the status of P1.2 in bit location 06 and the status of P1.3 in bit location 07.

Solution:

```
     CLR  06         ;clear bit address 06
     CLR  07         ;clear bit address 07
     JNB  P1.2,OVER  ;check bit P1.2,if 0 then jump
     SETB 06         ;if P1.2=1,set bit location 06 to 1
OVER:JNB  P1.3,NEXT  ;check bit P1.3, if 0 then jump
     SETB 07         ;if P1.3=1, set bit location 07 to 1
NEXT:...
```

Example 5-18

Write a program to save the status of bit P1.7 on RAM address bit 05.

Solution:

```
        MOV  C,P1.7      ;get bit from port
        MOV  05,C        ;save bit
```

Example 5-19

Write a program to get the status of bit pin P1.7 and send it to pin P2.0.

Solution:

```
HERE:   MOV  C,P1.7      ;get bit from port
        MOV  P2.0,C      ;send bit to port
        SJMP HERE        ;repeat forever
```

Using BIT directive

The BIT directive is a widely used directive to assign the bit-address-able I/O and RAM locations. The BIT directive allows a program to assign the I/O or RAM bit at the beginning of the program, making it easier to modify them. For the use of BIT directive, see Examples 5-20 through 5-23.

Example 5-20

Assume that bit P2.3 is an input and represents the condition of an oven. If it goes high, it means that the oven is hot. Monitor the bit continuously. Whenever it goes high, send a low-to-high pulse to port P1.5 to turn on a buzzer.

Solution:

```
OVEN_HOT  BIT  P2.3
BUZZER    BIT  P1.5

HERE:JNB    OVEN_HOT,HERE ;keep monitoring for HOT
     ACALL DELAY          ;
     CPL    BUZZER        ;sound the buzzer
     ACALL DELAY          ;
     SJMP   HERE
```

This is similar to Example 5-16, except the use of BIT directive allows us to assign the OVEN_HOT and BUZZER bit to any port. This way you do not have to search the program for them.

Example 5-21

An LED is connected to pin P1.7. Write a program to toggle the LED forever.

Solution:

```
LED       BIT    P.7      ;using BIT directive
HERE:     CPL    LED      ;toggle LED
          LCALL  DELAY    ;delay
          SJMP   HERE     ;repeat forever
```

Example 5-22

A switch is connected to pin P1.7 and an LED to pin P2.0. Write a program to get the status of the switch and send it to the LED.

Solution:

```
SW        BIT   P1.7    ;assign bit
LED       BIT   P2.0    ;assign bit
HERE:     MOV   C,SW    ;get the bit from the port
          MOV   LED,C   ;send the bit to the port
          SJMP  HERE    ;repeat forever
```

Example 5-23

Assume that RAM bit location 12H holds the status of whether there has been a phone call or not. If it is high, it means there has been a new call since it was checked the last time. Write a program to display "New Messages" on an LCD if bit RAM 12H is high. If it is low, the LCD should say "No New Messages."

Solution:

```
      PHONBIT BIT 12H
      MOV    C,PHONBIT    ;copy bit location 12H to carry
      JNC    NO           ;check to see if is high
      MOV    DPTR,#400H   ;yes, load address of message
      LCALL  DISPLAY      ;display message (see Chap. 12)
      SJMP   EXIT         ;get out
NO:   MOV    DPTR,#420H   ;load the address of No message
      LCALL  DISPLAY      ;display it
EXIT:                     ;exit

;-------------data to be displayed on LCD
      ORG    400H
YES_MG:  DB    "New Messages",0
      ORG    420H
NO_MG:   DB    "No New Messages",0
```

Using EQU directive

We can also use the EQU directive to assign addresses, as shown in the next few examples. Notice that in Example 5-24, the ports are defined by their names, while in Example 5-25, they are defined by their addresses.

Example 5-24

A switch is connected to pin P1.7. Write a program to check the status of the switch and make the following decision.
(a) If sw = 0, send "NO" to P2.
(b) If sw = 1, send "YES" to P2.

Solution:

```
        SW          EQU  P1.7
        MYDATA      EQU  P2

        HERE:       MOV  C,SW
                    JC   OVER
                    MOV  MYDATA,#'N'    ;SW=0, send "NO"
                    MOV  MYDATA,#'O'
                    SJMP HERE
        OVER:       MOV  MYDATA,#'Y'    ;SW=1, send "YES"
                    MOV  MYDATA,#'E'
                    MOV  MYDATA,#'S'
                    SJMP HERE
                    END
```

Example 5-25

A switch is connected to pin P1.7. Write a program to check the status of the switch and make the following decision.
(a) If sw = 0, send '0' to P2.
(b) If sw = 1, send '1' to P2.
Use EQU to designate the I/O ports.

Solution:

```
        SW          EQU  97H            ;P1.7 bit address
        MYDATA      EQU  0A0H           ;P2 address
        HERE:       MOV  C,SW
                    JC   OVER
                    MOV  MYDATA,#'0'    ;00110000 to P2
                    SJMP HERE
        OVER:       MOV  MYDATA,#'1'    ;00110001 to P2
                    SJMP HERE
                    END
```

REVIEW QUESTIONS

1. True or false. All I/O ports of the 8051 are bit-addressable.
2. True or false. All registers of the 8051 are bit-addressable.
3. True or false. All RAM locations of the 8051 are bit-addressable.
4. Indicate which of the following registers are bit-addressable.
   (a) A   (b) B   (c) R4   (d) PSW   (e) R7
5. Of the 128 bytes of RAM in the 8051, how many bytes are bit-addressable? List them.
6. How would you check to see whether bit D0 of R3 is high or low?
7. Find out to which byte each of the following bits belongs. Give the address of the RAM byte in hex.
   (a) SETB 20   (b) CLR 32   (c) SETB 12H
   (d) SETB 95H (e) SETB 0E6H
8. While bit addresses 00–7FH belong to _____, bit addresses 80–F7H belong to _____.
9. True or false. P0, P1, P2, and P3 are part of SFR.
10. True or false. Register ACC is bit-addressable.

5.4: EXTRA 128-BYTE ON-CHIP RAM IN 8052

The 8052 microprocessor is an enhanced version of the 8051. In recent years, the 8052 has replaced the 8051 due to many of its new features. DS89C430 is an example of 8052 architecture. One of the new features of the 8052 is an extra 128 bytes of on-chip RAM space. In other words, the 8051 has only 128 bytes of on-chip RAM, while the 8052 has 256 bytes of it. To understand it, first let's recall the following two facts from earlier discussion in this chapter and Chapter 2.

1. The 8051 has 128 bytes of on-chip RAM with addresses 00–7FH. They are used for (a) register banks (addresses 00–1FH), (b) bit-addressable RAM space (addresses 20–2FH), and (c) the scratch pad (addresses 30–7FH).

2. Another 128 bytes of on-chip RAM with addresses 80–FFH are designated as special function registers. Again, the SFRs are accessed by direct addressing mode as we saw earlier in this chapter.

In addition to the above two features, the 8052 has another 128 bytes of on-chip RAM with addresses 80–FFH. This extra 128 bytes of on-chip RAM is often called upper memory to distinguish it from the lower 128 bytes of 00–7FH. The only problem is, the address space 80–FFH is the same address space assigned to the SFRs. In other words, they are physically two separate memories, but they have the same addresses. This parallel address space in the 8052 forces us to use two different addressing modes to access them as described next.

1. To access the SFRs, we use direct addressing mode. The instruction "MOV 90H, #55H" is an example of accessing the SFR with direct addressing mode. Since 90H is the address of P1, this is same as "MOV P1, #55H".

2. To access the upper 128 bytes, we use the indirect addressing mode, which uses R0 and R1 registers as pointers. Therefore, instructions "MOV @R0, A" and "MOV @R1, A" are employed to access the upper memory as long as registers R0 and R1 have values of 80H or higher. For example, the following codes will put 55H into address 90H of the upper 128 bytes of RAM.

```
MOV R0,#90H  ;load the upper memory address
MOV @R0,#55H ;put 55H into an address pointed to
             ;by R0 reg.
```

Figure 5-4 shows the parallel space shared between the SFR and the upper 128 bytes of RAM in the 8052. Example 5-26 shows how to access the upper 128 bytes of on-chip RAM in the 8052 microprocessor.

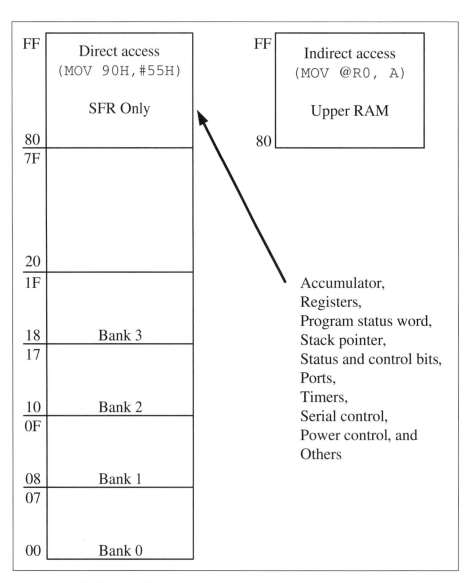

Figure 5-4. 8052 On-Chip RAM Address Space

Example 5-26

Write a program for the 8052 to put 55H into the upper RAM locations of 90–99H.

Solution:

```
      ORG   0
      MOV   A,#55H
      MOV   R2,#10
      MOV   R0,#90H  ;access the upper 128 bytes of on-chip RAM
BACK:MOV   @R0,A    ;use indirect addressing mode
      INC   R0
      DJNZ  R2,BACK  ;repeat for all locations
      SJMP  $        ;stay here
      END
```

Run the above program on your simulator and examine the upper memory to see the result. (See Figures 5-5 and 5-6 for screenshots.)

For data to be processed in the code space of ROM, see Example 5-27.

Example 5-27

Assume that the on-chip ROM has a message. Write a program to copy it from code space into the upper memory space starting at address 80H. Also, as you place a byte in upper RAM, give a copy to P0.

Solution:

```
      ORG   0
      MOV   DPTR,#MYDATA
      MOV   R1,#80H     ;access the upper 128 bytes of on-chip RAM
B1:   CLR   A
      MOVC  A,@A+DPTR   ;copy from code ROM space
      MOV   @R1,A       ;store in upper RAM space
      MOV   P0,A        ;give a copy to P0
      JZ    EXIT        ;exit if last byte
      INC   DPTR        ;increment DPTR
      INC   R1          ;increment R1
      SJMP  B1          ;repeat until the last byte
EXIT: SJMP  $           ;stay here when finished
;-----------
      ORG   300H
MYDATA: DB  "The Promise of World Peace",0
      END
```

Run the above program on your simulator and examine the upper memory to see the result.

Simulators and Data RAM space

All the major 8051/52 simulators have ways of showing the data RAM contents. Figures 5-5 and 5-6 show some of them.

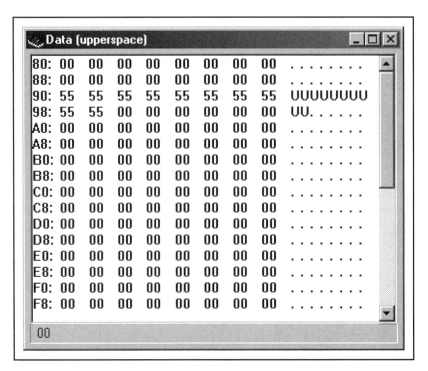

Figure 5-5. Franklin Software's ProView Upper Memory for the 8052

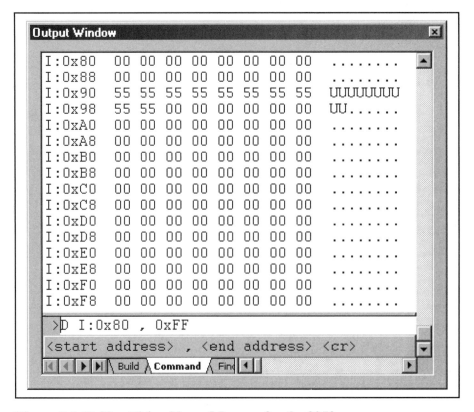

Figure 5-6. Keil's μVision Upper Memory for the 8052

REVIEW QUESTIONS

1. True or false. The 8052 is an upgraded version of the 8051.
2. True or false. The 8052 has a total of 256 bytes of on-chip RAM in addition to the SFRs.
3. True or false. The extra 128 bytes of RAM in the 8052 is physically the same RAM as the SFR.
4. Give the address for the upper RAM of the 8052.
5. Show how to put value 99H into RAM location F6H of upper RAM in the 8052.

SUMMARY

This chapter described the five addressing modes of the 8051. Immediate addressing mode uses a constant for the source operand. Register addressing mode involves the use of registers to hold data to be manipulated. Direct or register indirect addressing modes can be used to access data stored in either RAM or in registers of the 8051. Direct addressing mode is also used to manipulate the stack. Register indirect addressing mode uses a register as a pointer to the data. The advantage of this is that it makes addressing dynamic rather than static. Indexed addressing mode is widely used in accessing data elements of look-up table entries located in the program ROM space of the 8051.

A group of registers called the SFRs (special function registers) can be accessed by their names or their addresses. We also discussed the bit-addressable ports, registers, and RAM locations and showed how to use single-bit instructions to access them directly.

PROBLEMS

5.1 AND 5.2: IMMEDIATE AND REGISTER ADDRESSING MODES/ ACCESSING MEMORY USING VARIOUS ADDRESSING MODES

1. Which of the following are invalid uses of immediate addressing mode?
       (a) MOV A,#24H   (b) MOV R1,30H   (c) MOV R4,#60H
2. Identify the addressing mode for each of the following.
       (a) MOV B,#34H   (b) MOV A,50H   (c) MOV R2,07
       (d) MOV R3,#0   (e) MOV R7,0   (f) MOV R6,#7FH
       (g) MOV R0,A   (h) MOV B,A   (i) MOV A,@R0
       (j) MOV R7,A   (k) MOV A,@R1
3. Indicate the address assigned to each of the following.
       (a) R0 of bank 0   (b) ACC   (c) R7 of bank 0
       (d) R3 of bank 2   (e) B   (f) R7 of bank 3
       (g) R4 of bank 1   (h) DPL   (i) R6 of bank 1
       (j) R0 of bank 3   (k) DPH   (l) P0
4. Which register bank shares space with the stack?
5. In accessing the stack, we must use _____ addressing mode.

6. What does the following instruction do?
   "MOV A,0F0H"
7. What does the following instruction do?
   "MOV A,1FH"
8. Write code to push R0, R1, and R3 of bank 0 onto the stack and pop them back into R5, R6, and R7 of bank 3.
9. Which registers are allowed to be used for register indirect addressing mode when accessing data in RAM?
10. Write a program to copy FFH into RAM locations 50H to 6FH.
11. Write a program to copy 10 bytes of data starting at ROM address 400H to RAM locations starting at 30H.
12. Write a program to find y where $y = x^2 + 2x + 5$, and x is between 0 and 9.
13. Write a program to add the following data and store the result in RAM location 30H.

```
         ORG   200H
MYDATA:  DB    06,09,02,05,07
```

5.3: BIT ADDRESSES FOR I/O AND RAM

14. "SETB A" is a(n) _____ (valid, invalid) instruction.
15. "CLR A" is a(n) _____ (valid, invalid) instruction.
16. "CPL A" is a(n) _____ (valid, invalid) instruction.
17. Which I/O ports of P0, P1, P2, and P3 are bit-addressable?
18. Which registers of the 8051 are bit-addressable?
19. Which of the following instructions are valid? If valid, indicate which bit is altered.

   (a) SETB P1   (b) SETB P2.3   (c) CLR ACC.5
   (d) CLR 90H   (e) SETB B.4   (f) CLR 80H
   (g) CLR PSW.3   (h) CLR 87H

20. Write a program to generate a square wave with 75% duty cycle on bit P1.5.
21. Write a program to generate a square wave with 80% duty cycle on bit P2.7.
22. Write a program to monitor P1.4. When it goes high, the program will generate a sound (square wave of 50% duty cycle) on pin P2.7.
23. Write a program to monitor P2.1. When it goes low, the program will send the value 55H to P0.
24. What bit addresses are assigned to P0?
25. What bit addresses are assigned to P1?
26. What bit addresses are assigned to P2?
27. What bit addresses are assigned to P3?
28. What bit addresses are assigned to the PCON register?
29. What bit addresses are assigned to the TCON register?
30. What bit addresses are assigned to register A?
31. What bit addresses are assigned to register B?
32. What bit addresses are assigned to register PSW?
33. The following are bit addresses. Indicate where each one belongs.
   (a) 85H   (b) 87H   (c) 88H   (d) 8DH   (e) 93H   (f) A5H
   (g) A7H   (h) B3H   (i) D4H   (j) D7H   (k) F3H
34. Write a program to save registers A and B on R3 and R5 of bank 2, respectively.

35. Give another instruction for "CLR C".
36. In Problem 19, assemble each instruction and state if there is any difference between them.
37. Show how you would check whether the OV flag is low.
38. Show how you would check whether the CY flag is high.
39. Show how you would check whether the P flag is high.
40. Show how you would check whether the AC flag is high.
41. Give the bit addresses assigned to the flag bit of CY, P, AC, and OV.
42. Of the 128 bytes of RAM locations in the 8051, how many of them are assigned a bit address as well? Indicate which bytes those are.
43. Indicate the bit addresses assigned to RAM locations 20H to 2FH.
44. The byte addresses assigned to the 128 bytes of RAM are _____ to _____.
45. The byte addresses assigned to the SFR are _____ to _____.
46. Indicate the bit addresses assigned to both of the following. Is there a gap between them?
    (a) RAM locations 20H to 2FH   (b) SFR
47. The following are bit addresses. Indicate where each one belongs.
    (a) 05H   (b) 47H   (c) 18H   (d) 2DH   (e) 53H   (f) 15H
    (g) 67H   (h) 55H   (i) 14H   (j) 37H   (k) 7FH
48. True or false. The bit addresses of less than 80H are assigned to RAM locations 20–2FH.
49. True or false. The bit addresses of 80H and beyond are assigned to SFR.
50. Write instructions to save the CY flag bit in bit location 4.
51. Write instructions to save the AC flag bit in bit location 16H.
52. Write instructions to save the P flag bit in bit location 12H.
53. Write instructions to see whether the D0 and D1 bits of register A are high. If so, divide register A by 4.
54. Write a program to see whether the D7 bit of register A is high. If so, send a message to the LCD stating that ACC has a negative number.
55. Write a program to see whether the D7 bit of register B is low. If so, send a message to the LCD stating that register B has a positive number.
56. Write a program to set high all the bits of RAM locations 20H to 2FH using the following methods:
    (a) byte addresses   (b) bit addresses
57. Write a program to see whether the accumulator is divisible by 8.
58. Write a program to find the number of zeros in register R2.

5.4: EXTRA 128-BYTE ON-CHIP RAM IN 8052

59. What is the total number of bytes of RAM in the 8052 including the SFR registers? Contrast that with the 8051.
60. What addressing mode is used to access the SFR?
61. What addressing mode is used to access the upper 128 bytes of RAM in the 8052?
62. Give the address range of the lower and the upper 128 bytes of RAM in the 8052.
63. In the 8052, the SFR shares the address space with the _____ (lower, upper) 128 bytes of RAM.
64. In Question 63, discuss if they are physically the same memory.

65. Explain what is the difference between these two instructions.
    (a) MOV 80H,#99H   (b) MOV @R0,#99H if R0=80H

66. Which registers can be used to access the upper 128 bytes of RAM in the 8052?

67. Write a program to put 55H into RAM locations C0–CFH of upper memory.

68. Write a program to copy the contents of lower RAM locations 60–6FH to upper RAM locations D0–DFH.

ANSWERS TO REVIEW QUESTIONS

5.1: IMMEDIATE AND REGISTER ADDRESSING MODES

1. No
2. MOV R3,#10000000B
3. Source and destination registers' sizes do not match.
4. True
5. No

5.2: ACCESSING MEMORY USING VARIOUS ADDRESSING MODES

1. Direct; because there is no "#" sign
2. 02
3. 12H
4. E0H
5. R0 and R1

5.3: BIT ADDRESSES FOR I/O AND RAM

1. True
2. False
3. False
4. A, B, and PSW
5. 16 bytes are bit-addressable; they are from byte location 20H to 2FH.
6. MOV A,R3
   JNB ACC.0
7. For (a), (b), and (c) use Figure 5-1.   (a) RAM byte 22H, bit D4
   (b) RAM byte 24H, bit D0   (c) RAM byte 22H, bit D2
   For (d) and (e) use Figure 5-2.   (d) SETB P1.5   (e) SETB ACC.6
8. RAM bytes 20–2FH, special function registers.
9. True
10. True

5.4: EXTRA 128-BYTE ON-CHIP RAM IN 8052

1. True
2. True
3. False
4. 80–FFH
5. MOV A,#99H
   MOV R0,#0F6H
   MOV @R0,A

CHAPTER 6

ARITHMETIC, LOGIC INSTRUCTIONS, AND PROGRAMS

OBJECTIVES

Upon completion of this chapter, you will be able to:

>> Define the range of numbers possible in 8051 unsigned data.
>> Code addition and subtraction instructions for unsigned data.
>> Perform addition of BCD (binary coded decimal) data.
>> Code 8051 unsigned data multiplication and division instructions.
>> Code 8051 Assembly language logic instructions AND, OR, and EX-OR.
>> Use 8051 logic instructions for bit manipulation.
>> Use compare and jump instructions for program control.
>> Code 8051 rotate instruction and data serialization.
>> Explain the BCD system of data representation.
>> Contrast and compare packed and unpacked BCD data.
>> Code 8051 programs for ASCII and BCD data conversion.
>> Code 8051 programs to create and test the checksum byte.

This chapter describes all 8051 arithmetic and logic instructions. Program examples are given to illustrate the application of these instructions. In Section 6.1, we discuss instructions and programs related to addition, subtraction, multiplication, and division of unsigned numbers. Signed numbers are discussed in Section 6.2. In Section 6.3, we discuss the logic instructions AND, OR, and XOR, as well as the COMPARE instruction. The ROTATE instruction and data serialization are discussed in Section 6.4. In Section 6.5, we provide some real-world applications such as BCD and ASCII conversion and checksum byte testing.

6.1: ARITHMETIC INSTRUCTIONS

Unsigned numbers are defined as data in which all the bits are used to represent data, and no bits are set aside for the positive or negative sign. This means that the operand can be between 00 and FFH (0 to 255 decimal) for 8-bit data.

Addition of unsigned numbers

In the 8051, in order to add numbers together, the accumulator register (A) must be involved. The form of the ADD instruction is

```
ADD A, source    ;A = A + source
```

The instruction ADD is used to add two operands. The destination operand is always in register A, while the source operand can be a register, immediate data, or in memory. Remember that memory-to-memory arithmetic operations are never allowed in 8051 Assembly language. The instruction could change any of the AC, CY, or P bits of the flag register, depending on the operands involved. The effect of the ADD instruction on the overflow flag is discussed in Section 6.3 since it is used mainly in signed number operations. Look at Example 6-1.

Example 6-1

Show how the flag register is affected by the following instructions.

```
        MOV A,#0F5H          ;A=F5 hex
        ADD A,#0BH           ;A=F5+0B=00
```

Solution:

```
      F5H        1111 0101
  +   0BH    +   0000 1011
     100H        0000 0000
```

After the addition, register A (destination) contains 00 and the flags are as follows:

CY = 1 since there is a carry out from D7.
P = 0 because the number of 1s is zero (an even number).
AC = 1 since there is a carry from D3 to D4.

Addition of individual bytes

Chapter 2 contained a program that added 5 bytes of data. The sum was purposely kept less than FFH, the maximum value an 8-bit register can hold. To calculate the sum of any number of operands, the carry flag should be checked after the addition of each operand. Example 6-2 uses R7 to accumulate carries as the operands are added to A.

Analysis of Example 6-2

Three iterations of the loop are shown below. Tracing of the program is left to the reader as an exercise.

1. In the first iteration of the loop, 7DH is added to A with CY = 0 and R7 = 00, and the counter R2 = 04.

2. In the second iteration of the loop, EBH is added to A, which results in A = 68H and CY = 1. Since a carry occurred, R7 is incremented. Now the counter R2 = 03.

3. In the third iteration, C5H is added to A, which makes A = 2DH. Again a carry occurred, so R7 is incremented again. Now counter R2 = 02.

At the end when the loop is finished, the sum is held by registers A and R7, where A has the low byte and R7 has the high byte.

Example 6-2

Assume that RAM locations 40–44 have the following values. Write a program to find the sum of the values. At the end of the program, register A should contain the low byte and R7 the high byte. All values are in hex.

```
40=(7D)
41=(EB)
42=(C5)
43=(5B)
44=(30)
```

Solution:

```
        MOV  R0,#40H   ;load pointer
        MOV  R2,#5     ;load counter
        CLR  A         ;A=0
        MOV  R7,A      ;clear R7
AGAIN:  ADD  A,@R0     ;add the byte pointer to A by R0
        JNC  NEXT      ;if CY=0 don't accumulate carry
        INC  R7        ;keep track of carries
NEXT:   INC  R0        ;increment pointer
        DJNZ R2,AGAIN  ;repeat until R2 is zero
```

Example 6-3

Write a program to add two 16-bit numbers. The numbers are 3CE7H and 3B8DH. Place the sum in R7 and R6; R6 should have the lower byte.

Solution:

```
CLR   C          ;make CY=0
MOV   A,#0E7H     ;load the low byte now A=E7H
ADD   A,#8DH      ;add the low byte now A=74H and CY=1
MOV   R6,A        ;save the low byte of the sum in R6
MOV   A,#3CH      ;load the high byte
ADDC  A,#3BH      ;add with the carry
                 ;3B + 3C + 1 = 78(all in hex)
MOV   R7,A        ;save the high byte of the sum
```

ADDC and addition of 16-bit numbers

When adding two 16-bit data operands, we need to be concerned with the propagation of a carry from the lower byte to the higher byte. The instruction ADDC (add with carry) is used on such occasions. For example, look at the addition of 3CE7H + 3B8DH, as shown below.

```
      1
    3C  E7
+   3B  8D
    78  74
```

When the first byte is added (E7 + 8D = 74, CY = 1). The carry is propagated to the higher byte, which results in 3C + 3B + 1 = 78 (all in hex). Example 6-3 shows the above steps in an 8051 program.

BCD number system

BCD stands for binary coded decimal. BCD is needed because in everyday life we use the digits 0 to 9 for numbers, not binary or hex numbers. Binary representation of 0 to 9 is called BCD (see Table 6-1). In computer literature one encounters two terms for BCD numbers: (1) unpacked BCD and (2) packed BCD. We describe each one next.

Unpacked BCD

In unpacked BCD, the lower 4 bits of the number represent the BCD number, and the rest of the bits are 0. For example, "0000 1001" and "0000 0101" are unpacked BCD for 9 and 5, respectively. Unpacked BCD requires 1 byte of memory or an 8-bit register to contain it.

Table 6-1. BCD Code

Digit	BCD
0	0000
1	0001
2	0010
3	0011
4	0100
5	0101
6	0110
7	0111
8	1000
9	1001

Packed BCD

In packed BCD, a single byte has two BCD numbers in it, one in the lower 4 bits, and one in the upper 4 bits. For example, "0101 1001" is packed BCD for 59H. It takes only 1 byte of memory to store the packed BCD operands. And so one reason to use packed BCD is that it is twice as efficient in storing data.

There is a problem with adding BCD numbers, which must be corrected. The problem is that after adding packed BCD numbers, the result is no longer BCD. Look at the following.

```
MOV A,#17H
ADD A,#28H
```

Adding these two numbers gives 0011 1111B (3FH), which is not BCD! A BCD number can only have digits from 0000 to 1001 (or 0 to 9). In other words, adding two BCD numbers must give a BCD result. The result above should have been 17 + 28 = 45 (0100 0101). To correct this problem, the programmer must add 6 (0110) to the low digit: 3F + 06 = 45H. The same problem could have happened in the upper digit (e.g., in 52H + 87H = D9H). Again to solve this problem, 6 must be added to the upper digit (D9H + 60H = 139H) to ensure that the result is BCD (52 + 87 = 139). This problem is so pervasive that most microprocessors such as the 8051 have an instruction to deal with it. In the 8051, the instruction "DA A" is designed to correct the BCD addition problem. This is discussed next.

DA instruction

The DA (decimal adjust for addition) instruction in the 8051 is provided to correct the aforementioned problem associated with BCD addition. The mnemonic "DA" has as its only operand the accumulator "A." The DA instruction will add 6 to the lower nibble or higher nibble if needed; otherwise, it will leave the result alone. The following example will clarify these points.

```
MOV   A,#47H    ;A=47H first BCD operand
MOV   B,#25H    ;B=25 second BCD operand
ADD   A,B       ;hex(binary) addition (A=6CH)
DA    A         ;adjust for BCD addition (A=72H)
```

After the program is executed, register A will contain 72H (47 + 25 = 72). The "DA" instruction works only on A. In other words, while the source can be an operand of any addressing mode, the destination must be in register A in order for DA to work. It also needs to be emphasized that DA must be used after the addition of BCD operands and that BCD operands can never have any digit greater than 9. In other words, A–F digits are not allowed. It is also important to note that DA works only after an ADD instruction; it will not work after the INC (increment) instruction.

Summary of DA action

After an ADD or ADDC instruction,

1. If the lower nibble (4 bits) is greater than 9, or if AC = 1, add 0110 to the lower 4 bits.
2. If the upper nibble is greater than 9, or if CY = 1, add 0110 to the upper 4 bits.

In reality there is no other use for the AC (auxiliary carry) flag bit except for BCD addition and correction. For example, adding 29H and 18H will result in 41H, which is incorrect as far as BCD is concerned.

	Hex		BCD	
	29		0010 1001	
+	18	+	0001 1000	
	41		0100 0001	AC=1
+	6	+	0110	
	47		0100 0111	

Since AC = 1 after the addition, "DA A" will add 6 to the lower nibble. The final result is in BCD format. See Example 6-4.

Example 6-4

Assume that 5 BCD data items are stored in RAM locations starting at 40H, as shown below. Write a program to find the sum of all the numbers. The result must be in BCD.

```
40=(71)
41=(11)
42=(65)
43=(59)
44=(37)
```

Solution:

```
            MOV   R0,#40H     ;load pointer
            MOV   R2,#5       ;load counter
            CLR   A           ;A=0
            MOV   R7,A        ;clear R7
AGAIN:      ADD   A,@R0       ;add the byte pointer to A by R0
            DA    A           ;adjust for BCD
            JNC   NEXT        ;if CY=0 don't accumulate carry
            INC   R7          ;keep track of carries
NEXT:       INC   R0          ;increment pointer
            DJNZ  R2,AGAIN    ;repeat until R2 is zero
```

Subtraction of unsigned numbers

```
SUBB A, source ;A = A - source - CY
```

In many microprocessors, there are two different instructions for subtraction: SUB and SUBB (subtract with borrow). In the 8051 we have only SUBB. To make SUB out of SUBB, we have to make CY = 0 prior to the execution of the instruction. Therefore, there are two cases for the SUBB instruction: (1) with CY = 0 and (2) with CY = 1. First, we examine the case where CY = 0 prior to the execution of SUBB. Notice that we use the CY (carry flag) flag for the borrow.

SUBB (subtract with borrow) when CY = 0

In subtraction, the 8051 microprocessors (indeed, all modern CPUs) use the 2's complement method. Although every CPU contains adder circuitry, it would be too cumbersome (and take too many transistors) to design separate subtracter circuitry. For this reason, the 8051 uses adder circuitry to perform the subtraction command. Assuming that the 8051 is executing a simple subtract instruction and that CY = 0 prior to the execution of the instruction, one can summarize the steps of the hardware of the CPU in executing the SUBB instruction for unsigned numbers, as follows.

1. Take the 2's complement of the subtrahend (source operand).
2. Add it to the minuend (A).
3. Invert the carry.

These three steps are performed for every SUBB instruction by the internal hardware of the 8051 CPU, regardless of the source of the operands, provided that the addressing mode is supported. After these three steps, the result is obtained and the flags are set. Example 6-5 illustrates the three steps.

Example 6-5

Show the steps involved in the following.

```
    CLR   C           ;make CY=0
    MOV   A,#3FH       ;load 3FH into A (A = 3FH)
    MOV   R3,#23H      ;load 23H into R3 (R3 = 23H)
    SUBB  A,R3         ;subtract A - R3, place result in A
```

Solution:

```
    A  =  3F   0011 1111      0011 1111
    R3 =  23   0010 0011    + 1101 1101  (2's complement)
          1C                1 0001 1100
                            0  CF=0 (step 3)
```

The flags would be set as follows: CY = 0, AC = 0, and the programmer must look at the carry flag to determine if the result is positive or negative.

If the CY = 0 after the execution of SUBB, the result is positive; if CY = 1, the result is negative and the destination has the 2's complement of the result. Normally, the result is left in 2's complement, but the CPL (complement) and INC instructions can be used to change it. The CPL instruction performs the 1's complement of the operand; then the operand is incremented (INC) to get the 2's complement. See Example 6-6.

SUBB (subtract with borrow) when CY = 1

This instruction is used for multibyte numbers and will take care of the borrow of the lower operand. If CY = 1 prior to executing the SUBB instruction, it also subtracts 1 from the result. See Example 6-7.

Example 6-6

Analyze the following program:
```
      CLR   C
      MOV   A,#4CH      ;load A with value 4CH (A=4CH)
      SUBB  A,#6EH      ;subtract 6E from A
      JNC   NEXT        ;if CY=0 jump to NEXT target
      CPL   A           ;if CY=1 then take 1's complement
      INC   A           ;and increment to get 2's complement
NEXT:MOV   R1,A         ;save A in R1
```

Solution:

Following are the steps for "SUBB A, #6EH":

```
     4C         0100 1100                0100 1100
  -  6E         0110 1110   2's comp = 1001 0010
    -22                              0 1101 1110
```
CY = 1, the result is negative, in 2's complement.

Example 6-7

Analyze the following program:

```
      CLR   C             ;CY = 0
      MOV   A,#62H        ;A = 62H
      SUBB  A,#96H        ;62H - 96H = CCH with CY = 1
      MOV   R7,A          ;save the result
      MOV   A,#27H        ;A=27H
      SUBB  A,#12H        ;27H - 12H - 1 = 14H
      MOV   R6,A          ;save the result
```

Solution:

After the SUBB, A = 62H – 96H = CCH and the carry flag is set high indicating there is a borrow. Since CY = 1, when SUBB is executed the second time A = 27H – 12H – 1 = 14H. Therefore, we have 2762H – 1296H = 14CCH.

UNSIGNED MULTIPLICATION AND DIVISION

In multiplying or dividing two numbers in the 8051, the use of registers A and B is required since the multiplication and division instructions work only with these two registers. We first discuss multiplication.

Multiplication of unsigned numbers

The 8051 supports byte-by-byte multiplication only. The bytes are assumed to be unsigned data. The syntax is as follows:

```
MUL AB     ;A x B, place 16-bit result in B and A
```

In byte-by-byte multiplication, one of the operands must be in register A, and the second operand must be in register B. After multiplication, the result is in the A and B registers; the lower byte is in A, and the upper byte is in B. The following example multiplies 25H by 65H. The result is a 16-bit data that is held by the A and B registers. See Table 6-2.

```
MOV  A,#25H    ;load 25H to reg. A
MOV  B,#65H    ;load 65H in reg. B
MUL  AB        ;25H * 65H = E99 where
               ;B = 0EH and A = 99H
```

Division of unsigned numbers

In the division of unsigned numbers, the 8051 supports byte over byte only. The syntax is as follows.

```
DIV AB     ;divide A by B
```

When dividing a byte by a byte, the numerator must be in register A and the denominator must be in B. After the DIV instruction is performed, the quotient is in A and the remainder is in B. See the following example and Table 6-3.

```
MOV  A,#95     ;load 95 into A
MOV  B,#10     ;load 10 into B
DIV  AB        ;now A = 09 (quotient) and
               ;B = 05(remainder)
```

Table 6-2. Unsigned Multiplication Summary (MUL AB)

Multiplication	Operand 1	Operand 2	Result
byte × byte	A	B	A = low byte, B = high byte

Note: Multiplication of operands larger than 8 bits takes some manipulation. It is left to the reader to experiment with.

Table 6-3. Unsigned Division Summary (`DIV AB`)

Division	Numerator	Denominator	Quotient	Remainder
byte / byte	A	B	A	B

(If B = 0, then OV = 1 indicating an error)

Notice the following points for instruction "DIV AB".

1. This instruction always makes CY = 0 and OV = 0 if the denominator is not 0.
2. If the denominator is 0 (B = 0), OV = 1 indicates an error, and CY = 0. The standard practice in all microprocessors when dividing a number by 0 is to indicate in some way the invalid result of infinity. In the 8051, the OV (overflow) flag is set to 1.

An application for DIV instructions

There are times when an ADC (analog-to-digital converter) is connected to a port and the ADC represents some quantity such as temperature or pressure. The 8-bit ADC provides data in hex in the range of 00–FFH. This hex data must be converted to decimal. We do that by dividing it by 10 repeatedly, saving the remainders as shown in Examples 6-8 and 6-9.

Example 6-8

Write a program (a) to make P1 an input port, (b) to get a byte of hex data in tl range of 00–FFH from P1 and convert it to decimal. Save the digits in R7, R6, an R5, where the least significant digit is in R7.

Solution:

```
    MOV   A,#0FFH
    MOV   P1,A        ;make P1 an input port
    MOV   A,P1        ;read data from P1
    MOV   B,#10       ;B=0A hex (10 dec)
    DIV   AB          ;divide by 10
    MOV   R7,B        ;save lower digit
    MOV   B,#10       ;
    DIV   AB          ;divide by 10 once more
    MOV   R6,B        ;save the next digit
    MOV   R5,A        ;save the last digit
```

The input value from P1 is in the hex range of 00–FFH or in binary 00000000 11111111. This program will not work if the input data is in BCD. In other wor this program converts from binary to decimal. To convert a single decimal digit ASCII format, we OR it with 30H as shown in Sections 6.4 and 6.5.

Example 6-9

Analyze the program in Example 6-8, assuming that P1 has a value of FDH for data.

Solution:

To convert a binary (hex) value to decimal, we divide it by 10 repeatedly until the quotient is less than 10. After each division the remainder is saved. In the case of an 8-bit binary such as FDH we have 253 decimal as shown below (all in hex).

```
            Quotient   Remainder
FD/0A=      19         3 (low digit)
19/0A=      2          5 (middle digit)
                       2 (high digit)
```

Therefore, we have FDH = 253. In order to display this data it must be converted to ASCII, which is described in a later section in this chapter.

REVIEW QUESTIONS

1. In multiplication of two bytes in the 8051, we must place one byte in register _____ and the other in register _____.
2. In unsigned byte-by-byte multiplication, the product will be placed in register(s) _____.
3. Is "MUL A,R1" a valid 8051 instruction? Explain your answer.
4. In byte/byte division, the numerator must be placed in register_____ and the denominator in register_____.
5. In unsigned byte/byte division, the quotient will be placed in register_____ and the remainder in register_____.
6. Is "DIV A,R1" a valid 8051 instruction? Explain your answer.
7. The instruction "ADD A, source" places the sum in _____.
8. Why is the following ADD instruction illegal?
   "ADD R1,R2"
9. Rewrite the instruction above in correct form.
10. The instruction "ADDC A, source" places the sum in _____.
11. Find the value of the A and CY flags in each of the following.
    (a) MOV A,#4FH   (b)   MOV A,#9CH
        ADD A,#0B1H   ADD A,#63H
12. Show how the CPU would subtract 05H from 43H.
13. If CY = 1, A = 95H, and B = 4FH prior to the execution of "SUBB A,B", what will be the contents of A after the subtraction?

6.2: SIGNED NUMBER CONCEPTS AND ARITHMETIC OPERATIONS

All data items used so far have been unsigned numbers, meaning that the entire 8-bit operand was used for the magnitude. Many applications require signed data. In this section, the concept of signed numbers is discussed along with related instructions. If your applications do not involve signed numbers, you can bypass this section.

Concept of signed numbers in computers

In everyday life, numbers are used that could be positive or negative. For example, a temperature of 5 degrees below zero can be represented as –5, and 20 degrees above zero as +20. Computers must be able to accommodate such numbers. To do that, computer scientists have devised the following arrangement for the representation of signed positive and negative numbers: The most significant bit (MSB) is set aside for the sign (+ or –), while the rest of the bits are used for the magnitude. The sign is represented by 0 for positive (+) numbers and 1 for negative (–) numbers. Signed byte representation is discussed below.

Signed 8-bit operands

In signed byte operands, D7 (MSB) is the sign and D0 to D6 are set aside for the magnitude of the number. If D7 = 0, the operand is positive, and if D7 = 1, it is negative.

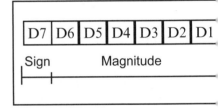

Figure 6-1. 8-Bit Signed Operand

Positive numbers

The range of positive numbers that can be represented by the format shown in Figure 6-1 is 0 to +127. If a positive number is larger than +127, a 16-bit size operand must be used. Since the 8051 does not support 16-bit data, we will not discuss it.

```
0      0000 0000
+1     0000 0001
. . .  . . .
+5     0000 0101
. . .  . . .
+127   0111 1111
```

Negative numbers

For negative numbers, D7 is 1; however, the magnitude is represented in its 2's complement. Although the assembler does the conversion, it is still important to understand how the conversion works. To convert to negative number representation (2's complement), follow these steps.

1. Write the magnitude of the number in 8-bit binary (no sign).
2. Invert each bit.
3. Add 1 to it.

Examples 6-10–6-12 demonstrate these three steps.

Example 6-10

Show how the 8051 would represent –5.

Solution:

Observe the following steps.

```
1.    0000 0101      5 in 8-bit binary
2.    1111 1010      invert each bit
3.    1111 1011      add 1 (which becomes FB in hex)
```

Therefore –5 = FBH, the signed number representation in 2's complement for –5.

Example 6-11

Show how the 8051 would represent –34H.

Solution:

Observe the following steps.

```
1.    0011 0100      34H given in binary
2.    1100 1011      invert each bit
3.    1100 1100      add 1 (which is CC in hex)
```

Therefore –34 = CCH, the signed number representation in 2's complement for 34H.

Example 6-12

Show how the 8051 would represent –128.

Solution:

Observe the following steps.

```
.     1000 0000      128 in 8-bit binary
.     0111 1111      invert each bit
.     1000 0000      add 1 (which becomes 80 in hex)
```

Therefore –128 = 80H, the signed number representation in 2's complement for 128.

From the examples, it is clear that the range of byte-sized negative numbers is –1 to –128. The following lists byte-sized signed number ranges:

Decimal	Binary	Hex
-128	1000 0000	80
-127	1000 0001	81
-126	1000 0010	82
. . .	. . . .	. .
-2	1111 1110	FE
-1	1111 1111	FF
0	0000 0000	00
+1	0000 0001	01
+2	0000 0010	02
. .	. . . .	. .
+127	0111 1111	7F

The above explains the mystery behind the relative address of –128 to +127 in the short jump discussed in Chapter 3.

Overflow problem in signed number operations

When using signed numbers, a serious problem arises that must be dealt with. This is the overflow problem. The 8051 indicates the existence of an error by raising the OV flag, but it is up to the programmer to take care of the erroneous result. The CPU understands only 0s and 1s and ignores the human convention of positive and negative numbers. What is an overflow? If the result of an operation on signed numbers is too large for the register, an overflow has occurred and the programmer must be notified. Look at Example 6-13.

In this example, +96 is added to +70 and the result according to the CPU was –90. Why? The reason is that the result was larger than what A could contain. Like all other 8-bit registers, A could only contain up to +127. The

---

Example 6-13

Examine the following code and analyze the result.

```
        MOV   A,#+96        ;A = 0110 0000 (A = 60H)
        MOV   R1,#+70       ;R1 = 0100 0110 (R1 = 46H)
        ADD   A,R1          ;A = 1010 0110
                            ;A = A6H = -90 decimal, INVALID
```

Solution:

```
    +96   0110 0000
+   +70   0100 0110
+   166   1010 0110   and OV=1
```

According to the CPU, the result is –90, which is wrong. The CPU sets OV = 1 indicate the overflow.

---

designers of the CPU created the overflow flag specifically for the purpose of informing the programmer that the result of the signed number operation is erroneous.

When is the OV flag set?

In 8-bit signed number operations, OV is set to 1 if either of the following two conditions occurs:

1. There is a carry from D6 to D7 but no carry out of D7 (CY = 0).
2. There is a carry from D7 out (CY = 1) but no carry from D6 to D7.

In other words, the overflow flag is set to 1 if there is a carry from D6 to D7 or from D7 out, but not both. This means that if there is a carry both from D6 to D7 and from D7 out, OV = 0. In Example 6-13, since there is only a carry from D6 to D7 and no carry from D7 out, OV = 1. Study Examples 6-14–16 to understand the overflow flag in signed arithmetic.

Example 6-14

Observe the following, noting the role of the OV flag.

```
MOV   A,#-128    ;A = 1000 0000 (A = 80H)
MOV   R4,#-2     ;R4 = 1111 1110 (R4 = FEH)
ADD   A,R4       ;A = 0111 1110 (A=7EH=+126, invalid)
```

Solution:

```
  -128      1000 0000
+   -2      1111 1110
  -130      0111 1110   and OV=1
```

According to the CPU, the result is +126, which is wrong (OV = 1).

Example 6-15

Observe the following, noting the OV flag.

```
MOV   A,#-2      ;A=1111 1110 (A=FEH)
MOV   R1,#-5     ;R1=1111 1011 (R1=FBH)
ADD   A,R1       ;A=1111 1001 (A=F9H=-7,correct,OV=0)
```

Solution:

```
  -2       1111 1110
+ -5       1111 1011
  -7       1111 1001   and OV = 0
```

According to the CPU, the result is –7, which is correct (OV = 0).

Example 6-16

Examine the following, noting the role of OV.

```
    MOV   A,#+7       ;A=0000 0111 (A=07H)
    MOV   R1,#+18     ;R1=0001 0010(R1=12H)
    ADD   A,R1        ;A=0001 1001 (A=19H=+25, correct,OV=0)
```

Solution:

```
      7    0000 0111
  +  18    0001 0010
     25    0001 1001   and OV = 0
```

According to the CPU, this is +25, which is correct (OV = 0)

From the examples, we conclude that in any signed number addition, OV indicates whether the result is valid or not. If OV = 1, the result is erroneous; if OV = 0, the result is valid. We can state emphatically that in unsigned number addition we must monitor the status of CY (carry flag), and in signed number addition, the OV (overflow) flag must be monitored by the programmer. In the 8051, instructions such as JNC and JC allow the program to branch right after the addition of unsigned numbers, as we saw in Section 6.1. There is no such instruction for the OV flag. However, this can be achieved by "JB PSW.2" or "JNB PSW.2" since PSW, the flag register, is a bit-addressable register. This is discussed later in this chapter.

Instructions to create 2's complement

The 8051 does not have a special instruction to make the 2's complement of a number. To do that, we can use the CPL instruction and ADD, as shown next.

```
    CPL   A    ; 1's complement (Invert)
    ADD   A,#1 ; add 1 to make 2's complement
```

REVIEW QUESTIONS

1. In an 8-bit operand, bit _____ is used for the sign bit.
2. Convert –16H to its 2's complement representation.
3. The range of byte-sized signed operands is – _____ to + _____.
4. Show +9 and –9 in binary.
5. Explain the difference between a carry and an overflow.

6.3: LOGIC AND COMPARE INSTRUCTIONS

Apart from I/O and arithmetic instructions, logic instructions are some of the most widely used instructions. In this section, we cover Boolean logic instructions such as AND, OR, exclusive-or (XOR), and complement. We will also study the compare instruction.

al AND Function

s		Output
Y		X AND Y
0		0
1		0
0		0
1		1

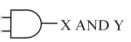

—X AND Y

AND

    ANL destination,source ;dest = dest AND source

This instruction will perform a logical AND on the two operands and place the result in the destination. The destination is normally the accumulator. The source operand can be a register, in memory, or immediate. See Appendix A for more on the addressing modes for this instruction. The ANL instruction for byte-size operands has no effect on any of the flags. The ANL instruction is often used to mask (set to 0) certain bits of an operand. See Example 6-17.

al OR Function

s		Output
Y		X OR Y
0		0
1		1
0		1
1		1

—X OR Y

OR

    ORL destination,source   ;dest = dest OR source

The destination and source operands are ORed, and the result is placed in the destination. The ORL instruction can be used to set certain bits of an operand to 1. The destination is normally the accumulator. The source operand can be a register, in memory, or immediate. See Appendix A for more on the addressing modes supported by this instruction. The ORL instruction for byte-size operands has no effect on any of the flags. See Example 6-18.

---

ample 6-17

ow the results of the following.

```
    MOV   A,#35H    ;A = 35H
    ANL   A,#0FH    ;A = A AND 0FH (now A = 05)
```

lution:

```
    35H           0011 0101
    0FH           0000 1111
    05H           0000 0101        35H AND 0FH = 05H
```

Example 6-18

Show the results of the following.

```
MOV  A,#04          ;A = 04
ORL  A,#30H         ;A = A OR 30H (now A = 34H)
```

Solution:

```
04H          0000 0100
30H          0011 0000
34H          0011 0100          04H OR 30H = 34H
```

XOR

Logical XOR Funct

```
XRL destination,source     ;dest = dest
XOR source
```

This instruction will perform the XOR operation on the two operands and place the result in the destination. The destination is normally the accumulator. The source operand can be a register, in memory, or immediate. See Appendix A for the addressing modes of this instruction. The XRL instruction for byte-size operands has no effect on any of the flags. See Examples 6-19 and 6-20.

XRL can also be used to see if two registers have the same value. "XRL A,R1" will exclusive-or register A and register R1, and put the result in A. If both registers have the same value, 00 is placed in A. Then we can use the JZ instruction to make a decision based on the result. See Example 6-20.

Inputs		Out
X	Y	X XC
0	0	0
0	1	1
1	0	1
1	1	0

X ⊕ Y → X XC

Example 6-19

Show the results of the following.

```
MOV    A,#54H
XRL    A,#78H
```

Solution:

```
54H          0101 0100
78H          0111 1000
2CH          0010 1100          54H XOR 78H = 2CH
```

Example 6-20

The XRL instruction can be used to clear the contents of a register by XORing with itself. Show how "XRL A, A" clears A, assuming that A = 45H.

Solution:

```
45H          0100 0101
45H          0100 0101
00           0000 0000          XOR a number with itself = 0
```

Example 6-21

Read and test P1 to see whether it has the value 45H. If it does, send 99H to P2; otherwise, it stays cleared.

Solution:

```
        MOV    P2,#00      ;clear P2
        MOV    P1,#0FFH    ;make P1 an input port
        MOV    R3,#45H     ;R3=45H
        MOV    A,P1        ;read P1
        XRL    A,R3
        JNZ    EXIT        ;jump if A has value other than 0
        MOV    P2,#99H
EXIT:...
```

In the program in Example 6-21, notice the use of the JNZ instruction. JNZ and JZ test the contents of the accumulator only. In other words, there is no such thing as a zero flag in the 8051.

Another widely used application of XRL is to toggle bits of an operand. For example, to toggle bit 2 of register A, we could use the following code. This code causes D2 of register A to change to the opposite value, while all the other bits remain unchanged.

```
    XRL   A,#04H     ;EX-OR   A with 0000 0100
```

cal Inverter	
t	**Output**
	NOT X
	1
	0
—▷∘— NOT X	

CPL A (complement accumulator)

This instruction complements the contents of register A. The complement action changes the 0s to 1s and the 1s to 0s. This is also called *1's complement*.

```
    MOV   A,#55H
    CPL   A     ;now A=AAH
    ;01010101 becomes 10101010 (AAH)
```

To get the 2's complement, all we have to do is to add 1 to the 1's complement. See Example 6-22. In other words, there is no 2's complement

xample 6-22

ind the 2's complement of the value 85H.

olution:

```
        MOV   A,#85H                85H = 1000 0101
        CPL   A          ;1's comp. 1'S = 0111 1010
        ADD   A,#1       ;2's comp.        + 1
                                    0111 1011 = 7BH
```

instruction in the 8051. Notice that in complementing a byte, the data must be in register A. Although the CPL instruction cannot be used to complement R0–R7, it does work on P0–P3 ports. See Appendix A for which addressing mode is available for the CPL instruction.

Compare instruction

The 8051 has an instruction for the compare operation. It has the following syntax.

```
CJNE destination,source,relative address
```

In the 8051, the actions of comparing and jumping are combined into a single instruction called CJNE (compare and jump if not equal). The CJNE instruction compares two operands, and jumps if they are not equal. In addition, it changes the CY flag to indicate if the destination operand is larger or smaller. It is important to notice that the operands themselves remain unchanged. For example, after the execution of the instruction "CJNE A,#67H,NEXT", register A still has its original value. This instruction compares register A with value 67H and jumps to the target address NEXT only if register A has a value other than 67H. See Examples 6-23 and 6-24.

In CJNE, the destination operand can be in the accumulator or in one of the Rn registers. The source operand can be in a register, in memory, or immediate. See Appendix A for the addressing modes of this instruction. This instruction affects the carry flag only. CY is changed as shown in Table 6-4.

Table 6-4. Carry Flag Setting For CJNE Instruction

Compare	Carry Fl
destination ≥ source	CY = 0
destination < source	CY = 1

Example 6-23

Examine the following code, then answer the following questions.

```
        MOV   A,#55H
        CJNE  A,#99H,NEXT
        . . .
NEXT:         . . .
```

(a) Will it jump to NEXT?
(b) What is in A after the CJNE instruction is executed?

Solution:

(a) Yes, it jumps because 55H and 99H are not equal.
(b) A = 55H, its original value before the comparison.

Example 6-24

Write a code to determine if register A contains the value 99H. If so, make R1 = FFH; otherwise, make R1 = 0.

Solution:

```
      MOV   R1,#0             ;clear R1
      CJNE  A,#99H,NEXT       ;if A not equal to 99, then jump
      MOV   R1,#0FFH          ;they are equal, make R1 = FFH
NEXT:...                      ;not equal so R1 = 0
OVER:...
```

The following code shows how the comparison works for all possible conditions.

```
                CJNE  R5,#80,NOT_EQUAL   ;check R5 for 80
                ...                      ;R5=80
NOT_EQUAL:  JNC   NEXT                   ;jump if R5>80
                ...                      ;R5<80
NEXT:           ...
```

Notice in the CJNE instruction that any Rn register can be compared with an immediate value. There is no need for register A to be involved. Also notice that CY is always checked for cases of greater or less than, but only after it is determined that they are not equal. See Examples 6-25 through 6-27.

Example 6-25

Assume that P1 is an input port connected to a temperature sensor. Write a program to read the temperature and test it for the value 75. According to the test results, place the temperature value into the registers indicated by the following.

If T = 75   then A = 75
If T < 75   then R1 = T
If T > 75   then R2 = T

Solution:

```
            MOV  P1,#0FFH       ;make P1 an input port
            MOV  A,P1           ;read P1 port, temperature
            CJNE A,#75,OVER     ;jump if A not equal to 75
            SJMP EXIT           ;A=75, exit
OVER:       JNC  NEXT           ;if CY=0 then A>75
            MOV  R1,A           ;CY=1, A<75, save in R1
            SJMP EXIT           ;and exit
NEXT:       MOV  R2,A           ;A>75, save it in R2
EXIT:       ...
```

Example 6-26

Write a program to monitor P1 continuously for the value 63H. It should stop monitoring only if P1 = 63H.

Solution:

```
        MOV  P1,#0FFH      ;make P1 an input port
HERE:   MOV  A,P1          ;get P1
        CJNE A,#63,HERE    ;keep monitoring unless P1=63H
```

Example 6-27

Assume internal RAM memory locations 40H–44H contain the daily temperature for five days, as shown below. Search to see if any of the values equals 65. If value 65 does exist in the table, give its location to R4; otherwise, make R4 = 0.

40H=(76)   41H=(79)   42H=(69)   43H=(65)   44H=(62)

Solution:

```
            MOV  R4,#0        ;R4=0
            MOV  R0,#40H      ;load pointer
            MOV  R2,#05       ;load counter
BACK:       MOV  A,@R0        ;get the byte from RAM
            CJNE A,#65,NEXT   ;compare RAM data with 65
            MOV  A,R0         ;if 65, save address
            MOV  R4,A
            SJMP EXIT         ;and exit
NEXT:       INC  R0           ;otherwise increment pointer
            DJNZ R2,BACK      ;keep checking until count=0
EXIT:       SJMP EXIT
```

The compare instruction is really a subtraction, except that the values of the operands do not change. Flags are changed according to the execution of the SUBB instruction. It must be emphasized again that in the CJNE instruction, the operands are not affected, regardless of the result of the comparison. Only the CY flag is affected. This is despite the fact that CJNE uses the subtract operation to set or reset the CY flag.

REVIEW QUESTIONS

1. Find the contents of register A after the following code in each case.
    (a) MOV A,#37H   (b) MOV A,#37H   (c) MOV A,#37H
        ANL A,#0CAH   ORL A,#0CAH   XRL A,#0CAH
2. To mask certain bits of the accumulator, we must ANL it with _____.
3. To set certain bits of the accumulator, to 1, we must ORL it with _____.
4. XRLing an operand with itself results in _____.
5. True or false. The CJNE instruction alters the contents of its operands.

---

6. What value must R4 have in order for the following instruction not to jump?

```
CJNE  R4,#53,OVER
```

7. Find the contents of register A after execution of the following code.

```
CLR  A
ORL  A,#99H
CPL  A
```

6.4: ROTATE INSTRUCTION AND DATA SERIALIZATION

In many applications, there is a need to perform a bitwise rotation of an operand. In the 8051, the rotation instructions RL, RR, RLC, and RRC are designed specifically for that purpose. They allow a program to rotate the accumulator right or left. We explore the rotate instructions next since they are widely used in many different applications. In the 8051, to rotate a byte the operand must be in register A. There are two type of rotations. One is a simple rotation of the bits of A, and the other is a rotation through the carry. Each is explained below.

Rotating the bits of A right or left

```
RR   A      ;rotate right A
```

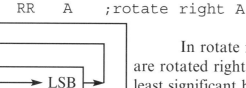

In rotate right, the 8 bits of the accumulator are rotated right one bit, and bit D0 exits from the least significant bit and enters into D7 (most significant bit). See the code and diagram.

```
MOV  A,#36H    ;A=0011 0110
RR   A         ;A=0001 1011
RR   A         ;A=1000 1101
RR   A         ;A=1100 0110
RR   A         ;A=0110 0011
```

```
RL   A         ;rotate left A
```

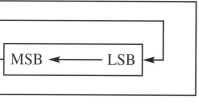

In rotate left, the 8 bits of the accumulator are rotated left one bit, and bit D7 exits from the MSB (most significant bit) and enters into D0 (least significant bit). See the code and diagram.

```
MOV  A,#72H    ;A=0111 0010
RL   A         ;A=1110 0100
RL   A         ;A=1100 1001
```

Notice that in the RR and RL instructions no flags are affected.

Rotating through the carry

There are two more rotate instructions in the 8051. They involve the carry flag. Each is shown next.

```
RRC  A                 ;rotate right through carry
```

In RRC A, as bits are rotated
from left to right, they exit the LSB to the
carry flag, and the carry flag enters the
MSB. In other words, in RRC A the LSB
is moved to CY and CY is moved to the
MSB. In reality, the carry flag acts as if
it is part of register A, making it a 9-bit
register.

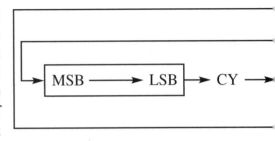

```
CLR  C           ;make CY=0
MOV  A,#26H      ;A=0010 0110
RRC  A           ;A=0001 0011 CY=0
RRC  A           ;A=0000 1001 CY=1
RRC  A           ;A=1000 0100 CY=1


RLC  A                 ;rotate left through carry
```

In RLC A, as bits are shifted from
right to left they exit the MSB and enter
the carry flag, and the carry flag enters
the LSB. In other words, in RCL the
MSB is moved to CY and CY is moved
to the LSB. See the following code and
diagram.

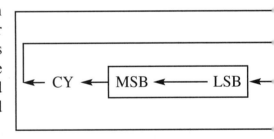

```
SETB C           ;make CY=1
MOV  A,#15H      ;A=0001 0101
RLC  A           ;A=0010 1011 CY=0
RLC  A           ;A=0101 0110 CY=0
RLC  A           ;A=1010 1100 CY=0
RLC  A           ;A=0101 1000 CY=1
```

Serializing data

Serializing data is a way of sending a byte of data one bit at a time
through a single pin of microprocessor. There are two ways to transfer a byte
of data serially:

1. Using the serial port. In using the serial port, programmers have very limited control over the sequence of data transfer. The details of serial port data transfer are discussed in Chapter 10.

2. The second method of serializing data is to transfer data one bit at a time and control the sequence of data and spaces in between them. In many new generation devices such as LCD, ADC, and ROM, the serial versions of these devices are becoming popular since they take less space on a printed circuit board. We discuss this important topic next.

Serializing a byte of data

Serializing data is one of the most widely used applications of the rotate instruction. We showed in Chapter 5 how the CY flag status can be moved to any pin of ports P0–P3. Using that concept and the rotate instruction, we transfer a byte of data serially (one bit at a time). Repeating the following sequence 8 times will transfer an entire byte, as shown in Example 6-28.

```
RRC   A           ;move the bit to CY
MOV   P1.3,C      ;output carry as data bit
```

Example 6-28

Write a program to transfer value 41H serially (one bit at a time) via pin P2.1. Put two highs at the start and end of the data. Send the byte LSB first.

Solution:

```
        MOV A,#41H
        SETB P2.1       ;high
        SETB P2.1       ;high
        MOV R5, #8
HERE:RRC   A
        MOV    P2.1,C    ;send the carry bit to P2.1
        DJNZ R5, HERE
        SETB P2.1       ;high
        SETB P2.1       ;high
```

Example 6-29

Write a program to bring in a byte of data serially one bit at a time via pin P2.7 and save it in register R2. The byte comes in with the LSB first.

Solution:

```
      MOV R5, #8
HERE:MOV  C,P2.7     ; bring in bit
      RRC  A
      DJNZ R5, HERE
      MOV  R2,A        ;save it
```

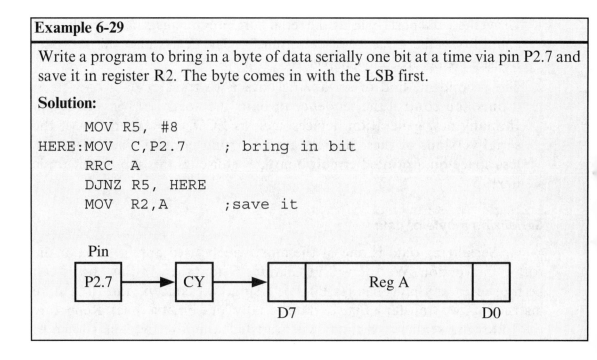

Example 6-29 shows how to bring in a byte of data serially one bit at a time. We will see how to use these concepts in Chapter 13 for a serial ADC chip.

Single-bit operations with CY

Aside from the fact that the carry flag is altered by arithmetic and logic instructions, in the 8051 there are also several instructions by which the CY flag can be manipulated directly. These instructions are listed in Table 6-5.

Of the instructions in Table 6-5, we have shown the use of JNC, CLR, and SETB in many examples in the last few chapters. Examples 6-30–6-33 give simple applications of the instructions in Table 6-5, including some dealing with the logic operations AND and OR.

Example 6-30

Write a program to save the status of bits P1.2 and P1.3 on RAM bit locations 6 and 7, respectively.

Solution:

```
            MOV C,P1.2     ;save status of P1.2 on CY
            MOV 06,C       ;save carry in RAM bit location 06
            MOV C,P1.3     ;save status of P1.3 on CY
            MOV 07,C       ;save carry in RAM bit location 07
```

Table 6-5. Carry Bit-Related Instructions

Instruction	Function
SETB C	make CY = 1
CLR C	clear carry bit (CY = 0)
CPL C	complement carry bit
MOV b,C	copy carry status to bit location (CY = b)
MOV C,b	copy bit location status to carry (b = CY)
JNC target	jump to target if CY = 0
JC target	jump to target if CY = 1
ANL C,bit	AND CY with bit and save it on CY
ANL C,/bit	AND CY with inverted bit and save it on CY
ORL C,bit	OR CY with bit and save it on CY
ORL C,/bit	OR CY with inverted bit and save it on CY

Example 6-31

Assume that bit P2.2 is used to control an outdoor light and bit P2.5 a light inside a building. Show how to turn on the outside light and turn off the inside one.

Solution:

```
SETB C           ;CY = 1
ORL  C,P2.2      ;CY = P2.2 ORed with CY
MOV  P2.2,C      ;turn it "on" if not already "on"
CLR  C           ;CY = 0
ANL  C,P2.5      ;CY = P2.5 ANDed with CY
MOV  P2.5,C      ;turn it off if not already off
```

Example 6-32

Write a program that finds the number of 1s in a given byte.

Solution:

```
        MOV  R1,#0       ;R1 keeps the number of 1s
        MOV  R7,#8       ;counter = 08 rotate 8 times
        MOV  A,#97H      ;find the number of 1s in 97H
AGAIN:  RLC  A           ;rotate it through the CY once
        JNC  NEXT        ;check for CY
        INC  R1          ;if CY=1 then add one to count
NEXT:   DJNZ R7,AGAIN    ;go through this 8 times
```

Before:	D7–D4	D3–D0	After: SWAP	D3–D0	D7–D4

Before:	0111	0010	After: SWAP	0010	0111

Example 6-33

(a) Find the contents of register A in the following code.
(b) In the absence of a SWAP instruction, how would you exchange the nibbles?
    Write a simple program to show the process.

Solution:

(a)
```
    MOV  A,#72H      ;A = 72H
    SWAP A           ;A = 27H
```

(b)
```
    MOV  A,#72H      ;A=0111 0010
    RL   A           ;A=1110 0100
    RL   A           ;A=1100 1001
    RL   A           ;A=1001 0011
    RL   A           ;A=0010 0111
```

SWAP A

Another useful instruction is the SWAP instruction. It works only on the accumulator. It swaps the lower nibble and the higher nibble. In other words, the lower 4 bits are put into the higher 4 bits, and the higher 4 bits are put into the lower 4 bits. See the diagrams below and Example 6-33.

REVIEW QUESTIONS

1. What is the value of register A after each of the following instructions?
```
    MOV  A,#25H
    RR   A
    RR   A
    RR   A
    RR   A
```

2. What is the value of register A after each of the following instructions?
```
    MOV  A,#A2H
    RL   A
    RL   A
    RL   A
    RL   A
```

3. What is the value of register A after each of the following instructions?
```
CLR   A
SETB  C
RRC   A
SETB  C
RRC   A
```

4. Why does "RLC R1" give an error in the 8051?
5. What is in register A after the execution of the following code?
```
MOV   A,#85H
SWAP  A
ANL   A,#0F0H
```

6. Find the status of the CY flag after the following code.
```
        CLR   A
        ADD   A,#0FFH
        JNC   OVER
        CPL   C
OVER:         ...
```

7. Find the status of the CY flag after the following code.
```
        CLR   C
        JNC   OVER
        SETB  C
OVER:         ....
```

8. Find the status of the CY flag after the following code.
```
        CLR   C
        JC    OVER
        CPL   C
OVER:         ....
```

9. Show how to save the status of P2.7 in RAM bit location 31.
10. Show how to move the status of RAM bit location 09 to P1.4.

6.5: BCD, ASCII, AND OTHER APPLICATION PROGRAMS

In this section, we provide some real-world examples on how to use arithmetic and logic instructions. We will see their applications in real-world devices covered in future chapters. For example, many newer microprocessors have a real-time clock (RTC), where the time and date are kept even when the power is off. These microprocessors provide the time and date in BCD. However, to display them they must be converted to ASCII. Next, we show the application of logic and rotate instructions in the conversion of BCD and ASCII.

ASCII numbers

On ASCII keyboards, when the key "0" is activated, "011 0000" (30H) is provided to the computer. Similarly, 31H (011 0001) is provided for the key "1," and so on, as shown in Table 6-6.

It must be noted that although ASCII is standard in the United States (and many other countries), BCD numbers are universal. Since the keyboard, printers, and monitors all use ASCII, how does data get converted from ASCII to BCD, and vice versa? These are the subjects covered next.

Packed BCD to ASCII conversion

Many systems have what is called a *real-time clock* (RTC). The RTC provides the time of day (hour, minute, second) and the date (year, month, day) continuously, regardless of whether the power is on or off (see Chapter 16). However, this data is provided in packed BCD. For this data to be displayed on a device such as an LCD, or to be printed by the printer, it must be in ASCII format.

To convert packed BCD to ASCII, it must first be converted to unpacked BCD. Then the unpacked BCD is tagged with 011 0000 (30H). The following demonstrates converting from packed BCD to ASCII. See also Example 6-34.

```
Packed BCD      Unpacked BCD        ASCII
29H             02H   & 09H         32H   & 39H
0010 1001       0000 0010 &         0011 0010 &
                0000 1001           0011 1001
```

ASCII to packed BCD conversion

To convert ASCII to packed BCD, it is first converted to unpacked BCD (to get rid of the 3), and then combined to make packed BCD. For example, for 4 and 7 the keyboard gives 34 and 37, respectively. The goal is

Table 6-6. ASCII Code for Digits 0–9

Key	ASCII (hex)	Binary	BCD (unpacked)
0	30	011 0000	0000 0000
1	31	011 0001	0000 0001
2	32	011 0010	0000 0010
3	33	011 0011	0000 0011
4	34	011 0100	0000 0100
5	35	011 0101	0000 0101
6	36	011 0110	0000 0110
7	37	011 0111	0000 0111
8	38	011 1000	0000 1000
9	39	011 1001	0000 1001

Example 6-34

Assume that register A has packed BCD. Write a program to convert packed BCD to two ASCII numbers and place them in R2 and R6.

Solution:

```
MOV  A,#29H       ;A=29H, packed BCD
MOV  R2,A         ;keep a copy of BCD data in R2
ANL  A,#0FH       ;mask the upper nibble(A=09)
ORL  A,#30H       ;make it an ASCII, A=39H ('9')
MOV  R6,A         ;save it (R6=39H ASCII char)
MOV  A,R2         ;A=29H, get the original data
ANL  A,#0F0H      ;mask the lower nibble(A=20)
RR   A            ;rotate right
RR   A            ;rotate right
RR   A            ;rotate right
RR   A            ;rotate right, (A=02)
ORL  A,#30H       ;A=32H, ASCII char '2'
MOV  R2,A         ;save ASCII char in R2
```

Of course, in the above code we can replace all the "RR A" instructions with a single "SWAP A" instruction.

to produce 47H or "0100 0111," which is packed BCD. This process is illustrated next.

Key	ASCII	Unpacked BCD	Packed BCD
4	34	00000100	
7	37	00000111	01000111 or 47H

```
MOV    A, #'4'    ;A=34H, hex for ASCII char 4
ANL    A, #0FH    ;mask upper nibble (A=04)
SWAP   A          ;A=40H
MOV    B, A
MOV    A, #'7'    ;R1=37H, hex for ASCII char 7
ANL    A, #0FH    ;mask upper nibble (R1=07)
ORL    A, B       ;A=47H, packed BCD
```

After this conversion, the packed BCD numbers are processed and the result will be in packed BCD format. As we saw earlier in this chapter, a special instruction—"DA A"—requires that data be in packed BCD format.

Using a look-up table for ASCII

In some applications, it is much easier to use a look-up table to get the ASCII character we need. This is a widely used concept in interfacing a keyboard to the microprocessor. This is shown in Example 6-35.

Example 6-35

Assume that the lower three bits of P1 are connected to three switches. Write a program to send the following ASCII characters to P2 based on the status of the switches.

000	'0'
001	'1'
010	'2'
011	'3'
100	'4'
101	'5'
110	'6'
111	'7'

Solution:

```
        MOV   DPTR,#MYTABLE
        MOV   A,P1        ;get SW status
        ANL   A,#07H      ;mask all but lower 3 bits
        MOVC  A,@A+DPTR   ;get the data from look-up table
        MOV   P2,A        ;display value
        SJMP  $           ;stay here
;    - - - - - - - - - - - - - - - - - - - -
        ORG   400H
MYTABLE DB    '0','1','2','3','4','5','6','7'
        END
```

You can easily modify this program for the hex values of 0–F, which are supplied by 4x4 keyboards. See Chapter 12 for a keyboard example.

Checksum byte in ROM

To ensure the integrity of the ROM contents, every system must perform the checksum calculation. The process of checksum will detect any corruption of the contents of ROM. One of the causes of ROM corruption is current surge, which occurs either when the system is turned on or during operation. To ensure data integrity in ROM, the checksum process uses what is called a *checksum byte*. The checksum byte is an extra byte that is tagged to the end of a series of bytes of data. To calculate the checksum byte of a series of bytes of data, the following steps can be taken.

1. Add the bytes together and drop the carries.
2. Take the 2's complement of the total sum; this is the checksum byte, which becomes the last byte of the series.

To perform the checksum operation, add all the bytes, including the checksum byte. The result must be zero. If it is not zero, one or more bytes of data have been changed (corrupted). To clarify these important concepts, see Example 6-36.

Example 6-36

Assume that we have 4 bytes of hexadecimal data: 25H, 62H, 3FH, and 52H.
(a) Find the checksum byte, (b) perform the checksum operation to ensure data integrity, and (c) if the second byte 62H has been changed to 22H, show how checksum detects the error.

Solution:

(a) Find the checksum byte.

```
      25H
  +   62H
  +   3FH
  +   52H
     118H     (Dropping the carry of 1, we have 18H. Its 2's complement is E8H.
              Therefore, the checksum byte is E8H.)
```

(b) Perform the checksum operation to ensure data integrity.

```
      25H
  +   62H
  +   3FH
  +   52H
  +   E8H
     200H     (Dropping the carries, we get 00, indicating that data is not corrupted.)
```

(c) If the second byte 62H has been changed to 22H, show how checksum detects the error.

```
      25H
  +   22H
  +   3FH
  +   52H
  +   E8H
     1C0H     (Dropping the carry, we get C0H, which is not 00, and that means data
              is corrupted.)
```

Checksum program in modules

The checksum generation and testing program is given in modular form. We have divided the program into several modules (subroutines or subprograms). Dividing a program into several modules (called functions in C programming) allows us to use its modules in other applications. It is common practice to divide a program into several modules, test each module, and put them into a library. The checksum program shown next has three modules: It (a) gets the data from code ROM, (b) calculates the checksum byte, and (c) tests the checksum byte for any data error. Each of these modules can be used in other applications.

Checksum program

```
;CALCULATING AND TESTING CHECKSUM BYTE


DATA_ADDR    EQU 400H
COUNT        EQU 4
RAM_ADDR     EQU 30H


;-----------main program
        ORG 0
        ACALL COPY_DATA
        ACALL CAL_CHKSUM
        ACALL TEST_CHKSUM
        SJMP   $


;--------copying data from code ROM to data RAM
COPY_DATA:
        MOV  DPTR,#DATA_ADDR    ;load data address
        MOV  R0,#RAM_ADDR ;load RAM data address
        MOV  R2,#COUNT     ;load counter
H1:     CLR  A             ;clear accumulator
        MOVC A,@A+DPTR     ;bring in data from code ROM
        MOV  @R0,A         ;save it in RAM
        INC  DPTR          ;increment DPTR
        INC  R0            ;increment R0
        DJNZ R2,H1         ;repeat for all
        RET


;-----calculating checksum byte
CAL_CHKSUM:
        MOV  R1,#RAM_ADDR ;load data address
        MOV  R2,#COUNT     ;load count
        CLR  A             ;clear accumulator
H2:     ADD  A,@R1         ;add bytes and ignore carries
        INC  R1            ;increment R1
        DJNZ R2,H2         ;repeat for all
        CPL  A             ;1's complement
        INC  A             ;2's complement(checksum byte)
        MOV  @R1,A         ;save it in data RAM
        RET


;----------testing checksum byte
TEST_CHKSUM:
        MOV  R1,#RAM_ADDR ;load data address
        MOV  R2,#COUNT+1   ;load counter
        CLR  A             ;clear accumulator
H3:     ADD  A,@R1         ;add bytes and ignore carries
        INC  R1            ;increment R1
        DJNZ R2,H3         ;repeat for all
        JZ   G_1           ;is result zero? then good
        MOV  P1,#'B'       ;if not, data is bad
        SJMP OVER
G_1:    MOV  P1,#'G'       ;data is not corrupted
OVER:   RET


;----------my data in code ROM
        ORG 400H
MYBYTE: DB   25H,62H,3FH,52H
        END
```

Binary (hex) to ASCII conversion

Many ADC (analog-to-digital converter) chips provide output data in binary (hex). To display the data on an LCD or PC screen, we need to convert it to ASCII. The following code shows the binary-to-ASCII conversion program. Notice that the subroutine gets a byte of 8-bit binary (hex) data from P1 and converts it to decimal digits, and the second subroutine converts the decimal digits to ASCII digits and saves them. We are saving the low digit in the lower address location and the high digit in the higher address location. This is referred to as the little-endian convention, that is, low byte to low location and high byte to high location. All Intel products use the little-endian convention.

Binary-to-ASCII conversion program

```
;CONVERTING BIN(HEX) TO ASCII

RAM_ADDR    EQU 40H
ASCI_RSULT  EQU 50H
COUNT       EQU 3
;----------main program
      ORG 0
      ACALL BIN_DEC_CONVRT
      ACALL DEC_ASCI_CONVRT
      SJMP  $

;-----Converting BIN(HEX) TO DEC (00-FF TO 000-255)
BIN_DEC_CONVRT:
      MOV R0,#RAM_ADDR ;save DEC digits in these RAM loca-
tions
      MOV A,P1          ;read data from P1
      MOV B,#10         ;B=0A hex (10 dec)
      DIV AB            ;divide by 10
      MOV @R0,B         ;save lower digit
      INC R0
      MOV B,#10
      DIV AB            ;divide by 10 once more
      MOV @R0,B         ;save the next digit
      INC R0
      MOV @R0,A         ;save the last digit
      RET
;---------Converting DEC digits to displayable ASCII digits
DEC_ASCI_CONVRT:
      MOV R0,#RAM_ADDR     ;addr of DEC data
      MOV R1,#ASCI_RSULT   ;addr of ASCII data
      MOV R2,#3            ;count
BACK: MOV A,@R0            ;get DEC digit
      ORL A,#30H           ;make it an ASCII digit
      MOV @R1,A            ;save it
      INC R0               ;next digit
      INC R1               ;next
      DJNZ R2,BACK         ;repeat until the last one
      RET
;-------------------------------------------------
      END
```

REVIEW QUESTIONS

1. For the following decimal numbers, give the packed BCD and unpacked BCD representations.
   (a) 15   (b) 99
2. Show the binary and hex formats for "76" and its BCD version.
3. Does the register A have BCD data after the following instruction is executed?

   ```
   MOV  A,#54
   ```
4. 67H in BCD when converted to ASCII is ____H and ____H.
5. Does the following convert unpacked BCD in register A to ASCII?

   ```
   MOV  A,#09
   ADD  A,#30H
   ```
6. The checksum byte method is used to test data integrity in ____ (RAM, ROM).
7. Find the checksum byte for the following hex values: 88H, 99H, AAH, BBH, CCH, DDH.
8. True or false. If we add all the bytes, including the checksum byte, and the result is FFH, there is no error in the data.

SUMMARY

This chapter discussed arithmetic instructions for both signed and unsigned data in the 8051. Unsigned data uses all 8 bits of the byte for data, making a range of 0 to 255 decimal. Signed data uses 7 bits for data and 1 for the sign bit, making a range of –128 to +127 decimal.

Binary coded decimal (BCD) data represents the digits 0 through 9. Both packed and unpacked BCD formats were discussed. The 8051 contains special instructions for arithmetic operations on BCD data.

In coding arithmetic instructions for the 8051, special attention has to be given to the possibility of a carry or overflow condition.

This chapter also defined the logic instructions AND, OR, XOR, and complement. In addition, 8051 Assembly language instructions for these functions were described. Compare and jump instructions were described as well. These functions are often used for bit manipulation purposes.

The rotate and swap instructions of the 8051 are used in many applications such as serial devices. This chapter also described checksum byte data checking, BCD and ASCII formats, and conversions.

PROBLEMS

6.1: ARITHMETIC INSTRUCTIONS

1. Find the CY and AC flags for each of the following.

(a)
```
MOV A,#3FH
ADD A,#45H
```
       (b)
```
MOV A,#99H
ADD A,#58H
```

(c)	MOV A,#0FFH	(d)	MOV A,#0FFH
	SETB C		ADD A,#1
	ADDC A,#00		
(e)	MOV A,#0FEH	(f)	CLR C
	SETB C		MOV A,#0FFH
	ADDC A,#01		ADDC A,#01
			ADDC A,#0

2. Write a program to add all the digits of your ID number and save the result in R3. The result must be in BCD.

3. Write a program to add the following numbers and save the result in R2, R3. The data is stored in on-chip ROM.

```
        ORG   250H
MYDATA:  DB   53,94,56,92,74,65,43,23,83
```

4. Modify Problem 3 to make the result in BCD.

5. Write a program to (a) write the value 55H to RAM locations 40H–4FH, and (b) add all these RAM locations' contents together, and save the result in RAM locations 60H and 61H.

6. State the steps that the SUBB instruction will go through for each of the following.
   (a) 23H–12H   (b) 43H–53H   (c) 99–99

7. For Problem 6, write a program to perform each operation.

8. True or false. The "DA A" instruction works on register A and it must be used after the ADD and ADDC instructions.

9. Write a program to add 897F9AH to 34BC48H and save the result in RAM memory locations starting at 40H.

10. Write a program to subtract 197F9AH from 34BC48H and save the result in RAM memory locations starting at 40H.

11. Write a program to add BCD 197795H to 344548H and save the BCD result in RAM memory locations starting at 40H.

12. Show how to perform 77 × 34 in the 8051.

13. Show how to perform 77 ÷ 3 in the 8051.

14. True or false. The MUL and DIV instructions work on any register of the 8051.

15. Write a program with three subroutines to (a) transfer the following data from on-chip ROM to RAM locations starting at 30H, (b) add them and save the result in 70H, and (c) find the average of the data and store it in R7. Notice that the data is stored in a code space of on-chip ROM.

```
        ORG   250H
MYDATA:  DB   3,9,6,9,7,6,4,2,8
```

6.2: SIGNED NUMBER CONCEPTS AND ARITHMETIC OPERATIONS

16. Show how the following are represented by the assembler.
   (a) –23   (b) +12   (c) –28
   (d) +6FH   (e) –128   (f) +127

17. The memory addresses in computers are _____ (signed, unsigned) numbers.

18. Write a program for each of the following and indicate the status of the OV flag for each.
(a) (+15) + (–12)   (b) (–123) + (–127)
(c) (+25H) + (+34H)   (d) (–127) + (+127)
19. Explain the difference between the CY and OV flags and where each one is used.
20. Explain when the OV flag is raised.
21. Which register holds the OV flag?
22. How do you detect the OV flag in the 8051? How do you detect the CY flag?

6.3: LOGIC AND COMPARE INSTRUCTIONS

23. Assume that these registers contain the following: A = F0, B = 56, and R1 = 90. Perform the following operations. Indicate the result and the register where it is stored.
    Note: The operations are independent of each other.
    (a) ANL A,#45H   (b) ORL A,B
    (c) XRL A,#76H   (d) ANL A,R1
    (e) XRL A,R1   (f) ORL A,R1
    (g) ANL A,#0FFH   (h) ORL A,#99H
    (i) XRL A,#0EEH   (j) XRL A,#0AAH
24. Find the contents of register A after each of the following instructions.
    (a) MOV A,#65H   (b) MOV A,#70H
          ANL A,#76H   ORL A,#6BH
    (c) MOV A,#95H   (d) MOV A,#5DH
          XRL A,#0AAH   MOV R3,#78H
                             ANL A,R3
    (e) MOV A,#0C5H   (f) MOV A,#6AH
          MOV R6,#12H   MOV R4,#6EH
          ORL A,R6   XRL A,R4
    (g) MOV A,#37H
          ORL A,#26H
25. True or false. In using the CJNE instruction, we must use the accumulator as the destination.
26. Is the following a valid instruction?
    "CJNE R4,#67,HERE"
27. Does the 8051 have a "CJE" (compare and jump if equal) instruction?
28. Indicate the status of CY after CJNE is executed in each of the following cases.
    (a) MOV   A,#25H   (b) MOV   A,#0FFH
          CJNE A,#44H,OVER   CJNE A,#6FH,NEXT
    (c) MOV   A,#34   (d) MOV   R1,#0
          CJNE A,#34,NEXT   CJNE R1,#0,NEXT
    (e) MOV   R5,#54H   (f) MOV   A,#0AAH
          CJNE R5,#0FFH,NEXT   ANL   A,#55H
                               CJNE A,#00,NEXT
29. In Problem 28, indicate whether or not the jump happens for each case.

6.4: ROTATE INSTRUCTION AND DATA SERIALIZATION

30. Find the contents of register A after each of the following is executed.

```
(a) MOV    A,#56H        (b) MOV    A,#39H
    SWAP  A                  CLR    C
    RR    A                  RLA
    RR    A                  RLA
(c) CLR   C            (d) SETB   C
    MOV   A,#4DH             MOV    A,#7AH
    SWAP  A                  SWAP   A
    RRC   A                  RLC    A
    RRC   A                  RLC    A
    RRC   A
```

31. Show the code to replace the SWAP code
    (a) using the rotate right instructions.
    (b) using the rotate left instructions.
32. Write a program that finds the number of zeros in an 8-bit data item.
33. Write a program that finds the position of the first high in an 8-bit data item. The data is scanned from D0 to D7. Give the result for 68H.
34. Write a program that finds the position of the first high in an 8-bit data item. The data is scanned from D7 to D0. Give the result for 68H.
35. A stepper motor uses the following sequence of binary numbers to move the motor. How would you generate them?

    1100,0110,0011,1001

6.5: BCD, ASCII, AND OTHER APPLICATION PROGRAMS

36. Write a program to convert a series of packed BCD numbers to ASCII. Assume that the packed BCD is located in ROM locations starting at 300H. Place the ASCII codes in RAM locations starting at 40H.

```
            ORG 300H
MYDATA:    DB    76H,87H,98H,43H
```

37. Write a program to convert a series of ASCII numbers to packed BCD. Assume that the ASCII data is located in ROM locations starting at 300H. Place the BCD data in RAM locations starting at 60H.

```
            ORG 300H
MYDATA:    DB    "87675649"
```

38. Write a program to get an 8-bit binary number from P1, convert it to ASCII, and save the result in RAM locations 40H, 41H, and 42H. What is the result if P1 has 1000 1101 binary as input?
39. Find the result at points (1), (2), and (3) in the following code.

```
            CJNE A,#50,NOT_EQU
            ...                    ;point (1)
NOT_EQU:    JC    NEXT
            ...                    ;point (2)
NEXT:       ...                    ;point (3)
```

40. Assume that the lower four bits of P1 are connected to four switches. Write a program to send the following ASCII characters to P2 based on the status of the switches.

0000	'0'
0001	'1'
0010	'2'
0011	'3'
0100	'4'
0101	'5'
0110	'6'
0111	'7'
1000	'8'
1001	'9'
1010	'A'
1011	'B'
1100	'C'
1101	'D'
1110	'E'
1111	'F'

41. Find the checksum byte for the following ASCII message: "Hello"
42. True or false. If we add all the bytes, including the checksum byte, and the result is 00H, then there is no error in the data.
43. Write a program: (a) to get the data "Hello, my fellow World citizens" from code ROM, (b) to calculate the check sum byte, and (c) to test the checksum byte for any data error.
44. Give three reasons you should write your programs in modules.
45. To display data on LCD or PC monitors, it must be in _____ (BIN, BCD, ASCII).
46. Assume that the lower four bits of P1 are connected to four switches. Write a program to send the following ASCII characters to P2 based on the status of the switches. Do not use the look-up table method.

0000	'0'
0001	'1'
0010	'2'
0011	'3'
0100	'4'
0101	'5'
0110	'6'
0111	'7'
1000	'8'
1001	'9'

ANSWERS TO REVIEW QUESTIONS

6.1: ARITHMETIC INSTRUCTIONS

1. A, B
2. A, B
3. No. We must use registers A and B for this operation.
4. A, B
5. A, B
6. We must use registers A and B for this operation.
7. A, the accumulator
8. We must use register A for this operation.
9. ```
   MOV       A,R1
   ADD       A,R2
   ```
10. A, the accumulator
11. (a) A = 00 and CY = 1   (b) A = FF and CY = 0
12.
```
    43H   0100 0011                           0100 0011
   -05H   0000 0101  2's complement  +  1111 1011
    3EH   0011 1110
```
13. A = 95H – 4FH – 1 = 45H

6.2: SIGNED NUMBER CONCEPTS AND ARITHMETIC OPERATIONS

1. D7
2. 16H is 00010110 in binary and its 2's complement is 1110 1010 or
   −16H = EA in hex.
3. −128 to +127
4. +9 = 00001001 and −9 = 11110111 or F7 in hex.
5. An overflow is a carry into the sign bit (D7), but the carry is a carry out of register (D7).

6.3: LOGIC AND COMPARE INSTRUCTIONS

1. (a) 02   (b) FFH   (c) FDH
2. Zeros
3. One
4. All zeros
5. False
6. #53
7. 66H

6.4: ROTATE INSTRUCTION AND DATA SERIALIZATION

1. 52H
2. 2AH
3. C0H
4. Because all the rotate instructions work with the accumulator only
5. 50H
6. CY = 0
7. CY = 0
8. CY = 1
9. ```
   MOV C,P2.7      ;save status of P2.7 on CY
   MOV 31,C        ;save carry in RAM bit location 06
   ```
10. ```
    MOV C,9         ;save status of RAM bit 09 in CY
    MOV P1.4,C      ;save carry in P1.4
    ```
    ```

6.5: BCD, ASCII, AND OTHER APPLICATION PROGRAMS

1. (a) 15H = 0001 0101 packed BCD, 0000 0001,0000 0101 unpacked BCD
    (b) 99H = 1001 1001 packed BCD, 0000 1001,0000 1001 unpacked BCD
2. 3736H = 00110111 00110110B
    and in BCD we have 76H = 0111 0110B
3. No. We need to write it 54H (with the H) or 01010100B to make it in BCD. The value 54 without the "H" is interpreted as 36H by the assembler.
4. 36H, 37H
5. Yes, since A = 39H
6. ROM
7. 88H + 99H + AAH + BBH + CCH + DDH = 42FH. Dropping the carries we have 2FH, and its 2's complement is D1H.
8. False

CHAPTER 7

8051 PROGRAMMING IN C

OBJECTIVES

Upon completion of this chapter, you will be able to:

>> Examine the C data type for the 8051.
>> Code 8051 C programs for time delay and I/O operations.
>> Code 8051 C programs for I/O bit manipulation.
>> Code 8051 C programs for logic and arithmetic operations.
>> Code 8051 C programs for ASCII and BCD data conversion.
>> Code 8051 C programs for binary (hex) to decimal conversion.
>> Code 8051 C programs to use the 8051 code space.
>> Code 8051 C programs for data serialization.

Compilers produce hex files that we download into the ROM of the microprocessor. The size of the hex file produced by the compiler is one of the main concerns of microprocessor programmers, for two reasons:

1. Microprocessors have limited on-chip ROM.
2. The code space for the 8051 is limited to 64K bytes.

How does the choice of programming language affect the compiled program size? While Assembly language produces a hex file that is much smaller than C, programming in Assembly language is tedious and time consuming. C programming, on the other hand, is less time consuming and much easier to write, but the hex file size produced is much larger than if we used Assembly language. The following are some of the major reasons for writing programs in C instead of Assembly:

1. It is easier and less time consuming to write in C than Assembly.
2. C is easier to modify and update.
3. You can use code available in function libraries.
4. C code is portable to other microprocessors with little or no modification.

The study of C programming for the 8051 is the main topic of this chapter. In Section 7.1, we discuss data types and time delays. I/O programming is discussed in Section 7.2. The logic operations AND, OR, XOR, inverter, and shift are discussed in Section 7.3. Section 7.4 describes ASCII and BCD conversions and checksums. In Section 7.5, we show how 8051 C compilers use the program (code) ROM space for data. Finally, Section 7.6 examines data serialization for the 8051.

7.1: DATA TYPES AND TIME DELAY IN 8051 C

In this section, we first discuss C data types for the 8051 and then provide code for time delay functions.

C data types for the 8051

Since one of the goals of 8051 C programmers is to create smaller hex files, it is worthwhile to reexamine C data types for the 8051. In other words, a good understanding of C data types for the 8051 can help programmers to create smaller hex files. In this section, we focus on the specific C data types that are most useful and widely used for the 8051 microprocessor.

Unsigned char

Since the 8051 is an 8-bit microprocessor, the character data type is the most natural choice for many applications. The unsigned char is an 8-bit data type that takes a value in the range of 0–255 (00–FFH). It is one of the most widely used data types for the 8051. In many situations, such as setting a counter value, where there is no need for signed data we should use the unsigned char instead of the signed char. Remember that C compilers use the signed char as the default if we do not put the keyword *unsigned* in front of the char (see Example 7-1). We can also use the unsigned char data type for a string of ASCII characters, including extended ASCII characters. Example 7-2 shows a string of ASCII characters. See Example 7-3 for toggling ports.

In declaring variables, we must pay careful attention to the size of the data and try to use unsigned char instead of int. Because the 8051 has a limited number of registers and data RAM locations, using the int in place of the char data type can lead to a larger size hex file. Such a misuse of the data types in compilers such as Microsoft Visual C++ for x86 IBM PCs is not a significant issue.

Example 7-1

Write an 8051 C program to send values 00–FF to port P1.

Solution:

```
#include <reg51.h>
void main(void)
  {
     unsigned char z;
     for(z=0;z<=255;z++)
        P1=z;
  }
```

Run the above program on your simulator to see how P1 displays values 00–FFH in binary.

Example 7-2

Write an 8051 C program to send hex values for ASCII characters of 0, 1, 2, 3, 4, 5, A, B, C, and D to port P1.

Solution:

```
#include <reg51.h>
void main(void)
  {
     unsigned char mynum[]= "012345ABCD";
     unsigned char z;
     for(z=0;z<=10;z++)
        P1=mynum[z];
  }
```

Run the above program on your simulator to see how P1 displays values 30H, 31H, 32H, 33H, 34H, 35H, 41H, 42H, 43H, and 44H, the hex values for ASCII 0, 1, 2, and so on.

Example 7-3

Write an 8051 C program to toggle all the bits of P1 continuously.

Solution:

```
// Toggle P1 forever
#include <reg51.h>
void main(void)
    {
    for(;;)         //repeat forever
       {
        P1=0x55;    //0x indicates the data is in hex (binary)
        P1=0xAA;
       }
    }
```

Run the above program on your simulator to see how P1 toggles continuously. Examine the asm code generated by the C compiler.

Signed char

The signed char is an 8-bit data type that uses the most significant bit (D7 of D7–D0) to represent the – or + value. As a result, we have only 7 bits for the magnitude of the signed number, giving us values from –128 to +127. In situations where + and – are needed to represent a given quantity such as temperature, the use of the signed char data type is a must.

Again notice that if we do not use the keyword *unsigned,* the default is the signed value. For that reason,we should stick with the unsigned char unless the data needs to be represented as signed numbers. See Example 7-4.

Example 7-4

Write an 8051 C program to send values of –4 to +4 to port P1.

Solution:

```
//sign numbers
#include <reg51.h>
void main(void)
    {
    char mynum[]= {+1,-1,+2,-2,+3,-3,+4,-4};
    unsigned char z;
    for(z=0;z<=8;z++)
       P1=mynum [z];
    }
```

Run the above program on your simulator to see how P1 displays values of 1, FFH, 2, FEH, 3, FDH, and 4, FCH, the hex values for +1, –1, +2, –2, and so on.

Unsigned int

The unsigned int is a 16-bit data type that takes a value in the range of 0 to 65535 (0000–FFFFH). In the 8051, unsigned int is used to define 16-bit variables such as memory addresses. It is also used to set counter values of more than 256. Since the 8051 is an 8-bit microprocessor and the int data type takes two bytes of RAM, we must not use the int data type unless we have to. Since registers and memory accesses are in 8-bit chunks, the misuse of int variables will result in a larger hex file. Such misuse is not a big deal in PCs with 256 megabytes of memory, 32-bit Pentium registers and memory accesses, and a bus speed of 133 MHz. However, for 8051 programming, do not use unsigned int in places where unsigned char will do the job. Of course the compiler will not generate an error for this misuse, but the overhead in hex file size is noticeable. Also in situations where there is no need for signed data (such as setting counter values), we should use unsigned int instead of signed int. This gives a much wider range for data declaration. Again, remember that the C compiler uses signed int as the default if we do not use the keyword *unsigned.*

Signed int

Signed int is a 16-bit data type that uses the most significant bit (D15 of D15–D0) to represent the – or + value. As a result, we have only 15 bits for the magnitude of the number, or values from –32,768 to +32,767.

Sbit (single bit)

The *sbit* keyword is a widely used 8051 C data type designed specifically to access single-bit addressable registers. It allows access to the single bits of the SFR registers. As we saw in Chapter 5, some of the SFRs are bit-addressable. Among the SFRs that are widely used and are also bit-addressable are ports P0–P3. We can use sbit to access the individual bits of the ports, as shown in Example 7-5.

Example 7-5

Write an 8051 C program to toggle bit D0 of the port P1 (P1.0) 50,000 times.

Solution:

```
#include <reg51.h>
sbit MYBIT = P1^0;      //notice that sbit is
                        //declared outside of main
void main(void)
  {
    unsigned int z;
    for (z=0; z<=50000; z++)
      {
        MYBIT = 0;
        MYBIT = 1;
      }
  }
```

Run the above program on your simulator to see how P1.0 toggles continuously.

Bit and sfr

The bit data type allows access to single bits of bit-addressable memory spaces 20–2FH. Notice that while the sbit data type is used for bit-addressable SFRs, the bit data type is used for the bit-addressable section of RAM space 20–2FH. To access the byte-size SFR registers, we use the sfr data type. We will see the use of sbit, bit, and sfr data types in the next section. See Table 7-1.

Time delay

There are two ways to create a time delay in 8051 C:

1. Using a simple `for` loop
2. Using the 8051 timers

In either case, when we write a time delay we must use the oscilloscope to measure the duration of our time delay. Next, we use the `for` loop to create time delays. Discussion of the use of the 8051 timer to create time delays is postponed until Chapter 9.

In creating a time delay using a `for` loop, we must be mindful of three factors that can affect the accuracy of the delay.

1. The 8051 design: The original 8051 microprocessor was designed in 1980. Since then, both the fields of IC technology and microprocessor architectural design have seen great advancements. As we saw in Chapter 3, the number of machine cycles and the number of clock periods per machine cycle vary among different versions of the 8051/52 microprocessor. While the original 8051/52 design used 12 clock periods per machine cycle, many of the newer generations of the 8051 use fewer clocks per machine cycle. For example, the DS5000 uses 4 clock periods per machine cycle, while the DS89C4x0 uses only 1 clock per machine cycle.

2. The crystal frequency connected to the X1–X2 input pins: The duration of the clock period for the machine cycle is a function of this crystal frequency.

3. Compiler choice: The third factor that affects the time delay is the compiler used to compile the C program. When we program in Assembly language, we can control the exact instructions and their sequences used in the DELAY subroutine. In the case of C programs, it is the C compiler that converts the C

Table 7-1. Some Widely Used Data Types for 8051 C

Data Type	Size in Bits	Data Range/Usage
unsigned char	8-bit	0 to 255
char (signed)	8-bit	–128 to +127
unsigned int	16-bit	0 to 65535
int (signed)	16-bit	–32,768 to +32,767
sbit	1-bit	SFR bit-addressable only
bit	1-bit	RAM bit-addressable only
sfr	8-bit	RAM addresses 80–FFH only

statements and functions to Assembly language instructions. As a result, different compilers produce different code. In other words, if we compile a given 8051 C program with different compilers, each compiler produces different hex code.

For the above reasons, when we write time delays for C, we must use the oscilloscope to measure the exact duration. Look at Examples 7-6 through 7-8.

Example 7-6

Write an 8051 C program to toggle bits of P1 continuously forever with some delay.

Solution:

```c
// Toggle P1 forever with some delay in between "on" and "off".
#include <reg51.h>
void main(void)
    {
        unsigned int x;
        for(;;)                         //repeat forever
          {
            P1=0x55;
            for(x=0;x<40000;x++);   //delay size unknown
            P1=0xAA;
            for(x=0;x<40000;x++);
          }
    }
```

Example 7-7

Write an 8051 C program to toggle bits of P1 ports continuously with a 250 ms delay.

Solution:

This program is tested for the DS89C4x0 with XTAL = 11.0592 MHz.

```c
#include <reg51.h>
void MSDelay(unsigned int);
void main(void)
    {
        while(1)    //repeat forever
          {
            P1=0x55;
            MSDelay(250);
            P1=0xAA;
            MSDelay(250);
          }
    }
void MSDelay(unsigned int itime)
    {
        unsigned int i, j;
        for(i=0;i<itime;i++)
          for(j=0;j<1275;j++);
    }
```

Run the above program on your Trainer and use the oscilloscope to measure the delay.

Example 7-8

Write an 8051 C program to toggle all the bits of P0 and P2 continuously with a 250 ms delay.

Solution:

```c
//This program is tested for the DS89C4x0 with XTAL = 11.0592 MHz
#include <reg51.h>
void MSDelay(unsigned int);
void main(void)
    {
    while(1)      //another way to do it forever
        {
        P0=0x55;
        P2=0x55;
        MSDelay(250);
        P0=0xAA;
        P2=0xAA;
        MSDelay(250);
        }
    }
void MSDelay(unsigned int itime)
    {
    unsigned int i, j;
    for(i=0;i<itime;i++)
        for(j=0;j<1275;j++);
    }
```

REVIEW QUESTIONS

1. Give the magnitude of the unsigned char and signed char data types.
2. Give the magnitude of the unsigned int and signed int data types.
3. If we are declaring a variable for a person's age, we should use the ___ data type.
4. True or false. Using a for loop to create a time delay is not recommended if you want your code be portable to other 8051 versions.
5. Give three factors that can affect the delay size.

7.2: I/O PROGRAMMING IN 8051 C

In this section, we look at C programming of the I/O ports for the 8051. We look at both byte and bit I/O programming.

Byte size I/O

As we stated in Chapter 4, ports P0–P3 are byte-accessible. We use the P0–P3 labels as defined in the 8051/52 C header file. Examples 7-9–7-11 provide a better understanding of how ports are accessed in 8051 C.

Example 7-9

LEDs are connected to bits P1 and P2. Write an 8051 C program that shows the count from 0 to FFH (0000 0000 to 1111 1111 in binary) on the LEDs.

Solution:

```c
#include <reg51.h>
#define LED P2              //notice how we can define P2
void main(void)
  {
    P1=00;                  //clear P1
    LED=0;                  //clear P2
    for(;;)                 //repeat forever
      {
        P1++;               //increment P1
        LED++;              //increment P2
      }
  }
```

Example 7-10

Write an 8051 C program to get a byte of data from P1, wait 1/2 second, and then send it to P2.

Solution:

```c
#include <reg51.h>
void MSDelay(unsigned int);
void main(void)
  {
    unsigned char mybyte;
    P1=0xFF;                    //make P1 an input port
    while(1)
      {
        mybyte=P1;              //get a byte from P1
        MSDelay(500);
        P2=mybyte;              //send it to P2
      }
  }

void MSDelay(unsigned int itime)
  {
    unsigned int i, j;
    for(i=0;i<itime;i++)
      for(j=0;j<1275;j++);
  }
```

Example 7-11

Write an 8051 C program to get a byte of data from P0. If it is less than 100, send it to P1; otherwise, send it to P2.

Solution:

```c
#include <reg51.h>
void main(void)
  {
    unsigned char mybyte;
    P0=0xFF;                //make P0 an input port
    while(1)
      {
        mybyte=P0;          //get a byte from P0
        if(mybyte<100)
          P1=mybyte;        //send it to P1 if less than 100
        else
          P2=mybyte;        //send it to P2 if more than 100
      }
  }
```

Bit-addressable I/O programming

The I/O ports of P0–P3 are bit-addressable. We can access a single bit without disturbing the rest of the port. We use the sbit data type to access a single bit of P0–P3. One way to do that is to use the Px^y format where x is the port 0, 1, 2, or 3, and y is the bit 0–7 of that port. For example, P1^7 indicates P1.7. When using this method, you need to include the reg51.h file. Study Examples 7-12–7-15 to become familiar with the syntax.

Example 7-12

Write an 8051 C program to toggle only bit P2.4 continuously without disturbing the rest of the bits of P2.

Solution:

```c
//toggling an individual bit
#include <reg51.h>
sbit mybit = P2^4;      //notice the way single bit is declared
void main(void)
{
  while(1)
    {
      mybit=1;          //turn on P2.4
      mybit=0;          //turn off P2.4
    }
}
```

Example 7-13

Write an 8051 C program to monitor bit P1.5. If it is high, send 55H to P0; otherwise, send AAH to P2.

Solution:

```c
#include <reg51.h>
sbit mybit = P1^5;      //notice the way single bit is declared
void main(void)
  {
     mybit=1;            //make mybit an input
     while(1)
       {
          if(mybit==1)
            P0=0x55;
          else
            P2=0xAA;
       }
  }
```

Example 7-14

A door sensor is connected to the P1.1 pin, and a buzzer is connected to P1.7. Write an 8051 C program to monitor the door sensor, and when it opens, sound the buzzer. You can sound the buzzer by sending a square wave of a few hundred Hz.

Solution:

```c
#include <reg51.h>
void MSDelay(unsigned int);
sbit Dsensor = P1^1;  //notice the way single bit is defined
sbit Buzzer = P1^7;
void main(void)
  {
     Dsensor=1;         //make P1.1 an input
     while(Dsensor==1)
       {
          buzzer=0;
          MSDelay(200);
          buzzer=1;
          MSDelay(200);
       }
  }

void MSDelay(unsigned int itime)
  {
     unsigned int i, j;
     for(i=0;i<itime;i++)
       for(j=0;j<1275;j++);
  }
```

Example 7-15

The data pins of an LCD are connected to P1. The information is latched into the LCD whenever its Enable pin goes from high to low. Write an 8051 C program to send "The Earth is but One Country" to this LCD.

Solution:

```
#include <reg51.h>
#define LCDData P1              //LCDData declaration
sbit En=P2^0;                   //the enable pin
void main(void)
   {
      unsigned char message[ ]= "The Earth is but One Country";
      unsigned char z;
      for(z=0;z<28;z++)         //send all the 28 characters
        {
         LCDData=message[z];
         En=1;                  //a high-
         En=0;                  //-to-low pulse to latch the LCD data
        }
   }
```

Run the above program on your simulator to see how P1 displays each character of the message. Meanwhile, monitor bit P2.0 after each character is issued.

Accessing SFR addresses 80–FFH

Another way to access the SFR RAM space 80–FFH is to use the sfr data type. This is shown in Example 7-16. We can also access a single bit of any SFR if we specify the bit address as shown in Example 7-17. Both the bit and byte addresses for the P0–P3 ports are given in Table 7-2. Notice in Examples 7-16 and 7-17 that there is no #include <reg51.h> statement. This allows us to access any byte of the SFR RAM space 80–FFH. This is a method widely used for the new generation of 8051 microprocessors, and we will use it in future chapters.

Table 7-2. Single-Bit Addresses of Ports

P0	Address	P1	Address	P2	Address	P3	Address	Port's B
P0.0	80H	P1.0	90H	P2.0	A0H	P3.0	B0H	D0
P0.1	81H	P1.1	91H	P2.1	A1H	P3.1	B1H	D1
P0.2	82H	P1.2	92H	P2.2	A2H	P3.2	B2H	D2
P0.3	83H	P1.3	93H	P2.3	A3H	P3.3	B3H	D3
P0.4	84H	P1.4	94H	P2.4	A4H	P3.4	B4H	D4
P0.5	85H	P1.5	95H	P2.5	A5H	P3.5	B5H	D5
P0.6	86H	P1.6	96H	P2.6	A6H	P3.6	B6H	D6
P0.7	87H	P1.7	97H	P2.7	A7H	P3.7	B7H	D7

Example 7-16

Write an 8051 C program to toggle all the bits of P0, P1, and P2 continuously with a 250 ms delay. Use the sfr keyword to declare the port addresses.

Solution:

```c
// Accessing Ports as SFRs using the sfr data type
sfr P0 = 0x80;              //declaring P0 using sfr data type
sfr P1 = 0x90;
sfr P2 = 0xA0;
void MSDelay(unsigned int);
void main(void)
   {
      while(1)                  //do it forever
        {
          P0=0x55;
          P1=0x55;
          P2=0x55;
          MSDelay(250);     //250 ms delay
          P0=0xAA;
          P1=0xAA;
          P2=0xAA;
          MSDelay(250);
        }
   }

void MSDelay(unsigned int itime)
   {
     unsigned int i, j;
     for(i=0;i<itime;i++)
       for(j=0;j<1275;j++);
   }
```

Example 7-17

Write an 8051 C program to turn bit P1.5 on and off 50,000 times.

Solution:

```c
sbit MYBIT = 0x95;  //another way to declare bit P1^5
void main(void)
   {
     unsigned int z;
     for(z=0;z<50000;z++)
       {
          MYBIT=1;
          MYBIT=0;
       }
   }
```

Example 7-18

Write an 8051 C program to get the status of bit P1.0, save it, and send it to P2.7 continuously.

Solution:

```
#include <reg51.h>
sbit inbit = P1^0;
sbit outbit = P2^7;        //sbit is used to declare SFR bits
bit membit;                //notice we use bit to declare
                           //bit-addressable memory

void main(void)
  {
    while(1)
      {
          membit=inbit;    //get a bit from P1.0
          outbit=membit;   //and send it to P2.7
      }
  }
```

Using bit data type for bit-addressable RAM

The sbit data type is used for bit-addressable SFR registers only. Sometimes we need to store some data in a bit-addressable section of the data RAM space 20–2FH. To do that, we use the bit data type, as shown in Example 7-18.

REVIEW QUESTIONS

1. The address of P1 is _____.
2. Write a short program that toggles all bits of P2.
3. Write a short program that toggles only bit P1.0.
4. True or false. The sbit data type is used for both SFR and RAM single-bit addressable locations.
5. True or false. The bit data type is used only for RAM single-bit addressable locations.

7.3: LOGIC OPERATIONS IN 8051 C

One of the most important and powerful features of the C language is its ability to perform bit manipulation. Because many books on C do not cover this important topic, it is appropriate to discuss it in this section. This section describes the action of bit-wise logic operators and provides some examples of how they are used.

Bit-wise operators in C

While every C programmer is familiar with the logical operators AND (&&), OR (||), and NOT (!), many C programmers are less familiar with the bit-wise operators AND (&), OR (|), EX-OR (^), Inverter (~), Shift Right (>>), and Shift Left (<<). These bit-wise operators are widely used in software engineering for embedded systems and control; consequently, understanding and mastery of them are critical in microprocessor-based system design and interfacing. See Table 7-3.

The following shows some examples using the C logical operators.

1. 0x35 & 0x0F = 0x05   /* ANDing */
2. 0x04 | 0x68 = 0x6C   /* ORing: */
3. 0x54 ^ 0x78 = 0x2C   /* XORing */
4. ~0x55 = 0xAA   /* Inverting 55H */

Examples 7-19 and 7-20 show the use of bit-wise operators.

```
0011 0101
0000 1111 0X0 5
_____
00000101
```

Table 7-3. Bit-wise Logic Operators for C

		AND	OR	EX-OR	Inverter
A	B	A&B	A|B	A^B	Y=~B
0	0	0	0	0	1
0	1	0	1	1	0
1	0	0	1	1	
1	1	1	1	0	

Example 7-19

Run the following program on your simulator and examine the results.

Solution:

```
#include <reg51.h>
void main (void)
  {
    P0= 0x35 & 0x0F;      //ANDing
    P1= 0x04 | 0x68;      //ORing
    P2= 0x54 ^ 0x78;      //XORing
    P0= ~0x55;            //inversing
    P1= 0x9A >> 3;        //shifting right 3 times
    P2= 0x77 >> 4;        //shifting right 4 times
    P0= 0x6 << 4;         //shifting left 4 times
  }
```

Example 7-20

Write an 8051 C program to toggle all the bits of P0 and P2 continuously with a 250 ms delay. Use the inverting operator.

Solution:

The program below is tested for the DS89C4x0 with XTAL = 11.0592 MHz.

```c
#include <reg51.h>
void MSDelay(unsigned int);
void main(void)
    {
        P0=0x55;
        P2=0x55;
        while(1)
            {
                P0=~P0;
                P2=~P2;
                MSDelay(250);
            }
    }

void MSDelay(unsigned int itime)
    {
        unsigned int i, j;
        for(i=0;i<itime;i++)
            for(j=0;j<1275;j++);
    }
```

Bit-wise shift operation in C

There are two bit-wise shift operators in C: (1) shift right (>>) and (2) shift left (<<).

Their format in C is as follows:

data >> number of bits to be shifted right
data << number of bits to be shifted left

The following shows some examples of shift operators in C.

1. 0x9A >> 3= 0x13   /* shifting right 3 times */
2. 0x77 >> 4 = 0x07   /* shifting right 4 times */
3. 0x6 << 4 = 0x60   /* shifting left 4 times */

Examples 7-21–7-23 show how the bit-wise operators are used in the 8051 C.

Example 7-21

Write an 8051 C program to toggle all the bits of P0, P1, and P2 continuously with a 250 ms delay. Use the Ex-OR operator.

Solution:

The program below is tested for the DS89C4x0 with XTAL = 11.0592 MHz.

```c
#include <reg51.h>
void MSDelay(unsigned int);
void main(void)
{
    P0=0x55;
    P1=0x55;
    P2=0x55;
    while(1)
    {
        P0=P0^0xFF;
        P1=P1^0xFF;
        P2=P2^0xFF;
        MSDelay(250);
    }
}

void MSDelay(unsigned int itime)
{
    unsigned int i, j;
    for(i=0;i<itime;i++)
        for(j=0;j<1275;j++);
}
```

Example 7-22

Write an 8051 C program to get bit P1.0 and send it to P2.7 after inverting it.

Solution:

```c
#include <reg51.h>
sbit inbit=P1^0;
sbit outbit=P2^7;      //sbit is used declare port (SFR) bits
bit membit;            //notice this is bit-addressable memory
void main(void)
{
    while(1)
    {
        membit=inbit;      //get a bit from P1.0
        outbit=~membit;    //invert it and send it to P2.7
    }
}
```

Example 7-23

Write an 8051 C program to read the P1.0 and P1.1 bits and issue an ASCII character to P0 according to the following table.

P1.1	P1.0	
0	0	send '0' to P0
0	1	send '1' to P0
1	0	send '2' to P0
1	1	send '3' to P0

Solution:

```c
#include <reg51.h>
void main(void)
    {
    unsigned char z;
    z=P1;                       //read P1
    z=z&0x3;                    //mask the unused bits
    switch(z)                   //make decision
        {
        case(0):
          {
            P0='0';             //issue ASCII 0
            break;
          }
        case(1):
          {
            P0='1';             //issue ASCII 1
            break;
          }
        case(2):
          {
            P0='2';             //issue ASCII 2
            break;
          }
        case(3):
          {
            P0='3';             //issue ASCII 3
            break;
          }
        }
    }
```

REVIEW QUESTIONS

1. Find the content of P1 after the following C code in each case.
   (a) P1=0x37&0xCA; (b) P1=0x37|0xCA; (c) P1=0x37^0xCA;
2. To mask certain bits, we must AND them with _____.
3. To set high certain bits, we must OR them with _____.
4. Ex-ORing a value with itself results in _____.
5. Find the contents of P2 after execution of the following code.
   ```c
   P2=0;
   P2=P2|0x99;
   P2=~P2;
   ```

7.4: DATA CONVERSION PROGRAMS IN 8051 C

Recall that BCD numbers were discussed in Chapter 6. As stated there, Many newer microprocessors have a real-time clock (RTC) that keeps track of the time and date even when the power is off. Very often the RTC provides the time and date in packed BCD. However, to display them they must be converted to ASCII. In this section, we show the application of logic and rotate instructions in the conversion of BCD and ASCII.

ASCII numbers

On ASCII keyboards, when the key "0" is activated, "011 0000" (30H) is provided to the computer. Similarly, 31H (011 0001) is provided for the key "1," and so on, as shown in Table 7-4.

Packed BCD to ASCII conversion

The RTC provides the time of day (hour, minute, second) and the date (year, month, day) continuously, regardless of whether the power is on or off. However, this data is provided in packed BCD. To convert packed BCD to ASCII, it must first be converted to unpacked BCD. Then the unpacked BCD is tagged with 011 0000 (30H). The following demonstrates converting from packed BCD to ASCII. See also Example 7-24.

```
Packed BCD       Unpacked BCD          ASCII
0x29             0x02, 0x09            0x32, 0x39
00101001         00000010,00001001     00110010,00111001
```

ASCII to packed BCD conversion

To convert ASCII to packed BCD, it is first converted to unpacked BCD (to get rid of the 3), and then combined to make packed BCD. For example, 4

Table 7-4. ASCII Code for Digits 0–9

Key	ASCII (hex)	Binary	BCD (unpacked)
0	30	011 0000	0000 0000
1	31	011 0001	0000 0001
2	32	011 0010	0000 0010
3	33	011 0011	0000 0011
4	34	011 0100	0000 0100
5	35	011 0101	0000 0101
6	36	011 0110	0000 0110
7	37	011 0111	0000 0111
8	38	011 1000	0000 1000
9	39	011 1001	0000 1001

and 7 on the keyboard give 34H and 37H, respectively. The goal is to produce 47H or "0100 0111", which is packed BCD.

Key	ASCII	Unpacked BCD	Packed BCD
4	34	00000100	
7	37	00000111	01000111 or 47H

After this conversion, the packed BCD numbers are processed and the result will be in packed BCD format. Chapter 16 discusses the RTC chip and uses the BCD and ASCII conversion programs shown in Examples 7-24 and 7-25. See Examples 7-24 and 7-25.

Example 7-24

Write an 8051 C program to convert packed BCD 0x29 to ASCII and display the bytes on P1 and P2.

Solution:

```
#include <reg51.h>
void main(void)
    {
    unsigned char x, y, z;
    unsigned char mybyte = 0x29;
    x = mybyte & 0x0F;          //mask lower 4 bits
    P1 =   x | 0x30;            //make it ASCII
    y = mybyte & 0xF0;          //mask upper 4 bits
    y = y >> 4;                 //shift it to lower 4 bits
    P2 = y | 0x30;              //make it ASCII
    }
```

Example 7-25

Write an 8051 C program to convert ASCII digits of '4' and '7' to packed BCD and display them on P1.

Solution:

```
#include <reg51.h>
void main(void)
    {
    unsigned char bcdbyte;
    unsigned char w='4';
    unsigned char z='7';
    w = w & 0x0F;     //mask 3
    w = w << 4;       //shift left to make upper BCD digit
    z = z & 0x0F;     //mask 3
    bcdbyte = w | z;  //combine to make packed BCD
    P1 = bcdbyte;
    }
```

Checksum byte in ROM

To ensure the integrity of ROM contents, every system must perform the checksum calculation. The process of checksum will detect any corruption of the contents of ROM. One of the causes of ROM corruption is current surge, which occurs either when the system is turned on or during operation. To ensure data integrity in ROM, the checksum process uses what is called a *checksum byte*. The checksum byte is an extra byte that is tagged to the end of a series of bytes of data. To calculate the checksum byte of a series of bytes of data, the following steps can be taken.

1. Add the bytes together and drop the carries.
2. Take the 2's complement of the total sum. This is the checksum byte, which becomes the last byte of the series.

To perform the checksum operation, add all the bytes, including the checksum byte. The result must be zero. If it is not zero, one or more bytes of data have been changed (corrupted). To clarify these important concepts, see Examples 7-26–7-28.

Example 7-26

Assume that we have 4 bytes of hexadecimal data: 25H, 62H, 3FH, and 52H. (a) Find the checksum byte, (b) perform the checksum operation to ensure data integrity, and (c) if the second byte 62H has been changed to 22H, show how checksum detects the error.

Solution:

(a)   Find the checksum byte.

```
        25H
    +   62H
    +   3FH
    +   52H
       118H  (Dropping the carry of 1 and taking the 2's complement, we get E8H.)
```

(b)   Perform the checksum operation to ensure data integrity.

```
        25H
    +   62H
    +   3FH
    +   52H
    +   E8H
       200H  (Dropping the carries we get 00, which means data is not corrupted.)
```

(c)   If the second byte 62H has been changed to 22H, show how checksum detects the error.

```
        25H
    +   22H
    +   3FH
    +   52H
    +   E8H
       1C0H  (Dropping the carry, we get C0H, which means data is corrupted.)
```

Example 7-27

Write an 8051 C program to calculate the checksum byte for the data given in Example 7-26.

Solution:
```c
#include <reg51.h>
void main(void)
   {
      unsigned char mydata[] = {0x25,0x62,0x3F,0x52};
      unsigned char sum=0;
      unsigned char x;
      unsigned char chksumbyte;
      for(x=0;x<4;x++)
        {
           P2=mydata[x];            //issue each byte to P2
           sum=sum+mydata[x];       //add them together
           P1=sum;                  //issue the sum to P1
        }
      chksumbyte=~sum+1;            //make 2's complement
      P1=chksumbyte;               //show the checksum byte
   }
```

Single-step the above program on the 8051 simulator and examine the contents of P1 and P2. Notice that each byte is put on P1 as they are added together.

Example 7-28

Write an 8051 C program to perform step (b) of Example 7-26. If data is good, send ASCII character 'G' to P0. Otherwise send 'B' to P0.

Solution:
```c
#include <reg51.h>
void main(void)
   {
      unsigned char mydata[]={0x25,0x62,0x3F,0x52,0xE8};
      unsigned char chksum=0;
      unsigned char x;
      for(x=0;x<5;x++)
         chksum=chksum+mydata[x];   //add them together
      if(chksum==0)
         P0='G';
      else
         P0='B';
   }
```

Binary (hex) to decimal and ASCII conversion in 8051 C

The `printf` function is part of the standard I/O library in C and can do many things, including converting data from binary (hex) to decimal, or vice versa. But printf takes a lot of memory space and increases your hex file substantially. For this reason, in systems based on the 8051 microprocessor, it is better to write your own conversion function instead of using printf.

One of the most widely used conversions is the binary to decimal conversion. In devices such as ADC (analog-to-digital conversion) chips, the data is provided to the microprocessor in binary. In some RTCs, data, such as time and dates are also provided in binary. In order to display binary data, we need to convert it to decimal and then to ASCII. Since the hexadecimal format is a convenient way of representing binary data, we refer to the binary data as hex. The binary data 00–FFH converted to decimal will give us 000 to 255. One way to do that is to divide it by 10 and keep the remainder, as was shown in Chapter 6. For example, 11111101 or FDH is 253 in decimal. The following is one version of an algorithm for conversion of hex (binary) to decimal:

	Quotient	Remainder
FD/0A	19	3 (low digit) LSD
19/0A	2	5 (middle digit)
		2 (high digit) (MSD)

Example 7-29 shows the C program for that algorithm.

Example 7-29

Write an 8051 C program to convert 11111101 (FD hex) to decimal and display the digits on P0, P1, and P2.

Solution:

```
#include <reg51.h>
void main(void)
  {
     unsigned char x, binbyte, d1, d2, d3;
     binbyte = 0xFD;          //binary(hex) byte
     x = binbyte / 10;        //divide by 10
     d1 = binbyte % 10;       //find remainder (LSD)
     d2 = x % 10;             //middle digit
     d3 = x / 10;             //most significant digit (MSD)
     P0 = d1;
     P1 = d2;
     P2 = d3;
  }
```

REVIEW QUESTIONS

1. For the following decimal numbers, give the packed BCD and unpacked BCD representations.
   (a) 15   (b) 99
2. Show the binary and hex formats for "76" and its BCD version.
3. 67H in BCD when converted to ASCII is ____H and ____H.
4. Does the following convert unpacked BCD in register A to ASCII?
   `mydata = 0x09 + 0x30;`
5. Why is the use of packed BCD preferable to ASCII?
6. Which one takes more memory space: packed BCD or ASCII?
7. In Question 6, which is more universal?
8. Find the checksum byte for the following values: 22H, 76H, 5FH, 8CH, 99H.
9. To test data integrity, we add them together, including the checksum byte. Then drop the carries. The result must be equal to ____ if the data is not corrupted.
10. An ADC provides an input of 0010 0110. What happens if we output that to the screen?

7.5: ACCESSING CODE ROM SPACE IN 8051 C

Using the code (program) space for predefined data is the widely used option in the 8051, as we saw in Chapter 5. In that chapter we saw how to use the Assembly language instruction MOVC to access the data stored in the 8051 code space. In this chapter, we explore the same concept for 8051 C.

RAM data space versus code data space

In the 8051, we have three spaces to store data. They are as follows:

1. The 128 bytes of RAM space with address range 00–7FH. (In the 8052, it is 256 bytes.) We can read (from) or write (into) this RAM space directly or indirectly using the R0 and R1 registers, as we saw in Chapter 5.
2. The 64K bytes of code (program) space with addresses of 0000–FFFFH. This 64K bytes of on-chip ROM space is used for storing programs (opcodes) and therefore is directly under the control of the program counter (PC). We can use the "MOVC A, @A+DPTR" Assembly language instruction to access it for data (see Chapter 5). There are two problems with using this code space for data. First, since it is ROM memory, we can burn our predefined data and tables into it. But we cannot write into it during the execution of the program. The second problem is that the more of this code space we use for data, the less is left for our program code. For example, if we have an 8051 chip such as DS89C4x0 with only 16K bytes of on-chip ROM, and we use 4K bytes of it to store some look-up table, only 12K bytes is left for the code program. For some applications this can be a problem. For this reason, Intel created another memory space called *external memory* especially for data. This is discussed next very briefly and we postpone the full discussion to Chapter 14.

3. The 64K bytes of external memory, which can be used for both RAM and ROM. This 64K bytes is called external since we must use the MOVX Assembly language instruction to access it. At the time the 8051 was designed, the cost of on-chip ROM was very high; therefore, Intel used all the on-chip ROM for code but allowed connection to external RAM and ROM. In other words, we have a total of 128K bytes of memory space since the off-chip or external memory space of 64K bytes plus the 64K bytes of on-chip space provides you a total of 128K bytes of memory space. We will discuss the external memory expansion and how to access it for both Assembly and C in Chapter 14.

Next, we discuss on-chip RAM and ROM space usage by the 8051 C compiler. We have used the Proview32 C compiler to verify the concepts discussed next. Use the compiler of your choice to verify these concepts.

RAM data space usage by the 8051 C compiler

In Assembly language programming, as shown in Chapters 2 and 5, the 128 bytes of RAM space is used mainly by register banks and the stack. Whatever remains is used for scratch pad RAM. The 8051 C compiler first allocates the first 8 bytes of the RAM to bank 0 and then some RAM to the stack. Then it starts to allocate the rest to the variables declared by the C program. While in Assembly the default starting address for the stack is 08, the C compiler moves the stack's starting address to somewhere in the range of 50–7FH. This allows us to allocate contiguous RAM locations to array elements. See Figure 7-1.

In cases where the program has individual variables in addition to array elements, the 8051 C compiler allocates RAM locations in the following order:

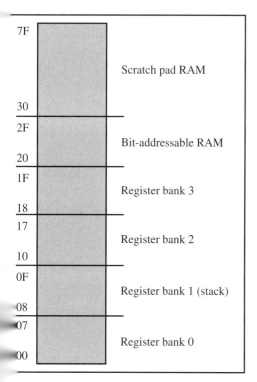

1. Bank 0   addresses 0–7
2. Individual variables   addresses 08 and beyond
3. Array elements   addresses right after variables
4. Stack   addresses right after array elements

You can verify the above order by running Example 7-30 on your 8051 C simulator and examining the contents of the data RAM space. Remember that array elements need contiguous RAM locations and that limits the size of the array due to the fact that we have only 128 bytes of RAM for everything. In the case of Example 7-31, the array elements are limited to around 100. Run Example 7-31 on your 8051 C simulator and examine the RAM space allocation. Keep changing the size of the array and monitor the RAM space to see what happens.

7F
Scratch pad RAM
30
2F
Bit-addressable RAM
20
1F
Register bank 3
18
17
Register bank 2
10
0F
Register bank 1 (stack)
08
07
Register bank 0
00

Figure 7-1. RAM Allocation in the 8051

Example 7-30

Compile and single-step the following program on your 8051 simulator. Examine the contents of the 128-byte RAM space to locate the ASCII values.

Solution:

```
#include <reg51.h>
void main(void)
  {
    unsigned char mynum[]= "ABCDEF";   //This uses RAM space
                                       //to store data
    unsigned char z;
    for(z=0;z<=6;z++)
      P1=mynum [z];
  }
```

Run the above program on your 8051 simulator and examine the RAM space to locate values 41H, 42H, 43H, 44H, and so on, the hex values for ASCII letters 'A,' 'B,' 'C,' and so on.

Example 7-31

Write, compile, and single-step the following program on your 8051 simulator. Examine the contents of the code space to locate the values.

Solution:

```
#include <reg51.h>
void main(void)
  {
    unsigned char mydata[100];   //100 byte space in RAM
    unsigned char x,z=0;
    for(x=0;x<100;x++)
      {
        z--;                         //count down
        mydata[x]=z;                 //save it in RAM
        P1=z;                        //give a copy to P1 too
      }
  }
```

Run the above program on your 8051 simulator and examine the data RAM space to locate values FFH, FEH, FDH, and so on in RAM.

The 8052 RAM data space

Intel added some new features to the 8051 microprocessor and called it the 8052. One of the new features was an extra 128 bytes of RAM space. That means that the 8052 has 256 bytes of RAM space instead of 128 bytes. Remember that the 8052 is code-compatible with the 8051. This means that any program written for the 8051 will run on the 8052, but not the other way around since some features of the 8052 do not exist in the 8051. The extra 128 bytes of RAM helps the 8051/52 C compiler to manage its registers and resources much more effectively. Since the vast majority of the new versions of the 8051, such as DS89C4x0, are really based on 8052 architecture, you should compile your C programs for the 8052 microprocessor. We do that by (1) using the reg52.h header file and (2) choosing the 8052 option when compiling the program.

Accessing code data space in 8051 C

In all our 8051 C examples so far, byte-size variables were stored in the 128 bytes of RAM. To make the C compiler use the code space instead of the RAM space, we need to put the keyword *code* in front of the variable declaration. The following are some examples:

```
code unsigned char mynum[]= "012345ABCD";  //use code space
code unsigned char weekdays=7, month=0x12; //use code space
```

Example 7-32 shows how to use code space for data in 8051 C.

Compiler variations

Look at Example 7-33. It shows three different versions of a program that sends the string "HELLO" to the P1 port. Compile each program with the 8051 C compiler of your choice and compare the hex file size. Then compile each program on a different 8051 C compiler, and examine the hex file size to see the effectiveness of your C compiler. See www.MicroDigitalEd.com for 8051 C compilers.

Example 7-32

Compile and single-step the following program on your 8051 simulator. Examine the contents of the code space to locate the ASCII values.

Solution:
```
#include <reg51.h>
void main(void)
  {
    code unsigned char mynum[]= "ABCDEF";  //uses code space
                                           //for data
    unsigned char z;
    for(z=0;z<=6;z++)
      P1=mynum[z];
  }
```

Run the above program on your 8051 simulator and examine the code space to locate values 41H, 42H, 43H, 44H, and so on, the hex values for ASCII characters of 'A,' 'B,' 'C,' and so on.

Example 7-33

Compare and contrast the following programs and discuss the advantages and disadvantages of each one.

(a)
```
#include <reg51.h>
void main(void)
  {
    P1='H';
    P1='E';
    P1='L';
    P1='L';
    P1='O';
  }
```

(b)
```
#include <reg51.h>
void main(void)
  {
    unsigned char mydata[]="HELLO";
    unsigned char z;
    for(z=0;z<=5;z++)
      P1=mydata[z];
  }
```

(c)
```
#include <reg51.h>
void main(void)
  {
    //Notice Keyword code
    code unsigned char mydata[]="HELLO";
    unsigned char z;
    for(z=0;z<=5;z++)
      P1=mydata[z];
  }
```

Solution:

All the programs send out "HELLO" to P1, one character at a time, but they do it in different ways. The first one is short and simple, but the individual characters are embedded into the program. If we change the characters, the whole program changes. It also mixes the code and data together. The second one uses the RAM data space to store array elements, and therefore the size of the array is limited. The third one uses a separate area of the code space for data. This allows the size of the array to be as long as you want if you have the on-chip ROM. However, the more code space you use for data, the less space is left for your program code. Both programs (b) and (c) are easily upgradable if we want to change the string itself or make it longer. That is not the case for program (a).

REVIEW QUESTIONS

1. The 8051 has ____ bytes of data RAM, while the 8052 has ____ bytes.
2. The 8051 has ____ K bytes of code space and ____ K bytes of external data space.
3. True or false. The code space can be used for data but the external data space cannot be used for code.
4. Which space would you use to declare the following values for 8051 C?
   (a) the number of days in the week
   (b) the number of months in a year
   (c) a counter for a delay
5. In 8051 C, we should not use more than 100 bytes of the RAM data space for variables. Why?

7.6: DATA SERIALIZATION USING 8051 C

Serializing data is a way of sending a byte of data one bit at a time through a single pin of microprocessor. There are two ways to transfer a byte of data serially:

1. Using the serial port. When using the serial port, the programmer has very limited control over the sequence of data transfer. The detail of serial port data transfer is discussed in Chapter 10.

2. The second method of serializing data is to transfer data one bit a time and control the sequence of data and spaces in between them. In many new generation devices such as LCD, ADC, and ROM, the serial versions are becoming popular since they take less space on a printed circuit board.

Examine Examples 7-34–7-37 to see how data serialization is done in 8051 C.

Example 7-34

Write a C program to send out the value 44H serially one bit at a time via P1.0. The LSB should go out first.

Solution:

```
//SERIALIZING DATA VIA P1.0 (SHIFTING RIGHT)
#include <reg51.h>
sbit P1b0 = P1^0;
sbit regALSB = ACC^0;
void main(void)
  {
    unsigned char conbyte = 0x44;
    unsigned char x;
    ACC = conbyte;
    for(x=0; x<8; x++)
      {
        P1b0 = regALSB;
        ACC = ACC >> 1;
      }
  }
```

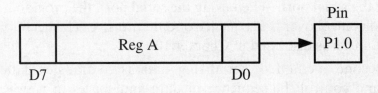

Example 7-35

Write a C program to send out the value 44H serially one bit at a time via P1.0. The MSB should go out first.

Solution:

```
//SERIALIZING DATA VIA P1.0 (SHIFTING LEFT)
#include <reg51.h>
sbit P1b0 =  P1^0;
sbit regAMSB = ACC^7;
void main(void)
  {
    unsigned char conbyte = 0x44;
    unsigned char x;
    ACC = conbyte;
    for(x=0; x<8; x++)
      {
        P1b0 = regAMSB;
        ACC = ACC << 1;
      }
  }
```

Example 7-36

Write a C program to bring in a byte of data serially one bit at a time via P1.0. The LSB should come in first.

Solution:

```c
//BRINGING IN DATA VIA P1.0 (SHIFTING RIGHT)
#include <reg51.h>
sbit P1b0  =   P1^0;
sbit ACCMSB = ACC^7;
void main(void)
  {
     unsigned char conbyte = 0x44;
     unsigned char x;
     for(x=0; x<8; x++)
       {
          ACCMSB = P1b0;
          ACC = ACC >> 1;
       }
     P2=ACC;
  }
```

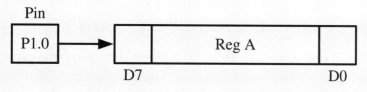

Example 7-37

Write a C program to bring in a byte of data serially one bit at a time via P1.0. The MSB should come in first.

Solution:

```c
//BRINGING DATA IN VIA P1.0 (SHIFTING LEFT)
#include <reg51.h>
sbit P1b0 = P1^0;
sbit regALSB = ACC^0;
void main(void)
  {
     unsigned char x;
     for(x=0; x<8; x++)
       {
          regALSB = P1b0;
          ACC = ACC << 1;
       }
     P2=ACC;
  }
```

SUMMARY

This chapter dealt with 8051 C programming, especially I/O programming and time delays in 8051 C. We also showed the logic operators AND, OR, XOR, and complement. In addition, some applications for these operators were discussed. This chapter also described BCD and ASCII formats and conversions in 8051 C. We also compared and contrasted the use of code space and RAM data space in 8051 C. The widely used technique of data serialization was also discussed.

RECOMMENDED WEB LINKS

See the following websites for 8051 C compilers:

- www.MicroDigitalEd.com
- www.8052.com

PROBLEMS

7.1: DATA TYPES AND TIME DELAY IN 8051 C

1. Indicate what data type you would use for each of the following variables:
   (a) the temperature
   (b) the number of days in a week
   (c) the number of days in a year
   (d) the number of months in a year
   (e) the counter to keep the number of people getting on a bus
   (f) the counter to keep the number of people going to a class
   (g) an address of 64K bytes RAM space
   (h) the voltage
   (i) a string for a message to welcome people to a building
2. Give the hex value that is sent to the port for each of the following C statements:
   (a) P1=14;   (b) P1=0x18;   (c) P1='A';   (d) P1=7;
   (e) P1=32;   (f) P1=0x45;   (g) P1=255;   (h) P1=0x0F;
3. Give three factors that can affect time delay code size in the 8051 microprocessor.
4. Of the three factors in Problem 3, which one can be set by the system designer?
5. Can the programmer set the number of clock cycles used to execute an instruction? Explain your answer.
6. Explain why various 8051 C compilers produce different hex file sizes.

7.2: I/O PROGRAMMING IN 8051 C

7. What is the difference between the sbit and bit data types?
8. Write an 8051 C program to toggle all bits of P1 every 200 ms.
9. Use your 8051 C compiler to see the shortest time delay that you can produce.
10. Write a time delay function for 100 ms.
11. Write an 8051 C program to toggle only bit P1.3 every 200 ms.
12. Write an 8051 C program to count up P1 from 0 to 99 continuously.

7.3: LOGIC OPERATIONS IN 8051 C

13. Indicate the data on the ports for each of the following.
    Note: The operations are independent of each other.
    (a) `P1=0xF0&0x45;`   (b) `P1=0xF0&0x56;`
    (c) `P1=0xF0^0x76;`   (d) `P2=0xF0&0x90;`
    (e) `P2=0xF0^0x90;`   (f) `P2=0xF0|0x90;`
    (g) `P2=0xF0&0xFF;`   (h) `P2=0xF0|0x99;`
    (i) `P2=0xF0^0xEE;`   (j) `P2=0xF0^0xAA;`
14. Find the contents of the port after each of the following operations.
    (a) `P1=0x65&0x76;`   (b) `P1=0x70|0x6B;`
    (c) `P2=0x95^0xAA;`   (d) `P2=0x5D&0x78;`
    (e) `P2=0xC5|0x12;`   (f) `P0=0x6A^0x6E;`
    (g) `P1=0x37|0x26;`
15. Find the port value after each of the following is executed.
    (a) `P1=0x65>>2;`   (b) `P2=0x39<<2;`
    (c) `P1=0xD4>>3;`   (d) `P1=0xA7<<2;`
16. Show the C code to swap 0x95 to make it 0x59.
17. Write a C program that finds the number of zeros in an 8-bit data item.
18. A stepper motor uses the following sequence of binary numbers to move the motor. How would you generate them in 8051 C?
    `1100,0110,0011,1001`

7.4: DATA CONVERSION PROGRAMS IN 8051 C

19. Write a program to convert the following series of packed BCD numbers to ASCII. Assume that the packed BCD is located in data RAM.
    `76H,87H,98H,43H`
20. Write a program to convert the following series of ASCII numbers to packed BCD. Assume that the ASCII data is located in data RAM.
    `"8767"`
21. Write a program to get an 8-bit binary number from P1, convert it to ASCII, and save the result if the input is packed BCD of 00–0x99. Assume P1 has 1000 1001 binary as input.

7.5: ACCESSING CODE ROM SPACE IN 8051 C

22. Indicate what memory (embedded, data RAM, or code ROM space) you would use for the following variables:
    (a) the temperature
    (b) the number of days in week
    (c) the number of days in a year
    (d) the number of months in a year
    (e) the counter to keep the number of people getting on a bus
    (f) the counter to keep the number of people going to a class
    (g) an address of 64K bytes RAM space
    (h) the voltage
    (i) a string for a message to welcome people to building
23. Discuss why the total size of your 8051 C variables should not exceed 100 bytes.
24. Why do we use the ROM code space for video game characters and shapes?
25. What is the drawback of using RAM data space for 8051 C variables?
26. What is the drawback of using ROM code space for 8051 C data?
27. Write an 8051 C program to send your first and last names to P2. Use ROM code space.

ANSWERS TO REVIEW QUESTIONS

7.1: DATA TYPES AND TIME DELAY IN 8051 C

1. 0 to 255 for unsigned char and –128 to +127 for signed char
2. 0 to 65,535 for unsigned int and –32,768 to +32,767 for signed int
3. Unsigned char
4. True
5. (a) Crystal frequency of 8051 system, (b) 8051 machine cycle timing, and (c) compiler use for 8051 C

7.2: I/O PROGRAMMING IN 8051 C

1. 90H
2.
```
#include <reg51.h>
void main()
  {
     P2 = 0x55;
     P2 = 0xAA
  }
```
3.
```
#include <reg51.h>
sbit P10bit = P1^0;
void main()
  {
     P10bit = 0;
     P10bit = 1;
  }
```
4. False, only to SFR bit
5. True

7.3: LOGIC OPERATIONS IN 8051 C

1. (a) 02   (b) FFH   (c) FDH
2. Zeros
3. One
4. All zeros
5. 66H

7.4: DATA CONVERSION PROGRAMS IN 8051 C

1. (a) 15H = 0001 0101 packed BCD, 0000 0001,0000 0101 unpacked BCD
    (b) 99H = 1001 1001 packed BCD, 0000 1001,0000 1001 unpacked BCD
2. 3736H = 00110111 00110110B
    and in BCD we have 76H = 0111 0110B
3. 36H, 37H
4. Yes, since A = 39H
5. Space savings
6. ASCII
7. ASCII
8. 21CH
9. 00
10. First convert from binary to decimal, then to ASCII, then send to screen.

7.5: ACCESSING CODE ROM SPACE IN 8051 C

1. 128, 256
2. 64K, 64K
3. True
4. (a) data space, (b) data space, (c) RAM space
5. The compiler starts storing variables in code space.

CHAPTER 8

8051 HARDWARE CONNECTION AND INTEL HEX FILE

OBJECTIVES

Upon completion of this chapter, you will be able to:

>> Explain the purpose of each pin of the 8051 microprocessor.
>> Show the hardware connection of the 8051 chip.
>> Explain how to design an 8051-based system.
>> Show the design of the DS89C4x0 Trainer.
>> Code the test program in Assembly and C for testing the DS89C4x0.
>> Show how to delete programs from DS89C4x0 flash ROM using PC HyperTerminal.
>> Show how to download programs into a DS89C4x0 system using PC HyperTerminal.
>> Explain the Intel hex file.

This chapter describes the process of physically connecting and testing 8051-based systems. In the first section, we describe the function of the pins of 8051 chip. The second section shows the hardware connection for an 8051 Trainer using the DS89C4x0 (DS89C430/40/50) chip. It also shows how to download programs into a DS89C4x0-based system using PC HyperTerminal. In Section 8.3, we explain the characteristics of the Intel hex file.

8.1: PIN DESCRIPTION OF THE 8051

Although 8051 family members (e.g., 8751, 89C51, 89C52, DS89C4x0) come in different packages, such as DIP (dual in-line package), QFP (quad flat package), and LLC (leadless chip carrier), they all have 40 pins that are dedicated to various functions such as I/O, $\overline{RD}$, $\overline{WR}$, address, data, and interrupts. It must be noted that some companies provide a 20-pin version of the 8051 with a reduced number of I/O ports for less demanding applications. However, since the vast majority of developers use the 40-pin chip, we will concentrate on that. Figure 8-1 shows the pins for the 8051/52. For the 8052 chip, some of the pins have extra functions and they will be discussed as we study them.

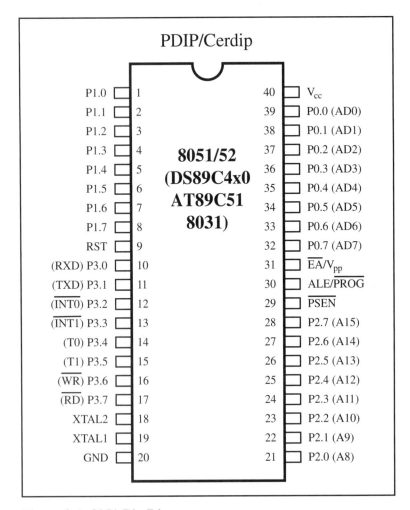

Figure 8-1. 8051 Pin Diagram

Examining Figure 8-1, note that of the 40 pins, a total of 32 pins are set aside for the four ports P0, P1, P2, and P3, where each port takes 8 pins. The rest of the pins are designated as V_{cc}, GND, XTAL1, XTAL2, RST, $\overline{EA}$, $\overline{PSEN}$, and ALE. Of these pins, six (V_{cc}, GND, XTAL1, XTAL2, RST, and $\overline{EA}$) are used by all members of the 8051 and 8031 families. In other words, they must be connected in order for the system to work, regardless of whether the microprocessor is of the 8051 or 8031 family. The other two pins, $\overline{PSEN}$ and ALE, are used mainly in 8031-based systems. We first describe the function of each pin. Ports are discussed separately.

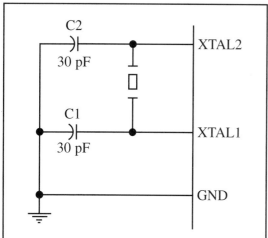

Figure 8-2(a). XTAL Connection to 8051

V_{cc}

Pin 40 provides supply voltage to the chip. The voltage source is +5V.

GND

Pin 20 is the ground.

XTAL1 and XTAL2

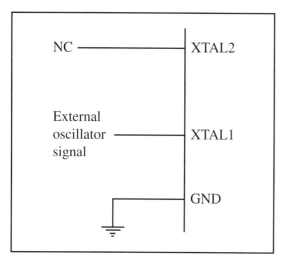

Figure 8-2(b). XTAL Connection to an External Clock Source

The 8051 has an on-chip oscillator but requires an external clock to run it. Most often a quartz crystal oscillator is connected to inputs XTAL1 (pin 19) and XTAL2 (pin 18). The quartz crystal oscillator connected to XTAL1 and XTAL2 also needs two capacitors of 30 pF value. One side of each capacitor is connected to the ground, as shown in Figure 8-2(a).

It must be noted that there are various speeds of the 8051 family. Speed refers to the maximum oscillator frequency connected to XTAL. For example, a 12-MHz chip must be connected to a crystal with 12-MHz frequency or less. Likewise, a 20-MHz microprocessor requires a crystal frequency of no more than 20 MHz. When the 8051 is connected to a crystal oscillator and is powered up, we can observe the frequency on the XTAL2 pin using the oscilloscope.

If you decide to use a frequency source other than a crystal oscillator, such as a TTL oscillator, it will be connected to XTAL1; XTAL2 is left unconnected, as shown in Figure 8-2(b).

RST

Pin 9 is the RESET pin. It is an input and is active high (normally low). Upon applying a high pulse to this pin, the microprocessor will reset and terminate all activities. This is often referred to as a *power-on reset*. Activating a power-on reset will cause all values in the registers to be lost. It will set program counter (PC) to all 0s.

Figures 8-3(a) and (b) show two ways of connecting the RST pin to the power-on reset circuitry. Figure 8-3(b) uses a momentary switch for reset circuitry.

In order for the RESET input to be effective, it must have a minimum duration of 2 machine cycles. In other words, the high pulse must be high for a minimum of 2 machine cycles before it is allowed to go low. Here is what the Intel manual says about the Reset circuitry:

> When power is turned on, the circuit holds the RST pin high for an amount of time that depends on the capacitor value and the rate at which it charges. To ensure a valid reset the RST pin must be held high long enough to allow the oscillator to start up plus two machine cycles.

Although, an 8.2K-ohm resistor and a 10-μF capacitor will take care of the vast majority of the cases, you still need to check the data sheet for the 8051 you are using.

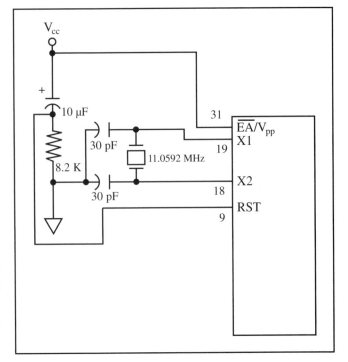

Figure 8-3(a). Power-On RESET Circuit

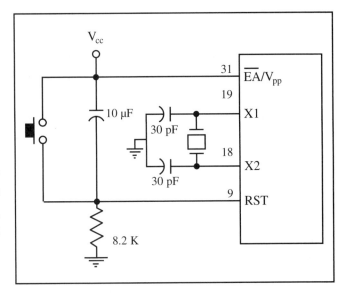

Figure 8-3(b). Power-On RESET with Momentary Switch

EA

The 8051 family members, such as the 8751/52, 89C51/52, or DS89C4x0, all come with on-chip ROM to store programs. In such cases, the $\overline{EA}$ pin is connected to V_{cc}. For family members such as the 8031 and 8032 in which there is no on-chip ROM, code is stored on an external ROM and is fetched by the 8031/32. Therefore, for the 8031 the $\overline{EA}$ pin must be connected to GND to indicate that the code is stored externally. $\overline{EA}$, which stands for "external access," is pin number 31 in the DIP packages. It is an input pin and must be connected to either V_{cc} or GND. In other words, it cannot be left unconnected.

In Chapter 14, we will show how the 8031 uses this pin along with $\overline{PSEN}$ to access programs stored in ROM memory located outside the 8031. In

8051 chips with on-chip ROM, such as the 8751/52, 89C51/52, or DS89C4x0, $\overline{EA}$ is connected to V_{cc}, as we will see in the next section.

The pins discussed so far must be connected no matter which family member is used. The next two pins are used mainly in 8031-based systems and are discussed in more detail in Chapter 14. The following is a brief description of each.

PSEN

This is an output pin. $\overline{PSEN}$ stands for "program store enable." In an 8031-based system in which an external ROM holds the program code, this pin is connected to the OE pin of the ROM. See Chapter 14 to see how this is used.

ALE

ALE (address latch enable) is an output pin and is active high. When connecting an 8031 to external memory, port 0 provides both address and data. In other words, the 8031 multiplexes address and data through port 0 to save pins. The ALE pin is used for demultiplexing the address and data by connecting to the G pin of the 74LS373 chip. This is discussed in detail in Chapter 14.

Ports 0, 1, 2, and 3

As shown in Figure 8-1 (and discussed in Chapter 4), the four ports P0, P1, P2, and P3 each use 8 pins, making them 8-bit ports. All the ports upon RESET are configured as input, since P0–P3 have value FFH on them. The following is a summary of features of P0–P3 based on the materials in Chapter 4.

P0

As shown in Figure 8-1, port 0 is also designated as AD0–AD7, allowing it to be used for both address and data. When connecting an 8051/31 to an external memory, port 0 provides both address and data. The 8051 multiplexes address and data through port 0 to save pins. ALE indicates if P0 has address or data. When ALE = 0, it provides data D0–D7, but when ALE = 1 it has address A0–A7. Therefore, ALE is used for demultiplexing address and data with the help of a 74LS373 latch, as we will see in Chapter 14. In the 8051-based systems where there is no external memory connection, the pins of P0 must be connected externally to a 10K-ohm pull-up resistor. This is due to the fact that P0 is an open drain, unlike P1, P2, and P3. *Open drain* is a term used for MOS chips in the same way that *open collector*

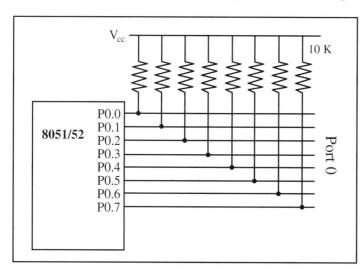

Figure 8-4. Port 0 with Pull-Up Resistors

is used for TTL chips. In many systems using the 8751, 89C51, or DS89C4x0 chips, we normally connect P0 to pull-up resistors. See Figure 8-4. With external pull-up resistors connected to P0, it can be used as a simple I/O port, just like P1 and P2. In contrast to port 0, ports P1, P2, and P3 do not need any pull-up resistors since they already have pull-up resistors internally. Upon reset, ports P1, P2, and P3 are configured as input ports.

P1 and P2

In 8051-based systems with no external memory connection, both P1 and P2 are used as simple I/O. However, in 8031/51-based systems with external memory connections, port 2 must be used along with P0 to provide the 16-bit address for the external memory. As shown in Figure 8-1, port 2 is also designated as A8–A15, indicating its dual function. Since an 8031/51 is capable of accessing 64K bytes of external memory, it needs a path for the 16 bits of the address. While P0 provides the lower 8 bits via A0–A7, it is the job of P2 to provide bits A8–A15 of the address. In other words, when the 8031/51 is connected to external memory, P2 is used for the upper 8 bits of the 16-bit address, and it cannot be used for I/O. This is discussed in detail in Chapter 14.

From the discussion so far, we conclude that in systems based on 8051 microprocessors, we have three ports, P0, P1, and P2, for I/O operations. This should be enough for most microprocessor applications. That leaves port 3 for interrupts as well as other signals, as we will see next.

Port 3

Port 3 occupies a total of 8 pins, pins 10 through 17. It can be used as input or output. P3 does not need any pull-up resistors, the same as P1 and P2 did not. Although port 3 is configured as an input port upon reset, this is not the way it is most commonly used. Port 3 has the additional function of providing some extremely important signals such as interrupts. Table 8-1 provides these alternate functions of P3. This information applies to both 8051 and 8031 chips.

P3.0 and P3.1 are used for the RxD and TxD serial communication signals. Refer Chapter 10 to see how they are connected. Bits P3.2 and P3.3 are set aside for external interrupts, and are discussed in Chapter 11. Bits P3.4 and P3.5 are used for Timers 0 and 1, and are discussed in Chapter 9. Finally, P3.6 and P3.7 are used to provide the $\overline{WR}$ and $\overline{RD}$ signals of external memory connections. Chapter 14 discusses how they are used in 8031-based systems. In systems based on the 8051, pins 3.6 and 3.7 are used for I/O while the rest of the pins in port 3 are normally used in the alternate function role.

Table 8-1. Port 3 Alternate Functions

P3 Bit	Function	Pin
P3.0	RxD	10
P3.1	TxD	11
P3.2	$\overline{INT0}$	12
P3.3	$\overline{INT1}$	13
P3.4	T0	14
P3.5	T1	15
P3.6	$\overline{WR}$	16
P3.7	$\overline{RD}$	17

Table 8-2. RESET Value of Some 8051 Registers

Register	Reset Value (hex)
PC	0000
DPTR	0000
ACC	00
PSW	00
SP	07
B	00
P0–P3	FF

Program counter value upon reset

Activating a power-on reset will cause all values in the registers to be lost. Table 8-2 provides a partial list of 8051 registers and their values after power-on reset. From Table 8-2, we note that the value of the program counter is 0 upon reset, forcing the CPU to fetch the first opcode from ROM memory location 0000. This means that we must place the first byte of opcode in ROM location 0 because that is where the CPU expects to find the first instruction.

Machine cycle and crystal frequency

As we discussed in Chapter 3, the 8051, one or more machine cycles are used to execute an instruction. The period of machine cycle (MC) varies among the different versions of 8051 from 12 clocks in the AT89C51 to 1 clock in the DS89C4x0 chip. See Table 8-3 and Example 8-1. The frequency of the crystal oscillator connected to the X–X2 pins dictates the speed of the clock used in the machine cycle. From Table 8-3, we can conclude that using the same crystal frequency of 12 MHz for both the AT89C51 and DS89C4x0 chips gives performance almost 12 times better from the DS89C4x0 chip. The reason we say "almost" is that the number of machine cycles it takes to execute an instruction is not the same for the AT89C51 and DS89C4x0 chips, as we discussed in Chapter 3. See Example 8-1.

Table 8-3. Clocks per Machine Cycle for Various 8051 Versions

Chip (Maker)	Clocks per Machine Cycle
AT89C51/52 (Atmel)	12
P89C54X2 (Phillips)	6
DS5000 (Maxim/Dallas Semiconductor)	4
DS89C4x0 (Maxim/Dallas Semiconductor)	1

Example 8-1

Find the machine cycle for the following chips if XTAL = 11.0592 MHz:
(a) AT89C51 (b) DS89C4x0 (c) DS5000.

Solution:

1/11.0592 MHz = 90.42 ns
(a) MC = 12×90.42 ns = 1.085 μs
(b) MC = 1×90.42 ns = 90.42 ns
(c) MC = 4×90.42 ns = 361.68 ns

REVIEW QUESTIONS

1. A given AT89C51 chip has a speed of 16 MHz. What is the range of frequency that can be applied to the XTAL1 and XTAL2 pins?
2. Which pin is used to inform the 8051 that the on-chip ROM contains the program?
3. Upon power-up, the program counter has a value of _____.
4. Upon power-up, the 8051 fetches the first opcode from ROM address location _____.
5. Which 8051 port needs pull-up resistors to function as an I/O port?

8.2: DESIGN AND TEST OF DS89C4x0 TRAINER

In this section, we show connections for 8051-based systems using chips such as the AT89C51 and DS89C4x0. If you decide to wire-wrap one of these, make sure that you read Appendix B on wire wrapping.

AT89C51/52-based trainer connection

In systems based on an AT89C51/52-type microprocessor, you need a ROM burner to burn your program into the microprocessor. For the AT89C51, the ROM burner can erase the flash ROM in addition to burning a program into it. In the case of the 8751, you also need an EPROM erasure tool since it uses UV-EPROM. To burn the 8751, you need to erase its contents first, which takes approximately 20 minutes for UV-EPROM. For the AT89C51, this is not required since it has flash ROM.

Figure 8.5 shows the minimum connection for the 8751 or 89C51-based system. Notice that "EA=V_{cc}" indicates that an 8751 or 89C51 has on-chip ROM for the program. Also notice the P0 connection to pull-up resistors to ensure the availability of P0 for I/O operations. If you need to use a momentary switch for RESET, refer to Figure 8-3(b).

DS89C4x0 family

The DS89C4x0 chip from Maxim/Dallas Semiconductor is an 8051 type microprocessor with on-chip flash ROM. It also has a built-in loader allowing it to download programs into the chip via the serial port, therefore eliminating any need for an external ROM burner. This important feature makes the DS89C4x0 chip an ideal candidate for 8051-based home development systems.

DS89C4x0 flash ROM size

While all DS89C4x0 chips share the same features, they come with different amounts of on-chip ROM. Table 8-4

Table 8-4. On-Chip Flash ROM Size for the DS89C4x0 Family from Maxim/Dallas Semiconductor.

Chip	On-Chip ROM Size (Flash)
DS89C430	16K bytes
DS89C440	32K bytes
DS89C450	64K bytes

Source: www.maxim-ic.com

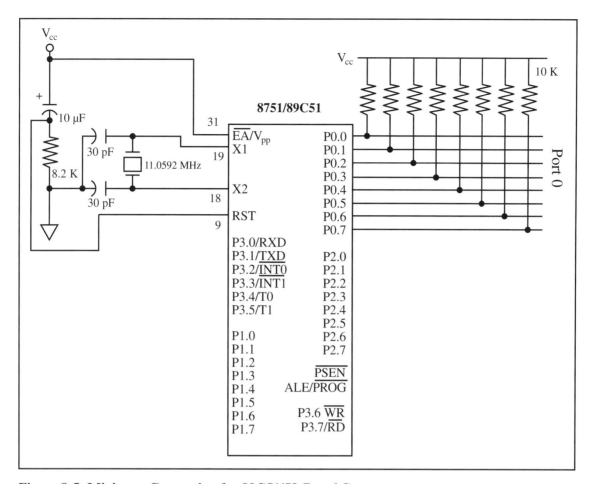

Figure 8-5. Minimum Connection for 89C51/52-Based Systems

shows the on-chip ROM size for various DS89C4x0 chips. Refer to the website www.maxim-ic.com for further information. Notice that while the AT89C51 comes with 4K bytes of on-chip ROM and the AT89C52 comes with 8K bytes, the DS89C4x0 has 16K bytes of on-chip ROM. Also notice that the DS89C430 is a replacement for the DS89C420 with the bugs fixed. See Example 8-2.

Example 8-2

Find the address space for the on-chip ROM of the following chips:
(a) AT89C51, (b) AT89C52, and (c) DS89C430.

Solution:

(a) AT89C51 has 4K bytes of on-chip ROM. That gives us $4 \times 1024 = 4,096$ bytes. Converting the 4096 to hex, we get 1000H. Therefore, the address space is 0000–0FFFH.

(b) AT89C52 has 8K bytes of on-chip ROM. That gives us $8 \times 1024 = 8,192$ bytes. Converting the 8,192 to hex, we get 2000H. Therefore, the address space is 0000–1FFFH.

(c) DS89C430 has 16K bytes of on-chip ROM. That gives us $16 \times 1024 = 16,384$ bytes. Converting the 16,384 to hex, we get 4000H. Therefore, the address space is 0000–3FFFH.

Key features of the DS89C4x0

The following are some of the key features of the DS89C4x0 chip taken from the Maxim/Dallas Semiconductor website (http://www.maxim-ic.com). We will look at many of these features and show how to use them in future chapters.

1. 80C52 compatible
   - (a) 8051 pin- and instruction-set compatible
   - (b) Four bidirectional I/O ports
   - (c) Three 16-bit timer counters
   - (d) 256 bytes scratchpad RAM
2. On-chip flash memory
   - (a) 16KB for DS89C430
   - (b) 32KB for DS89C440
   - (c) 64KB for DS89C450
3. In-system programmable through the serial port

   1KB SRAM for MOVX
4. ROMSIZE Feature
   - (a) Selects internal program memory size from 0 to 64K
   - (b) Allows access to entire external memory map
   - (c) Dynamically adjustable by software
5. High-speed architecture
   - (a) 1 clock per machine cycle
   - (b) DC to 33MHz operation
   - (c) Single-cycle instruction in 30 ns
   - (d) Optional variable length MOVX to access fast/slow peripherals
6. Two full-duplex serial ports
7. Programmable watchdog timer
8. 13 interrupt sources (six external)
9. Five levels of interrupt priority
10. Power-fail reset
11. Early warning power-fail interrupt

DS89C4x0 Trainer connection

We selected the DS89C4x0 for an 8051 Trainer because it is inexpensive but powerful, and one can easily wire-wrap it to be used at work and home. The connection for the DS89C4x0 Trainer is shown in Figure 8-6.

If you decide not to wire-wrap the trainer yourself, you can buy this DS89C4x0-based trainer from the www.MicroDigitalEd.com website.

Using the DS89C4x0 for development is more advantageous than using the 8751 or 89C51 system for the following two major reasons.

1. Using the DS89C4x0 for an 8051 microprocessor allows us to program the chip without any need for a ROM burner. Because not everyone has access to a ROM burner, the DS89C4x0 is an ideal home-development system.

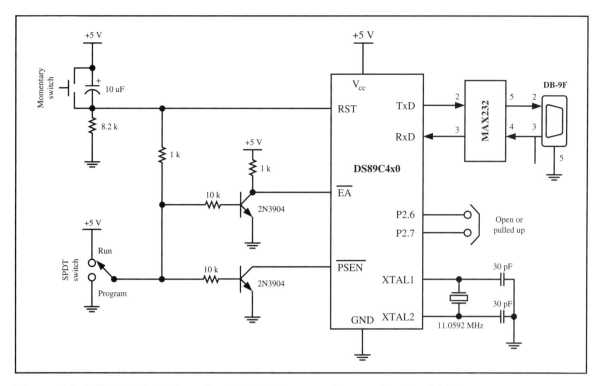

Figure 8-6. DS89C4x0 Trainer (for MAX232 connection, see Section 10.2)

The advantage of the DS89C4x0 is that it can be programmed via the COM port of a PC (x86 IBM or compatible PC) while it is in the system. Contrast this with the 89C51 system in which you must remove the chip, program it, and install it back in the system every time you want to change the program contents of the on-chip ROM. This results in a much longer development time for the 89C51 system compared with the DS89C4x0 system.

2. The two serial ports on the DS89C4x0 allow us to use one for PC interfacing with the chip and the other for data acquisition.

Notice from Figure 8-6 that the reset circuitry and serial port connections are the same as in any 8051-based system. However, the extra circuitry needed for programming are two transistors, a switch, and 10K and 1K-ohm resistors. In fact, you can add these components to your 8751/89C51 system and use it as a DS89C4x0 system by simply plugging a DS89C4x0 chip in the socket. The switch allows you to select between the program and run options. We can load our program into the DS89C4x0 by setting the switch to V_{cc}, and run the program by setting it to Gnd.

Figure 8-6 shows the connection for the 8051 Trainer from www. MicroDigitalEd.com. The trainer provided by this website has both of the serial ports connected and accessible via two DB-9 connectors. It also has 8 LEDs and 8 switches along with the P0–P3 ports, all of which are accessible via terminal blocks. It also comes with an on-board power regulator.

Communicating with the DS89C4x0 Trainer

After we build our DS89C4x0-based system, we can communicate with it using the HyperTerminal software. HyperTerminal comes with Microsoft Windows NT, 2000, and XP. For Windows Vista and 7 use Tera Terminal.

Using HyperTerminal with the DS89C4x0

Assuming that your serial cable has a DB-9 connector on both ends, we take the following steps to establish communication between the DS89C4x0 Trainer and HyperTerminal. See Figure 8-7.

1. With the trainer's power off, connect the COM1 port on the back of your PC to one end of the serial cable.
2. The other end of the serial cable is connected to the DB-9 connection on the DS89C4x0 Trainer designated as SERIAL#0. After you connect your DS89C4x0 Trainer to your PC, power up the trainer. Set the switch to the program position.
3. In Windows Accessories, click on HyperTerminal. (If you get a modem installation option, choose "No.")
4. Type a name, and click OK (or HyperTerminal will not let you go on).
5. For "Connect Using" select COM1 and click OK. Choose COM2 if COM1 is used by the mouse.
6. Pick 9600 baud rate, 8-bit data, no parity bit, and 1 stop bit.
7. Change the "Flow Control" to NONE or Xon/Xoff, and click OK. (Definitely do not choose the hardware option.)
8. Now you are in Windows HyperTerminal, and when you press the ENTER key a couple of times, the DS89C4x0 will respond with the following message: DS89C4x0 LOADER VERSION 1.0 COPYRIGHT (C) 2000 DALLAS SEMICONDUCTOR>

If you do not see ">" after pressing the ENTER key several times, go through the above steps one more time. Then, if you do not get ">", you need to check your hardware connections, such as the MAX232/233. See the end of this section for some troubleshooting tips.

Loading and running a program with the DS89C4x0 Trainer

After we get the ">" from the DS89C4x0, we are ready to load the program into it and run. First, make sure that the file you are loading is in Intel hex format. The Intel hex format is provided by your 8051 assembler/compiler. More about Intel hex format is given in the next section.

Erase command for the DS89C4x0

To reload the DS89C4x0 chip with another program, we first need to erase its contents. The K (Klean) command will erase the entire contents of the

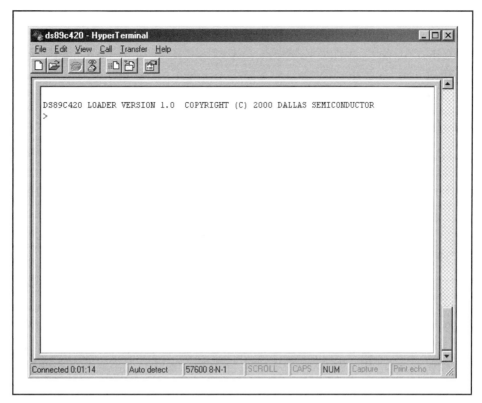

Figure 8-7. Screen Capture from HyperTerminal for DS89C4x0 Trainer

flash ROM of the chip. Remember that you must use the ">K" command to erase the ROM before you can reload any program. You can verify the operation of the ">K" command by using the Dump command to display ROM contents on screen. You should see all FFs in all the locations of ROM after applying the ">K" command.

Go to www.MicroDigitalEd.com to see the above steps presented with screenshots. The website also shows how to use Tera Terminal with Windows Vista and Windows 7 since HyperTerminal is no longer provided with the Windows Vista and 7.

Loading the program

After making sure that you have the switch on the program position and you have the ">" prompt on your screen, go through the following steps to load a program:

1. At the ">" prompt, enter L (L is for Load). Example: ">L" and press Enter.

2. In HyperTerminal, click on the Transfer menu option. Click on Send Text File.

3. Select your file from your disk. Example: "C:test.hex"

4. Wait until the loading is complete. The appearance of the "GGGG>" prompt indicates that the loading is good and finished.

5. Now use D to dump the contents of the flash ROM of the DS89C4x0 onto the screen. Example: >D 00 4F

The dump will give you the opcodes and operands of all the instructions in your program. You can compare this information with the information provided by the list file. In the next section, we will examine the Intel hex file and compare it with the list file of the test program.

Running the program

Change the switch to the run position, press the reset button on the DS89C4x0 system, and the program will execute. Use a logic probe (or scope) to see the P0, P1, and P2 bits toggle "on" and "off" continuously with some delay in between the "on" and "off" states.

Test program for the DS89C4x0 in Assembly and C

To test your DS89C4x0 hardware connection, we can run a simple test in which all the bits of P0, P1, and P2 toggle continuously with some delay in between the "on" and "off" states. The programs for testing the trainer in both Assembly and C are provided below. Notice that the time delay is for a DS89C4x0 based on the 11.0592 MHz crystal frequency. This time delay must be modified for the AT89C51/52 chips since DS89C4x0 uses a machine cycle of 1 clock period instead of the 12 clock periods used by the AT89C51/52 chip.

Trainer test program in Assembly

```
            ORG 0H
MAIN:       MOV P0, #55H
            MOV P1, #55H
            MOV P2, #55H
            MOV R5, #250
            ACALL MSDELAY
            MOV P0, #0AAH
            MOV P1, #0AAH
            MOV P2, #0AAH
            MOV R5, #250
            ACALL MSDELAY
            SJMP MAIN
;--------- 250 MILLISECOND DELAY ---
MSDELAY:
HERE3:      MOV R4, #35
HERE2:      MOV R3, #79
HERE1:      DJNZ R3, HERE1
            DJNZ R4, HERE2
            DJNZ R5, HERE3
            RET
            END MAIN
```

Trainer test program in C

```c
#include <reg51.h>
void MSDelay(unsigned int);
void main(void)
  {
    while(1)                 //repeat forever
      {
        P0=0x55;             //send value to port
        P1=0x55;
        P2=0x55;
        MSDelay(250);        //call 250 ms function
        P0 = 0xAA;           //set value to port
        P1 = 0xAA;
        P2 = 0xAA;
        MSDelay(250);        //call 250 ms function
      }
  }

void MSDelay(unsigned int itime)
  {
  unsigned int i, j;
  for(i=0;i<itime;i++)
    for(j=0;j<1275;j++);
  }
```

DS89C4x0 commands

There are many commands embedded into the DS89C4x0 loader. The most widely used among them are L, K, and D. Here is the summary of their operations.

L   Loads standard ASCII Intel hex formatted data into flash memory.
K   Erases the entire contents of flash memory.
D   <begin> <end>   Dumps the Intel hex file.

We have shown the use of the L (load), K (klean), and D (dump) commands earlier. A complete list of commands and error messages can be obtained from www.MicroDigitalEd.com.

Some troubleshooting tips

Running the test program on your DS89Cx0-based trainer (or 8051 system) should toggle all the I/O bits with some delay. If your system does not work, follow these steps to find the problem.

1. With the power off, check your connection for all pins, especially V_{cc} and GND.

2. Check RST (pin #9) using an oscilloscope. When the system is powered up, pin #9 is low. Upon pressing the momentary switch it goes high. Make sure the momentary switch is connected properly.

---

3. Observe the XTAL2 pin on the oscilloscope while the power is on. You should see a crude square wave. This indicates that the crystal oscillator is good.

4. If all the above steps pass inspection, check the contents of the on-chip ROM starting at memory location 0000. It must be the same as the opcodes provided by the list file of Figure 8-8. Your assembler produces the list file, which lists the opcodes and operands on the left side of the assembly instructions. This must match exactly the contents of your on-chip ROM if the proper steps were taken in burning and loading the program into the on-chip ROM.

REVIEW QUESTIONS

1. True or false. The DS89C4x0 is an 8052 chip.
2. Which pin is used for reset?
3. What is the status of the reset pin when it is not activated?
4. What kind of ROM is used in the DS89C4x0 chip?
5. The loader for the DS89C4x0 works with the _____ (serial, parallel) port.
6. Give two reasons that the DS89C4x0 is preferable over 89C51 chips.
7. In the DS89C4x0 Trainer, what is the role of the Prog/Run switch?
8. What is the highest frequency that we can connect to the DS89C4x0?
9. True or false. The DS89C4x0 can download the file into its ROM only if it is in Intel hex file format.
10. Which command is used to erase the contents of ROM in the DS89C4x0 chip?
11. Which command is used to load the ROM in the DS89C4x0 chip?
12. Which command is used to dump the contents of ROM in the DS89C4x0 chip?

8.3: EXPLAINING THE INTEL HEX FILE

Intel hex file is a widely used file format designed to standardize the loading of executable machine codes into a ROM chip. Therefore, loaders that come with every ROM burner (programmer) support the Intel hex file format. While in many newer Windows-based assemblers the Intel hex file is produced automatically (by selecting the right setting), in a DOS-based PC you need a utility called OH (object-to-hex) to produce that. In the DOS environment, the object file is fed into the linker program to produce the abs file; then the abs file is fed into the OH utility to create the Intel hex file. While the abs file is used by systems that have a monitor program, the hex file is used only by the loader of an EPROM programmer to load it into the ROM chip.

Program list file for test program

The list file for the test program is given in Figure 8-8. The LOC and OBJ fields in Figure 8-8 must be noted. The location is the address where the opcodes (object codes) are placed. The LOC and OBJ information is used to create the hex file. Next, we will analyze the hex file belonging to the list file of Figure 8-8.

```
LOC   OBJ        LINE
0000             1                      ORG  0H
0000  758055     2      MAIN:           MOV  P0, #55H
0003  759055     3                      MOV  P1, #55H
0006  75A055     4                      MOV  P2, #55H
0009  7DFA       5                      MOV  R5, #250
000B  111C       6                      ACALL MSDELAY
000D  7580AA     7                      MOV  P0, #0AAH
0010  7590AA     8                      MOV  P1, #0AAH
0013  75A0AA     9                      MOV  P2, #0AAH
0016  7DFA       10                     MOV  R5, #250
0018  111C       11                     ACALL MSDELAY
001A  80E4       12                     SJMP MAIN
                 13  ;--- THE 250 MILLISECOND DELAY.
                 14     MSDELAY:
001C  7C23       15     HERE3:          MOV  R4, #35
001E  7B4F       16     HERE2:          MOV  R3,#79
0020  DBFE       17     HERE1:          DJNZ R3, HERE1
0022  DCFA       18                     DJNZ R4, HERE2
0024  DDF6       19                     DJNZ R5, HERE3
0026  22         20                     RET
                 21                     END
```

Figure 8-8. List File For Test Program (Assembly)

Analyzing Intel hex file

Figure 8-9 shows the Intel hex file for the test program whose list file is given in Figure 8-8. Since the ROM burner (loader) uses the hex file to download the opcode into ROM, the hex file must provide the following: (1) the number of bytes of information to be loaded, (2) the information itself, and

```
:10000000758055759055575A0557DFA111C7580AA9F
:100010007590AA75A0AA7DFA111C80E47C237B4F01
:07002000DBFEDCFADDF62235
:00000001FF
```

Separating the fields, we get the following:

:CC	AAAA	TT	DDDDDDDDDDDDDDDDDDDDDDDDDDDDDDDD	SS
:10	0000	00	75805575905575A0557DFA111C7580AA	9F
:10	0010	00	7590AA75A0AA7DFA111C80E47C237B4F	01
:07	0020	00	DBFEDCFADDF622	35
:00	0000	01	FF	

Figure 8-9. Intel Hex File Test Program as Provided by the Assembler

(3) the starting address where the information must be placed. Each line of the hex file consists of six parts. In Figure 8-9, we have separated the parts to make it easier to analyze. The following describes each part.

1. ":" Each line starts with a colon.

2. CC, the count byte. This tells the loader how many bytes are in the line. CC can range from 00 to 16 (10 in hex).

3. AAAA is for the address. This is a 16-bit address. The loader places the first byte of data into this memory address.

4. TT is for type. This field is either 00 or 01. If it is 00, it means that there are more lines to come after this line. If it is 01, it means that this is the last line and the loading should stop after this line.

5. DD......D is the real information (data or code). There is a maximum of 16 bytes in this part. The loader places this information into successive memory locations of ROM.

6. SS is a single byte. This last byte is the checksum byte of everything in that line. The checksum byte is used for error checking. Checksum bytes are discussed in detail in Chapters 6 and 7. Notice that the checksum byte at the end of each line represents everything in that line and not just the data portion.

Now, compare the data portion of the Intel hex file in Figure 8-9 with the information under the OBJ field of the list file in Figure 8-8. Notice that they are identical, as they should be. The extra information is added by the Intel hex file formatter. You can run the C language version of the test program and verify its operation. Your C compiler will provide you both the list file and the Intel hex file if you want to explore the Intel hex file concept.

Examine Examples 8-3 to 8-5 to gain an insight into the Intel hex file.

Example 8-3

From Figure 8-9, analyze the six parts of line 3.

Solution:

After the colon (:) we have 07, which means that 7 bytes of data are in this line. 0020H is the address at which the data starts. Next, 00 means that this is not the last line of the record. Then the data, which is 7 bytes, is as follows: DB FE DC FA DD F6 22. Finally, the last byte, 35, is the checksum byte.

Example 8-4

Verify the checksum byte for line 3 of Figure 8-9. Verify also that the information is not corrupted.

Solution:

$07 + 00 + 20 + 00 + DB + FE + DC + FA + DD + F6 + 22 = 5CBH$. Dropping the carries (5) gives CBH, and its 2's complement is 35H, which is the last byte of line 3. If we add all the information in line 3, including the checksum byte, and drop the carries we should get 00.

$07 + 00 + 20 + 00 + DB + FE + DC + FA + DD + F6 + 22 + 35 = 600H$

Compare the data portion of the Intel hex file of Figure 8-9 with the opcodes in the list file of the test program given in Figure 8-8. Do they match?

Solution:

In the first line of Figure 8-9, the data portion starts with 75H, which is the opcode for the instruction "MOV", as shown in the list file of Figure 8-8. The last byte of the data in line 3 of Figure 8-9 is 22, which is the opcode for the "RET" instruction in the list file of Figure 8-8.

REVIEW QUESTIONS

1. True or false. The Intel hex file uses the checksum byte method to ensure data integrity.
2. The first byte of a line in the Intel hex file represents ____.
3. The last byte of a line in the Intel hex file represents ____.
4. In the TT field of the Intel hex file, we have 00. What does it indicate?
5. Find the checksum byte for the following values: 22H, 76H, 5FH, 8CH, 99H.
6. In Question 5, add all the values and the checksum byte. What do you get?

SUMMARY

This chapter began by describing the function of each pin of the 8051. The four ports of the 8051, P0, P1, P2, and P3, each use 8 pins, making them 8-bit ports. These ports can be used for input or output. Port 0 can be used for either address or data. Port 3 can be used to provide interrupt and serial communication signals. Then the design of the DS89C4x0-based trainer was shown. We also explained the Intel hex format.

RECOMMENDED WEB LINKS

See the following website for the DS89C4x0 and other trainers:

- www.MicroDigitalEd.com

For Microsoft Windows Vista and 7, we must use Tera Terminal since they no longer come with HyperTerminal. See the following website for using Tera Terminal in place of HyperTerminal:

- www.MicroDigitalEd.com

PROBLEMS

8.1: PIN DESCRIPTION OF THE 8051

1. The 8051 DIP package is a ____-pin package.
2. Which pins are assigned to V_{cc} and GND?
3. In the 8051, how many pins are designated as I/O port pins?
4. The crystal oscillator is connected to pins ____ and ____ .
5. If an 8051 is rated as 25 MHz, what is the maximum frequency that can be connected to it?
6. Indicate the pin number assigned to RST in the DIP package.
7. RST is an _____ (input, output) pin.
8. The RST pin is normally _____ (low, high) and needs a _____ (low, high) signal to be activated.
9. What are the contents of the program counter upon RESET of the 8051?
10. What are the contents of the SP register upon RESET of the 8051?
11. What are the contents of the A register upon RESET of the 8051?
12. Find the machine cycle for the following crystal frequencies connected to X1 and X2.
    (a) 12 MHz   (b) 20 MHz   (c) 25 MHz   (d) 30 MHz
13. $\overline{EA}$ stands for _____ and is an_____ (input, output) pin.
14. For 8051 family members with on-chip ROM such as the 8751 and the 89C51, pin $\overline{EA}$ is connected to ____ (V_{cc}, GND).
15. $\overline{PSEN}$ is an _____ (input, output) pin.
16. ALE is an _____ (input, output) pin.
17. ALE is used mainly in systems based on the _____ (8051, 8031).
18. How many pins are designated as P0 and what are those in the DIP package?
19. How many pins are designated as P1 and what are those in the DIP package?
20. How many pins are designated as P2 and what are those in the DIP package?
21. How many pins are designated as P3 and what are those in the DIP package?
22. Upon RESET, all the bits of ports are configured as _____ (input, output).
23. In the 8051, which port needs a pull-up resistor to be used as I/O?
24. Which port of the 8051 does not have any alternate function and can be used solely for I/O?

8.2: DESIGN AND TEST OF DS89C40 TRAINER

25. Write a program to get 8-bit data from P1 and send it to ports P0, P2, and P3.
26. Write a program to get 8-bit data from P2 and send it to ports P0 and P1.
27. In P3, which pins are for RxD and TxD?
28. At what memory location does the 8051 wake up upon RESET? What is the implication of that?
29. Write a program to toggle all the bits of P1 and P2 continuously
    (a) using AAH and 55H (b) using the CPL instruction.

30. What is the address of the last location of on-chip ROM for the AT89C51?
31. What is the address of the last location of on-chip ROM for the DS89C430?
32. What is the address of the last location of on-chip ROM for the DS89C440?
33. What is the address of the last location of on-chip ROM for the DS89C450?
34. What is the fastest frequency that DS89C4x0 can run on?
35. What is the slowest frequency that DS89C4x0 can run on?
36. Calculate the machine cycle time for the DS89C430 if XTAL = 33 MHz.
37. Before we reprogram the DS89C4x0 we must _____ (dump, erase) the flash ROM.
38. True or false. In order to download the hex file into the DS89C4x0, it must be in the Intel hex file format.
39. Give two features of the DS89C4x0 that earlier 8051 and 8052 chips do not have.
40. After downloading a program, the DS89C4x0 gives the message ">GGGG". What does it mean?

8.3: EXPLAINING THE INTEL HEX FILE

41. Analyze the six parts of line 1 of Figure 8-9.
42. Analyze the six parts of line 2 of Figure 8-9.
43. Verify the checksum byte for line 1 of Figure 8-9 and also verify that the information is not corrupted.
44. Verify the checksum byte for line 2 of Figure 8-9 and also verify that the information is not corrupted.
45. Reassemble the test program with ORG address of 100H and analyze the Intel hex file.
46. Reassemble the test program with ORG address of 300H and compare the Intel hex file with the results of Problem 45.
47. Write a program to toggle all the bits of P1 and P2 continuously with no delay and analyze the Intel hex file.

ANSWERS TO REVIEW QUESTIONS

8.1: PIN DESCRIPTION OF THE 8051

1. From 0 to 16 MHz, but no more than 16 MHz
2. EA
3. PC = 0000
4. 0000
5. Port 0

8.2: DESIGN AND TEST OF DS89C4X0 TRAINER

1. True
2. Pin 9
3. Low
4. Flash
5. Serial
6. (a) It comes with a loader inside the chip and (b) it has two serial ports.
7. The SW allows to load the program or to run it.

---

8. 33 MHz
9. True
10. >K
11. >L
12. >D

8.3: EXPLAINING INTEL THE HEX FILE

1. True
2. The number of bytes of data in the line
3. Checksum byte
4. 00 means this is not the last line and there are more lines of data to be followed.
5. 22H + 76H + 5FH + 8CH + 99H = 21CH. Dropping the carries we have 1CH and its 2's complement is E4H.
6. 22H + 76H + 5FH + 8CH + 99H + E4 = 300H. Dropping the carries we have 00, which means data is not corrupted.

CHAPTER 9

8051 TIMER PROGRAMMING IN ASSEMBLY AND C

OBJECTIVES

Upon completion of this chapter, you will be able to:

>> List the timers of the 8051 and their associated registers.
>> Describe the various modes of the 8051 timers.
>> Program the 8051 timers in Assembly and C to generate time delays.
>> Program the 8051 counters in Assembly and C as event counters.

The 8051 has two timers/counters. They can be used either as timers to generate a time delay or as counters to count events happening outside the microprocessor. In Section 9.1, we see how these timers are used to generate time delays. In Section 9.2, we show how they are used as event counters. In Section 9.3, we use C language to program the 8051 timers.

9.1: PROGRAMMING 8051 TIMERS

The 8051 has two timers: Timer 0 and Timer 1. They can be used either as timers or as event counters. In this section, we first discuss the timers' registers and then show how to program the timers to generate time delays.

Basic registers of the timer

Both Timer 0 and Timer 1 are 16 bits wide. Since the 8051 has an 8-bit architecture, each 16-bit timer is accessed as two separate registers of low byte and high byte. Each timer is discussed separately.

Timer 0 registers

The 16-bit register of Timer 0 is accessed as low byte and high byte. The low-byte register is called TL0 (Timer 0 low byte) and the high-byte register is referred to as TH0 (Timer 0 high byte). These registers can be accessed like any other register, such as A, B, R0, R1, or R2. For example, the instruction "MOV TL0,#4FH" moves the value 4FH into TL0, the low byte of Timer 0. These registers can also be read like any other register. For example, "MOV R5,TH0" saves TH0 (high byte of Timer 0) in R5. See Figure 9-1.

Timer 1 registers

Timer 1 is also 16 bits, and its 16-bit register is split into two bytes, referred to as TL1 (Timer 1 low byte) and TH1 (Timer 1 high byte). These registers are accessible in the same way as the registers of Timer 0. See Figure 9-2.

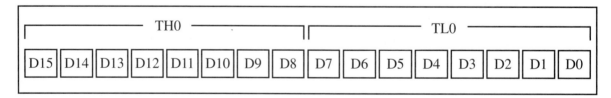

Figure 9-1. Timer 0 Registers

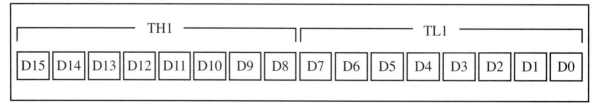

Figure 9-2. Timer 1 Registers

TMOD (timer mode) register

Both timers 0 and 1 use the same register, called TMOD, to set the various timer operation modes. TMOD is an 8-bit register in which the lower 4 bits are set aside for Timer 0 and the upper 4 bits for Timer 1. In each case, the lower 2 bits are used to set the timer mode and the upper 2 bits to specify the operation. These options are discussed next.

M1, M0

M0 and M1 select the timer mode. As shown in Figure 9-3, there are three modes: 0, 1, and 2. Mode 0 is a 13-bit timer, mode 1 is a 16-bit timer, and mode 2 is an 8-bit timer. We will concentrate on modes 1 and 2 since they are the ones used most widely. We will soon describe the characteristics of these modes, after describing the rest of the TMOD register. See Example 9-1.

C/T (clock/timer)

This bit in the TMOD register is used to decide whether the timer is used as a delay generator or an event counter. If C/T = 0, it is used as a timer for time delay generation. The clock source for the time delay is the crystal frequency of the 8051. This section is concerned with this choice. The timer's use as an event counter is discussed in the next section.

(MSB)							(LSB)
GATE	C/T	M1	M0	GATE	C/T	M1	M0
Timer 1				Timer 0			

GATE Gating control when set. The timer/counter is enabled only when the INTx pin is high and the TRx control pin is set. When cleared, the timer is enabled whenever the TRx control bit is set.

C/T Timer or counter selected cleared for timer operation (input from internal system clock). Set for counter operation (input from Tx input pin).

M1 Mode bit 1

M0 Mode bit 0

M1	M0	Mode	Operating Mode
0	0	0	13-bit timer mode
			8-bit timer/counter THx with TLx as 5-bit prescaler
0	1	1	16-bit timer mode
			16-bit timer/counters THx and TLx are cascaded; there is no prescaler
1	0	2	8-bit auto-reload
			8-bit auto-reload timer/counter; THx holds a value that is to be reloaded into TLx each time it overflows.
1	1	3	Split timer mode

Figure 9-3. TMOD Register

Indicate which mode and which timer are selected for each of the following:
(a) MOV TMOD,#01H (b) MOV TMOD,#20H   (c) MOV TMOD,#12H.

Solution:

We convert the values from hex to binary. From Figure 9-3, we have:

(a) TMOD = 00000001, mode 1 of Timer 0 is selected.
(b) TMOD = 00100000, mode 2 of Timer 1 is selected.
(c) TMOD = 00010010, mode 2 of Timer 0, and mode 1 of
                     Timer 1 are selected.

Clock source for timer

As you know, every timer needs a clock pulse to tick. What is the source of the clock pulse for the 8051 timers? If C/T = 0, the crystal frequency attached to the 8051 is the source of the clock for the timer. This means that the size of the crystal frequency attached to the 8051 also decides the speed at which the 8051 timer ticks. The frequency for the timer is always 1/12th the frequency of the crystal attached to the 8051. See Example 9-2.

Example 9-2

Find the timer's clock frequency and its period for various 8051-based systems, with the following crystal frequencies.
(a)   12 MHz
(b)   16 MHz
(c)   11.0592 MHz

Solution:

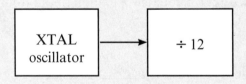

(a) $1/12 \times 12$ MHz = 1 MHz and T = 1/1 MHz = 1 μs

(b) $1/12 \times 16$ MHz = 1.333 MHz and T = 1/1.333 MHz = .75 μs

(c) $1/12 \times 11.0592$ MHz = 921.6 kHz;
    T = 1/921.6 kHz = 1.085 μs

Note that 8051 timers use 1/12 of XTAL frequency, regardless of machine cycle time.

Although various 8051-based systems have an XTAL frequency of 10 MHz to 40 MHz, we will concentrate on the XTAL frequency of 11.0592 MHz. The reason behind such an odd number has to do with the baud rate for serial communication of the 8051. XTAL = 11.0592 MHz allows the 8051 system to communicate with the IBM PC with no errors, as we will see in Chapter 10.

GATE

The other bit of the TMOD register is the GATE bit. Notice in the TMOD register of Figure 9-3 that both timers 0 and 1 have the GATE bit. What is its purpose? Every timer has a means of starting and stopping. Some timers do this by software, some by hardware, and some have both software and hardware controls. The timers in the 8051 have both. The start and stop of the timer are controlled by way of software by the TR (timer start) bits TR0 and TR1. This is achieved by the instructions "SETB TR1" and "CLR TR1" for Timer 1, and "SETB TR0" and "CLR TR0" for Timer 0. The SETB instruction starts it, and it is stopped by the CLR instruction. These instructions start and stop the timers as long as GATE = 0 in the TMOD register. The hardware way of starting and stopping the timer by an external source is achieved by making GATE = 1 in the TMOD register. However, to avoid further confusion for now, we will make GATE = 0, meaning that no external hardware is needed to start and stop the timers. In using software to start and stop the timer where GATE = 0, all we need are the instructions "SETB TRx" and "CLR TRx". The use of external hardware to stop or start the timer is discussed in Chapter 11 when interrupts are discussed.

Now that we have this basic understanding of the role of the TMOD register, we will look at the timers' modes and how they are programmed to create a time delay. Because modes 1 and 2 are so widely used, we describe each of them in detail. See Example 9-3.

Mode 1 programming

The following are the characteristics and operations of mode 1:

1. It is a 16-bit timer; therefore, it allows values of 0000 to FFFFH to be loaded into the timer's registers TL and TH.

2. After TH and TL are loaded with a 16-bit initial value, the timer must be started. This is done by "SETB TR0" for Timer 0 and "SETB TR1" for Timer 1.

Example 9-3

Find the value for TMOD if we want to program Timer 0 in mode 2, use 8051 XTAL for the clock source, and use instructions to start and stop the timer.

Solution:

TMOD   = 0000 0010   Timer 0, mode 2,
                     C/T = 0 to use XTAL clock source, and
                     gate = 0 to use internal (software)
                     start and stop method.

---

3. After the timer is started, it starts to count up. It counts up until it reaches its limit of FFFFH. When it rolls over from FFFFH to 0000, it sets high a flag bit called TF (timer flag). This timer flag can be monitored. When this timer flag is raised, one option would be to stop the timer with the instructions "CLR TR0" or "CLR TR1" for Timer 0 and Timer 1, respectively. Again, it must be noted that each timer has its own timer flag: TF0 for Timer 0 and TF1 for Timer 1.

4. After the timer reaches its limit and rolls over, in order to repeat the process the registers TH and TL must be reloaded with the original value, and TF must be reset to 0.

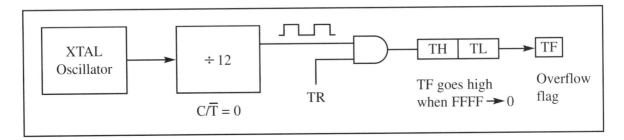

Steps to program in mode 1

To generate a time delay using the timer's mode 1, the following steps are taken. To clarify these steps, see Example 9-4.

1. Load the TMOD value register indicating which timer (Timer 0 or Timer 1) is to be used and which timer mode (0 or 1) is selected.

2. Load registers TL and TH with initial count values.

3. Start the timer.

4. Keep monitoring the timer flag (TF) with the "JNB TFx, target" instruction to see if it is raised. Get out of the loop when TF becomes high.

5. Stop the timer.

6. Clear the TF flag for the next round.

7. Go back to Step 2 to load TH and TL again.

To calculate the exact time delay and the square wave frequency generated on pin P1.5, we need to know the XTAL frequency. See Example 9-5.

From Example 9-6, we can develop a formula for delay calculations using mode 1 (16-bit) of the timer for a crystal frequency of XTAL = 11.0592 MHz. This is given in Figure 9-4. The scientific calculator in the Accessories

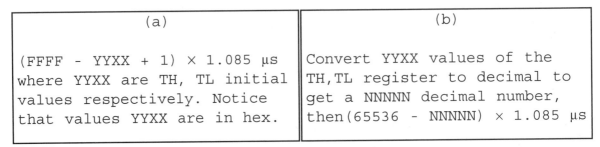

Figure 9-4. Timer Delay Calculation for XTAL = 11.0592 MHz: (a) in Hex; (b) in Decimal

Example 9-4

In the following program, we are creating a square wave of 50% duty cycle (with equal portions high and low) on the P1.5 bit. Timer 0 is used to generate the time delay. Analyze the program.

```
            MOV    TMOD,#01      ;Timer 0, mode 1(16-bit mode)
HERE:       MOV    TL0,#0F2H     ;TL0 = F2H, the Low byte
            MOV    TH0,#0FFH     ;TH0 = FFH, the High byte
            CPL    P1.5          ;toggle P1.5
            ACALL  DELAY
            SJMP   HERE          ;load TH, TL again
;--------delay using Timer 0
DELAY:
            SETB   TR0           ;start Timer 0
AGAIN:      JNB    TF0,AGAIN     ;monitor Timer 0 flag until
                                 ;it rolls over
            CLR    TR0           ;stop Timer 0
            CLR    TF0           ;clear Timer 0 flag
            RET
```

Solution:

In the above program notice the following steps.

1. TMOD is loaded.
2. FFF2H is loaded into TH0–TL0.
3. P1.5 is toggled for the high and low portions of the pulse.
4. The DELAY subroutine using the timer is called.
5. In the DELAY subroutine, Timer 0 is started by the "SETB TR0" instruction.
6. Timer 0 counts up with the passing of each clock, which is provided by the crystal oscillator. As the timer counts up, it goes through the states of FFF3, FFF4, FFF5, FFF6, FFF7, FFF8, FFF9, FFFA, FFFB, and so on until it reaches FFFFH. One more clock rolls it to 0, raising the timer flag (TF0 = 1). At that point, the JNB instruction falls through.
7. Timer 0 is stopped by the instruction "CLR TR0". The DELAY subroutine ends, and the process is repeated.

Notice that to repeat the process, we must reload the TL and TH registers and start the timer again.

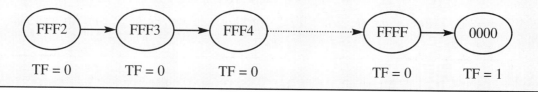

Example 9-5

In Example 9-4, calculate the amount of time delay in the DELAY subroutine generated by the timer. Assume that XTAL = 11.0592 MHz.

Solution:

The timer works with a clock frequency of 1/12 of the XTAL frequency; therefore, we have 11.0592 MHz / 12 = 921.6 kHz as the timer frequency. As a result, each clock has a period of T = 1 / 921.6 kHz = 1.085 μs. In other words, Timer 0 counts up each 1.085 μs resulting in delay = number of counts × 1.085 μs.

The number of counts for the rollover is FFFFH − FFF2H = 0DH (13 decimal). However, we add one to 13 because of the extra clock needed when it rolls over from FFFF to 0 and raises the TF flag. This gives 14 × 1.085 μs = 15.19 μs for half the pulse. For the entire period T = 2 × 15.19 μs = 30.38 μs gives us the time delay generated by the timer.

Example 9-6

In Example 9-5, calculate the frequency of the square wave generated on pin P1.5.

Solution:

In the time delay calculation of Example 9-5, we did not include the overhead due to instructions in the loop. To get a more accurate timing, we need to add clock cycles due to the instructions in the loop. To do that, we use the machine cycles from Table A-1 in Appendix A, as shown below.

```
                                     Cycles
HERE:       MOV    TL0,#0F2H            2
            MOV    TH0,#0FFH            2
            CPL    P1.5                 1
            ACALL  DELAY               2
            SJMP   HERE                 2
;----------delay using Timer 0
DELAY:
            SETB   TR0                  1
AGAIN:      JNB    TF0,AGAIN           14
            CLR    TR0                  1
            CLR    TF0                  1
            RET                         2
                            Total      28
```

T = 2 × 28 × 1.085 μs = 60.76 μs and F = 16458.2 Hz.

Note that 8051 timers use 1/12 of XTAL frequency, regardless of machine cycle time.

directory of Microsoft Windows can help you to find the TH, TL values. This calculator supports decimal, hex, and binary calculations.

In Examples 9-7 and 9-8, we did not reload TH and TL since it was a single pulse. Look at Example 9-9 to see how the reloading works in mode 1.

Example 9-7

Find the delay generated by Timer 0 in the following code, using both of the methods of Figure 9-4. Do not include the overhead due to instructions.

```
              CLR    P2.3          ;clear P2.3
              MOV    TMOD,#01      ;Timer 0, mode 1(16-bit mode)
HERE:         MOV    TL0,#3EH      ;TL0 = 3EH, Low byte
              MOV    TH0,#0B8H     ;TH0 = B8H, High byte
              SETB   P2.3          ;SET high P2.3
              SETB   TR0           ;start Timer 0
AGAIN:        JNB    TF0,AGAIN     ;monitor Timer 0 flag
              CLR    TR0           ;stop Timer 0
              CLR    TF0           ;clear Timer 0 flag for
                                   ;next round
              CLR    P2.3
```

Solution:

(a) (FFFF – B83E + 1) = 47C2H = 18370 in decimal and 18370×1.085 μs = 19.93145 ms.

(b) Since TH – TL = B83EH = 47166 (in decimal), we have 65536 – 47166 = 18370. This means that the timer counts from B83EH to FFFFH. This plus rolling over to 0 goes through a total of 18370 clock cycles, where each clock is 1.085 μs in duration. Therefore, we have 18370×1.085 μs = 19.93145 ms as the width of the pulse.

Example 9-8

Modify TL and TH in Example 9-7 to get the largest time delay possible. Find the delay in ms. In your calculation, exclude the overhead due to the instructions in the loop.

Solution:

To get the largest delay, we make TL and TH both 0. This will count up from 0000 to FFFFH and then roll over to 0.

```
              CLR    P2.3          ;clear P2.3
              MOV    TMOD,#01      ;Timer 0, mode 1(16-bit mode)
HERE:         MOV    TL0,#0        ;TL0 = 0, Low byte
              MOV    TH0,#0        ;TH0 = 0, High byte
              SETB   P2.3          ;SET P2.3 high
              SETB   TR0           ;start Timer 0
AGAIN:        JNB    TF0,AGAIN     ;monitor Timer 0 flag
              CLR    TR0           ;stop Timer 0
              CLR    TF0           ;clear Timer 0 flag
              CLR    P2.3
```

Making TH and TL both 0 means that the timer will count from 0000 to FFFFH, and then roll over to raise the TF flag. As a result, it goes through a total of 65536 states. Therefore, we have delay = $(65536 - 0) \times 1.085$ μs = 71.1065 ms.

Example 9-9

The following program generates a square wave on pin P1.5 continuously using Timer 1 for a time delay. Find the frequency of the square wave if XTAL = 11.0592 MHz. In your calculation do not include the overhead due to instructions in the loop.

```
        MOV   TMOD,#10H      ;Timer 1, mode 1(16-bit)
AGAIN:  MOV   TL1,#34H       ;TL1 = 34H, Low byte
        MOV   TH1,#76H       ;TH1 = 76H, High byte
                             ;(7634H = timer value)
        SETB  TR1            ;start Timer 1
BACK:   JNB   TF1,BACK       ;stay until timer rolls over
        CLR   TR1            ;stop Timer 1
        CPL   P1.5           ;comp. P1.5 to get hi, lo
        CLR   TF1            ;clear Timer 1 flag
        SJMP  AGAIN          ;reload timer since Mode 1
                             ;is not auto-reload
```

Solution:

In the above program notice the target of SJMP. In mode 1, the program must reload the TH, TL register every time if we want to have a continuous wave. Here is the calculation.

Since FFFFH – 7634H = 89CBH + 1 = 89CCH and 89CCH = 35276 clock count. 35276 × 1.085 μs = 38.274 ms for half of the square wave. The entire square wave length is 38.274 × 2 = 76.548 ms and has a frequency = 13.064 Hz.

Also notice that the high and low portions of the square wave pulse are equal. In the above calculation, the overhead due to all the instructions in the loop is not included.

Finding values to be loaded into the timer

Assuming that we know the amount of timer delay we need, the question is how to find the values needed for the TH, TL registers. To calculate the values to be loaded into the TL and TH registers, look at Examples 9-10 through 9-12 where we use crystal frequency of 11.0592 MHz for the 8051 system.

Assuming XTAL = 11.0592 MHz from Example 9-10, we can use the following steps for finding the TH, TL registers' values.

1. Divide the desired time delay by 1.085 μs.

2. Perform 65536 – n, where n is the decimal value we got in Step 1.

3. Convert the result of Step 2 to hex, where $yyxx$ is the initial hex value to be loaded into the timer's registers.

4. Set TL = xx and TH = yy.

Example 9-10

Assume that XTAL = 11.0592 MHz. What value do we need to load into the timer's registers if we want to have a time delay of 5 ms? Show the program for Timer 0 to create a pulse width of 5 ms on P2.3.

Solution:

Since XTAL = 11.0592 MHz, the counter counts up every 1.085 μs. This means that out of many 1.085 μs intervals we must make a 5 ms pulse. To get that, we divide one by the other. We need 5 ms / 1.085 μs = 4608 clocks. To achieve that we need to load into TL and TH the value 65536 – 4608 = 60928 = EE00H. Therefore, we have TH = EE and TL = 00.

```
            CLR     P2.3            ;clear P2.3
            MOV     TMOD,#01        ;Timer 0, mode 1 (16-bit mode)
HERE:       MOV     TL0,#0          ;TL0 = 0, Low byte
            MOV     TH0,#0EEH       ;TH0 = EE( hex), High byte
            SETB    P2.3            ;SET P2.3 high
            SETB    TR0             ;start Timer 0
AGAIN:      JNB     TF0,AGAIN       ;monitor Timer 0 flag
                                    ;until it rolls over
            CLR     P2.3            ;clear P2.3
            CLR     TR0             ;stop Timer 0
            CLR     TF0             ;clear Timer 0 flag
```

Example 9-11

Assuming that XTAL = 11.0592 MHz, write a program to generate a square wave of 2 kHz frequency on pin P1.5.

Solution:

This is similar to Example 9-10, except that we must toggle the bit to generate the square wave. Look at the following steps.
(a) T = 1 / f = 1 / 2 kHz = 500 μs the period of the square wave.
(b) 1/2 of it for the high and low portions of the pulse is 250 μs.
(c) 250 μs / 1.085 μs = 230 and 65536 – 230 = 65306, which in hex is FF1AH.
(d) TL = 1AH and TH = FFH, all in hex. The program is as follows.

```
            MOV     TMOD,#10H       ;Timer 1, mode 1(16-bit)
AGAIN:      MOV     TL1,#1AH        ;TL1=1AH, Low byte
            MOV     TH1,#0FFH       ;TH1=FFH, High byte
            SETB    TR1             ;start Timer 1
BACK:       JNB     TF1,BACK        ;stay until timer rolls over
            CLR     TR1             ;stop Timer 1
            CPL     P1.5            ;complement P1.5 to get hi, lo
            CLR     TF1             ;clear Timer 1 flag
            SJMP    AGAIN           ;reload timer since mode 1
                                    ;is not auto-reload
```

Example 9-12

Assuming XTAL = 11.0592 MHz, write a program to generate a square wave of 50 Hz frequency on pin P2.3.

Solution:

Look at the following steps.
(a) T = 1 / 50 Hz = 20 ms, the period of the square wave.
(b) 1/2 of it for the high and low portions of the pulse = 10 ms
(c) 10 ms / 1.085 μs = 9216 and 65536 – 9216 = 56320 in decimal, and in hex it is DC00H.
(d) TL = 00 and TH = DC (hex)

The program follows.

```
        MOV   TMOD,#10H   ;Timer 1, mode 1 (16-bit)
AGAIN:  MOV   TL1,#00     ;TL1 = 00, Low byte
        MOV   TH1,#0DCH   ;TH1 = DCH, High byte
        SETB  TR1         ;start Timer 1
BACK:   JNB   TF1,BACK    ;stay until timer rolls over
        CLR   TR1         ;stop Timer 1
        CPL   P2.3        ;comp. P2.3 to get hi, lo
        CLR   TF1         ;clear Timer 1 flag
        SJMP  AGAIN       ;reload timer since mode 1
                          ;is not auto-reload
```

Generating a large time delay

As we have seen in the examples so far, the size of the time delay depends on two factors: (a) the crystal frequency and (b) the timer's 16-bit register in mode 1. Both of these factors are beyond the control of the 8051 programmer. We saw earlier that the largest time delay is achieved by making both TH and TL zero. What if that is not enough? Example 9-13 shows how to achieve large time delays.

Using Windows calculator to find TH, TL

The scientific calculator in Microsoft Windows is a handy and easy-to-use tool to find the TH, TL values. Assume that we would like to find the TH, TL values for a time delay that uses 35,000 clocks of 1.085 μs. The following steps show the calculation.

1. Bring up the scientific calculator in MS Windows and select decimal.

2. Enter 35,000.

3. Select hex. This converts 35,000 to hex, which is 88B8H.

4. Select +/– to give –35000 decimal (7748H).

5. The lowest two digits (48) of this hex value are for TL and the next two (77) are for TH. We ignore all the Fs on the left since our number is 16-bit data.

Example 9-13

Examine the following program and find the time delay in seconds. Exclude the overhead due to the instructions in the loop.

```
            MOV     TMOD,#10H       ;Timer 1, mode 1(16-bit)
            MOV     R3,#200         ;counter for multiple delay
AGAIN:      MOV     TL1,#08H        ;TL1 = 08, Low byte
            MOV     TH1,#01H        ;TH1 = 01, High byte
            SETB    TR1             ;start Timer 1
BACK:       JNB     TF1,BACK        ;stay until timer rolls over
            CLR     TR1             ;stop Timer 1
            CLR     TF1             ;clear Timer 1 flag
            DJNZ    R3,AGAIN        ;if R3 not zero then
                                    ;reload timer
```

Solution:

TH – TL = 0108H = 264 in decimal and 65536 – 264 = 65272. Now 65272 × 1.085 μs = 70.820 ms, and for 200 of them we have 200 × 70.820 ms = 14.164024 seconds.

Mode 0

Mode 0 is exactly like mode 1 except that it is a 13-bit timer instead of 16-bit. The 13-bit counter can hold values between 0000 to 1FFFH in TH – TL. Therefore, when the timer reaches its maximum of 1FFH, it rolls over to 0000, and TF is raised.

Mode 2 programming

The following are the characteristics and operations of mode 2.

1. It is an 8-bit timer; therefore, it allows only values of 00 to FFH to be loaded into the timer's register TH.

2. After TH is loaded with the 8-bit value, the 8051 gives a copy of it to TL. Then the timer must be started. This is done by the instruction "SETB TR0" for Timer 0 and "SETB TR1" for Timer 1. This is just like mode 1.

3. After the timer is started, it starts to count up by incrementing the TL register. It counts up until it reaches its limit of FFH. When it rolls over from FFH to 00, it sets high the TF (timer flag). If we are using Timer 0, TF0 goes high; if we are using Timer 1, TF1 is raised.

4. When the TL register rolls from FFH to 0 and TF is set to 1, TL is reloaded automatically with the original value kept by the TH register. To repeat the

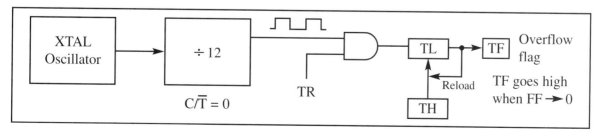

process, we must simply clear TF and let it go without any need by the programmer to reload the original value. This makes mode 2 an auto-reload, in contrast with mode 1 in which the programmer has to reload TH and TL.

It must be emphasized that mode 2 is an 8-bit timer. However, it has an auto-reloading capability. In auto-reload, TH is loaded with the initial count and a copy of it is given to TL. This reloading leaves TH unchanged, still holding a copy of the original value. This mode has many applications, including setting the baud rate in serial communication, as we will see in Chapter 10.

Steps to program in mode 2

To generate a time delay using the timer's mode 2, take the following steps.

1. Load the TMOD value register indicating which timer (Timer 0 or Timer 1) is to be used, and select the timer mode (mode 2).

2. Load the TH registers with the initial count value.

3. Start the timer.

4. Keep monitoring the timer flag (TF) with the "JNB TFx, target" instruction to see whether it is raised. Get out of the loop when TF goes high.

5. Clear the TF flag.

6. Go back to Step 4, since mode 2 is auto-reload.

Example 9-14 illustrates these points. To achieve a larger delay, we can use multiple registers as shown in Example 9-15. See also Examples 9-16 and 9-17.

Example 9-14

Assuming that XTAL = 11.0592 MHz, find (a) the frequency of the square wave generated on pin P1.0 in the following program and (b) the smallest frequency achievable in this program, and the TH value to do that.

```
            MOV    TMOD,#20H      ;T1/mode 2/8-bit/auto-reload
            MOV    TH1,#5         ;TH1 = 5
            SETB   TR1            ;start Timer 1
BACK:       JNB    TF1,BACK       ;stay until timer rolls over
            CPL    P1.0           ;comp. P1.0 to get hi, lo
            CLR    TF1            ;clear Timer 1 flag
            SJMP   BACK           ;mode 2 is auto-reload
```

Solution:

(a) First notice the target address of SJMP. In mode 2 we do not need to reload TH since it is auto-reload. Now (256 − 05) × 1.085 µs = 251 × 1.085 µs = 272.33 µs is the high portion of the pulse. Since it is a 50% duty cycle square wave, the period T is twice that; as a result T = 2 × 272.33 µs = 544.67 µs and the frequency = 1.83597 kHz.

(b) To get the smallest frequency, we need the largest T and that is achieved when TH = 00. In that case, we have T = 2 × 256 × 1.085 µs = 555.52 µs and the frequency = 1.8 kHz.

Example 9-15

Find the frequency of a square wave generated on pin P1.0.

Solution:

```
            MOV    TMOD,#2H        ;Timer 0, mode 2
                                   ;(8-bit, auto-reload)
            MOV    TH0,#0          ;TH0=0
AGAIN:      MOV    R5,#250         ;count for multiple delay
            ACALL  DELAY
            CPL    P1.0            ;toggle P1.0
            SJMP   AGAIN           ;repeat
DELAY:      SETB   TR0             ;start Timer 0
BACK:       JNB    TF0,BACK        ;stay until timer rolls over
            CLR    TR0             ;stop Timer 0
            CLR    TF0             ;clear TF for next round
            DJNZ   R5,DELAY
            RET
```

$T = 2 (250 \times 256 \times 1.085 \ \mu s) = 138.88$ ms and frequency = 72 Hz.

Example 9-16

Assuming that we are programming the timers for mode 2, find the value (in hex) loaded into TH for each of the following cases.

(a) MOV   TH1,#-200   (b) MOV   TH0,#-60
(c) MOV   TH1,#-3   (d) MOV   TH1,#-12
(e) MOV   TH0,#-48

Solution:

You can use the Windows scientific calculator to verify the results provided by the assembler. In Windows calculator, select decimal and enter 200. Then select hex, then +/– to get the TH value. Remember that we only use the right two digits and ignore the rest since our data is an 8-bit data. The following is what we get.

Decimal	*2's Complement (TH Value)*
–200	38H
–60	C4H
–3	FDH
–12	F4H
–48	D0H

Example 9-17

Find (a) the frequency of the square wave generated in the following code and (b) the duty cycle of this wave.

```
            MOV   TMOD,#2H        ;Timer 0, mode 2
                                  ;(8-bit, auto-reload)
            MOV   TH0,#-150       ;TH0 = 6AH = 2's comp of -150
AGAIN:      SETB  P1.3            ;P1.3 = 1
            ACALL DELAY
            ACALL DELAY
            CLR   P1.3            ;P1.3 = 0
            ACALL DELAY
            SJMP  AGAIN
DELAY:
            SETB  TR0             ;start Timer 0
BACK:       JNB   TF0,BACK        ;stay until timer rolls over
            CLR   TR0             ;stop Timer 0
            CLR   TF0             ;clear TF for next round
            RET
```

Solution:

For the TH value in mode 2, the conversion is done by the assembler as long as we enter a negative number. This also makes the calculation easy. Since we are using 150 clocks, we have time for the DELAY subroutine = 150×1.085 μs = 162 μs. The high portion of the pulse is twice that of the low portion (66% duty cycle). Therefore, we have T = high portion + low portion = 325.5 μs + 162.25 μs = 488.25 μs and frequency = 2.048 kHz.

Assemblers and negative values

Since the timer is 8-bit in mode 2, we can let the assembler calculate the value for TH. For example, in "MOV TH1,#-100", the assembler will calculate the –100 = 9C, and makes THl = 9C in hex. This makes our job easier.

Notice that in many of the time delay calculations we have ignored the clocks caused by the overhead instructions in the loop. To get a more accurate time delay, and hence frequency, you need to include them. If you use a digital scope and you don't get exactly the same frequency as the one we have calculated, it is because of the overhead associated with those instructions.

In this section, we used the 8051 timer for time delay generation. However, a more powerful and creative use of these timers is to use them as event counters. We discuss this use of the counter next.

REVIEW QUESTIONS

1. How many timers do we have in the 8051?
2. Each timer has _____ registers that are ___ bits wide.
3. TMOD register is a(n) ___-bit register.

4. True or false. The TMOD register is a bit-addressable register.
5. Indicate the selection made in the instruction "MOV TMOD, #20H".
6. In mode 1, the counter rolls over when it goes from ____ to ____.
7. In mode 2, the counter rolls over when it goes from ____ to ____.
8. In the instruction "MOV TH1, #-200", find the hex value for the TH register.
9. To get a 2-ms delay, what number should be loaded into TH, TL using mode 1? Assume that XTAL = 11.0592 MHz.
10. To get a 100-µs delay, what number should be loaded into the TH register using mode 2? Assume XTAL = 11.0592 MHz.

9.2: COUNTER PROGRAMMING

In the last section, we used the timer/counter of the 8051 to generate time delays. These timers can also be used as counters counting events happening outside the 8051. The use of the timer/counter as an event counter is covered in this section. As far as the use of a timer as an event counter is concerned, everything that we have talked about in programming the timer in the last section also applies to programming it as a counter, except the source of the frequency. When the timer/counter is used as a timer, the 8051's crystal is used as the source of the frequency. When it is used as a counter, however, it is a pulse outside the 8051 that increments the TH, TL registers. In counter mode, notice that the TMOD and TH, TL registers are the same as for the timer discussed in the last section; they even have the same names. The timer's modes are the same as well.

C/T bit in TMOD register

Recall from the last section that the C/T bit in the TMOD register decides the source of the clock for the timer. If C/T = 0, the timer gets pulses from the crystal. By contrast, when C/T = 1, the timer is used as a counter and gets its pulses from outside the 8051. Therefore, when C/T = 1, the counter counts up as pulses are fed from pins 14 and 15. These pins are called T0 (Timer 0 input) and T1 (Timer 1 input). Notice that these two pins belong to port 3. In the case of Timer 0, when C/T = 1, pin P3.4 provides the clock pulse and the counter counts up for each clock pulse coming from that pin. Similarly, for Timer 1, when C/T = 1 each clock pulse coming in from pin P3.5 makes the counter count up. See Table 9-1.

Table 9-1. Port 3 Pins Used for Timers 0 and 1

Pin	Port Pin	Function	Description
14	P3.4	T0	Timer/Counter 0 external input
15	P3.5	T1	Timer/Counter 1 external input

(MSB)   (LSB)

GATE	C/T	M1	M0	GATE	C/T	M1	M0
Timer 1				Timer 0			

In Example 9-18, we use Timer 1 as an event counter where it counts up as clock pulses are fed into pin 3.5. These clock pulses could represent the number of people passing through an entrance, or the number of wheel rotations, or any other event that can be converted to pulses.

In Example 9-18, the TL data was displayed in binary. In Example 9-19, the TL registers are converted to ASCII to be displayed on an LCD. See Figures 9-5 through 9-7 and Example.

Example 9-18

Assuming that clock pulses are fed into pin T1, write a program for counter 1 in mode 2 to count the pulses and display the state of the TL1 count on P2.

Solution:

```
        MOV   TMOD,#01100000B    ;counter 1, mode 2,C/T=1
                                 ;external pulses
        MOV   TH1,#0             ;clear TH1
        SETB  P3.5               ;make T1 input
AGAIN:  SETB  TR1                ;start the counter
BACK:   MOV   A,TL1              ;get copy of count TL1
        MOV   P2,A               ;display it on port 2
        JNB   TF1,BACK           ;keep doing it if TF=0
        CLR   TR1                ;stop the counter 1
        CLR   TF1                ;make TF=0
        SJMP  AGAIN              ;keep doing it
```

Notice in the above program the role of the instruction "SETB P3.5". Although ports are set up for input when the 8051 is powered up, we still make P3.5 an input port (by making it high) to make sure it is an input since some other programs could have used it as an output. In other words, we must configure (set high) the T1 pin (pin P3.5) to allow pulses to be fed into it.

P2 is connected to eight LEDs and input T1 to pulse.

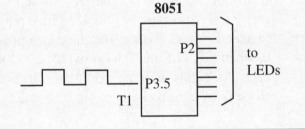

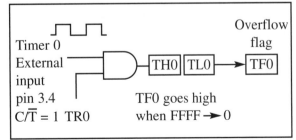

Figure 9-5(a). Timer 0 with External Input (Mode 1)

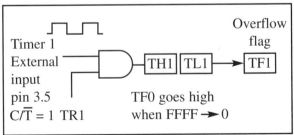

Figure 9-5(b). Timer 1 with External Input (Mode 1)

Example 9-19

Assume that a 1-Hz frequency pulse is connected to input pin 3.4. Write a program to display counter 0 on an LCD. Set the initial value of TH0 to –60.

Solution:

To display the TL count on an LCD, we must convert 8-bit binary data to ASCII. See Chapter 6 for data conversion.

```
          ACALL   LCD_SET_UP      ;initialize the LCD
          MOV     TMOD,#00000110B ;counter 0,mode 2,C/T=1
          MOV     TH0,#-60        ;counting 60 pulses
          SETB    P3.4            ;make T0 as input
AGAIN:    SETB    TR0             ;starts the counter
BACK:     MOV     A,TL0           ;get copy of count TL0
          ACALL   CONV            ;convert in R2, R3, R4
          ACALL   DISPLAY         ;display on LCD
          JNB     TF0,BACK        ;loop if TF0=0
          CLR     TR0             ;stop the counter 0
          CLR     TF0             ;make TF0=0
          SJMP    AGAIN           ;keep doing it

;converting 8-bit binary to ASCII
;upon return, R4, R3, R2 have ASCII data (R2 has LSD)

CONV:     MOV     B,#10           ;divide by 10
          DIV     AB
          MOV     R2,B            ;save low digit
          MOV     B,#10           ;divide by 10 once more
          DIV     AB
          ORL     A,#30H          ;make it ASCII
          MOV     R4,A            ;save MSD
          MOV     A,B
          ORL     A,#30H          ;make 2nd digit an ASCII
          MOV     R3,A            ;save it
          MOV     A,R2
          ORL     A,#30H          ;make 3rd digit an ASCII
          MOV     R2,A            ;save the ASCII
          RET
```

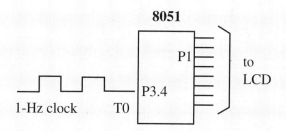

By using 60 Hz we can generate seconds, minutes, hours.

Note that on the first round, it starts from 0, since on RESET, TL0 = 0.
To solve this problem, load TL0 with –60 at the beginning of the program.

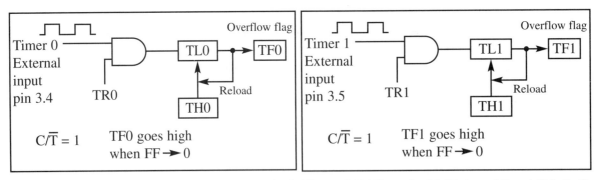

Figure 9-6. Timer 0 with External Input (Mode 2) Figure 9-7. Timer 1 with External Input (Mode 2)

As another example of the application of the timer with C/T = 1, we can feed an external square wave of 60 Hz frequency into the timer. The program will generate the second, the minute, and the hour out of this input frequency and display the result on an LCD. This will be a nice digital clock, but not a very accurate one.

Before we finish this chapter, we need to state two important points.

1. You might think that the use of the instruction "JNB TFx,target" to monitor the raising of the TFx flag is a waste of the microprocessor's time. You are right. There is a solution to this: the use of interrupts. By using interrupts we can go about doing other things with the microprocessor. When the TF flag is raised it will inform us. This important and powerful feature of the 8051 is discussed in Chapter 11.

2. You might wonder to what register TR0 and TR1 belong. They belong to a register called TCON, which is discussed next.

Table 9-2. Equivalent Instructions for the Timer Control Register (TCON)

For Timer 0

SETB TR0	=	SETB TCON.4	
CLR TR0	=	CLR TCON.4	

SETB TF0	=	SETB TCON.5	
CLR TF0	=	CLR TCON.5	

For Timer 1

SETB TR1	=	SETB TCON.6	
CLR TR1	=	CLR TCON.6	

SETB TF1	=	SETB TCON.7	
CLR TF1	=	CLR TCON.7	

TCON: Timer/Counter Control Register

TF1	TR1	TF0	TR0	IE1	IT1	IE0	IT0

TCON register

In the examples so far we have seen the use of the TR0 and TR1 flags to turn on or off the timers. These bits are part of a register called TCON (timer control). This register is an 8-bit register. As shown in Table 9-2, the upper four bits are used to store the TF and TR bits of both Timer 0 and Timer 1. The lower four bits are set aside for controlling the interrupt bits, which will be discussed in Chapter 11. We must notice that the TCON register is a bit-addressable register. Instead of using instructions such as "SETB TR1" and "CLR TR1", we could use "SETB TCON.6" and "CLR TCON.6", respectively. Table 9-2 shows replacements of some of the instructions we have seen so far.

The case of GATE = 1 in TMOD

Before we finish this section, we need to discuss another case of the GATE bit in the TMOD register. All discussion so far has assumed that GATE = 0. When GATE = 0, the timer is started with instructions "SETB TR0" and "SETB TR1" for Timers 0 and 1, respectively. What happens if the GATE bit in TMOD is set to 1? As can be seen in Figures 9-8 and 9-9, if GATE = 1, the start and stop of the timer are done externally through pins P3.2 and P3.3 for Timers 0 and 1, respectively. This is in spite of the fact that TRx is turned on by the "SETB TRx" instruction. This allows us to start or stop the timer externally at any time via a simple switch. This hardware way of controlling the stop and start of the timer can have many applications. For example, assume that an 8051 system is used in a product to sound an alarm every second using Timer 0, perhaps in addition to many other things. Timer 0 is turned on by the software method of using the "SETB TR0" instruction and is beyond the control of the

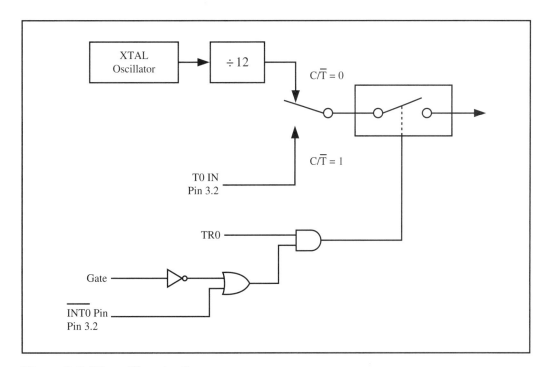

Figure 9-8. Timer/Counter 0

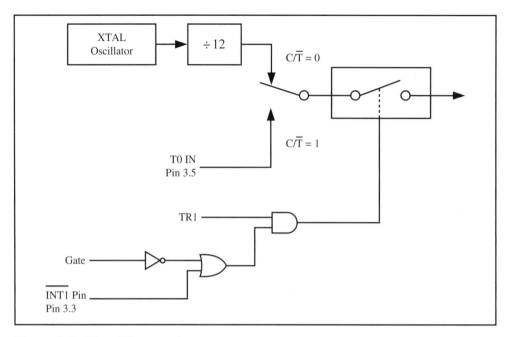

Figure 9-9. Timer/Counter 1

user of that product. However, a switch connected to pin P3.2 can be used to turn on and off the timer, thereby shutting down the alarm.

REVIEW QUESTIONS

1. Who provides the clock pulses to 8051 timers if C/T = 0?
2. Who provides the clock pulses to 8051 timers if C/T = 1?
3. Does the discussion in Section 9.1 apply to timers if C/T = 1?
4. What must be done to allow P3.4 to be used as an input for T1, and why?
5. What is the equivalent of the following instruction?
   "SETB TCON.6"

9.3: PROGRAMMING TIMERS 0 AND 1 IN 8051 C

In Chapter 7, we showed some examples of C programming for the 8051. In this section, we study C programming for the 8051 timers. As we saw in the examples in Chapter 7, the general-purpose registers of the 8051, such as R0–R7, A, and B, are under the control of the C compiler and are not accessed directly by C statements. In the case of SFRs, the entire RAM space of 80–FFH is accessible directly using 8051 C statements. As an example of accessing the SFRs directly, we saw how to access ports P0–P3 in Chapter 7. Here, we discuss how to access the 8051 timers directly using C statements.

Accessing timer registers in C

In 8051 C, we can access the timer registers TH, TL, and TMOD directly using the reg51.h header file. This is shown in Example 9-20. It also shows how to access the TR and TF bits.

Example 9-20

Write an 8051 C program to toggle all the bits of port P1 continuously with some delay in between. Use Timer 0, 16-bit mode to generate the delay.

Solution:

```
#include <reg51.h>
void T0Delay(void);
void main(void)
  {
    while(1)              //repeat forever
     {
        P1=0x55;          //toggle all bits of P1
        T0Delay();        //delay size unknown
        P1=0xAA;          //toggle all bits of P1
        T0Delay();
     }
  }

void T0Delay()
  {
      TMOD=0x01;          //Timer 0, Mode 1
      TL0=0x00;           //load TL0
      TH0=0x35;           //load TH0
      TR0=1;              //turn on T0
      while(TF0==0);      //wait for TF0 to roll over
      TR0=0;              //turn off T0
      TF0=0;              //clear TF0
  }
```

FFFFH — 3500H = CAFFH = 51967 + 1 = 51968

$51968 \times 1.085\ \mu s = 56.384\ ms$ is the approximate delay.

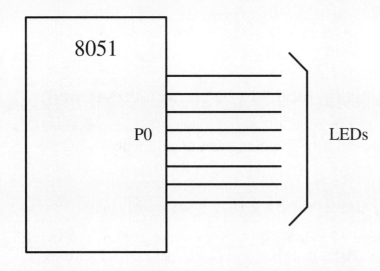

Calculating delay length using timers

As we mentioned in Chapter 7, the delay length depends on three factors: (a) the crystal frequency, (b) the number of clocks per machine cycle, and (c) the C compiler. The original 8051 used 1/12 of the crystal oscillator frequency as 1 machine cycle. In other words, each machine cycle is equal to 12 clock periods of the crystal frequency connected to the X1–X2 pins. The time it takes for the 8051 to execute an instruction is one or more machine cycles, as shown in Appendix A. To speed up the 8051, many recent versions of the 8051 have reduced the number of clocks per machine cycle from 12 to 4, or even 1. For example, the AT89C51/52 uses 12, while the DS5000 uses 4 clocks, and the DS89C4x0 uses only 1 clock per machine cycle. As we mentioned earlier in this chapter, the 8051 timers also use the crystal frequency as the clock source. The frequency for the timer is always 1/12th the frequency of the crystal attached to the 8051, regardless of the 8051 version. In other words, for the AT89C51/52, DS5000, or DS89C4x0 the duration of the time to execute an instruction varies, but they all use 1/12th of the crystal's oscillator frequency for the clock source to the timers. This is done in order to maintain compatibility with the original 8051 since many designers use timers to create time delay. This is an important point and needs to be emphasized. The C compiler is a factor in the delay size since various 8051 C compilers generate different hex code sizes. This explains why the timer delay duration is unknown for Example 9-20 since none of the other factors mentioned is specified.

Delay duration for the AT89C51/52 and DS89C4x0 chips

As we stated before, there is a major difference between the AT89C51 and DS89C4x0 chips in terms of the time it takes to execute a single instruction. Although the DS89C4x0 executes instructions 12 times faster than the AT89C51 chip, they both still use Osc/12 clock for their timers. The faster execution time for the instructions will have an impact on your delay length. To verify this very important point, compare parts (a) and (b) of Example 9-21 since they have been tested on these two chips with the same speed and C compiler.

Timers 0 and 1 delay using mode 1 (16-bit nonauto–reload)

Examples 9-21 and 9-22 show 8051 C programming of the timers 0 and 1 in mode 1 (16-bit nonauto–reload). Examine them to get familiar with the syntax.

Timers 0 and 1 delay using mode 2 (8-bit auto-reload)

Examples 9-23 through 9-25 show 8051 C programming of timers 0 and 1 in mode 2 (8-bit auto-reload). Study these examples to get familiar with the syntax.

Example 9-21

Write an 8051 C program to toggle only bit P1.5 continuously every 50 ms. Use Timer 0, mode 1 (16-bit) to create the delay. Test the program (a) on the AT89C51 and (b) on the DS89C4x0.

Solution:

```c
#include <reg51.h>
void T0M1Delay(void);
sbit mybit=P1^5;
void main(void)
  {
    while(1)
      {
        mybit=~mybit;   //toggle P1.5
        T0M1Delay();    //Timer 0, mode 1(16-bit)
      }
  }
```

(a) Tested for AT89C51, XTAL=11.0592 MHz, using the Proview32 compiler

```c
void T0M1Delay(void)
  {
    TMOD=0x01;          //Timer 0, mode 1(16-bit)
    TL0=0xFD;           //load TL0
    TH0=0x4B;           //load TH0
    TR0=1;              //turn on T0
    while(TF0==0);      //wait for TF0 to roll over
    TR0=0;              //turn off T0
    TF0=0;              //clear TF0
  }
```

(b) Tested for DS89C4x0, XTAL=11.0592 MHz, using the Proview32 compiler

```c
void T0M1Delay(void)
  {
    TMOD=0x01;          //Timer 0, mode 1(16-bit)
    TL0=0xFD;           //load TL0
    TH0=0x4B;           //load TH0
    TR0=1;              //turn on T0
    while(TF0==0);      //wait for TF0 to roll over
    TR0=0;              //turn off T0
    TF0=0;              //clear TF0
  }
```

FFFFH — 4BFDH = B402H = 46082 + 1 = 46083

Timer delay = 46083 × 1.085 μs = 50 ms

Example 9-22

Write an 8051 C program to toggle all bits of P2 continuously every 500 ms. Use Timer 1, mode 1 to create the delay.

Solution:

//tested for DS89C4x0, XTAL = 11.0592 MHz, using the Proview32 compiler

```c
#include <reg51.h>
void T1M1Delay(void);
void main(void)
  {
    unsigned char x;
    P2=0x55;
    while(1)
      {
        P2=~P2;         //toggle all bits of P2
        for(x=0;x<20;x++)
          T1M1Delay();
      }
  }

void T1M1Delay(void)
  {
    TMOD=0x10;          //Timer 1, mode 1(16-bit)
    TL1=0xFE;           //load TL1
    TH1=0xA5;           //load TH1
    TR1=1;              //turn on T1
    while(TF1==0);      //wait for TF1 to roll over
    TR1=0;              //turn off T1
    TF1=0;              //clear TF1
  }
```

A5FEH = 42494 in decimal

65536 − 42494 = 23042

$23042 \times 1.085 \ \mu s = 25$ ms and 20×25 ms $= 500$ ms

Note that 8051 timers use 1/12 of XTAL frequency, regardless of machine cycle time.

Example 9-23

Write an 8051 C program to toggle only pin P1.5 continuously every 250 ms. Use Timer 0, mode 2 (8-bit auto-reload) to create the delay.

Solution:

//tested for DS89C4x0, XTAL = 11.0592 MHz, using the Proview32 compiler

```c
#include <reg51.h>
void T0M2Delay(void);
sbit mybit=P1^5;
void main(void)
   {
      unsigned char x, y;
      while(1)
         {
            mybit=~mybit;              //toggle P1.5
            for(x=0;x<250;x++)         //due to for loop overhead
               for(y=0;y<36;y++)       //we put 36 and not 40
                  T0M2Delay();
         }
   }

void T0M2Delay(void)
   {
      TMOD=0x02;            //Timer 0, mode 2(8-bit auto-reload)
      TH0=-23;             //load TH0(auto-reload value)
      TR0=1;               //turn on T0
      while(TF0==0);       //wait for TF0 to roll over
      TR0=0;               //turn off T0
      TF0=0;               //clear TF0
   }
```

$256 — 23 = 233$

$23 \times 1.085\ \mu s = 25\ \mu s$
$25\ \mu s \times 250 \times 40 = 250\ ms$ by calculation.

However, the scope output does not give us this result. This is due to overhead of the for loop in C. To correct this problem, we put 36 instead of 40.

Example 9-24

Write an 8051 C program to create a frequency of 2500 Hz on pin P2.7. Use Timer 1, mode 2 to create the delay.

Solution:

//tested for DS89C4x0, XTAL = 11.0592 MHz, using the Proview32 compiler

```
#include <reg51.h>
void T1M2Delay(void);
sbit mybit=P2^7;
void main(void)
  {
    unsigned char x;
    while(1)
      {
        mybit=~mybit;       //toggle P2.7
          T1M2Delay();
      }
  }

void T1M2Delay(void)
  {
    TMOD=0x20;              //Timer 1, mode 2(8-bit auto-reload)
    TH1=-184;              //load TH1(auto-reload value)
    TR1=1;                //turn on T1
    while(TF1==0);        //wait for TF1 to roll over
    TR1=0;               //turn off T1
    TF1=0;              //clear TF1
  }
```

1 / 2500 Hz = 400 μs
400 μs / 2 = 200 μs
200 μs / 1.085 μs = 184

Example 9-25

A switch is connected to pin P1.2. Write an 8051 C program to monitor sw and create the following frequencies on pin P1.7:

SW=0:   500 Hz

SW=1:   750 Hz

Use Timer 0, mode 1 for both of them.

Solution:

```c
//tested for AT89C51/52, XTAL = 11.0592 MHz, using the Proview32 compiler
#include <reg51.h>
sbit mybit=P1^5;
sbit SW=P1^7;
void T0M1Delay(unsigned char);
void main(void)
  {
    SW=1;                     //make P1.7 an input
    while(1)
      {
        mybit=~mybit;         //toggle P1.5
        if(SW==0)             //check switch
          T0M1Delay(0);
        else
          T0M1Delay(1);
      }
  }
void T0M1Delay(unsigned char c)
  {
    TMOD=0x01;
    if(c==0)
      {
        TL0=0x67;             //FC67
        TH0=0xFC;
      }
    else
      {
        TL0=0x9A;             //FD9A
        TH0=0xFD;
      }
    TR0=1;
    while(TF0==0);
    TR0=0;
    TF0=0;
  }
```

FC67H = 64615

65536 — 64615 = 921

921 × 1.085 μs = 999.285 μs

1 / (999.285 μs × 2) = 500 Hz

C programming of timers 0 and 1 as counters

In Section 9.2, we showed how to use timers 0 and 1 as event counters. A timer can be used as a counter if we provide pulses from outside the chip instead of using the frequency of the crystal oscillator as the clock source. By feeding pulses to the T0 (P3.4) and T1 (P3.5) pins, we turn Timer 0 and Timer 1 into counter 0 and counter 1, respectively. Study Examples 9-26 through 9-29 to see how timers 0 and 1 are programmed as counters using the C language.

Example 9-26

Assume that a 1-Hz external clock is being fed into pin T1 (P3.5). Write a C program for counter 1 in mode 2 (8-bit auto-reload) to count up and display the state of the TL1 count on P1. Start the count at 0H.

Solution:

```
#include <reg51.h>
sbit T1 = P3^5;
void main(void)
   {
      T1=1;                  //make T1 an input
      TMOD=0x60;             //
      TH1=0;                 //set count to 0

      while(1)               //repeat forever
        {
          do
           {
              TR1=1;         //start timer
              P1=TL1;        //place value on pins
           }
          while(TF1==0);     //wait here
          TR1=0;             //stop timer
          TF1=0;             //clear flag
        }
   }
```

P1 is connected to 8 LEDs.
T1 (P3.5) is connected to a
1-Hz external clock.

Example 9-27

Assume that a 1-Hz external clock is being fed into pin T0 (P3.4). Write a C program for counter 0 in mode 1 (16-bit) to count the pulses and display the TH0 and TL0 registers on P2 and P1, respectively.

Solution:

```c
#include <reg51.h>

void main(void)
  {
    T0=1;                   //make T0 an input
    TMOD=0x05;              //
    TL0=0;                  //set count to 0
    TH0=0;                  //set count to 0

    while(1)                //repeat forever
      {
        do
          {
            TR0=1;          //start timer
            P1=TL0;         //place value on pins
            P2=TH0;         //
          }
        while(TF0==0);      //wait here
        TR0=0;              //stop timer
        TF0=0;
      }
  }
```

1-Hz clock   T0 P3.4

8051

P1

P1 and
P2 to
LEDs

Example 9-28

Assume that a 2-Hz external clock is being fed into pin T1 (P3.5). Write a C program for counter 0 in mode 2 (8-bit auto-reload) to display the count in ASCII. The 8-bit binary count must be converted to ASCII. Display the ASCII digits (in binary) on P0, P1, and P2 where P0 has the least significant digit. Set the initial value of TH0 to 0.

Solution:

To display the TL1 count, we must convert 8-bit binary data to ASCII. See Chapter 7 for data conversion. The ASCII values will be shown in binary. For example, '9' will show as 00111001 on ports.

```c
#include <reg51.h>
void BinToASCII(unsigned char);
void main()
  {
     unsigned char value;
     T1=1;
     TMOD=0x06;
     TH0=0;

     while(1)
       {
         do
          {
             TR0=1;
             value=TL0;
             BinToASCII(value);
          }
         while(TF0==0);
         TR0=0;
         TF0=0;
       }
  }

void BinToASCII(unsigned char value)        //see Chapter 7
  {
     unsigned char x,d1,d2,d3;
     x = value / 10;
     d1 = value % 10
     d2 = x % 10;
     d3 = x / 10
     P0 = 30 | d1;
     P1 = 30 | d2;
     P2 = 30 | d3
  }
```

Example 9-29

Assume that a 60-Hz external clock is being fed into pin T0 (P3.4). Write a C program for counter 0 in mode 2 (8-bit auto-reload) to display the seconds and minutes on P1 and P2, respectively.

Solution:

```
#include <reg51.h>
void ToTime(unsigned char);
void main()
  {
    unsigned char val;
    T0=1;
    TMOD=0x06;                    //T0, mode 2, counter
    TH0=-60;                      //sec = 60 pulses
    while(1)
      {
        do
          {
            TR0=1;
            sec=TL0;
            ToTime(val);
          }
        while(TF0==0);
        TR0=0;
        TF0=0;
      }
  }

void ToTime(unsigned char val)
  {
    unsigned char sec, min;
    min = value / 60;
    sec = value % 60;
    P1 = sec;
    P2 = min;
  }
```

By using 60 Hz, we can generate seconds, minutes, and hours.

REVIEW QUESTIONS

1. Who provides the clock pulses to 8051 timers if C/T = 0?
2. Indicate the selection made in the statement "TMOD = 0x20".
3. In mode 1, the counter rolls over when it goes from _____ to _____.
4. In mode 2, the counter rolls over when it goes from _____ to _____.
5. In the statement "TH1 = -200", find the hex value for the TH register.
6. TF0 and TF1 are part of register _____.
7. In Question 6, is the register bit-addressable?
8. Show how to monitor the TF1 flag for high in 8051 C.

SUMMARY

The 8051 has two timers/counters. When used as timers they can generate time delays. When used as counters they can serve as event counters. This chapter showed how to program the timers/counters for various modes.

The two timers are accessed as two 8-bit registers: TL0 and TH0 for Timer 0, and TL1 and TH1 for Timer 1. Both timers use the TMOD register to set timer operation modes. The lower 4 bits of TMOD are used for Timer 0 and the upper 4 bits are used for Timer 1.

There are different modes that can be used for each timer. Mode 0 sets the timer as a 13-bit timer, mode 1 sets it as a 16-bit timer, and mode 2 sets it as an 8-bit timer.

When the timer/counter is used as a timer, the 8051's crystal is used as the source of the frequency; when it is used as a counter, however, it is a pulse outside the 8051 that increments the TH, TL registers.

PROBLEMS

9.1: PROGRAMMING 8051 TIMERS

1. How many timers do we have in the 8051?
2. The timers of the 8051 are _____-bit and are designated as _____ and
   _____.
3. The registers of Timer 0 are accessed as _____ and _____.
4. The registers of Timer 1 are accessed as _____ and _____.
5. In Questions 3 and 4, are the registers bit-addressable?
6. The TMOD register is a(n) ____-bit register.
7. What is the job of the TMOD register?
8. True or false. TMOD is a bit-addressable register.
9. Find the TMOD value for both Timer 0 and Timer 1, mode 2, software start/stop (gate = 0), with the clock coming from the 8051's crystal.
10. Find the frequency and period used by the timer if the crystal attached to the 8051 has the following values.
    (a) XTAL = 11.0592 MHz   (b) XTAL = 20 MHz
    (c) XTAL = 24 MHz   (d) XTAL = 30 MHz

11. Indicate the size of the timer for each of the following modes.
    (a) mode 0   (b) mode 1   (c) mode 2
12. Indicate the rollover value (in hex and decimal) of the timer for each of the following modes.
    (a) mode 0   (b) mode 1   (c) mode 2
13. Indicate when the TF1 flag is raised for each of the following modes.
    (a) mode 0   (b) mode 1   (c) mode 2
14. True or false. Both Timer 0 and Timer 1 have their own TF.
15. True or false. Both Timer 0 and Timer 1 have their own timer start (TR).
16. Assuming XTAL = 11.0592 MHz, indicate when the TF0 flag is raised for the following program.

```
MOV   TMOD,#01
MOV   TL0,#12H
MOV   TH0,#1CH
SETB  TR0
```

17. Assuming that XTAL = 16 MHz, indicate when the TF0 flag is raised for the following program.

```
MOV   TMOD,#01
MOV   TL0,#12H
MOV   TH0,#1CH
SETB  TR0
```

18. Assuming that XTAL = 11.0592 MHz, indicate when the TF0 flag is raised for the following program.

```
MOV   TMOD,#01
MOV   TL0,#10H
MOV   TH0,#0F2H
SETB  TR0
```

19. Assuming that XTAL = 20 MHz, indicate when the TF0 flag is raised for the following program.

```
MOV   TMOD,#01
MOV   TL0,#12H
MOV   TH0,#1CH
SETB  TR0
```

20. Assume that XTAL = 11.0592 MHz. Find the TH1,TL1 value to generate a time delay of 2 ms. Timer 1 is programmed in mode 1.
21. Assume that XTAL = 16 MHz. Find the TH1,TL1 value to generate a time delay of 5 ms. Timer 1 is programmed in mode 1.
22. Assuming that XTAL = 11.0592 MHz, program Timer 0 to generate a time delay of 2.5 ms.
23. Assuming that XTAL = 11.0592 MHz, program Timer 1 to generate a time delay of 0.2 ms.
24. Assuming that XTAL = 20 MHz, program Timer 1 to generate a time delay of 100 ms.
25. Assuming that XTAL = 11.0592 MHz and that we are generating a square wave on pin P1.2, find the lowest square wave frequency that we can generate using mode 1.

26. Assuming that XTAL = 11.0592 MHz and that we are generating a square wave on pin P1.2, find the highest square wave frequency that we can generate using mode 1.

27. Assuming that XTAL = 16 MHz and that we are generating a square wave on pin P1.2, find the lowest square wave frequency that we can generate using mode 1.

28. Assuming that XTAL = 16 MHz and that we are generating a square wave on pin P1.2, find the highest square wave frequency that we can generate using mode 1.

29. In mode 2 assuming that TH1 = F1H, indicate which states timer 2 goes through until TF1 is raised. How many states is that?

30. Program Timer 1 to generate a square wave of 1 kHz. Assume that XTAL = 11.0592 MHz.

31. Program Timer 0 to generate a square wave of 3 kHz. Assume that XTAL = 11.0592 MHz.

32. Program Timer 0 to generate a square wave of 0.5 kHz. Assume that XTAL = 20 MHz.

33. Program Timer 1 to generate a square wave of 10 kHz. Assume that XTAL = 20 MHz.

34. Assuming that XTAL = 11.0592 MHz, show a program to generate a 1-second time delay. Use any timer you want.

35. Assuming that XTAL = 16 MHz, show a program to generate a 0.25-second time delay. Use any timer you want.

36. Assuming that XTAL = 11.0592 MHz and that we are generating a square wave on pin P1.3, find the lowest square wave frequency that we can generate using mode 2.

37. Assuming that XTAL = 11.0592 MHz and that we are generating a square wave on pin P1.3, find the highest square wave frequency that we can generate using mode 2.

38. Assuming that XTAL = 16 MHz and that we are generating a square wave on pin P1.3, find the lowest square wave frequency that we can generate using mode 2.

39. Assuming that XTAL = 16 MHz and that we are generating a square wave on pin P1.3, find the highest square wave frequency that we can generate using mode 2.

40. Find the value (in hex) loaded into TH in each of the following.

(a)	MOV	TH0,#-12	(b)		MOV	TH0,#-22
(c)	MOV	TH0,#-34	(d)		MOV	TH0,#-92
(e)	MOV	TH1,#-120	(f)		MOV	TH1,#-104
(g)	MOV	TH1,#-222	(h)		MOV	TH1,#-67

41. In Problem 40, indicate by what number the machine cycle frequency of 921.6 kHz (XTAL = 11.0592 MHz) is divided.

42. In Problem 41, find the time delay for each case from the time the timer starts to the time the TF flag is raised.

9.2: COUNTER PROGRAMMING

43. To use the timer as an event counter, we must set the C/T bit in the TMOD register to _____ (low, high).
44. Can we use both of the timers as event counters?
45. For counter 0, which pin is used to input clocks?
46. For counter 1, which pin is used to input clocks?
47. Program Timer 1 to be an event counter. Use mode 1 and display the binary count on P1 and P2 continuously. Set the initial count to 20,000.
48. Program Timer 0 to be an event counter. Use mode 2 and display the binary count on P2 continuously. Set the initial count to 20.
49. Program Timer 1 to be an event counter. Use mode 2 and display the decimal count on P2, P1, and P0 continuously. Set the initial count to 99.
50. The TCON register is a(n) _____-bit register.
51. True or false. The TCON register is not a bit-addressable register.
52. Give another instruction to perform the action of "SETB TR0".

9.3: PROGRAMMING TIMERS 0 AND 1 IN 8051 C

53. Program Timer 0 in C to generate a square wave of 3 kHz. Assume that XTAL = 11.0592 MHz.
54. Program Timer 1 in C to generate a square wave of 3 kHz. Assume that XTAL = 11.0592 MHz.
55. Program Timer 0 in C to generate a square wave of 0.5 kHz. Assume that XTAL = 11.0592 MHz.
56. Program Timer 1 in C to generate a square wave of 0.5 kHz. Assume that XTAL = 11.0592 MHz.
57. Program Timer 1 in C to be an event counter. Use mode 1 and display the binary count on P1 and P2 continuously. Set the initial count to 20,000.
58. Program Timer 0 in C to be an event counter. Use mode 2 and display the binary count on P2 continuously. Set the initial count to 20.

ANSWERS TO REVIEW QUESTIONS

9.1: PROGRAMMING 8051 TIMERS

1. Two
2. 2, 8
3. 8
4. False
5. 0010 0000 indicates Timer 1, mode 2, software start and stop, and using XTAL for frequency.
6. FFFFH to 0000
7. FFH to 00
8. −200 is 38H; therefore, TH1 = 38H
9. 2 ms/1.085 μs = 1843 = 0733H where TH = F8H and TL = CDH (negative of 0733H)
10. 100 ms/1.085 μs = 92 or 5CH; therefore, TH = A4H (negative of 5CH)

9.2: COUNTER PROGRAMMING

1. The crystal attached to the 8051
2. The clock source for the timers comes from pins T0 and T1.
3. Yes
4. We must use the instruction "SETB P3.4" to configure the T1 pin as input, which allows the clocks to come from an external source.
5. SETB TR1

9.3: PROGRAMMING TIMERS 0 AND 1 IN 8051 C

1. The crystal attached to the 8051
2. Timer 2, mode 2, 8-bit auto-reload
3. FFFFH to 0
4. FFH to 0
5. 38H
6. TMOD
7. Yes
8. While (TF1==0);

CHAPTER 10

8051 SERIAL PORT PROGRAMMING IN ASSEMBLY AND C

OBJECTIVES

Upon completion of this chapter, you will be able to:

>> Contrast and compare serial versus parallel communication.
>> List the advantages of serial communication over parallel.
>> Explain serial communication protocol.
>> Contrast synchronous versus asynchronous communication.
>> Contrast half- versus full-duplex transmission.
>> Explain the process of data framing.
>> Describe data transfer rate and bps rate.
>> Define the RS232 standard.
>> Explain the use of the MAX232 and MAX233 chips.
>> Interface the 8051 with an RS232 connector.
>> Discuss the baud rate of the 8051.
>> Describe serial communication features of the 8051.
>> Program the 8051 serial port in Assembly and C.
>> Program the second serial port of DS89C4x0 in Assembly and C.

Computers transfer data in two ways: parallel and serial. In parallel data transfers, often eight or more lines (wire conductors) are used to transfer data to a device that is only a few feet away. Examples of parallel transfers are printers and hard disks; each uses cables with many wire strips. Although in such cases a lot of data can be transferred in a short amount of time by using many wires in parallel, the distance cannot be great. To transfer to a device located many meters away, the serial method is used. In serial communication, the data is sent one bit at a time, in contrast to parallel communication, in which the data is sent a byte or more at a time. Serial communication of the 8051 is the topic of this chapter. The 8051 has serial communication capability built into it, thereby making possible fast data transfer using only a few wires.

In this chapter, we first discuss the basics of serial communication. In Section 10.2, 8051 interfacing to RS232 connectors via MAX232 line drivers is discussed. Serial port programming of the 8051 is discussed in Section 10.3. The second serial port of DS89C4x0 is programmed in Section 10.4. Section 10.5 covers 8051 C programming for serial ports #0 and #1.

10.1: BASICS OF SERIAL COMMUNICATION

When a microprocessor communicates with the outside world, it provides the data in byte-sized chunks. In some cases, such as printers, the information is simply grabbed from the 8-bit data bus and presented to the 8-bit data bus of the printer. This can work only if the cable is not too long, since long cables diminish and even distort signals. Furthermore, an 8-bit data path is expensive. For these reasons, serial communication is used for transferring data between two systems located at distances of hundreds of feet to millions of miles apart. Figure 10-1 diagrams serial versus parallel data transfers.

The fact that serial communication uses a single data line instead of the 8-bit data line of parallel communication not only makes it much cheaper but also enables two computers located in two different cities to communicate over the telephone.

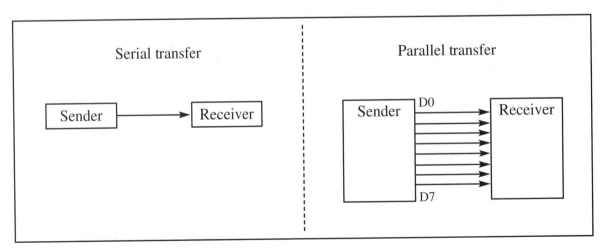

Figure 10-1. Serial versus Parallel Data Transfer

For serial data communication to work, the byte of data must be converted to serial bits using a parallel-in-serial-out shift register; then it can be transmitted over a single data line. This also means that at the receiving end there must be a serial-in-parallel-out shift register to receive the serial data and pack them into a byte. Of course, if data is to be transferred on the telephone line, it must be converted from 0s and 1s to audio tones, which are sinusoidal-shaped signals. This conversion is performed by a peripheral device called a *modem*, which stands for "modulator/demodulator."

When the distance is short, the digital signal can be transferred as it is on a simple wire and requires no modulation. This is how IBM PC keyboards transfer data to the motherboard. However, for long-distance data transfers using communication lines such as a telephone, serial data communication requires a modem to *modulate* (convert from 0s and 1s to audio tones) and *demodulate* (converting from audio tones to 0s and 1s).

Serial data communication uses two methods, asynchronous and synchronous. The *synchronous* method transfers a block of data (characters) at a time, while the *asynchronous* method transfers a single byte at a time. It is possible to write software to use either of these methods, but the programs can be tedious and long. For this reason, there are special IC chips made by many manufacturers for serial data communications. These chips are commonly referred to as UART (universal asynchronous receiver-transmitter) and USART (universal synchronous-asynchronous receiver-transmitter). The 8051 chip has a built-in UART, which is discussed in detail in Section 10.3.

Half- and full-duplex transmission

In data transmission if the data can be transmitted and received, it is a *duplex* transmission. This is in contrast to *simplex* transmissions such as with printers, in which the computer only sends data. Duplex transmissions can be half or full duplex, depending on whether or not the data transfer can be simultaneous. If data is transmitted one way at a time, it is referred to as *half duplex*. If the data can go both ways at the same time, it is *full duplex*. Of course, full duplex requires two wire conductors for the data lines (in addition to the signal ground), one for transmission and one for reception in order to transfer and receive data simultaneously. See Figure 10-2.

Asynchronous serial communication and data framing

The data coming in at the receiving end of the data line in a serial data transfer is all 0s and 1s; it is difficult to make sense of the data unless the sender and receiver agree on a set of rules, a *protocol*, on how the data is packed, how many bits constitute a character, and when the data begins and ends.

Start and stop bits

Asynchronous serial data communication is widely used for character-oriented transmissions, while block-oriented data transfers use the synchronous method. In the asynchronous method, each character is placed between

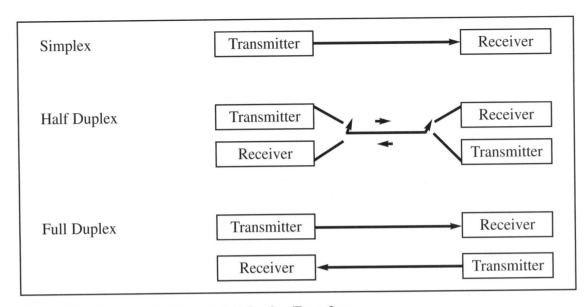

Figure 10-2. Simplex, Half-, and Full-Duplex Transfers

start and stop bits. This is called *framing*. In data framing for asynchronous communications, the data, such as ASCII characters, are packed between a start bit and a stop bit. The start bit is always one bit, but the stop bit can be one or two bits. The start bit is always a 0 (low) and the stop bit(s) is 1 (high). For example, look at Figure 10-3 in which the ASCII character "A" (8-bit binary 0100 0001) is framed between the start bit and a single stop bit. Notice that the LSB is sent out first.

Notice in Figure 10-3 that when there is no transfer, the signal is 1 (high), which is referred to as *mark*. The 0 (low) is referred to as *space*. Notice that the transmission begins with a start bit followed by D0, which is the LSB, then the rest of the bits until the MSB (D7), and finally, the one stop bit indicating the end of the character "A."

In asynchronous serial communications, peripheral chips and modems can be programmed for data that is 7- or 8-bits wide. This is in addition to the number of stop bits, 1 or 2. While in older systems ASCII characters were 7-bit, in recent years, due to the extended ASCII characters, 8-bit data has become common. In some older systems, due to the slowness of the receiving mechanical device, two stop bits were used to give the device sufficient time to organize itself before transmission of the next byte. In modern PCs, however, the use of one stop bit is standard. Assuming that we are transferring a text

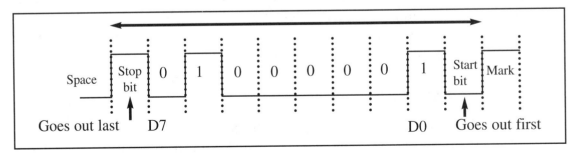

Figure 10-3. Framing ASCII "A" (41H)

file of ASCII characters using one stop bit, we have a total of 10 bits for each character: 8 bits for the ASCII code and 1 bit each for the start and stop bits. Therefore, for each 8-bit character there are an extra 2 bits, which gives 20% overhead.

In some systems, the parity bit of the character byte is included in the data frame in order to maintain data integrity. This means that for each character (7- or 8-bit, depending on the system) we have a single parity bit in addition to start and stop bits. The parity bit is odd or even. In the case of an odd-parity bit, the number of data bits, including the parity bit, has an odd number of 1s. Similarly, in an even-parity bit system, the total number of bits, including the parity bit, is even. For example, the ASCII character "A," binary 0100 0001, has 0 for the even-parity bit. UART chips allow programming of the parity bit for odd-, even-, and no-parity options.

Data transfer rate

The rate of data transfer in serial data communication is stated in *bps* (bits per second). Another widely used terminology for bps is *baud rate*. However, the baud and bps rates are not necessarily equal. This is due to the fact that baud rate is the modem terminology and is defined as the number of signal changes per second. In modems a single change of signal sometimes transfers several bits of data. As far as the conductor wire is concerned, the baud rate and bps are the same, and for this reason in this book we use the terms *bps* and *baud* interchangeably.

The data transfer rate of a given computer system depends on communication ports incorporated into that system. For example, the early IBM PC/XT could transfer data at the rate of 100 to 9600 bps. In recent years, however, Pentium-based PCs transfer data at rates as high as 56K bps. It must be noted that in asynchronous serial data communication, the baud rate is generally limited to 100,000 bps.

RS232 standards

To allow compatibility among data communication equipment made by various manufacturers, an interfacing standard called RS232 was set by the Electronics Industries Association (EIA) in 1960. In 1963, it was modified and called RS232A. RS232B and RS232C were issued in 1965 and 1969, respectively. In this book, we refer to it simply as RS232. Today, RS232 is the most widely used serial I/O interfacing standard. This standard is used in PCs and numerous types of equipment. However, since the standard was set long before the advent of the TTL logic family, its input and output voltage levels are not TTL-compatible. In RS232, a 1 is represented by −3 to −25 V, while a 0 bit is +3 to +25 V, making −3 to +3 undefined. For this reason, to connect any RS232 to a microprocessor system we must use voltage converters such as MAX232 to convert the TTL logic levels to the RS232 voltage levels, and vice versa. MAX232 IC chips are commonly referred to as line drivers. RS232 connection to MAX232 is discussed in Section 10.2.

RS232 pins

Table 10-1 provides the pins and their labels for the original RS232 cable, commonly referred to as the DB-25 connector. In labeling, DB-25P refers to the plug connector (male) and DB-25S is for the socket connector (female). See Figure 10-4.

Since not all the pins are used in PC cables, IBM introduced the DB-9 version of the serial I/O standard, which uses 9 pins only, as shown in Table 10-2. The DB-9 pins are shown in Figure 10-5.

Data communication classification

Current terminology classifies data communication equipment as DTE (data terminal equipment) or DCE (data communication equipment). DTE refers to terminals and computers that send and receive data, while DCE refers to communication equipment, such as modems, that are responsible for transferring the data. Notice that all the RS232 pin function definitions of Tables 10-1 and 10-2 are from the DTE point of view.

The simplest connection between a PC and microprocessor requires a minimum of three pins, TxD, RxD, and ground, as shown in Figure 10-6. Notice in the figure that the RxD and TxD pins are interchanged.

Examining RS232 handshaking signals

To ensure fast and reliable data transmission between two devices, the data transfer must be coordinated. Just as in the case of the printer, because the receiving device in serial

Table 10-1. RS232 Pins (DB-25)

Pin	Description
1	Protective ground
2	Transmitted data (TxD)
3	Received data (RxD)
4	Request to send ($\overline{\text{RTS}}$)
5	Clear to send ($\overline{\text{CTS}}$)
6	Data set ready ($\overline{\text{DSR}}$)
7	Signal ground (GND)
8	Data carrier detect ($\overline{\text{DCD}}$)
9/10	Reserved for data testing
11	Unassigned
12	Secondary data carrier detect
13	Secondary clear to send
14	Secondary transmitted data
15	Transmit signal element timing
16	Secondary received data
17	Receive signal element timing
18	Unassigned
19	Secondary request to send
20	Data terminal ready ($\overline{\text{DTR}}$)
21	Signal quality detector
22	Ring indicator
23	Data signal rate select
24	Transmit signal element timing
25	Unassigned

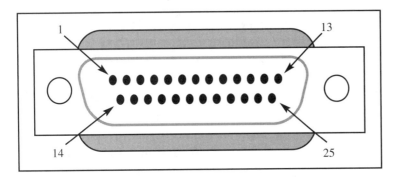

Figure 10-4. The Original RS232 Connector DB-25 (No Longer in Use)

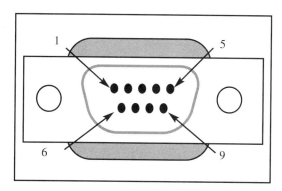

Figure 10-5. DB-9 9-Pin Connector

Table 10-2. IBM PC DB-9 Signals

Pin	Description
1	Data carrier detect ($\overline{\text{DCD}}$)
2	Received data (RxD)
3	Transmitted data (TxD)
4	Data terminal ready (DTR)
5	Signal ground (GND)
6	Data set ready ($\overline{\text{DSR}}$)
7	Request to send ($\overline{\text{RTS}}$)
8	Clear to send ($\overline{\text{CTS}}$)
9	Ring indicator (RI)

data communication may have no room for the data, there must be a way to inform the sender to stop sending data. Many of the pins of the RS 232 connector are used for handshaking signals. Their descriptions are provided below only as a reference and they can be bypassed since they are not supported by the 8051 UART chip.

1. DTR (data terminal ready). When a terminal (or a PC COM port) is turned on, after going through a self-test, it sends out signal DTR to indicate that it is ready for communication. If there is something wrong with the COM port, this signal will not be activated. This is an active-low signal and can be used to inform the modem that the computer is alive and kicking. This is an output pin from DTE (PC COM port) and an input to the modem.

2. DSR (data set ready). When DCE (modem) is turned on and has gone through the self-test, it asserts DSR to indicate that it is ready to communicate. Thus, it is an output from the modem (DCE) and input to the PC (DTE). This is an active-low signal. If for any reason the modem cannot make a connection to the telephone, this signal remains inactive, indicating to the PC (or terminal) that it cannot accept or send data.

3. RTS (request to send). When the DTE device (such as a PC) has a byte to transmit, it asserts RTS to signal the modem that it has a byte of data to transmit. RTS is an active-low output from the DTE and an input to the modem.

4. CTS (clear to send). In response to RTS, when the modem has room for storing the data it is to receive, it sends out signal CTS to the DTE (PC) to indicate that it can receive the data now. This input signal to the DTE is used by the DTE to start transmission.

5. DCD (carrier detect, or DCD, data carrier detect). The modem asserts signal DCD to inform the DTE (PC) that a valid carrier has been detected and that contact between it and the other modem is established. Therefore, DCD is an output from the modem and an input to the PC (DTE).

6. RI (ring indicator). An output from the modem (DCE) and an input to a PC (DTE) indicates that the telephone is ringing. It goes on and off in synchronization with the ringing sound. Of the six handshake signals, this is the least often

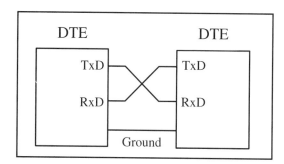

Figure 10-6. Null Modem Connection

used, due to the fact that modems take care of answering the phone. However, if the PC is in charge of answering the phone, this signal can be used.

From the above description, PC and modem communication can be summarized as follows: While signals DTR and DSR are used by the PC and modem, respectively, to indicate that they are alive and well, it is RTS and CTS that actually control the flow of data. When the PC wants to send data it asserts RTS, and in response, if the modem is ready (has room) to accept the data, it sends back CTS. If, for lack of room, the modem does not activate CTS, the PC will deassert DTR and try again. RTS and CTS are also referred to as hardware control flow signals.

This concludes the description of the most important pins of the RS232 handshake signals plus TxD, RxD, and ground. Ground is also referred to as SG (signal ground).

x86 PC COM ports

The x86 PCs (based on x86 microprocessors) used to have two COM ports. Both COM ports were RS232-type connectors. The COM ports were designated as COM 1 and COM 2. In recent years, one of these has been replaced with the USB port, and COM 1 is the only serial port available, if any. We can connect 8051 serial port to the COM 1 port of a PC for serial communication experiments. In the absence of a COM port, we can use COM-to-USB converter module.

With this background in serial communication, we are ready to look at the 8051. In the next section, we discuss the physical connection of the 8051 and RS232 connector, and in Section 10.3, we show how to program the 8051 serial communication port.

REVIEW QUESTIONS

1. The transfer of data using parallel lines is _____ (faster, slower) but _____ (more expensive, less expensive).
2. True or false. Sending data to a printer is duplex.
3. True or false. In full duplex we must have two data lines, one for transfer and one for receive.
4. The start and stop bits are used in the _____ (synchronous, asynchronous) method.
5. Assuming that we are transmitting the ASCII letter "E" (0100 0101 in binary) with no parity bit and one stop bit, show the sequence of bits transferred serially.
6. In Question 5, find the overhead due to framing.
7. Calculate the time it takes to transfer 10,000 characters as in Question 5 if we use 9600 bps. What percentage of time is wasted due to overhead?
8. True or false. RS232 is not TTL-compatible.
9. What voltage levels are used for binary 0 in RS232?
10. True or false. The 8051 has a built-in UART.
11. On the back of x86 PCs, we normally have ____ COM port connectors.
12. The PC COM ports are designated by DOS and Windows as ___ and ____.

10.2: 8051 CONNECTION TO RS232

In this section, the details of the physical connections of the 8051 to RS232 connectors are given. As stated in Section 10.1, the RS232 standard is not TTL-compatible; therefore, it requires a line driver such as the MAX232 chip to convert RS232 voltage levels to TTL levels, and vice versa. The interfacing of 8051 with RS232 connectors via the MAX232 chip is the main topic of this section.

RxD and TxD pins in the 8051

The 8051 has two pins that are used specifically for transferring and receiving data serially. These two pins are called TxD and RxD and are part of the port 3 group (P3.0 and P3.1). Pin 11 of the 8051 (P3.1) is assigned to TxD and pin 10 (P3.0) is designated as RxD. These pins are TTL-compatible; therefore, they require a line driver to make them RS232 compatible. One such line driver is the MAX232 chip. This is discussed next.

MAX232

Since the RS232 is not compatible with today's microprocessors and microprocessors, we need a line driver (voltage converter) to convert the RS232's signals to TTL voltage levels that will be acceptable to the 8051's TxD and RxD pins. One example of such a converter is MAX232 from Maxim Corp. (www.maxim-ic.com). The MAX232 converts from RS232 voltage levels to TTL voltage levels, and vice versa. One advantage of the MAX232 chip is that it uses a +5 V power source which is the same as the source voltage for the 8051. In other words, with a single +5 V power supply we can power both the 8051 and MAX232, with no need for the dual power supplies that are common in many older systems.

The MAX232 has two sets of line drivers for transferring and receiving data, as shown in Figure 10-7. The line drivers used for TxD are called T1 and T2, while the line drivers for RxD are designated as R1 and R2. In many applications,

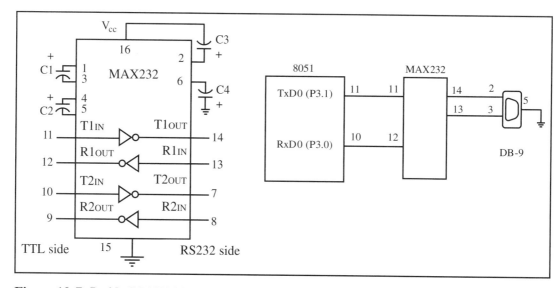

Figure 10-7. Inside MAX232 and Its Connection to the 8051 (Null Modem)

CHAPTER 10: 8051 SERIAL PORT PROGRAMMING　　　　　　　　**317**

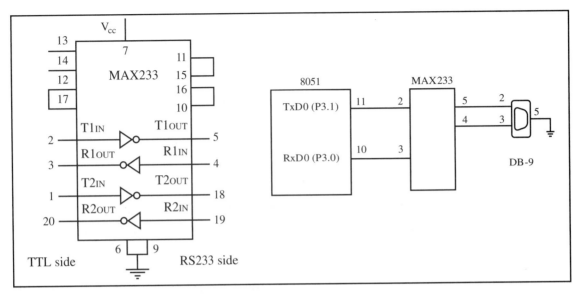

Figure 10-8. Inside MAX233 and Its Connection to the 8051 (Null Modem)

only one of each is used. For example, T1 and R1 are used together for TxD and RxD of the 8051, and the second set is left unused. Notice in MAX232 that the T1 line driver has a designation of T1in and T1out on pin numbers 11 and 14, respectively. The T1in pin is the TTL side and is connected to TxD of the micro-processor, while T1out is the RS232 side that is connected to the RxD pin of the RS232 DB connector. The R1 line driver has a designation of R1in and R1out on pin numbers 13 and 12, respectively. The R1in (pin 13) is the RS232 side that is connected to the TxD pin of the RS232 DB connector, and R1out (pin 12) is the TTL side that is connected to the RxD pin of the microprocessor. See Figure 10-7. Notice the null modem connection where RxD for one is TxD for the other.

MAX232 requires four capacitors ranging from 1 to 22 μF. The most widely used value for these capacitors is 22 μF.

MAX233

To save board space, some designers use the MAX233 chip from Maxim. The MAX233 performs the same job as the MAX232 but eliminates the need for capacitors. However, the MAX233 chip is much more expensive than the MAX232. Notice that MAX233 and MAX232 are not pin compatible. You cannot take a MAX232 out of a board and replace it with a MAX233. See Figure 10-8 for MAX233 with no capacitor used.

REVIEW QUESTIONS

1. True or false. The PC COM port connector is the RS232 type.
2. Which pins of the 8051 are set aside for serial communication, and what are their functions?
3. What are line drivers such as MAX232 used for?
4. MAX232 can support ____ lines for TxD and ____ lines for RxD.
5. What is the advantage of the MAX233 over the MAX232 chip?

Table 10-3. PC Baud Rates

10.3: 8051 SERIAL PORT PROGRAMMING IN ASSEMBLY

110
150
300
600
1200
2400
4800
9600
19200

In this section, we discuss the serial communication registers of the 8051 and show how to program them to transfer and receive data serially. Since IBM PC/compatible computers are so widely used to communicate with 8051-based systems, we will emphasize serial communications of the 8051 with the COM port of the PC. To allow data transfer between the PC and an 8051 system without any error, we must make sure that the baud rate of the 8051 system matches the baud rate of the PC's COM port. Some of the baud rates supported by PC BIOS are listed in Table 10-3. You can examine these baud rates by going to the Windows HyperTerminal program and clicking on the Communication Settings option. The HyperTerminal program comes with Windows. HyperTerminal supports baud rates much higher than the ones listed in Table 10-3.

Baud rate in the 8051

The 8051 transfers and receives data serially at many different baud rates. The baud rate in the 8051 is programmable. This is done with the help of Timer 1. Before we discuss how to do that, we will look at the relationship between the crystal frequency and the baud rate in the 8051.

As discussed in previous chapters, the 8051 divides the crystal frequency by 12 to get the machine cycle frequency. In the case of XTAL = 11.0592 MHz, the machine cycle frequency is 921.6 kHz (11.0592 MHz / 12 = 921.6 kHz). The 8051's serial communication UART circuitry divides the machine cycle frequency of 921.6 kHz by 32 once more before it is used by Timer 1 to set the baud rate. Therefore, 921.6 kHz divided by 32 gives 28,800 Hz. This is the number we will use throughout this section to find the Timer 1 value to set the baud rate. When Timer 1 is used to set the baud rate it must be programmed in mode 2, that is 8-bit, auto-reload. To get baud rates compatible with the PC, we must load TH1 with the values shown in Table 10-4. Example 10-1 shows how to verify the data in Table 10-4.

Table 10-4. Timer 1 TH1 Register Values for Various Baud Rates

Baud Rate	TH1 (Decimal)	TH1 (Hex)
9600	−3	FD
4800	−6	FA
2400	−12	F4
1200	−24	E8

Note: XTAL = 11.0592 MHz.

Example 10-1

With XTAL = 11.0592 MHz, find the TH1 value needed to have the following baud rates: (a) 9600 (b) 2400 (c) 1200.

Solution:

With XTAL = 11.0592 MHz, we have:

The machine cycle frequency of the 8051 = 11.0592 MHz / 12 = 921.6 kHz, and 921.6 kHz / 32 = 28,800 Hz is the frequency provided by UART to Timer 1 to set baud rate.

(a) 28,800 / 3 = 9600   where −3 = FD (hex) is loaded into TH1
(b) 28,800 / 12 = 2400   where −12 = F4 (hex) is loaded into TH1
(c) 28,800 / 24 = 1200   where −24 = E8 (hex) is loaded into TH1

Notice that 1/12th of the crystal frequency divided by 32 is the default value upon activation of the 8051 RESET pin. We can change this default setting. This is explained at the end of this chapter.

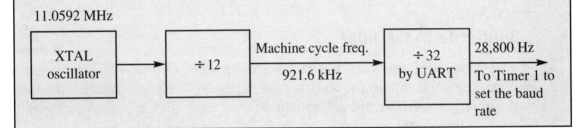

SBUF register

SBUF is an 8-bit register used solely for serial communication in the 8051. For a byte of data to be transferred via the TxD line, it must be placed in the SBUF register. Similarly, SBUF holds the byte of data when it is received by the 8051's RxD line. SBUF can be accessed like any other register in the 8051. Look at the following examples of how this register is accessed:

```
MOV SBUF,#'D'       ;load SBUF=44H, ASCII for 'D'
MOV SBUF,A          ;copy accumulator into SBUF
MOV A,SBUF          ;copy SBUF into accumulator
```

The moment a byte is written into SBUF, it is framed with the start and stop bits and transferred serially via the TxD pin. Similarly, when the bits are received serially via RxD, the 8051 deframes it by eliminating the stop and start bits, making a byte out of the data received, and then placing it in the SBUF.

SCON (serial control) register

The SCON register is an 8-bit register used to program the start bit, stop bit, and data bits of data framing, among other things.

The following describes various bits of the SCON register.

SM0	SM1	SM2	REN	TB8	RB8	TI	RI

SM0	SCON.7	Serial port mode specifier.
SM1	SCON.6	Serial port mode specifier.
SM2	SCON.5	Used for multiprocessor communication. (Make it 0.)
REN	SCON.4	Set/cleared by software to enable/disable reception.
TB8	SCON.3	Not widely used.
RB8	SCON.2	Not widely used.
TI	SCON.1	Transmit interrupt flag. Set by hardware at the beginning of the stop bit in mode 1. Must be cleared by software.
RI	SCON.0	Receive interrupt flag. Set by hardware halfway through the stop bit time in mode 1. Must be cleared by software.

Figure 10-9. SCON Serial Port Control Register (Bit-Addressable)
Note: Make SM2, TB8, and RB8 = 0.

SM0, SM1

SM0 and SM1 are D7 and D6 of the SCON register, respectively. These two bits determine the framing of data by specifying the number of bits per character, and the start and stop bits. They take the following combinations.

SM0	*SM1*	
0	0	Serial Mode 0
0	1	Serial Mode 1, 8-bit data, 1 stop bit, 1 start bit
1	0	Serial Mode 2
1	1	Serial Mode 3

Of the four serial modes, only mode 1 is of interest to us. Further explanation for the other three modes is in Appendix A.2. They are rarely used today. In the SCON register, when serial mode 1 is chosen, the data framing is 8 bits, 1 stop bit, and 1 start bit, which makes it compatible with the COM port of IBM/compatible PCs. More importantly, serial mode 1 allows the baud rate to be variable and is set by Timer 1 of the 8051. In serial mode 1, for each character a total of 10 bits are transferred, where the first bit is the start bit, followed by 8 bits of data, and finally 1 stop bit.

SM2

SM2 is the D5 bit of the SCON register. This bit enables the multiprocessing capability of the 8051 and is beyond the discussion of this chapter. For our applications, we will make SM2 = 0 since we are not using the 8051 in a multiprocessor environment.

REN

The REN (receive enable) bit is D4 of the SCON register. The REN bit is also referred to as SCON.4 since SCON is a bit-addressable register. When the REN bit is high, it allows the 8051 to receive data on the RxD pin of the

8051. As a result if we want the 8051 to both transfer and receive data, REN must be set to 1. By making REN = 0, the receiver is disabled. Making REN = 1 or REN = 0 can be achieved by the instructions "SETB SCON.4" and "CLR SCON.4", respectively. Notice that these instructions use the bit-addressable features of register SCON. This bit can be used to block any serial data reception and is an extremely important bit in the SCON register.

TB8

TB8 (transfer bit 8) is bit D3 of SCON. It is used for serial modes 2 and 3. We make TB8 = 0 since it is not used in our applications.

RB8

RB8 (receive bit 8) is bit D2 of the SCON register. In serial mode 1, this bit gets a copy of the stop bit when an 8-bit data is received. This bit (as is the case for TB8) is rarely used anymore. In all our applications we will make RB8 = 0. Like TB8, the RB8 bit is also used in serial modes 2 and 3.

TI

TI (transmit interrupt) is bit D1 of the SCON register. This is an extremely important flag bit in the SCON register. When the 8051 finishes the transfer of the 8-bit character, it raises the TI flag to indicate that it is ready to transfer another byte. The TI bit is raised at the beginning of the stop bit. We will discuss its role further when programming examples of data transmission are given.

RI

RI (receive interrupt) is the D0 bit of the SCON register. This is another extremely important flag bit in the SCON register. When the 8051 receives data serially via RxD, it gets rid of the start and stop bits and places the byte in the SBUF register. Then it raises the RI flag bit to indicate that a byte has been received and should be picked up before it is lost. RI is raised halfway through the stop bit, and we will soon see how this bit is used in programs for receiving data serially.

Programming the 8051 to transfer data serially

In programming the 8051 to transfer character bytes serially, the following steps must be taken.

1. The TMOD register is loaded with the value 20H, indicating the use of Timer 1 in mode 2 (8-bit auto-reload) to set the baud rate.
2. The TH1 is loaded with one of the values in Table 10-4 to set the baud rate for serial data transfer (assuming XTAL = 11.0592 MHz).
3. The SCON register is loaded with the value 50H, indicating serial mode 1, where an 8-bit data is framed with start and stop bits.
4. TR1 is set to 1 to start Timer 1.
5. TI is cleared by the "CLR TI" instruction.

6. The character byte to be transferred serially is written into the SBUF register.
7. The TI flag bit is monitored with the use of the instruction "JNB TI,xx" to see if the character has been transferred completely.
8. To transfer the next character, go to Step 5.

Example 10-2 shows a program to transfer data serially at 4800 baud. Example 10-3 shows how to transfer "YES" continuously.

Importance of the TI flag

To understand the importance of the role of TI, look at the following sequence of steps that the 8051 goes through in transmitting a character via TxD.

Example 10-2

Write a program for the 8051 to transfer letter "A" serially at 4800 baud, continuously.

Solution:

```
        MOV    TMOD,#20H   ;Timer 1, mode 2(auto-reload)
        MOV    TH1,#-6     ;4800 baud rate
        MOV    SCON,#50H   ;8-bit, 1 stop, REN enabled
        SETB   TR1         ;start Timer 1
AGAIN:  MOV    SBUF,#"A"   ;letter "A" to be transferred
HERE:   JNB    TI,HERE     ;wait for the last bit
        CLR    TI          ;clear TI for next char
        SJMP   AGAIN       ;keep sending A
```

Example 10-3

Write a program to transfer the message "YES" serially at 9600 baud, 8-bit data, 1 stop bit. Do this continuously.

Solution:

```
        MOV    TMOD,#20H ;Timer 1, mode 2
        MOV    TH1,#-3   ;9600 baud
        MOV    SCON,#50H ;8-bit, 1 stop bit, REN enabled
        SETB   TR1       ;start Timer 1
AGAIN:  MOV    A,#"Y"    ;transfer "Y"
        ACALL  TRANS
        MOV    A,#"E"    ;transfer "E"
        ACALL  TRANS
        MOV    A,#"S"    ;transfer "S"
        ACALL  TRANS
        SJMP   AGAIN     ;keep doing it
;-----serial data transfer subroutine
TRANS:  MOV    SBUF,A    ;load SBUF
HERE:   JNB    TI,HERE   ;wait for last bit to transfer
        CLR    TI        ;get ready for next byte
        RET
```

---

1. The byte character to be transmitted is written into the SBUF register.
2. The start bit is transferred.
3. The 8-bit character is transferred one bit at a time.
4. The stop bit is transferred. It is during the transfer of the stop bit that the 8051 raises the TI flag (TI = 1), indicating that the last character was transmitted and it is ready to transfer the next character.
5. By monitoring the TI flag, we make sure that we are not overloading the SBUF register. If we write another byte into the SBUF register before TI is raised, the untransmitted portion of the previous byte will be lost. In other words, when the 8051 finishes transferring a byte, it raises the TI flag to indicate it is ready for the next character.
6. After SBUF is loaded with a new byte, the TI flag bit must be forced to 0 by the "CLR TI" instruction in order for this new byte to be transferred.

From the above discussion, we conclude that by checking the TI flag bit, we know whether or not the 8051 is ready to transfer another byte. More importantly, it must be noted that the TI flag bit is raised by the 8051 itself when it finishes the transfer of data, whereas it must be cleared by the programmer with an instruction such as "CLR TI". It also must be noted that if we write a byte into SBUF before the TI flag bit is raised, we risk the loss of a portion of the byte being transferred. The TI flag bit can be checked by the instruction "JNB TI, . . ." or we can use an interrupt. In Chapter 11, we will show how to use interrupts to transfer data serially, and avoid tying down the microprocessor with instructions such as "JNB TI, xx".

Programming the 8051 to receive data serially

In the programming of the 8051 to receive character bytes serially, the following steps must be taken.

1. The TMOD register is loaded with the value 20H, indicating the use of Timer 1 in mode 2 (8-bit auto-reload) to set the baud rate.
2. TH1 is loaded with one of the values in Table 10-4 to set the baud rate (assuming XTAL = 11.0592 MHz).
3. The SCON register is loaded with the value 50H, indicating serial mode 1, where 8-bit data is framed with start and stop bits and receive enable is turned on.
4. TR1 is set to 1 to start Timer 1.
5. RI is cleared with the "CLR RI" instruction.
6. The RI flag bit is monitored with the use of the instruction "JNB RI, xx" to see if an entire character has been received yet.
7. When RI is raised, SBUF has the byte. Its contents are moved into a safe place.
8. To receive the next character, go to Step 5.

Example 10-4

Program the 8051 to receive bytes of data serially, and put them in P1. Set the baud rate at 4800, 8-bit data, and 1 stop bit.

Solution:

```
        MOV   TMOD,#20H   ;Timer 1, mode 2(auto-reload)
        MOV   TH1,#-6     ;4800 baud
        MOV   SCON,#50H   ;8-bit, 1 stop, REN enabled
        SETB  TR1         ;start Timer 1
HERE:   JNB   RI,HERE     ;wait for char to come in
        MOV   A,SBUF      ;save incoming byte in A
        MOV   P1,A        ;send to port 1
        CLR   RI          ;get ready to receive next byte
        SJMP  HERE        ;keep getting data
```

Examples 10-4 and 10-5 show the coding of the above steps.

Importance of the RI flag bit

In receiving bits via its RxD pin, the 8051 goes through the following steps.

1. It receives the start bit indicating that the next bit is the first bit of the character byte it is about to receive.

2. The 8-bit character is received one bit at a time. When the last bit is received, a byte is formed and placed in SBUF.

3. The stop bit is received. When receiving the stop bit the 8051 makes RI = 1, indicating that an entire character byte has been received and must be picked up before it gets overwritten by an incoming character.

4. By checking the RI flag bit when it is raised, we know that a character has been received and is sitting in the SBUF register. We copy the SBUF contents to a safe place in some other register or memory before it is lost.

5. After the SBUF contents are copied into a safe place, the RI flag bit must be forced to 0 by the "CLR RI" instruction in order to allow the next received character byte to be placed in SBUF. Failure to do this causes loss of the received character.

From the above discussion, we conclude that by checking the RI flag bit we know whether or not the 8051 has received a character byte. If we fail to copy SBUF into a safe place, we risk the loss of the received byte. More importantly, it must be noted that the RI flag bit is raised by the 8051, but it must be cleared by the programmer with an instruction such as "CLR RI". It also must be noted that if we copy SBUF into a safe place before the RI flag bit is raised, we risk copying garbage. The RI flag bit can be checked by the instruction "JNB RI,xx" or by using an interrupt, as we will see in Chapter 11.

Example 10-5

Assume that the 8051 serial port is connected to the COM port of the IBM PC, and on the PC we are using the HyperTerminal program to send and receive data serially. P1 and P2 of the 8051 are connected to LEDs and switches, respectively. Write an 8051 program to (a) send to the PC the message "We Are Ready," (b) receive any data sent by the PC and put it on LEDs connected to P1, and (c) get data on switches connected to P2 and send it to the PC serially. The program should perform part (a) once, but parts (b) and (c) continuously. Use the 4800 baud rate.

Solution:

```
            ORG    0
            MOV    P2,#0FFH        ;make P2 an input port
            MOV    TMOD,#20H       ;Timer 1, mode 2(auto-reload)
            MOV    TH1,#0FAH       ;4800 baud rate
            MOV    SCON,#50H       ;8-bit,1 stop, REN enabled
            SETB   TR1             ;start Timer 1
            MOV    DPTR,#MYDATA    ;load pointer for message
H_1:        CLR    A
            MOVC   A,@A+DPTR       ;get the character
            JZ     B_1             ;if last character get out
            ACALL  SEND            ;otherwise call transfer
            INC    DPTR            ;next one
            SJMP   H_1             ;stay in loop
B_1:        MOV    A,P2            ;read data on P2
            ACALL  SEND            ;transfer it serially
            ACALL  RECV            ;get the serial data
            MOV    P1,A            ;display it on LEDs
            SJMP   B_1             ;stay in loop indefinitely
;---------------serial data transfer. ACC has the data
SEND:       MOV    SBUF,A          ;load the data
H_2:        JNB    TI,H_2          ;stay here until last bit gone
            CLR    TI              ;get ready for next char
            RET                    ;return to caller
;---------------receive data serially in ACC
RECV:       JNB    RI,RECV         ;wait here for char
            MOV    A,SBUF          ;save it in ACC
            CLR    RI              ;get ready for next char
            RET                    ;return to caller
;---------------The message
MYDATA:     DB     "We Are Ready",0
            END
```

8051

```
                        P1 >----- LED
    To ----- TxD
    PC
    COM
    port ----- RxD      P2 <----- SW
```

Doubling the baud rate in the 8051

There are two ways to increase the baud rate of data transfer in the 8051.

1. Use a higher-frequency crystal.
2. Change a bit in the PCON register, shown below.

Option 1 is not feasible in many situations since the system crystal is fixed. More importantly, it is not feasible because the new crystal may not be compatible with the IBM PC serial COM port's baud rate. Therefore, we will explore option 2. There is a software way to double the baud rate of the 8051 while the crystal frequency is fixed. This is done with the register called PCON (power control). The PCON register is an 8-bit register. Of the 8 bits, some are unused, and some are used for the power control capability of the 8051. The bit that is used for the serial communication is D7, the SMOD (serial mode) bit. When the 8051 is powered up, D7 (SMOD bit) of the PCON register is zero. We can set it to high by software and thereby double the baud rate. The following sequence of instructions must be used to set high D7 of PCON, since it is not a bit-addressable register:

```
MOV   A,PCON        ;place a copy of PCON in ACC
SETB  ACC.7         ;make D7=1
MOV   PCON,A        ;now SMOD=1 without
                    ;changing any other bits
```

To see how the baud rate is doubled with this method, we show the role of the SMOD bit (D7 bit of the PCON register), which can be 0 or 1. We discuss each case.

Baud rates for SMOD = 0

When SMOD = 0, the 8051 divides 1/12 of the crystal frequency by 32 and uses that frequency for Timer 1 to set the baud rate. In the case of XTAL = 11.0592 MHz, we have:

```
Machine cycle freq. = 11.0592 MHz / 12 = 921.6 kHz
and
921.6 kHz / 32 = 28,800 Hz since SMOD = 0
```

This is the frequency used by Timer 1 to set the baud rate. This has been the basis of all the examples so far since it is the default when the 8051 is powered up. The baud rate for SMOD = 0 was listed in Table 10-4.

Baud rates for SMOD = 1

With the fixed crystal frequency, we can double the baud rate by making SMOD = 1. When the SMOD bit (D7 of the PCON register) is set to 1, 1/12 of

Table 10-5. Baud Rate Comparison for SMOD = 0 and SMOD = 1

TH1 (Decimal)	(Hex)	SMOD = 0	SMOD = 1
–3	FD	9,600	19,200
–6	FA	4,800	9,600
–12	F4	2,400	4,800
–24	E8	1,200	2,400

Note: XTAL = 11.0592 MHz.

XTAL is divided by 16 (instead of 32) and that is the frequency used by Timer 1 to set the baud rate. In the case of XTAL = 11.0592 MHz, we have:

```
Machine cycle freq. = 11.0592 MHz / 12 = 921.6 kHz
and
921.6 kHz / 16 = 57,600 Hz since SMOD = 1
```

This is the frequency used by Timer 1 to set the baud rate.

Table 10-5 shows that the values loaded into TH1 are the same for both cases; however, the baud rates are doubled when SMOD = 1. See Examples 10-6 through 10-10 to clarify the data given in Table 10-5.

Example 10-6

Assuming that XTAL = 11.0592 MHz for the following program, state (a) what this program does, (b) compute the frequency used by Timer 1 to set the baud rate, and (c) find the baud rate of the data transfer.

```
        MOV    A,PCON      ;A = PCON
        SETB   ACC.7       ;make D7 = 1
        MOV    PCON,A      ;SMOD = 1, double baud rate
                           ;with same XTAL freq.
        MOV    TMOD,#20H   ;Timer 1, mode 2(auto-reload)
        MOV    TH1,-3      ;19200 (57,600 / 3 = 19200 baud rate
                           ;since SMOD=1)
        MOV    SCON,#50H   ;8-bit data,1 stop bit, RI enabled
        SETB   TR1         ;start Timer 1
        MOV    A,#"B"      ;transfer letter B
A_1:    CLR    TI          ;make sure TI=0
        MOV    SBUF,A      ;transfer it
H_1:    JNB    TI,H_1      ;stay here until the last bit is gone
        SJMP   A_1         ;keep sending "B" again and again
```

Solution:

(a) This program transfers ASCII letter B (01000010 binary) continuously.
(b) With XTAL = 11.0592 MHz and SMOD = 1 in the above program, we have:

11.0592 MHz / 12 = 921.6 kHz machine cycle frequency
921.6 kHz / 16 = 57,600 Hz frequency used by Timer 1 to set the baud rate
57,600 Hz / 3 = 19,200 baud rate

Example 10-7

Find the TH1 value (in both decimal and hex) to set the baud rate to each of the following: (a) 9600 (b) 4800 if SMOD = 1. Assume that XTAL = 11.0592 MHz.

Solution:

With XTAL = 11.0592 MHz and SMOD = 1, we have Timer 1 frequency = 57,600 Hz.
(a) 57,600 / 9600 = 6; therefore, TH1 = −6 or TH1 = FAH.
(b) 57,600 / 4800 = 12; therefore, TH1 = −12 or TH1 = F4H.

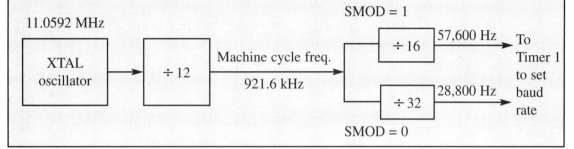

Example 10-8

Find the baud rate if TH1 = −2, SMOD = 1, and XTAL = 11.0592 MHz. Is this baud rate supported by IBM/compatible PCs?

Solution:

With XTAL = 11.0592 MHz and SMOD = 1, we have Timer 1 frequency = 57,600 Hz. The baud rate is 57,600 / 2 = 28,800. This baud rate is not supported by the BIOS of the PCs; however, the PC can be programmed to do data transfer at such a speed. Also, HyperTerminal in Windows supports this and other baud rates.

Interrupt-based data transfer

By now you might have noticed that it is a waste of the microprocessor's time to poll the TI and RI flags. In order to avoid wasting the microprocessor's time, we use interrupts instead of polling. In Chapter 11, we will show how to use interrupts to program the 8051's serial communication port.

REVIEW QUESTIONS

1. Which timer of the 8051 is used to set the baud rate?
2. If XTAL = 11.0592 MHz, what frequency is used by the timer to set the baud rate?
3. Which mode of the timer is used to set the baud rate?
4. With XTAL = 11.0592 MHz, what value should be loaded into TH1 to have a 9600 baud rate? Give the answer in both decimal and hex.
5. To transfer a byte of data serially, it must be placed in register _____.
6. SCON stands for _____ and it is a(n) ____-bit register.

Example 10-9

Assume a switch is connected to pin P1.7. Write a program to monitor its status and send two messages to serial port continuously as follows:

If sw=0, send "NO"

If sw=1, send "YES"

Assume XTAL = 11.0592 MHz, 9600 baud, 8-bit data, and 1 stop bit.

Solution:

```
          SW1     EQU   P1.7
          ORG     0H                  ;starting position
MAIN:     MOV     TMOD,#20H
          MOV     TH1,#-3             ;9600 baud rate
          MOV     SCON,#50H
          SETB    TR1                 ;start timer
          SETB    SW1                 ;make SW an input
S1:       JB      SW1,NEXT            ;check SW status
          MOV     DPTR,#MESS1         ;if SW=0 display "NO"
FN:       CLR     A
          MOVC    A,@A+DPTR           ;read the value
          JZ      S1                  ;check for end of line
          ACALL   SENDCOM             ;send value to serial port
          INC     DPTR                ;move to next value
          SJMP    FN                  ;repeat
NEXT:     MOV     DPTR,#MESS2         ;if SW=1 display "YES"
LN:       CLR     A
          MOVC    A,@A+DPTR           ;read the value
          JZ      S1                  ;check for end of line
          ACALL   SENDCOM             ;send value to serial port
          INC     DPTR                ;move to next value
          SJMP    LN                  ;repeat
;-------------------
SENDCOM:  MOV     SBUF,A              ;place value in buffer
HERE:     JNB     TI,HERE             ;wait until transmitted
          CLR     TI                  ;clear
          RET                         ;return
;-------------------
MESS1:    DB      "NO",0
MESS2:    DB      "YES",0
          END
```

7. Which register is used to set the data size and other framing information such as the stop bit?

8. True or false. SCON is a bit-addressable register.

9. When is TI raised?

10. Which register has the SMOD bit, and what is its status when the 8051 is powered up?

Example 10-10

Write a program to send the message "The Earth is but One Country" to serial port. Assume a sw is connected to pin P1.2. Monitor its status and set the baud rate as follows:

sw = 0, 4800 baud rate

sw = 1, 9600 baud rate

Assume XTAL = 11.0592 MHz, 8-bit data, and 1 stop bit.

Solution:

```
          SW      BIT P1.2
          ORG     0H                ;Starting position
MAIN:
          MOV     TMOD,#20H
          MOV     TH1,#-6           ;4800 baud rate (default)
          MOV     SCON,#50H
          SETB    TR1
          SETB    SW                ;make SW an input
S1:       JNB     SW,SLOWSP         ;check SW status
          MOV     A,PCON            ;read PCON
          SETB    ACC.7             ;set SMOD High for 9600
          MOV     PCON,A            ;write PCON
          SJMP    OVER              ;send message
SLOWSP:   MOV     A,PCON            ;read PCON
          CLR     ACC.7             ;make SMOD Low for 4800
          MOV     PCON,A            ;write PCON
OVER:     MOV     DPTR,#MESS1       ;load address to message
FN:       CLR     A
          MOVC    A,@A+DPTR         ;read value
          JZ      S1                ;check for end of line
          ACALL   SENDCOM           ;send value to the serial port
          INC     DPTR              ;move to next value
          SJMP    FN                ;repeat


;-------------
SENDCOM:
          MOV     SBUF,A            ;place value in buffer
HERE:     JNB     TI,HERE           ;wait until transmitted
          CLR     TI                ;clear
          RET                       ;return


;-------------------
MESS1:    DB      "The Earth is but One Country",0
          END
```

10.4: PROGRAMMING THE SECOND SERIAL PORT

Many of the new generations of the 8051 microprocessors come with two serial ports. The DS89C4x0 and DS80C320 are among them. In this section, we show the programming of the second serial port of the DS89C4x0 chip.

DS89C4x0 second serial port

The second serial port of the DS89C4x0 uses pins P1.2 and P1.3 for the Rx and Tx lines, respectively. See Figure 10-10. The MDE8051 Trainer (available from www.MicroDigitalEd.com) uses the DS89C4x0 chip and comes with two serial ports already installed. It also uses the MAX232 for the RS232 connection to DB9. The connections for the RS232 to the DS89C4x0 of the MDE8051 Trainer are shown in Figure 10-11. Notice that the first and second serial ports are designated as Serial #0 and Serial #1, respectively.

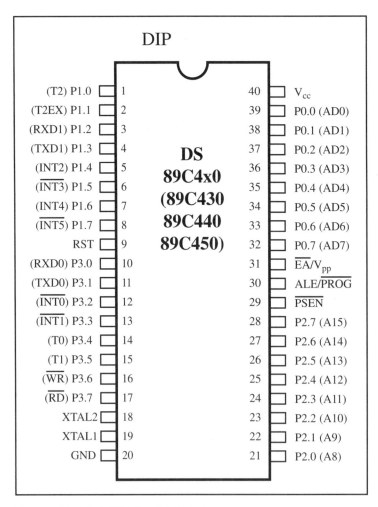

Figure 10-10. DS89C4x0 Pin Diagram
Note: Notice P1.2 and P1.3 pins are used by Rx and Tx lines of the second serial port.

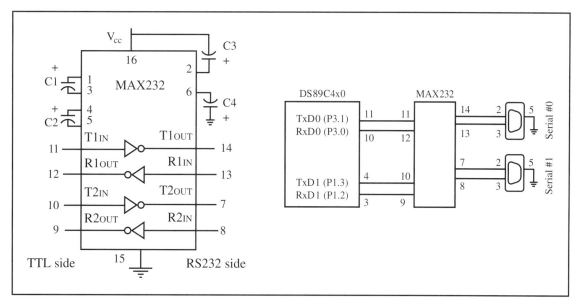

Figure 10-11. Inside MAX232 and Its Connection to the DS89C4x0

Addresses for all SCON and SBUF registers

All the programs we have seen so far in this chapter assume the use of the first serial port as the default serial port since every version of the 8051 comes with at least one serial port. The SCON, SBUF, and PCON registers of the 8051 are part of the special function registers. The address for each of the SFRs is shown in Table 10-6. Notice that SCON has address 98H, SBUF has address 99H, and finally PCON is assigned the 87H address. The first serial port is supported by all assemblers and C compilers in the market for the 8051. If you examine the list file for 8051 Assembly language programs, you will see that these labels are replaced with their SFR addresses. The second serial port is not implemented by all versions of the 8051/52 microprocessor. Only a few versions of the 8051/52, such as the DS89C4x0, come with the second serial port. As a result, the second serial port uses some reserved SFR addresses for the SCON and SBUF registers and there is no universal agreement among the makers as to which addresses should be used. In the case of the DS89C4x0, the SFR addresses of C0H and C1H are set aside for SBUF and SCON, as shown in Table 10-6. The DS89C4x0 technical documentation refers to these registers as SCON1 and SBUF1 since the first ones are designated as SCON0 and SBUF0.

Table 10-6. SFR Byte Addresses for DS89C4x0 Serial Ports

SFR	First Serial Port	Second Serial Port
SCON (byte address)	SCON0 = 98H	SCON1 = C0H
SBUF (byte address)	SBUF0 = 99H	SBUF1 = C1H
TL (byte address)	TL1 = 8BH	TL1 = 8BH
TH (byte address)	TH1 = 8DH	TH1 = 8DH
TCON (byte address)	TCON0 = 88H	TCON0 = 88H
PCON (byte address)	PCON = 87H	PCON = 87H

Table 10-7. SFR Addresses for the DS89C4x0

Symbol	Name	Address
ACC*	Accumulator	E0H
B*	B register	F0H
PSW*	Program status word	D0H
SP	Stack pointer	81H
DPTR	Data pointer 2 bytes	
DPL	Low byte	82H
DPH	High byte	83H
P0*	Port 0	80H
P1*	Port 1	90H
P2*	Port 2	0A0H
P3*	Port 3	B0H
IP*	Interrupt priority control	B8H
IE*	Interrupt enable control	A8H
TMOD	Timer/counter mode control	89H
TCON*	Timer/counter control	88H
T2CON*	Timer/counter 2 control	C8H
T2MOD	Timer/counter mode control	C9H
TH0	Timer/counter 0 high byte	8CH
TL0	Timer/counter 0 low byte	8AH
TH1	Timer/counter 1 high byte	8DH
TL1	Timer/counter 1 low byte	8BH
TH2	Timer/counter 2 high byte	CDH
TL2	Timer/counter 2 low byte	CCH
RCAP2H	T/C 2 capture register high byte	CBH
RCAP2L	T/C 2 capture register low byte	CAH
SCON0*	Serial control (first serial port)	98H
SBUF0	Serial data buffer (first serial port)	99H
PCON	Power control	87H
SCON1*	Serial control (second serial port)	C0H
SBUF1	Serial data buffer (second serial port)	C1H

* Bit-addressable

Programming the second serial port using timer 1

While each serial port has its own SCON and SBUF registers, both ports can use Timer 1 for setting the baud rate. Indeed, upon reset, the DS89C4x0 chip uses Timer 1 for setting the baud rate of both serial ports. Since the older 8051 assemblers do not support this new second serial port, we need to define

SM0	SM1	SM2	REN	TB8	RB8	TI	RI

Bits	**Bit Addresses**		
	Serial #0	**Serial #1**	
SM0	SCON0.7 = 9FH	SCON1.7 = C7H	Serial port mode specifier
SM1	SCON0.6 = 9EH	SCON1.6 = C6H	Serial port mode specifier
SM2	SCON0.5 = 9DH	SCON1.5 = C5H	Multiprocessor communication.
REN	SCON0.4 = 9CH	SCON1.4 = C4H	Enable/disable reception
TB8	SCON0.3 = 9BH	SCON1.3 = C3H	Not widely used
RB8	SCON0.2 = 9AH	SCON1.2 = C2H	Not widely used
TI	SCON0.1 = 99H	SCON1.1 = C1H	Transmit interrupt flag
RI	SCON0.0 = 98H	SCON1.0 = C0H	Receive interrupt flag
Note:	Make SM2, TB8, and RB8 = 0.		

Figure 10-12. SCON0 and SCON1 Bit Addresses (TI and RI Bits Must be Noted)

them as shown in Example 10-11. Notice that in both C and Assembly, SBUF and SCON refer to the SFR registers of the first serial port. To avoid confusion, in DS89C4x0 programs we use SCON0 and SBUF0 for the first and SCON1 and SBUF1 for the second serial ports. For this reason, the MDE8051 Trainer designates the serial ports as Serial #0 and Serial #1 in order to comply with this designation. See Examples 10-12 through 10-14.

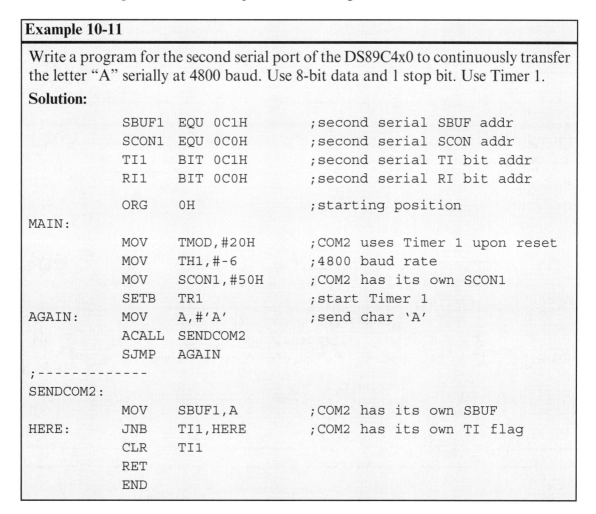

Example 10-11

Write a program for the second serial port of the DS89C4x0 to continuously transfer the letter "A" serially at 4800 baud. Use 8-bit data and 1 stop bit. Use Timer 1.

Solution:

```
          SBUF1   EQU   0C1H      ;second serial SBUF addr
          SCON1   EQU   0C0H      ;second serial SCON addr
          TI1     BIT   0C1H      ;second serial TI bit addr
          RI1     BIT   0C0H      ;second serial RI bit addr

          ORG     0H              ;starting position
MAIN:
          MOV     TMOD,#20H       ;COM2 uses Timer 1 upon reset
          MOV     TH1,#-6         ;4800 baud rate
          MOV     SCON1,#50H      ;COM2 has its own SCON1
          SETB    TR1             ;start Timer 1
AGAIN:    MOV     A,#'A'          ;send char 'A'
          ACALL   SENDCOM2
          SJMP    AGAIN

;-------------
SENDCOM2:
          MOV     SBUF1,A         ;COM2 has its own SBUF
HERE:     JNB     TI1,HERE        ;COM2 has its own TI flag
          CLR     TI1
          RET
          END
```

Example 10-12

Write a program to send the text string "Hello" to Serial #1. Set the baud rate at 9600, 8-bit data, and 1 stop bit.

Solution:

```
        SCON1  EQU  0C0H
        SBUF1  EQU  0C1H
        TI1    BIT  0C1H
        ORG    0H                  ;starting position
        MOV    TMOD,#20H
        MOV    TH1,#-3             ;9600 baud rate
        MOV    SCON1,#50H
        SETB   TR1
        MOV    DPTR,#MESS1         ;display "Hello"
FN:     CLR    A
        MOVC   A,@A+DPTR           ;read value
        JZ     S1                  ;check for end of line
        ACALL  SENDCOM2            ;send to serial port
        INC    DPTR                ;move to next value
        SJMP   FN
S1:     SJMP   S1
SENDCOM2:
        MOV    SBUF1,A             ;place value in buffer
HERE1:  JNB    TI1,HERE1           ;wait until transmitted
        CLR    TI1                 ;clear
        RET
MESS1:  DB     "Hello",0
        END
```

Example 10-13

Program the second serial port of the DS89C4x0 to receive bytes of data serially and put them on P1. Set the baud rate at 4800, 8-bit data, and 1 stop bit.

Solution:

```
        SBUF1 EQU 0C1H    ;second serial SBUF addr
        SCON1 EQU 0C0H    ;second serial SCON addr
        RI1 BIT 0C0H      ;second serial RI bit addr
        ORG 0H            ;starting position
        MOV TMOD,#20H     ;COM2 uses Timer 1 upon reset
        MOV TH1,#-6       ;4800 baud rate
        MOV SCON1,#50H    ;COM2 has its own SCON1
        SETB TR1          ;start Timer 1
HERE:   JNB RI1,HERE      ;wait for data to come in
        MOV A,SBUF1       ;save data
        MOV P1,A          ;display on P1
        CLR RI1
        SJMP HERE
        END
```

Example 10-14

Assume that a switch is connected to pin P2.0.
Write a program to monitor the switch and perform the following:
   (a) If sw = 0, send the message "Hello" to the Serial #0 port.
   (b) If sw = 1, send the message "Goodbye" to the Serial #1 port.

Solution:

```
          SCON1  EQU  0C0H
          TI1    BIT  0C1H
          SW1    BIT  P2.0
          ORG    0H                  ;starting position
          MOV    TMOD,#20H
          MOV    TH1,#-3             ;9600 baud rate
          MOV    SCON,#50H
          MOV    SCON1,#50H
          SETB   TR1
          SETB   SW1                 ;make SW1 an input
S1:       JB     SW1,NEXT            ;check SW1 status
          MOV    DPTR,#MESS1         ;if SW1=0 display "Hello"
FN:       CLR    A
          MOVC   A,@A+DPTR           ;read value
          JZ     S1                  ;check for end of line
          ACALL  SENDCOM1            ;send to serial port
          INC    DPTR                ;move to next value
          SJMP   FN
NEXT:     MOV    DPTR,#MESS2         ;if SW1=1 display "Goodbye"
LN:       CLR    A
          MOVC   A,@A+DPTR           ;read value
          JZ     S1                  ;check for end of line
          ACALL  SENDCOM2            ;send to serial port
          INC    DPTR                ;move to next value
          SJMP   LN

SENDCOM1:
          MOV    SBUF,A              ;place value in buffer
HERE:     JNB    TI,HERE            ;wait until transmitted
          CLR    TI                  ;clear
          RET

SENDCOM2:
          MOV    SBUF1,A             ;place value in buffer
HERE1:    JNB    TI1,HERE1          ;wait until transmitted
          CLR    TI1                 ;clear
          RET

MESS1:    DB     "Hello",0
MESS2:    DB     "Goodbye",0
          END
```

REVIEW QUESTIONS

(All questions refer to the DS89C4x0 chip.)
1. Upon reset, which timer is used to set the baud rate for Serial #0 and Serial #1?
2. Which pins are used for the second serial ports?
3. With XTAL = 11.0592 MHz, what value should be loaded into TH1 to have a 28,800 baud rate? Give the answer in both decimal and hex.
4. To transfer a byte of data via the second serial port, it must be placed in register _____.
5. SCON1 refers to _____ and it is a(n) ____-bit register.
6. Which register is used to set the data size and other framing information such as the stop bit for the second serial port?

10.5: SERIAL PORT PROGRAMMING IN C

This section shows C programming of the serial ports for the 8051/52 and DS89C4x0 chips.

Transmitting and receiving data in 8051 C

As we stated in the last chapter, the SFR registers of the 8051 are accessible directly in 8051 C compilers by using the reg51.h file. Examples 10-15 through 10-19 show how to program the serial port in 8051 C. Connect your 8051 Trainer to the PC's COM port and use HyperTerminal to test the operation of these examples.

Example 10-15

Write a C program for the 8051 to transfer the letter "A" serially at 4800 baud continuously. Use 8-bit data and 1 stop bit.

Solution:
```
#include <reg51.h>
void main(void)
  {
    TMOD=0x20;              //use Timer 1,8-BIT auto-reload
    TH1=0xFA;              //4800 baud rate
    SCON=0x50;
    TR1=1;
    while(1)
      {
        SBUF='A';          //place value in buffer
        while(TI==0);
        TI=0;
      }
  }
```

Example 10-16

Write an 8051 C program to transfer the message "YES" serially at 9600 baud, 8-bit data, 1 stop bit. Do this continuously.

Solution:

```c
#include <reg51.h>
void SerTx(unsigned char);
void main(void)
  {
    TMOD=0x20;            //use Timer 1,8-BIT auto-reload
    TH1=0xFD;            //9600 baud rate
    SCON=0x50;
    TR1=1;               //start timer
    while(1)
      {
        SerTx('Y');
        SerTx('E');
        SerTx('S');
      }
  }
void SerTx(unsigned char x)
  {
    SBUF=x;              //place value in buffer
    while(TI==0);        //wait until transmitted
    TI=0;
  }
```

Example 10-17

Program the 8051 in C to receive bytes of data serially and put them in P1. Set the baud rate at 4800, 8-bit data, and 1 stop bit.

Solution:

```c
#include <reg51.h>
void main (void)
  {
    unsigned char mybyte;
    TMOD=0x20;                       //use Timer 1,8-BIT auto-reload
    TH1=0xFA;                       //4800 baud rate
    SCON=0x50;
    TR1=1;                          //start timer
    while(1)                        //repeat forever
      {
        while(RI==0);               //wait to receive
        mybyte=SBUF;                //save value
        P1=mybyte;                  //write value to port
        RI=0;
      }
  }
```

Example 10-18

Write an 8051 C program to send two different strings to the serial port. Assuming that sw is connected to pin P2.0, monitor its status and make a decision as follows:
  If sw = 0, send your first name
  If sw = 1, send your last name
Assume XTAL = 11.0592 MHz, baud rate of 9600, 8-bit data, 1 stop bit.

Solution:

```c
#include <reg51.h>
sbit MYSW=P2^0;                     //input switch
void main(void)
  {
    unsigned char z;
    unsigned char fname[]="ALI";
    unsigned char lname[]="SMITH";
    TMOD=0x20;                      //use Timer 1,8-BIT auto-reload
    TH1=0xFD;                       //9600 baud rate
    SCON=0x50;
    TR1=1;                          //start timer
    if(MYSW==0)                     //check switch
      {
        for(z=0;z<3;z++)            //write name
          {
            SBUF=fname[z];          //place value in buffer
            while(TI==0);           //wait for transmit
            TI=0;
          }
      }
    else
      {
        for(z=0;z<5;z++)            //write name
          {
            SBUF=lname[z];          //place value in buffer
            while(TI==0);           //wait for transmit
            TI=0;
          }
      }
  }
```

Example 10-19

Write an 8051 C program to send the two messages "Normal Speed" and "High Speed" to the serial port. Assuming that sw is connected to pin P2.0, monitor its status and set the baud rate as follows:

sw = 0, 28,800 baud rate

sw = 1, 56K baud rate

Assume that XTAL = 11.0592 MHz for both cases.

Solution:

```
#include <reg51.h>
sbit MYSW=P2^0;                         //input switch
void main(void)
  {
    unsigned char z;
    unsigned char Mess1[]="Normal Speed";
    unsigned char Mess2[]="High Speed";
    TMOD=0x20;                          //use Timer 1,8-BIT auto-reload
    TH1=0xFF;                           //28,800 for normal speed
    SCON=0x50;
    TR1=1;                              //start timer
    if(MYSW==0)
      {
        for(z=0;z<12;z++)
          {
            SBUF=Mess1[z];              //place value in buffer
            while(TI==0);              //wait for transmit
            TI=0;
          }
      }
    else
      {
        PCON=PCON|0x80;                 //for high speed of 56K
        for(z=0;z<10;z++)
          {
            SBUF=Mess2[z];              //place value in buffer
            while(TI==0);              //wait for transmit
            TI=0;
          }
      }
  }
```

8051 C compilers and the second serial port

Since many C compilers do not support the second serial port of the DS89C4x0 chip, we have to declare the byte addresses of the new SFR registers using the sfr keyword. Table 10-6 and Figure 10-12 provide the SFR byte and bit addresses for the DS89C4x0 chip. Examples 10-20 and 10-21 show C versions of Examples 10-11 and 10-13 in Section 10.4.

Notice in both Examples 10-20 and 10-21 that we are using Timer 1 to set the baud rate for the second serial port. Upon reset, Timer 1 is the default for the second serial port of the DS89C4x0 chip.

Example 10-20

Write a C program for the DS89C4x0 to transfer letter "A" serially at 4800 baud continuously. Use the second serial port with 8-bit data and 1 stop bit. We can only use Timer 1 to set the baud rate.

Solution:

```
#include <reg51.h>
sfr SBUF1=0xC1;
sfr SCON1=0xC0;
sbit TI1=0xC1;
void main(void)
    {
    TMOD=0x20;              //use Timer 1 for 2nd serial port
    TH1=0xFA;               //4800 baud rate
    SCON1=0x50;             //use 2nd serial port SCON1 register
    TR1=1;                  //start timer
    while(1)
        {
        SBUF1='A';          //use 2nd serial port SBUF1 register
        while(TI1==0);      //wait for transmit
        TI1=0;
        }
    }
```

Example 10-21

Program the DS89C4x0 in C to receive bytes of data serially via the second serial port and put them in P1. Set the baud rate at 9600, 8-bit data, and 1 stop bit. Use Timer 1 for baud rate generation.

Solution:

```c
#include <reg51.h>
sfr SBUF1=0xC1;
sfr SCON1=0xC0;
sbit RI1=0xC0;
void main(void)
  {
    unsigned char mybyte;
    TMOD=0x20;            //use Timer 1,8-BIT auto-reload
    TH1=0xFD;             //9600
    SCON1=0x50;          //use SCON1 of 2nd serial port
    TR1=1;
    while(1)
      {
        while(RI1==0);   //monitor RI1 of 2nd serial port
        mybyte=SBUF1;    //use SBUF1 of 2nd serial port
        P2=mybyte;       //place value on port
        RI1=0;
      }
  }
```

REVIEW QUESTIONS

1. How are the SFR registers accessed in C?
2. True or false. C compilers support the second serial port of the DS89C4x0 chip.
3. Registers SBUF and SCON are declared in C using the _____ keyword.

SUMMARY

This chapter began with an introduction to the fundamentals of serial communication. Serial communication, in which data is sent one bit a time, is used when data is sent over significant distances since in parallel communication, where data is sent a byte or more a time, great distances can cause distortion of the data. Serial communication has the additional advantage of allowing transmission over phone lines. Serial communication uses two methods: synchronous and asynchronous. In synchronous communication, data is sent in blocks of bytes; in asynchronous, data is sent in bytes. Data communication can be simplex (can send but cannot receive), half duplex (can send and receive, but not at the same time), or full duplex (can send and receive at the same time). RS232 is a standard for serial communication connectors.

The 8051's UART was discussed. We showed how to interface the 8051 with an RS232 connector and change the baud rate of the 8051. In addition, we described the serial communication features of the 8051, and programmed the 8051 for serial data communication. We also showed how to program the second serial port of the DS89C4x0 chip in Assembly and C.

PROBLEMS

10.1: BASICS OF SERIAL COMMUNICATION

1. Which is more expensive, parallel or serial data transfer?
2. True or false. 0- and 5-V digital pulses can be transferred on the telephone without being converted (modulated).
3. Show the framing of the letter ASCII "Z" (0101 1010), no parity, 1 stop bit.
4. If there is no data transfer and the line is high, it is called _____ (mark, space).
5. True or false. The stop bit can be 1, 2, or none at all.
6. Calculate the overhead percentage if the data size is 7, 1 stop bit, no parity.
7. True or false. The RS232 voltage specification is TTL compatible.
8. What is the function of the MAX 232 chip?
9. True or false. DB-25 and DB-9 are pin compatible for the first 9 pins.
10. How many pins of the RS232 are used by the IBM serial cable, and why?
11. True or false. The longer the cable, the higher the data transfer baud rate.
12. State the absolute minimum number of signals needed to transfer data between two PCs connected serially. What are those signals?
13. If two PCs are connected through the RS232 without the modem, they are both configured as a _____ (DTE, DCE) -to- _____ (DTE, DCE) connection.
14. State the nine most important signals of the RS232.
15. Calculate the total number of bits transferred if 200 pages of ASCII data are sent using asynchronous serial data transfer. Assume a data size of 8 bits, 1 stop bit, and no parity. Assume each page has 80x25 of text characters.
16. In Problem 15, how long will the data transfer take if the baud rate is 9,600?

10.2: 8051 CONNECTION TO RS232

17. The MAX232 DIP package has _____ pins.
18. For the MAX232, indicate the V_{cc} and GND pins.
19. The MAX233 DIP package has ____ pins.
20. For the MAX233, indicate the V_{cc} and GND pins.
21. Is the MAX232 pin compatible with the MAX233?
22. State the advantages and disadvantages of the MAX232 and MAX233.
23. MAX232/233 has ____ line driver(s) for the RxD wire.
24. MAX232/233 has ____ line driver(s) for the TxD wire.
25. Show the connection of pins TxD and RxD of the 8051 to a DB-9 RS232 connector via the second set of line drivers of MAX232.
26. Show the connection of the TxD and RxD pins of the 8051 to a DB-9 RS232 connector via the second set of line drivers of MAX233.

27. Show the connection of the TxD and RxD pins of the 8051 to a DB-25 RS232 connector via MAX232.

28. Show the connection of the TxD and RxD pins of the 8051 to a DB-25 RS232 connector via MAX233.

10.3: 8051 SERIAL PORT PROGRAMMING IN ASSEMBLY

29. Which of the following baud rates are supported by the BIOS of 486/ Pentium PCs?
    (a) 4,800   (b) 3,600   (c) 9,600
    (d) 1,800   (e) 1,200   (f) 19,200

30. Which timer of the 8051 is used for baud rate programming?

31. Which mode of the timer is used for baud rate programming?

32. What is the role of the SBUF register in serial data transfer?

33. SBUF is a(n) ____-bit register.

34. What is the role of the SCON register in serial data transfer?

35. SCON is a(n) ____-bit register.

36. For XTAL = 11.0592 MHz, find the TH1 value (in both decimal and hex) for each of the following baud rates.
    (a) 9,600   (b) 4,800   (c) 1,200   (d) 300   (e) 150

37. What is the baud rate if we use "MOV TH1,#-1" to program the baud rate?

38. Write an 8051 program to transfer serially the letter "Z" continuously at a 1,200 baud rate.

39. Write an 8051 program to transfer serially the message "The earth is but one country and mankind its citizens" continuously at a 57,600 baud rate.

40. When is the TI flag bit raised?

41. When is the RI flag bit raised?

42. To which register do RI and TI belong? Is that register bit-addressable?

43. What is the role of the REN bit in the SCON register?

44. In a given situation we cannot accept reception of any serial data. How do you block such a reception with a single instruction?

45. To which register does the SMOD bit belong? State its role in the rate of data transfer.

46. Is the SMOD bit high or low when the 8051 is powered up?

In the following questions, the baud rates are not compatible with the COM ports of the PC (x86 IBM/compatible).

47. Find the baud rate for the following if XTAL = 16 MHz and SMOD = 0.
    (a) MOV TH1,#-10   (b) MOV TH1,#-25
    (c) MOV TH1,#-200   (d) MOV TH1,#-180

48. Find the baud rate for the following if XTAL = 24 MHz and SMOD = 0.
    (a) MOV TH1,#-15   (b) MOV TH1,#-24
    (c) MOV TH1,#-100   (d) MOV TH1,#-150

49. Find the baud rate for the following if XTAL = 16 MHz and SMOD = 1.
    (a) MOV TH1,#-10   (b) MOV TH1,#-25
    (c) MOV TH1,#-200   (d) MOV TH1,#-180

50. Find the baud rate for the following if XTAL = 24 MHz and SMOD = 1.
    (a) MOV TH1,#-15   (b) MOV TH1,#-24
    (c) MOV TH1,#-100   (d) MOV TH1,#-150

10.4: PROGRAMMING THE SECOND SERIAL PORT

51. Upon reset, which timer of the 8051 is used?
52. Which timer of the DS89C4x0 is used to set the baud rate for the second serial port?
53. Which mode of the timer is used for baud rate programming of the second serial port?
54. What is the role of the SBUF1 register in serial data transfer?
55. SBUF1 is a(n) ____-bit register.
56. What is the role of the SCON1 register in serial data transfer?
57. SCON1 is a(n) ____-bit register.
58. For XTAL = 11.0592 MHz, find the TH1 value (in both decimal and hex) for each of the following baud rates.
    (a) 9,600   (b) 4,800   (c) 1,200   (d) 300   (e) 150
59. Write a program for DS89C4x0 to transfer serially the letter "Z" continuously at a 1,200 baud rate. Use the second serial port.
60. Write a program for DS89C4x0 to transfer serially the message "The earth is but one country and mankind its citizens" continuously at a 57,600 baud rate. Use the second serial port.
61. When is the TI1 flag bit raised?

10.5: SERIAL PORT PROGRAMMING IN C

62. Write an 8051 C program to transfer serially the letter "Z" continuously at a 1,200 baud rate.
63. Write an 8051 C program to transfer serially the message "The earth is but one country and mankind its citizens" continuously at a 57,600 baud rate.
64. Write a C program for DS89C4z0 to transfer serially the letter "Z" continuously at a 1,200 baud rate. Use the second serial port.
65. Write a C program for the DS89C4x0 to transfer serially the message "The earth is but one country and mankind its citizens" continuously at a 57,600 baud rate. Use the second serial port.

ANSWERS TO REVIEW QUESTIONS

10.1: BASICS OF SERIAL COMMUNICATION

1. Faster, more expensive
2. False; it is simplex.
3. True
4. Asynchronous
5. With 0100 0101 binary, the bits are transmitted in the sequence:
   (a) 0 (start bit) (b) 1 (c) 0 (d) 1 (e) 0 (f) 0 (g) 0 (h) 1 (i) 0 (j) 1 (stop bit)
6. 2 bits (one for the start bit and one for the stop bit). Therefore, for each 8-bit character, a total of 10 bits is transferred.

7. $10000 \times 10 = 100000$ bits total bits transmitted. $100000 / 9600 = 10.4$ seconds; $2 / 10 = 20\%$.
8. True
9. +3 to +25 V
10. True
11. 2
12. COM 1 and COM 2

10.2: 8051 CONNECTION TO RS232

1. True
2. Pins 10 and 11. Pin 11 is for TxD and pin 10 for RxD.
3. They are used for converting from RS232 voltage levels to TTL voltage levels and vice versa.
4. 2, 2
5. It does not need the four capacitors that MAX232 must have.

10.3: 8051 SERIAL PORT PROGRAMMING IN ASSEMBLY

1. Timer 1
2. 28,800 Hz
3. Mode 2
4. −3 or FDH since $28,800/3 = 9,600$
5. SBUF
6. Serial control, 8
7. SCON
8. True
9. During transfer of stop bit
10. PCON; it is low upon RESET.

10.4: PROGRAMMING THE SECOND SERIAL PORT

1. Timer 1
2. Pins P1.2 and P1.3
3. −1 of FFH
4. SBUF1
5. Serial control 1, 8
6. SCON1

10.5: SERIAL PORT PROGRAMMING IN C

1. By using the `reg51.h` file
2. False
3. sfr

CHAPTER 11

INTERRUPTS PROGRAMMING IN ASSEMBLY AND C

OBJECTIVES

Upon completion of this chapter, you will be able to:

>> Contrast and compare interrupts versus polling.
>> Explain the purpose of the ISR (interrupt service routine).
>> List the six interrupts of the 8051.
>> Explain the purpose of the interrupt vector table.
>> Enable or disable 8051/52 interrupts.
>> Program the 8051/52 timers using interrupts.
>> Describe the external hardware interrupts of the 8051/52.
>> Contrast edge-triggered with level-triggered interrupts.
>> Program the 8051 for interrupt-based serial communication.
>> Define the interrupt priority of the 8051.
>> Program 8051/52 interrupts in C.

In this chapter, we explore the concept of the interrupt and interrupt programming. In Section 11.1, the basics of 8051 interrupts are discussed. In Section 11.2, interrupts belonging to Timers 0 and 1 are discussed. External hardware interrupts are discussed in Section 11.3, while the interrupt related to serial communication is presented in Section 11.4. In Section 11.5, we cover interrupt priority in the 8051/52. Finally, C programming of 8051 interrupts is covered in Section 11.6.

11.1: 8051 INTERRUPTS

In this section, first we examine the difference between polling and interrupts and then describe the various interrupts of the 8051.

Interrupts versus polling

A single microprocessor can serve several devices. There are two ways to do that: interrupts or polling. In the *interrupt* method, whenever any device needs its service, the device notifies the microprocessor by sending it an interrupt signal. Upon receiving an interrupt signal, the microprocessor interrupts whatever it is doing and serves the device. The program associated with the interrupt is called the *interrupt service routine* (ISR) or *interrupt handler*. In *polling*, the microprocessor continuously monitors the status of a given device; when the status condition is met, it performs the service. After that, it moves on to monitor the next device until each one is serviced. Although polling can monitor the status of several devices and serve each of them as certain conditions are met, it is not an efficient use of the microprocessor. The advantage of interrupts is that the microprocessor can serve many devices (not all at the same time, of course); each device can get the attention of the microprocessor based on the priority assigned to it. The polling method cannot assign priority since it checks all devices in a round-robin fashion. More importantly, in the interrupt method the microprocessor can also ignore (mask) a device request for service. This is again not possible with the polling method. The most important reason that the interrupt method is preferable is that the polling method wastes much of the microprocessor's time by polling devices that do not need service. So in order to avoid tying down the microprocessor, interrupts are used. For example, in discussing timers in Chapter 9, we used the instruction "JNB TF, target", and waited until the timer rolled over, and while we were waiting we could not do anything else. That is a waste of the microprocessor's time that could have been used to perform some useful tasks. In the case of the timer, if we use the interrupt method, the microprocessor can go about doing other tasks, and when the TF flag is raised the timer will interrupt the microprocessor in whatever it is doing.

Interrupt service routine

For every interrupt, there must be an interrupt service routine (ISR), or interrupt handler. When an interrupt is invoked, the microprocessor runs the interrupt service routine. For every interrupt, there is a fixed location in memory that holds the address of its ISR. The group of memory locations set aside to hold the addresses of ISRs is called the interrupt vector table, shown in Table 11-1.

Steps in executing an interrupt

Upon activation of an interrupt, the microprocessor goes through the following steps.

1. It finishes the instruction it is executing and saves the address of the next instruction (PC) on the stack.

2. It also saves the current status of all the interrupts internally (i.e., not on the stack).

3. It jumps to a fixed location in memory called the interrupt vector table that holds the address of the interrupt service routine.

4. The microprocessor gets the address of the ISR from the interrupt vector table and jumps to it. It starts to execute the interrupt service subroutine until it reaches the last instruction of the subroutine, which is RETI (return from interrupt).

5. Upon executing the RETI instruction, the microprocessor returns to the place where it was interrupted. First, it gets the program counter (PC) address from the stack by popping the top two bytes of the stack into the PC. Then it starts to execute from that address.

Notice from Step 5 the critical role of the stack. For this reason, we must be careful in manipulating the stack contents in the ISR. Specifically, in the ISR, just as in any CALL subroutine, the number of pushes and pops must be equal.

Six interrupts in the 8051

In reality, only five interrupts are available to the user in the 8051, but many manufacturers' data sheets state that there are six interrupts since they include reset. The six interrupts in the 8051 are allocated as follows.

1. Reset. When the reset pin is activated, the 8051 jumps to address location 0000. This is the power-up reset discussed in Chapter 4.

Table 11-1. Interrupt Vector Table for the 8051

Interrupt	ROM Location (Hex)	Pin	Flag Clearing
Reset	0000	9	Auto
External hardware interrupt 0 (INT0)	0003	P3.2 (12)	Auto
Timer 0 interrupt (TF0)	000B		Auto
External hardware interrupt 1 (INT1)	0013	P3.3 (13)	Auto
Timer 1 interrupt (TF1)	001B		Auto
Serial COM interrupt (RI and TI)	0023		Programmer clears it

2. Two interrupts are set aside for the timers: one for Timer 0 and one for Timer 1. Memory locations 000BH and 001BH in the interrupt vector table belong to Timer 0 and Timer 1, respectively.

3. Two interrupts are set aside for hardware external hardware interrupts. Pin numbers 12 (P3.2) and 13 (P3.3) in port 3 are for the external hardware interrupts INT0 and INT1, respectively. These external interrupts are also referred to as EX1 and EX2. Memory locations 0003H and 0013H in the interrupt vector table are assigned to INT0 and INT1, respectively.

4. Serial communication has a single interrupt that belongs to both receive and transmit. The interrupt vector table location 0023H belongs to this interrupt.

Notice in Table 11-1 that a limited number of bytes is set aside for each interrupt. For example, a total of 8 bytes from location 0003 to 0000A is set aside for INT0, external hardware interrupt 0. Similarly, a total of 8 bytes from location 000BH to 0012H is reserved for TF0, Timer 0 interrupt. If the service routine for a given interrupt is short enough to fit in the memory space allocated to it, it is placed in the vector table; otherwise, an LJMP instruction is placed in the vector table to point to the address of the ISR. In that case, the rest of the bytes allocated to that interrupt are unused. In the next three sections, we will see many examples of interrupt programming that clarify these concepts.

From Table 11-1, also notice that only three bytes of ROM space are assigned to the reset pin. They are ROM address locations 0, 1, and 2. Address location 3 belongs to external hardware interrupt 0. For this reason, in our program we put the LJMP as the first instruction and redirect the processor away from the interrupt vector table, as shown in Figure 11-1. In the next section, we will see how this works in the context of some examples.

Enabling and disabling an interrupt

Upon reset, all interrupts are disabled (masked), meaning that none will be responded to by the microprocessor if they are activated. The interrupts must be enabled by software in order for the microprocessor to respond

```
          ORG   0     ;wake-up ROM reset location
          LJMP MAIN ;bypass interrupt vector table

;---- the wake-up program
          ORG   30H
MAIN:

          ....
          END
```

Figure 11-1. Redirecting the 8051 from the Interrupt Vector Table at Power-up

D7							D0
EA	--	ET2	ES	ET1	EX1	ET0	EX0

EA   IE.7   Disables all interrupts. If EA = 0, no interrupt is acknowledged. If EA = 1, each interrupt source is individually enabled or disabled by setting or clearing its enable bit.

--   IE.6   Not implemented, reserved for future use.*

ET2   IE.5   Enables or disables Timer 2 overflow or capture interrupt (8052 only).

ES   IE.4   Enables or disables the serial port interrupt.

ET1   IE.3   Enables or disables Timer 1 overflow interrupt.

EX1   IE.2   Enables or disables external interrupt 1.

ET0   IE.1   Enables or disables Timer 0 overflow interrupt.

EX0   IE.0   Enables or disables external interrupt 0.

Figure 11-2. IE (Interrupt Enable) Register
*User software should not write 1s to reserved bits. These bits may be used in future flash microprocessors to invoke new features.

to them. There is a register called IE (interrupt enable) that is responsible for enabling (unmasking) and disabling (masking) the interrupts. Figure 11-2 shows the IE register. Note that IE is a bit-addressable register.

From Figure 11-2, notice that bit D7 in the IE register is called EA (enable all). This must be set to 1 in order for the rest of the register to take effect. D6 is unused. D5 is used by the 8052. The D4 bit is for the serial interrupt, and so on.

Steps in enabling an interrupt

To enable an interrupt, we take the following steps:

1. Bit D7 of the IE register (EA) must be set to high to allow the rest of the register to take effect.

2. If EA = 1, interrupts are enabled and will be responded to if their corresponding bits in IE are high. If EA = 0, no interrupt will be responded to, even if the associated bit in the IE register is high.

To understand this important point, look at Example 11-1.

Show the instructions to (a) enable the serial interrupt, Timer 0 interrupt, and external hardware interrupt 1 (EX1), and (b) disable (mask) the Timer 0 interrupt, then (c) show how to disable all the interrupts with a single instruction.

Solution:

```
(a)    MOV IE,#10010110B    ;enable serial, Timer 0, EX1
```
Since IE is a bit-addressable register, we can use the following instructions to access individual bits of the register.
```
(b)    CLR IE.1             ;mask(disable) Timer 0 interrupt only
(c)    CLR IE.7             ;disable all interrupts
```
Another way to perform the "MOV IE,#10010110B" instruction is by using single-bit instructions as shown below.
```
SETB IE.7          ;EA=1, Global enable
SETB IE.4          ;enable serial interrupt
SETB IE.1          ;enable Timer 0 interrupt
SETB IE.2          ;enable EX1
```

REVIEW QUESTIONS

1. Of the interrupt and polling methods, which one avoids tying down the microprocessor?
2. Besides reset, how many interrupts do we have in the 8051?
3. In the 8051, what memory area is assigned to the interrupt vector table? Can the programmer change the memory space assigned to the table?
4. What are the contents of register IE upon reset, and what do these contents mean?
5. Show the instruction to enable the EX0 and Timer 0 interrupts.
6. Which pin of the 8051 is assigned to the external hardware interrupt INT1?
7. What address in the interrupt vector table is assigned to the INT1 and Timer 1 interrupts?

11.2: PROGRAMMING TIMER INTERRUPTS

In Chapter 9 we discussed how to use Timer 0 and Timer 1 with the polling method. In this section, we use interrupts to program the 8051 timers. Please review Chapter 9 before you study this section.

Roll-over timer flag and interrupt

In Chapter 9 we stated that the timer flag (TF) is raised when the timer rolls over. In that chapter, we also showed how to monitor TF with the instruction "JNB TF, target". In polling TF, we have to wait until the TF is raised. The problem with this method is that the microprocessor is tied down while waiting for TF to be raised and cannot do any thing else.

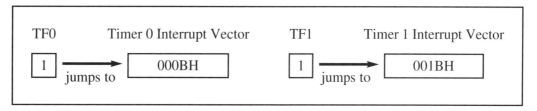

Figure 11-3. TF Interrupt

Using interrupts solves this problem and avoids tying down the controller. If the timer interrupt in the IE register is enabled, whenever the timer rolls over, TF is raised, and the microprocessor is interrupted in whatever it is doing, and jumps to the interrupt vector table to service the ISR. In this way, the microprocessor can do other things until it is notified that the timer has rolled over. See Figure 11-3 and Example 11-2.

    Notice the following points about the program in Example 11-2.

1. We must avoid using the memory space allocated to the interrupt vector table. Therefore, we place all the initialization codes in memory starting at

---

Example 11-2

Write a program that continuously gets 8-bit data from P0 and sends it to P1 while simultaneously creating a square wave of 200 μs period on pin P2.1. Use Timer 0 to create the square wave. Assume that XTAL = 11.0592 MHz.

Solution:

We will use Timer 0 in mode 2 (auto-reload). TH0 = 100/1.085 μs = 92.

```
;--Upon wake-up go to main, avoid using memory space ;allocat-
ed to Interrupt Vector Table
        ORG   0000H
        LJMP  MAIN          ;bypass interrupt vector table
;
;--ISR for Timer 0 to generate square wave
        ORG   000BH         ;Timer 0 interrupt vector table
        CPL   P2.1          ;toggle P2.1 pin
        RETI                ;return from ISR
;
;--The main program for initialization
        ORG   0030H         ;after vector table space
MAIN:   MOV   TMOD,#02H     ;Timer 0, mode 2(auto-reload)
        MOV   P0,#0FFH      ;make P0 an input port
        MOV   TH0,#-92      ;TH0=A4H for -92
        MOV   IE,#82H       ;IE=10000010(bin) enable Timer 0
        SETB  TR0           ;Start Timer 0
BACK:   MOV   A,P0          ;get data from P0
        MOV   P1,A          ;issue it to P1
        SJMP  BACK          ;keep doing it
                            ;loop unless interrupted by TF0
        END
```

30H. The LJMP instruction is the first instruction that the 8051 executes when it is powered up. LJMP redirects the controller away from the interrupt vector table.

2. The ISR for Timer 0 is located starting at memory location 000BH since it is small enough to fit the address space allocated to this interrupt.

3. We enabled the Timer 0 interrupt with "MOV IE,#10000010B" in MAIN.

4. While the P0 data is brought in and issued to P1 continuously, whenever Timer 0 is rolled over, the TF0 flag is raised, and the microprocessor gets out of the "BACK" loop and goes to 0000BH to execute the ISR associated with Timer 0.

5. In the ISR for Timer 0, notice that there is no need for a "CLR TF0" instruction before the RETI instruction. This is because the 8051 clears the TF flag internally upon jumping to the interrupt vector table.

In Example 11-2, the interrupt service routine was short enough that it could be placed in memory locations allocated to the Timer 0 interrupt. However, that is not always the case. See Example 11-3.

Notice that the low portion of the pulse is created by the 14 MC (machine cycles) where each MC = 1.085 μs and 14 × 1.085 μs = 15.19 μs.

REVIEW QUESTIONS

1. True or false. There is only a single interrupt in the interrupt vector table assigned to both Timer 0 and Timer 1.
2. What address in the interrupt vector table is assigned to Timer 0?
3. Which bit of IE belongs to the timer interrupt? Show how both are enabled.
4. Assume that Timer 1 is programmed in mode 2, TH1 = F5H, and the IE bit for Timer 1 is enabled. Explain how the interrupt for the timer works.
5. True or false. The last two instructions of the ISR for Timer 0 are:

```
CLR  TF0
RETI
```

11.3: PROGRAMMING EXTERNAL HARDWARE INTERRUPTS

The 8051 has two external hardware interrupts. Pin 12 (P3.2) and pin 13 (P3.3) of the 8051, designated as INT0 and INT1, are used as external hardware interrupts. Upon activation of these pins, the 8051 gets interrupted in whatever it is doing and jumps to the vector table to perform the interrupt service routine. In this section, we study these two external hardware interrupts of the 8051 with some examples.

Example 11-3

Rewrite Example 11-2 to create a square wave that has a high portion of 1085 μs and a low portion of 15 μs. Assume XTAL = 11.0592 MHz. Use Timer 1.

Solution:

Since 1085 μs is 1000 × 1.085, we need to use mode 1 of Timer 1.

```
;--Upon wake-up go to main, avoid using memory space
;--allocated to Interrupt Vector Table
          ORG   0000H
          LJMP  MAIN          ;bypass interrupt vector table
;
;--ISR for Timer 1 to generate square wave
          ORG   001BH         ;Timer 1 interrupt vector table
      LJMP  ISR_T1        ;jump to ISR
;
;--The main program for initialization
          ORG   0030H         ;after vector table
MAIN:     MOV   TMOD,#10H     ;Timer 1, mode 1
          MOV   P0,#0FFH      ;make P0 an input port
          MOV   TL1,#018H     ;TL1=18 the Low byte of -1000
          MOV   TH1,#0FCH     ;TH1=FC the High byte of -1000
          MOV   IE,#88H       ;IE=10001000 enable Timer 1 int.
          SETB  TR1           ;start Timer 1
BACK:     MOV   A,P0          ;get data from P0
          MOV   P1,A          ;issue it to P1
          SJMP  BACK          ;keep doing it
;
;--Timer 1 ISR. Must be reloaded since not auto-reload
ISR_T1:   CLR   TR1           ;stop Timer 1
          CLR   P2.1          ;P2.1=0, start of low portion
          MOV   R2,#4         ;                         2 MC
HERE:     DJNZ  R2,HERE       ;4x2 machine cycle(MC)    8 MC
          MOV   TL1,#18H      ;load T1 Low byte value   2 MC
          MOV   TH1,#0FCH     ;load T1 High byte value  2 MC
          SETB  TR1           ;starts Timer 1           1 MC
          SETB  P2.1          ;P2.1=1, back to high     1 MC
          RETI                ;return to main
          END
```

External interrupts INT0 and INT1

There are only two external hardware interrupts in the 8051: INT0 and INT1. They are located on pins P3.2 and P3.3 of port 3, respectively. The interrupt vector table locations 0003H and 0013H are set aside for INT0 and INT1, respectively. See Figure 11-4. As mentioned in Section 11.1, they are enabled and disabled using the IE register. How are they activated? There are two types of activation for the external hardware interrupts: (1) level triggered and (2) edge triggered. Let's look at each one. First, we see how the level-triggered interrupt works. See Example 11-4.

Example 11-4

Write a program to generate a square wave of 50 Hz frequency on pin P1.2. This is similar to Example 9-12 except that it uses an interrupt for Timer 0. Assume that XTAL = 11.0592 MHz.

Solution:

```
                ORG   0
                LJMP  MAIN
                ORG   000BH           ;ISR for Timer 0
                CPL   P1.2            ;complement P1.2
                MOV   TL0,#00         ;reload timer values
                MOV   TH0,#0DCH
                RETI                  ;return from interrupt
                ORG   30H             ;starting location for prog.
;------main program for initialization
MAIN:           MOV   TMOD,#00000001B ;Timer 0, Mode 1
                MOV   TL0,#00
                MOV   TH0,#0DCH
                MOV   IE,#82H          ;enable Timer 0 interrupt
                SETB  TR0              ;start timer
HERE:           SJMP  HERE             ;stay here until interrupted
                END
```

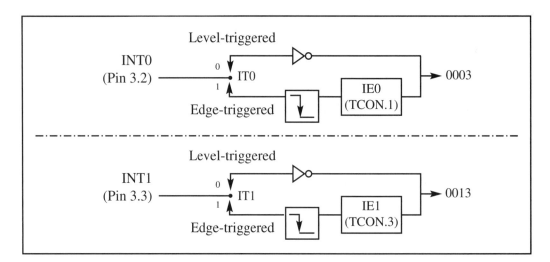

Figure 11-4. Activation of INT0 and INT1

Level-triggered interrupt

In the level-triggered mode, INT0 and INT1 pins are normally high (just like all I/O port pins) and if a low-level signal is applied to them, it triggers the interrupt. Then the microprocessor stops whatever it is doing and jumps to the interrupt vector table to service that interrupt. This is called a *level-triggered* or *level-activated* interrupt and is the default mode upon reset of the 8051. The low-level signal at the INT pin must be removed before the execution of the last instruction of the interrupt service routine, RETI; otherwise, another interrupt will be generated. In other words, if the low-level interrupt signal is not removed before the ISR is finished, it is interpreted as another interrupt and the 8051 jumps to the vector table to execute the ISR again. Look at Example 11-5.

Example 11-5

Assume that the INT1 pin is connected to a switch that is normally high. Whenever it goes low, it should turn on an LED. The LED is connected to P1.3 and is normally off. When it is turned on it should stay on for a fraction of a second. As long as the switch is pressed low, the LED should stay on.

Solution:

```
            ORG   0000H
            LJMP  MAIN               ;bypass interrupt vector table
;--ISR for hardware interrupt INT1 to turn on the LED
            ORG   0013H              ;INT1 ISR
            SETB  P1.3               ;turn on LED
            MOV   R3,#255            ;load counter
BACK:       DJNZ  R3,BACK            ;keep LED on for a while
            CLR   P1.3               ;turn off the LED
            RETI                     ;return from ISR
;--MAIN program for initialization
            ORG   30H
MAIN:       MOV   IE,#10000100B      ;enable external INT1
HERE:       SJMP  HERE               ;stay here until interrupted
            END
```

Pressing the switch will turn the LED on. If it is kept activated, the LED stays on.

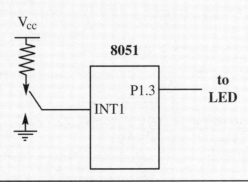

In this program, the microprocessor is looping continuously in the HERE loop. Whenever the switch on INT1 (pin P3.3) is activated, the microprocessor gets out of the loop and jumps to vector location 0013H. The ISR for INT1 turns on the LED, keeps it on for a while, and turns it off before it returns. If by the time it executes the RETI instruction the INT1 pin is still low, the microprocessor initiates the interrupt again. Therefore, to end this problem, the INT1 pin must be brought back to high by the time RETI is executed.

Sampling the low-level triggered interrupt

Pins P3.2 and P3.3 are used for normal I/O unless the INT0 and INT1 bits in the IE registers are enabled. After the hardware interrupts in the IE register are enabled, the controller keeps sampling the INT*n* pin for a low-level signal once each machine cycle. According to one manufacturer's data sheet, "the pin must be held in a low state until the start of the execution of ISR. If the INT*n* pin is brought back to a logic high before the start of the execution of ISR there will be no interrupt." However, upon activation of the interrupt due to the low level, it must be brought back to high before the execution of RETI. Again, according to one manufacturer's data sheet, "If the INT*n* pin is left at a logic low after the RETI instruction of the ISR, another interrupt will be activated after one instruction is executed." Therefore, to ensure the activation of the hardware interrupt at the INT*n* pin, make sure that the duration of the low-level signal is around 4 machine cycles, but no more. This is due to the fact that the level-triggered interrupt is not latched. Thus the pin must be held in a low state until the start of the ISR execution. See Figure 11-5.

Edge-triggered interrupts

As stated before, upon reset the 8051 makes INT0 and INT1 low-level triggered interrupts. To make them edge-triggered interrupts, we must program the bits of the TCON register. The TCON register holds, among other bits, the IT0 and IT1 flag bits that determine level- or edge-triggered mode of the hardware interrupts. IT0 and IT1 are bits D0 and D2 of the TCON register, respectively. They are also referred to as TCON.0 and

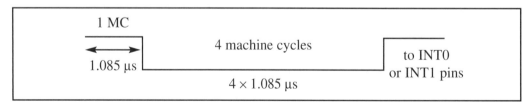

Figure 11-5. Minimum Duration of the Low-Level Triggered Interrupt (XTAL = 11.0592 MHz)
Note: On RESET, IT0 (TCON.0) and IT1 (TCON.2) are both low, making external interrupts level-triggered.

TCON.2 since the TCON register is bit-addressable. Upon reset, TCON.0 (IT0) and TCON.2 (IT1) are both 0s, meaning that the external hardware interrupts of INT0 and INT1 pins are low-level triggered. By making the TCON.0 and TCON.2 bits high with instructions such as "SETB TCON.0" and "SETB TCON.2", the external hardware interrupts of INT0 and INT1 become edge-triggered. For example, the instruction "SETB CON.2" makes INT1 what is called an *edge-triggered interrupt*, in which, when a high-to-low signal is applied to pin P3.3, the controller will be interrupted and forced to jump to location 0013H in the vector table to service the ISR (assuming that the interrupt bit is enabled in the IE register).

Look at Example 11-6. Notice that the only difference between this program and the program in Example 11-5 is in the first line of MAIN where the instruction "SETB TCON.2" makes INT1 an edge-triggered interrupt. When the falling edge of the signal is applied to pin INT1, the LED will be turned on momentarily. The LED's on-state duration depends on the time delay inside the ISR for INT1. To turn on the LED again, another high-to-low pulse must be applied to pin 3.3. This is the opposite of Example 11-5. In Example 11-5, due to the level-triggered nature of the interrupt, as long as INT1 is kept at a low level, the LED is kept in the on state. But in this example, to turn on the LED again, the INT1 pulse must be brought back high and then forced low to create a falling edge to activate the interrupt.

Example 11-6

Assuming that pin 3.3 (INT1) is connected to a pulse generator, write a program in which the falling edge of the pulse will send a high to P1.3, which is connected to an LED (or buzzer). In other words, the LED is turned on and off at the same rate as the pulses are applied to the INT1 pin. This is an edge-triggered version of Example 11-5.

Solution:

```
      ORG   0000H
      LJMP  MAIN
;--ISR for hardware interrupt INT1 to turn on the LED
      ORG   0013H              ;INT1 ISR
      SETB  P1.3               ;turn on the LED
      MOV   R3,#255
BACK: DJNZ  R3,BACK            ;keep the LED on for a while
      CLR   P1.3               ;turn off the LED
      RETI                     ;return from ISR
;--MAIN program for initialization
      ORG   30H
MAIN: SETB  TCON.2             ;make INT1 edge-trigger interrupt
      MOV   IE,#10000100B      ;enable External INT1
HERE: SJMP  HERE               ;stay here until interrupted
      END
```

Sampling the edge-triggered interrupt

Before ending this section, we need to answer the question of how often the edge-triggered interrupt is sampled. In edge-triggered interrupts, the external source must be held high for at least one machine cycle, and then held low for at least one machine cycle to ensure that the transition is seen by the microprocessor.

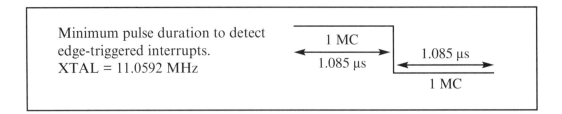

Minimum pulse duration to detect edge-triggered interrupts. XTAL = 11.0592 MHz

The falling edge is latched by the 8051 and is held by the TCON register. The TCON.1 and TCON.3 bits hold the latched falling edge of pins INT0 and INT1, respectively. TCON.1 and TCON.3 are also called IE0 and IE1, respectively, as shown in Figure 11-6. They function as interrupt-in-service flags. When an interrupt-in-service flag is raised, it indicates to the external world that the interrupt is being serviced and no new interrupt on this INTn pin will be responded to until this service is finished. This is just like the busy signal you get if calling a telephone number that is in use. Regarding the IT0 and IT1 bits in the TCON register, the following two points must be emphasized.

1. The first point is that when the ISRs are finished (i.e., upon execution of instruction RETI), these bits (TCON.1 and TCON.3) are cleared, indicating that the interrupt is finished and the 8051 is ready to respond to another interrupt on that pin. For another interrupt to be recognized, the pin must go back to a logic high state and be brought back low to be considered an edge-triggered interrupt.

2. The second point is that while the interrupt service routine is being executed, the INTn pin is ignored, no matter how many times it makes a high-to-low transition. In reality, one of the functions of the RETI instruction is to clear the corresponding bit in the TCON register (TCON.1 or TCON.3). This informs us that the service routine is no longer in progress and has finished being serviced. For this reason, TCON.1 and TCON.3 in the TCON register are called interrupt-in-service flags. The interrupt-in-service flag goes high whenever a falling edge is detected at the INT pin, and stays high during the entire execution of the ISR. It is only cleared by RETI, the last instruction of the ISR. Because of this, there is no need for an instruction such as "CLR TCON.1" (or "CLR TCON.3" for INT1) before the RETI in the ISR associated with the hardware interrupt INT0. As we will see in the next section, this is not the case for the serial interrupt.

D7							D0
TF1	TR1	TF0	TR0	IE1	IT1	IE0	IT0

TF1 TCON.7   Timer 1 overflow flag. Set by hardware when timer/counter 1 overflows. Cleared by hardware as the processor vectors to the interrupt service routine.

TR1 TCON.6   Timer 1 run control bit. Set/cleared by software to turn timer/counter 1 on/off.

TF0 TCON.5   Timer 0 overflow flag. Set by hardware when timer/counter 0 overflows. Cleared by hardware as the processor vectors to the service routine.

TR0 TCON.4   Timer 0 run control bit. Set/cleared by software to turn timer/counter 0 on/off.

IE1 TCON.3   External interrupt 1 edge flag. Set by CPU when the external interrupt edge (H-to-L transition) is detected. Cleared by CPU when the interrupt is processed.
Note: This flag does not latch low-level triggered interrupts.

IT1 TCON.2   Interrupt 1 type control bit. Set/cleared by software to specify falling edge/low-level triggered external interrupt.

IE0 TCON.1   External interrupt 0 edge flag. Set by CPU when external interrupt (H-to-L transition) edge is detected. Cleared by CPU when interrupt is processed.
Note: This flag does not latch low-level triggered interrupts.

IT0 TCON.0   Interrupt 0 type control bit. Set/cleared by software to specify falling edge/low-level triggered external interrupt.

Figure 11-6. TCON (Timer/Counter) Register (Bit-addressable)

More about the TCON register

Next, we look at the TCON register more closely to understand its role in handling interrupts. Figure 11-6 shows the bits of the TCON register.

IT0 and IT1

TCON.0 and TCON.2 are referred to as IT0 and IT1, respectively. These two bits set the low-level or edge-triggered modes of the external hardware interrupts of the INT0 and INT1 pins. They are both 0 upon reset, which makes them

---

Example 11-7

What is the difference between the RET and RETI instructions? Explain why we cannot use RET instead of RETI as the last instruction of an ISR.

Solution:

Both perform the same actions of popping off the top two bytes of the stack into the program counter, and making the 8051 return to where it left off. However, RETI also performs an additional task of clearing the interrupt-in-service flag, indicating that the servicing of the interrupt is over and the 8051 now can accept a new interrupt on that pin. If you use RET instead of RETI as the last instruction of the interrupt service routine, you simply block any new interrupt on that pin after the first interrupt, since the pin status would indicate that the interrupt is still being serviced. In the cases of TF0, TF1, TCON.1, and TCON.3, they are cleared by the execution of RETI.

---

low-level triggered. The programmer can make either of them high to make the external hardware interrupt edge-triggered. In a given system based on the 8051, once they are set to 0 or 1 they will not be altered again since the designer has fixed the interrupt as either edge- or level-triggered. See Example 11-7.

IE0 and IE1

TCON.1 and TCON.3 are referred to as IE0 and IE1, respectively. These bits are used by the 8051 to keep track of the edge-triggered interrupt only. In other words, if the IT0 and IT1 are 0, meaning that the hardware interrupts are low-level triggered, IE0 and IE1 are not used at all. The IE0 and IE1 bits are used by the 8051 only to latch the high-to-low edge transition on the INT0 and INT1 pins. Upon the edge transition pulse on the INT0 (or INT1) pin, the 8051 marks (sets high) the IEx bit in the TCON register, jumps to the vector in the interrupt vector table, and starts to execute the ISR. While it is executing the ISR, no H-to-L pulse transition on the INT0 (or INT1) is recognized, thereby preventing any interrupt inside the interrupt. Only the execution of the RETI instruction at the end of the ISR will clear the IEx bit, indicating that a new H-to-L pulse will activate the interrupt again. From this discussion, we can see that the IE0 and IE1 bits are used internally by the 8051 to indicate whether or not an interrupt is in use. In other words, the programmer is not concerned with these bits since they are solely for internal use.

TR0 and TR1

These are the D4 (TCON.4) and D6 (TCON.6) bits of the TCON register. We were introduced to these bits in Chapter 9. They are used to start or stop timers 0 and 1, respectively. Although we have used syntax such as "SETB TRx" and "CLR Trx", we could have used instructions such as "SETB TCON.4" and "CLR TCON.4" since TCON is a bit-addressable register.

TF0 and TF1

These are the D5 (TCON.5) and D7 (TCON.7) bits of the TCON register. We were introduced to these bits in Chapter 9. They are used by timers 0 and 1,

---

respectively, to indicate if the timer has rolled over. Although we have used the syntax "JNB TFx, target" and "CLR Trx", we could have used instructions such as "JNB TCON.5, target" and "CLR TCON.5" since TCON is bit-addressable.

REVIEW QUESTIONS

1. True or false. There is a single interrupt in the interrupt vector table assigned to both external hardware interrupts IT0 and IT1.
2. What address in the interrupt vector table is assigned to INT0 and INT1? How about the pin numbers on port 3?
3. Which bit of IE belongs to the external hardware interrupts? Show how both are enabled.
4. Assume that the IE bit for the external hardware interrupt EX1 is enabled and is active low. Explain how this interrupt works when it is activated.
5. True or false. Upon reset, the external hardware interrupt is low-level triggered.
6. In Question 5, how do we make sure that a single interrupt is not recognized as multiple interrupts?
7. True or false. The last two instructions of the ISR for INT0 are:
```
        CLR   TCON.1
        RETI
```

11.4: PROGRAMMING THE SERIAL COMMUNICATION INTERRUPT

In Chapter 10, we studied the serial communication of the 8051. All examples in that chapter used the polling method. In this section, we explore interrupt-based serial communication, which allows the 8051 to do many things, in addition to sending and receiving data from the serial communication port.

RI and TI flags and interrupts

As you may recall from Chapter 10, TI (transmit interrupt) is raised when the last bit of the framed data, the stop bit, is transferred, indicating that the SBUF register is ready to transfer the next byte. RI (receive interrupt) is raised when the entire frame of data, including the stop bit, is received. In other words, when the SBUF register has a byte, RI is raised to indicate that the received byte needs to be picked up before it is lost (overrun) by new incoming serial data. As far as serial communication is concerned, all the above concepts apply equally when using either polling or an interrupt. The only difference is in how the serial communication needs are served. In the polling method, we wait for the flag (TI or RI) to be

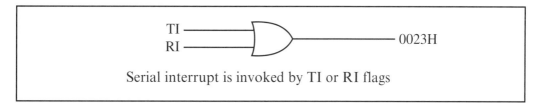

Serial interrupt is invoked by TI or RI flags

Figure 11-7. Single Interrupt for Both TI and RI

---

raised; while we wait we cannot do anything else. In the interrupt method, we are notified when the 8051 has received a byte, or is ready to send the next byte; we can do other things while the serial communication needs are served.

In the 8051, only one interrupt is set aside for serial communication. See Figure 11-7. This interrupt is used to both send and receive data. If the interrupt bit in the IE register (IE.4) is enabled, that is, when RI or TI is raised, the 8051 gets interrupted and jumps to memory address location 0023H to execute the ISR. In that ISR, we must examine the TI and RI flags to see which one caused the interrupt and respond accordingly. See Example 11-8.

Example 11-8

Write a program in which the 8051 reads data from P1 and writes it to P2 continuously while giving a copy of it to the serial COM port to be transferred serially. Assume that XTAL = 11.0592 MHz. Set the baud rate at 9600.

Solution:

```
                ORG    0
                LJMP   MAIN
                ORG    23H
                LJMP   SERIAL            ;jump to serial interrupt ISR
                ORG    30H
MAIN:           MOV    P1,#0FFH          ;make P1 an input port
                MOV    TMOD,#20H         ;timer 1, mode 2(auto-reload)
                MOV    TH1,#0FDH         ;9600 baud rate
                MOV    SCON,#50H         ;8-bit, 1 stop, REN enabled
                MOV    IE,#10010000B     ;enable serial interrupt
                SETB   TR1               ;start timer 1
BACK:           MOV    A,P1              ;read data from port 1
                MOV    SBUF,A            ;give a copy to SBUF
                MOV    P2,A              ;send it to P2
                SJMP   BACK              ;stay in loop indefinitely
;
;------------------Serial Port ISR
                ORG    100H
SERIAL:         JB     TI,TRANS          ;jump if TI is high
                MOV    A,SBUF            ;otherwise due to receive
                CLR    RI                ;clear RI since CPU does not
                RETI                     ;return from ISR
TRANS:          CLR    TI                ;clear TI since CPU does not
                RETI                     ;return from ISR
                END
```

In the above program, notice the role of TI and RI. The moment a byte is written into SBUF it is framed and transferred serially. As a result, when the last bit (stop bit) is transferred the TI is raised, which causes the serial interrupt to be invoked since the corresponding bit in the IE register is high. In the serial ISR, we check for both TI and RI since both could have invoked the interrupt. In other words, there is only one interrupt for both transmit and receive.

Use of serial COM in the 8051

In the vast majority of applications, the serial interrupt is used mainly for receiving data and is never used for sending data serially. This is like receiving a telephone call, where we need a ring to be notified. If we need to make a phone call there are other ways to remind ourselves and so no need for ringing. In receiving the phone call, however, we must respond immediately no matter what we are doing or we will miss the call. Similarly, we use the serial interrupt to receive incoming data so that it is not lost. Look at Example 11-9.

Clearing RI and TI before the RETI instruction

Notice in Example 11-9 that the last instruction before the RETI is the clearing of the RI or TI flags. This is necessary since there is only one interrupt for both receive and transmit, and the 8051 does not know who generated it;

Example 11-9

Write a program in which the 8051 gets data from P1 and sends it to P2 continuously while incoming data from the serial port is sent to P0. Assume that XTAL = 11.0592 MHz. Set the baud rate at 9600.

Solution:

```
           ORG   0
           LJMP  MAIN
           ORG   23H
           LJMP  SERIAL          ;jump to serial ISR
           ORG   30H
MAIN:      MOV   P1,#0FFH         ;make P1 an input port
           MOV   TMOD,#20H        ;timer 1, mode 2(auto-reload)
           MOV   TH1,#0FDH        ;9600 baud rate
           MOV   SCON,#50H        ;8-bit,1 stop, REN enabled
           MOV   IE,#10010000B    ;enable serial interrupt
           SETB  TR1              ;start Timer 1
BACK:      MOV   A,P1             ;read data from port 1
           MOV   P2,A             ;send it to P2
           SJMP  BACK             ;stay in loop indefinitely
;------------------SERIAL PORT ISR
           ORG   100H
SERIAL:    JB    TI,TRANS         ;jump if TI is high
           MOV   A,SBUF           ;otherwise due to receive
           MOV   P0,A             ;send incoming data to P0
           CLR   RI               ;clear RI since CPU doesn't
           RETI                   ;return from ISR
TRANS:     CLR   TI               ;clear TI since CPU doesn't
           RETI                   ;return from ISR
           END
```

Example 11-10

Write a program using interrupts to do the following:
(a) Receive data serially and send it to P0.
(b) Have port P1 read and transmitted serially, and a copy given to P2.
(c) Make Timer 0 generate a square wave of 5 kHz frequency on P0.1.
Assume that XTAL = 11.0592 MHz. Set the baud rate at 4800.

Solution:

```
            ORG    0
            LJMP   MAIN
            ORG    000BH              ;ISR for Timer 0
            CPL    P0.1               ;toggle P0.1
            RETI                      ;return from ISR
            ORG    23H
            LJMP   SERIAL             ;jump to serial int. ISR
            ORG    30H
MAIN:       MOV    P1,#0FFH           ;make P1 an input port
            MOV    TMOD,#22H          ;timer 0&1,mode 2, auto-reload
            MOV    TH1,#0F6H          ;4800 baud rate
            MOV    SCON,#50H          ;8-bit, 1 stop, REN enabled
            MOV    TH0,#-92           ;for 5 KHz wave
            MOV    IE,#10010010B      ;enable serial, timer 0 int.
            SETB   TR1                ;start timer 1
            SETB   TR0                ;start timer 0
BACK:       MOV    A,P1               ;read data from port 1
            MOV    SBUF,A             ;give a copy to SBUF
            MOV    P2,A               ;write it to P2
            SJMP   BACK               ;stay in loop indefinitely


;-------------------SERIAL PORT ISR
            ORG    100H
SERIAL:     JB     TI,TRANS           ;jump if TI is high
            MOV    A,SBUF             ;otherwise due to received
            MOV    P0,A               ;send serial data to P0
            CLR    RI                 ;clear RI since CPU does not
            RETI                      ;return from ISR
TRANS:      CLR    TI                 ;clear TI since CPU does not
            RETI                      ;return from ISR
            END
```

therefore, it is the job of the ISR to clear the flag. Contrast this with the external and timer interrupts where it is the job of the 8051 to clear the interrupt flags. By contrast, in serial communication the RI (or TI) must be cleared by the programmer using software instructions such as "CLR TI" and "CLR RI" in the ISR. See Example 11-10. Notice that the last two instructions of the ISR are clearing the flag, followed by RETI.

Table 11-2. Interrupt Flag Bits for the 8051/52

Interrupt	Flag	SFR Register Bit
External 0	IE0	TCON.1
External 1	IE1	TCON.3
Timer 0	TF0	TCON.5
Timer 1	TF1	TCON.7
Serial port	TI	SCON.1
Timer 2	TF2	T2CON.7 (AT89C52)
Timer 2	EXF2	T2CON.6 (AT89C52)

Before finishing this section notice the list of all interrupt flags given in Table 11-2. While the TCON register holds four of the interrupt flags, in the 8051 the SCON register has the RI and TI flags.

REVIEW QUESTIONS

1. True or false. There is a single interrupt in the interrupt vector table assigned to both the TI and RI interrupts.
2. What address in the interrupt vector table is assigned to the serial interrupt?
3. Which bit of the IE register belongs to the serial interrupt? Show how it is enabled.
4. Assume that the IE bit for the serial interrupt is enabled. Explain how this interrupt gets activated and also explain its actions upon activation.
5. True or false. Upon reset, the serial interrupt is active and ready to go.
6. True or false. The last two instructions of the ISR for the receive interrupt are:
   ```
   CLR   RI
   RETI
   ```
7. Answer Question 6 for the send interrupt.

11.5: INTERRUPT PRIORITY IN THE 8051/52

The next topic that we must deal with is what happens if two interrupts are activated at the same time? Which of these two interrupts is responded to first? Interrupt priority is the main topic of discussion in this section.

Interrupt priority upon reset

When the 8051 is powered up, the priorities are assigned according to Table 11-3. From Table 11-3, we see, for example, that if external hardware interrupts 0 and 1 are activated at the same time, external interrupt 0 (INT0) is responded to first. Only after INT0 has been serviced is INT1 serviced, since INT1 has the lower priority. In reality, the priority scheme in the table is nothing but an internal polling sequence in which the 8051 polls the interrupts in the sequence listed in Table 11-3 and responds accordingly.

Table 11-3. 8051/52 Interrupt Priority Upon Reset

Highest to Lowest Priority	
External Interrupt 0	(INT0)
Timer Interrupt 0	(TF0)
External Interrupt 1	(INT1)
Timer Interrupt 1	(TF1)
Serial Communication	(RI + TI)
Timer 2 (8052 only)	**TF2**

Example 11-11

Discuss what happens if interrupts INT0, TF0, and INT1 are activated at the same time. Assume priority levels were set by the power-up reset and that the external hardware interrupts are edge-triggered.

Solution:

If these three interrupts are activated at the same time, they are latched and kept internally. Then the 8051 checks all five interrupts according to the sequence listed in Table 11-3. If any is activated, it services it in sequence. Therefore, when the above three interrupts are activated, IE0 (external interrupt 0) is serviced first, then Timer 0 (TF0), and finally IE1 (external interrupt 1).

Setting interrupt priority with the IP register

We can alter the sequence of Table 11-3 by assigning a higher priority to any one of the interrupts. This is done by programming a register called IP (interrupt priority). Figure 11-8 shows the bits of the IP register. Upon power-up reset, the IP register contains all 0s, making the priority sequence based on Table 11-3. To give a higher priority to any of the interrupts, we make the corresponding bit in the IP register high. Look at Examples 11-11 and 11-12.

Another point that needs to be clarified is the interrupt priority when two or more interrupt bits in the IP register are set to high. In this case, while these interrupts have a higher priority than others, they are serviced according to the sequence of Table 11-3. See Example 11-13.

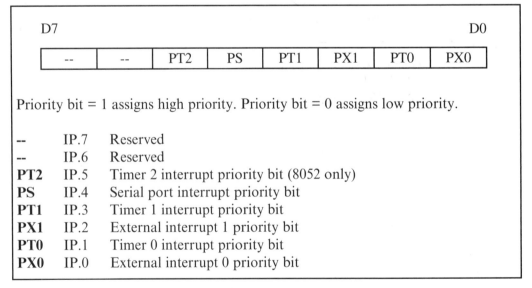

Figure 11-8. Interrupt Priority Register (Bit-addressable)
User software should never write 1s to unimplemented bits, since they may be used in future products.

Example 11-12

(a) Program the IP register to assign the highest priority to INT1 (external interrupt 1), then (b) discuss what happens if INT0, INT1, and TF0 are activated at the same time. Assume that the interrupts are both edge-triggered.

Solution:

(a) `MOV IP,#00000100B ;IP.2=1 to assign INT1 higher priority`
The instruction "`SETB IP.2`" also will do the same thing as the above line since IP is bit-addressable.

(b) The instruction in Step (a) assigned a higher priority to INT1 than the others; therefore, when INT0, INT1, and TF0 interrupts are activated at the same time, the 8051 services INT1 first, then it services INT0, then TF0. This is due to the fact that INT1 has a higher priority than the other two because of the instruction in Step (a). The instruction in Step (a) makes both the INT0 and TF0 bits in the IP register 0. As a result, the sequence in Table 11-3 is followed, which gives a higher priority to INT0 over TF0.

Interrupt inside an interrupt

What happens if the 8051 is executing an ISR belonging to an interrupt and another interrupt is activated? In such cases, a high-priority interrupt can interrupt a low-priority interrupt. This is an interrupt inside an interrupt. In the 8051 a low-priority interrupt can be interrupted by a higher-priority interrupt, but not by another low-priority interrupt. Although all the interrupts are latched and kept internally, no low-priority interrupt can get the immediate attention of the CPU until the 8051 has finished servicing the high-priority interrupts.

Triggering the interrupt by software

There are times when we need to test an ISR by way of simulation. This can be done with simple instructions to set the interrupts high and thereby

Example 11-13

Assume that after reset, the interrupt priority is set by the instruction "`MOV IP, #00001100B`". Discuss the sequence in which the interrupts are serviced.

Solution:

The instruction "`MOV IP,#00001100B`" (B is for binary) sets the external interrupt 1 (INT1) and Timer 1 (TF1) to a higher priority level compared with the rest of the interrupts. However, since they are polled according to Table 11-3, they will have the following priority.

Highest Priority	External Interrupt 1	(INT1)
	Timer Interrupt 1	(TF1)
	External Interrupt 0	(INT0)
	Timer Interrupt 0	(TF0)
Lowest Priority	Serial Communication	(RI + TI)

cause the 8051 to jump to the interrupt vector table. For example, if the IE bit for Timer 1 is set, an instruction such as "SETB TF1" will interrupt the 8051 in whatever it is doing and force it to jump to the interrupt vector table. In other words, we do not need to wait for Timer 1 to roll over to have an interrupt. We can cause an interrupt with an instruction that raises the interrupt flag.

REVIEW QUESTIONS

1. True or false. Upon reset, all interrupts have the same priority.
2. What register keeps track of interrupt priority in the 8051? Is it a bit-addressable register?
3. Which bit of IP belongs to the serial interrupt priority? Show how to assign it the highest priority.
4. Assume that the IP register contains all 0s. Explain what happens if both INT0 and INT1 are activated at the same time.
5. Explain what happens if a higher-priority interrupt is activated while the 8051 is serving a lower-priority interrupt (i.e., executing a lower-priority ISR).

11.6: INTERRUPT PROGRAMMING IN C

So far all the programs in this chapter have been written in Assembly. In this section, we show how to program the 8051/52's interrupts in 8051 C language. In reading this section, it is assumed that you already know the material in the first two sections of this chapter.

8051 C interrupt numbers

The 8051 C compilers have extensive support for the 8051 interrupts with two major features as follows:

1. They assign a unique number to each of the 8051 interrupts, as shown in Table 11-4.
2. It can also assign a register bank to an ISR. This avoids code overhead due to the pushes and pops of the R0–R7 registers.

Example 11-14 shows how a simple interrupt is written in 8051 C. See also Examples 11-15 through 11-17.

Table 11-4. 8051/52 Interrupt Numbers in C

Interrupt	Name	Numbers Used by 8051 C
External Interrupt 0	(INT0)	0
Timer Interrupt 0	(TF0)	1
External Interrupt 1	(INT1)	2
Timer Interrupt 1	(TF1)	3
Serial Communication	(RI + TI)	4
Timer 2 (8052 only)	(TF2)	5

Example 11-14

Write a C program that continuously gets a single bit of data from P1.7 and sends it to P1.0, while simultaneously creating a square wave of 200 µs period on pin P2.5. Use timer 0 to create the square wave. Assume that XTAL = 11.0592 MHz.

Solution:

We will use Timer 0 in mode 2 (auto-reload). One half of the period is 100 µs, 100/1.085 µs = 92, and TH0 = 256 – 92 = 164 or A4H

```c
#include <reg51.h>

sbit SW     = P1^7;
sbit IND    = P1^0;
sbit WAVE   = P2^5;

void timer0(void) interrupt 1
  {
    WAVE = ~WAVE;      //toggle pin
  }

void main()
  {
    SW = 1;            //make switch input
    TMOD = 0x02;
    TH0 = 0xA4;        //TH0 = -92
    IE = 0x82;         //enable interrupts for timer 0
    while(1)
      {
        IND = SW;      //send switch to LED
      }
  }
```

200 µs / 2 = 100 µs

100 µs / 1.085 µs = 92

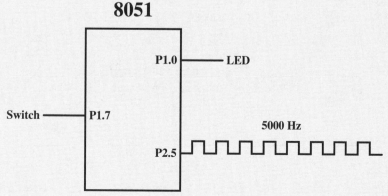

Example 11-15

Write a C program that continuously gets a single bit of data from P1.7 and sends it to P1.0 in the main, while simultaneously (a) creating a square wave of 200 μs period on pin P2.5, and (b) sending letter 'A' to the serial port. Use Timer 0 to create the square wave. Assume that XTAL = 11.0592 MHz. Use the 9600 baud rate.

Solution:

We will use Timer 0 in mode 2 (auto-reload). TH0 = 100/1.085 μs = –92, which is A4H

```c
#include <reg51.h>

sbit SW    = P1^7;
sbit IND   = P1^0;
sbit WAVE  = P2^5;

void timer0(void) interrupt 1
  {
     WAVE = ~WAVE;       //toggle pin
  }

void serial0() interrupt 4
  {
     if(TI == 1)
       {
          SBUF = 'A';  //send A to serial port
          TI = 0;      //clear interrupt
       }
     else
       {
          RI = 0;      //clear interrupt
       }
  }

void main()
  {
     SW = 1;            //make switch input
     TH1 = -3;          //9600 baud
     TMOD = 0x22;       //mode 2 for both timers
     TH0 = 0xA4;        //-92=A4H for timer 0
     SCON = 0x50;
     TR0 = 1;
     TR1 = 1;                    //start timer
     IE = 0x92;         //enable interrupt for T0
     while(1)           //stay here
       {
          IND = SW;     //send switch to LED
       }
  }
```

Example 11-16

Write a C program using interrupts to do the following:
(a) Receive data serially and send it to P0.
(b) Read port P1, transmit data serially, and give a copy to P2.
(c) Make Timer 0 generate a square wave of 5 kHz frequency on P0.1.
Assume that XTAL = 11.0592 MHz. Set the baud rate at 4800.

Solution:

```c
#include <reg51.h>
sbit WAVE = P0^1;

void timer0() interrupt 1
  {
    WAVE = ~WAVE;            //toggle pin
  }

void serial0() interrupt 4
  {
    if(TI == 1)
      {
        TI = 0;             //clear interrupt
      }
    else
      {
        P0 = SBUF;          //put value on pins
        RI = 0;             //clear interrupt
      }
  }

void main()
  {
    unsigned char x;
    P1 = 0xFF;              //make P1 an input
    TMOD = 0x22;
    TH1 = 0xF6;             //4800 baud rate
    SCON = 0x50;
    TH0 = 0xA4;             //5 kHz has T = 200 µs
    IE = 0x92;              //enable interrupts
    TR1 = 1;                //start timer 1
    TR0 = 1;                //start timer 0
    while(1)
      {
        x = P1;            //read value from pins
        SBUF = x;          //put value in buffer
        P2 = x;            //write value to pins
      }
  }
```

Example 11-17

Write a C program using interrupts to do the following:

(a) Generate a 10000 Hz frequency on P2.1 using T0 8-bit auto-reload.

(b) Use Timer 1 as an event counter to count up a 1-Hz pulse and display it on P0. The pulse is connected to EX1.

Assume that XTAL = 11.0592 MHz. Set the baud rate at 9600.

Solution:

```c
#include <reg51.h>

sbit WAVE = P2^1;
unsigned char cnt;

void timer0() interrupt 1
   {
      WAVE = ~WAVE;            //toggle pin
   }
void timer1() interrupt 3
   {
      cnt++;                   //increment counter
      P0 = cnt;                //display value on pins
   }

void main()
   {
      cnt = 0;                 //set counter to zero
      TMOD = 0x42;
      TH0 = 0x-46;             //10000 Hz
      IE = 0x86;               //enable interrupts
      TR0 = 1;                 //start timer 0
      TR1 = 1;                 //start timer 1
      while(1);                //wait until interrupted
   }
```

1/10000 Hz = 100 µs

100 µs/2 = 50 µs

50 µs/1.085 µs = 46

SUMMARY

An interrupt is an external or internal event that interrupts the microprocessor to inform it that a device needs its service. Every interrupt has a program associated with it called the ISR, or interrupt service routine. The 8051 has six interrupts, five of which are user-accessible. The interrupts are for reset: two for the timers, two for external hardware interrupts, and a serial communication interrupt. The 8052 has an additional interrupt for Timer 2.

The 8051 can be programmed to enable or disable an interrupt, and the interrupt priority can be altered. This chapter showed how to program 8051/52 interrupts in both Assembly and C languages.

PROBLEMS

11.1: 8051 INTERRUPTS

1. Which technique, interrupt or polling, avoids tying down the microprocessor?
2. Including reset, how many interrupts does the 8051 have?
3. In the 8051, what memory area is assigned to the interrupt vector table?
4. True or false. The 8051 programmer cannot change the memory space assigned to the interrupt vector table.
5. What memory address in the interrupt vector table is assigned to INT0?
6. What memory address in the interrupt vector table is assigned to INT1?
7. What memory address in the interrupt vector table is assigned to Timer 0?
8. What memory address in the interrupt vector table is assigned to Timer 1?
9. What memory address in the interrupt vector table is assigned to the serial COM interrupt?
10. Why do we put an LJMP instruction at address 0?
11. What are the contents of the IE register upon reset, and what do these values mean?
12. Show the instruction to enable the EX1 and Timer 1 interrupts.
13. Show the instruction to enable every interrupt of the 8051.
14. Which pin of the 8051 is assigned to the external hardware interrupts INT0 and INT1?
15. How many bytes of address space in the interrupt vector table are assigned to the INT0 and INT1 interrupts?
16. How many bytes of address space in the interrupt vector table are assigned to the Timer 0 and Timer 1 interrupts?
17. To put the entire interrupt service routine in the interrupt vector table, it must be no more than _____ bytes in size.
18. True or false. The IE register is not a bit-addressable register.
19. With a single instruction, show how to disable all the interrupts.
20. With a single instruction, show how to disable the EX1 interrupt.
21. True or false. Upon reset, all interrupts are enabled by the 8051.
22. In the 8051, how many bytes of ROM space are assigned to the reset interrupt, and why?

11.2: PROGRAMMING TIMER INTERRUPTS

23. True or false. For both Timer 0 and Timer 1, there is an interrupt assigned to it in the interrupt vector table.

24. What address in the interrupt vector table is assigned to Timer 1?

25. Which bit of IE belongs to the Timer 0 interrupt? Show how it is enabled.

26. Which bit of IE belongs to the Timer 1 interrupt? Show how it is enabled.

27. Assume that Timer 0 is programmed in mode 2, TH1 = F0H, and the IE bit for Timer 0 is enabled. Explain how the interrupt for the timer works.

28. True or false. The last two instructions of the ISR for Timer 1 are:

```
        CLR   TF1
        RETI
```

29. Assume that Timer 1 is programmed for mode 1, TH0 = FFH, TL1 = F8H, and the IE bit for Timer 1 is enabled. Explain how the interrupt is activated.

30. If Timer 1 is programmed for interrupts in mode 2, explain when the interrupt is activated.

31. Write a program to create a square wave of T = 160 ms on pin P2.2 while the 8051 is sending out 55H and AAH to P1 continuously.

32. Write a program in which every 2 seconds, the LED connected to P2.7 is turned on and off four times, while the 8051 is getting data from P1 and sending it to P0 continuously. Make sure the on and off states are 50 ms in duration.

11.3: PROGRAMMING EXTERNAL HARDWARE INTERRUPTS

33. True or false. A single interrupt is assigned to each of the external hardware interrupts EX0 and EX1.

34. What address in the interrupt vector table is assigned to INT0 and INT1? How about the pin numbers on port 3?

35. Which bit of IE belongs to the EX0 interrupt? Show how it is enabled.

36. Which bit of IE belongs to the EX1 interrupt? Show how it is enabled.

37. Show how to enable both external hardware interrupts.

38. Assume that the IE bit for external hardware interrupt EX0 is enabled and is low-level triggered. Explain how this interrupt works when it is activated. How can we make sure that a single interrupt is not interpreted as multiple interrupts?

39. True or false. Upon reset, the external hardware interrupt is edge-triggered.

40. In Question 39, how do we make sure that a single interrupt is not recognized as multiple interrupts?

41. Which bits of TCON belong to EX0?

42. Which bits of TCON belong to EX1?

43. True or false. The last two instructions of the ISR for INT1 are:

```
        CLR   TCON.3
        RETI
```

44. Explain the role of TCON.0 and TCON.2 in the execution of external interrupt 0.

45. Explain the role of TCON.1 and TCON.3 in the execution of external interrupt 1.
46. Assume that the IE bit for external hardware interrupt EX1 is enabled and is edge-triggered. Explain how this interrupt works when it is activated. How can we make sure that a single interrupt is not interpreted as multiple interrupts?
47. Write a program using interrupts to get data from P1 and send it to P2 while Timer 0 is generating a square wave of 3 kHz.
48. Write a program using interrupts to get data from P1 and send it to P2 while Timer 1 is turning on and off the LED connected to P0.4 every second.
49. Explain the difference between the low-level and edge-triggered interrupts.
50. How do we make the hardware interrupt edge-triggered?
51. Which interrupts are latched, low-level or edge-triggered?
52. Which register keeps the latched interrupt for INT0 and INT1?

11.4: PROGRAMMING THE SERIAL COMMUNICATION INTERRUPT

53. True or false. There are two interrupts assigned to interrupts TI and RI.
54. What address in the interrupt vector table is assigned to the serial interrupt? How many bytes are assigned to it?
55. Which bit of the IE register belongs to the serial interrupt? Show how it is enabled.
56. Assume that the IE bit for the serial interrupt is enabled. Explain how this interrupt gets activated and also explain its working upon activation.
57. True or false. Upon reset, the serial interrupt is blocked.
58. True or false. The last two instructions of the ISR for the receive interrupt are:
```
CLR   TI
RETI
```
59. Answer Question 58 for the receive interrupt.
60. Assuming that the interrupt bit in the IE register is enabled, when TI is raised, what happens subsequently?
61. Assuming that the interrupt bit in the IE register is enabled, when RI is raised, what happens subsequently?
62. Write a program using interrupts to get data serially and send it to P2 while Timer 0 is generating a square wave of 5 kHz.
63. Write a program using interrupts to get data serially and send it to P2 while Timer 0 is turning the LED connected to P1.6 on and off every second.

11.5: INTERRUPT PRIORITY IN THE 8051/52

64. True or false. Upon reset, EX1 has the highest priority.
65. What register keeps track of interrupt priority in the 8051? Explain its role.
66. Which bit of IP belongs to the EX2 interrupt priority? Show how to assign it the highest priority.
67. Which bit of IP belongs to the Timer 1 interrupt priority? Show how to assign it the highest priority.
68. Which bit of IP belongs to the EX1 interrupt priority? Show how to assign it the highest priority.

69. Assume that the IP register has all 0s. Explain what happens if both INT0 and INT1 are activated at the same time.
70. Assume that the IP register has all 0s. Explain what happens if both TF0 and TF1 are activated at the same time.
71. If both TF0 and TF1 in the IP are set to high, what happens if both are activated at the same time?
72. If both INT0 and INT1 in the IP are set to high, what happens if both are activated at the same time?
73. Explain what happens if a low-priority interrupt is activated while the 8051 is serving a higher-priority interrupt.

ANSWERS TO REVIEW QUESTIONS

11.1: 8051 INTERRUPTS

1. Interrupts
2. 5
3. Address locations 0000 to 25H. No. They are set when the processor is designed.
4. All 0s means that all interrupts are masked, and as a result no interrupts will be responded to by the 8051.
5. MOV IE,#10000011B
6. P3.3, which is pin 13 on the 40-pin DIP package
7. 0013H for INT1 and 001BH for Timer 1

11.2: PROGRAMMING TIMER INTERRUPTS

1. False. There is an interrupt for each of the timers, Timer 0 and Timer 1.
2. 000BH
3. Bits D1 and D3 and "MOV IE,#10001010B" will enable both of the timer interrupts.
4. After Timer 1 is started with instruction "SETB TR1", the timer will count up from F5H to FFH on its own while the 8051 is executing other tasks. Upon rolling over from FFH to 00, the TF1 flag is raised, which will interrupt the 8051 in whatever it is doing and force it to jump to memory location 001BH to execute the ISR belonging to this interrupt.
5. False. There is no need for "CLR TF0" since the RETI instruction does that for us.

11.3: PROGRAMMING EXTERNAL HARDWARE INTERRUPTS

1. False. There is an interrupt for each of the external hardware interrupts of INT0 and INT1.
2. 0003H and 0013H. The pins numbered 12 (P3.2) and 13 (P3.3) on the DIP package.
3. Bits D0 and D2 and "MOV IE,#10000101B" will enable both of the external hardware interrupts.
4. Upon application of a low pulse (4 machine cycles wide) to pin P3.3, the 8051 is interrupted in whatever it is doing and jumps to ROM location 0013H to execute the ISR.
5. True
6. Make sure that the low pulse applied to pin INT1 is no wider than 4 machine cycles. Or, make sure that the INT1 pin is brought back to high by the time the 8051 executes the RETI instruction in the ISR.
7. False. There is no need for the "CLR TCON.0" since the RETI instruction does that for us.

11.4: PROGRAMMING THE SERIAL COMMUNICATION INTERRUPT

1. True. There is only one interrupt for both the transfer and receive.
2. 23H
3. Bit D4 (IE.4) and "MOV IE,#10010000B" will enable the serial interrupt.
4. The RI (receive interrupt) flag is raised when the entire frame of data, including the stop bit, is receive. As a result, the receive byte is delivered to the SBUF register and the 8051 jumps to memory location 0023H to execute the ISR belonging to this interrupt. In the serial COM interrupt service routine, we must save the SBUF contents before it is lost by the incoming data.
5. False
6. True. We must do it since the RETI instruction will not do it for the serial interrupt.
7.   CLR   TI
    RETI

11.5: INTERRUPT PRIORITY IN THE 8051/52

1. False. They are assigned priority according to Table 11-3.
2. IP (interrupt priority) register. Yes, it is bit-addressable.
3. Bit D4 (IP.4) and the instruction "MOV IP,#00010000B" will do it.
4. If both are activated at the same time, INT0 is serviced first since it has a higher priority. After INT0 is serviced, INT1 is serviced, assuming that the external interrupts are edge-triggered and H-to-L transitions are latched. In the case of low-level triggered interrupts, if both are activated at the same time, the INT0 is serviced first; then after the 8051 has finished servicing the INT0, it scans the INT0 and INT1 pins again, and if the INT1 pin is still high, it will be serviced.
5. We have an interrupt inside an interrupt, meaning that the lower-priority interrupt is put on hold and the higher one is serviced. After servicing this higher-priority interrupt, the 8051 resumes servicing the lower-priority ISR.

CHAPTER 12

LCD AND KEYBOARD INTERFACING

OBJECTIVES

Upon completion of this chapter, you will be able to:

>> List reasons that LCDs are gaining widespread use, replacing LEDs.
>> Describe the functions of the pins of a typical LCD.
>> List instruction command codes for programming an LCD.
>> Interface an LCD to the 8051.
>> Program an LCD in Assembly and C.
>> Explain the basic operation of a keyboard.
>> Describe the key press and detection mechanisms.
>> Interface a 4x4 keypad to the 8051 using C and Assembly.

This chapter explores some real-world applications of the 8051. We explain how to interface the 8051 to devices such as an LCD and a keyboard. In Section 12.1, we show LCD interfacing with the 8051. In Section 12.2, keyboard interfacing with the 8051 is shown. We use C and Assembly for both sections.

12.1: LCD INTERFACING

This section describes the operation modes of LCDs, then describes how to program and interface an LCD to an 8051 using Assembly and C.

LCD operation

In recent years, the LCD is finding widespread use replacing LEDs (seven-segment LEDs or other multisegment LEDs). This is due to the following reasons:

1. The declining prices of LCDs.
2. The ability to display numbers, characters, and graphics. This is in contrast to LEDs, which are limited to numbers and a few characters.
3. Incorporation of a refreshing controller into the LCD, thereby relieving the CPU of the task of refreshing the LCD. By contrast, the LED must be refreshed by the CPU (or in some other way) to keep displaying the data.
4. Ease of programming for characters and graphics.

LCD pin descriptions

The LCD discussed in this section has 14 pins. The function of each pin is given in Table 12-1. Figure 12-1 shows the pin positions for various LCDs.

V_{CC}, V_{SS}, and V_{EE}

While V_{CC} and V_{SS} provide +5 V and ground, respectively, V_{EE} is used for controlling LCD contrast.

RS, register select

There are two very important registers inside the LCD. The RS pin is used for their selection as follows. If RS = 0, the instruction command code register is selected, allowing the user to send a command such as clear display or cursor at home. If RS = 1, the data register is selected, allowing the user to send data to be displayed on the LCD.

Table 12-1. Pin Descriptions for LCD

Pin	Symbol	I/O	Description
1	V_{SS}	--	Ground
2	V_{CC}	--	+5 V power supply
3	V_{ee}	--	Power supply to control contrast
4	RS	I	RS = 0 to select command register, RS = 1 to select data register
5	R/W	I	R/W = 0 for write, R/W = 1 for read
6	E	I	Enable
7	DB0	I/O	The 8-bit data bus
8	DB1	I/O	The 8-bit data bus
9	DB2	I/O	The 8-bit data bus
10	DB3	I/O	The 8-bit data bus
11	DB4	I/O	The 8-bit data bus
12	DB5	I/O	The 8-bit data bus
13	DB6	I/O	The 8-bit data bus
14	DB7	I/O	The 8-bit data bus

Table 12-2. LCD Command Codes Code Command to LCD Instruction (Hex) Register

Code	Command to LCD Instruction Register
1	Clear display screen
2	Return home
4	Decrement cursor (shift cursor to left)
6	Increment cursor (shift cursor to right)
5	Shift display right
7	Shift display left
8	Display off, cursor off
A	Display off, cursor on
C	Display on, cursor off
E	Display on, cursor blinking off
F	Display on, cursor blinking
10	Shift cursor position to left
14	Shift cursor position to right
18	Shift the entire display to the left
1C	Shift the entire display to the right
80	Force cursor to beginning of 1st line
C0	Force cursor to beginning of 2nd line
38	2 lines and 5x7 matrix

R/W, read/write

R/W input allows the user to write information to the LCD or read information from it. R/W = 1 when reading; R/W = 0 when writing.

E, enable

The enable pin is used by the LCD to latch information presented to its data pins. When data is supplied to data pins, a high-to-low pulse must be applied to this pin in order for the LCD to latch in the data present at the data pins. This pulse must be a minimum of 450 ns wide.

D0–D7

The 8-bit data pins, D0–D7, are used to send information to the LCD or read the contents of the LCD's internal registers.

To display letters and numbers, we send ASCII codes for the letters A–Z, a–z, and numbers 0–9 to these pins while making RS = 1.

There are also instruction command codes that can be sent to the LCD to clear the display or force the cursor to the home position or blink the cursor. Table 12-2 lists the instruction command codes.

We also use RS = 0 to check the busy flag bit to see if the LCD is ready to receive information. The busy flag is D7 and can be read when R/W = 1 and RS = 0, as follows: if R/W = 1, RS = 0. When D7 = 1 (busy flag = 1), the LCD

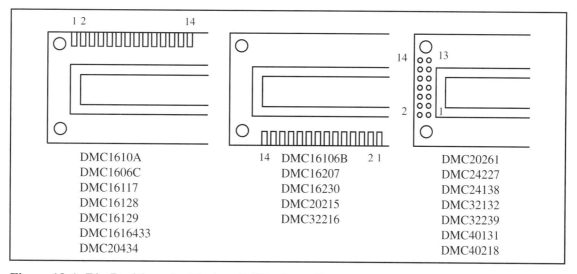

Figure 12-1. Pin Positions for Various LCDs from Optrex

is busy taking care of internal operations and will not accept any new information. When D7 = 0, the LCD is ready to receive new information. (*Note:* It is recommended to check the busy flag before writing any data to the LCD.)

Sending commands and data to LCDs with a time delay

To send any of the commands from Table 12-2 to the LCD, make pin RS = 0. For data, make RS = 1. Then send a high-to-low pulse to the E pin to enable the internal latch of the LCD. This is shown in Program 12-1. See Figure 12-2 for LCD connections.

```
;calls a time delay before sending next data/command
; P1.0-P1.7 are connected to LCD data pins D0-D7
; P2.0 is connected to RS pin of LCD
; P2.1 is connected to R/W pin of LCD
; P2.2 is connected to E pin of LCD
        ORG    0H
        MOV    A,#38H          ;init. LCD 2 lines,5x7 matrix
        ACALL  COMNWRT         ;call command subroutine
        ACALL  DELAY           ;give LCD some time
        MOV    A,#0EH          ;display on, cursor on
        ACALL  COMNWRT         ;call command subroutine
        ACALL  DELAY           ;give LCD some time
        MOV    A,#01           ;clear LCD
        ACALL  COMNWRT         ;call command subroutine
        ACALL  DELAY           ;give LCD some time
        MOV    A,#06H          ;shift cursor right
        ACALL  COMNWRT         ;call command subroutine
        ACALL  DELAY           ;give LCD some time
        MOV    A,#84H          ;cursor at line 1,pos. 4
        ACALL  COMNWRT         ;call command subroutine
        ACALL  DELAY           ;give LCD some time
        MOV    A,#'N'          ;display letter N
        ACALL  DATAWRT         ;call display subroutine
        ACALL  DELAY           ;give LCD some time
        MOV    A,#'O'          ;display letter O
        ACALL  DATAWRT         ;call display subroutine
AGAIN:  SJMP   AGAIN           ;stay here
COMNWRT:                       ;send command to LCD
        MOV    P1,A            ;copy reg A to port1
        CLR    P2.0            ;RS=0 for command
        CLR    P2.1            ;R/W=0 for write
        SETB   P2.2            ;E=1 for high pulse
        ACALL  DELAY           ;give LCD some time
        CLR    P2.2            ;E=0 for H-to-L pulse
        RET
DATAWRT:                       ;write data to LCD
        MOV    P1,A            ;copy reg A to port1
        SETB   P2.0            ;RS=1 for data
        CLR    P2.1            ;R/W=0 for write
```

Program 12-1. Communicating with LCD Using a Delay (*continued*)

```
              SETB    P2.2              ;E=1 for high pulse
              ACALL   DELAY             ;give LCD some time
              CLR     P2.2              ;E=0 for H-to-L pulse
              RET
DELAY:        MOV     R3,#50            ;50 or higher for fast CPUs
HERE2:        MOV     R4,#255           ;R4=255
HERE:         DJNZ    R4,HERE           ;stay until R4 becomes 0
              DJNZ    R3,HERE2
              RET
              END
```

Program 12-1. (*continued*)

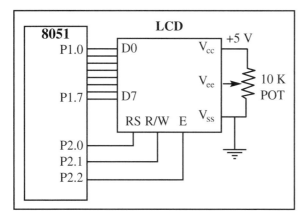

Figure 12-2. LCD Connections

Sending code or data to the LCD with checking busy flag

The above code showed how to send commands to the LCD without checking the busy flag. Notice that we must put a long delay between issuing data or commands to the LCD. However, a much better way is to monitor the busy flag before issuing a command or data to the LCD. This is shown in Program 12-2.

```
;Check busy flag before sending data, command to LCD
;P1=data pin,P2.0=RS,P2.1=R/W,P2.2=E pins
              MOV     A,#38H            ;init. LCD 2 lines,5x7 matrix
              ACALL   COMMAND           ;issue command
              MOV     A,#0EH            ;LCD on, cursor on
              ACALL   COMMAND           ;issue command
              MOV     A,#01H            ;clear LCD command
              ACALL   COMMAND           ;issue command
              MOV     A,#06H            ;shift cursor right
              ACALL   COMMAND           ;issue command
              MOV     A,#86H            ;cursor: line 1, pos. 6
              ACALL   COMMAND           ;command subroutine
              MOV     A,#'N'            ;display letter N
              ACALL   DATA_DISPLAY
              MOV     A,#'O'            ;display letter O
              ACALL   DATA_DISPLAY
HERE:         SJMP    HERE              ;STAY HERE
COMMAND:      ACALL   READY             ;is LCD ready?
              MOV     P1,A              ;issue command code
              CLR     P2.0              ;RS=0 for command
              CLR     P2.1              ;R/W=0 to write to LCD
```

Program 12-2. Communicating with LCD Using the Busy Flag (*continued*)

CHAPTER 12: LCD AND KEYBOARD INTERFACING   387

```
                SETB    P2.2            ;E=1 for H-to-L pulse
                CLR     P2.2            ;E=0 ,latch in
                RET
DATA_DISPLAY:
                ACALL   READY           ;is LCD ready?
                MOV     P1,A            ;issue data
                SETB    P2.0            ;RS=1 for data
                CLR     P2.1            ;R/W=0 to write to LCD
                SETB    P2.2            ;E=1 for H-to-L pulse
                ACALL   DELAY           ;give LCD some time
                CLR     P2.2            ;E=0, latch in
                RET
READY:          SETB    P1.7            ;make P1.7 input port
                CLR     P2.0            ;RS=0 access command reg
                SETB    P2.1            ;R/W=1 read command reg
;read command reg and check busy flag
BACK:           CLR     P2.2            ;E=0 for L-to-H pulse
                ACALL   DELAY           ;give LCD some time
                SETB    P2.2            ;E=1 L-to-H pulse
```

Program 12-2. (*continued*)

Notice in the above program that the busy flag is D7 of the command register. To read the command register we make R/W = 1 and RS = 0, and a L-to-H pulse for the E pin will provide us the command register. After reading the command register, if bit D7 (the busy flag) is high, the LCD is busy and no information (command or data) should be issued to it. Only when D7 = 0 can we send data or commands to the LCD. Notice in this method that no time delays are used since we are checking the busy flag before issuing commands or data to the LCD. Contrast the Read and Write timing for the LCD in Figures 12-3 and 12-4. Note that the E line is negative-edge triggered for the write, while it is positive-edge triggered for the read.

LCD data sheet

In the LCD, one can put data at any location. The following shows address locations and how they are accessed.

RS	R/W	DB7	DB6	DB5	DB4	DB3	DB2	DB1	DB0
0	0	1	A	A	A	A	A	A	A

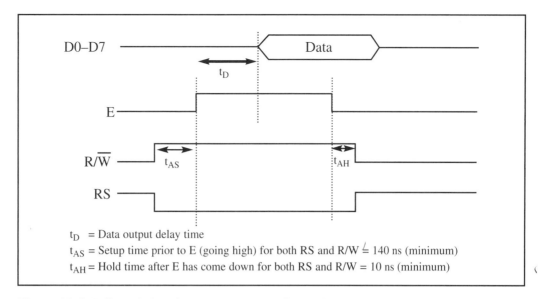

t_D = Data output delay time
t_{AS} = Setup time prior to E (going high) for both RS and R/W = 140 ns (minimum)
t_{AH} = Hold time after E has come down for both RS and R/W = 10 ns (minimum)

Figure 12-3. LCD Timing for Read (L-to-H for E line)
Note: Read requires an L-to-H pulse for the E pin.

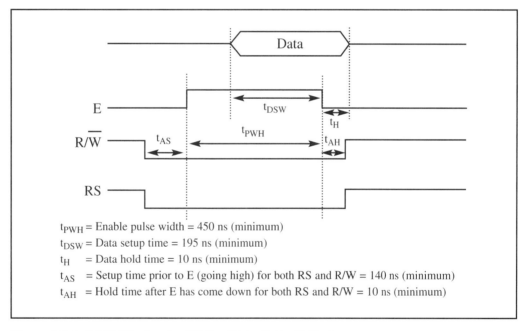

t_{PWH} = Enable pulse width = 450 ns (minimum)
t_{DSW} = Data setup time = 195 ns (minimum)
t_H = Data hold time = 10 ns (minimum)
t_{AS} = Setup time prior to E (going high) for both RS and R/W = 140 ns (minimum)
t_{AH} = Hold time after E has come down for both RS and R/W = 10 ns (minimum)

Figure 12-4. LCD Timing for Write (H-to-L for E line)

CHAPTER 12: LCD AND KEYBOARD INTERFACING 389

Table 12-3. LCD Addressing

	DB7	DB6	DB5	DB4	DB3	DB2	DB1	DB0
Line 1 (min)	1	0	0	0	0	0	0	0
Line 1 (max)	1	0	1	0	0	1	1	1
Line 2 (min)	1	1	0	0	0	0	0	0
Line 2 (max)	1	1	1	0	0	1	1	1

where AAAAAAA = 0000000 to 0100111 for line 1 and AAAAAAA = 1000000 to 1100111 for line 2. See Table 12-3.

The upper address range can go as high as 0100111 for the 40-character-wide LCD, while for the 20-character-wide LCD it goes up to 010011 (19 decimal = 10011 binary). Notice that the upper range 0100111 (binary) = 39 decimal, which corresponds to locations 0 to 39 for the LCDs of 40x2 size.

From the above discussion, we can get the addresses of cursor positions for various sizes of LCDs. See Figure 12-5 for the cursor addresses for common types of LCDs. Note that all the addresses are in hex. Table 12-4 provides a detailed list of LCD commands and instructions. Table 12-2 is extracted from this table.

```
16 x 2 LCD    80    81    82    83    84    85    86 through 8F
              C0    C1    C2    C3    C4    C5    C6 through CF

20 x 1 LCD    80    81    82    83    through 93

20 x 2 LCD    80    81    82    83    through 93
              C0    C1    C2    C3    through D3

20 x 4 LCD    80    81    82    83    through 93
              C0    C1    C2    C3    through D3
              94    95    96    97    through A7
              D4    D5    D6    D7    through E7

40 x 2 LCD    80    81    82    83    through A7
              C0    C1    C2    C3    through E7
```

Figure 12-5. Cursor Addresses for Some LCDs
Note: All data is in hex.

Table 12-4. List of LCD Instructions

Instruction	RS	R/W	DB7	DB6	DB5	DB4	DB3	DB2	DB1	DB0	Description	Execution Time (Max)
Clear Display	0	0	0	0	0	0	0	0	0	1	Clears entire display and sets DD RAM address 0 in address counter	1.64 ms
Return Home	0	0	0	0	0	0	0	0	1	-	Sets DD RAM address 0 as address counter. Also returns display being shifted to original position. DD RAM contents remain unchanged.	1.64 ms
Entry Mode Set	0	0	0	0	0	0	0	1	1/D	S	Sets cursor move direction and specifies shift of display. These operations are performed during data write and read.	40 µs
Display On/ Off Control	0	0	0	0	0	0	1	D	C	B	Sets On/Off of entire display (D), cursor On/Off (C), and blink of cursor position character (B).	40 µs
Cursor or Display Shift	0	0	0	0	0	1	S/C	R/L	-	-	Moves cursor and shifts display without changing DD RAM contents.	40 µs
Function Set	0	0	0	0	1	DL	N	F	-	-	Sets interface data length (DL), number of display lines (L), and character font (F).	40 µs
Set CG RAM Address	0	0	0	1	AGC						Sets CG RAM address. CG RAM data is sent and received after this setting.	40 µs
Set DD RAM Address	0	0	1	ADD							Sets DD RAM address. DD RAM data is sent and received after this setting.	40 µs
Read Busy Flag & Address	0	1	BF	AC							Reads busy flag (BF) indicating internal operation is being performed and reads address counter contents.	40 µs
Write Data CG or DD RAM	1	0	Write Data								Writes data into DD or CG RAM.	40 µs
Read Data CG or DD RAM	1	1	Read Data								Reads data from DD or CG RAM.	40 µs

Notes:

1. Execution times are maximum times when fcp or fosc is 250 kHz.
2. Execution time changes when frequency changes. For example, when fcp or fosc is 270 kHz:

    40 µs × 250 / 270 = 37 µs.
3. Abbreviations:

DD RAM	Display data RAM
CG RAM	Character generator RAM
ACC	CG RAM address
ADD	DD RAM address, corresponds to cursor address
AC	Address counter used for both DD and CG RAM addresses.
1/D = 1	Increment	1/D = 0 Decrement
S = 1	Accompanies display shift
S/C = 1	Display shift;	S/C = 0 Cursor move
R/L = 1	Shift to the right;	R/L = 0 Shift to the left
DL = 1	8 bits, DL = 0: 4 bits
N = 1	1line, N = 0 : 1 line
F = 1	5 x 10 dots, F = 0 : 5 x 7 dots
BF = 1	Internal operation;	BF = 0 Can accept instruction

Sending information to LCD using MOVC instruction

Program 12-3 shows how to use the MOVC instruction to send data and commands to an LCD. For an 8051 C version of LCD programming, see Examples 12-1 and 12-2.

```
;calls a time delay before sending next data/command
; P1.0-P1.7=D0-D7, P2.0=RS, P2.1=R/W, P2.2=E pins
            ORG    0
            MOV    DPTR,#MYCOM
C1:         CLR    A
            MOVC   A,@A+DPTR
            ACALL  COMNWRT        ;call command subroutine
            ACALL  DELAY          ;give LCD some time
            JZ     SEND_DAT
            INC    DPTR
            SJMP   C1
SEND_DAT:   MOV    DPTR,#MYDATA
D1:         CLR    A
            MOVC   A,@A+DPTR
            ACALL  DATAWRT        ;call command subroutine
            ACALL  DELAY          ;give LCD some time
            INC    DPTR
            JZ     AGAIN
            SJMP   D1
AGAIN:      SJMP   AGAIN          ;stay here
COMNWRT:                          ;send command to LCD
            MOV    P1,A           ;SEND COMND to P1
            CLR    P2.0           ;RS=0 for command
            CLR    P2.1           ;R/W=0 for write
            SETB   P2.2           ;E=1 for high pulse
            ACALL  DELAY          ;give LCD some time
            CLR    P2.2           ;E=0 for H-to-L
            RET
DATAWRT:
            MOV    P1,A           ;SEND DATA to P1
            SETB   P2.0           ;RS=1 for data
            CLR    P2.1           ;R/W=0 for write
            SETB   P2.2           ;E=1 for high pulse
            ACALL  DELAY          ;give LCD some time
            CLR    P2.2           ;E=0 for H-to-L pulse
            RET
DELAY:      MOV    R3,#250        ;LONG DELAY FOR fast CPUs
HERE2:      MOV    R4,#255        ;
HERE:       DJNZ   R4,HERE        ;
            DJNZ   R3,HERE2
            RET
            ORG    300H
MYCOM:      DB     38H,0EH,01,06,84H,0    ;commands and null
MYDATA:     DB     "HELLO",0              ;data and null
            END
```

Program 12-3. Sending Information to LCD with MOVC Instruction.

Example 12-1

Write an 8051 C program to send letters 'M,' 'D,' and 'E' to the LCD using delays.

Solution:

```
#include <reg51.h>
sfr ldata = 0x90;                    //P1=LCD data pins (Fig. 12-2)
sbit rs = P2^0;
sbit rw = P2^1;
sbit en = P2^2;
void main()
   {
   lcdcmd(0x38);
   MSDelay(250);
   lcdcmd(0x0E);
   MSDelay(250);
   lcdcmd(0x01);
   MSDelay(250);
   lcdcmd(0x06);
   MSDelay(250);
   lcdcmd(0x86);                     //line 1, position 6
   MSDelay(250);
   lcddata('M');
   MSDelay(250);
   lcddata('D');
   MSDelay(250);
   lcddata('E');
   }

void lcdcmd(unsigned char value)
   {
   ldata = value;                    // put the value on the pins
   rs = 0;
   rw = 0;
   en = 1;                           // strobe the enable pin
   MSDelay(1);
   en = 0;
   return;
   }

void lcddata(unsigned char value)
   {
   ldata = value;                    // put the value on the pins
   rs = 1;
   rw = 0;
   en = 1;                           // strobe the enable pin
   MSDelay(1);
   en = 0;
   return;
   }

void MSDelay(unsigned int itime)
   {
   unsigned int i, j;
   for(i=0;i<itime;i++)
     for(j=0;j<1275;j++);
   }
```

Example 12-2

Repeat Example 12-1 using the busy flag method.

Solution:

```c
#include <reg51.h>
sfr ldata = 0x90;                        //P1=LCD data pins (Fig. 12-2)
sbit rs = P2^0;
sbit rw = P2^1;
sbit en = P2^2;
sbit busy = P1^7;
void main()
  {
    lcdcmd(0x38);
    lcdcmd(0x0E);
    lcdcmd(0x01);
    lcdcmd(0x06);
    lcdcmd(0x86);                        //line 1, position 6
    lcddata('M');
    lcddata('D');
    lcddata('E');
  }

void lcdcmd(unsigned char value)
  {
    lcdready();                          //check the LCD busy flag
    ldata = value;                       //put the value on the pins
    rs = 0;
    rw = 0;
    en = 1;                              //strobe the enable pin
    MSDelay(1);
    en = 0;
    return;
  }

void lcddata(unsigned char value)
  {
    lcdready();                          //check the LCD busy flag
    ldata = value;                       //put the value on the pins
    rs = 1;
    rw = 0;
    en = 1;                              //strobe the enable pin
    MSDelay(1);
    en = 0;
    return;
  }

void lcdready()
  {
    busy = 1;                            //make the busy pin an input
    rs = 0;
    rw = 1;
    while(busy==1)                       //wait here for busy flag
      {
        en = 0;                          //strobe the enable pin
        MSDelay(1);
        en = 1;
      }
    return;
  }
```

Example 12-2 (*Continued*)

```
void MSDelay(unsigned int itime)
{
    unsigned int i, j;
    for(i=0;i<itime;i++)
       for(j=0;j<1275;j++);
}
```

REVIEW QUESTIONS

1. The RS pin is an _____ (input, output) pin for the LCD.
2. The E pin is an _____ (input, output) pin for the LCD.
3. The E pin requires an _____ (H-to-L, L-to-H) pulse to latch in information at the data pins of the LCD.
4. For the LCD to recognize information at the data pins as data, RS must be set to _____ (high, low).
5. Give the command codes for line 1, first character, and line 2, first character.

12.2: KEYBOARD INTERFACING

Keyboards and LCDs are the most widely used input/output devices of the 8051, and a basic understanding of them is essential. In this section, we first discuss keyboard fundamentals, along with key press and key detection mechanisms. Then we show how a keyboard is interfaced to an 8051.

Interfacing the keyboard to the 8051

At the lowest level, keyboards are organized in a matrix of rows and columns. The CPU accesses both rows and columns through ports; therefore, with two 8-bit ports, an 8 x 8 matrix of keys can be connected to a microprocessor. When a key is pressed, a row and a column make a contact; otherwise, there is no connection between rows and columns. In IBM PC keyboards, a single microprocessor (consisting of a microprocessor, RAM and EPROM, and several ports all on a single chip) takes care of hardware and software interfacing of the keyboard. In such systems, it is the function of programs stored in the EPROM of the microprocessor to scan the keys continuously, identify which one has been activated, and present it to the motherboard. In this section, we look at the mechanism by which the 8051 scans and identifies the key.

Scanning and identifying the key

Figure 12-6 shows a 4 x 4 matrix connected to two ports. The rows are connected to an output port and the columns are connected to an input port. If no key has been pressed, reading the input port will yield 1s for all columns since they are all connected to high (V_{CC}). If all the rows are grounded and a key is

---

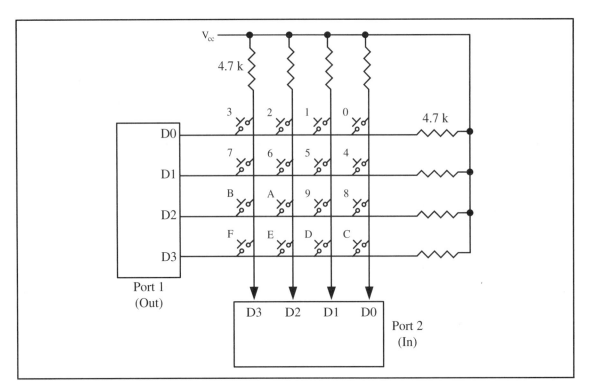

Figure 12-6. Matrix Keyboard Connection to Ports

pressed, one of the columns will have 0 since the key pressed provides the path to ground. It is the function of the microprocessor to scan the keyboard continuously to detect and identify the key pressed. How it is done is explained next.

Grounding rows and reading the columns

To detect a pressed key, the microprocessor grounds all rows by providing 0 to the output latch, and then it reads the columns. If the data read from the columns is D3–D0 = 1111, no key has been pressed and the process continues until a key press is detected. However, if one of the column bits has a zero, this means that a key press has occurred. For example, if D3–D0 = 1101, this means that a key in the D1 column has been pressed. After a key press is detected, the microprocessor will go through the process of identifying the key. Starting with the top row, the microprocessor grounds it by providing a low to row D0 only; then it reads the columns. If the data read is all 1s, no key in that row is activated and the process is moved to the next row. It grounds the next row, reads the columns, and checks for any zero. This process continues until the row is identified. After identification of the row in which the key has been pressed, the next task is to find out which column the pressed key belongs to. This should be easy since the microprocessor knows at any time which row and column are being accessed. Look at Example 12-3.

Program 12-4 is the 8051 Assembly language program for detection and identification of key activation. In this program, it is assumed that P1 and

Example 12-3

From Figure 12-6, identify the row and column of the pressed key for each of the following.

(a) D3–D0 = 1110 for the row, D3–D0 = 1011 for the column

(b) D3–D0 = 1101 for the row, D3–D0 = 0111 for the column

Solution:

From Figure 12-6, the row and column can be used to identify the key.

(a) The row belongs to D0 and the column belongs to D2; therefore, key number 2 was pressed.

(b) The row belongs to D1 and the column belongs to D3; therefore, key number 7 was pressed.

```
;Keyboard subroutine. This program sends the ASCII code ;for
pressed key to P0.1
;P1.0-P1.3 connected to rows P2.0-P2.3 connected to columns
        MOV   P2,#0FFH            ;make P2 an input port
K1:     MOV   P1,#0               ;ground all rows at once
        MOV   A,P2            ;read all col. ensure all keys open
        ANL   A,#00001111B        ;masked unused bits
        CJNE  A,#00001111B,K1     ;check till all keys released
K2:     ACALL DELAY               ;call 20 ms delay
        MOV   A,P2                ;see if any key is pressed
        ANL   A,#00001111B        ;mask unused bits
        CJNE  A,#00001111B,OVER   ;key pressed, await closure
        SJMP  K2                  ;check if key pressed
OVER:   ACALL DELAY               ;wait 20 ms debounce time
        MOV   A,P2                ;check key closure
        ANL   A,#00001111B        ;mask unused bits
        CJNE  A,#00001111B,OVER1  ;key pressed, find row
        SJMP  K2                  ;if none, keep polling
OVER1:  MOV   P1,#11111110B       ;ground row 0
        MOV   A,P2                ;read all columns
        ANL   A,#00001111B        ;mask unused bits
        CJNE  A,#00001111B,ROW_0  ;key row 0, find the col.
        MOV   P1,#11111101B       ;ground row 1
        MOV   A,P2                ;read all columns
        ANL   A,#00001111B        ;mask unused bits
        CJNE  A,#00001111B,ROW_1  ;key row 1, find the col.
        MOV   P1,#11111011B       ;ground row 2
        MOV   A,P2                ;read all columns
        ANL   A,#00001111B        ;mask unused bits
        CJNE  A,#00001111B,ROW_2  ;key row 2, find the col.
        MOV   P1,#11110111B       ;ground row 3
        MOV   A,P2                ;read all columns
```

Program 12-4. Keyboard Program (*continued*)

```
            ANL    A,#00001111B          ;mask unused bits
            CJNE   A,#00001111B,ROW_3    ;key row 3, find the col.
            LJMP   K2                    ;if none, false input, repeat

ROW_0:  MOV    DPTR,#KCODE0          ;set DPTR=start of row 0
        SJMP   FIND                 ;find col. key belongs to
ROW_1:  MOV    DPTR,#KCODE1          ;set DPTR=start of row 1
        SJMP   FIND                 ;find col. key belongs to
ROW_2:  MOV    DPTR,#KCODE2          ;set DPTR=start of row 2
        SJMP   FIND                 ;find col. key belongs to
ROW_3:  MOV    DPTR,#KCODE3          ;set DPTR=start of row 3
FIND:   RRC    A                    ;see if any CY bit is low
        JNC    MATCH                ;if zero, get the ASCII code
        INC    DPTR                 ;point to next col. address
        SJMP   FIND                 ;keep searching
MATCH:  CLR    A                    ;set A=0 (match is found)
        MOVC   A,@A+DPTR            ;get ASCII code from table
        MOV    P0,A                 ;display pressed key
        LJMP   K1
;ASCII LOOK-UP TABLE FOR EACH ROW
        ORG    300H
KCODE0: DB     '0','1','2','3'             ;ROW 0
KCODE1: DB     '4','5','6','7'             ;ROW 1
KCODE2: DB     '8','9','A','B'             ;ROW 2
KCODE3: DB     'C','D','E','F'             ;ROW 3
        END
```

Program 12-4. (*continued*)

P2 are initialized as output and input, respectively. Program 12-4 goes through the following four major stages:

1. To make sure that the preceding key has been released, 0s are output to all rows at once, and the columns are read and checked repeatedly until all the columns are high. When all columns are found to be high, the program waits for a short amount of time before it goes to the next stage of waiting for a key to be pressed.

2. To see if any key is pressed, the columns are scanned over and over in an infinite loop until one of them has a 0 on it. Remember that the output latches connected to rows still have their initial zeros (provided in stage 1), making them grounded. After the key press detection, the microprocessor waits 20 ms for the bounce and then scans the columns again. This serves two functions: (a) it ensures that the first key press detection was not an erroneous one due to a spike noise, and (b) the 20-ms delay prevents the same key press from being interpreted as a multiple key press. If after the 20-ms delay the key is still pressed, it goes to the next stage to detect which row it belongs to; otherwise, it goes back into the loop to detect a real key press.

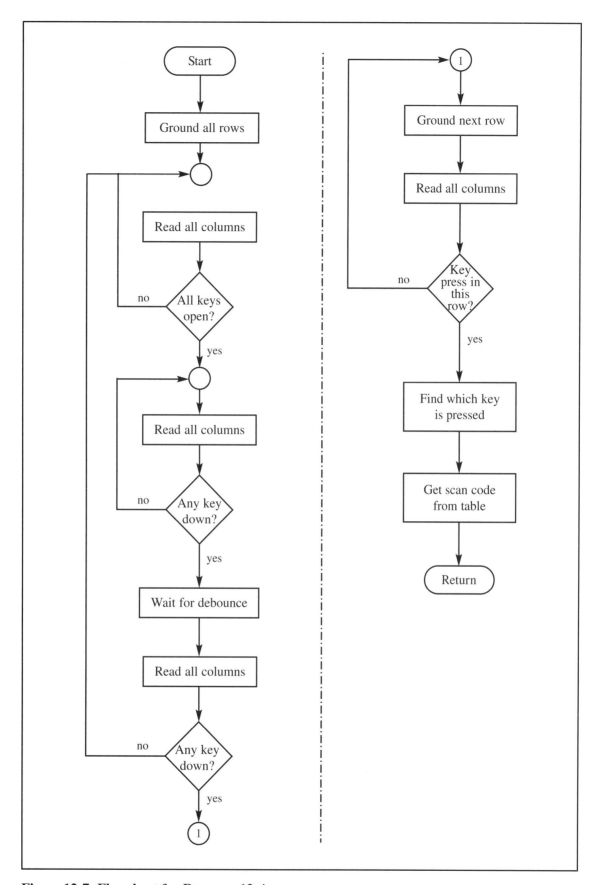

Figure 12-7. Flowchart for Program 12-4

3. To detect which row the key press belongs to, the microprocessor grounds one row at a time, reading the columns each time. If it finds that all columns are high, this means that the key press cannot belong to that row; therefore, it grounds the next row and continues until it finds the row the key press belongs to. Upon finding the row that the key press belongs to, it sets up the starting address for the look-up table holding the scan codes (or the ASCII value) for that row and goes to the next stage to identify the key.

4. To identify the key press, the microprocessor rotates the column bits, one bit at a time, into the carry flag and checks to see if it is low. Upon finding the zero, it pulls out the ASCII code for that key from the look-up table; otherwise, it increments the pointer to point to the next element of the look-up table. Figure 12-7 flowcharts this process.

Example 12-4

Write a C program to read the keypad and send the result to the first serial port.
P1.0–P1.3 connected to rows
P2.0–P1.3 connected to columns
Configure the serial port for 9600 baud, 8-bit, and 1 stop bit.

Solution:
```c
#include <reg51.h>

#define COL  P2                  //define ports for easier reading
#define ROW  P1

void MSDelay(unsigned int value);
void SerTX(unsigned char);

unsigned char keypad[4][4] =      {'0','1','2','3',
                                   '4','5','6','7',
                                   '8','9','A','B',
                                   'C','D','E','F'};

void main()
  {
    unsigned char colloc, rowloc;

     TMOD = 0x20;                 //timer 1, mode 2
     TH1 = -3;                    //9600 baud
     SCON = 0x50;                 //8-bit, 1 stop bit
     TR1 = 1;                     //start timer 1

   //keyboard routine. This sends the ASCII
   //code for pressed key to the serial port
   COL = 0xFF;                    //make P2 an input port
   while(1)                       //repeat forever
     {
     do
       {
       ROW = 0x00;                //ground all rows at once
       colloc = COL;              //read the columns
       colloc &= 0x0F;            //mask used bits
       } while(colloc != 0x0F);   //check until all keys released
```

Example 12-4 (*Continued*)

```
do
  {
  do
    {
    MSDelay(20);               //call delay
    colloc = COL;              //see if any key is pressed
    colloc &= 0x0F;            //mask unused bits
    } while(colloc == 0x0F);//keep checking for keypress

  MSDelay(20);                 //call delay for debounce
  colloc = COL;                //read columns
  colloc &= 0x0F;              //mask unused bits
  } while(colloc == 0x0F);     //wait for keypress

  while(1)
    {
    ROW = 0xFE;                //ground row 0
    colloc = COL;              //read columns
    colloc &= 0x0F;            //mask unused bits
    if(colloc != 0x0F)         //column detected
      {
        rowloc = 0;            //save row location
        break;                //exit while loop
      }

    ROW = 0xFD;                //ground row 1
    colloc = COL;              //read columns
    colloc &= 0x0F;            //mask unused bits
    if(colloc != 0x0F)         //column detected
      {
        rowloc = 1;            //save row location
        break;                //exit while loop
      }

    ROW = 0xFB;                //ground row 2
    colloc = COL;              //read columns
    colloc &= 0x0F;            //mask unused bits
    if(colloc != 0x0F)         //column detected
      {
        rowloc = 2;            //save row location
        break;                //exit while loop
      }

    ROW = 0xF7;                //ground row 3
    colloc = COL;              //read columns
    colloc &= 0x0F;            //mask unused bits
    rowloc = 3;                //save row location
    break;                    //exit while loop
    }

  //check column and send result to the serial port
  if(colloc == 0x0E)
    SerTX(keypad[rowloc][0]);
  else if(colloc == 0x0D)
    SerTX(keypad[rowloc][1]);
  else if(colloc == 0x0B)
    SerTX(keypad[rowloc][2]);
```

Example 12-4 (*Continued*)

```
        else
          SerTX(keypad[rowloc][3]);
        }

    }

void SerTX(unsigned char x)
    {
      SBUF = x;                 //place value in buffer
      while(TI==0);             //wait until transmitted
      TI = 0;                   //clear flag
    }

void MSDelay(unsigned int value)
    {
      unsigned int x, y;
      for(x=0;x<1275;x++)
        for(y=0;y<value;y++);
    }
```

While the key press detection is standard for all keyboards, the process for determining which key is pressed varies. The look-up table method shown in Program 12-4 can be modified to work with any matrix up to 8 x 8. Figure 12-7 provides the flowchart for Program 12-4 for scanning and identifying the pressed key.

There are IC chips such as National Semiconductor's MM74C923 that incorporate keyboard scanning and decoding all in one chip. Such chips use combinations of counters and logic gates (no microprocessor) to implement the underlying concepts presented in Program 12-4. Example 12-4 shows keypad programming in 8051 C.

REVIEW QUESTIONS

1. True or false. To see if any key is pressed, all rows are grounded.
2. If D3–D0 = 0111 is the data read from the columns, which column does the pressed key belong to?
3. True or false. Key press detection and key identification require two different processes.
4. In Figure 12-6, if the rows are D3–D0 = 1110 and the columns are D3–D0 = 1110, which key is pressed?
5. True or false. To identify the pressed key, one row at a time is grounded.

SUMMARY

This chapter showed how to interface real-world devices such as LCDs and keypads to the 8051. First, we described the operation modes of LCDs, then described how to program the LCD by sending data or commands to it via its interface to the 8051.

Keyboards are one of the most widely used input devices for 8051 projects. This chapter also described the operation of keyboards, including key press and detection mechanisms. Then the 8051 was shown interfacing with a keyboard. 8051 programs were written to return the ASCII code for the pressed key.

RECOMMENDED WEB LINKS

Optrex is one of the largest manufacturer of LCDs. You can obtain datasheets from its website:

- www.optrex.com.

LCDs can be purchased from the following websites:

- www.digikey.com
- www.jameco.com
- www.elexp.com

PROBLEMS

12.1: LCD INTERFACING

1. The LCD discussed in this section has _____ (4, 8) data pins.
2. Describe the function of pins E, R/W, and RS in the LCD.
3. What is the difference between the V_{CC} and V_{EE} pins on the LCD?
4. "Clear LCD" is a _____ (command code, data item) and its value is ___ hex.
5. What is the hex value of the command code for "display on, cursor on"?
6. Give the state of RS, E, and R/W when sending a command code to the LCD.
7. Give the state of RS, E, and R/W when sending data character "Z" to the LCD.
8. Which of the following is needed on the E pin in order for a command code (or data) to be latched in by the LCD?
   (a) H-to-L pulse (b) L-to-H pulse
9. True or false. For the above to work, the value of the command code (data) must already be at the D0–D7 pins.
10. There are two methods of sending streams of characters to the LCD: (1) checking the busy flag, or (2) putting some time delay between sending each character without checking the busy flag. Explain the difference and the advantages and disadvantages of each method. Also explain how we monitor the busy flag.
11. For a 16x2 LCD, the location of the last character of line 1 is 8FH (its command code). Show how this value was calculated.
12. For a 16x2 LCD, the location of the first character of line 2 is C0H (its command code). Show how this value was calculated.

---

13. For a 20x2 LCD, the location of the last character of line 2 is 93H (its command code). Show how this value was calculated.
14. For a 20x2 LCD, the location of the third character of line 2 is C2H (its command code). Show how this value was calculated.
15. For a 40x2 LCD, the location of the last character of line 1 is A7H (its command code). Show how this value was calculated.
16. For a 40x2 LCD, the location of the last character of line 2 is E7H (its command code). Show how this value was calculated.
17. Show the value (in hex) for the command code for the 10th location, line 1 on a 20x2 LCD. Show how you got your value.
18. Show the value (in hex) for the command code for the 20th location, line 2 on a 40x2 LCD. Show how you got your value.
19. Rewrite the COMNWRT subroutine. Assume connections P1.4 = RS, P1.5 = R/W, P1.6 = E.
20. Repeat Problem 19 for the data write subroutine. Send the string "Hello" to the LCD by checking the busy flag. Use the instruction MOVC.

12.2: KEYBOARD INTERFACING

21. In reading the columns of a keyboard matrix, if no key is pressed we should get all _____ (1s, 0s).
22. In Figure 12-6, to detect the key press, which of the following is grounded?
    (a) all rows   (b) one row at time   (c) both (a) and (b)
23. In Figure 12-6, to identify the key pressed, which of the following is grounded?
    (a) all rows   (b) one row at time   (c) both (a) and (b)
24. For Figure 12-6, indicate the column and row for each of the following.
    (a) D3–D0 = 0111   (b) D3–D0 = 1110
25. Indicate the steps to detect the key press.
26. Indicate the steps to identify the key pressed.
27. Indicate an advantage and a disadvantage of using an IC chip for keyboard scanning and decoding instead of using a microprocessor.
28. What is the best compromise for the answer to Problem 27?

ANSWERS TO REVIEW QUESTIONS

12.1: LCD INTERFACING

1. Input
2. Input
3. H-to-L
4. High
5. 80H and C0H

12.2: KEYBOARD INTERFACING

1. True
2. Column 3
3. True
4. 0
5. True

CHAPTER 13

ADC, DAC, AND SENSOR INTERFACING

OBJECTIVES

Upon completion of this chapter, you will be able to:

>> Interface ADC (analog-to-digital converter) chips to the 8051.
>> Interface temperature sensors to the 8051.
>> Explain the process of data acquisition using ADC chips.
>> Describe factors to consider in selecting an ADC chip.
>> Describe the function of the pins of 804/809/848 ADC chips.
>> Describe the function of the pins of the MAX1112 serial ADC chip.
>> Interface serial ADC chips to the 8051.
>> Program serial and parallel ADC chips in 8051 C and Assembly.
>> Describe the basic operation of a DAC (digital-to-analog converter) chip.
>> Interface a DAC chip to the 8051.
>> Program a DAC chip to produce a sine wave on an oscilloscope.
>> Program DAC chips in 8051 C and Assembly.
>> Explain the function of precision IC temperature sensors.
>> Describe signal conditioning and its role in data acquisition.

This chapter explores some more real-world devices such as ADCs (analog-to-digital converters), DACs (digital-to-analog converters), and sensors. We will also explain how to interface the 8051 to these devices. In Section 13.1, we describe analog-to-digital converter (ADC) chips. We will study the 8-bit parallel ADC chips ADC0804, ADC0808/0809, and ADC0848 We will also look at the serial ADC chip MAX1112. The characteristics of DAC chips are discussed in Section 13.2. In Section 13.3, we show the interfacing of sensors and discuss the issue of signal conditioning.

13.1: PARALLEL AND SERIAL ADC

This section will explore interfacing of both parallel and serial ADC chips to microprocessors. First, we describe the ADC0804 chip, then show how to interface it to the 8051. Then we examine the ADC0808/0809 and ADC0848 characteristics and show how to interface them to the 8051. At the end of this section, we describe the serial ADC chip MAX1112 and program it in both C and Assembly.

ADC devices

Analog-to-digital converters are among the most widely used devices for data acquisition. Digital computers use binary (discrete) values, but in the physical world everything is analog (continuous). Temperature, pressure (wind or liquid), humidity, and velocity are a few examples of physical quantities that we deal with every day. A physical quantity is converted to electrical (voltage, current) signals using a device called a *transducer*. Transducers are also referred to as *sensors*. Sensors for temperature, velocity, pressure, light, and many other natural quantities produce an output that is voltage (or current). Therefore, we need an analog-to-digital converter to translate the analog signals to digital numbers so that the microprocessor can read and process them. An ADC has *n*-bit resolution where *n* can be 8, 10, 12, 16 or even 24 bits. The higher-resolution ADC provides a smaller step size, where *step size* is the smallest change that can be discerned by an ADC. This is shown in Table 13-1. In this chapter, we examine several 8-bit ADC chips. In addition to resolution, conversion time is another major factor in judging an ADC. *Conversion time* is

Table 13-1. Resolution versus Step Size for ADC

n-bit	Number of Steps	Step Size (mV)
8	256	5/256 = 19.53
10	1024	5/1024 = 4.88
12	4096	5/4096 = 1.2
16	65536	5/65536 = 0.076

Notes: V_{cc} = 5 V

Step size (resolution) is the smallest change that can be discerned by an ADC.

defined as the time it takes for an ADC to convert the analog input to a digital (binary) number. The ADC chips are either parallel or serial. In parallel ADC, we have eight or more pins dedicated to bringing out the binary data, but in serial ADC we have only one pin for data out. Serial ADCs are discussed at the end of this section.

ADC0804 chip

The ADC0804 IC is an 8-bit parallel ADC in the family of the ADC0800 series from National Semiconductor (www.national.com). It is also available from many other manufacturers. It works with +5 V and has a resolution of 8 bits. In the ADC0804, the conversion time varies depending on the clocking signals applied to the CLK IN pin, but it cannot be faster than 110 μs. The following is the ADC0804 pin description.

CS

Chip select is an active-low input used to activate the ADC0804 chip. To access the ADC0804, this pin must be low.

RD (read)

This is an input signal and is active low. The ADC converts the analog input to its binary equivalent and holds it in an internal register. RD is used to get the converted data out of the ADC0804 chip. When CS = 0, if a high-to-low pulse is applied to the RD pin, the 8-bit digital output shows up at the D0–D7 data pins. The RD pin is also referred to as output enable (OE).

WR (write; a better name might be "start conversion")

This is an active-low input used to inform the ADC0804 to start the conversion process. If CS = 0 when WR makes a low-to-high transition, the ADC0804 starts converting the analog input value of V_{in} to an 8-bit digital number. The amount of time it takes to convert varies depending on the CLK IN and CLK R values explained below. When the data conversion is complete, the INTR pin is forced low by the ADC0804.

CLK IN and CLK R

CLK IN is an input pin connected to an external clock source when an external clock is used for timing. However, the 804 has an internal clock generator. To use the internal clock generator (also called self-clocking) of the ADC0804, the CLK IN and CLK R pins are connected to a capacitor and a resistor, as shown in Figure 13-1. In that case, the clock frequency is determined by the equation:

$$ f = \frac{1}{1.1\, RC} $$

Typical values are R = 10K ohms and C = 150 pF. Substituting in the above equation, we get f = 606 kHz. In that case, the conversion time is 110 μs.

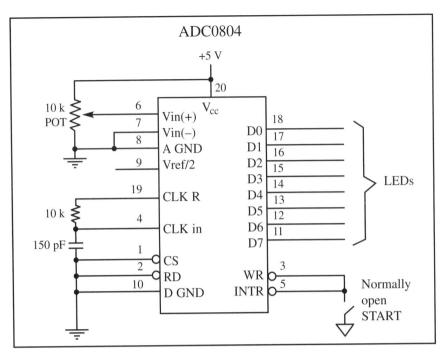

Figure 13-1. ADC0804 Chip (Testing ADC0804 in Free Running Mode)

INTR (interrupt; a better name might be "end of conversion")

This is an output pin and is active low. It is a normally high pin and when the conversion is finished, it goes low to signal the CPU that the converted data is ready to be picked up. After INTR goes low, we make CS = 0 and send a high-to-low pulse to the RD pin to get the data out of the ADC0804 chip.

V_{in} (+) and V_{in} (−)

These are the differential analog inputs where $V_{in} = V_{in} (+) - V_{in} (-)$. Often the $V_{in} (-)$ pin is connected to ground and the $V_{in} (+)$ pin is used as the analog input to be converted to digital.

V_{CC}

This is the +5 V power supply. It is also used as a reference voltage when the $V_{ref}/2$ input (pin 9) is open (not connected). This is discussed next.

$V_{ref}/2$

Pin 9 is an input voltage used for the reference voltage. If this pin is open (not connected), the analog input voltage for the ADC0804 is in the range of 0 to 5 V (the same as the V_{cc} pin). However, there are many applications where the analog input applied to V_{in} needs to be other than the 0 to +5 V range. $V_{ref}/2$ is used to implement analog input voltages other than 0 to 5 V. For example, if the analog input range needs to be 0 to 4 V, $V_{ref}/2$ is connected to 2 V. Table 13-2 shows the V_{in} range for various $V_{ref}/2$ inputs.

Table 13-2. $V_{ref}/2$ Relation to V_{in} Range (ADC0804)

$V_{ref}/2$ (V)	V_{in} (V)	Step Size (mV)
Not connected*	0 to 5	5/256 = 19.53
2.0	0 to 4	4/255 = 15.62
1.5	0 to 3	3/256 = 11.71
1.28	0 to 2.56	2.56/256 = 10

Notes: V_{cc} = 5 V

*When not connected (open), $V_{ref}/2$ is measured at 2.5 V for V_{cc} = 5 V.

Step size (resolution) is the smallest change that can be discerned by an ADC.

D0–D7

D0–D7 (D7 is the MSB) are the digital data output pins since ADC0804 is a parallel ADC chip. These are tri-state buffered and the converted data is accessed only when CS = 0 and RD is forced low. To calculate the output voltage, use the following formula.

$$D_{out} = \frac{V_{in}}{step\ size}$$

where D_{out} = digital data output (in decimal), V_{in} = analog input voltage, and step size (resolution) is the smallest change, which is $(2 \times V_{ref}/2)/256$ for ADC0804.

Analog ground and digital ground

These are the input pins providing the ground for both the analog signal and the digital signal. Analog ground is connected to the ground of the analog V_{in} while digital ground is connected to the ground of the V_{cc} pin. The reason that we have two ground pins is to isolate the analog V_{in} signal from transient voltages caused by digital switching of the output D0–D7. Such isolation contributes to the accuracy of the digital data output. In our discussion, both are connected to the same ground; however, in the real world of data acquisition, the analog and digital grounds are handled separately.

From this discussion, we conclude that the following steps must be followed for data conversion by the ADC0804 chip.

1. Make CS = 0 and send a low-to-high pulse to pin WR to start the conversion.

2. Keep monitoring the INTR pin. If INTR is low, the conversion is finished and we can go to the next step. If INTR is high, keep polling until it goes low.

3. After the INTR has become low, we make CS = 0 and send a high-to-low pulse to the RD pin to get the data out of the ADC0804 IC chip. The timing for this process is shown in Figure 13-2.

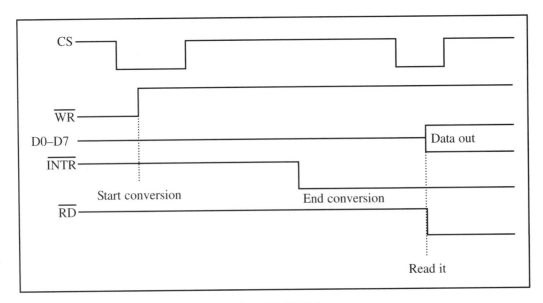

Figure 13-2. Read and Write Timing for ADC0804

Note: CS is set to low for both $\overline{RD}$ and $\overline{WR}$ pulses.

Clock source for ADC0804

The speed at which an analog input is converted to the digital output depends on the speed of the CLK input. According to the ADC0804 data sheets, the typical operating frequency is approximately 640 kHz at 5 V. Figures 13-3 and 13-4 show two ways of providing clock to the ADC0804. In Figure 13-4, notice that the clock in for the ADC0804 is coming from the crystal of the microprocessor. Since this frequency is too high, we use D flip-flops (74LS74) to divide the frequency. A single D flip-flop divides the frequency by 2 if we connect its $\overline{Q}$ to the D input. For a higher-frequency crystal, you can use four flip-flops.

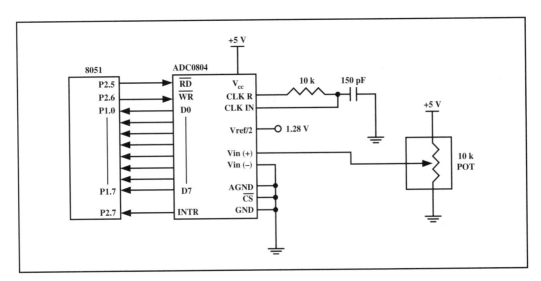

Figure 13-3. 8051 Connection to ADC0804 with Self-Clocking

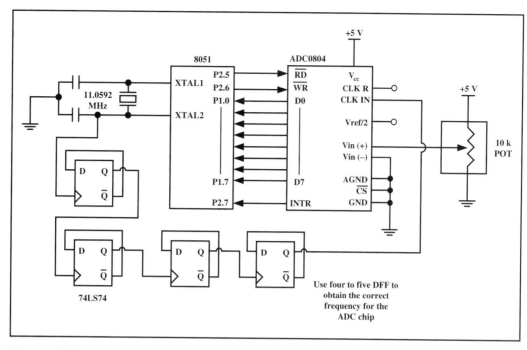

Figure 13-4. 8051 Connection to ADC0804 with Clock from XTAL2 of the 8051

Programming ADC0804 in Assembly

Examine the ADC0804 connection to the 8051 in Figure 13-4. The following program monitors the INTR pin and brings an analog input into register A. It then calls hex-to-ASCII conversion and data display subroutines.

```
        RD      BIT P2.5        ;RD
        WR      BIT P2.6        ;WR (start conversion)
        INTR    BIT P2.7        ;end-of-conversion
        MYDATA  EQU P1          ;P1.0-P1.7=D0-D7 of the ADC804
        MOV     P1,#0FFH        ;make P1 = input
        SETB    INTR
BACK:   CLR     WR              ;WR=0
        SETB    WR              ;WR=1 L-to-H to start conversion
HERE:   JB      INTR,HERE       ;wait for end of conversion
        CLR     RD              ;conversion finished,enable RD
        MOV     A,MYDATA        ;read the data
        ACALL   CONVERSION      ;hex-to-ASCII conversion(Chap 6)
        ACALL   DATA_DISPLAY    ;display the data(Chap 12)
        SETB    RD              ;make RD=1 for next round
        SJMP    BACK
```

For hex-to-ASCII conversion and data display, see Chapters 6 and 12, respectively.

CHAPTER 13: ADC, DAC, AND SENSOR INTERFACING

The 8051 C version of the above program is given below.

```c
#include <reg51.h>
sbit RD = P2^5;
sbit WR = P2^6;
sbit INTR = P2^7;
sfr MYDATA = P1;
void main()
  {
    unsigned char value;
    MYDATA = 0xFF;          //make P1 and input
    INTR = 1;               //make INTR and input
    RD = 1;                 //set RD high
    WR = 1;                 //set WR high
    while(1)
     {
        WR = 0;             //send WR pulse
        WR = 1;             //L-to-H(Start Conversion)
        while(INTR == 1);   //wait for EOC
        RD = 0;             //send RD pulse
        value = MYDATA;     //read value
        ConvertAndDisplay(value);   //(Chap 7 and 12)
        RD = 1;
     }
  }
```

ADC0808/0809 chip with eight analog channels

Another useful chip is the ADC0808/0809 from National Semiconductor. See Figure 13-5. While the ADC0804 has only one analog input, this chip has eight of them. The ADC0808/0809 chip allows us to monitor up to eight different analog inputs using only a single chip. Notice that the ADC0808/0809 has an 8-bit data output just like the ADC0804. The eight analog input channels are multiplexed and selected according to Table 13-3 using three address pins, A, B, and C.

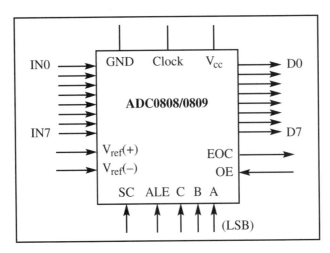

Figure 13-5. ADC0808/0809

CHAPTER 13: ADC, DAC, AND SENSOR INTERFACING

Table 13-3. ADC0808/0809 Analog Channel Selection

Selected Analog Channel	C	B	A
IN0	0	0	0
IN1	0	0	1
IN2	0	1	0
IN3	0	1	1
IN4	1	0	0
IN5	1	0	1
IN6	1	1	0
IN7	1	1	1

In the ADC0808/0809, $V_{ref}(+)$ and $V_{ref}(-)$ set the reference voltage. If $V_{ref}(-)$ = Gnd and $V_{ref}(+)$ = 5 V, the step size is 5 V/256 = 19.53 mV. Therefore, to get a 10 mV step size we need to set $V_{ref}(+)$ = 2.56 V and $V_{ref}(-)$ = Gnd. From Figure 13-5, notice the ALE (address latch enable) pin. We use A, B, and C addresses to select IN0–IN7, and activate ALE to latch in the address. SC is for start conversion. SC is the same as the WR pin in other ADC chips. EOC is for end-of-conversion, and OE is for output enable (READ). The EOC and OE are the same as the INTR and RD pins respectively. Table 13-4 shows the step size relation to the V_{ref} voltage. Notice that there is no $V_{ref}/2$ in the ADC0808/0809 chip.

Steps to program the ADC0808/0809

The following are steps to get data from an ADC0808/0809.

1. Select an analog channel by providing bits to A, B, and C addresses according to Table 13-3.
2. Activate the ALE (address latch enable) pin. It needs an L-to-H pulse to latch in the address. See Figure 13-6.
3. Activate SC (start conversion) by an L-to-H pulse to initiate conversion.
4. Monitor EOC (end of conversion) to see whether conversion is finished. H-to-L output indicates that the data is converted and is ready to be picked up. If we do not use EOC, we can read the converted digital data after a

Table 13-4. V_{ref} Relation to V_{in} Range for ADC0808/0809

V_{ref} (V)	V_{in} (V)	Step Size (mV)
Not connected	0 to 5	5/256 = 19.53
4.0	0 to 4	4/255 = 15.62
3.0	0 to 3	3/256 = 11.71
2.56	0 to 2.56	2.56/256 = 10
2.0	0 to 2	2/256 = 7.81
1	0 to 1	1/256 = 3.90

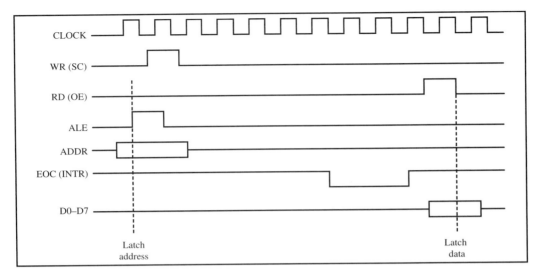

Figure 13-6. Selecting a Channel and Read Timing for ADC0809

brief time delay. The delay size depends on the speed of the external clock we connect to the CLK pin. Notice that the EOC is the same as the INTR pin in other ADC chips.

5. Activate OE (output enable) to read data out of the ADC chip. An L-to-H pulse to the OE pin will bring digital data out of the chip. Also notice that the OE is the same as the RD pin in other ADC chips.

Notice in the ADC0808/0809 that there is no self-clocking and the clock must be provided from an external source to the CLK pin. Although the speed of conversion depends on the frequency of the clock connected to the CLK pin, it cannot be faster than 100 microseconds.

Figure 13-7 shows the connections for the following programs.

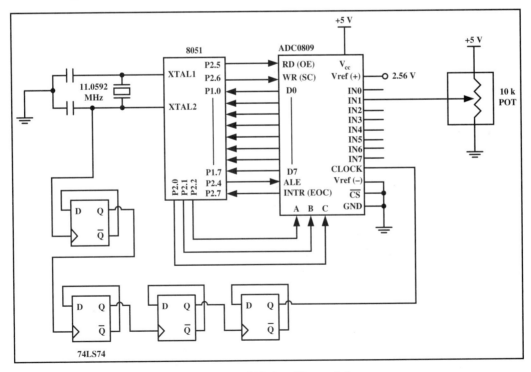

Figure 13-7. 8051 Connection to ADC0809 for Channel 1

Programming ADC0808/0809 in Assembly

```
              ALE    BIT P2.4
              OE     BIT P2.5
              SC     BIT P2.6
              EOC    BIT P2.7
              ADDR_A BIT P2.0
              ADDR_B BIT P2.1
              ADDR_C BIT P2.2
              MYDATA EQU P1
              ORG    0H
              MOV    MYDATA,#0FFH      ;make P1 an input
              SETB   EOC               ;make EOC an input
              CLR    ALE               ;clear ALE
              CLR    SC                ;clear WR
              CLR    OE                ;clear RD
BACK:
              CLR    ADDR_C            ;C=0
              CLR    ADDR_B            ;B=0
              SETB   ADDR_A            ;A=1 (Select Channel 1)
              ACALL  DELAY             ;make sure the addr is stable
              SETB   ALE               ;latch address
              ACALL  DELAY             ;delay for fast DS89C4x0 Chip
              SETB   SC                ;start conversion
              ACALL  DELAY
              CLR    ALE
              CLR    SC


HERE:
              JB     EOC, HERE         ;wait until done
HERE1:
              JNB    EOC, HERE1        ;wait until done
              SETB   OE                ;enable RD
              ACALL  DELAY             ;wait
              MOV    A,MYDATA          ;read data
              CLR    OE                ;clear RD for next time
              ACALL  CONVERSION        ;hex to ASCII (Chap 6)
              ACALL  DATA_DISPLAY      ;display the data (Chap 12)
              SJMP   BACK
```

Programming ADC0808/0809 in C

```c
#include <reg51.h>
sbit ALE = P2^4;
sbit OE = P2^5;
sbit SC = P2^6;
sbit EOC = P2^7;
sbit ADDR_A = P2^0;
sbit ADDR_B = P2^1;
sbit ADDR_C = P2^2;
sfr  MYDATA = P1;
```

CHAPTER 13: ADC, DAC, AND SENSOR INTERFACING   415

```
void main()
  {
    unsigned char value;
    MYDATA = 0xFF;                  //make P1 an input
    EOC = 1;                        //make EOC an input
    ALE = 0;                        //clear ALE
    OE = 0;                         //clear OE
    SC = 0;                         //clear SC
    while(1)
      {
        ADDR_C = 0;                 //C=0
        ADDR_B = 0;                 //B=0
        ADDR_A = 1;                 //A=1 (Select Channel 1)
        MSDelay(1);                 //delay for fast DS89C4x0
        ALE = 1;
        MSDelay(1);
        SC = 1;
        MSDelay(1);
        ALE = 0;
        SC = 0;                     //start conversion
        while(EOC==1);              //wait for data conversion
        while(EOC==0);
        OE = 1;                     //enable RD
        MSDelay(1);
        value = MYDATA;             //get the data
        OE = 0;                     //disable RD for next round
        ConvertAndDisplay(value);   //Chap 7 & 12
      }
  }
```

ADC0848 interfacing

The ADC0848 IC is another analog-to-digital converter in the family of the ADC0800 series from National Semiconductor Corp. Data sheets for this chip can be found at its website, www.national. com. From there, go to Products > Analog-Data Acquisition > A-to-D Converter-General Purpose.

The ADC0848 has a resolution of 8 bits. It is an eight-channel ADC, thereby allowing it to monitor up to eight different analog inputs. See Figure 13-8. The ADC0844 chip in the same family has four channels. The following describes the pins of the ADC0848.

CS

Chip select is an active-low input used to activate the 848 chip. To access the 848, this pin must be low.

RD (read)

RD is an input signal and is active low. ADC converts the analog input to its binary equivalent and

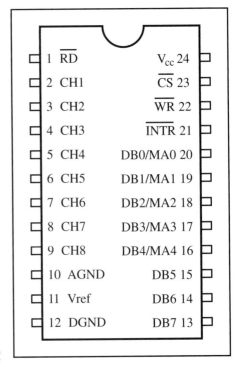

Figure 13-8. ADC0848 Chip

Table 13-5. ADC0848 Vref versus Step Size

V_{ref}(V)	Step Size (mV)
5	19.53 (5V/256)
4	15.62 (4V/256)
2.56	10 (2.56V/256)
1.26	5
0.64	2.5

Note: Step size = V_{ref}/256.

holds it in an internal register. RD is used to get the converted data out of the 848 chip. When CS = 0, if the RD pin is asserted low, the 8-bit digital output shows up at the D0–D7 data pins. The RD pin is also referred to as output enable (OE).

V_{ref}

V_{ref} is an input voltage used for the reference voltage. The voltage connected to this pin dictates the step size. For the ADC0848, the step size is V_{ref}/256 since it is an 8-bit ADC and 2 to the power of 8 gives us 256 steps. See Table 13-5. For example, if the analog input range needs to be 0 to 4 V, V_{ref} is connected to 4 V. That gives 4 V/256 = 15.62 mV for the step size. In another case, if we need a step size of 10 mV, then V_{ref} = 2.56 V, since 2.56 V/256 = 10 mV.

DB0–DB7

DB0–DB7 are the digital data output pins. With a D0–D7 output, the 848 must be an 8-bit ADC. The step size, which is the smallest change, is dictated by the number of digital outputs and the V_{ref} voltage. To calculate the output voltage, we use the following formula:

$$D_{out} = \frac{V_{in}}{step\ size}\ \ 2.5$$

where D_{out} = digital data output (in decimal), V_{in} = analog input voltage, and step size (resolution) is the smallest change, which is V_{ref}/256 for an 8-bit ADC. See Example 13-1 for clarification. Notice that D0–D7 are tri-state buffered and that the converted data is accessed only when CS = 0 and a low pulse is applied to the RD pin. Also, notice the dual role of pins D0–D7. They are also used to send in the channel address. This is discussed next.

Example 13-1

For a given ADC0848, we have V_{ref} = 2.56 V. Calculate the D0–D7 output if the analog input is: (a) 1.7 V and (b) 2.1 V.

Solution:

Since the step size is 2.56/256 = 10 mV, we have the following.
(a) D_{out} = 1.7 V/10 mV = 170 in decimal, which gives us 10101011 in binary for D7–D0.
(b) D_{out} = 2.1 V/10 mV = 210 in decimal, which gives us 11010010 in binary for D7–D0.

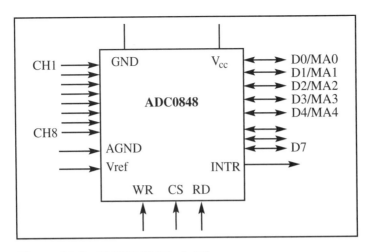

Figure 13-9. ADC0848 Block Diagram

MA0–MA4 (multiplexed address)

The ADC0848 uses multiplexed address/data pins to select the channel. Notice in Figure 13-9 that a portion of the DB0–DB7 pins are also designated as MA0–MA4. The D0–D7 pins are inputs when the channel's address is sent in. However, when the converted data is being read, D0–D7 are outputs. While the use of multiplexed address/data saves some pins, it makes I/O interfacing more difficult as we will soon see.

WR (write; a better name might be "start conversion")

This is an input into the ADC0848 chip and plays two important roles: (1) It latches the address of the selected channel present on the D0–D7 pins, and (2) it informs the ADC0848 to start the conversion of the analog input at that channel. If CS = 0 when WR makes a low-to-high transition, the ADC0848 latches in the address of the selected channel and starts converting the analog input value to an 8-bit digital number. The amount of time it takes to convert is a maximum of 40 µs for the ADC0848. The conversion time is set by an internal clock.

CH1–CH8

CH1–CH8 are eight channels of the V_{in} analog inputs. In what is called single-ended mode, each of the eight channels can be used for analog V_{in}, where the AGND (analog ground) pin is used as a ground reference for all the channels. These eight channels of input allow us to read eight different analog signals, but not all at the same time since there is only a single D0–D7 output. We select the input channel by using the MA0–MA4 multiplexed address pins according to Table 13-6. In Table 13-6, notice that MA4 = low and MA3 = high for single-ended mode. The ADC0848 can also be used in differential mode. In differential mode, two channels, such as CH1 and CH2, are paired together for the $V_{in}(+)$ and $V_{in}(-)$ differential analog inputs. In that case V_{in} = CH1(+) − CH2(−) is the differential analog input. To use ADC0848 in differential mode, MA4 = don't care and MA3 is set to low. For more on this, see the ADC0848 data sheet on the www.national.com website.

Table 13-6. ADC0848 Analog Channel Selection (Single-Ended Mode)

Selected Analog Channel	MA4	MA3	MA2	MA1	MA0
CH1	0	1	0	0	0
CH2	0	1	0	0	1
CH3	0	1	0	1	0
CH4	0	1	0	1	1
CH5	0	1	1	0	0
CH6	0	1	1	0	1
CH7	0	1	1	1	0
CH8	0	1	1	1	1

Note: Channel is selected when CS = 0, RD = 1, and an L-to-H pulse is applied to WR.

V_{CC}

V_{cc} is the +5 V power supply.

AGND, DGND (analog ground and digital ground)

Both are input pins providing the ground for both the analog signal and the digital signal. Analog ground is connected to the ground of the analog V_{in} while digital ground is connected to the ground of the V_{CC} pin. The reason that we have two ground pins is to isolate the analog V_{in} signal from transient voltages caused by digital switching of the output D0–D7. Such isolation contributes to the accuracy of the digital data output. Notice that in the single-ended mode the voltage at the channel is the analog input and AGND is the reference for the V_{in}. In our discussion, both the AGND and DGND are connected to the same ground; however, in the real world of data acquisition, the analog and digital grounds are handled separately.

INTR (interrupt; a better name might be "end of conversion")

This is an output pin and is active low. It is a normally high pin and when the conversion is finished, it goes low to signal the CPU that the converted data is ready to be picked up. After INTR goes low, we make CS = 0 and apply a low pulse to the RD pin to get the binary data out of the ADC0848 chip. See Figure 13-10.

Selecting an analog channel

The following are the steps we need to take for data conversion by the ADC0848 chip.

1. While CS = 0 and RD = 1 provide the address of the selected channel (see Table 13-6) to the DB0–DB7 pins, and apply a low-to-high pulse to the WR pin to latch in the address and start the conversion. The channel's addresses are 08H for CH1, 09H for CH2, 0AH for CH3, and so on, as

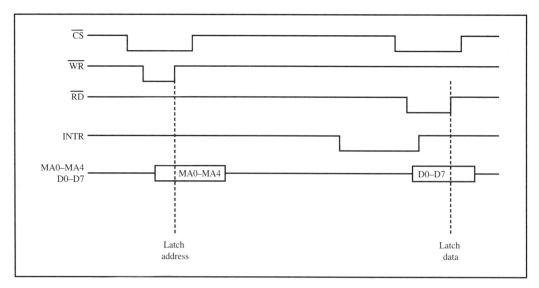

Figure 13-10. Selecting a Channel and Read Timing for the ADC0848

shown in Table 13-6. Notice that this process not only selects the channel, but also starts the conversion of the analog input at the selected channel.

2. While WR = 1 and RD = 1 keep monitoring the INTR pin. When INTR goes low, the conversion is finished and we can go to the next step. If INTR is high, we keep the ADC0848 polling until it goes low, signalling end-of-conversion.

3. After the INTR has become low, we must make CS = 0, WR = 1, and apply a low pulse to the RD pin to get the data out of the 848 IC chip.

ADC0848 connection to 8051

The following is a summary of the connection between the 8051 and the ADC0848, as shown in Figure 13-11.

P1.0–P1.7 D0–D7 of ADC:	Channel selection (out), data read (in)
P2.7 to INTR	P2.7 as input
P2.6 to WR	P2.6 as output
P2.5 to RD	P2.5 as output

Notice the following facts about Figure 13-11.

1. P2 is an output when we select a channel, and it is an input when we read the converted data.

2. We can monitor the INTR pin of the ADC for end-of-conversion or we can wait a few milliseconds and then read the converted data.

Displaying ADC0848 data

In order to display the ADC result on a screen or LCD, it must be converted to ASCII. To convert it to ASCII, however, it must first be converted to decimal. To convert a 00–FF hex value to decimal, we keep dividing it by 10 until the remainder is less than 10. Each time we divide it by 10 we keep the

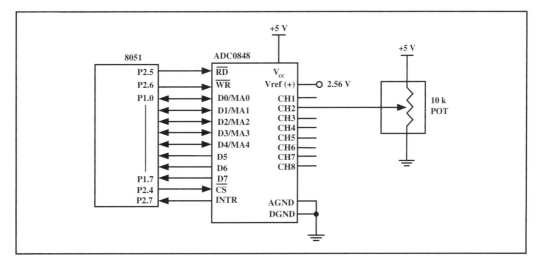

Figure 13-11. 8051 Connection to ADC0848 for Channel 2

quotient as one of our decimal digits. In the case of an 8-bit data, dividing it by 10 twice will do the job. For example, if we have FFH it will become 255 in decimal. To convert from decimal to ASCII format, we OR each digit with 30H (see Chapter 6). Now all we have to do is to send the digits to the PC screen using a serial port, or send them to the LCD, as was shown in Chapter 12.

Programming ADC0848 in Assembly

The following program selects channel 2, reads the data, and calls conversion and display subroutines.

```
        CS    BIT  P2.4
        RD    BIT  P2.5
        WR    BIT  P2.6
        INTR  BIT  P2.7
        ORG   0H
        SETB  INTR            ;make INTR an input
        SETB  CS              ;set Chip Select high
        SETB  RD              ;set Read high
        SETB  WR              ;set Write high
BACK:
        MOV   P1,#09H         ;Chan 2 address(Table 13-6)
        NOP                   ;wait
        CLR   CS              ;chip select (CS=0)
        CLR   WR              ;write = LOW
        NOP                   ;make pulse width wide enough
        NOP                   ;for DS89C4x0 you might need a delay
        SETB  WR              ;latch the address and start conv
        SETB  CS              ;de-select the chip
        MOV   P1,#0FFH        ;make P1 an input
HERE:
        JB    INTR,HERE       ;wait for EOC
        CLR   CS              ;chip select (CS=0)
        CLR   RD              ;read RD=0
        NOP                   ;make pulse width wide enough
        NOP
        SETB  RD              ;bring out digital data
```

```
        MOV    A,P1              ;get the value
        SETB   CS               ;de-select for next round
        ACALL  CONVERT          ;convert to ASCII (Chap 6)
        ACALL  DATA_DISPLAY     ;display the data (Chap 12)
        SJMP   BACK
```

Programming ADC0848 in C

The following program selects channel 2, reads the data, and calls conversion and display subroutines.

```c
#include <reg51.h>
sbit CS = P2^4;
sbit WR = P2^5;
sbit RD = P2^6;
sbit INTR = P2^7;

void main()
  {
    unsigned char value;
    INTR = 1;               //make INTR an input
    CS = 1;
    WR = 1;
    RD = 1;
    while(1)
      {
        P1 = 0x09;          //Chan 2 addr see Table 13-6
        CS = 0;             //chip select
        WR = 0;             //write=LOW
        Delay();            //make pulse wide enough
        WR = 1;             //L-to-H to latch addr
        CS = 1;             //de-select
        P1 = 0xFF;          //make P1 an input
        while(INTR==1);     //wait for EOC
        CS = 0;             //chip select
        RD = 0;             //read
        Delay();
        RD = 1;             //read the data
        value = P1;         //get the value
        CS = 1;
        ConvertAndDisplay(value);   //Chap 7 & 12
      }
  }
```

Serial ADC chips

All the ADC chips we have discussed so far have been of the parallel type. The D0–D7 data pins of the ADC0848/0808/0809/0804 provide an 8-bit parallel data path between the ADC chip and the CPU. In the case of the 16-bit parallel ADC chip, we need 16 pins for the data path. In recent years, for many applications where space is a critical issue, using such a large number of pins for data is not feasible. For this reason, serial devices such as the serial ADC are becoming widely used. Next, we examine the MAX1112 serial ADC chip from Maxim Corporation (www.maxim-ic.com) and show how to interface it with the microprocessor.

MAX1112 ADC

The MAX1112 is an eight-bit serial ADC chip with eight channels of analog input. It has a single D_{OUT} pin to bring out the digital data after it has been converted. It is compatible with a popular SPI and Microwire serial standard. The following are descriptions of the MAX1112 pins (see Figure 13-12).

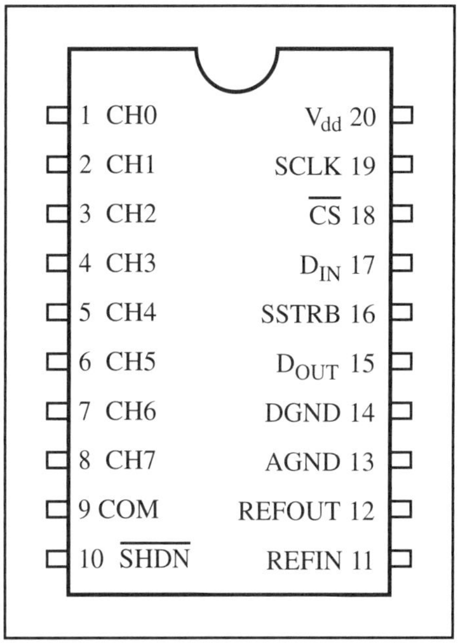

CH0–CH7

CH0–CH7 are eight channels of the analog inputs. In the single-ended mode, each of the channels can be used for an analog input where the COM pin is used as a ground reference for all the channels. In single-ended mode, eight channels of input allow us to read eight different analog inputs. We select the input channel by sending in the control byte via the DIN pin. In differential mode, we have four sets of two-channel differentials. CH0 and CH1 go together, and CH2–CH3, and so on. See Figure 13-13.

Figure 13-12. MAX1112 Chip

Pin assignments:
- 1 CH0
- 2 CH1
- 3 CH2
- 4 CH3
- 5 CH4
- 6 CH5
- 7 CH6
- 8 CH7
- 9 COM
- 10 $\overline{SHDN}$
- V_{dd} 20
- SCLK 19
- $\overline{CS}$ 18
- D_{IN} 17
- SSTRB 16
- D_{OUT} 15
- DGND 14
- AGND 13
- REFOUT 12
- REFIN 11

COM

Ground reference for the analog input in single-ended mode.

CS

Chip select is an active-low input used to select the MAX1112 chip. To send in the control byte via the D_{IN} pin, CS must be low. When CS is high, the D_{OUT} is high impedance.

SCLK

Serial clock input. SCLK is used to bring data out and send in the control byte, one bit at a time.

D_OUT

Serial data out. The digital data is clocked out one bit at a time on the H-to-L edge (falling edge) of SCLK.

D_IN

Serial data in the control byte is clocked in one bit at a time on the L-to-H edge (rising edge) of SCLK.

SSTRB

Serial strobe output. In internal clock mode this indicates end-of-conversion. It goes high when the conversion is complete.

V_{DD}

V_{DD} is the +5 V power supply.

AGND, DGND (analog ground and digital ground)

Both are input pins providing ground for both the analog and the digital signals.

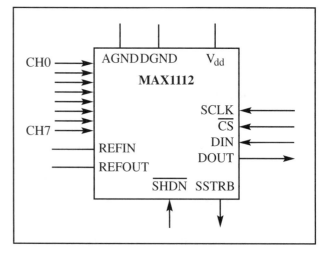

Figure 13-13. MAX1112 Serial ADC Block Diagram

SHDN

Shutdown is an input and is normally not connected (or is connected to V_{DD}). If low, the ADC is shut down to save power. This is shut down by hardware. The control byte causes shutdown by software.

REFIN

Reference voltage input. This voltage dictates the step size.

REFOUT

Internal Reference Generator output. A 1 μF bypass capacitor is placed between this pin and AGND.

MAX1112 control byte

The MAX1112 chip has eight channels of analog inputs that are selected using a control byte. The control byte is fed into the MAX1112 serially one bit at a time via the D_{IN} pin with the help of SCLK. The control byte must be sent in with the MSB (most significant bit) going in first. The MSB of the control byte is high to indicate the start of the control byte, as shown in Figure 13-14.

REFIN voltage and step size

The step size for the MAX1112 depends on the voltage connected to the REFIN pin. In unipolar mode, with V_{DD} = 5 V, we get 4.096 V for full-scale if the REFIN pin is connected to the AGND with a 1-μF capacitor. That gives us a 16-mV step size since 4.096 V/256 = 16mV. To get a 10-mV step size, we need to connect the REFIN pin to a 2.56 V external voltage source, since 2.56 V/256 = 10 mV. According to the MAX1112 data sheet, the external reference voltage must be between 1 V and V_{DD}. Notice the lower limit for the reference voltage. See Figure 13-15.

Start	SEL2	SLE1	SEL0	UN/BIP	SGL/DF	PD1	PD0

Start The MSB (D7) must be high to define the beginning of the control byte. It must be sent in first.

SEL2 SEL1 SEL0 CHANNEL SELECTION (single-ended mode)

SEL2	SEL1	SEL0	
0	0	0	CHAN0
0	0	1	CHAN1
0	1	0	CHAN2
0	1	1	CHAN3
1	0	0	CHAN4
1	0	1	CHAN5
1	1	0	CHAN6
1	1	1	CHAN7

UNI/BIP 1 = unipolar: Digital data output is binary 00–FFH.
0 = bipolar: Digital data output is in 2's complement.

SGL/DIF 1 = single-ended: eight channels of single-ended with COM as reference.
0 = differential: Two channels (e.g., CH0–CH1) are differential.

PD1 1 = fully operational
0 = power-down: Power down to save power using software.

PD0 1 = external clock mode: The conversion speed is dictated by SCLK.
0 = internal clock mode: The conversion speed is dictated internally, and the SSTRB pin goes high to indicate end-of-conversion.

Figure 13-14. MAX1112 Control Byte

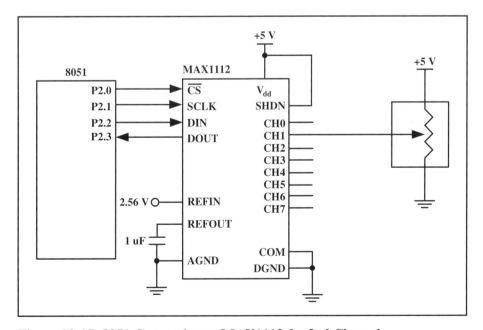

Figure 13-15. 8051 Connection to MAX1112 for 2nd Channel

Example 13-2

Find the MAX1112 control byte for (a) CH0 and (b) CH3. Assume single-ended, unipolar, internal clock, and fully operational modes.

Solution:

From Figure 13-14, we have the following:
(a) 10001110 (8E in hex)   (b) 10111110 (BE in hex)

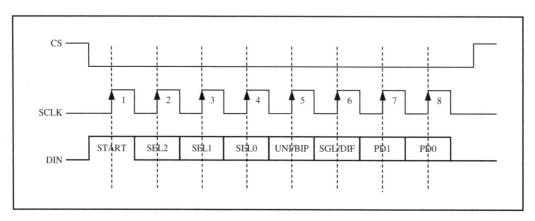

Figure 13-16. MAX1112 Internal Clock Mode Timing Diagram: Sending Control Byte into MAX1112

Selecting a channel

We select the analog input channel using the control byte. See Example 13-2. Notice that the MSB (D7) of the control byte must be high.

The control byte is fed into the DIN pin one bit at a time using SCLK. The DIN pin clocks in the control byte on the rising edge of SCLK, as shown in Figure 13-16.

```
;Assembly Code for sending in control byte in
;MAX1112, see Figure 13-15
      CS   BIT P2.0
      SCLK BIT P2.1
      DIN  BIT P2.2
      DOUT BIT P2.3

      MOV   A,#9EH        ;channel 1 selection
      MOV   R3,#8         ;load count
      CLR   CS            ;CS=0
      CLR   C
H1:   RLC   A             ;give bit to CY
      MOV   DIN,C         ;send bit to DIN
      CLR   SCLK          ;low SCLK for L-H pulse
      ACALL DELAY         ;delay
      SETB  SCLK          ;latch data, see Fig 13-16
      ACALL DELAY         ;delay
      DJNZ  R3,H1         ;repeat for all 8 bits
      SETB  CS            ;deselect ADC, conversion starts
      CLR   SCLK          ;SCLK=0 during conversion
```

```
//C Code for sending in control byte for MAX1112 ADC
#include <reg51.h>
sbit  CS = P2^0;              //see Figure 13-15
sbit  SCLK = P2^1;
sbit  DIN = P2^2;
sbit  DOUT = P2^3;
sbit  MSBRA =  ACC^7;
void main(void)
  {
     unsigned char conbyte=0x9E;        //Chan 1
     unsigned char x;
     ACC=conbyte;
     CS=0;
     for(x=0; x<8; x++)
       {
          SCLK=0;
          DIN=MSBRA;             //Send D7 of Reg A to Din
          Delay();
          SCLK=1;                //latch in the bit
          Delay();
          ACC = ACC << 1;        //next bit
       }
     CS=1;                       //deselect MAX1112
     SCLK=0;                     //Make SCLK low during conversion
  }
```

Start conversion and end of conversion for MAX1112

When the last bit of the control byte, PD0, is sent in, the conversion starts, and SSTRB goes low. The end-of-conversion state is indicated by SSTRB going high, which happens 55 μs after PD0 is clocked in. We can either wait 55 μs, or monitor SSTRB before we get the digital data out of the ADC chip. Next, we show how to get digital data out of the MAX1112.

Reading out digital data

The 8-bit converted digital data is brought out of the MAX1112 via the D_{OUT} pin using SCLK. As we apply a negative-edge pulse to the SCLK pin, the 8-bit digital data is read out one bit at a time with the MSB (D7) coming out first. The SSTRB goes high to indicate that the conversion is finished. According to the MAX1112 data sheet, "after SSTRB goes high, the second falling edge of SCLK produces the MSB" of converted data at the D_{OUT} pin. In other words, we need 9 pulses to get data out. To bring data out, CS must be low. See Figure 13-17.

The following is Assembly code for reading out digital data in the MAX1112:

```
CS    BIT    P2.0
SCLK  BIT    P2.1
DIN   BIT    P2.2
DOUT  BIT    P2.3
```

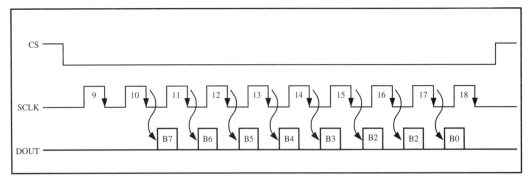

Figure 13-17. MAX1112 Internal Clock Mode Timing Diagram: Reading ADC Data Byte from MAX1112

```
        SETB   DOUT          ;make it an input
        CLR    CS            ;CS=0
        SETB   SCLK
        ACALL  DELAY         ;need delay for DS89C4x0
        CLR    SCLK          ;first H-to-L
        ACALL  DLELAY        ;read data out on 2ND H-to-L
        CLR    A
        MOV    R3,#8         ;
H2:     SETB   SCLK          ;
        ACALL  DELAY         ;need delay for DS89C4x0
        CLR    SCLK          ;H-to-L pulse to get bit out
        ACALL  DELAY ;
        MOV    C,DOUT        ;move bit to CY flag
        RLC    A             ;bring in the bit
        DJNZ   R3,H2         ;repeat for all 8 bits
        SETB   CS            ;CS=1
        MOV    P1,A          ;send converted data to P1
```

```c
//C Code for reading data in MAX1112
#include <reg51.h>
sbit CS = P2^0;
sbit SCLK = P2^1;
sbit DIN = P2^2;
sbit DOUT = P2^3;
sbit LSBRA = ACC^0;

void main(void)
  {
    unsigned char x;
    CS=0;                 //select max1112
    SCLK=1;               //an extra H-to-L pulse
    Delay();
    SCLK=0;
    Delay();
    for(x=0; x<8; x++)    //get all 8 bits
      {
        SCLK=1;
        Delay();
```

```
         SCLK=0;
         Delay()
         LSBRA=DOUT;          //bring in bit from DOUT
                              //pin to D0 of Reg A
         ACC = ACC << 1;      //keep shifting data
                              //for all 8 bits
      }
   CS=1;                      //deselect ADC
   P1=ACC;                    //display data on P1
   }
```

MAX1112 program in Assembly

```
;The following program selects the channel and
;reads the ADC data
      CS    BIT P2.0
      SCLK  BIT P2.1
      DIN   BIT P2.2
      DOUT  BIT P2.3

      ORG   0H
;sending in control byte
MAIN: MOV   A,#9EH       ;channel 1
      MOV   R3,#8        ;load count
      CLR   CS           ;CS=0
H1:   RLC   A            ;give bit to CY
      MOV   DIN,C        ;send bit to DIN
      CLR   SCLK         ;low SCLK for L-H pulse
      ACALL DELAY        ;delay
      SETB  SCLK         ;latch data
      ACALL DELAY        ;delay
      DJNZ  R3,H1        ;repeat for all 8 bits
      SETB  CS           ;deselect ADC, conv starts
      CLR   SCLK         ;SCLK=0 during conversion
      SETB  DOUT         ;make it an input
;Reading data out
      CLR   CS           ;CS=0
      SETB  SCLK
      ACALL DELAY        ;need delay for DS89C4x0
      CLR   SCLK         ;first H-to-L
      ACALL DLELAY       ;read data out on 2ND H-L
      MOV   R3,#8        ;
H2:   SETB  SCLK         ;
      ACALL DELAY        ;need delay for DS89C4x0
      CLR   SCLK         ;H-to-L pulse to get bit out
      ACALL DELAY ;
      MOV   C,DOUT       ;move bit to CY flag
      RLC   A            ;bring in the bit
      DJNZ  R3,H2        ;repeat for all 8 bits
      SETB  CS           ;CS=1
      MOV   P1,A         ;display data on P1
      SJMP  MAIN         ;keep doing it
```

CHAPTER 13: ADC, DAC, AND SENSOR INTERFACING   429

MAX1112 program in C

```c
//The following program selects the channel and
//reads ADC data
#include <reg51.h>
sbit CS   = P2^0;
sbit SCLK = P2^1;
sbit DIN  = P2^2;
sbit DOUT = P2^3;
sbit MSBRA = ACC^7;
sbit LSBRA = ACC^0;

void main(void)
  {
    unsigned char conbyte=0x9E;      //Chan 1
    unsigned char x;
    while(1)
      {
      ACC=conbyte;              //select the channel
      CS=0;
      for(x=0; x<8; x++)
        {
          SCLK=0;
          DIN=MSBRA;            //send D7 of Reg A to Din
          Delay();
          SCLK=1;               //latch in the bit
          Delay();
          ACC = ACC << 1;    //next bit
        }
      CS=1;                     //deselect MAX1112
      SCLK=0;                   //Make SCLK low during conversion
      CS=0;                     //read the data
      SCLK=1;                   //an extra H-to-L pulse
      Delay();
      SCLK=0;                   //get all 8 bits
      Delay();
      for(x=0; x<8; x++)
        {
          SCLK=1;
          Delay();
          SCLK=0;
          Delay()
          LSBRA=DOUT;           //bring in bit from DOUT
                                //pin to D0 of Reg A
          ACC = ACC << 1;    //keep shifting data
                                //for all 8 bits
        }
      CS=1;                     //deselect ADC
      P1=ACC;                   //display data on P1
  }
```

REVIEW QUESTIONS

1. In the ADC0804, the INTR signal is an _____ (input, output).
2. In the ADC0804, to begin conversion, send a(n) _____ pulse to pin _____.
3. Which pin of the ADC0804 indicates end-of-conversion?
4. Both the ADC0804 and ADC0808/0809 are _____-bit converters.
5. Indicate the direction (out, in) for each of the following pins of the ADC0808/0809.
   (a) A, B, C   (b) SC   (c) EOC
6. In the ADC0848, the INTR signal is an _____ (input, output).
7. In the ADC0848, to begin conversion, send a(n)_____ pulse to _____.
8. Which pin of the ADC0848 indicates end-of-conversion?
9. The ADC0848 is a(n) _____-bit converter.
10. True or false. While the ADC0848 has eight pins for D_{OUT}, the MAX1112 has only one D_{OUT} pin.
11. Indicate the number of analog input channels for each of the following ADC chips.
    (a) ADC0804   (b) ADC0848   (c) MAX1112
12. Explain how to select analog input channel for the MAX1112.

13.2: DAC INTERFACING

This section will show how to interface a DAC (digital-to-analog converter) to the 8051. Then we demonstrate how to generate a sine wave on the scope using the DAC.

Digital-to-analog (DAC) converter

The digital-to-analog converter (DAC) is a device widely used to convert digital pulses to analog signals. In this section, we discuss the basics of interfacing a DAC to the 8051.

Recall from your digital electronics book the two methods of creating a DAC: binary weighted and R/2R ladder. The vast majority of integrated circuit DACs, including the MC1408 (DAC0808) used in this section, use the R/2R method since it can achieve a much higher degree of precision. The first criterion for judging a DAC is its resolution, which is a function of the number of binary inputs. The common ones are 8, 10, and 12 bits. The number of data bit inputs decides the resolution of the DAC since the number of analog output levels is equal to 2^n, where n is the number of data bit inputs. Therefore, an 8-input DAC such as the DAC0808 provides 256 discrete voltage (or current) levels of output. Similarly, the 12-bit DAC provides 4096 discrete voltage levels. There are also 16-bit DACs, but they are more expensive.

MC1408 DAC (or DAC0808)

In the MC1408 (DAC0808), the digital inputs are converted to current (I_{out}), and by connecting a resistor to the I_{out} pin, we convert the result to voltage. The total current provided by the I_{out} pin is a function of the binary numbers at the D0–D7 inputs of the DAC0808 and the reference current (I_{ref}), and is as follows:

$$I_{out} = I_{ref} \left(\frac{D7}{2} + \frac{D6}{4} + \frac{D5}{8} + \frac{D4}{16} + \frac{D3}{32} + \frac{D2}{64} + \frac{D1}{128} + \frac{D0}{256} \right)$$

Here, D0 is the LSB, D7 is the MSB for the inputs, and I_{ref} is the input current that must be applied to pin 14. The I_{ref} current is generally set to 2 mA. Figure 13-18 shows the generation of current reference (setting I_{ref} = 2 mA) by using the standard 5 V power supply and 1 K and 1.5 K-ohm standard resistors. Some DACs also use the zener diode (LM336), which overcomes any fluctuation associated with the power supply voltage. Now assuming that

---

Example 13-3

Assuming that R = 5K and I_{ref} = 2 mA, calculate V_{out} for the following binary inputs:
(a) 10011001 binary (99H)   (b) 11001000 (C8H).

Solution:

(a) I_{out} = 2 mA (153/256) = 1.195 mA and V_{out} = 1.195 mA × 5K = 5.975 V
(b) I_{out} = 2 mA (200/256) = 1.562 mA and V_{out} = 1.562 mA × 5K = 7.8125 V

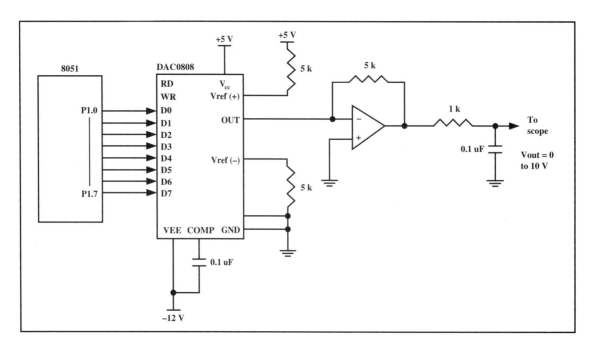

Figure 13-18. 8051 Connection to DAC0808

$I_{ref} = 2$ mA, if all the inputs to the DAC are high, the maximum output current is 1.99 mA (verify this for yourself). See Example 13-3.

Converting I_{out} to voltage in DAC0808

Ideally we connect the output pin I_{out} to a resistor, convert this current to voltage, and monitor the output on the scope. In real life, however, this can cause inaccuracy since the input resistance of the load where it is connected will also affect the output voltage. For this reason, the I_{ref} current output is isolated by connecting it to an op-amp such as the 741 with $R_f = 5$ K ohms for the feedback resistor. Assuming that R = 5 K ohms by changing the binary input, the output voltage changes as shown in Example 13-4.

Generating a sine wave

To generate a sine wave, we first need a table whose values represent the magnitude of the sine of angles between 0 and 360 degrees. The values for the sine function vary from −1.0 to +1.0 for 0- to 360-degree angles. Therefore, the table values are integer numbers representing the voltage magnitude for the sine of theta. This method ensures that only integer numbers are output to the DAC by the 8051 microprocessor. Table 13-7 shows the angles, the sine values, the voltage magnitudes, and the integer values representing the voltage magnitude for each angle (with 30-degree increments). To generate Table 13-7, we assumed the full-scale voltage of 10 V for DAC output (as designed in Figure 13-18). Full-scale output of the DAC is achieved when all the data inputs of the DAC are high. Therefore, to achieve the full-scale 10 V output, we use the following equation.

$$V_{out} = 5 \text{ V} + (5 \times \sin \theta)$$

V_{out} of DAC for various angles is calculated and shown in Table 13-7. See Example 13-5 for verification of the calculations.

To find the value sent to the DAC for various angles, we simply multiply the V_{out} voltage by 25.60 because there are 256 steps and full-scale V_{out} is 10 V. Therefore, 256 steps/10 V = 25.6 steps per volt. To further

---

Example 13-4

In order to generate a stair-step ramp, set up the circuit in Figure 13-18 and connect the output to an oscilloscope. Then write a program to send data to the DAC to generate a stair-step ramp.

Solution:

```
        CLR   A
AGAIN:  MOV   P1,A          ;send data to DAC
        INC   A             ;count from 0 to FFH
        ACALL DELAY         ;let DAC recover
        SJMP  AGAIN
```

Table 13-7. Angle versus Voltage Magnitude for Sine Wave

Angle θ (degrees)	Sin θ	V_{out} (Voltage Magnitude) $5\ V + (5\ V \times \sin \theta)$	Values Sent to DAC (Decimal) (Voltage Mag. $\times$ 25.6)
0	0	5	128
30	0.5	7.5	192
60	0.866	9.33	238
90	1.0	10	255
120	0.866	9.33	238
150	0.5	7.5	192
180	0	5	128
210	−0.5	2.5	64
240	−0.866	0.669	17
270	−1.0	0	0
300	−0.866	0.669	17
330	−0.5	2.5	64
360	0	5	128

Example 13-5

Verify the values given for the following angles: (a) 30°   (b) 60°.

Solution:

(a) $V_{out} = 5\ V + (5\ V \times \sin \theta) = 5\ V + 5 \times \sin 30° = 5\ V + 5 \times 0.5 = 7.5\ V$
    DAC input values = 7.5 V $\times$ 25.6 = 192 (decimal)
(b) $V_{out} = 5\ V + (5\ V \times \sin \theta) = 5\ V + 5 \times \sin 60° = 5\ V + 5 \times 0.866 = 9.33\ V$
    DAC input values = 9.33 V $\times$ 25.6 = 238 (decimal)

---

clarify this, look at the following code. This program sends the values to the DAC continuously (in an infinite loop) to produce a crude sine wave. See Figure 13-19.

```
AGAIN:      MOV DPTR,#TABLE
            MOV R2,#COUNT
BACK:       CLR A
            MOVC A,@A+DPTR
            MOV P1,A
            INC DPTR
            DJNZ R2,BACK
            SJMP AGAIN
            ORG 300
TABLE:      DB 128,192,238,255,238,192 ;see Table 13-7
            DB 128,64,17,0,17,64,128
;To get a better looking sine wave, regenerate
;Table 13-7 for 2-degree angles
```

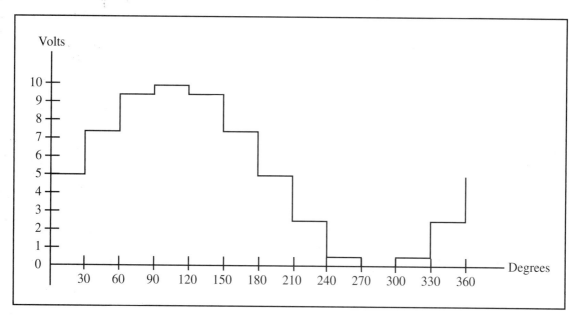

Figure 13-19. Angle versus Voltage Magnitude for Sine Wave

Programming DAC in C

```
#include <reg51.h>
sfr DACDATA = P1;
void main()
  {
    unsigned char WAVEVALUE[12] = {128,192,238,255,
                                   238,192,128,64,
                                   17,0,17,64};
    unsigned char x;
    while(1)
      {
      for(x=0;x<12;x++)
        {
          DACDATA = WAVEVALUE[x];
        }
      }
  }
```

REVIEW QUESTIONS

1. In a DAC, input is _____ (digital, analog) and output is _____ (digital, analog).
2. In an ADC, input is _____ (digital, analog) and output is _____ (digital, analog).
3. DAC0808 is a(n) ____-bit D-to-A converter.
4. (a) The output of DAC0808 is in _____ (current, voltage).
   (b) True or false. The output of DAC0808 is ideal to drive a motor.

13.3: SENSOR INTERFACING AND SIGNAL CONDITIONING

This section will show how to interface sensors to the microprocessor. We examine some popular temperature sensors and then discuss the issue of signal conditioning. Although we concentrate on temperature sensors, the principles discussed in this section are the same for other types of sensors such as light and pressure sensors.

Temperature sensors

Transducers convert physical data such as temperature, light intensity, flow, and speed to electrical signals. Depending on the transducer, the output produced is in the form of voltage, current, resistance, or capacitance. For example, temperature is converted to electrical signals using a transducer called a *thermistor*. A thermistor responds to temperature change by changing resistance, but its response is not linear, as seen in Table 13-8.

The complexity associated with writing software for such nonlinear devices has led many manufacturers to market a linear temperature sensor. Simple and widely used linear temperature sensors include the LM34 and LM35 series from National Semiconductor Corp. They are discussed next.

Table 13-8. Thermistor Resistance versus Temperature

Temperature (C)	Tf (K ohms)
0	29.490
25	10.000
50	3.893
75	1.700
100	0.817

From William Kleitz, *Digital Electronics*

LM34 and LM35 temperature sensors

The sensors of the LM34 series are precision integrated-circuit temperature sensors whose output voltage is linearly proportional to the Fahrenheit temperature. See Table 13-9. The LM34 requires no external calibration since it is internally calibrated. It outputs 10 mV for each degree of Fahrenheit temperature. Table 13-9 is a selection guide for the LM34.

Table 13-9. LM34 Temperature Sensor Series Selection Guide

Part	Temperature Range	Accuracy	Output Scale
LM34A	−50 F to +300 F	+2.0 F	10 mV/F
LM34	−50 F to +300 F	+3.0 F	10 mV/F
LM34CA	−40 F to +230 F	+2.0 F	10 mV/F
LM34C	−40 F to +230 F	+3.0 F	10 mV/F
LM34D	−32 F to +212 F	+4.0 F	10 mV/F

Note: Temperature range is in degrees Fahrenheit.

Table 13-10. LM35 Temperature Sensor Series Selection Guide

Part	Temperature Range	Accuracy	Output Scale
LM35A	−55 C to +150 C	+1.0 C	10 mV/C
LM35	−55 C to +150 C	+1.5 C	10 mV/C
LM35CA	−40 C to +110 C	+1.0 C	10 mV/C
LM35C	−40 C to +110 C	+1.5 C	10 mV/C
LM35D	0 C to +100 C	+2.0 C	10 mV/C

Note: Temperature range is in degrees Celsius.

The LM35 series sensors are precision integrated-circuit temperature sensors whose output voltage is linearly proportional to the Celsius (centigrade) temperature. The LM35 requires no external calibration since it is internally calibrated. It outputs 10 mV for each degree of centigrade temperature. Table 13-10 is the selection guide for the LM35. (For further information, see www.national.com.)

Signal conditioning and interfacing the LM35 to the 8051

Signal conditioning is widely used in the world of data acquisition. The most common transducers produce an output in the form of voltage, current, charge, capacitance, and resistance. However, we need to convert these signals to voltage in order to send input to an A-to-D converter. See Figure 13-20. This conversion (modification) is commonly called *signal conditioning*. See Figure 13-20. Signal conditioning can be a current-to-voltage conversion or a signal amplification. For example, the thermistor changes resistance with temperature. The change of resistance must be translated into voltages in order to be of any use to an ADC. Look at the case of connecting an LM35 to an ADC0848. Since the ADC0848 has 8-bit resolution with a maximum of 256 (2^8) steps and the LM35 (or LM34) produces 10 mV for every degree of temperature change, we can condition V_{in} of the ADC0848 to produce a V_{out} of 2560 mV (2.56 V) for full-scale output. Therefore, in order to produce the full-scale V_{out} of 2.56 V for the ADC0848, we need to set V_{ref} = 2.56. This makes V_{out} of the ADC0848 correspond directly to the temperature as monitored by the LM35. See Table 13-11.

Figure 13-21 shows the connection of a temperature sensor to the ADC0848. Notice that we use the LM336-2.5 zener diode to fix the voltage across the 10 K pot at 2.5 V. The use of the LM336-2.5 should overcome any fluctuations in the power supply.

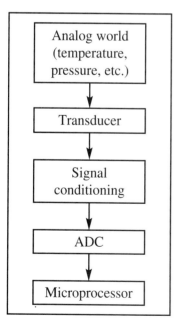

Figure 13-20. Getting Data From the Analog World

Table 13-11. Temperature versus V_{out} for ADC0848

Temp. (C)	V_{in} (mV)	V_{out} (D7–D0)
0	0	0000 0000
1	10	0000 0001
2	20	0000 0010
3	30	0000 0011
10	100	0000 1010
30	300	0001 1110

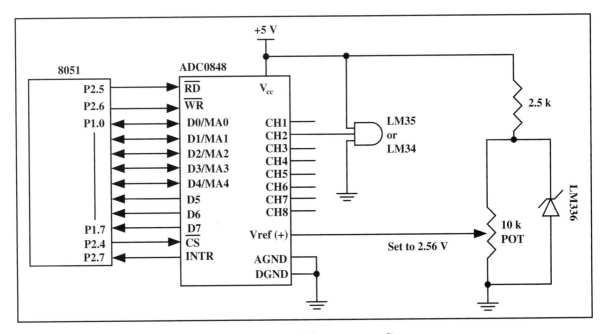

Figure 13-21. 8051 Connection to ADC0848 and Temperature Sensor

Reading and displaying temperature

The following two programs show code for displaying temperature in both Assembly and C. The programs correspond to Figure 13-21.

```
;Program 13-1
;Assembly code to read temperature, convert it,
;and put it on P0 with some delay
      RD    BIT P2.5      ;RD
      WR    BIT P2.6      ;WR (start conversion)
      INTR  BIT P2.7      ;end-of-conversion
      MYDATA      EQU P1  ;P1.0-P1.7=D0-D7 of the ADC0848
      MOV  P1,#0FFH       ;make P1 = input
      SETB INTR
BACK: CLR  WR             ;WR=0
      SETB WR             ;WR=1 L-to-H to start conversion
HERE: JB   INTR,HERE      ;wait for end of conversion
      CLR  RD             ;conversion finished,enable RD
      MOV  A,MYDATA       ;read the data from ADC0848
      ACALL CONVERSION          ;hex-to-ASCII conversion
```

```
        ACALL DATA_DISPLAY      ;display the data
        SETB  RD                ;make RD=1 for next round
        SJMP  BACK
CONVERSION:
        MOV   B,#10
        DIV   AB
        MOV   R7,B              ;least significant byte
        MOV   B,#10
        DIV   AB
        MOV   R6,B
        MOV   R5,A              ;most significant byte
        RET

DATA_DISPLAY
        MOV   P0,R7
        ACALL DELAY
        MOV   P0,R6
        ACALL DELAY
        MOV   P0,R5
        ACALL DELAY
        RET


//Program 13-2
//C code to read temp from ADC0848, convert it to
//decimal, and put it on P0 with some delay
#include <reg51.h>
sbit RD = P2^5;
sbit WR = P2^6;
sbit INTR = P2^7;
sfr MYDATA = P1;        //P1 connected to D0-D7 of '848
void ConvertAndDisplay(unsigned char value);
void MSDelay(unsigned int value);
void main()
   {
     MYDATA = 0xFF;          //make P1 and input
     INTR = 1;               //make INTR and input
     RD = 1;                 //set RD high
     WR = 1;                 //set WR high
     while(1)
       {
         WR = 0;             //send WR pulse
         WR = 1;
         while(INTR == 1);   //wait for EOC
         RD = 0;             //send RD pulse
         value = MYDATA;     //read value from ADC0848
         ConvertAndDisplay(value);
         RD = 1;
       }
   }

void ConvertAndDisplay(unsigned char value)
   {
     unsigned char x,d1,d2,d3;
     x=value/10;
     d1=value%10;
```

```
      d2=x%10
      d3=x/10
      P0=d1;                    //LSByte
      MSDelay(250);
      P0=d2;
      MSDelay(250);
      P0=d3;                    //MSByte
      MSDelay(250);
  }

void MSDelay(unsigned int value)
  {
    unsigned char x,y;
    for(x=0;x<value;x++)
      for(y=0;y<1275;y++);
  }
```

REVIEW QUESTIONS

1. True or false. The transducer must be connected to signal conditioning circuitry before it is sent to the ADC.
2. The LM35 provides _____ mV for each degree of _____ (Fahrenheit, Celsius) temperature.
3. The LM34 provides ____ mV for each degree of _____ (Fahrenheit, Celsius) temperature.
4. Why do we set the V_{ref} of ADC0848 to 2.56 V if the analog input is connected to the LM35?
5. In Question 4, what is the temperature if the ADC output is 0011 1001?

SUMMARY

This chapter showed how to interface real-world devices such as DAC chips, ADC chips, and sensors to the 8051. First, we discussed both parallel and serial ADC chips, then described how to interface them to the 8051 and program it in both Assembly and C. Next, we explored the DAC chip and showed how to interface it to the 8051. In the last section we studied sensors. We also discussed the relation between the analog world and a digital device, and described signal conditioning, an essential feature of data acquisition systems.

PROBLEMS

13.1: PARALLEL AND SERIAL ADC

1. Give the status of CS and WR in order to start conversion for the ADC0804.
2. Give the status of CS and WR in order to get data from the ADC0804.
3. In the ADC0804, what happens to the converted analog data? How do we know if the ADC is ready to provide us the data?

4. In the ADC0804, what happens to the old data if we start conversion again before we pick up the last data?
5. In the ADC0804, INTR is an _____ (input, output) signal. What is its function in the ADC0804?
6. For an ADC0804 chip, find the step size for each of the following $V_{ref}/2$ values.
   (a) $V_{ref}/2 = 1.28$ V (b) $V_{ref}/2 = 1$ V   (c) $V_{ref}/2 = 1.9$ V
7. In the ADC0804, what should be the $V_{ref}/2$ value for a step size of 20 mV?
8. In the ADC0804, what should be the $V_{ref}/2$ value for a step size of 5 mV?
9. In the ADC0804, what is the role of pins $V_{in}(+)$ and $V_{in}(-)$?
10. With a step size of 19.53 mV, what is the analog input voltage if all outputs are 1?
11. With $V_{ref}/2 = 0.64$ V, find the V_{in} for the following outputs.
    (a) D7–D0 = 11111111 (b) D7–D0 = 10011001 (c) D7–D0 = 1101100
12. True or false. ADC0804 is an 8-bit ADC.
13. Which of the following ADC sizes provide the best resolution?
    (a) 8-bit (b) 10-bit (c) 12-bit (d) 16-bit (e) They are all the same.
14. In Question 13, which provides the smallest step size?
15. Calculate the step size for the following ADCs, if V_{ref} is 5 V.
    (a) 8-bit (b) 10-bit (c) 12-bit (d) 16-bit
16. True or false. ADC0808/0809 is an 8-bit ADC.
17. Indicate the direction (in, out) for each of the following ADC0808/0809 pins.
    (a) SC   (b) EOC   (c) A, B, C
    (d) ALE   (e) OE   (f) IN0–IN7
    (g) D0–D7
18. Explain the role of the ALE pin in the ADC0808/0809 and show how to select channel 5 analog input.
19. In the ADC0808/0809, assume $V_{ref}(-)$ = Gnd. Give the $V_{ref}(+)$ voltage value if we want the following step sizes:
    (a) 20 mV   (b) 5 mV   (c) 10 mV
    (d) 15 mV   (e) 2 mV   (f) 25 mV
20. In the ADC0808/0809, assume $V_{ref}(-)$ = Gnd. Find the step size for the following values of $V_{ref}(+)$:
    (a) 1.28 V   (b) 1 V   (c) 0.64 V
21. True or false. ADC0848 is an 8-bit ADC.
22. Give the status of CS and WR in order to start conversion for the ADC0848.
23. Give the status of CS and WR in order to get data from the ADC0848.
24. In the ADC0848, what happens to the converted analog data? How do we know that the ADC is ready to provide us the data?
25. In the ADC0848, what happens to the old data if we start conversion again before we pick up the last data?
26. In the ADC0848, INTR is an _____ (input, output) signal. What is its function in the ADC0848?
27. For an ADC0848 chip, find the step size for each of the following V_{ref}.
    (a) $V_{ref} = 1.28$ V   (b) $V_{ref} = 1$ V   (c) $V_{ref} = 1.9$ V

---

28. In the ADC0848, what should be the Vref value if we want a step size of 20 mV?
29. In the ADC0848, what should be the Vref value if we want a step size of 5 mV?
30. In the ADC0848, how is the analog channel selected?
31. With a step size of 19.53 mV, what is the analog input voltage if all outputs are 1?
32. With $V_{ref} = 1.28V$, find the V_{in} for the following outputs.
    (a) D7–D0 = 11111111 (b) D7–D0 = 10011001 (c) D7–D0 = 1101100
33. True or false. MAX1112 is an 8-bit ADC.
34. Indicate the direction (in, out) for each of the following MAX1112 pins.
    (a) CS   (b) DOUT   (c) COM
    (d) DIN   (e) SCLK   (f) CHAN0–CHAN7
    (g) SSTRB
35. For MAX1112, give the status of CS in order to get data out.
36. For MAX1112, give the status of CS when sending in the control byte.
37. For MAX1112, give the control byte for CHAN2, CHAN5, and CHAN7. Assume single-ended, unipolar, internal clock, and fully operational modes.
38. For MAX1112 chip, find the step size for each of the following REFIN provided externally.
    (a) REFIN = 1.28 V (b) REFIN = 1 V (c) REFIN = 1.9 V
39. In the MAX1112, how is the analog channel selected?
40. In the MAX1112, what should be the REFIN value if we want a step size of 5 mV?
41. With REFIN = 1.28 V, find the V_{in} for the following outputs.
    (a) D7–D0 = 11111111 (b) D7–D0 = 10011001 (c) D7–D0 = 1101100
42. The control byte is sent in on the _____ (positive edge/negative edge) of the SCLK signal.
43. Converted digital data is brought out on the _____ (positive edge/negative edge) of the SCLK signal.
44. What is the lowest REFIN value?
45. It takes _____ SCLKs to send in the control byte.
46. It takes _____ SCLKs to bring out digital data for one channel after the conversion is completed.
47. When does the conversion start in the MAX1112?
48. How do we recognize end-of-conversion in the MAX1112?
49. What is the step size if REFIN is connected to AGND with REFOUT?
50. In single-ended mode, which pin is used for ground reference for CHAN0–CHAN7?

13.2: DAC INTERFACING

51. True or false. DAC0808 is the same as DAC1408.
52. Find the number of discrete voltages provided by the n-bit DAC for the following.
    (a) $n = 8$ (b) $n = 10$ (c) $n = 12$

53. For DAC1408, if I_{ref} = 2 mA show how to get the I_{out} of 1.99 when all inputs are high.
54. Find the I_{out} for the following inputs. Assume I_{ref} = 2 mA for DAC0808.
    (a) 1001|1001   (b) 1100|1100   (c) 1110|1110
    (d) 0010|0010   (e) 0000|1001   (f) 1000|1000
55. To get a smaller step, we need a DAC with _____ (more, fewer) digital inputs.
56. To get full-scale output, what should be the inputs for DAC?

13.3: SENSOR INTERFACING AND SIGNAL CONDITIONING

57. What does it mean when it is said that a given sensor has a linear output?
58. The LM34 sensor produces _____ mV for each degree of temperature.
59. What is signal conditioning?
60. What is the purpose of the LM336 zener diode around the pot setting the V_{ref} in Figure 13-21?

ANSWERS TO REVIEW QUESTIONS

13.1: PARALLEL AND SERIAL ADC

1. Output
2. L-to-H, WR
3. INTR
4. 8
5. (a) all in (b) in (c) out
6. Output
7. L-to-H, WR
8. INTR
9. 8
10. True
11. (a) 1 (b) 8 (c) 8
12. We send the control byte to the DIN pin one bit at a time.

13.2: DAC INTERFACING

1. (a) Digital, analog.   (b) Analog, digital
2. 8
3. (a) current   (b) true

13.3: SENSOR INTERFACING AND SIGNAL CONDITIONING

1. True
2. 10, Celsius.
3. 10, Fahrenheit.
4. Since ADC0848 is an 8-bit ADC, it gives us 256 steps, and 2.56 V/256 = 10 mV. LM35 produces 10 mV for each degree of temperature which matches the ADC's step size.
5. 00111001 = 57, which indicates it is 57 degrees.

CHAPTER 14

8051 INTERFACING TO EXTERNAL MEMORY

OBJECTIVES

Upon completion of this chapter, you will be able to:

>> Explain how to interface ROM with the 8031/51/52.
>> Explain how to use both on-chip and off-chip memory with the 8051/52.
>> Code 8051 Assembly and C programs accessing the 64K-byte data memory space.
>> Show how to access the 1K-byte RAM of the DS89C4x0 in Assembly and C.

In this chapter, we discuss how to interface the 8031/51/52 to external memory. In Section 14.1, we explore 8031/51/52 interfacing with external ROM. In Section 14.2, we discuss 8031/51/52 interfacing with external RAM. We will also examine the 1K-byte SRAM of the DS89C4x0 chip. In Section 14.3, we will show how to access external data memory in C.

14.1: 8031/51 INTERFACING WITH EXTERNAL ROM

As discussed in Chapter 1, the 8031 chip is a ROMless version of the 8051. In other words, it is exactly like any member of the 8051 family such as the 8751 or 89C51 as far as executing the instructions and features are concerned, but it has no on-chip ROM. Therefore, to make the 8031 execute 8051 code, it must be connected to external ROM memory containing the program code. In this section, we look at interfacing the 8031 microprocessor with external ROM. Before we discuss this topic, one might wonder why someone would want to use the 8031 when they could buy an 8751, 89C51, or DS5000. The reason is that all these chips have a limited amount of on-chip ROM. Therefore, in many systems where the on-chip ROM of the 8051 is not sufficient, the use of an 8031 is ideal since it allows the program size to be as large as 64K bytes. Although the 8031 chip itself is much cheaper than other family members, an 8031-based system is much more expensive since the ROM containing the program code is connected externally and requires more supporting circuitry, as we explain next. First, we review some of the pins of the 8031/51 used in external memory interfacing. See Figure 14-1.

EA pin

As shown in Chapter 4, for 8751/89C51/DS5000-based systems, we connect the EA pin to V_{cc} to indicate that the program code is stored in the microprocessor's on-chip ROM. To indicate that the program code is stored in external ROM, this pin must be connected to GND. This is the case for the 8051-based system. In fact, there are times when, due to repeated burning and erasing of on-chip ROM, its UV-EPROM is no longer working. In such cases, one can also use the 8751 (or 89C51 or any 8051) as the 8031. All we have to do is to connect the EA pin to ground and connect the chip to external ROM containing the program code.

P0 and P2 role in providing addresses

Since the PC (program counter) of the 8031/51 is 16-bit, it is capable of accessing up to 64K bytes of program code. In the 8031/51, port 0 and port 2 provide the 16-bit address to access external memory. Of these two ports, P0 provides the lower 8 bit addresses A0–A7, and P2 provides the upper 8-bit addresses A8–A15. More importantly, P0 is also used to provide the 8-bit data bus D0–D7. In other words, pins P0.0–P0.7 are used for both the address and data paths. This is called address/data multiplexing in chip design. Of course, the reason Intel used address/data multiplexing in the 8031/51 is to save pins.

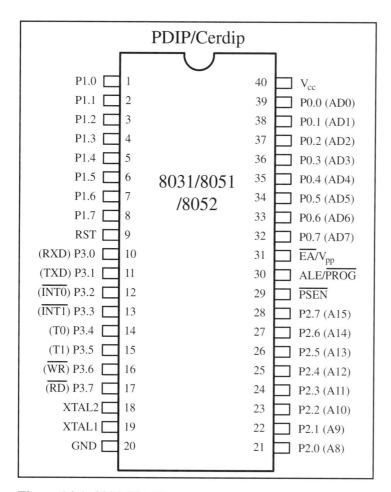

Figure 14-1. 8051 Pin Diagram

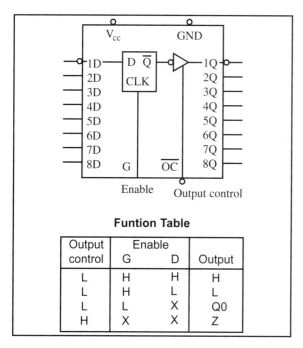

Figure 14-2. 74LS373 D Latch

Source: Reprinted by permission of Texas Instruments, Copyright Texas Instruments, 1988.

How do we know when P0 is used for the data path and when it is used for the address path? This is the job of the ALE (address latch enable) pin. ALE is an output pin for the 8031/51 microprocessor. Therefore, when ALE = 0, the 8031 uses P0 for the data path, and when ALE = 1, it uses it for the address path. As a result, to extract the addresses from the P0 pins we connect P0 to a 74LS373 latch (see Figure 14-2) and use the ALE pin to latch the address as shown in Figure 14-3. This extracting of addresses from P0 is called address/data demultiplexing.

From Figure 14-3, it is important to note that normally ALE = 0, and P0 is used as a data bus, sending data out or bringing data in. Whenever the 8031/51 wants to use P0 as an address bus, it puts the addresses A0–A7 on the P0 pins and activates ALE = 1 to indicate that P0 has the addresses. See Figure 14-4.

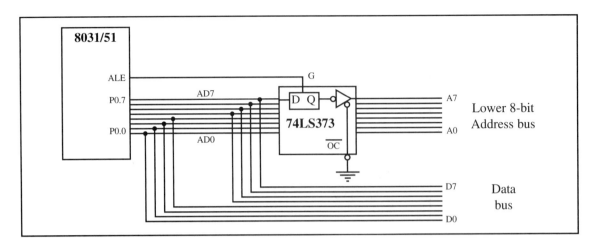

Figure 14-3. Address/Data Multiplexing

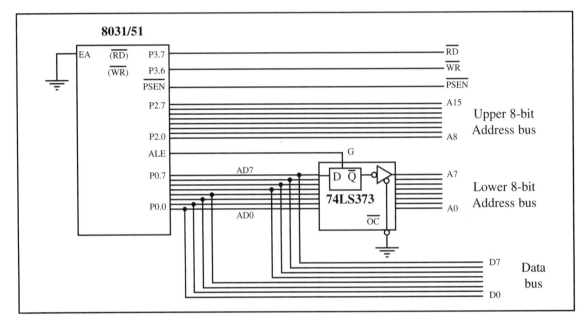

Figure 14-4. Data, Address, and Control Buses for the 8031

(For reset and crystal connection, see Chapter 4.)

PSEN

Another important signal for the 8031/51 is the PSEN (program store enable) signal. PSEN is an output signal for the 8031/51 microprocessor and must be connected to the OE pin of a ROM containing the program code. In other words, to access external ROM containing program code, the 8031/51 uses the PSEN signal. It is important to emphasize the role of EA and PSEN when connecting the 8031/51 to external ROM. When the EA pin is connected to GND, the 8031/51 fetches opcode from external ROM by using PSEN. Notice in Figure 14-5 the connection of the PSEN pin to the OE pin of ROM. In systems based on the 8751/89C51/DS5000 where EA is connected to V_{CC}, these chips do not activate the PSEN pin. This indicates that the on-chip ROM contains program code.

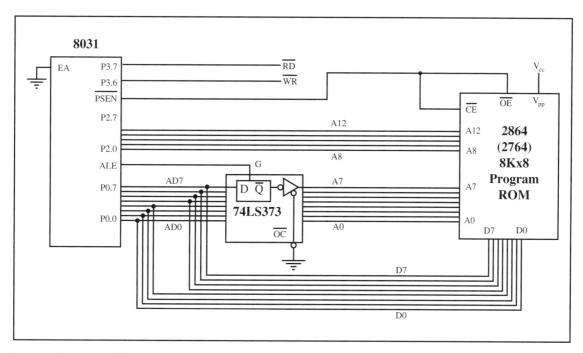

Figure 14-5. 8031 Connection to External Program ROM

On-chip and off-chip code ROM

In systems where the external ROM contains the program code, burning the program into ROM leaves the microprocessor chip untouched. This is preferable in some applications due to flexibility. In such applications, the software is updated via the serial or parallel ports of the x86 PC. This is especially the case during software development and this method is widely used in many 8051-based trainers and emulators.

On-chip and off-chip code ROM

In all our examples of 8051-based systems so far, we used either the on-chip ROM or the off-chip ROM for the program code. There are times that we want to use both of them. Is this possible? The answer is yes. For example, in an 8751 (or 89C51) system we could use the on-chip ROM for the boot code, and an external ROM (using NV-RAM) will contain the user's program. In this way, the system boot code resides on-chip and the user's programs are downloaded into off-chip NV-RAM. In such a system we still have EA = V_{cc}, meaning that upon reset the 8051 executes the on-chip program first; then, when it reaches the end of the on-chip ROM it switches to external ROM for the rest of the program code. Many 8051 trainers are designed using this method. Again, notice that this is done automatically by the 8051. For example, in an 8751 (89C51) system with both on-chip and off-chip ROM code where EA = V_{cc}, the controller fetches opcodes starting at address 0000, and then goes on to address 0FFF (the last location of on-chip ROM). Then the program counter generates address 1000H and is automatically directed to the external ROM containing the program code. See Examples 14-1 and 14-2. Figure 14-6 shows the memory configuration.

Example 14-1

Discuss the program ROM space allocation for each of the following cases.
(a) EA = 0 for the 8751 (89C51) chip.
(b) EA = V_{CC} with both on-chip and off-chip ROM for the 8751.
(c) EA = V_{CC} with both on-chip and off-chip ROM for the 8752.

Solution:

(a) When EA = 0, the EA pin is strapped to GND, and all program fetches are directed to external memory regardless of whether or not the 8751 has some on-chip ROM for program code. This external ROM can be as high as 64K bytes with address space of 0000–FFFFH. In this case, an 8751 (89C51) is the same as the 8031 system.
(b) With the 8751 (89C51) system where EA = V_{CC}, the microprocessor fetches the program code of addresses 0000–0FFFH from on-chip ROM since it has 4K bytes of on-chip program ROM and any fetches from addresses 1000H–FFFFH are directed to external ROM.
(c) With the 8752 (89C52) system where EA = V_{CC}, the microprocessor fetches the program code of addresses 0000–1FFFH from on-chip ROM since it has 8K bytes of on-chip program ROM and any fetches from addresses 2000H–FFFFH are directed to external ROM.

Example 14-2

Discuss the role of the PSEN pin in accessing on-chip and off-chip program codes.

Solution:

In the process of fetching the internal on-chip program code, the PSEN pin is not used and is never activated. However, PSEN is used for all external program fetches. In Figure 14-11, notice that PSEN is also used to activate the CE pin of the program ROM.

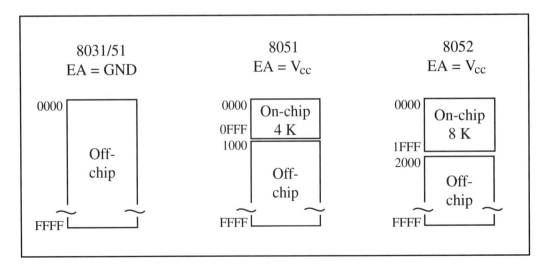

Figure 14-6. On-chip and Off-chip Program Code Access

REVIEW QUESTIONS

1. If EA = GND, indicate from what source the program code is fetched.
2. If EA = V$_{cc}$, indicate from what source the program code is fetched.
3. Which port of the 8051 is used for address/data multiplexing?
4. Which port of the 8051 provides D0–D7?
5. Which port of the 8051 provides A0–A7?
6. Which port of the 8051 provides A8–A15?
7. True or false. In accessing externally stored program code, the PSEN signal is always activated.

14.2: 8051 DATA MEMORY SPACE

So far in this book, all our discussion about memory space has involved program code. We have stated that the program counter in the 8051 is 16-bit and therefore can access up to 64K bytes of program code. In Chapter 6, we showed how to place data in the code space and used the instruction "MOVC A, @A+DPTR" to get the data. The MOVC instruction, where C stands for code, indicates that data is located in the code space of the 8051. In the 8051 family there is also a separate data memory space. In this section, we describe the data memory space of the 8051 and show how to access it in Assembly.

Data memory space

In addition to its code space, the 8051 family also has 64K bytes of data memory space. In other words, the 8051 has 128K bytes of address space of which 64K bytes are set aside for program code and the other 64K bytes are set aside for data. Program space is accessed using the program counter to locate and fetch instructions, but the data memory space is accessed using the DPTR register and an instruction called MOVX, where X stands for external (meaning that the data memory space must be implemented externally).

External ROM data

To connect the 8031/51 to external ROM containing data, we use RD (pin P3.7). See Figure 14-7. Notice the role of signals PSEN and RD. For the ROM containing the program code, PSEN is used to fetch the code. For the ROM containing data, the RD signal is used to fetch the data. To access the external data memory space, we must use the instruction MOVX as described next.

MOVX instruction

MOVX is a widely used instruction allowing access to external data memory space. This is true regardless of which member of the 8051 family is used. To bring externally stored data into the CPU, we use the instruction "MOVX A, @DPTR". This instruction will read the byte of data pointed to by register DPTR and store it in the accumulator. In applications where a large data space is needed, the look-up table method is widely used. See Examples 14-3 and 14-4 for the use of MOVX.

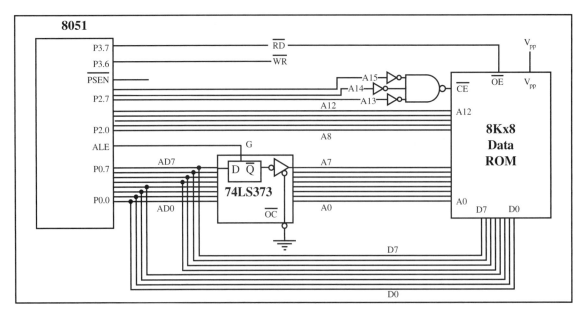

Figure 14-7. 8051 Connection to External Data ROM

Example 14-3

An external ROM uses the 8051 data space to store the look-up table (starting at 1000H) for DAC data. Write a program to read 30 bytes of these data and send them to P1.

Solution:
```
MYXDATA   EQU   1000H
COUNT     EQU   30
          . . .
          MOV   DPTR,#MYXDATA    ;pointer to external data
          MOV   R2,#COUNT        ;counter
AGAIN:    MOVX  A,@DPTR          ;get byte from external mem
          MOV   P1,A             ;issue it to P1
          INC   DPTR             ;next location
          DJNZ  R2,AGAIN         ;until all are read
```

Example 14-4

External data ROM has a look-up table for the squares of numbers 0–9. Since the internal RAM of the 8031/51 has a shorter access time, write a program to copy the table elements into internal RAM starting at address 30H. The look-up table address starts at address 0 of external ROM.

Solution:
```
TABLE     EQU   000H
RAMTBLE   EQU   30H
COUNT     EQU   10
          . . .
          MOV   DPTR,#TABLE      ;pointer to external data
          MOV   R5,#COUNT        ;counter
          MOV   R0,#RAMTBLE      ;pointer to internal RAM
BACK:     MOVX  A,@DPTR          ;get byte from external mem
          MOV   @R0,A            ;store it in internal RAM
          INC   DPTR             ;next data location
          INC   R0               ;next RAM location
          DJNZ  R5,BACK          ;until all are read
```

Example 14-5

Show the design of an 8031-based system with 8K bytes of program ROM and 8K bytes of data ROM.

Solution:

Figure 14-8 shows the design. Notice the role of PSEN and RD in each ROM. For program ROM, PSEN is used to activate both OE and CE. For data ROM, we use RD to activate OE, while CE is activated by a simple decoder.

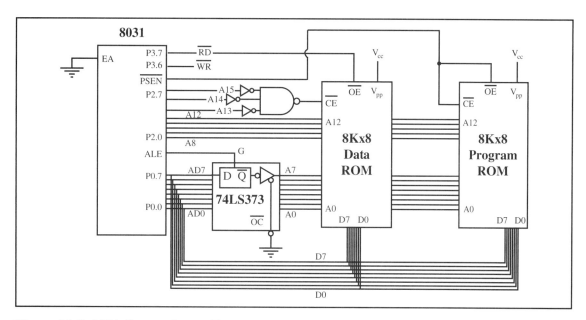

Figure 14-8. 8031 Connection to External Data ROM and External Program ROM

Contrast Example 14-4 with Example 5-8. In that example, the table elements are stored in the program code space of the 8051 and we used the instruction "MOVC" to access each element. Although both "MOVC A, @A+DPTR" and "MOVX A, @DPTR" look very similar, one is used to get data in the code space and the other is used to get data in the data space of the microprocessor. Example 14-5 shows an 8031-based system with both data and program ROM.

From the discussion so far, we conclude that while we can use internal RAM and registers located inside the CPU for storage of data, any additional memory space for read/write data must be implemented externally. This is discussed further next.

External data RAM

To connect the 8051 to an external SRAM, we must use both RD (P3.7) and WR (P3.6). This is shown in Figure 14-9.

MOVX instruction

In writing data to external data RAM, we use the instruction "MOVX @DPTR, A" where the contents of register A are written to external RAM

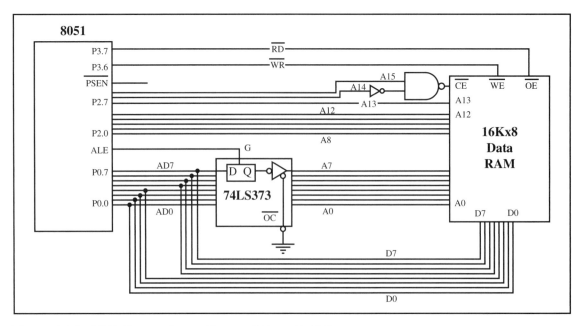

Figure 14-9. 8051 Connection to External Data RAM

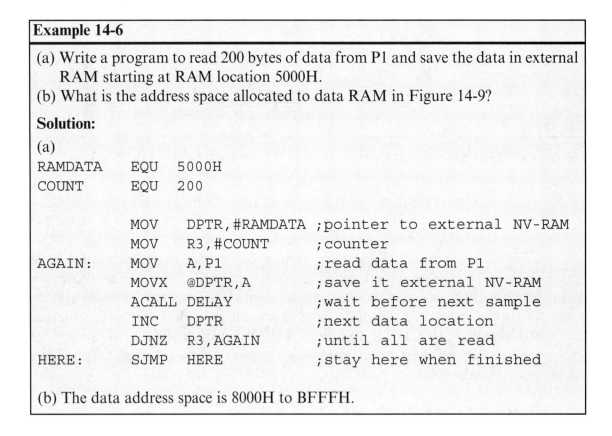

Example 14-6

(a) Write a program to read 200 bytes of data from P1 and save the data in external RAM starting at RAM location 5000H.

(b) What is the address space allocated to data RAM in Figure 14-9?

Solution:

(a)

```
RAMDATA    EQU   5000H
COUNT      EQU   200

           MOV   DPTR,#RAMDATA  ;pointer to external NV-RAM
           MOV   R3,#COUNT      ;counter
AGAIN:     MOV   A,P1           ;read data from P1
           MOVX  @DPTR,A        ;save it external NV-RAM
           ACALL DELAY          ;wait before next sample
           INC   DPTR           ;next data location
           DJNZ  R3,AGAIN       ;until all are read
HERE:      SJMP  HERE           ;stay here when finished
```

(b) The data address space is 8000H to BFFFH.

whose address is pointed to by the DPTR register. This has many applications, especially where we are collecting a large number of bytes of data. In such applications, as we collect data we must store them in NV-RAM so that when power is lost we do not lose the data. See Example 14-6 and Figure 14-9.

A single external ROM for code and data

Assume that we have an 8031-based system connected to a single 64Kx8 (27512) external ROM chip. This single external ROM chip is used for both program code and data storage. For example, the space 0000–7FFFH is allocated to program code, and address space D000H–FFFFH is set aside for data. In accessing the data, we use the MOVX instruction. How do we connect the PSEN and RD signals to such a ROM? Note that PSEN is used to access the external code space and the RD signal is used to access the external data space. To allow a single ROM chip to provide both program code space and data space, we use an AND gate to signal the OE pin of the ROM chip as shown in Figure 14-10.

8031 system with ROM and RAM

There are times that we need program ROM, data ROM, and data RAM in a system. This is shown in Example 14-7.

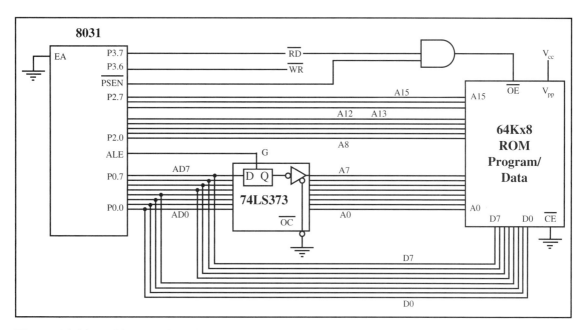

Figure 14-10. A Single ROM for Both Program and Data

Example 14-7

Assume that we need an 8031 system with 16KB of program space, 16KB of data ROM starting at 0000, and 16K of NV-RAM starting at 8000H. Show the design using a 74LS138 for the address decoder.

Solution:

The solution is diagrammed in Figure 14-11. Notice that there is no need for a decoder for program ROM, but we need a 74LS138 decoder for data ROM and RAM. Also notice that G1 = V_{cc}, G2A = GND, G2B = GND, and the C input of the 74LS138 is also grounded since we use Y0–Y3 only.

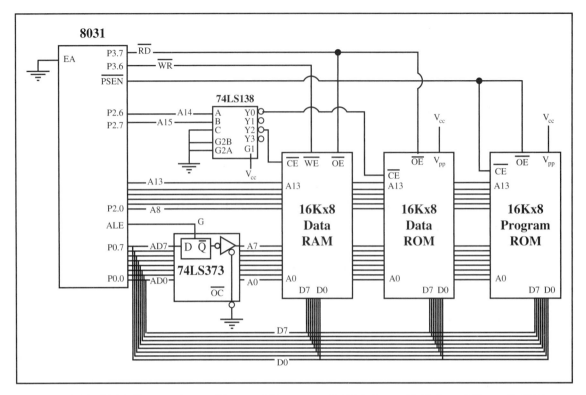

Figure 14-11. 8031 Connection to External Program ROM, Data RAM, and Data ROM

Interfacing to large external memory

In some applications, we need a large amount (256K bytes, for example) of memory to store data. However, the 8051 can support only 64K bytes of external data memory since DPTR is 16-bit. To solve this problem, we connect A0–A15 of the 8051 directly to the external memory's A0–A15 pins and use some of the P1 pins to access the 64K-byte blocks inside the single 256Kx8 memory chip. This is shown in Example 14-8 and illustrated in Figure 14-12.

Accessing 1K-byte SRAM in Assembly

The DS89C4x0 chip family has 1K byte of SRAM, which is accessible by using the MOVX instruction. Next, we will show how to access this 1K byte of SRAM in Assembly language. The C versions of these programs are given in the next section.

1k byte of SRAM in DS89C4X0

The DS89C4x0 family (DS89C30/40/50) comes with 1K byte of SRAM embedded into the chip. See Table 14-1. This is in addition to the 256 bytes of RAM that comes with any 8052 chip such as the DS89C4x0. This 1K byte (1KB) of SRAM can be very useful in many applications, especially for C compilers that need to store data variables. Another case in which this

Example 14-8

In a certain application, we need 256K bytes of NV-RAM to store data collected by an 8051 microprocessor. (a) Show the connection of an 8051 to a single 256Kx8 NV-RAM chip. (b) Show how various blocks of this single chip are accessed.

Solution:

(a) The 256Kx8 NV-RAM has 18 address pins (A0–A17) and 8 data lines. As shown in Figure 14-12, A0–A15 go directly to the memory chip while A16 and A17 are controlled by P1.0 and P1.1, respectively. Also notice that chip select of external RAM is connected to P1.2 of the 8051.

(b) The 256K bytes of memory are divided into four blocks, and each block is accessed as follows:

Chip Select **P1.2**	*A17* **P1.1**	*A16* **P1.0**	**Block Address Space**
0	0	0	00000H-0FFFFH
0	0	1	10000H-1FFFFH
0	1	0	20000H-2FFFFH
0	1	1	30000H-3FFFFH
1	x	x	External RAM disabled

For example, to access the 20000H–2FFFFH address space, we need the following:

```
CLR   P1.2          ;enable external RAM
MOV   DPTR,#0        ;start of 64K memory block
CLR   P1.0          ;A16=0
SETB  P1.1          ;A17=1 for 20000H block
MOV   A,SBUF        ;get data from serial port
MOVX  @DPTR,A       ;save data in block 20000H addr.
INC   DPTR          ;next location
...
```

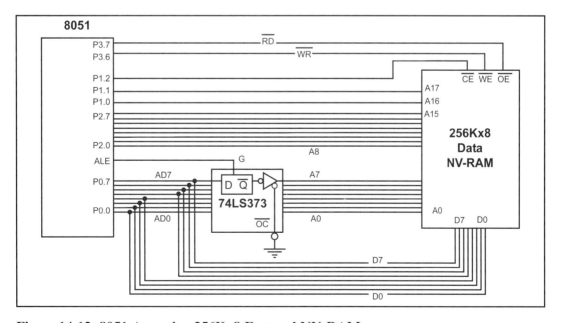

Figure 14-12. 8051 Accessing 256Kx8 External NV-RAM

Table 14-1. DS89C4x0 Family from Maxim/Dallas Semiconductor

Part No.	On-chip ROM (Flash)	On-chip RAM	On-chip SRAM Accessed by MOVX
DS89C430	16KB	256B	1KB
DS89C440	32KB	256B	1KB
DS89C450	64KB	256B	1KB

1K-byte RAM can be put to great use is the tiny RTOS (real time operating systems) designed for the 8051 family. To access this 1K byte of SRAM in the DS89C4x0 chip, we must use the MOVX instruction. Notice that while accessing the 256 bytes of RAM in the 8052, we use either direct or register-indirect addressing modes, but to access the data stored in this 1KB of RAM, we must use the MOVX instruction. Upon power-on reset, the access to the 1KB SRAM is blocked. In order to access it, we must enable some bits in the SFR registers called PMR (power management register). The PMR is an SFR register and is located at address C4H. The SFR location C4H is one of the reserved byte spaces of the 8052 used by Dallas Semiconductor for PMR. The PMR bits related to the 1KB SRAM are shown in Figure 14-13. Examine the information in Figure 14-13 very carefully. The 1KB SRAM is not accessible upon reset. This is the default state that allows us to interface the DS89C4x0 chip to external data memory, just like any member of the 8051/52 family. To access the 1KB SRAM, we must make PMR bits DEM0 = 1 and DME1 = 0. In that case, any MOVX address of 0000–03FFH will go to the on-chip 1KB SRAM and all other addresses are directed to the external data memory. That means that if we want to add external data memory

1	0	0	0	0	0	DME1	DME0

DME1	DME0	Data Memory Address Range	Memory Access
0	0	0000–FFFFH	External Data Memory (Default) (after every reset)
X	1	0000–03FFH	Internal SRAM Data Memory
		0400–FFFFH	External Data Memory
1	0	Reserved	Reserved

Figure 14-13. PMR Register Bits for 1K-byte SRAM of DS89C4x0 Chip
Note: Power management register (PMR) is an SFR in the DS89C4x0 family and is located at address C4H.

to the DS89C4x0 chip, we must designate it as 0400–FFFFH since the first 1K-byte space is already taken by the 1KB SRAM, assuming that the proper bits in the PMR are enabled. Again, it must be emphasized that upon reset, access to the 1KB SRAM is blocked, and can be accessed only if we set the proper bits in the PMR register. This must be done every time we power up the DS89C4x0-based system. Study Examples 14-9–14-11 to see how we access this 1KB SRAM.

REVIEW QUESTIONS

1. The 8051 has a total of ___ bytes of memory space for both program code and data.
2. All the data memory space of the 8051 is _____ (internal, external).
3. True or false. In the 8051, program code must be read-only memory.
4. True or false. In the 8051, data memory can be read or write memory.
5. Explain the role of pins PSEN, RD, and WR in accessing external memory.
6. True or false. Every 8051 chip comes with 1KB of SRAM.
7. True or false. Upon reset, access to the 1KB SRAM of the DS89C4x0 is blocked.

Example 14-9

Write a program (a) to enable access to the 1KB SRAM of the DS89C4x0, (b) put the ASCII numbers '0,' '1,' and '2' in SRAM, and (c) read the same data from SRAM and send each one to ports P0, P1, and P2, respectively.

Solution:

```
MYXDATA EQU 000H
COUNT EQU 5
IDATA EQU 40H
        ORG    0
        MOV    A,0C4h          ;read PMR register
        SETB   ACC.0           ;make DME0=1
        MOV    0C4H,A          ;enable 1KB SRAM
        MOV    DPTR,#MYXDATA
        MOV    A,#'0'
        MOVX   @DPTR,A
        MOVX   A,@DPTR,A
        MOV    P0,A
        INC    DPTR
        MOV    A,#'1'
        MOVX   @DPTR,A
        MOVX   A,@DPTR,A
        MOV    P1,A
        INC    DPTR
        MOV    A,#'2'
        MOVX   @DPTR,A
        MOVX   A,@DPTR,A
        MOV    P2,A
        END
```

Example 14-10

Write a program (a) to enable access to the 1KB SRAM of the DS89C4x0, and (b) transfer a block of data from RAM locations 40–44H into the 1K SRAM.

Solution:

Assume that we have the following data in the RAM location (256-byte space) starting at 40H:

$$40 = (7D) \quad 41 = (96) \quad 42 = (C5) \quad 43 = (12) \quad 44 = (83)$$

```
        MYXDATA EQU 000H
        COUNT EQU 5
        IDATA EQU 40H
              ORG   0
              MOV   A,0C4h         ;read PMR register
              SETB  ACC.0          ;make DME0=1
              MOV   0C4H,A         ;enable 1KB SRAM
              MOV   DPTR,#MYXDATA  ;pointer to 1KB SRAM
              MOV   R2,#COUNT      ;counter
              MOV   R0,#IDATA      ;LOAD POINTER
AGAIN:        MOV   A,@R0          ;get a byte
              MOVX  A,@DPTR        ;save it in 1KB SRAM
              INC   R0             ;NEXT
              INC   DPTR           ;next location
              DJNZ  R2,AGAIN       ;until all are read
              END
```

Example 14-11

Write a program in Assembly (a) to enable access to the 1KB SRAM of the DS89C4x0, (b) move a block of data from code space of the DS89C4x0 chip into 1KB SRAM, and (c) then read the same data from RAM and send it to the serial port of the 8051 one byte at a time.

Solution:

```
DATA_ADDR   EQU   400H        ;code data
COUNT       EQU   5           ;message size
RAM_ADDR    EQU   40H         ;8051 internal RAM address
        ORG   0
        ACALL COPY_1          ;copy from code ROM to internal RAM
        MOV   A,0C4H          ;read PMR of DS89C4x0
        SETB  ACC.0           ;enable PMR bit for 1K SRAM
        MOV   0C4H,A          ;write it to PMR of DS89C4x0
        ACALL COPY_2          ;copy from internal RAM to 1KB SRAM
        MOV   TMOD,#20H       ;set up serial port
        MOV   TH1,#-3         ;9600 baud rate
        MOV   SCON,#50H
        SETB  TR1
        ACALL COPY_COM        ;copy from 1KB SRAM to serial port
        SJMP  $               ;stay here

COPY_1:
        MOV   DPTR,#DATA_ADDR
        MOV   R0,#RAM_ADDR
        MOV   R2,#COUNT
```

Example 14-11 (*Continued*)

```
H1:    CLR   A
       MOVC  A,@A+DPTR
       MOV   @R0,A
       INC   DPTR
       INC   R0
       DJNZ  R2,H1
       RET

;--------transfer data from internal RAM to external RAM
COPY_2:
       MOV   DPTR,#0          ;DS89C4x0 1KB addr
       MOV   R0,#RAM_ADDR
       MOV   R2,#COUNT
H2:    MOV   A,@R0            ;get a byte from internal RAM
       MOVX  @DPTR,A          ;store it in 1KB SRAM of DS89C4x0
       INC   DPTR
       INC   R0
       DJNZ  R2,H2
       RET

;---------data transfer from 1KB SRAM to serial port
COPY_COM:
       MOV   DPTR,#0          ;DS89C4x0 1KB addr
       MOV   R2,#COUNT
H3:    MOVX  A,@DPTR          ;get a byte from 1KB SRAM space
       ACALL SERIAL           ;send it to com port
       INC   DPTR
       DJNZ  R2,H3
       RET

;-----------send data to serial port
SERIAL:
       MOV   SBUF,A
H4:    JNB   TI,H4
       CLR   TI
       RET
;----data in code space
       ORG   400H
MYBYTE:    DB     "HELLO"
       END
```

14.3: ACCESSING EXTERNAL DATA MEMORY IN 8051 C

In Chapter 7, we showed how to place fixed data into the code space using 8051 C. In that chapter, we also showed how to access fixed data stored in the code space of the 8051 family. In this section, we show how to access the external data space of the 8051 family using C language. To access the external data space (RAM or ROM) of the 8051 using C, we use XBYTE[loc] where loc is an address in the range of 0000–FFFFH. Example 14-12 shows how to write some data to external RAM addresses starting at 0. Notice that the XBYTE function is part of the absacc.h header file. Examine Examples 14-13 and 14-14 to gain some mastery of accessing external data memory using C.

Example 14-12

Write a C program (a) to store ASCII letters 'A' to 'E' in external RAM addresses starting at 0, then (b) get the same data from the external RAM and send it to P1 one byte at a time.

Solution:

```
#include <reg51.h>
#include <absacc.h> //notice the header file for XBYTE

void main(void)
  {
    unsigned char x;
    XBYTE[0]='A';  //write ASCII 'A' to External RAM location 0
    XBYTE[1]='B';  //write ASCII 'B' to External RAM location 1
    XBYTE[2]='C';  //write ASCII 'C' to External RAM location 2
    XBYTE[3]='D';
    XBYTE[4]='E';
    for(x=0;x<5;x++)
        P1=XBYTE[x];   //read external RAM data and send it to
P1
  }
```

Run the above program on your 8051 simulator and examine the contents of xdata to verify the result.

Example 14-13

An external ROM uses the 8051 data space to store the look-up table (starting at 100H) for DAC data. Write a C program to read 30 bytes of table data and send it to P1.

Solution:

```
#include <reg51.h>
#include <absacc.h>  //notice the header file for XBYTE

void main(void)
  {
    unsigned char count;
    for(count=0;count<30;count++)
      P1=XBYTE[0x100+count];
  }
```

Accessing DS89C4x0's 1KB SRAM in C

In Section 14.2, we discussed how to access the 1KB SRAM of the DS89C4x0 chip using Assembly language. Examples 14-15 and 14-16 will show the 8051 C version of some of the Assembly programs.

Example 14-14

Assume that we have an external RAM with addresses 0000–2FFFH for a given 8051-based system. (a) Write a C program to move the message "Hello" into external RAM, and (b) read the same data in external RAM and send it to the serial port.

Solution:

```
#include <reg51.h>
#include <absacc.h>   //notice the header file for XBYTE

unsigned char msg[5]="Hello";

void main(void)
  {
    unsigned char x;
    TMOD = 0x20;   //USE TIMER 1,8-BIT AUTO-RELOAD
    TH1  = 0xFD;   //9600
    SCON = 0x50;
    TR1  = 1;

    for(x=0;x<5;x++)
      XBYTE[0x000+x] = msg[x];

    for(x=0;x<5;x++)
      {
        SBUF = XBYTE[0x000+x];
        while(TI==0);
        TI=0;
      }
  }
```

Example 14-15

Write a C program (a) to enable access to the 1KB SRAM of the DS89C4x0, (b) put the ASCII letters 'A,' 'B,' and 'C' in SRAM, and (c) read the same data from SRAM and send each one to ports P0, P1, and P2.

Solution:

```
#include <reg51.h>
#include <absacc.h>   //notice the header file for XBYTE
sfr PMRREG = 0xC4;
void main(void)
  {
    unsigned char x;
    PMRREG = 0x81;
    XBYTE[0]='A';   //write ASCII 'A' to External RAM location 0
    XBYTE[1]='B';   //write ASCII 'B' to External RAM location 1
    XBYTE[2]='C';   //write ASCII 'C' to External RAM location 2
```

Example 14-15 (*Continued*)

```
    for(x=0;x<3;x++)
      {
        P0=XBYTE[x];  //read ext RAM data and send it to P0
        P1=XBYTE[x];  //read ext RAM data and send it to P1
        P2=XBYTE[x];  //read ext RAM data and send it to P2
      }
  }
```
Note: This is the C version of an earlier example.

Example 14-16

Write a C program to (a) enable access to the 1KB SRAM of the DS89C4x0, (b) move a block of data from the code space of the DS89C420 chip into 1KB SRAM, then (c) read the same data from SRAM and send it to the serial port of the 8051 one byte at a time.

Solution:

```
#include <reg51.h>
#include <absacc.h>            //needed for external data space
sfr PMRREG = 0xC4;            //PMR reg address in DS89C4x0

void main(void)
  {
    code unsigned char msg[]= "HELLO";      //data in code space
    unsigned char x;
    PMRREG = PMRREG | 0x1;       //enable 1KB SRAM bit in PMR reg
    TMOD = 0x20;                 //serial port set up
    TH1  = 0xFD;                 //9600 baud rate
    SCON = 0x50;
    TR1  = 1;

    for(x=0; x<5;x++)  //transfer data from code area to 1KB SRAM
      {
        XBYTE[0x0+x]  = msg[x];
      }
    for(x=0; x<5;x++)  //send data from 1KB SRAM to serial port
      {
        SBUF = XBYTE[0x0+x];
        while(TI==0);
        TI=0;
      }

    while(1);                              //and stay here forever
  }
```
Note: This is the C version of Example 14-11.

SUMMARY

This chapter described memory interfacing with 8031/51-based systems. RAM and ROM memories were interfaced with 8031 systems, and programs were written to access code and data stored on these external memories. The 64KB of external data space of the 8051 was discussed, and programs were written in both Assembly and C to access them. Finally, the 1KB SRAM memory of the DS89C4x0 chip was explored and we showed how to access it in both Assembly and C.

PROBLEMS

14.1: 8031/51 INTERFACING WITH EXTERNAL ROM

1. In a certain 8031 system, the starting address is 0000H and it has only 16K bytes of program memory. What is the ending address of this system?
2. When the 8031 CPU is powered up, at what address does it expect to see the first opcode?
3. In an 8031/51 microprocessor, RD and WR are pins ___ and ___, respectively. They belong to port ____. Which bits of this port?
4. The 8051 supports a maximum of _____ K bytes of program memory space.
5. True or false. For any member of the 8051 family, if EA = Gnd the microprocessor fetches program code from external ROM.
6. True or false. For any member of the 8051 family, if EA = V_{cc} the microprocessor fetches program code from internal (on-chip) ROM.
7. For which of the following must we have external memory for program code?
   (a) 8751   (b) 89C51   (c) 8031   (d) 8052
8. For which of the following is external memory for program code optional?
   (a) 8751   (b) 89C51   (c) 8031   (d) 8052
9. In the 8051, which port provides the A0–A7 address bits?
10. In the 8051, which port provides the A8–A15 address bits?
11. In the 8051, which port provides the D0–D7 data bits?
12. Explain the difference between ALE = 0 and ALE = 1.
13. RD is pin _____ of P3, and WR is pin ____ of P3. What about PSEN?
14. Which of the following signals must be used in fetching program code from external ROM?
   (a) RD   (b) WR   (c) PSEN
15. For the 8031-based system with external program ROM, when the microprocessor is powered up, it expects to find the first instruction at address _____ of program ROM. Is this internal or external ROM?
16. In an 8051 with 16K bytes of on-chip program ROM, explain what happens if EA = V_{cc}.
17. True or false. For the 8051 the program code must be read-only memory. In other words, the memory code space of the 8051 is read-only memory.
18. Indicate when PSEN is used. Is it used in accessing on-chip code ROM or external (off-chip) code ROM?

14.2: 8051 DATA MEMORY SPACE

19. Indicate when RD and WR are used. Are they used in accessing external data memory?
20. The 8051 supports a maximum of _____ K bytes of data memory space.
21. Which of the following signals must be used in fetching data from external data ROM?
    (a) RD   (b) WR   (c) PSEN   (d) both (a) and (b)
22. For each of the following, indicate if it is active low or active high.
    (a) PSEN   (b) RD   (c) WR
23. True or false. For the 8051, the data memory space can belong to ROM or RAM.
24. Explain the difference between the MOVX and MOVC instructions.
25. Write a program to transfer 20 bytes of data from external data ROM to internal RAM. The external data ROM address is 2000H, and internal RAM starts at 60H.
26. Write a program in Assembly to transfer 30 bytes of data from internal data RAM to external RAM. The external data RAM address is 6000H, and internal RAM starts at 40H.
27. Write a program in Assembly to transfer 50 bytes of data from external data ROM to external data RAM. The external data ROM address is 3000H, and the external data RAM starts at 8000H.
28. Write a program in Assembly to transfer 50 bytes of data from external data ROM to 1KB SRAM of DS89C4x0. The external data ROM address is 3000H, and the SRAM data starts at 0000H.
29. Write a program in Assembly to transfer 50 bytes of data from 1KB SRAM of DS89C4x0 to P1 one byte at a time every second. The SRAM data starts at 0200H.
30. Give the address of the PMR and its contents upon reset.
31. Which 8051 version has 1KB SRAM?
32. For the DS89C4x0, the 1KB SRAM is _____ (available, blocked) upon reset.
33. What memory space is available for expansion if DME0 = 0 and DME1 = 0?
34. What memory space is available for expansion if DME0 = 1 and DME1 = 0?

14.3: ACCESSING EXTERNAL DATA MEMORY IN 8051 C

35. Write a program in C to transfer 20 bytes of data from external data ROM to internal RAM. The external data ROM address is 2000H, and internal RAM starts at 60H.
36. Write a program in C to transfer 30 bytes of data from internal data RAM to external RAM. The external data RAM address is 6000H, and internal RAM starts at 40H.
37. Write a program in C to transfer 50 bytes of data from external data ROM to external data RAM. The external data ROM address is 3000H, and the external data RAM starts at 8000H.

38. Write a program in C to transfer 50 bytes of data from external data ROM to 1KB SRAM of DS89C4x0. The external data ROM address is 3000H, and the SRAM data starts at 0000H.

39. Write a program in C to transfer 100 bytes of data from 1KB SRAM of DS89C4x0 to P1 one byte at a time every second. The SRAM data starts at 0200H.

ANSWERS TO REVIEW QUESTIONS

14.1: 8031/51 INTERFACING WITH EXTERNAL ROM

1. From external ROM (i.e., off-chip)
2. From internal ROM (i.e., on-chip)
3. P0
4. P0
5. P0
6. P2
7. True

14.2: 8051 DATA MEMORY SPACE

1. 128K
2. External
3. True
4. True
5. Only PSEN is used to access external ROM containing program code, but when accessing external data memory we must use RD and WR signals. In other words, RD and WR are only for external data memory and are never used for external program ROM.
6. False
7. True

CHAPTER 15

RELAY, OPTOISOLATOR, AND STEPPER MOTOR

OBJECTIVES

Upon completion of this chapter, you will be able to:

>> Describe the basic operation of a relay.
>> Interface the 8051 with a relay.
>> Describe the basic operation of an optoisolator.
>> Interface the 8051 with an optoisolator.
>> Describe the basic operation of a stepper motor.
>> Interface the 8051 with a stepper motor.
>> Code 8051 programs to control and operate a stepper motor.
>> Define stepper motor operation in terms of step angle, steps per revolution, tooth pitch, rotation speed, and RPM.

This chapter discusses stepper motor control and shows 8051 interfacing with relays, optoisolators, and stepper motors. In Section 15.1, the basics of relays and optoisolators are described. Then we show their interfacing with the 8051. In Section 15.2, stepper motor interfacing with the 8051 is shown. We use both Assembly and C in our programming examples.

15.1: RELAYS AND OPTOISOLATORS

This section begins with an overview of the basic operations of electro-mechanical relays, solid-state relays, reed switches, and optoisolators. Then we describe how to interface them to the 8051. We use both Assembly and C language programs to demonstrate their control.

Electromechanical relays

A *relay* is an electrically controllable switch widely used in industrial controls, automobiles, and appliances. It allows the isolation of two separate sections of a system with two different voltage sources. For example, a +5V system can be isolated from a 120V system by placing a relay between them. One such relay is called an electromechanical (or electromagnetic) relay (EMR) as shown in Figure 15-1. The EMRs have three components: the coil, spring, and contacts. In Figure 15-1, a digital +5V on the left side can control a 12V motor on the right side without any physical contact between them. When current flows through the coil, a magnetic field is created around the coil (the coil is energized), which causes the armature to be attracted to the coil. The armature's contact acts like a switch and closes or opens the circuit. When the coil is not energized, a spring pulls the armature to its normal state of open or closed. In the block diagram for electromechanical relays, we do not show the spring, but it does exist internally. There are all types of relays for all kinds of applications. In choosing a relay, the following characteristics need to be considered:

1. The contacts can be normally open (NO) or normally closed (NC). In the NC type, the contacts are closed when the coil is not energized. In the NO, the contacts are open when the coil is unenergized.

2. There can be one or more contacts. For example, we can have SPST (single pole, single throw), SPDT (single pole, double throw), and DPDT (double pole, double throw) relays.

3. The voltage and current needed to energize the coil. The voltage can vary from a few volts to 50 volts, while the current can be from a few mA to 20 mA. The relay has a minimum voltage, below which the coil will not be energized. This minimum voltage is called the "pull-in" voltage. In the data sheet for relays we might not see current, but rather coil resistance. The V/R will give you the pull-in current. For example, if the coil voltage is 5 V and the coil resistance is 500 ohms, we need a minimum of 10 mA (5V/500 ohms = 10 mA) pull-in current.

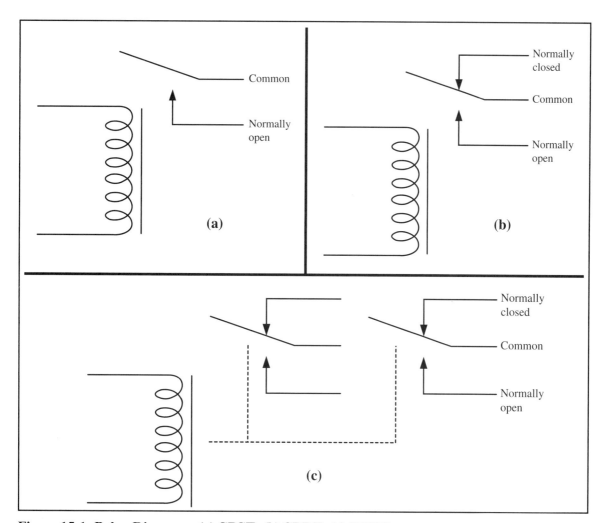

Figure 15-1. Relay Diagrams: (a) SPST; (b) SPDT; (c) DPDT

4. The maximum DC/AC voltage and current that can be handled by the contacts. This is in the range of a few volts to hundreds of volts, while the current can be from a few amps to 40A or more, depending on the relay. Notice the difference between this voltage/current specification and the voltage/current needed for energizing the coil. The fact that one can use such a small amount of voltage/current on one side to handle a large amount of voltage/current on the other side is what makes relays so widely used in industrial controls. Examine Table 15-1 for some relay characteristics.

Table 15-1. Selected DIP Relay Characteristics

Part No.	Contact Form	Coil Volts	Coil Ohms	Contact Volts-Current
106462CP	SPST-NO	5VDC	500	100VDC-0.5A
138430CP	SPST-NO	5VDC	500	100VDC-0.5A
106471CP	SPST-NO	12VDC	1000	100VDC-0.5A
138448CP	SPST-NO	12VDC	1000	100VDC-0.5A
129875CP	DPDT	5VDC	62.5	30VDC-1A

Source: www.Jameco.com

Driving a relay

Digital systems and microprocessor pins lack sufficient current to drive the relay. While the relay's coil needs around 10 mA to be energized, the microprocessor's pin can provide a maximum of 1–2 mA current. For this reason, we place a driver, such as the ULN2803, or a power transistor between the microprocessor and the relay as shown in Figure 15-2.

The following program turns the lamp on and off shown in Figure 15-2 by energizing and de-energizing the relay every second.

```
        ORG 0H
MAIN:
        SETB  P1.0
        MOV   R5, #55
        ACALL DELAY
        CLR   P1.0
        MOV   R5, #55
        ACALL DELAY
        SJMP  MAIN
DELAY:
H1:     MOV   R4,#100
H2:     MOV   R3,#253
H3:     DJNZ  R3, H3
        DJNZ  R4, H2
        DJNZ  R5, H1
        RET
        END
```

Solid-state relay

Another widely used relay is the solid-state relay (SSR). In this relay, there is no coil, spring, or mechanical contact switch. The entire relay is made out of semiconductor materials. Because no mechanical parts are involved in solid-state relays, their switching response time is much faster than that of

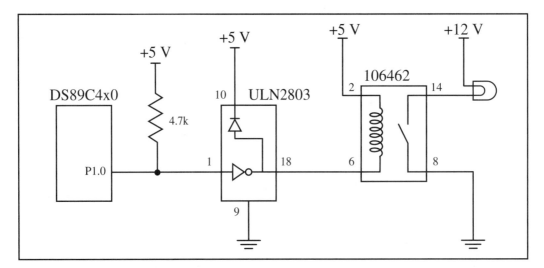

Figure 15-2. DS89C4x0 Connection to Relay

Table 15-2. Selected Solid-State Relay Characteristics

Part No.	Contact Style	Control Volts	Contact Volts	Contact Current
143058CP	SPST	4-32VDC	240VAC	3A
139053CP	SPST	3-32VDC	240VAC	25A
162341CP	SPST	3-32VDC	240VAC	10A
172591CP	SPST	3-32VDC	60VDC	2A
175222CP	SPST	3-32VDC	60VDC	4A
176647CP	SPST	3-32VDC	120VDC	5A

Source: (www.Jameco.com)

electromechanical relays. Another problem with the electromechanical relay is its life expectancy. The life cycle for the electromechanical relay can vary from a few hundred thousands to a few million operations. Wear and tear on the contact points can cause the relay to malfunction after a while. Solid-state relays have no such limitations. Extremely low input current and small packaging make solid-state relays ideal for microprocessor and logic control switching. They are widely used in controlling pumps, solenoids, alarms, and other power applications. Some solid-state relays have a phase control option, which is ideal for motor-speed control and light-dimming applications. Figure 15-3 shows control of a fan using a solid-state relay.

Reed switch

Another popular switch is the reed switch (see Figure 14-4). When the reed switch is placed in a magnetic field, the contact is closed. When the magnetic field is removed, the contact is forced open by its spring. The reed switch is ideal for moist and marine environments where it can be submerged in fuel or water. They are also widely used in dirty and dusty atmospheres since they are tightly sealed.

Optoisolator

In some applications, we use an optoisolator (also called optocoupler) to isolate two parts of a system. An example is driving a motor. Motors can produce what is called back EMF, a high-voltage spike produced by a sudden change of

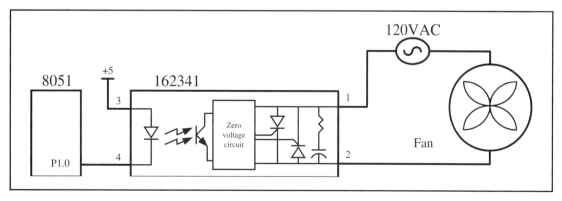

Figure 15-3. 8051 Connection to a Solid-State Relay

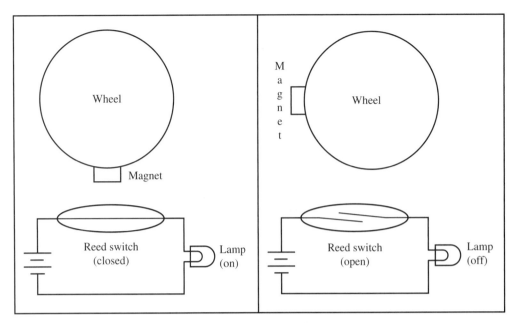

Figure 15-4. Reed Switch and Magnet Combination

current as indicated in the V = Ldi/dt formula. In situations such as printed circuit board design, we can reduce the effect of this unwanted voltage spike (called ground bounce) by using decoupling capacitors (see Appendix C). In systems that have inductors (coil winding), such as motors, decoupling capacitor or a diode will not do the job. In such cases we use optoisolators. An optoisolator has an LED (light-emitting diode) transmitter and a photosensor receiver, separated from each other by a gap. When current flows through the diode, it transmits a signal light across the gap and the receiver produces the same signal with the same phase but a different current and amplitude. See Figure 15-5. Optoisolators

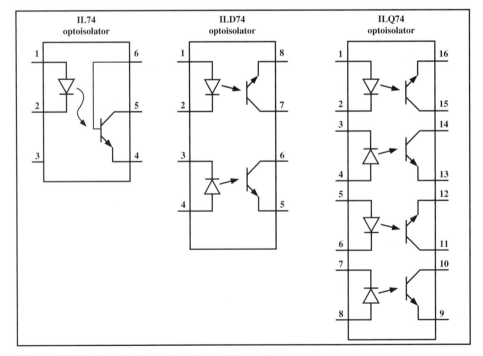

Figure 15-5. Optoisolator Package Examples

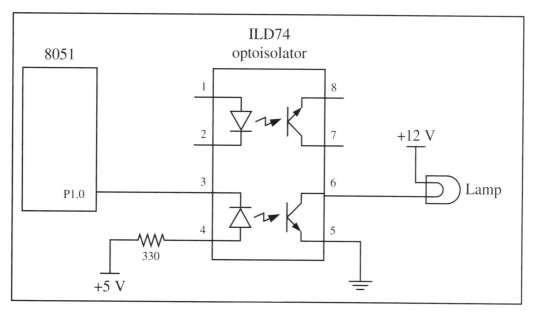

Figure 15-6. Controlling a Lamp via Optoisolator

are also widely used in communication equipment such as modems. This allows a computer to be connected to a telephone line without risk of damage from power surges. The gap between the transmitter and receiver of optoisolators prevents the electrical current surge from reaching the system.

Interfacing an optoisolator

The optoisolator comes in a small IC package with four or more pins. There are also packages that contain more than one optoisolator. When placing an optoisolator between two circuits, we must use two separate voltage sources, one for each side, as shown in Figure 15-6. Unlike relays, no drivers need to be placed between the microprocessor/digital output and the optoisolators.

REVIEW QUESTIONS

1. Give one application where would you use a relay.
2. Why do we place a driver between the microprocessor and the relay?
3. What is an NC relay?
4. Why are relays that use coils called electromechanical relays?
5. What is the advantage of a solid-state relay over EMR?
6. What is the advantage of an optoisolator over an EM relay?

15.2: STEPPER MOTOR INTERFACING

This section begins with an overview of the basic operation of stepper motors. Then we describe how to interface a stepper motor to the 8051. Finally, we use Assembly language programs to demonstrate control of the angle and direction of stepper motor rotation.

Stepper motors

A *stepper motor* is a widely used device that translates electrical pulses into mechanical movement. In applications such as disk drives, dot matrix printers, and robotics, the stepper motor is used for position control. Stepper motors commonly have a permanent magnet *rotor* (also called the *shaft*) surrounded by a *stator* (see Figure 15-7). There are also steppers called variable reluctance *stepper motors* that do not have a PM rotor. The most common stepper motors have four stator windings that are paired with a center-tapped common as shown in Figure 15-8. This type of stepper motor is commonly referred to as a *four-phase* or unipolar stepper motor. The center tap allows a change of current direction in each of two coils when a winding is grounded, thereby resulting in a polarity change of the stator. Notice that while a conventional motor shaft runs freely, the stepper motor shaft moves in a fixed repeatable increment, which allows one to move it to a precise position. This repeatable fixed movement is possible as a result of basic magnetic theory where poles of the same polarity repel and opposite poles attract. The direction of the rotation is dictated by the stator poles. The stator poles are determined by the current sent through the wire coils. As the direction of the current is changed, the polarity is also changed causing the reverse motion of the rotor. The stepper motor discussed here has a total of six leads: four leads representing the four stator windings and two commons for the center-tapped leads. As the sequence of power is applied to each stator winding, the rotor will rotate. There are several widely used sequences where each has a different degree of precision. Table 15-3 shows a two-phase, four-step stepping sequence.

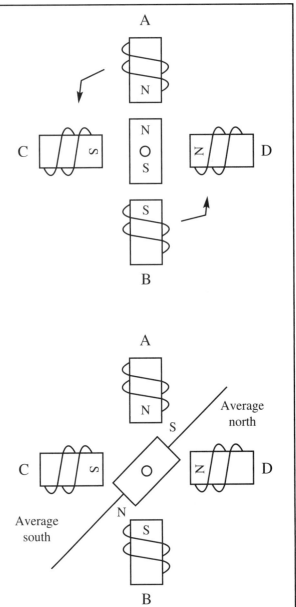

Figure 15-7. Rotor Alignment

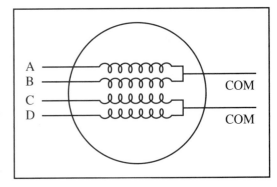

Figure 15-8. Stator Windings Configuration

Table 15-3. Normal Four-Step Sequence

Clockwise	Step #	Winding A	Winding B	Winding C	Winding D	Counter clockwise
	1	1	0	0	1	
	2	1	1	0	0	
	3	0	1	1	0	
	4	0	0	1	1	

It must be noted that although we can start with any of the sequences in Table 15-3, once we start we must continue in the proper order. For example, if we start with step 3 (0110), we must continue in the sequence of steps 4, 1, 2, and so on.

Table 15-4. Stepper Motor Step Angles

Step Angle	Steps per Revolution
0.72	500
1.8	200
2.0	180
2.5	144
5.0	72
7.5	48
15	24

Step angle

How much movement is associated with a single step? This depends on the internal construction of the motor, in particular the number of teeth on the stator and the rotor. The *step angle* is the minimum degree of rotation associated with a single step. Various motors have different step angles. Table 15-4 shows some step angles for various motors. In Table 15-4, notice the term *steps per revolution*. This is the total number of steps needed to rotate one complete rotation or 360 degrees (e.g., 180 steps × 2 degrees = 360).

It must be noted that perhaps contrary to one's initial impression, a stepper motor does not need more terminal leads for the stator to achieve smaller steps. All the stepper motors discussed in this section have four leads for the stator winding and two COM wires for the center tap. Although some manufacturers set aside only one lead for the common signal instead of two, they always have four leads for the stators. Next, we discuss some associated terminology in order to understand the stepper motor further.

Steps per second and rpm relation

The relation between rpm (revolutions per minute), steps per revolution, and steps per second is as follows.

$$Steps\ per\ second = \frac{rpm \times steps\ per\ revolution}{60}$$

The four-step sequence and number of teeth on rotor

The switching sequence shown earlier in Table 15-3 is called the four-step switching sequence since after four steps the same two windings will be "ON." How much movement is associated with these four steps? After completing every four steps, the rotor moves only one tooth pitch. Therefore, in a stepper motor with 200 steps per revolution, the rotor has 50 teeth since $4 \times 50 = 200$ steps are needed to complete one revolution (see Example 15-1). This leads to the conclusion that the minimum step angle is always a function of the

---

Example 15-1

Describe the 8051 connection to the stepper motor of Figure 15-9 and code a program to rotate it continuously.

Solution:

The following steps show the 8051 connection to the stepper motor and its programming.

1. Use an ohmmeter to measure the resistance of the leads. This should identify which COM leads are connected to which winding leads.
2. The common wire(s) are connected to the positive side of the motor's power supply. In many motors, +5 V is sufficient.
3. The four leads of the stator winding are controlled by four bits of the 8051 port (P1.0–P1.3). However, since the 8051 lacks sufficient current to drive the stepper motor windings, we must use a driver such as the ULN2003 to energize the stator. Instead of the ULN2003, we could have used transistors as drivers, as shown in Figure 15-9. However, notice that if transistors are used as drivers, we must also use diodes to take care of inductive current generated when the coil is turned off. One reason that using the ULN2003 is preferable to the use of transistors as drivers is that the ULN2003 has an internal diode to take care of back EMF.

```
            MOV   A,#66H      ;load step sequence
BACK:       MOV   P1,A        ;issue sequence to motor
            RR    A           ;rotate right clockwise
            ACALL DELAY       ;wait
            SJMP  BACK        ;keep going

            . . .

DELAY
            MOV   R2,#100
H1:         MOV   R3,#255
H2:         DJNZ  R3,H2
            DJNZ  R2,H1
            RET
```

Change the value of DELAY to set the speed of rotation.

We can use the single-bit instructions SETB and CLR instead of RR A to create the sequences.

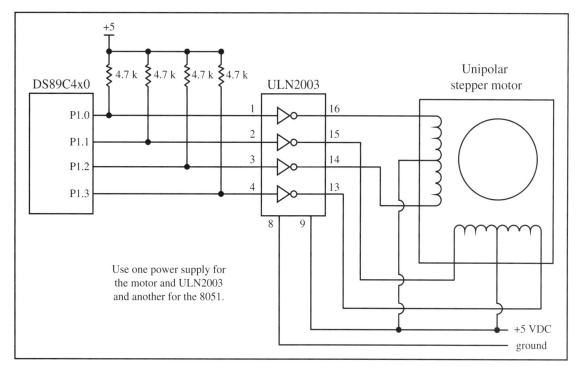

Figure 15-9. 8051 Connection to Stepper Motor

number of teeth on the rotor. In other words, the smaller the step angle, the more teeth the rotor passes. See Example 15-2.

From Example 15-2, one might wonder what happens if we want to move 45 degrees, since the steps are 2 degrees each. To allow for finer resolutions, all stepper motors allow what is called an *eight-step* switching sequence. The eight-step sequence is also called *half-stepping,* since in the eight-step sequence each step is half of the normal step angle. For example, a motor with a two-degree step angle can be used as a one-degree step angle if the sequence of Table 15-5 is applied.

Motor speed

The motor speed, measured in steps per second (steps/s), is a function of the switching rate. Notice in Example 15-1 that by changing the length of the time delay loop, we can achieve various rotation speeds.

Example 15-2

Give the number of times the four-step sequence in Table 15-3 must be applied to a stepper motor to make an 80-degree move if the motor has a two-degree step angle.

Solution:

A motor with a two-degree step angle has the following characteristics:

Step angle:	2 degrees	Steps per revolution:	180
Number of rotor teeth:	45	Movement per four-step sequence:	8 degrees

To move the rotor 80 degrees, we need to send 10 consecutive four-step sequences, since 10×4 steps $\times 2$ degrees = 80 degrees.

Table 15-5. Half-Step eight-Step Sequence

Clockwise	Step #	Winding A	Winding B	Winding C	Winding D	Counter clockwise
	1	1	0	0	1	
	2	1	0	0	0	
	3	1	1	0	0	
	4	0	1	0	0	
	5	0	1	1	0	
	6	0	0	1	0	
	7	0	0	1	1	
	8	0	0	0	1	

Holding torque

The following is a definition of holding torque: "With the motor shaft at standstill or zero rpm condition, the amount of torque, from an external source, required to break away the shaft from its holding position. This is measured with rated voltage and current applied to the motor." The unit of torque is ounce-inch (or kg-cm).

Wave drive four-step sequence

In addition to the eight-step and the four-step sequences discussed earlier, there is another sequence called the wave drive four-step sequence. It is shown in Table 15-6. Notice that the eight-step sequence of Table 15-5 is simply the combination of the wave drive four-step and normal four-step sequences shown in Tables 15-6 and 15-3, respectively. Experimenting with the wave drive four-step is left to the reader.

Unipolar versus bipolar stepper motor interface

There are three common types of stepper motor interfacing: universal, unipolar, and bipolar. They can be identified by the number of connections to the motor. A universal stepper motor has eight, while the unipolar has six and the bipolar has four. The universal stepper motor can be configured for all three modes, while the unipolar can be either unipolar or bipolar. Obviously

Table 15-6. Wave Drive Four-Step Sequence

Clockwise	Step #	Winding A	Winding B	Winding C	Winding D	Counter clockwise
	1	1	0	0	0	
	2	0	1	0	0	
	3	0	0	1	0	
	4	0	0	0	1	

Table 15-7. Selected Stepper Motor Characteristics

Part No.	Step Angle	Drive System	Volts	Phase Resistance	Current
151861CP	7.5	unipolar	5 V	9 ohms	550 mA
171601CP	3.6	unipolar	7 V	20 ohms	350 mA
164056CP	7.5	bipolar	5 V	6 mA	800 mA

Source: (www.Jameco.com)

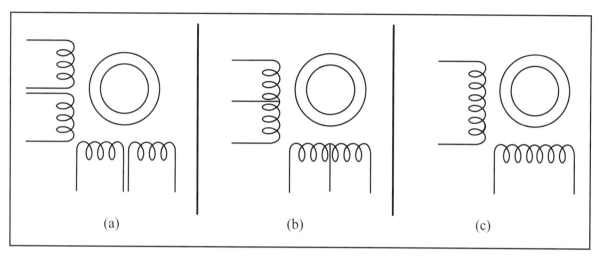

Figure 15-10. Common Stepper Motor Types: (a) Universal; (b) Unipolar; (c) Bipolar

the bipolar cannot be configured for universal nor unipolar mode. Table 15-7 shows selected stepper motor characteristics. Figure 15-10 shows the basic internal connections of all three type of configurations.

Unipolar stepper motors can be controlled using the basic interfacing shown in Figure 15-11, whereas the bipolar stepper requires H-Bridge circuitry. Bipolar stepper motors require a higher operational current than the unipolar; the advantage of this is a higher holding torque.

Using transistors as drivers

Figure 15-11 shows an interface to a unipolar stepper motor using transistors. Diodes are used to reduce the back EMF spike created when the coils are energized and de-energized, similar to the electromechanical relays discussed earlier. TIP transistors can be used to supply higher current to the motor. Table 15-8 shows the common industrial Darlington transistors. These transistors can accommodate higher voltages and currents.

Controlling stepper motor via optoisolator

In the first section of this chapter, we examined the optoisolator and its use. Optoisolators are widely used to isolate the stepper motor's EMF voltage and keep it from damaging the digital/microprocessor system. This is shown in Figure 15-12. See also Example 15-3.

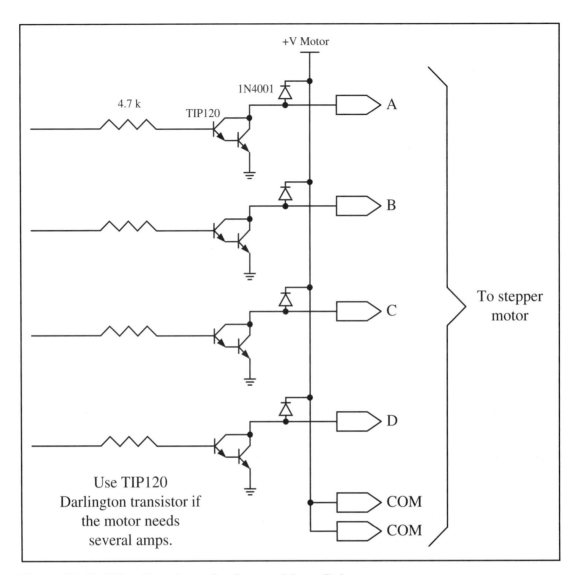

Figure 15-11. Using Transistors for Stepper Motor Driver

Table 15-8. Darlington Transistor Listing

NPN	PNP	Vceo (volts)	Ic (amps)	hfe (common)
TIP110	TIP115	60	2	1000
TIP111	TIP116	80	2	1000
TIP112	TIP117	100	2	1000
TIP120	TIP125	60	5	1000
TIP121	TIP126	80	5	1000
TIP122	TIP127	100	5	1000
TIP140	TIP145	60	10	1000
TIP141	TIP146	80	10	1000
TIP142	TIP147	100	10	1000

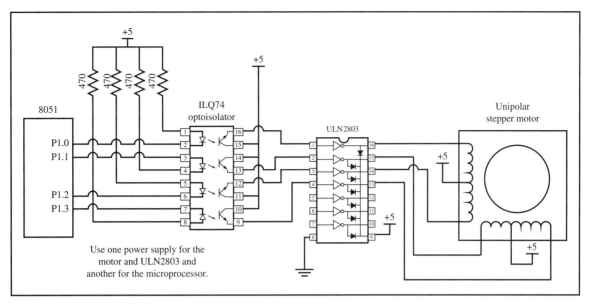

Figure 15-12. Controlling Stepper Motor via Optoisolator

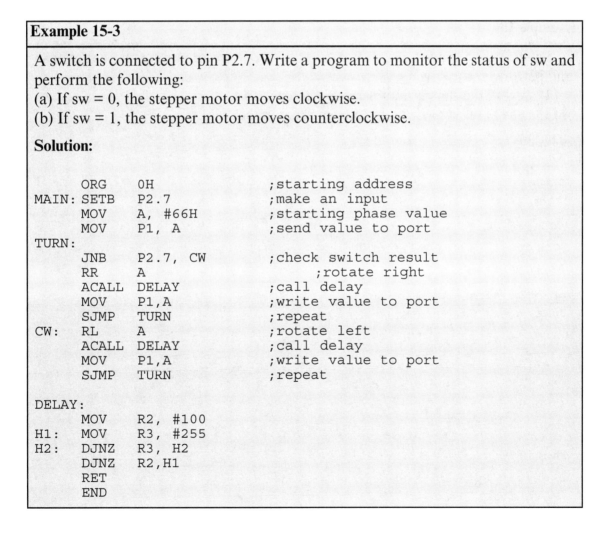

Example 15-3

A switch is connected to pin P2.7. Write a program to monitor the status of sw and perform the following:
(a) If sw = 0, the stepper motor moves clockwise.
(b) If sw = 1, the stepper motor moves counterclockwise.

Solution:

```
       ORG    0H              ;starting address
MAIN:  SETB   P2.7            ;make an input
       MOV    A, #66H         ;starting phase value
       MOV    P1, A           ;send value to port
TURN:
       JNB    P2.7, CW        ;check switch result
       RR     A                    ;rotate right
       ACALL  DELAY           ;call delay
       MOV    P1,A            ;write value to port
       SJMP   TURN            ;repeat
CW:    RL     A               ;rotate left
       ACALL  DELAY           ;call delay
       MOV    P1,A            ;write value to port
       SJMP   TURN            ;repeat

DELAY:
       MOV    R2, #100
H1:    MOV    R3, #255
H2:    DJNZ   R3, H2
       DJNZ   R2,H1
       RET
       END
```

Stepper motor control with 8051 C

The 8051 C version of the stepper motor control is given below (see Example 15-4). In this program, we could have used << (shift left) and >> (shift right) as was shown in Chapter 7.

```c
#include <reg51.h>
void main()
  {
    while(1)
      {
        P1 = 0x66;
        MSDelay(100);
        P1 = 0xCC;
        MSDelay(100);
        P1 = 0x99;
        MSDelay(100);
        P1 = 0x33;
        MSDelay(100);
      }
  }
```

Example 15-4

A switch is connected to pin P2.7. Write a C program to monitor the status of sw and perform the following:
(a) If sw = 0, the stepper motor moves clockwise.
(b) If sw = 1, the stepper motor moves counterclockwise.

Solution:

```c
#include <reg.h>
sbit SW=P2^7;

void main()
  {
    SW = 1;
    while(1)
      {
        if(SW == 0)
          {
            P1 = 0x66;
            MSDelay(100);
            P1 = 0xCC;
            MSDelay(100);
            P1 = 0x99;
            MSDelay(100);
            P1 = 0x33;
            MSDelay(100);
          }
        else
          {
            P1 = 0x66;
            MSDelay(100);
```

Example 15-4 (*Continued*)

```
            P1 = 0x33;
            MSDelay(100);
            P1 = 0x99;
            MSDelay(100);
            P1 = 0xCC;
            MSDelay(100);
        }
    }
}

void MSDelay(unsigned int value)
{
    unsigned int x, y;
    for(x=0;x<1275;x++)
        for(y=0;y<value;y++);
}
```

REVIEW QUESTIONS

1. Give the four-step sequence of a stepper motor if we start with 0110.
2. A stepper motor with a step angle of 5 degrees has _____ steps per revolution.
3. Why do we put a driver between the microprocessor and the stepper motor?

SUMMARY

This chapter continued showing how to interface the 8051 with real-world devices. Devices covered in this chapter were the relay, optoisolator, and stepper motor.

First, the basic operation of relays and optoisolators was defined, along with key terms used in describing and controlling their operations. Then the 8051 was interfaced with a stepper motor. The stepper motor was then controlled via an optoisolator using 8051 Assembly and C programming languages.

PROBLEMS

15.1: RELAYS AND OPTOISOLATORS

1. True or false. The minimum voltage needed to energize a relay is the same for all relays.
2. True or false. The minimum current needed to energize a relay depends on the coil resistance.
3 Give the advantages of a solid-state relay over an EM relay.
4. True or false. In relays, the energizing voltage is the same as the contact voltage.
5. Find the current needed to energize a relay if the coil resistance is 1200 ohms and the coil voltage is 5 V.

6. Give two applications for an optoisolator.
7 Give the advantages of an optoisolator over an EM relay.
8. Of the EM relay and solid-state relay, which has the problem of back EMF?
9. True or false. The greater the coil resistance, the worse the back EMF voltage.
10. True or false. We should use the same voltage sources for both the coil voltage and contact voltage.

15.2: STEPPER MOTOR INTERFACING

11. If a motor takes 90 steps to make one complete revolution, what is the step angle for this motor?
12. Calculate the number of steps per revolution for a step angle of 7.5 degrees.
13. Finish the normal four-step sequence clockwise if the first step is 0011 (binary).
14. Finish the normal four-step sequence clockwise if the first step is 1100 (binary).
15. Finish the normal four-step sequence counterclockwise if the first step is 1001 (binary).
16. Finish the normal four-step sequence counterclockwise if the first step is 0110 (binary).
17. What is the purpose of the ULN2003 placed between the 8051 and the stepper motor? Can we use that for 3A motors?
18. Which of the following cannot be a sequence in the normal four-step sequence for a stepper motor?
    (a) CCH   (b) DDH   (c) 99H   (d) 33H
19. What is the effect of a time delay between issuing each step?
20. In Question 19, how can we make a stepper motor go faster?

ANSWERS TO REVIEW QUESTIONS

15.1: RELAYS AND OPTOISOLATORS

1. With a relay, we can use a 5 V digital system to control 12 V–120 V devices such as horns and appliances.
2. Since microprocessor/digital outputs lack sufficient current to energize the relay, we need a driver.
3. When the coil is not energized, the contact is closed.
4. When current flows through the coil, a magnetic field is created around the coil, which causes the armature to be attracted to the coil.
5. It is faster and needs less current to get energized.
6. It is smaller and can be connected to the microprocessor directly without a driver.

15.2: STEPPER MOTOR INTERFACING

1. 0110, 0011, 1001, 1100 for clockwise; and 0110, 1100, 1001, 0011 for counterclockwise
2. 72
3. Because the microprocessor pins do not provide sufficient current to drive the stepper motor.

CHAPTER 16

DS12887 RTC INTERFACING AND PROGRAMMING

OBJECTIVES

Upon completion of this chapter, you will be able to:

>> Explain how the real-time clock (RTC) chip works.
>> Explain the function of the DS12887 RTC pins.
>> Explain the function of the DS12887 RTC registers.
>> Understand the interfacing of the DS12887 RTC to the 8051.
>> Code programs in Assembly and C to access the RTC registers.
>> Code programs to display time and date in Assembly and C.
>> Understand the interrupt and alarm features of the DS12887.
>> Explore and program the alarm and interrupt features of the RTC.

This chapter shows the interfacing and programming of the DS12C887 real-time clock (RTC) chip. In Section 16.1, we describe DS12887 RTC pin functions and show its interfacing with the 8051. We also show how to program the DS12887 in Assembly language. The C programming of DS12887 is shown in Section 16.2. The alarm and SQW features of the DS12287 are discussed in Section 16.3.

16.1: DS12887 RTC INTERFACING

The real-time clock (RTC) is a widely used device that provides accurate time and date for many applications. Many systems such as the x86 IBM PC come with such a chip on the motherboard. The RTC chip in the x86 PC provides time components of hour, minute, and second, in addition to the date/calendar components of year, month, and day. The RTC chip uses an internal battery, which keeps the time and date even when the power is off. Although some 8051 family members, such as the DS5000T, come with the RTC already embedded into the chip, we have to interface the vast majority of them to an external RTC chip. One of the most widely used RTC chips is the DS12887 from Dallas Semiconductor/Maxim Corp. This chip is found in the vast majority of x86 PCs. The original IBM PC/AT used the MC14618B RTC from Motorola. The DS12887 is the replacement for that chip. It uses an internal lithium battery to keep operating for over 10 years in the absence of external power. According to the DS12887 data sheet from Maxim, it keeps track of "seconds, minutes, hours, days, day of week, date, month, and year with leap-year compensation valid up to year 2100." The above information is provided in both binary (hex) and BCD formats. The DS12887 supports both 12-hour and 24-hour clock modes with AM and PM in the 12-hour mode. It also supports the Daylight Savings Time option. The DS12887 uses CMOS technology to keep the power consumption low and it has the designation DS12C887, where C is for CMOS. The DS12887 has a total of 128 bytes of nonvolatile RAM. It uses 14 bytes of RAM for clock/calendar and control registers, and the other 114 bytes of RAM are for general-purpose data storage. In the x86 IBM PC, these 114 bytes of NV-RAM are used for the CMOS configuration, where the system setups are kept before the operating system takes over. Next, we describe the pins of the DS12887. See Figure 16-1.

V_{cc}

Pin 24 provides external supply voltage to the chip. The external voltage source is +5 V. When V_{cc} falls below the 3V level, the external source is switched off and the internal lithium battery provides power to the RTC. This nonvolatile capability of the

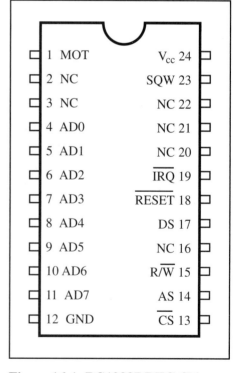

Figure 16-1. DS12887 RTC Chip

RTC prevents any loss of data. According to the DS12887 data sheet, "the RTC function continues to operate, and all of the RAM, time, calendar, and alarm memory locations remain non-volatile regardless of the level of the V_{cc} input." However, in order to access the registers via a program, the V_{cc} must be supplied externally. In other words, when external V_{cc} is applied, the device is fully accessible and data can be written and read. When V_{cc} falls below 4.25 V, the read and write to the chip are prevented, but the timekeeping and RAM contents are unaffected, since they are nonvolatile. **It must also be noted that "when V_{cc} is applied to the DS12887 and reaches a level of greater than 4.25V, the device becomes accessible after 200ms."**

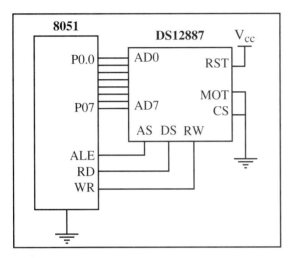

Figure 16-2. DS12887 Connection to 8051

GND

Pin 12 is the ground.

AD0–AD7

The multiplexed address/data pins provide both addresses and data to the chip. Addresses are latched into the DS12887 on the falling edge of the AS (ALE) signal. A simple way of connecting the DS12887 to the 8051 is shown in Figure 16-2. Notice that AD0–AD7 of the DS12887 are connected directly to P0 of the 8051 and there is no need for any 74xx373 latches, since the DS12887 provides the latch internally. To access the DS12887 in Figure 16-2, we use the MOVX instruction since it is mapped as external memory. We will discuss this shortly.

AS (ALE)

AS (address strobe) is an input pin. On the falling edge, it will cause the addresses to be latched into the DS12887. The AS pin is used for demultiplexing the address and data and is connected to the ALE pin of the 8051 chip.

MOT

This is an input pin that allows the choice between the Motorola and Intel microprocessor bus timings. The MOT pin is connected to GND for the Intel timing. That means when we connect DS12887 to the 8051, MOT = GND.

DS

Data strobe or read is an input. When MOT = GND for Intel timing, the DS pin is called the RD (read) signal and is connected to the RD pin of the 8051.

R/W

Read/Write is an input pin. When MOT = GND for the Intel timing, the R/W pin is called the WR (write) signal and is connected to the WR pin of the 8051.

CS

Chip select is an input pin and an active-low signal. During the read (RD) and write (WR) cycle time of Intel timing, the CS must be low in order to access the chip. It must be noted that the CS works only when the external V_{cc} is connected. In other words, "when V_{cc} falls below 4.25V, the chip-select input is internally forced to an inactive level regardless of the value of CS at the input pin." This is called the *write-protected state*. When the DS12887 is in write-protected state, all inputs are ignored.

IRQ

Interrupt request is an output pin and an active-low signal. To use IRQ, the interrupt-enable bits in register B must be set high. The interrupt feature of the DS12287 is discussed in Section 16.3.

SQW

Square wave is an output pin. We can program the DS12887 to provide up to 15 different square waves. The frequency of the square wave is set by programming register A and is discussed in Section 16.3.

RESET

Pin 18 is the reset pin. It is an input and is active low (normally high). In most applications the reset pin is connected to the V_{cc} pin. In applications where this pin is used, it has no effect on the clock, calendar, or RAM if it is forced low. The low on this pin will cause the reset of the IRQ and clearing of the SQW pin, as we will see in Section 16.3.

Address map of the DS12887

The DS12887 has a total of 128 bytes of RAM space with addresses 00–7FH. The first 10 locations, 00–09, are set aside for RTC values of time, calendar, and alarm data. The next four bytes are used for the control and status registers. They are registers A, B, C, and D and are located at addresses 10–13 (0A–0D in hex). Notice that their hex addresses match their names. The next 114 bytes from addresses 0EH to 7FH are available for data storage. The entire 128 bytes of RAM are accessible directly for read or write except the following:

1. Registers C and D are read-only.
2. D7 bit of register A is read-only.
3. The high-order bit of the seconds byte is read-only.

Figure 16-3 shows the address map of the DS12887.

Time, calendar, and alarm address locations and modes

The byte addresses 0–9 are set aside for the time, calendar, and alarm data. Table 16-1 shows their address locations and modes. Notice the data is available in both binary (hex) and BCD formats.

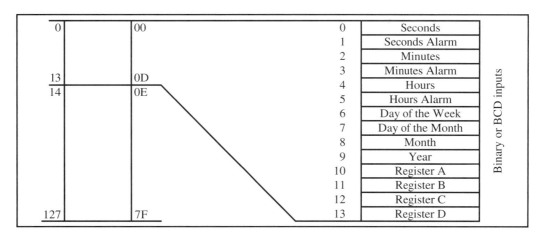

Figure 16-3. DS12887 Address Map

Turning on the oscillator for the first time

The DS12887 is shipped with the internal oscillator turned off in order to save the lithium battery. We need to turn on the oscillator before we use the timekeeping features of the DS12887. To do that, bits D6–D4 of register A must be set to value 010. See Figure 16-4 for details of register A.

The following code shows how to access the DS12887's register A and is written for the connection in Figure 16-2. In Figure 16-2, the DS12887 is using the external memory space of the 8051 and is mapped to address space of 00–7FH since CS = 0. See Chapter 14 for a discussion of external memory in the 8051. For the programs in this chapter, we use instruction "MOVX A, @ R0" since the address is only 8-bit. In the case of a 16-bit address, we must use

Table 16-1. DS12887 Address Location for Time, Calendar, and Alarm

Address Location	Function	Decimal Range	Data Mode Range Binary (hex)	BCD
0	Seconds	0–59	00–3B	00–59
1	Seconds Alarm	0–59	00–3B	00–59
2	Minutes	0–59	00–3B	00–59
3	Minutes Alarm	0–59	00–3B	00–59
4	Hours, 12-Hour Mode	1–12	01–0C AM	01–12 AM
	Hours, 12-Hour Mode	1–12	81–8C PM	81–92 PM
	Hours, 24-Hour Mode	0–23	0–17	0–23
5	Hours Alarm, 12-Hour	1–12	01–0C AM	01–12 AM
	Hours Alarm, 12-Hour	1–12	81–8C PM	81–92 PM
	Hours Alarm, 24-Hour	0–23	0–17	0–23
6	Day of the Week, Sun = 1	1–7	01–07	01–07
7	Day of the Month	1–31	01–1F	01–31
8	Month	1–12	01–0C	01–12
9	Year	0–99	00–63	00–99

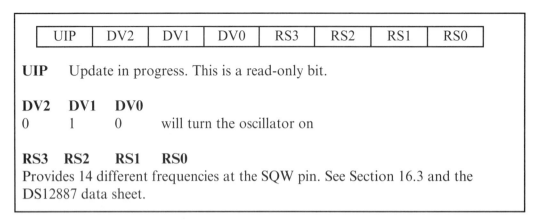

UIP	DV2	DV1	DV0	RS3	RS2	RS1	RS0

UIP   Update in progress. This is a read-only bit.

DV2 DV1 DV0
0   1   0   will turn the oscillator on

RS3 RS2   RS1   RS0
Provides 14 different frequencies at the SQW pin. See Section 16.3 and the DS12887 data sheet.

Figure 16-4. Register A Bits for Turning on the DS12887's Oscillator

"MOVX A,@DPTR", as was shown in Chapter 14. Examine the following code to see how to access the DS12887 of Figure 16-2.

```
ACALL DELAY_200ms ;RTC NEEDS 200ms AFTER POWER-UP
MOV  R0,#10        ;R0=0AH,Reg A address
MOV  A,#20H        ;010 in D6-D4 to turn on osc.
MOVX @R0,A         ;send it to Reg A of DS12887
```

Setting the time

When we initialize the time or date, we need to set D7 of register B to 1. This will prevent any update at the middle of the initialization. After setting the time and date, we need to make D7 = 0 to make sure that the clock and time are updated. The update occurs once per second. The following code initializes the clock at 16:58:55 using the BCD mode and 24-hour clock mode with daylight savings time. See also Figure 16-5 for details of register B.

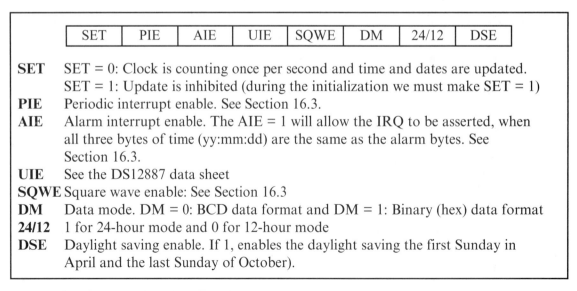

SET	PIE	AIE	UIE	SQWE	DM	24/12	DSE

SET   SET = 0: Clock is counting once per second and time and dates are updated.
           SET = 1: Update is inhibited (during the initialization we must make SET = 1)
PIE   Periodic interrupt enable. See Section 16.3.
AIE   Alarm interrupt enable. The AIE = 1 will allow the IRQ to be asserted, when all three bytes of time (yy:mm:dd) are the same as the alarm bytes. See Section 16.3.
UIE   See the DS12887 data sheet
SQWE Square wave enable: See Section 16.3
DM   Data mode. DM = 0: BCD data format and DM = 1: Binary (hex) data format
24/12 1 for 24-hour mode and 0 for 12-hour mode
DSE   Daylight saving enable. If 1, enables the daylight saving the first Sunday in April and the last Sunday of October).

Figure 16-5. Some Major Bits of Register B

```
;------WAIT 200msec FOR RTC TO BE READY AFTER POWER-UP
    ACALL DELAY_200ms
;------------TURNING ON THE RTC
    MOV   R0,#10      ;R0=0AH,Reg A address
    MOV   A,#20H      ;010 in D6-D4 to turn on osc.
    MOVX  @R0,A       ;send it to Reg A of DS12887
;--------------Setting the Time mode
    MOV   R0,#11      ;Reg B address
    MOV   A,#83H ;BCD,24hrs,Daylight saving,D7=1 No update
    MOVX  @R0,A       ;send it to Reg B
;----------Setting the Time
    MOV   R0,#0       ;point to seconds address
    MOV   A,#55H      ;seconds= 55H (BCD numbers need H)
    MOVX  @R0,A       ;set seconds
    MOV   R0,#02      ;point to minutes address
    MOV   A,#58H      ;minutes= 58
    MOVX  @R0,A       ;set minutes
    MOV   R0,#04      ;point to hours address
    MOV   A,#16H      ;hours=16
    MOVX  @R0,A       ;set hours
    MOV   R0,#11      ;Reg B address
    MOV   A,#03       ;D7=0 of reg B to allow update
    MOVX  @R0,A       ;send it to reg B
```

Setting the date

The following program shows how to set the date to October 19, 2004.
Notice that when we initialize time or date, we need to set D7 of register B to 1.

```
;------------TURNING ON THE RTC
        MOV   R0,#10      ;R0=0AH,Reg A address
        MOV   A,#20H      ;010 in D6-D4 to turn on osc
        MOVX  @R0,A       ;send it to Reg A of DS12887
;--------------Setting the Time mode
        MOV   R0,#11      ;Reg B address
        MOV   A,#83H      ;BCD,24 hrs, daylight saving
        MOVX  @R0,A       ;send it to Reg B
;----------Setting the DATE
        MOV   R0,#07      ;load pointer for DAY OF MONTH
        MOV   A,#19H      ; DAY=19H (BCD numbers need H)
        MOVX  @R0,A       ;set DAY OF MONTH
        ACALL DELAY       ;
        MOV   R0,#08      ;point to MONTH
        MOV   A,#10H      ;10=OCTOBER.
        MOVX  @R0,A       ;set MONTH
        ACALL DELAY       ;
        MOV   R0,#09      ;point to YEAR address
        MOV   A,#04       ;YEAR=04 FOR 2004
        MOVX  @R0,A       ;set YEAR to 2004
        ACALL DELAY
        MOV   R0,#11      ;Reg B address
        MOV   A,#03       ;D7=0 of reg B to allow update
        MOVX  @R0,A       ;send it to reg B
```

RTCs setting, reading, displaying time and date

The following is a complete Assembly code for setting, reading, and displaying the time and date. The times and dates are sent to the screen via the serial port after they are converted from BCD to ASCII.

```
;----RTCTIME.ASM: SETTING TIME,READING AND DISPLAYING IT
        ORG  0
        ACALL DELAY_200ms ;RTC needs 200ms upon power-up
;SERIAL PORT SET-UP
        MOV   TMOD,#20H
        MOV   SCON,#50H
        MOV   TH1,#-3     ;9600
        SETB  TR1
;------------TURNING ON THE RTC
        MOV   R0,#10      ;R0=0AH,Reg A address
        MOV   A,#20H      ;010 in D6-D4 to turn on osc.
        MOVX  @R0,A       ;send it to Reg A of DS12887
;--------------Setting the Time mode
        MOV   R0,#11      ;Reg B address
        MOV   A,#83H      ;BCD, 24 hrs, daylight saving
        MOVX  @R0,A       ;send it to Reg B
;----------Setting the DATE
        MOV   R0,#07      ;load pointer for DAY OF MONTH
        MOV   A,#24H      ; DAY=24H (BCD numbers need H)
        MOVX  @R0,A       ;set DAY OF MONTH
        ACALL DELAY       ;
        MOV   R0,#08      ;point to MONTH
        MOV   A,#10H      ; 10=OCTOBER.
        MOVX  @R0,A       ;set MONTH
        ACALL DELAY       ;
        MOV   R0,#09      ;point to YEAR address
        MOV   A,#04       ;YEAR=04 FOR 2004
        MOVX  @R0,A       ;set YEAR to 2004
        ACALL DELAY
        MOV   R0,#11      ;Reg B address
        MOV   A,#03       ;D7=0 of reg B to allow update
        MOVX  @R0,A       ;send it to reg B
;--------READ Time(HH:MM:SS), CONVERT IT AND DISPLAY IT
OV1:    MOV   A,#20H      ;ASCII for SPACE
        ACALL SERIAL
        MOV   R0,#4       ;point to HR loc
        MOVX  A,@R0       ;read hours
        ACALL DISPLAY
        MOV   A,#20H      ;send out SPACE
        ACALL SERIAL
        MOV   R0,#2       ;point to minute loc
        MOVX  A,@R0       ;read minute
        ACALL DISPLAY
        MOV   A,#20H      ;send out SPACE
        ACALL SERIAL
```

```
            MOV   R0,#0        ;point to seconds loc
            MOVX  A,@R0        ;read seconds
            ACALL DISPLAY
            MOV   A,#0AH       ;send out CR
            ACALL SERIAL
            MOV   A,#0DH       ;send LF
            ACALL SERIAL
            SJMP  OV1          ;read and display forever
;---------SMALL DELAY
DELAY:
            MOV   R7,#250
D1:         DJNZ  R7,D1
            RET
;-------------CONVERT BCD TO ASCII AND SEND IT TO SCREEN
DISPLAY:
            MOV   B,A
            SWAP  A
            ANL   A,#0FH
            ORL   A,#30H
            ACALL SERIAL
            MOV   A,B
            ANL   A,#0FH
            ORL   A,#30H
            ACALL SERIAL
            RET
;-----------
SERIAL:
            MOV   SBUF,A
S1:         JNB   TI,S1
            CLR   TI
            RET
;-----------
            END
```

The following shows how to read and display the date. You can replace the time display portion of the above program with the program below.

```
;--------READ DATE(YYYY:MM:MM), CONVERT IT AND DSIPLAY IT
OV2:        MOV   A,#20H       ;ASCII SPACE
            ACALL SERIAL
            MOV   A,#'2'       ;SEND OUT 2 (for 20)
            ACALL SERIAL
            MOV   A,#'0'       ;SEND OUT 0 (for 20)
            ACALL SERIAL
            MOV   R0,#09       ;point to year loc
            MOVX  A,@R0        ;read year
            ACALL DISPLAY
            MOV   A,#':'       ;SEND OUT : for yyyy:mm
            ACALL SERIAL
            MOV   R0,#08       ;point to month loc
            MOVX  A,@R0        ;read month
```

```
        ACALL DISPLAY
        ACALL DELAY
        MOV   A,#':'      ;SEND OUT : for mm:dd
        ACALL SERIAL
        MOV   R0,#07      ;point to DAY loc
        MOVX  A,@R0       ;read day
        ACALL DISPLAY
        ACALL DELAY
        MOV   A,#' '      ;send out SPACE
        ACALL SERIAL
        ACALL DELAY
        MOV   A,#' '      ;send out SPACE
        ACALL SERIAL
        ACALL DELAY
        MOV   A,#0AH      ;send out LF
        ACALL SERIAL
        MOV   A,#0DH      ;send CR
        ACALL SERIAL
        ACALL DELAY
        LJMP  OV2         ;display date forever
```

REVIEW QUESTIONS

1. True or false. All of the RAM contents of the DS12887 are nonvolatile.
2. How many bytes of RAM in the DS12887 are set aside for the clock and date?
3. How many bytes of RAM in the DS12887 are set aside for general-purpose applications?
4. True or false. The NV-RAM contents of the DS12887 can last up to 10 years without an external power source.
5. Which pin of the DS12887 is the same as the ALE pin in the 8051?
6. True or false. When the DS12887 is shipped, its oscillator is turned on.

16.2: DS12887 RTC PROGRAMMING IN C

In this section, we program the DS12887 in 8051 C language. Before you embark on this section, make sure that the basic concepts of the DS12887 chip covered in the first section are understood. Also, review external memory access using 8051 C, as discussed in Chapter 14.

Turning on the oscillator, setting the time and date in C

In Chapter 14, we discussed how to access external memory using 8051 C. We also discussed the details of the DS12887 in the previous section. In this section, we provide the C version of the programs given in the previous section. To access the DS12887 in Figure 16-2, we use the 8051 C command XBYTE[addr], where *addr* points to the external address location. Notice that XBYTE is part of the absacc.h library file. The following C program shows how to turn on the oscillator, and set the time and date for the configuration in Figure 16-2.

```
//RTC Time&Date initialization in C
#include <reg51.h>
#include <absacc.h>
void main(void)
  {
    Delay(200)        //RTC needs 200 ms upon power-up
    XBYTE[10]=0x20;   //turn on osc.
    XBYTE[11]=0x83;   //BCD, 24 hrs, daylight savings
    XBYTE[0]=0x55;    //SECOND=55h for BCD
    XBYTE[2]=0x58;    //MINUTE=58h for BCD
    XBYTE[4]=0x16;    //HOUR=16H for BCD
    XBYTE[7]=0x19;    //day=19h
    XBYTE[8]=0x10;    //month=10h for October
    XBYTE[9]=0x04;    //year=04
    XBYTE[11]=0x03;   //allow update
  }
```

Reading and displaying the time and date in C

The following C program shows how to read the time, convert it to ASCII, and send it to the PC screen via the serial port.

```
//Displaying Time and Date in C
#include <reg51.h>
#include <absacc.h>
void bcdconv(unsigned x);
void serial(unsigned x);
void main(void)
  {
    unsigned char hr,min,sec;
    TMOD=0x20;
    TH1=0xFD;              //9600 baud rate
    SCON=0x50;
    TR1=1;
    while(1)               //display time forever
        {
        hr=XBYTE[4];    //get hour
        bcdconv(hr);    //convert and display
        serial(':');    //send out : to separate
    min=XBYTE[2];    //get minute
        bcdconv(min);   //convert and display
        serial(':');    //send out : to separate
    sec=XBYTE[0];    //get second
        bcdconv(sec);   //convert and display
        serial(0x0D);   //send out CR
        serial(0x0A);   //send out Line feed
        }
    }
```

```
// convert BCD to ASCII and send it to serial
  void bcdconv(unsigned mybyte)     //see Chapter 7
  {
    unsigned char x,y,z;
    x=mybyte&0x0F;
    x=x|0x30;
    y=mybyte&0xF0;
    y=y>>4;
    y=y|0x30;
    serial(y);
    serial (x);
  }
//send out one char serially
  void serial(unsigned x)
  {
    SBUF=x;
    while(TI==0);
    TI=0;
  }
```

The following shows how to read and display the date in 8051 C. **You can replace the time display portion of the above program with the code below.**

```
;--------READ DATE(YYYY:MM:MM), CONVERT AND DISPLAY

while(1)                          //display date forever
        {
        serial('2');      //send out 2 for 20xx
        serial('0');      //send out 0 for 20xx
        yr=XBYTE[9];      //get year
        bcdconv(yr);      //convert and display
        serial(':');      //send out : to separate
        month=XBYTE[8];   //get month
        bcdconv(month);   //convert and display
        serial(':');      //send out : to separate
        day=XBYTE[7];     //get day
        bcdconv(sec);     //convert and display
        serial(0x0D);     //send out CR
        serial(0x0A);     //send out line feed
        }
```

REVIEW QUESTIONS

1. True or false. The time and date are not updated during the initialization of RTC.
2. What address range is used for the time and date?
3. Give the address of the first RAM location belonging to general-purpose applications.
4. Give the C statement to set the month to October.
5. Give the C statement to set the year to 2009.

16.3: ALARM, SQW, AND IRQ FEATURES OF THE DS12887 CHIP

In this section, we program the SQW, alarm, and interrupt features of the DS12887 chip using Assembly language. These powerful features of the DS12887 can be very useful in many real-world applications.

Programming the SQW feature

The SQW pin provides us a square wave output of various frequencies. The frequency is chosen by bits RS0–RS3 of register A, as shown in Figure 16-6. In addition to choosing the proper frequency, we must also enable the SQW bit in register B of the DS12887 (see Figures 16-7 and 16-8). This is shown below.

```
MOV    R0,#10        ;R0 = 0AH,reg A address
MOV    A,#2EH        ;turn on osc., 1110=RS4-RS0 4Hz SQW
MOVX   @R0,A         ;send it to Reg A of DS12887
MOV    R0,#11        ;R0 = 0BH, Reg B address
MOVX   A,@R0         ;get reg B of DS12887 to ACC
ACALL  DELAY         ;need delay for fast 8051
SETB   ACC.3         ;let 4Hz come out
MOVX   @R0,A         ;send it back to reg B
```

UIP	DV2	DV1	DV0	RS3	RS2	RS1	RS0

UIP Update in progress. This is a read-only bit.

DV2 DV1 DV0

0	1	0	will turn the oscillator on

RS3	RS2	RS1	RS0	SQW Output Frequency
0	0	0	0	None
0	0	0	1	256 Hz
0	0	1	0	128 Hz
0	0	1	1	8.192 kHz
0	1	0	0	4.096 kHz
0	1	0	1	2.048 kHz
0	1	1	0	1.024 kHz
0	1	1	1	512 Hz
1	0	0	0	256 Hz (repeat)
1	0	0	1	128 Hz (repeat)
1	0	1	0	64 Hz
1	0	1	1	32 Hz
1	1	0	0	16 Hz
1	1	0	1	8 Hz
1	1	1	0	4 Hz
1	1	1	1	2 Hz

Figure 16-6. Register A Bits for Frequencies Generated at the SQW Output Pin

SET	PIE	AIE	UIE	SQWE	DM	24/12	DSE

SET SET = 0: Clock is counting once per second, and time and dates are updated.
SET = 1: Update is inhibited (during the initialization we must make SET = 1).

PIE Periodic interrupt enable. If PIE = 1, upon generation of the periodic-interrupt, the IRQ pin of the DS12887 is asserted low. Therefore, IRQ becomes a hardware version of the PI bit in register C if we do not want to poll the PI bit. The rate of the periodic-interrupt is dictated by RS0–RS3 of register A. Remember that PIE allows the generation of a hardware interrupt version of bit PI in register C and has no effect on the periodic-interrupt generation. In other words, the PIE will simply direct the PI bit of register C into the IRQ output pin.

AIE Alarm interrupt enable. If AIE = 1, the IRQ pin will be asserted low when all three bytes of the real time (hh:mm:ss) are the same as the alarm bytes of hh:mm:ss. Also, if AIE = 1, the cases of once-per-second, once-per-minute, and once-per-hour will assert low the IRQ pin. Remember that AIE allows the generation of the hardware interrupt version of the AI bit in register C and has no effect on AI generation. In other words, the AIE will simply direct the AI bit of register C into the IRQ output pin.

UIE See the DS12887 data sheet.
SQWE Square wave enable: If SQWE = 1, the square wave frequency generated by the RS0–RS3 options of register A will show up on the SQW output pin of the DS12877 chip.
DM Data mode. DM = 0: BCD data format and DM = 1:binary (hex) data format
24/12 1 for 24-hour mode and 0 for 12-hour mode
DSE Daylight saving enable

Figure 16-7. PIE, AIE, and SQWE Bits of Register B

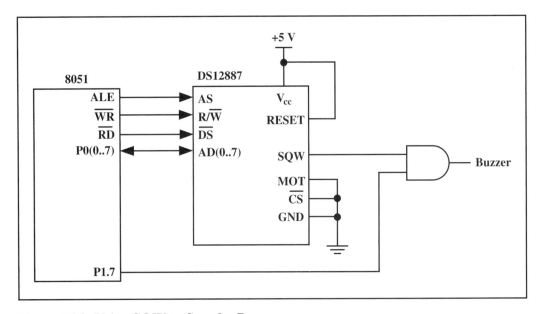

Figure 16-8. Using SQW to Sound a Buzzer

IRQ output pin and interrupt sources

Interrupt request (IRQ) is an output pin for the DS12887 RTC chip. It is an active-low signal. There are three possible sources that can activate the IRQ pin. They are (a) alarm interrupt, (b) periodic pulse interrupt, and (c) update interrupt. We can choose which source to activate the IRQ pin using the interrupt-enable bit in register B of the DS12887. In this section, we discuss the alarm and periodic interrupts and refer readers to the DS12887 data sheet for the update interrupt.

The alarm and IRQ output pin

The alarm interrupt can be programmed to occur at rates of (a) once per day, (b) once per hour, (c) once per minute, and (d) once per second. Next, we look at each of these.

Once-per-day alarm

Table 16-1 shows that address locations 1, 3, and 5 belong to the alarm seconds, alarm minutes, and alarm hours, respectively. To program the alarm for once per day, we write the desired time for the alarm into the hour, minute, and second RAM locations 1, 3, and 5. As the clock keeps the time, when all three bytes of hour, minute, and second for the real-time clock match the values in the alarm hour, minute, and second, the AF (alarm flag) bit in register C of the DS12887 will go high. We can poll the AF bit in register C, which is a waste of microprocessor resources, or allow the IRQ pin to be activated upon matching the alarm time with the real time. It must be noted that in order to use the IRQ pin of the DS12887 for an alarm, the interrupt-enable bit for alarm in register B (AIE) must be set high. How to enable the AIE bit in register B is shown shortly.

Once-per-hour alarm

To program the alarm for once per hour, we write value 11xxxxx into the alarm hour location of 5 only. Value 11xxxxx means any hex value of FCH to FFH. Very often we use value FFH.

Once-per-minute alarm

To program the alarm for once per minute, we write value FFH into both the alarm hour and alarm minute locations of 5 and 3.

Once-per-second alarm

To program the alarm for once per second, we write value FFH into all three locations of alarm hour, alarm minute, and alarm second.

Using IRQ of DS12877 to activate the 8051 interrupt

We can connect the IRQ of the DS12887 to the external interrupt pin of the 8051 (INT0). This allows us to perform a task once per day, once per minute, and so on. The following program will (a) sound the buzzer connected to SQW pin, and (b) will send the message "YES" to the serial port once per minute at exactly 8 seconds past the minute. The buzzer will stay on for 7 seconds before it is turned off. See Figure 16-9.

```
;-------SEND HELLO TO SCREEN 8 SEC PAST THE MINUTE
;-------USING ALRAM IRQ
     ORG  0
     LJMP MAIN        ;SOME INITIALIZATION
     ORG  03
     LJMP ISR_EX0     ;GO TO INTERRUPT SRVICE ROUTINE
     ORG  100H
MAIN:
     MOV  IE,#81H     ;INT0 (EX0) IS ENABLED
     SETB TCON.1      ;MAKE IT EDGE-TRIG
     MOV  TMOD,#20H   ;SERIAL PORT SET UP
     MOV  SCON,#50H
     MOV  TH1,#-3     ;9600
     SETB TR1
;-------TURNING ON THE RTC
     MOV  R0,#10      ;R0=0AH, Reg A address
     MOV  A,#2DH      ;010 in D6-D4 turn on osc.,SQW=8Hz
     MOVX @R0,A       ;send it to Reg A of DS12887
;-------------Setting the Time mode
     MOV  R0,#11      ;Reg B address
     MOV  A,#83H      ;BCD, 24hrs, daylight saving
     ACALL DELAY
     MOVX @R0,A       ;send it to Reg B
     ACALL DELAY
;----------Setting the Time
     PLACE THE CODE HERE
;----------Setting the Alarm Time
     MOV  R0,#1       ;pointer for alarm seconds address
     MOV  A,#08       ;8 SEC PAST THE MINUTE
     MOVX @R0,A       ;set seconds=8
     MOV  R0,#3       ;point to minutes address
     MOV  A,#0FFH     ;ONCE PER MINUTE
     MOVX @R0,A       ;
     MOV  R0,#5       ;
     MOV  A,#0FFH     ;FF FOR THE HOUR
     MOVX @R0,A       ;
     ACALL DELAY
     MOV  R0,#11      ;Reg B address
     MOV  A,#23H      ;D7=0 to update,AIE=1 to allow IRQ
     MOVX @R0,A       ;activate INT0 of 8051
;-------READING TIME
     PLACE READING TIME CODE HERE
;-------SERIAL TRANSFER
SERIAL:
     CLR  IE.7        ;DISABLE EXTERNAL INTERRUPT
     MOV  SBUF,A
S1:  JNB  TI,S1
```

```
        CLR  TI
        SETB IE.7        ;RE-ENABLE THE INTERRRUPT
        RET
;---ISR SENDS "YES" TO SCREEN AND SOUND THE BUZZER
        ORG 500H         ;the ISR for the IRQ of DS12887
ISR_EX0:
        MOV  R0,#12      ;Reg C address
        ACALL DELAY
        MOVX A,@R0       ;READING REG C WILL DISABLE THE IRQ
        MOV  R0,#11      ;Reg B address
        ACALL DELAY
        MOVX A,@R0
        ACALL DELAY
        SETB ACC.3       ;LET SQW COME OUT OF RTC
        SETB P1.7  ;ENABLE THE AND GATE TO SOUND BUZZER
        ACALL DELAY
        MOVX @R0,A
        MOV  A,#'Y'
        ACALL SERIAL
        MOV  A,#'E'
        ACALL SERIAL
        MOV  A,#'S'
        ACALL SERIAL
        ACALL DELAY_1    ;7 SEC DELAY TO HEAR THE BUZZER
        MOV  R0,#11      ;Reg B address
        ACALL DELAY
        MOVX A,@R0
        CLR  ACC.3       ;BLOCK SQW FROM COMING OUT OF RTC
        ACALL DELAY      ;SHORT DELAY TO LET RTC REST
        MOVX @R0,A       ;BEFORE ACCESSING IT AGAIN
        CLR  P1.7        ;TURN OFF THE AND GATE
        RETI             ;RETURN FROM INTERRUPT
```

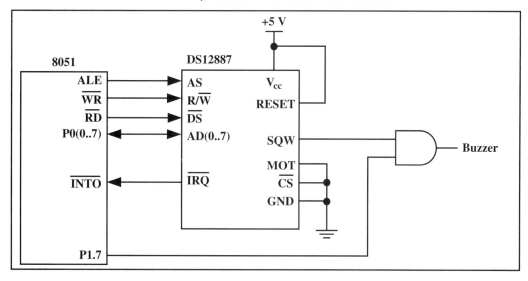

Figure 16-9. Using DS12887 IRQ to Activate an 8051 Interrupt

Regarding the last program, several points must be noted.

1. In the beginning of the program we enabled the external hardware inter-rupt and made it edge-triggered to match the IRQ of the DS12887.

2. In register B, the AIE bit was set high to allow an alarm interrupt.

3. In the serial subroutine, we disabled the external interrupt INT0 to prevent conflict with the TI flag.

4. In the ISR, we enabled the SQWE to allow a square wave to come out of the RTC chip in order to provide pulses to the buzzer. We disabled it at the end of ISR after 7 seconds duration in the DELAY_1 subroutine.

5. In the ISR, we also read the C register to prevent the occurrence of multiple interrupts from the same source. See Figure 16-10.

The periodic interrupt and IRQ output pin

The second source of interrupt is the periodic interrupt flag (PF). The periodic interrupt flag is part of register C. It will go high at a rate set by the RS3–RS0 bits of register A. This rate can be from once every 500 ms to once every 122 μs as shown in Figure 16-11. The PF becomes 1 when an edge is detected for the period. Just like alarm interrupt, the periodic interrupt can also be directed to the IRQ pin. To use IRQ, the interrupt-enable bits of PIE in register B must be set to 1. In other words, we can poll the PF bit of register C, which is a waste of the microprocessor's resources, or it can be directed to the hardware IRQ pin. If we set PIE = 1, the IRQ pin is asserted low when PF goes

IRQF	PF	AF	UF	0	0	0	0

IRQF = 1: if PF = PIE = 1 or AF = AIE = 1 or UF = UIE = 1
(PIE, AIE, and UIE are the bits of Register B.)

PF Periodic interrupt flag. Periodic interrupts can be generated at a rate of once every 500 ms to once every 122 μs. The rate is set by bits RS3–RS0 of register A. The PF becomes 1 when an edge is detected for the period. We can poll this or with the help of bit PIE of register B, the IRQ pin of DS12887 can be asserted low for the hardware interrupt version of this bit. This will be done if the PIF bit of Reg B is set to 1. That is, PF and PIE of register B together (if both are 1) will **allow IRQ to be asserted low**. Reading PF will clear it, and that is how we deassert the IRQ pin.

AF Alarm interrupt flag. The AF becomes 1 when the current real time matches the alarm time. AF and AIE of register B together (if both are 1) will **allow the IRQ to be asserted low** when all the three bytes of the real time (yy:mm:dd) are the same as the bytes in the alarm time. The AF also becomes 1 for cases of once per second, once per minute, and once per hour alarm. Reading AF will clear it and that is how we deassert the IRQ pin.

UF See the DS12887 data sheet.

Figure 16-10. Register C Bits for Interrupt Flag Sources

UIP	DV2	DV1	DV0	RS3	RS2	RS1	RS0

UIP   Update in progress. This is a read-only bit.

DV2 **DV1** **DV0**
0   1   0   will turn the oscillator on

RS3	RS2	RS1	RS0	Periodic Interrupt Rate	SQW Output Frequency
0	0	0	0	None	None
0	0	0	1	3.9062 ms	256 Hz
0	0	1	0	7.812 ms	128 Hz
0	0	1	1	122.070 µs	8.192 kHz
0	1	0	0	244.141 µs	4.096 kHz
0	1	0	1	488.281 µs	2.048 kHz
0	1	1	0	976.5625 µs	1.024 kHz
0	1	1	1	1.953125 ms	512 Hz
1	0	0	0	3.90625 ms	256 Hz
1	0	0	1	7.8125 ms	128 Hz
1	0	1	0	15.625 ms	64 Hz
1	0	1	1	31.25 ms	32 Hz
1	1	0	0	62.5 ms	16 Hz
1	1	0	1	125 ms	8 Hz
1	1	1	0	250 ms	4 Hz
1	1	1	1	500 ms	2 Hz

Figure 16-11. Register A Bits for Periodic Interrupt Rate

high. While the alarm interrupt gave us the options from once per day to once per second, the periodic interrupt gives us the option of subsecond interrupts. For example, we can write a program to send a message to the screen twice per second (2 Hz). The following code fragments show how to send the message "HELLO" to the screen twice per second using the periodic interrupt with the help of hardware IRQ (see Figure 16-9).

```
;-------sending HELLO to screen twice per second
      ORG   0
      LJMP  MAIN
      ORG   03
      LJMP  ISR_EX0
      ORG   100H
MAIN: MOV   IE,#81H    ;INT0 (EX0) IS ENABLED
      SETB  TCON.1     ;MAKE IT EDGE-TRIG
;SERIAL PORT SET-UP
      MOV   TMOD,#20H
      MOV   SCON,#50H
      MOV   TH1,#-3    ;9600
      SETB  TR1
```

```
;TURNING ON THE RTC
      MOV   R0,#10      ;R0=0AH,Reg A address
      MOV   A,#2FH      ;osc=on, Periodic of twice Per sec
      MOVX  @R0,A       ;send it to Reg A of DS12887

;------------Setting the Time mode
      MOV   R0,#11      ;Reg B address
      MOV   A,#83H      ;BCD, 24hrs, daylight saving
      ACALL DELAY
      MOVX  @R0,A       ;send it to Reg B
      ACALL DELAY
;----------Setting the Time
      MOV   R0,#0       ;load pointer for seconds address
      MOV   A,#55H      ;seconds=55H (BCD numbers need H)
      MOVX  @R0,A       ;set seconds to 31
      MOV   R0,#02      ;point to minutes address
      MOV   A,#56H      ;minutes=56 (BCD numbers need H)
      MOVX  @R0,A       ;set minutes
      MOV   R0,#04      ;point to hours address
      MOV   A,#16H      ;hours=16
      MOVX  @R0,A       ;set hours to 16
      ACALL DELAY
      MOV   R0,#11      ;Reg B address
      MOV   A,#43H      ;D7=0 to update,periodic INTR is ON
      MOVX  @R0,A
;--------READING TIME
OV1:  MOV   A,#20H      ;ASCII for SPACE
      ACALL SERIAL
      MOV   R0,#4       ;point to HR loc
      MOVX  A,@R0       ;read hours
      ACALL DISPLAY
      MOV   A,#20H      ;SEND OUT SPACE
      ACALL SERIAL
      MOV   R0,#2       ;point to minute loc
      MOVX  A,@R0       ;read minute
      ACALL DISPLAY
      MOV   A,#20H      ;send out SPACE
      ACALL SERIAL
      MOV   R0,#0       ;point to sec loc
      MOVX  A,@R0       ;read sec
      ACALL DISPLAY
      MOV   A,#0AH      ;send out CR
      ACALL SERIAL
      MOV   A,#0DH      ;send LF
      ACALL SERIAL
      SJMP  OV1         ;Read and display Time forever
;---------SMALL DELAY
```

```
DELAY:
      MOV  R7,#250
D1:   DJNZ R7,D1
      RET
;------------CONVERT BCD TO ASCII AND SEND IT TO SCREEN
DISPLAY:
      MOV  B,A
      SWAP A
      ANL  A,#0FH
      ORL  A,#30H
      ACALL SERIAL
      MOV  A,B
      ANL  A,#0FH
      ORL  A,#30H
      ACALL SERIAL
      RET
;------------------------
SERIAL:
      CLR  IE.7       ;DISABLE INT0 INTERRUPT
      MOV  SBUF,A
S1:   JNB  TI,S1
      CLR  TI
      SETB IE.7       ;RE-ENABLE INT0 INTERRUPT
      RET
;-----ISR TO SEND "HELLO" TO SCREEN TWICE PER SEC
      ORG 500H
ISR_EX0:
      MOV  R0,#12     ;Reg C address
      ACALL DELAY
      MOVX A,@R0      ;READING REG C WILL DISABLE
                      ;THE PERIODIC INTR
      MOV  A,#'H'
      ACALL SERIAL
      MOV  A,#'E'
      ACALL SERIAL
      MOV  A,#'L'
      ACALL SERIAL
      MOV  A,#'L'
      ACALL SERIAL
      MOV  A,#'O'
      ACALL SERIAL
      RETI
```

REVIEW QUESTIONS

1. Which bit of register B belongs to the SQW pin?
2. True or false. The IRQ out pin of DS12887 is active low.
3. Which bit of register B belongs to alarm interrupt?
4. Give the address locations for hh:mm:ss of the alarm.
5. If the source of activation for IRQ is alarm, then explain how the IRQ pin is activated.
6. What is the difference between the AF and AIE bits?
7. What is the difference between the PF and PIE bits?

SUMMARY

This chapter began by describing the function of each pin of the DS12887 RTC chip. The timing of AD0–AD7 of the DS12887 matches the timing of P0 of the 8051, eliminating the need for an external latch such as the 74LS373. The DS12887 can be used to provide a real-time clock and dates for many applications. Various features of the RTC were explained, and numerous programming examples were given.

PROBLEMS

16.1: DS12887 RTC INTERFACING

1. The DS12887 DIP package is a(n) _____-pin package.
2. Which pins are assigned to V_{cc} and GND?
3. In the DS12887, how many pins are designated as address/data pins?
4. True or false. The DS12887 needs an external crystal oscillator.
5. True or false. The DS12887's crystal oscillator is turned on when it is shipped.
6. In DS12887, what is the maximum year that it can provide?
7. Describe the functions of pins DS, AS, and MOT.
8. RESET is an _____ (input, output) pin.
9. The RESET pin is normally _____ (low, high) and needs a _____ (low, high) signal to be activated.
10. What are the contents of the DS12887 time and date registers if power to the V_{cc} pin is cut off?
11. DS pin stands for _____ and is an_____ (input, output) pin.
12. For the DS12887 chip, pin RESET is connected to _____ (V_{cc}, GND).
13. DS is an _____ (input, output) pin and it is connected to pin_____ of the 8051.
14. AS is an _____ (input, output) pin and it is connected to pin _____ of the 8051.
15. ALE of 8051 is connected to pin _____ of the DS12887.
16. IRQ is an _____ (input, output) pin.
17. SQW is an _____ (input, output) pin.

18. R/W is an _____ (input, output) pin.
19. DS12887 has a total of _____bytes of NV-RAM.
20. What are the contents of the DS12887 time and date registers if power to the V_cc pin is lost?
21. What are the contents of the general-purpose RAM locations if power to the V_cc is lost?
22. When does the DS12887 switch to its internal battery?
23. What are the addresses assigned to the real-time clock registers?
24. What are the addresses assigned to registers A–C?
25. Which register is used to set the AM/PM mode? Give the bit location of that register.
26. Which register is used to set the daylight savings mode? Give the bit location of that register.
27. At what memory location does the DS12887 store the year 2007?
28. What is the address of the last location of RAM for the DS12887?
29. Write a program to display the time in AM/PM mode.
30. Write a program to get the year data in BCD and send it to ports P1 and P2.
31. Write a program to get the hour and minute data in binary (hex) and send it to ports P1 and P2.
32. Write a program to set the time to 9:15:05 PM.
33. Write a program to set the time to 22:47:19.
34. Write a program to set the date to May 14, 2009.
35. On what day in October, is daylight savings time changed?

16.2: DS12887 RTC PROGRAMMING IN C

36. Write a C program to display the time in AM/PM mode.
37. Write a C program to get the year data in BCD and send it to ports P1 and P2.
38. Write a C program to get the hour and minute data in binary (hex) and send it to ports P1 and P2.
39. Write a C program to set the time to 9:15:05 PM.
40. Write a C program to set the time to 22:47:19.
41. Write a C program to set the date to May 14, 2009.
42. In Question 41, where did you get the 20H?

16.3: ALARM, SQW, AND IRQ FEATURES OF THE DS12887 CHIP

43. IRQ is an _____ (input, output) pin and active_____(low, high).
44. SQW is an _____ (input, output) pin.
45. Give the bit location of register B belonging to the alarm interrupt. Show how to enable it.
46. Give the bit location of register B belonging to the periodic interrupt. Show how to enable it.
47. Give the bit location of register C belonging to the alarm interrupt.
48. Give the bit location of register C belonging to the periodic interrupt.
49. What is the lowest frequency that we can create on the SQW pin?
50. What is the highest frequency that we can create on the SQW pin?

51. Give two sources of interrupt that can activate the IRQ pin.
52. What is the lowest period that we can use for the periodic interrupt?
53. What is the highest period that we can use for the periodic interrupt?
54. Why do we want to direct the PF (periodic interrupt) flag to IRQ?
55. Why do we want to direct the AF (alarm flag) to IRQ?
56. What is the difference between the PF and PIE bits?
57. What is the difference between the AF and AIE bits?
58. How do we allow the square wave to come out of the SQW pin?
59. Which register is used to set the frequency of the SQW pin?
60. Which register is used to set the periodic-interrupt duration?
61. Which register is used to set the once-per-second alarm interrupt?
62. Explain how the IRQ pin is activated due to the alarm interrupt.
63. Explain how the IRQ pin is activated due to the periodic interrupt.
64. Write a program to generate a 512 Hz square wave on the SQW pin.
65. Write a program to generate a 64 Hz square wave on the SQW pin.

ANSWERS TO REVIEW QUESTIONS

16.1: DS12887 RTC INTERFACING

1. True
2. 9
3. 114
4. True
5. AS
6. False

16.2: DS12887 RTC PROGRAMMING IN C

1. True
2. 0–9
3. 0EH (14 in decimal)
4. `XBYTE[8]=0x0A;`
5. `XBYTE[09]=0x09;` where the 20 part of 2009 is assumed.

16.3: ALARM, SWQ, AND IRQ FEATURES OF THE DS12887 CHIP

1. D3 of D0–D7
2. True
3. D5
4. Byte addresses of 1, 3, and 5
5. If the AIE bit of register B is set to 1, then the IRQ pin is activated. This happens due to the AF bit in register C going high when the alarm time and real time values match.
6. The AF bit in register C becomes high when the alarm time and real time values match, while the AIE bit of register B simply allows the AF to be directed to the IRQ pin.
7. The PF bit in register C becomes high when the edge is detected for the periodic interrupt, while the PIE bit of register B simply allows the PF to be directed to the IRQ pin.

CHAPTER 17

DC MOTOR CONTROL AND PWM

OBJECTIVES

Upon completion of this chapter, you will be able to:

>> Describe the basic operation of a DC motor.
>> Interface the 8051 with a DC motor.
>> Code 8051 programs to control and operate a DC motor.
>> Describe how PWM (pulse width modulation) is used to control motor speed.

This chapter discusses DC motor control and shows 8051 interfacing with DC motor. The characteristics of DC motors are discussed in Section 17.1, along with interfacing to the 8051. We will also discuss the topic of PWM (pulse width modulation). We use both Assembly and C in our programming examples.

17.1: DC MOTOR INTERFACING AND PWM

This section begins with an overview of the basic operation of DC motors. Then we describe how to interface a DC motor to the 8051. Finally, we use Assembly and C language programs to demonstrate the concept of pulse width modulation (PWM) and show how to control the speed and direction of a DC motor.

DC motors

A direct current (DC) motor is another widely used device that translates electrical pulses into mechanical movement. In the DC motor we have only + and – leads. Connecting them to a DC voltage source moves the motor in one direction. By reversing the polarity, the DC motor will move in the opposite direction. One can easily experiment with the DC motor. For example, small fans used in many motherboards to cool the CPU are run by DC motors. By connecting their leads to the + and – voltage source, the DC motor moves. While a stepper motor moves in steps of 1 to 15 degrees, the DC motor moves continuously. In a stepper motor, if we know the starting position we can easily count the number of steps the motor has moved and calculate the final position of the motor. This is not possible in a DC motor. The maximum speed of a DC motor is indicated in rpm and is given in the data sheet. The DC motor has two rpms: no-load and loaded. The manufacturer's data sheet gives the no-load rpm. The no-load rpm can be from a few thousand to tens of thousands. The rpm is reduced when moving a load and it decreases as the load is increased. For example, a drill turning a screw has a much lower rpm speed than when it is in the no-load situation. DC motors also have voltage and current ratings. The nominal voltage is the voltage for that motor under normal conditions, and can be from 1 to 150 V, depending on the motor. As we increase the voltage, the rpm goes up. The current rating is the current consumption when the nominal voltage is applied with no load and can be from 25 mA to a few amps. As the load increases, the rpm is decreased, unless the current or voltage provided to the motor is increased, which in turn increases the torque. With a fixed voltage, as the load increases, the current (power) consumption of a DC motor is increased. If we overload the motor it will stall, and that can damage the motor due to the heat generated by high current consumption.

Unidirection control

Figure 17-1 shows the DC motor rotation for clockwise (CW) and counterclockwise (CCW) rotations. See Table 17-1 for selected DC motors.

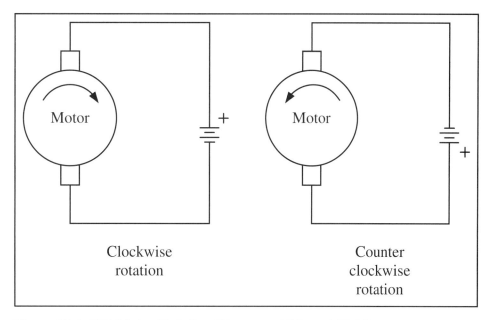

Figure 17-1. DC Motor Rotation (Permanent Magnet Field)

Bidirectional control

With the help of relays or some specially designed chips, we can change the direction of the DC motor rotation. Figures 17-2 through 17-5 show the basic concepts of H-Bridge control of DC motors.

Figure 17-2 shows the connection of an H-Bridge using simple switches. All the switches are open, which does not allow the motor to turn.

Figure 17-3 shows the switch configuration for turning the motor in one direction. When switches 1 and 4 are closed, current is allowed to pass through the motor.

Figure 17-4 shows the switch configuration for turning the motor in the opposite direction from the configuration of Figure 17-3. When switches 2 and 3 are closed, current is allowed to pass through the motor.

Figure 17-5 shows an invalid configuration. Current flows directly to ground, creating a short circuit. The same effect occurs when switches 1 and 3 are closed or switches 2 and 4 are closed.

Table 17-2 shows some of the logic configurations for the H-Bridge design.

Table 17-1. Selected DC Motor Characteristics

Part No.	Nominal Volts	Volt Range	Current	RPM	Torque
154915CP	3 V	1.5–3 V	0.070 A	5200	4.0 g-cm
154923CP	3 V	1.5–3 V	0.240 A	16000	8.3 g-cm
177498CP	4.5 V	3–14 V	0.150 A	10300	33.3 g-cm
181411CP	5 V	3–14 V	0.470 A	10000	18.8 g-cm

Source: (www.Jameco.com)

Table 17-2. Some H-Bridge Logic Configurations for Figure 17-2

Motor Operation	SW1	SW2	SW3	SW4
Off	Open	Open	Open	Open
Clockwise	Closed	Open	Open	Closed
Counterclockwise	Open	Closed	Closed	Open
Invalid	Closed	Closed	Closed	Closed

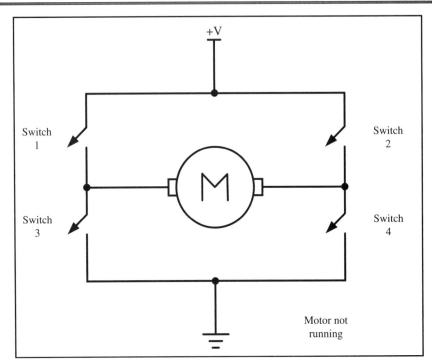

Figure 17-2. H-Bridge Motor Configuration

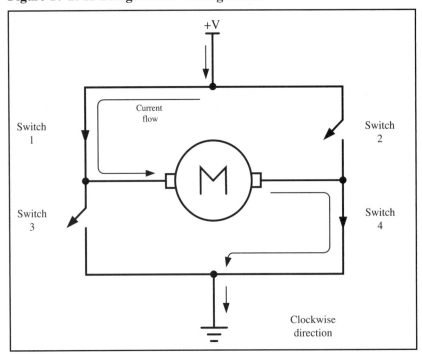

Figure 17-3. H-Bridge Motor Clockwise Configuration

CHAPTER 17: DC MOTOR CONTROL AND PWM

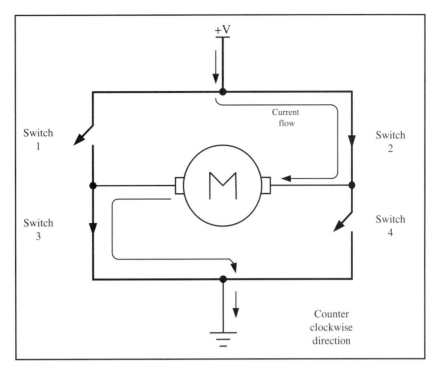

Figure 17-4. H-Bridge Motor Counterclockwise Configuration

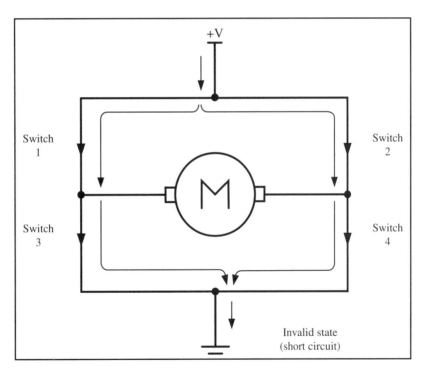

Figure 17-5. H-Bridge in an Invalid Configuration

H-Bridge control can be created using relays, transistors, or a single IC solution such as the L293. When using relays and transistors, you must ensure that invalid configurations do not occur.

Although we do not show the relay control of an H-Bridge, Example 17-1 shows a simple program to operate a basic H-Bridge.

Example 17-1

A switch is connected to pin P2.7. Using a simulator, write a program to monitor the status of sw and perform the following:

(a) If sw = 0, the DC motor moves clockwise.
(b) If sw = 1, the DC motor moves counterclockwise.

Solution:

```
        ORG 0H
MAIN:
        CLR   P1.0                ;switch 1
        CLR   P1.1                ;switch 2
        CLR   P1.2                ;switch 3
        CLR   P1.3                ;switch 4
        SETB  P2.7
MONITOR:
        JNB   P2.7, CLOCKWISE
        SETB  P1.0                ;switch 1
        CLR   P1.1                ;switch 2
        CLR   P1.2                ;switch 3
        SETB  P1.3                ;switch 4
        SJMP  MONITOR
CLOCKWISE:
        CLR   P1.0                ;switch 1
        SETB  P1.1                ;switch 2
        SETB  P1.2                ;switch 3
        CLR   P1.3                ;switch 4
        SJMP  MONITOR
        END
```

Note: View the results on your simulator. This example is for simulation only and should not be used on a connected system.

Figure 17-6 shows the connection of the L293 to an 8051. Be aware that the L293 will generate heat during operation. For sustained operation of the motor, use a heat sink. Example 17-2 shows control of the L293.

Pulse width modulation (PWM)

The speed of the motor depends on three factors: (a) load, (b) voltage, and (c) current. For a given fixed load, we can maintain a steady speed by using a method called *pulse width modulation* (PWM). By changing (modulating) the width of the pulse applied to the DC motor, we can increase or decrease the amount of power provided to the motor, thereby increasing or decreasing the motor speed. Notice that although the voltage has a fixed amplitude, it has a variable duty cycle. That means the wider the pulse, the higher the speed. PWM is so widely used in DC motor control that some microprocessors come with the PWM circuitry embedded in the chip. In such microprocessors, all we have to do is load the proper registers with the values of the high and low portions of the desired pulse, and the rest is taken care by the microprocessor. This allows the microprocessor to do other things. For microprocessors

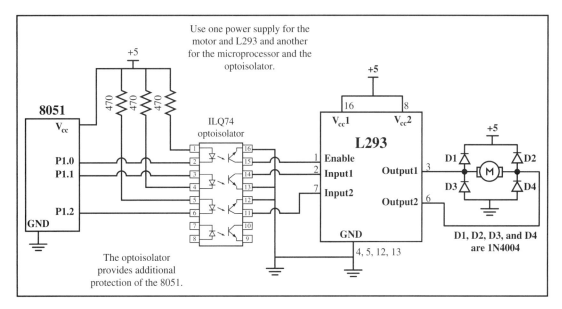

Figure 17-6. Bidirectional Motor Control Using an L293 Chip

without PWM circuitry, we must create the various duty cycle pulses using software, which prevents the microprocessor from doing other things. The ability to control the speed of the DC motor using PWM is one reason that DC motors are preferable over AC motors. AC motor speed is dictated by the AC frequency of the voltage applied to the motor and the frequency is generally fixed. As a result, we cannot control the speed of the AC motor when the load

---

Example 17-2

Figure 17-6 shows the connection of an L293. Add a switch to pin P2.7. Write a program to monitor the status of sw and perform the following:

(a) If sw = 0, the DC motor moves clockwise.
(b) If sw = 1, the DC motor moves counterclockwise.

Solution:

```
        ORG  0H
MAIN:
        CLR  P1.0
        CLR  P1.1
        CLR  P1.2
        SETB P2.7
MONITOR:
        SETB P1.0               ;enable the chip
        JNB  P2.7, CLOCKWISE
        CLR  P1.1               ;turn the motor counterclockwise
        SETB P1.2
        SJMP MONITOR
CLOCKWISE:
        SETB P1.1
        CLR  P1.2               ;turn motor clockwise
        SJMP MONITOR

        END
```

CHAPTER 17: DC MOTOR CONTROL AND PWM

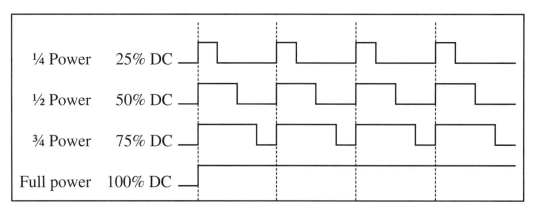

Figure 17-7. Pulse Width Modulation Comparison

is increased. As was shown earlier, we can also change the DC motor's direction and torque. See Figure 17-7 for PWM comparisons.

DC motor control with optoisolator

As we discussed in the first section of this chapter, the optoisolator is indispensable in many motor control applications. Figures 17-8 and 17-9 show the connections to a simple DC motor using a bipolar and a MOSFET transistor. Notice that the 8051 is protected from EMI created by motor brushes by using an optoisolator and a separate power supply.

Figures 17-8 and 17-9 show optoisolators for control of single directional motor control, and the same principle should be used for most motor applications. Separating the power supplies of the motor and logic will reduce the possibility of damage to the control circuitry.

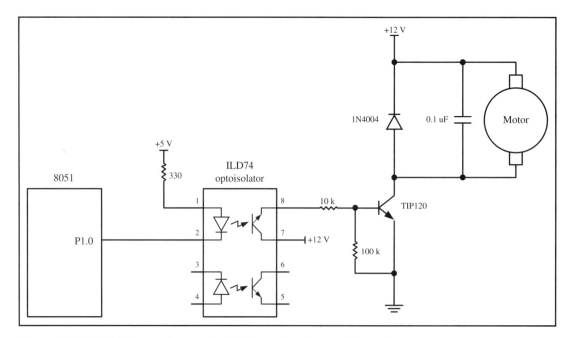

Figure 17-8. DC Motor Connection Using a Darlington Transistor

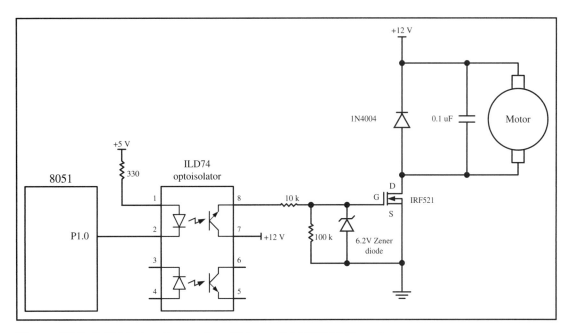

Figure 17-9. DC Motor Connection Using a MOSFET Transistor

Figure 17-8 shows the connection of a bipolar transistor to a motor. Protection of the control circuit is provided by the optoisolator. The motor and 8051 use separate power supplies. The separation of power supplies also allows the use of high-voltage motors. Notice that we use a decoupling capacitor across the motor; this helps reduce the EMI created by the motor. The motor is switched on by clearing bit P1.0.

Figure 17-9 shows the connection of a MOSFET transistor. The optoisolator protects the 8051 from EMI. The zener diode is required for the transistor to reduce gate voltage below the rated maximum value. See Example 17-3.

DC motor control and PWM using C

Examples 17-4 through 17-6 show the 8051 C version of the earlier programs controlling the DC motor.

Example 17-3

Refer to the figure in this example. Write a program to monitor the status of the switch and perform the following:

(a) If P2.7 = 1, the DC motor moves with 25% duty cycle pulse.
(b) If P2.7 = 0, the DC motor moves with 50% duty cycle pulse.

Solution:
```
      ORG 0H
MAIN:
      CLR P1.0                      ;turn off motor
      SETB P2.7
MONITOR:
      JNB P2.7, FIFTYPERCENT
      SETB P1.0                     ;high portion of pulse
```

Example 17-3 (*Continued*)

```
            MOV   R5, #25
            ACALL DELAY
            CLR   P1.0                    ;low portion of pulse
            MOV   R5, #75
            ACALL DELAY
            SJMP  MONITOR
FIFTYPERCENT:
            SETB  P1.0                    ;high portion of pulse
            MOV   R5, #50
            ACALL DELAY
            CLR   P1.0                    ;low portion of pulse
            MOV   R5, #50
            ACALL DELAY
            SJMP  MONITOR
DELAY:
H1:   MOV   R2, #100
H2:   MOV   R3, #255
H3:   DJNZ  R3, H3
            DJNZ  R2, H2
            DJNZ  R5, H1
            RET
            END
```

Example 17-4

Refer to Figure 17-6 for connection of the motor. A switch is connected to pin P2.7. Write a C program to monitor the status of sw and perform the following:

(a) If sw = 0, the DC motor moves clockwise.
(b) If sw = 1, the DC motor moves counterclockwise.

Solution:

```
#include <reg51.h>
sbit SW = P2^7;
sbit ENABLE = P1^0;
sbit MTR_1 = P1^1;
sbit MTR_2 = P1^2;
```

Example 17-4 (*Continued*)

```
void main()
  {
  SW = 1;
  ENABLE = 0;
  MTR_1 = 0;
  MTR_2 = 0;

  while(1)
    {
      ENABLE = 1;
      if(SW == 1)
        {
          MTR_0 = 1;
          MTR_1 = 0;
        }
      else
        {
          MTR_0 = 0;
          MTR_1 = 1;
        }
    }
  }
```

Example 17-5

Refer to the figure in this example. Write a C program to monitor the status of sw and perform the following:

(a) If sw = 0, the DC motor moves with 50% duty cycle pulse.
(b) If sw = 1, the DC motor moves with 25% duty cycle pulse.

Solution:

```
#include <reg51.h>
sbit SW = P2^7;
sbit MTR = P1^0;

void MSDelay(unsigned int value);
void main()
  {
  SW = 1;
  MTR = 0;
  while(1)
    {
      if(SW == 1)
        {
          MTR = 1;
          MSDelay(25);
          MTR = 0;
          MSDelay(75);
        }
      else
        {
          MTR = 1;
          MSDelay(50);
```

Example 17-5 (*Continued*)

```
            MTR = 0;
            MSDelay(50);
        }
    }
}
void MSDelay(unsigned int value)
{
    unsigned int x, y;
    for(x=0; x<1275; x++)
      for(y=0; y<value; y++);
}
```

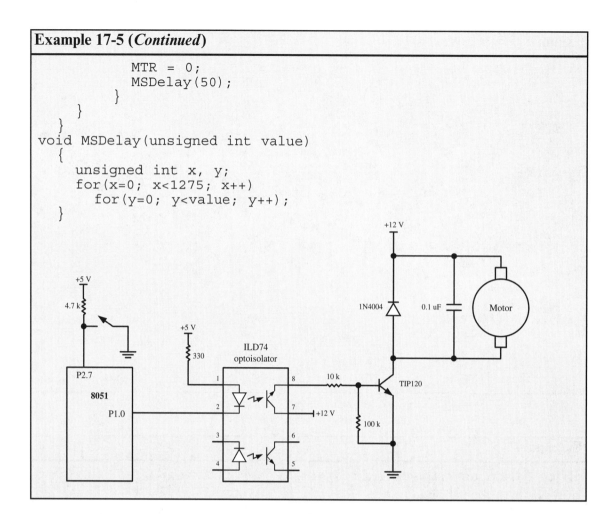

Example 17-6

Refer to Figure 17-8 for connection to the motor. Two switches are connected to pins P2.0 and P2.1. Write a C program to monitor the status of both switches and perform the following:

SW2(P2.7)	SW1(P2.6)	
0	0	DC motor moves slowly (25% duty cycle).
0	1	DC motor moves moderately (50% duty cycle).
1	0	DC motor moves fast (75% duty cycle).
1	1	DC motor moves very fast (100% duty cycle).

Solution:

```
#include <reg51.h>
sbit MTR = P1^0;
void MSDelay(unsigned int value);

void main()
{
  unsigned char z;
  P2 = 0xFF;
  z = P2;
  z = z & 0x03;
  MTR = 0;
  while(1)
```

Example 17-6 (*Continued*)

```
{
 switch(z)
   {
   case(0):
     {
       MTR = 1;
       MSDelay(25);
       MTR = 0;
       MSDelay(75);
       break;
     }
   case(1):
     {
       MTR = 1;
       MSDelay(50);
       MTR = 0;
       MSDelay(50);
       break;
     }
   case(2):
     {
       MTR = 1;
       MSDelay(75);
       MTR = 0;
       MSDelay(25);
       break;
     }
   default:
     MTR = 1;
   }
}
```

REVIEW QUESTIONS

1. True or false. The permanent magnet field DC motor has only two leads for + and – voltages.
2. True or false. Just like a stepper motor, one can control the exact angle of a DC motor's move.
3. Why do we put a driver between the microprocessor and the DC motor?
4. How do we change a DC motor's rotation direction?
5. What is stall in a DC motor?
6. True or false. PWM allows the control of a DC motor with the same phase, but different amplitude pulses.
7. The RPM rating given for the DC motor is for _____ (no-load, loaded).

SUMMARY

This chapter showed how to interface the 8051 with DC motors. A typical DC motor will take electronic pulses and convert them to mechanical motion. This chapter showed how to interface the 8051 with a DC motor. Then, simple Assembly and C programs were written to show the concept of PWM.

Control systems that require motors must be evaluated for the type of motor needed. For example, you would not want to use a stepper in a high-velocity application nor a DC motor for a low-speed, high-torque situation. The stepper motor is ideal in an open-loop positional system and a DC motor is better for a high-speed conveyer belt application. DC motors can be modified to operate in a closed-loop system by adding a shaft encoder, then using a microprocessor to monitor the exact position and velocity of the motor.

RECOMMENDED WEB LINKS

Some 8051 chips come with an on-chip PWM. Since there is no established standard for the PWM on the 8051, you must examine the data sheet for each chip to see the registers and addresses assigned to the PWM function.

See the following website for additional information on PWM and motor control:

- www.MicroDigitalEd.com

PROBLEMS

17.1: DC MOTOR INTERFACING AND PWM

1. Which motor is best for moving a wheel exactly 90 degrees?
2. True or false. Current dissipation of a DC motor is proportional to the load.
3. True or false. The rpm of a DC motor is the same for no-load and loaded.
4. The rpm given in data sheets is for _____ (no-load, loaded).
5. What is the advantage of DC motors over AC motors?
6. What is the advantage of stepper motors over DC motors?
7. True or false. Higher load on a DC motor slows it down if the current and voltage supplied to the motor are fixed.
8. What is PWM, and how is it used in DC motor control?
9. A DC motor is moving a load. How do we keep the rpm constant?
10. What is the advantage of placing an optoisolator between the motor and the microprocessor?

ANSWERS TO REVIEW QUESTIONS

17.1: DC MOTOR INTERFACING AND PWM

1. True
2. False
3. Since microprocessor/digital outputs lack sufficient current to drive the DC motor, we need a driver.
4. By reversing the polarity of voltages connected to the leads.
5. The DC motor is stalled if the load is beyond what it can handle.
6. False
7. No-load

CHAPTER 18

SPI AND I2C PROTOCOLS

OBJECTIVES

Upon completion of this chapter, you will be able to:

>> Understand the serial peripheral interface (SPI) protocol.
>> Explain how the SPI read and write operations work.
>> Examine the SPI pins SDO, SDI, CE, and SCLK.
>> Understand the inter-integrated circuit (I2C) protocol.
>> Explain how the I2C read and write operations work.
>> Examine the I2C pins SCK and SCL.

This chapter discusses the SPI and I2C buses. In Section 18.1, we examine the different pins of SPI protocol and then focus on the concept of clock polarity. We distinguish between single-byte read/write and multibyte burst read/ write. In Section 18.2, we describe the I2C bus and focus on I2C terminology and protocols.

18.1: SPI BUS PROTOCOL

The SPI (serial peripheral interface) is a bus interface connection incorporated into many devices such as ADC, DAC, and EEPROM. In this section, we examine the pins of the SPI bus and show how the read and write operations in the SPI work.

The SPI bus was originally developed by Motorola Corp. (now Freescale), but in recent years has become a widely used standard adapted by many semiconductor chip companies. SPI devices use only two pins for data transfer, called SDI (Din) and SDO (Dout), instead of the eight or more pins used in traditional buses. This reduction of data pins reduces the package size and power consumption drastically, making them ideal for many applications in which space is a major concern. The SPI bus has the SCLK (shift clock) pin to synchronize the data transfer between two chips. The last pin of the SPI bus is CE (chip enable), which is used to initiate and terminate the data transfer. The four pins SDI, SDO, SCLK, and CE make the SPI a four-wire interface. See Figure 18-1. In many chips, the SDI, SDO, SCLK, and CE signals are alternatively named as MOSI, MISO, SCK, and SS as shown in Figure 18-2 (compare with Figure 18-1). There is also a widely used standard called a *three-wire interface bus*. In a three-wire interface bus, we have SCLK and CE, and only a single pin for data transfer. The SPI four-wire bus can become a three-wire interface when the SDI and SDO data pins are tied together. However, there are some major differences between the SPI and three-wire devices in the

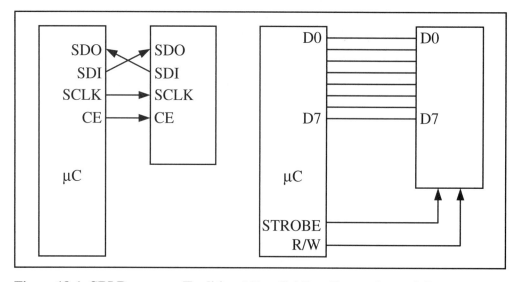

Figure 18-1. SPI Bus versus Traditional Parallel Bus Connection to Microprocessor

data transfer protocol. For that reason, a device must support the three-wire protocol internally in order to be used as a three-wire device. Many devices such as the DS1306 RTC (real-time clock) support both SPI and three-wire protocols.

How SPI works

SPI consists of two shift registers, one in the master and the other in the slave side. Also, there is a clock generator in the master side that generates the clock for the shift registers.

As you can see in Figure 18-2, the serial-out pin of the master shift register is connected to the serial-in pin of the slave shift register by MOSI (Master Out Slave In), and the serial-in pin of the master shift register is connected to the serial-out pin of the slave shift register by MISO (Master In Slave Out). The master clock generator provides clock to the shift registers in both the master and slave. The clock input of the shift registers can be falling or rising edge-triggered. This will be discussed shortly.

In SPI, the shift registers are 8 bits long. It means that after eight clock pulses, the contents of the two shift registers are interchanged. When the master wants to send a byte of data, it places the byte in its shift register and generates eight clock pulses. After eight clock pulses, the byte is transmitted to the other shift register. When the master wants to receive a byte of data, the slave side should place the byte in its shift register, and after eight clock pulses

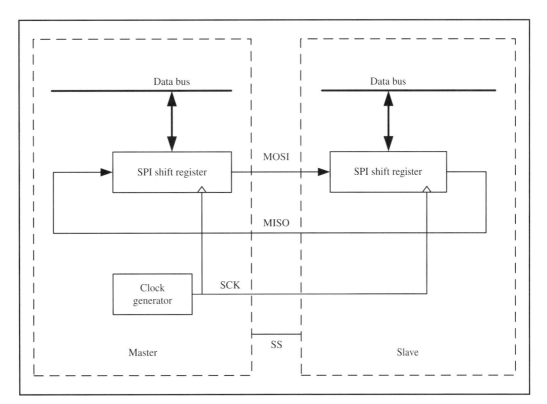

Figure 18-2. SPI Architecture

the data will be received by the master shift register. It must be noted that SPI is full duplex, meaning that it sends and receives data at the same time.

SPI read and write

In connecting a device with an SPI bus to a microprocessor, we use the microprocessor as the master while the SPI device acts as a slave. This means that the microprocessor generates the SCLK, which is fed to the SCLK pin of the SPI device. The SPI protocol uses SCLK to synchronize the transfer of information one bit at a time, where the most significant bit (MSB) goes in first. During the transfer, the CE must stay HIGH. The information (address and data) is transferred between the microprocessor and the SPI device in groups of 8 bits, where the address byte is followed immediately by the data byte. To distinguish between the read and write operations, the D7 bit of the address byte is always 1 for write, while for the read, the D7 bit is low, as we will see next.

Clock polarity and phase in SPI device

As in a UART (universal synchronous-asynchronous receiver-transmitter) communication where the transmitter and receiver must agree on a clock frequency, in SPI communication, the master and slave(s) must agree on the clock polarity and phase with respect to the data. Freescale names these two options as CPOL (clock polarity) and CPHA (clock phase), respectively, and most companies like Atmel have adopted that convention. At CPOL= 0 the base value of the clock is zero, while at CPOL = 1 the base value of the clock is one. CPHA = 0 means sample on the leading (first) clock edge, while CPHA = 1 means sample on the trailing (second) clock. Notice that if the base value of the clock is zero, the leading (first) clock edge is the rising edge but if the base value of the clock is one, the leading (first) clock edge is falling edge. See Table 18-1 and Figure 18-3.

Steps for writing data to an SPI device

In accessing SPI devices, we have two modes of operation: single-byte and multibyte. We will explain each one separately.

Table 18-1. SPI Clock Polarity and Phase

CPOL	CPHA	Data Read and Change Time	SPI Mode
0	0	Read on rising edge, changed on a falling edge	0
0	1	Read on falling edge, changed on a rising edge	1
1	0	Read on falling edge, changed on a rising edge	2
1	1	Read on rising edge, changed on a falling edge	3

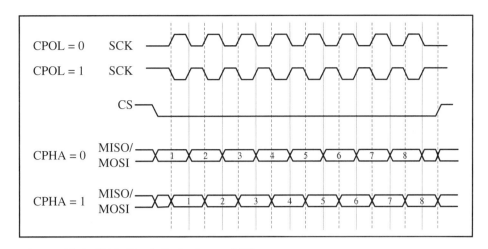

Figure 18-3. SPI Clock Polarity and Phase

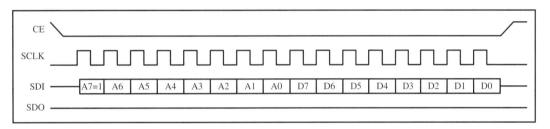

Figure 18-4. SPI Single-Byte Write Timing (Notice A7 = 1)

Single-byte write

The following steps are used to send (write) data in single-byte mode for SPI devices, as shown in Figure 18-4:

1. Make CE = 0 to begin writing.
2. The 8-bit address is shifted in, one bit at a time, with each edge of SCLK. Notice that A7 = 1 for the write operation, and the A7 bit goes in first.
3. After all 8 bits of the address are sent in, the SPI device expects to receive the data belonging to that address location immediately.
4. The 8-bit data is shifted in one bit at a time, with each edge of the SCLK.
5. Make CE = 1 to indicate the end of the write cycle.

Multibyte burst write

Burst mode writing is an effective means of loading consecutive locations. In burst mode, we provide the address of the first location, followed by the data for that location. From then on, while CE = 0, consecutive bytes are written to consecutive memory locations. In this mode, the SPI device internally increments the address location as long as CE is LOW. The following

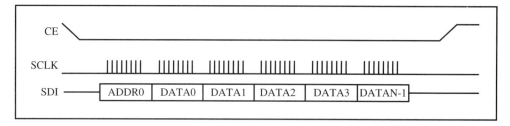

Figure 18-5. SPI Burst (Multibyte) Mode Writing

steps are used to send (write) multiple bytes of data in burst mode for SPI devices as shown in Figure 18-5:

1. Make CE = 0 to begin writing.
2. The 8-bit address of the first location is provided and shifted in, one bit at a time, with each edge of SCLK. Notice that A7 = 1 for the write operation, and the A7 bit goes in first.
3. The 8-bit data for the first location is provided and shifted in, one bit at a time, with each edge of the SCLK. From then on, we simply provide consecutive bytes of data to be placed in consecutive memory locations. In the process, CE must stay low to indicate that this is a burst mode multibyte write operation.
4. Make CE = 1 to end writing.

Steps for reading data from an SPI device

In reading SPI devices, we also have two modes of operation: single-byte and multibyte. We will explain each one separately.

Single-byte read

The following steps are used to get (read) data in single-byte mode from SPI devices, as shown in Figure 18-6:

1. Make CE = 0 to begin reading.
2. The 8-bit address is shifted in one bit at a time, with each edge of SCLK. Notice that A7 = 0 for the read operation, and the A7 bit goes in first.
3. After all 8 bits of the address are sent in, the SPI device sends out data belonging to that location.

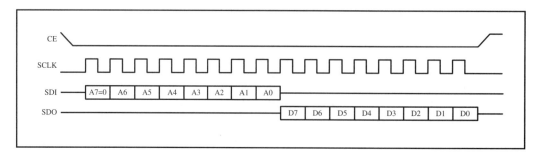

Figure 18-6. SPI Single-Byte Read Timing (Notice A7 = 0)

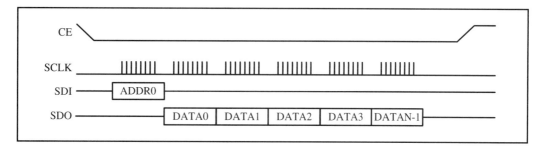

Figure 18-7. SPI Burst (Multibyte) Mode Reading

4. The 8-bit data is shifted out one bit at a time, with each edge of the SCLK.

5. Make CE = 1 to indicate the end of the read cycle.

Multibyte burst read

Burst mode reading is an effective means of bringing out the contents of consecutive locations. In burst mode, we provide the address of the first location only. From then on, while CE = 0, consecutive bytes are brought out from consecutive memory locations. In this mode, the SPI device internally increments the address location as long as CE is LOW. The following steps are used to get (read) multiple bytes of data in burst mode for SPI devices, as shown in Figure 18-7:

1. Make CE = 0 to begin reading.

2. The 8-bit address of the first location is provided and shifted in, one bit at a time, with each edge of SCLK. Notice that A7 = 0 for the read operation, and the A7 bit goes in first.

3. The 8-bit data for the first location is shifted out, one bit at a time, with each edge of the SCLK. From then on, we simply keep getting consecutive bytes of data belonging to consecutive memory locations. In the process, CE must stay LOW to indicate that this is a burst mode multibyte read operation.

4. Make CE = 1 to end reading.

REVIEW QUESTIONS

1. True or false. The SPI protocol writes and reads information in 8-bit chunks.
2. True or false. In SPI, the address is immediately followed by the data.
3. True or false. In an SPI write cycle, bit A7 of the address is LOW.
4. True or false. In an SPI write, the LSB goes in first.
5. State the difference between the single-byte and burst modes in terms of the CE signal.

18.2: I2C BUS PROTOCOL

The IIC (inter-integrated circuit) is a bus interface connection incorporated into many devices such as sensors, RTC, and EEPROM. The IIC is also referred to as I2C (I²C) or I square C in many technical literatures. In this section, we examine the pins of the I2C bus and focus on I2C terminology and protocols.

I2C bus

The I2C bus was originally developed by Philips, but in recent years has become a widely used standard adapted by many semiconductor chip companies. I2C is ideal for attaching low-speed peripherals to a motherboard or embedded system or anywhere that a reliable communication over a short distance is required. As we will see in this chapter, I2C provides a connection-oriented communication with acknowledge. I2C devices use only two pins for data transfer, instead of the eight or more pins used in traditional buses. They are called SCL (Serial Clock), which synchronize the data transfer between two chips, and SDA (Serial Data). This reduction of communication pins reduces the package size and power consumption drastically, making them ideal for many applications in which space is a major concern. These two pins, SDA and SCK, make the I2C a two-wire interface. In many application notes, I2C is referred to as *Two-Wire Serial Interface (TWI)*. In this chapter, we use I2C and TWI interchangeably.

I2C line electrical characteristics

I2C devices use only two bidirectional open-drain pins for data communication. To implement I2C, only a 4.7 kΩ pull-up resistor for each of bus lines is needed (see Figure 18-8). This implements a wired-AND, which is needed to implement I2C protocols. This means that if one or more devices pull the line to low (zero) level, the line state is zero and the level of line will be 1 only if none of devices pull the line to low level.

I2C nodes

Up to 120 different devices can share an I2C bus. Each of these devices is called a *node*. In I2C terminology, each node can operate as either master or slave. Master is a device that generates the clock for the system; it also initiates and terminates a transmission. Slave is the node that receives the clock and is addressed by the master. In I2C, both master and slave can receive or transmit data, so there are four modes of operation. They are master transmitter,

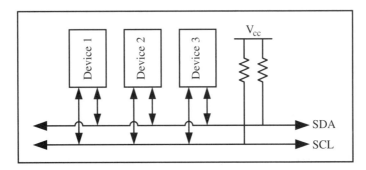

Figure 18-8. I2C Bus

Example 18-1

Give an example to show how a device (node) can have more than one mode of operation.

Solution:

If you connect a microprocessor to an EEPROM with I2C, the microprocessor does a master transmit operation to write to EEPROM. The microprocessor also does master receive operations to read from EEPROM. Notice that a node can do the operations of master and slave at different times.

master receiver, slave transmitter, and slave receiver. Notice that each node can have more than one mode of operation at different times, but it has only one mode of operation at a given time. See Example 18-1.

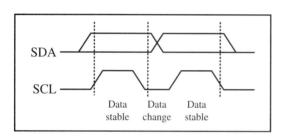

Figure 18-9. I2C Bit Format

Bit format

I2C is a synchronous serial protocol; each data bit transferred on the SDA line is synchronized by a high-to-low pulse of clock on the SCL line. According to I2C protocols, the data line cannot change when the clock line is high; it can change only when the clock line is low. See Figure 18-9. The STOP and START conditions are the only exceptions to this rule.

START and STOP conditions

As we mentioned earlier, I2C is a connection-oriented communication protocol. This means that each transmission is initiated by a START condition and is terminated by a STOP condition. Remember that the START and STOP conditions are generated by the master.

STOP and START conditions must be distinguished from bits of address or data. That is why they do not obey the bit format rule that we mentioned before.

START and STOP conditions are generated by keeping the level of the SCL line high and then changing the level of the SDA line. The START condition is generated by a high-to-low change in the SDA line when SCL is high. The STOP condition is generated by a low-to-high change in the SDA line when SCL is low. See Figure 18-10.

The bus is considered busy between each pair of START and STOP conditions, and no other master tries to take control of the bus when it is busy. If a master, which has the control of the

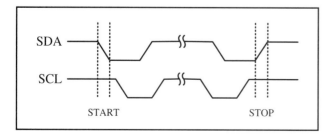

Figure 18-10. START and STOP Conditions

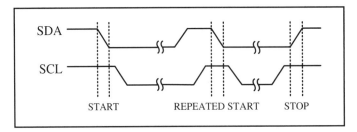

Figure 18-11. REPEATED START Condition

bus, wishes to initiate a new transfer and does not want to release the bus before starting the new transfer, it issues a new START condition between a pair of START and STOP conditions. It is called the REPEATED START condition. See Figure 18-11.

Example 18-2 shows why the REPEATED START condition is necessary.

Packet format in I2C

In I2C, each address or data to be transmitted must be framed in a packet. Each packet is 9 bits long. The first 8 bits are put on the SDA line by the transmitter, and the 9th bit is an acknowledge by the receiver or it may be NACK (not acknowledge). The clock is generated by the master, regardless of whether it is the transmitter or receiver. To get an acknowledge, the transmitter releases the SDA line during the 9th clock so that the receiver can pull the SDA line low to indicate an ACK. If the receiver doesn't pull the SDA line low, it is considered as NACK. See Figure 18-12.

In I2C, each packet may contain either address or data. Also notice that START condition + address packet + one or more data packet + STOP condition together form a complete data transfer. Next, we will study address

---

Example 18-2

Give an example to show when a master must use the REPEATED START condition. What will happen if the master does not use it?

Solution:

If you connect two microprocessors (micro A and micro B) and an EEPROM with I2C, and micro A wants to display the addition of the contents of addresses 0x34 and 0x35 of EEPROM, it has to use the REPEATED START condition. Let's see what may happen if micro A does not use the REPEATED START condition. micro A transmits a START condition, reads the content of address 0x34 of EEPROM into R1, and transmits a STOP condition to release the bus. Before micro A reads the contents of address 0x35 into R2, micro B seizes the bus and changes the contents of addresses 0x34 and 0x35 of EEPROM. Then micro A reads the content of address 0x35 into R2, adds it to R1, and displays the result on the LCD. The result on the LCD is neither the sum of the old values of addresses 0x34 and 0x35 nor the sum of the new values of addresses 0x34 and 0x35 of EEPROM!

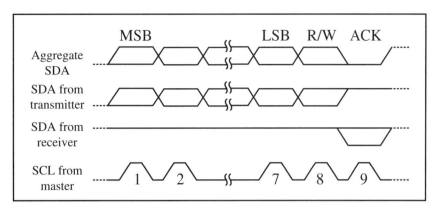

Figure 18-12. Packet Format in I2C

and data packet formats and how to combine them to make a complete transmission.

Address packet format

Like any other packets, all address packets transmitted on the I2C bus are 9 bits long. An address packet consists of seven address bits, one READ/WRITE control bit, and an acknowledge bit (see Figure 18-13).

Address bits are used to address a specific slave device on the bus. The 7-bit address lets the master address a maximum of 128 slaves on the bus, although the address 0000 000 is reserved for general call and all addresses of the format 1111 xxx are reserved. That means 119 (128 − 1 − 8) devices can share an I2C bus. In the I2C bus, the MSB of the address is transmitted first.

The 8th bit in the packet is the READ/WRITE control bit. If this bit is set, the master will read the next frame (Data) from the slave; otherwise, the master will write the next frame (Data) on the bus to the slave. When a slave detects its address on the bus, it knows that it is being addressed and it should acknowledge in the 9th SCL (ACK) cycle by changing SDA to zero. If the addressed slave is not ready or for any reason does not want to service the master, it should leave the SDA line high in the 9th clock cycle. This is considered to be NACK. In case of NACK, the master can transmit a STOP condition to terminate the transmission, or a REPEATED START condition to initiate a new transmission.

Example 18-3 shows how a master says that it wants to write to a slave.

An address packet consisting of a slave address and a READ is called SLA+R, while an address packet consisting of a slave address and a WRITE is called SLA+W.

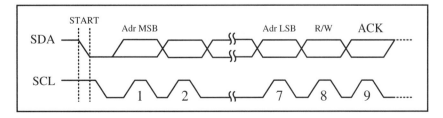

Figure 18-13. Address Packet Format in I2C

Example 18-3

Show how a master says that it wants to write to a slave with address 1001101.

Solution:

The following actions are performed by the master:

(1) The master puts a high-to-low pulse on SDA, while SCL is high to generate a start bit condition to start the transmission.

(2) The master transmits 10011010 into the bus. The first 7 bits (1001101) indicate the slave address, and the 8th bit (0) indicates a Write operation stating that the master will write the next byte (data) into the slave.

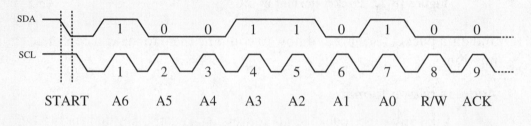

As we mentioned before, address 0000 000 is reserved for general call. This means that when a master transmits address 0000 000, all slaves respond by changing the SDA line to zero and wait to receive the data byte. This is useful when a master wants to transmit the same data byte to all slaves in the system. Notice that the general call address cannot be used to read data from slaves because no more than one slave is able to write to the bus at a given time.

Data packet format

Like other packets, data packets are 9 bits long too. The first 8 bits are a byte of data to be transmitted, and the 9th bit is ACK. If the receiver has received the last byte of data and there is no more data to be received, or the receiver cannot receive or process more data, it will signal a NACK by leaving the SDA line high. In data packets, like address packets, MSB is transmitted first.

Combining address and data packets into a transmission

In I2C, normally, a transmission is started by a START condition, followed by an address packet (SLA + R/W), one or more data packets, and finished by a STOP condition. Figure 18-14 shows a typical data transmission. Try to understand each element in the figure (see Example 18-4).

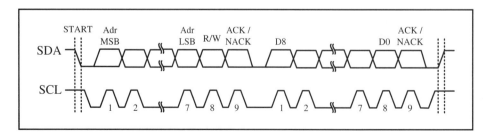

Figure 18-14. Typical Data Transmission

Example 18-4

Show how a master writes the value 11110000 to a slave with address 1001101.

Solution:

The following actions are performed by the master:

1. The master puts a high-to-low pulse on SDA, while SCL is high to generate a START condition to start the transmission.

2. The master transmits 10011010 into the bus. The first 7 bits (1001101) indicate the slave address, and the 8th bit (0) indicates the Write operation stating that the master will write the next byte (data) into the slave.

3. The slave pulls the SDA line low to signal an ACK to say that it is ready to receive the data byte.

4. After receiving the ACK, the master will transmit the data byte (1111000) on the SDA line (MSB first).

5. When the slave device receives the data it leaves the SDA line high to signal NACK. This informs the master that the slave received the last data byte and does not need any more data.

6. After receiving the NACK, the master will know that no more data should be transmitted. The master changes the SDA line when the SCL line is high to transmit a STOP condition and then releases the bus.

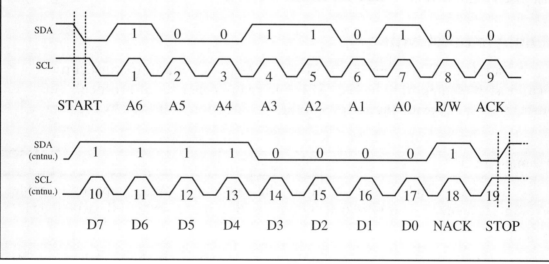

Clock stretching

One of the features of the I2C protocol is clock stretching. It is a kind of flow control. If an addressed slave device is not ready to process more data, it will stretch the clock by holding the clock line (SCL) low after receiving (or sending) a bit of data. Thus the master will not be able to raise the clock line (because devices are wire-ANDed) and will wait until the slave releases the SCL line to show it is ready to transfer the next bit. See Figure 18-15.

Arbitration

I2C protocol supports a multimaster bus system. This doesn't mean that more than one master can use the bus at the same time. Rather, each

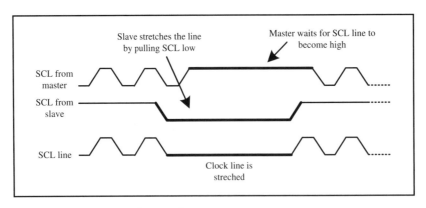

Figure 18-15. Clock Stretching

master waits for the current transmission to finish and then starts to use the bus. But it is possible that two or more masters initiate a transmission at about the same time. In this case the arbitration happens.

Each transmitter has to check the level of the bus and compare it with the level it expects; if it doesn't match, that transmitter has lost the arbitration and will switch to slave mode. In the case of arbitration, the winning master will continue its job. Notice that neither the bus is corrupted nor the data is lost. See Example 18-5.

Multibyte burst write

Burst mode writing is an effective means of loading consecutive locations. It is supported in I2C, SPI, and many other serial protocols. In burst mode, we provide the address of the first location, followed by the data

---

Example 18-5

Two masters, A and B, start at about the same time. What happens if master A wants to write to slave 0010 000 and master B wants to write to slave 0001 111?

Solution:

Master A will lose the arbitration in the third clock because the SDA line is different from the output of master A at the third clock. Master A switches to slave mode and leaves the bus after losing the arbitration.

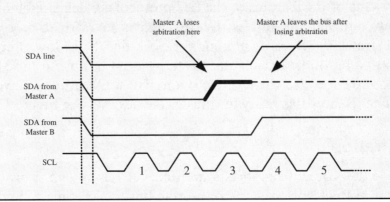

Start	Slave address	Write	ACK	First location address	ACK	Data byte #1	ACK	Data byte #2	ACK	Data byte #3	ACK	Stop
S	1111000	0	A	00001111	A	00000001	A	00000010	A	00000011	A	P

Figure 18-16. Multibyte Burst Write

for that location. From then on, consecutive bytes are written to consecutive memory locations. In this mode, the I2C device internally increments the address location as long as the STOP condition is not detected. The following steps are used to send (write) multiple bytes of data in burst mode for I2C devices.

1. Generate a START condition.
2. Transmit the slave address followed by zero (for write).
3. Transmit the address of the first location.
4. Transmit the data for the first location and from then on, simply provide consecutive bytes of data to be placed in consecutive memory locations.
5. Generate a STOP condition.

Figure 18-16 shows how to write 0x01, 0x02, and 0x03 to three consecutive locations starting from location 00001111 of slave 1111000.

Multibyte burst read

Burst mode reading is an effective way of bringing out the contents of consecutive locations. In burst mode, we provide the address of the first location only. From then on, contents are brought out from consecutive memory locations. In this mode, the I2C device internally increments the address location as long as the STOP condition is not detected. The following steps are used to get (read) multiple bytes of data using burst mode for I2C devices.

1. Generate a START condition.
2. Transmit the slave address followed by zero (for address write).
3. Transmit the address of the first location.
4. Generate a START (REPEATED START) condition.
5. Transmit the slave address followed by one (for read).
6. Read the data from the first location and from then on, bring contents out from consecutive memory locations.
7. Generate a STOP condition.

Figure 18-17 shows how to read three consecutive locations starting from location 00001111 of slave number 1111000.

Start	Slave address	Write	ACK	First location address	ACK	Start	Slave address	Read	ACK	Data byte #1	ACK	Data byte #2	ACK	Data byte #3	ACK	Stop
S	1111000	0	A	00001111	A	S	1111000	1	A	xxxxxxxx	A	xxxxxxxx	A	xxxxxxxx	A	P

Figure 18-17. Multibyte Burst Read

REVIEW QUESTIONS

1. True or false. I2C protocol is ideal for short distances.
2. How many bits are there in a frame? Which bit is for acknowledge?
3. True or false. START and STOP conditions are generated when the SDA is high.
4. What is the name of the flow control method in the I2C protocol?
5. What is the recommended value for the pull-up resistors in the I2C protocol?
6. True or false. After the arbitration of two masters, both of them must start transmission from the beginning.

SUMMARY

This chapter began by describing the SPI bus connection and protocol and then we discussed the I2C bus connection and protocol.

RECOMMENDED WEB LINKS

Some 8051 chips come with an on-chip SPI and I2C. Since there is no established standard for the SPI and I2C on the 8051, you must examine the data sheet for each chip to see the registers and addresses assigned to the SPI and I2C functions. See the following website for additional information on SPI and I2C.

• www.MicroDigitalEd.com

PROBLEMS

18.1: SPI BUS PROTOCOL

1. True or false. The SPI bus needs an external clock.
2. True or false. The SPI CE is active low.
3. True or false. The SPI bus has a single Din pin.
4. True or false. The SPI bus has multiple Dout pins.
5. True or false. When the SPI device is used as a slave, the SCLK is an input pin.
6. True or false. In SPI devices, data is transferred in 8-bit chunks.
7. True or false. In SPI devices, each bit of information (data, address) is transferred with a single clock pulse.

8. True or false. In SPI devices, the 8-bit data is followed by an 8-bit address.
9. In terms of data pins, what is the difference between the SPI and three-wire connections?
10. How does the SPI protocol distinguish between the read and write cycles?

18.2: I2C BUS PROTOCOL

1. True or false. The I2C bus needs an external clock.
2. True or false. The SDA pin is internally pulled up.
3. True or false. The I2C bus needs two wires to transfer data.
4. True or false. The SDA line is output for the master device.
5. True or false. When a device is used as a slave, the SCL is an input pin.
6. True or false. In I2C, the data frame is 8 bits long.
7. True or false. In I2C devices, each bit of information (data, address, ACK/NACK) is transferred with a single clock pulse.
8. True or false. In I2C devices, the 8-bit data is followed by an ACK/NACK.
9. In terms of data pins, what is the difference between the SPI and I2C connections?
10. How does the I2C protocol distinguish between the read and write cycles?

ANSWERS TO REVIEW QUESTIONS

18.1: SPI BUS PROTOCOL

1. True
2. True
3. False
4. False
5. In single-byte mode, after each byte, the CE pin must go HIGH before the next cycle. In burst mode, the CE pin stays LOW for the duration of the burst (multibyte) transfer.

18.2: I2C BUS PROTOCOL

1. True
2. 9 bits. The 9th bit
3. True
4. Clock stretching
5. 4.7 kΩ
6. False

APPENDIX A

8051 INSTRUCTIONS, TIMING, AND REGISTERS

OVERVIEW

In the first section of this appendix, we describe the instructions of the 8051 and give their formats with some examples. In many cases, more detailed programming examples will be given to clarify the instructions. These instructions will operate on any 8031, 8032, 8051, or 8052 microprocessor. This section concludes with a list of machine cycles (clock counts) for each 8051 instruction.

In the second section, a list of all the 8051 registers is provided for ease of reference for the 8051 programmer.

A.1: THE 8051 INSTRUCTION SET

ACALL target address

Function:	Absolute call
Flags:	None

ACALL stands for "absolute call." It calls subroutines with a target address within 2K bytes from the current program counter. See LCALL for more discussion on this.

ADD A, source byte

Function:	ADD
Flags:	OV, AC, CY

This adds the source byte to the accumulator (A), and places the result in A. Since register A is one byte in size, the source operands must also be one byte.

The ADD instruction is used for both signed and unsigned numbers. Each one is discussed separately.

Unsigned addition

In the addition of unsigned numbers, the status of CY, AC, and OV may change. The most important of these flags is CY. It becomes 1 when there is a carry from D7 out in 8-bit (D0–D7) operations. Some examples are as follows.

```
        MOV     A,#45H          ;A=45H
        ADD     A,#4FH          ;A=94H  (45H+4FH=94H)
                                ;CY=0,AC=1

        MOV     A,#0FEH         ;A=FEH
        MOV     R3,#75H         ;R3=75H
        ADD     A,R3            ;A=FE+75=73H
                                ;CY=1,AC=1

        MOV     A,#25H          ;A=25H
        ADD     A,#42H          ;A=67H  (25H+42H=67H)
                                ;CY=0,AC=0
```

Addressing modes

The following addressing modes are supported for the ADD instruction:

1. Immediate: `ADD A,#data`   `ADD A,#25H`
2. Register: `ADD A,Rn`   `ADD A,R3`

3. Direct: ADD A,direct

```
ADD A,30H ;add to A data in RAM loc. 30H
```

4. Register-indirect: ADD A,@Ri where i=0 or i=1 only

```
ADD A,@R0 ;add to A data pointed to by R0
ADD A,@R1 ;add to A data pointed to by R1
```

In the following example, the contents of RAM locations 50H to 5FH are added together, and the sum is saved in RAM locations 70H and 71H.

```
        CLR  A              ;A=0
        MOV  R0,#50H        ;source pointer
        MOV  R2,#16         ;counter
        MOV  R3,#0          ;clear R3
A_1:    ADD  A,@R0          ;ADD to A from source
        JNC  B_1            ;IF CY=0 go to next byte
        INC  R3             ;otherwise keep carries
B_1:    INC  R0             ;next location
        DJNZ R2,A_1         ;repeat for all bytes
        MOV  70H,A          ;save low byte of sum
        MOV  71H,R3         ;save high byte of sum
```

Notice in all the above examples that we ignored the status of the OV flag. Although ADD instructions do affect OV, it is in the context of signed numbers that the OV flag has any significance. This is discussed next.

Signed addition and negative numbers

In the addition of signed numbers, special attention should be given to the overflow flag (OV) since this indicates if there is an error in the result of the addition. There are two rules for setting OV in signed number operation. The overflow flag is set to 1:

1. If there is a carry from D6 to D7 and no carry from D7 out.
2. If there is a carry from D7 out and no carry from D6 to D7.
   Notice that if there is a carry both from D7 out and from D6 to D7, OV = 0.

```
        MOV   A,#+8        ;A=0000 1000
        MOV   R1,#+4       ;R1=0000 0100
        ADD   A,R1        ;A=0000 1100 OV=0,CY=0
```

Notice that D7 = 0 since the result is positive and OV = 0 since there is neither a carry from D6 to D7 nor any carry beyond D7. Since OV = 0, the result is correct [(+8) + (+4) = (+12)].

```
        MOV   A,#+66      ;A=0100 0010
        MOV   R4,#+69     ;R4=0100 0101
```

```
        ADD     A,R4        ;A=1000 0111 = -121
                            ;(INCORRECT) CY=0, D7=1, OV=1
```

In the above example, the correct result is +135 [(+66) + (+69) = (+135)], but the result was −121. OV = 1 is an indication of this error. Notice that D7 = 1 since the result is negative; OV = 1 since there is a carry from D6 to D7 and CY = 0.

```
        MOV     A,#-12      ;A=1111 0100
        MOV     R3,#+18     ;R3=0001 0010
        ADD     A,R3        ;A=0000 0110 (+6) correct
                            ;D7=0,OV=0, and CY=1
```

Notice above that the result is correct (OV = 0), since there is a carry from D6 to D7 and a carry from D7 out.

```
        MOV     A,#-30      ;A=1110 0010
        MOV     R0,#+14     ;R0=0000 1110
        ADD     A,R0        ;A=1111 0000 (-16, CORRECT)
                            ;D7=1,OV=0, CY=0
```

OV = 0 since there is no carry from D7 out nor any carry from D6 to D7.

```
        MOV     A,#-126     ;A=1000 0010
        MOV     R7,#-127    ;R7=1000 0001
        ADD     A,R7        ;A=0000 0011 (+3, WRONG)
                            ;D7=0, OV=1
```

CY = 1 since there is a carry from D7 out but no carry from D6 to D7.

From the above discussion, we conclude that while CY is important in any addition, OV is extremely important in signed number addition since it is used to indicate whether or not the result is valid. As we will see in instruction "DA A", the AC flag is used in the addition of BCD numbers. OV is used in DIV and MUL instructions as well. See the description of these two instructions for further details.

ADDC A, source byte

Function:	Add with carry
Flags:	OV, AC, CY

This will add the source byte to A, in addition to the CY flag (A = A + byte + CY). If CY = 1 prior to this instruction, CY is also added to A. If CY = 0 prior to the instruction, source is added to destination plus 0. This is used in multibyte additions. In the addition of 25F2H to 3189H, for example, we use the ADDC instruction as shown below.

```
CLR   C            ;CY=0
MOV   A,#89H       ;A=89H
ADDC  A,#0F2H      ;A=89H+F2H+0=17BH, A=7B, CY=1
MOV   R3,A         ;SAVE A
MOV   A,#31H
ADDC  A,#25H       ;A=31H+25H+1=57H
```

Therefore the result is:
$$\begin{array}{r} 25F2H \\ +3189H \\ \hline 577BH \end{array}$$

The addressing modes for ADDC are the same as for "ADD A,byte".

AJMP   target address

Function: Absolute jump
Flag: None

AJMP stands for "absolute jump." It transfers program execution to the target address unconditionally. The target address for this instruction must be within 2K bytes of program memory. See LJMP for more discussion on this.

ANL   dest-byte, source-byte

Function: Logical AND for byte variables
Flags: None affected

A	B	A AND B
0	0	0
0	1	0
1	0	0
1	1	1

This performs a logical AND on the operands, bit by bit, storing the result in the destination. Notice that both the source and destination values are byte-size only.

```
MOV   A,#39H    ;A=39H
ANL   A,#09H    ;A=39H ANDed with 09

39    0011 1001
09    0000 1001
09    0000 1001


MOV   A,#32H    ;A=32H   32   0011 0010
MOV   R4,#50H   ;R4=50H  50   0101 0000
ANL   A,R4      ;(A=10H) 10   0001 0000
```

For the ANL instruction, there are a total of six addressing modes. In four of them, the accumulator must be the destination. They are as follows:

1. Immediate: ANL A, #data

   ```
   ANL A,#25H
   ```

2. Register: ANL A, Rn

   ```
   ANL A,R3
   ```

3. Direct: ANL A, direct

   ```
   ANL A,30H ;AND A with data in RAM location 30H
   ```

4. Register-indirect:

   ```
   ANL A,@R0 ;AND A with data pointed to by R0
   ```

In the next two addressing modes, the destination is a direct address (a RAM location or one of the SFR registers), while the source is either A or immediate data.

5. ANL direct, #data

   Assume that RAM location 32H has the value 67H. Find its content after execution of the following code.

   ```
   ANL 32H,#44H
   44H  0100 0100
   67H  0110 0111
   44H  0100 0101    Therefore, it has 44H.
   ```

   Or look at these examples:

   ```
   ANL P1,#11111110B   ;mask P1.0(D0 of Port 1)
   ANL P1,#01111111B   ;mask P1.7(D7 of Port 1)
   ANL P1,#11110111B   ;mask P1.3(D3 of Port 1)
   ANL P1,#11111100B   ;mask P1.0 and P1.1
   ```

   The above instructions clear (mask) certain bits of the output port of P1.

6. ANL direct, A

   Find the contents of register B after the following:

   ```
   MOV B,#44H     ;B=44H
   MOV A,#67H     ;A=67H
   ANL 0F0H,A     ;A AND B(B is located at RAM F0H)
                  ;after the operation B=44H
   ```

Note: We cannot use this to mask bits of input ports! For example, "ANL A, P1" is incorrect!

ANL C, source-bit

Function:	Logical AND for bit variable
Flag:	CY

In this instruction, the carry flag bit is ANDed with a source bit and the result is placed in carry. Therefore, if source bit = 0, CY is cleared; otherwise, the CY flag remains unchanged.

Write code to clear the accumulator if bits P2.1 and P2.2 are both high; otherwise, make A = FFH.

```
        MOV  A,#0FFH    ;A=FFH
        MOV  C,P2.1     ;copy bit P2.1 to carry flag
        ANL  C,P2.2     ;and then
        JNC  B_1        ;jump if one of them is low
        CLR  A
B_1:
```

Another variation of this instruction involves the ANDing of the CY flag bit with the complement of the source bit. Its format is "ANL C,/bit". See the following example.

Clear A if P2.1 is high and P2.2 is low; otherwise, make A = FFH.
```
        MOV  A,#0FFH
        MOV  C,P2.1     ;get a copy of P2.1 bit
        ANL  C,/P2.2    ;AND P2.1 with complement of P2.2
        JNC  B_1
        CLR  A
B_1:
```

CJNE dest-byte, source-byte, target

Function: Compare and jump if not equal
Flag: CY

The magnitudes of the source byte and destination byte are compared. If they are not equal, it jumps to the target address.

Keep monitoring P1 indefinitely for the value of 99H. Get out only when P1 has the value 99H.

```
        MOV  P1,0FFH        ;make P1 an input port
BACK:   MOV  A,P1          ;read P1
        CJNE A,#99,BACK    ;keep monitoring
```

Notice that CJNE jumps only for the not-equal value. To find out if it is greater or less after the comparison, we must check the CY flag. Notice also that the CJNE instruction affects the CY flag only, and after the jump to the target address the carry flag indicates which value is greater, as shown here.

In the following example, P1 is read and compared with value 65. Then:

Dest < Source	CY = 1
Dest ≥ Source	CY = 0

1. If P1 is equal to 65, the accumulator keeps the result.

---

2. If P1 has a value less than 65, R2 has the result.

3. If P1 has a value greater than 65, it is kept by R3.

At the end of the program, A will contain the equal value, or R2 the smaller value, or R3 the greater value.

```
            MOV  A,P1               ;READ P1
            CJNE A,#65,NEXT         ;IS IT 65?
            SJMP EXIT               ;YES, A KEEPS IT, EXIT
NEXT:       JNC  OVER               ;NO
            MOV  R2,A               ;SAVE THE SMALLER IN R2
            SJMP EXIT               ;AND EXIT
OVER:       MOV  R3,A               ;SAVE THE LARGER IN R3
EXIT:
```

This instruction supports four addressing modes. In two of them, A is the destination.

1. Immediate: CJNE A, #data, target

   ```
   CJNE A,#96,NEXT         ;JUMP IF A IS NOT 96
   ```

2. Direct: CJNE A, direct, target

   ```
   CJNE A,40H,NEXT         ;JUMP IF A NOT =
   ;WITH THE VALUE HELD BY RAM LOC. 40H
   ```

Notice the absence of the "#" sign in the above instruction. This indicates RAM location 40H. Notice in this mode that we can test the value at an input port. This is a widely used application of this instruction. See the following:

```
            MOV  P1,#0FF            ;P1 is an input port
            MOV  A,#100            ;A = 100
HERE:       CJNE A,P1,HERE         ;WAIT HERE TIL P1 = 100
```

In the third addressing mode, any register, R0–R7, can be the destination.

3. Register: CJNE Rn, #data, target

   ```
   CJNE R5,#70,NEXT        ;jump if R5 is not 70
   ```

In the fourth addressing mode, any RAM location can be the destination. The RAM location is held by register R0 or R1.

4. Register-indirect: CJNE @Ri, #data, target

   ```
   CJNE @R1,#80,NEXT      ;jump if RAM
   ;location whose address is held by R1
   ;is not equal to 80
   ```

Notice that the target address can be no more than 128 bytes backward or 127 bytes forward, since it is a 2-byte instruction. For more on this, see SJMP.

CLR   A

Function: Clear accumulator

Flag: None are affected

This instruction clears register A. All bits of the accumulator are set to 0.

```
CLR  A
MOV  R0,A      ;clear R0
MOV  R2,A      ;clear R2
MOV  P1,A      ;clear port 1
```

CLR   bit

Function: Clear bit

This instruction clears a single bit. The bit can be the carry flag, or any bit-addressable location in the 8051. Here are some examples of its format:

```
CLR  C         ;CY=0
CLR  P2.4      ;CLEAR P2.5 (P2.5=0)
CLR  P1.7      ;CLEAR P1.7 (P1.7=0)
CLR  ACC.7     ;CLEAR D7 OF ACCUMULATOR (ACC.7=0)
```

CPL   A

Function: Complement accumulator

Flags: None are affected

This complements the contents of register A, the accumulator. The result is the 1's complement of the accumulator. That is, 0s become 1s and 1s become 0s.

```
        MOV A,#55H     ;A=01010101
AGAIN:  CPL A          ;complement reg. A
        MOV P1,A       ;toggle bits of P1
        SJMP AGAIN     ;continuously
```

CPL   bit

Function: Complement bit

This instruction complements a single bit. The bit can be any bit-addressable location in the 8051.

```
        SETB P1.0      ;set P1.0 high
AGAIN:  CPL P1.0       ;complement reg. bit
        SJMP AGAIN     ;continuously
```

Function: Decimal-adjust accumulator after addition
Flags: CY

This instruction is used after addition of BCD numbers to convert the result back to BCD. The data is adjusted in the following two possible cases.

1. It adds 6 to the lower 4 bits of A if it is greater than 9 or if AC = 1.

2. It also adds 6 to the upper 4 bits of A if it is greater than 9 or if CY = 1.

```
MOV    A,#47H    ;A=0100 0111
ADD    A,#38H    ;A=47H+38H=7FH, invalid BCD
DA     A         ;A=1000 0101=85H, valid BCD


  47H
+ 38H
  7FH    (invalid BCD)
+  6H    (after DA A)
  85H    (valid BCD)
```

In the above example, since the lower nibble was greater than 9, DA added 6 to A. If the lower nibble is less than 9 but AC = 1, it also adds 6 to the lower nibble. See the following example.

```
MOV    A,#29H      ;A=0010 1001
ADD    A,#18H      ;A=0100 0001 INCORRECT
DA     A           ;A=0100 0111 = 47H VALID BCD


  29H
+ 18H
  41H    (incorrect result in BCD)
+  6H
  47H    correct result in BCD
```

The same thing can happen for the upper nibble. See the following example.

```
MOV    A,#52H    ;A=0101 0010
ADD    A,#91H    ;A=1110 0011 INVALID BCD
DA     A         ;A=0100 0011 AND CY=1


  52H
+ 91H
  E3H         (invalid BCD)
+  6          (after DA A, adding to upper nibble)
 143H         valid BCD
```

Similarly, if the upper nibble is less than 9 and CY = 1, it must be corrected. See the following example.

```
MOV    A,#94H         ;A=1001 0100
ADD    A,#91H         ;A=0010 0101 INCORRECT
DA     A              ;A=1000 0101, VALID BCD
                      ;FOR 85,CY=1
```

It is possible that 6 is added to both the high and low nibbles. See the following example.

```
MOV    A,#54H         ;A=0101 0100
ADD    A,#87H         ;A=1101 1011 INVALID BCD
DA     A            ;A=0100 0001, CY=1 (BCD 141)
```

DEC   byte

Function:	Decrement
Flags:	None

This instruction subtracts 1 from the byte operand. Note that CY (carry/borrow) is unchanged even if a value 00 is decremented and becomes FF.
This instruction supports four addressing modes.

1. Accumulator: DEC A

    ```
    DEC A
    ```

2. Register: DEC Rn

    ```
    DEC R1 or DEC R3
    ```

3. Direct: DEC direct

    ```
    DEC 40H   ;dec byte in RAM location 40H
    ```

4. Register-indirect: DEC @Ri   ; where i = 0 or 1 only

    ```
    DEC @R0   ;decr. byte pointed to by R0
    ```

DIV   AB

Function:	Divide
Flags:	CY and OV

This instruction divides a byte accumulator by the byte in register B. It is assumed that both registers A and B contain an unsigned byte. After the division, the quotient will be in register A and the remainder in register B. If you divide by zero (i.e., set register B = 0 before the execution of "DIV AB"), the values in register A and B are undefined and the OV flag is set to high to indicate an invalid result. Notice that CY is always 0 in this instruction.

```
MOV A,#35
MOV B,#10
DIV AB              ;A=3  and B=5
```

```
MOV A,#97H
MOV B,#12H
DIV AB          ;A=8 and B=7
```

Notice in this instruction that the carry and OV flags are both cleared, unless we divide A by 0, in which case the result is invalid and OV = 1 to indicate the invalid condition.

DJNZ byte, target

Function: Decrement and jump if not zero
Flags: None

In this instruction a byte is decremented, and if the result is not zero it will jump to the target address.

Count from 1 to 20 and send the count to P1.

```
        CLR A           ;A=0
        MOV R2,#20      ;R2=20 counter
BACK:   INC A
        MOV P1,A
        DJNZ R2,BACK  ;repeat if R2 not = zero
```

The following two formats are supported by this instruction.

1. Register: DJNZ Rn,target (where n=0 to 7)

```
DJNZ R3,HERE
```

2. Direct: DJNZ direct,target

Notice that the target address can be no more than 128 bytes backward or 127 bytes forward, since it is a 2-byte instruction. For more on this, see SJMP.

INC   byte

Function: Increment
Flags: None

This instruction adds 1 to the register or memory location specified by the operand. Note that CY is not affected even if value FF is incremented to 00. This instruction supports four addressing modes.

1. Accumulator: INC A

```
INC A
```

2. Register: INC Rn

```
INC R1 or INC R5
```

3. Direct: INC direct

```
INC 30H  ;incr. byte in RAM loc. 30H
```

---

4. Register-indirect: INC @Ri (i = 0 or 1)

```
INC @R0  ;incr. byte pointed to by R0
```

INC   DPTR

Function:	Increment data pointer
Flags:	None

This instruction increments the 16-bit register DPTR (data pointer) by 1. Notice that DPTR is the only 16-bit register that can be incremented. Also notice that there is no decrement version of this instruction.

```
MOV  DPTR,#16FFH    ;DPTR=16FFH
INC  DPTR           ;now DPTR=1700H
```

JB   bit, target   also: JNB   bit, target

Function:	Jump if bit set	Jump if bit not set
Flags:	None	

These instructions are used to monitor a given bit and jump to a target address if a given bit is high or low. In the case of JB, if the bit is high it will jump, while for JNB if the bit is low it will jump. The given bit can be any of the bit-addressable bits of RAM, ports, or registers of the 8051.

Monitor bit P1.5 continuously. When it becomes low, send 55H to P2.

```
      SETB P1.5     ;make P1.5 an input bit
HERE: JB P1.5,HERE  ;stay here as long as P1.5=1
      MOV P2,#55H   ;since P1.5=0 send 55H to P2
```

See if register A has an even number. If so, make it odd.

```
      JB   ACC.0,NEXT    ;jump if it is odd
      INC A             ;it is even, make it odd
NEXT: ...
```

Monitor bit P1.4 continuously. When it becomes high, send 55H to P2.

```
      SETB P1.4     ;make P1.4 an input bit
HERE: JNB P1.4,HERE ;stay here as long as P1.4=0
      MOV P2,#55H   ;since P1.4=1 send 55H to P2
```

See if register A has an even number. If not, make it even.

```
      JNB  ACC.0,NEXT   ;jump if D0 is 0 (even)
      INC  A            ;D0=1, make it even
NEXT: ...
```

JBC   bit, target

Function: Jump if bit is set and clear bit
Flags: None

If the desired bit is high, it will jump to the target address; at the same time, the bit is cleared to zero.

The following instruction will jump to label NEXT if D7 of register A is high; at the same time D7 is cleared to zero.

```
JBC ACC.7,NEXT
MOV P1,A
...
```
NEXT:

Notice that the target address can be no more than 128 bytes backward or 127 bytes forward since it is a 2-byte instruction. For more on this, see SJMP.

JC   target

Function: Jump if CY = 1.
Flags: None

This instruction examines the CY flag; if it is high, it will jump to the target address.

JMP   @A+DPTR

Function: Jump indirect
Flags: None

The JMP instruction is an unconditional jump to a target address. The target address is provided by the total sum of register A and the DPTR register. Since this is not a widely used instruction, we will bypass further discussion of it.

JNB   bit, target

See JB and JNB.

JNC   target

Function: Jump if no carry (CY = 0)
Flags: None

This instruction examines the CY flag, and if it is zero it will jump to the target address.

Find the total sum of the bytes F6H, 98H, and 8AH. Save the carries in register R3.

```
            CLR     A               ;A=0
            MOV     R3,A            ;R3=0
            ADD     A,#0F6H
            JNC     OVER1
            INC     R3
OVER1:      ADD     A,#98H
            JNC     OVER2
            INC     R3
OVER2:      ADD     A,#8AH
            JNC     OVER3
            INC     R3
OVER3:
```

Notice that this is a 2-byte instruction and the target address cannot be farther than −128 to +127 bytes from the program counter. See J condition for more on this.

JNZ   target

Function:	Jump if accumulator is not zero
Flags:	None

This instruction jumps if register A has a value other than zero.

Search RAM locations 40H–4FH to find how many of them have the value 0.

```
            MOV     R5,16          ;set counter
            MOV     R3,#0          ;R3 holds number of 0s
            MOV     R1,#40H        ;address
BACK:       MOV     A,@R1          ;bring data to reg A
            JNZ     OVER
            INC     R3
OVER:       INC     R1             ;point to next location
            DJNZ    R5,BACK        ;repeat for all locations
```

The above program will bring the data into the accumulator and if it is zero, it increments counter R3. Notice that this is a 2-byte instruction; therefore, the target address cannot be more than −128 to +127 bytes away from the program counter. See J condition for further discussion on this.

JZ   target

> Function: Jump if A = zero
> Flags: None

This instruction examines the contents of the accumulator and jumps if it has value 0.

A string of bytes of data is stored in RAM locations starting at address 50H. The end of the string is indicated by the value 0. Send the values to P1 one by one with a delay between each.

```
        MOV   R0,#50H     ;address
BACK:   MOV   A,@R0       ;bring the value into reg A
        JZ    EXIT        ;end of string, exit
        MOV   P1,A        ;send it to P1
        ACALL DELAY
        INC   R0          ;point to next
        SJMP  BACK
EXIT:   ...
```

Notice that this is a 2-byte instruction; therefore, the target address cannot be more than –128 to +127 bytes away from the program counter. See J condition for further discussion on this.

J condition   target

> Function: Conditional jump

In this type of jump, control is transferred to a target address if certain conditions are met. The target address cannot be more than –128 to +127 bytes away from the current program counter.

JC	Jump carry	jump if CY = 1
JNC	Jump no carry	jump if CY = 0
JZ	Jump zero	jump if register A = 0
JNZ	Jump no zero	jump if register A is not 0
JNB bit	Jump no bit	jump if bit = 0
JB bit	Jump bit	jump if bit = 1
JBC bit	Jump bit clear bit	jump if bit = 1 and clear bit
DJNZ Rn,...	Decrement and jump if not zero	
CJNE A,#val,...	Compare A with value and jump if not equal	

Notice that all "J condition" instructions are short jumps, meaning that the target address cannot be more than –128 bytes backward or +127 bytes forward of the PC of the instruction following the jump (see SJMP). What happens if a programmer needs to use a "J condition" to go to a target address beyond the –128 to +127 range? The solution is to use the "J condition" along with the unconditional LJMP instruction, as shown below.

```
              ORG   100H
              ADD   A,R0
              JNC   NEXT
              LJMP  OVER        ;target more than 128 bytes away
NEXT:         ...
              ORG 300H
OVER:         ADD   A,R2
```

LCALL   16-bit address   also: ACALL   11-bit address

        Function: Transfers control to a subroutine
        Flags: None

There are two types of CALLs: ACALL and LCALL. In ACALL, the target address is within 2K bytes of the current program counter. To reach the target address in the 64K bytes maximum ROM space of the 8051, we must use LCALL. If calling a subroutine, the PC register (which has the address of the instruction after the ACALL) is pushed onto the stack, and the stack pointer (SP) is incremented by 2. Then the program counter is loaded with the new address and control is transferred to the subroutine. At the end of the procedure, when RET is executed, PC is popped off the stack, which returns control to the instruction after the CALL.

Notice that LCALL is a 3-byte instruction, in which one byte is the opcode, and the other two bytes are the 16-bit address of the target subroutine. ACALL is a 2-byte instruction, in which 5 bits are used for the opcode and the remaining 11 bits are used for the target subroutine address. An 11-bit address limits the range to 2K bytes.

LJMP 16-bit address   also: SJMP 8-bit address

        Function: Transfers control unconditionally to a new address.

In the 8051, there are two unconditional jumps: LJMP (long jump) and SJMP (short jump). Each is described next.

1. LJMP (long jump): This is a 3-byte instruction. The first byte is the opcode and the next two bytes are the target address. As a result, LJMP is used to jump to any address location within the 64K-byte code space of the 8051. Notice that the difference between LJMP and LCALL is that the CALL instruction will return and continue execution with the instruction following the CALL, whereas JMP will not return.

2. SJMP (short jump): This is a 2-byte instruction. The first byte is the opcode and the second byte is the signed number displacement, which is added to the program counter of the instruction following the SJMP to get the target address. Therefore, in this jump the target address must be within –128 to +127 bytes of the program counter of the instruction after the SJMP since a single byte of address can take values of +127 to –128. This address is often referred to as a *relative address* since the target address is –128 to +127 bytes relative to the program counter. In this

---

appendix, we have used the term *target address* instead of relative address only for the sake of simplicity.

Line 2 of the code below shows 803E as the object code for "SJMP OVER", which is a forward jump instruction. The 80H, located at address 100H, is the opcode for the SJMP, and 3EH, located at address 101H, is the relative address. The address is relative to the next address location, which is 102H. Adding 102H + F8H = 140H gives the target address of the "OVER" label.

```
LOC   OBJ        LINE
0100             1                ORG  100H
0100  803E       2                SJMP OVER
0140             3                ORG  140H
0140  7A0A       4    OVER:       MOV  R2,#10
0142  7B64       5    AGAIN:      MOV  R3,#100
0144  00         6    BACK:       NOP
0145  00         7                NOP
0146  DBFC       8                DJNZ R3,BACK
0148  80F8       9                SJMP AGAIN
```

Line 9 of the code above shows 80F8 for "SJMP AGAIN", which is a backward jump instruction. The 80H, located at address 148H, is the opcode for the SJMP, and F8H, located at address 149H, is the relative address. The address is relative to the next address location, which is 14AH. Therefore, adding 14AH + F8H = 142H gives the target address of the "AGAIN" label.

If the target address is beyond the –128 to +127 byte range, the assembler gives an error. All the conditional jumps are short jumps, as discussed next.

MOV dest-byte, source-byte

Function: Move byte variable
Flags: None

This copies a byte from the source location to the destination. There are 15 possible combinations for this instruction. They are as follows:

(a) Register A as the destination. This can have the following formats.
1. MOV A, #data
       MOV A,#25H   ; (A=25H)
2. MOV A, Rn
       MOV A,R3
3. MOV A, direct
       MOV A,30H ;A= data in 30H
4. MOV A, @Ri (i=0 or 1)
                 MOV A,@R0 ;A = data pointed to by R0
                 MOV A,@R1 ;A = data pointed to by R1
Notice that "MOV A,A" is invalid.

(b) Register A is the source. The destination can take the following forms.
    5. MOV Rn, A
    6. MOV direct, A
    7. MOV @Ri, A

(c) Rn is the destination.
    8. MOV Rn, #immediate
    9. MOV Rn, A
    10. MOV Rn, direct

(d) The destination is a direct address.
    11. MOV direct, #data
    12. MOV direct, @Ri
    13. MOV direct, A
    14. MOV direct, Rn
    15. MOV direct, direct

(d) Destination is an indirect address held by R0 or R1.
    16. MOV @Ri, #data
    17. MOV @Ri, A
    18. MOV @Ri, direct

MOV dest-bit, source-bit

Function: Move bit data

This MOV instruction copies the source bit to the destination bit. In this instruction, one of the operands must be the CY flag. Look at the following examples.

```
MOV  P1.2,C      ;copy carry bit to port bit P1.2
MOV  C,P2.5      ;copy port bit P2.5 to carry bit
```

MOV DPTR, #16-bit value

Function: Load data pointer
Flags: None

This instruction loads the 16-bit DPTR (data pointer) register with a 16-bit immediate value.

```
MOV  DPTR,#456FH         ;DPTR=456FH
MOV  DPTR,#MYDATA        ;load 16-bit address
                         ;assigned to MYDATA
```

Function:	Move code byte	
Flags:	None	

This instruction moves a byte of data located in program (code) ROM into register A. This allows us to put strings of data, such as look-up table elements, in the code space and read them into the CPU. The address of the desired byte in the code space (on-chip ROM) is formed by adding the original value of the accumulator to the 16-bit DPTR register.

Assume that an ASCII character string is stored in the on-chip ROM program memory starting at address 200H. Write a program to bring each character into the CPU and send it to P1 (port 1).

```
        ORG  100H
        MOV  DPTR,#200H      ;load data pointer
B1:     CLR  A               ;A=0
        MOVC A,@A+DPTR       ;move data at A+DPTR into A
        JZ   EXIT            ;exit if last (null) char
        MOV  P1,A            ;send character to P1
        INC  DPTR            ;next character
        SJMP B1              ;continue
EXIT:   ..


        ORG  200H
DATA:   DB   "The earth is but one country and"
        DB   "mankind its citizens","Baha'u'llah",0
        END
```

In the program above first A = 0 and then it is added to DPTR to form the address of the desired byte. After the MOVC instruction, register A has the character. Notice that the DPTR is incremented to point to the next character in the DATA table.

Look-up table SQUR has the squares of values between 0 and 9, and register R3 has the values of 0 to 9. Write a program to fetch the squares from the look-up table.

```
        MOV  DPTR,#SQUR      ;load pointer for table
        MOV  A,R3
        MOVC A,@A+DPTR

        ORG  100H
SQUR:   DB   0,1,4,9,16,25,36,49,64,81
```

Notice that the MOVC instruction transfers data from the internal ROM space of the 8051 into register A. This internal ROM space belongs to program (code) on-chip ROM of the 8051. To access off-chip memory, that is, memories connected externally, we use the MOVX instruction. See MOVX for further discussion.

MOVC   A, @A+PC

      Function: Move code byte
      Flags: None

This instruction moves a byte of data located in the program (code) area to A. The address of the desired byte of data is formed by adding the program counter register to the original value of the accumulator. Contrast this instruction with "MOVC A,@A+DPTR". Here the PC is used instead of DPTR to generate the data address.

Look-up table SQUR has the squares of values between 0 and 9, and register R3 has the values of 0 to 9. Write a program to fetch the squares from the table. Use the "MOVC A,@A+PC" instruction (this is a rewrite of an example of the previous instruction "MOVC A, @A+DPTR").

```
        MOV  A,R3
        INC  A
        MOVC A,@A+PC
        RET
SQUR:   DB   0,1,4,9,16,25,36,49,64,81
```

The following should be noted concerning the above code.

(a) The program counter, which is pointing to instruction RET, is added to register A to form the address of the desired data. In other words, the PC is incremented to the address of the next instruction before it is added to the original value of the accumulator.

(b) The role of "INC A" should be emphasized. We need instruction "INC A" to bypass the single byte of opcode belonging to the RET instruction.

(c) This method is preferable over "MOVC A,@A+DPTR" if we do not want to divide the program code space into two separate areas of code and data. As a result, we do not waste valuable on-chip code space located between the last byte of program (code) and the beginning of the data space where the look-up table is located.

MOVX   dest-byte, source-byte

Function: Move external
Flags: None

This instruction transfers data between external memory and register A. As discussed in Chapter 14, the 8051 has 64K bytes of data space in addition to the 64K bytes of code space. This data space must be connected externally. This instruction allows us to access externally connected memory. The address of external memory being accessed can be 16-bit or 8-bit as explained below.

(a) The 16-bit external memory address is held by the DPTR register.

```
MOVX  A,@DPTR
```

This moves into the accumulator a byte from external memory whose address is pointed to by DPTR. In other words, this brings data into the CPU (register A) from the off-chip memory of the 8051.

```
MOVX  @DPTR,A
```

This moves the contents of the accumulator to the external memory location, whose address is held by DPTR. In other words, this takes data from inside the CPU (register A) to memory outside the 8051.

(b) The 8-bit address of external memory is held by R0 or R1.

```
MOVX A,@Ri    ;where i = 0 or 1
```

This moves to the accumulator a byte from external memory, whose 8-bit address is pointed to by R0 (or R1 in MOVX A,@R1).

```
MOVX @Ri,A
```

This moves a byte from register A to an external memory location, whose 8-bit address is held by R0 (or R1 in MOVX @R1,A)
The 16-bit address version of this instruction is widely used to access external memory while the 8-bit version is used to access external I/O ports.

MUL AB

Function: Multiply $A \times B$
Flags: OV, CY

This multiplies an unsigned byte in A by an unsigned byte in register B. The result is placed in A and B where A has the lower byte and B has the higher byte.

```
        MOV  A,#5
        MOV  B,#7
        MUL  AB      ;A=35=23H, B=00

        MOV  A,#10
        MOV  B,#15
        MUL  AB      ;A=150=96H, B=00
```

This instruction always clears the CY flag; however, OV is changed according to the product. If the product is greater than FFH, OV = 1; otherwise, it is cleared (OV = 0).

```
        MOV  A,#25H
        MOV  B,#78H
        MUL  AB      ;A=58H, B=11H, CY=0, and OV=1
                     ;(25H x 78H = 1158H)

        MOV  A,#100
        MOV  B,#200
        MUL  AB      ;A=20H, B=4EH, OV=1, and CY=0
                     ;(100 x 200 = 20,000 = 4E20H)
```

NOP

Function: No operation
Flags: None

This performs no operation and execution continues with the next instruction. It is sometimes used for timing delays to waste clock cycles. This instruction only updates the program counter to point to the next instruction following NOP.

ORL dest-byte, source-byte

Function: Logical OR for byte variable
Flags: None

This performs a logical OR on the byte operands, bit by bit, and stores the result in the destination.

A	B	A OR B
0	0	0
0	1	1
1	0	1
1	1	1

```
        MOV   A,#39H    ;A=39H
        ORL   A,#09H    ;A=39H OR 09 (A=39H)
        39H   0011 1001
        09H   0000 1001
        39    0011 1001
```

```
MOV     A,#32H    ;A=32H
MOV     R4,#50H   ;R4=50H
ORL     A,R4      ;(A=72H)


32H     0011 0010
50H     0101 0000
72H     0111 0010
```

For the ORL instruction, there are a total of six addressing modes. In four of them, the accumulator must be the destination. They are as follows:

1. Immediate: ORL A, #data

    ```
    ORL A,#25H
    ```

2. Register: ORL A, Rx

    ```
    ORL A,R3
    ```

3. Direct: ORL A, direct

    ```
    ORL A, 30H ;OR A with data located in RAM 30H
    ```

4. Register-indirect: ORL A, @Rn

    ```
    ORL A,@R0  ;OR A with data pointed to by R0
    ```

In the next two addressing modes, the destination is a direct address (a RAM location or one of the SFR registers), while the source is either A or immediate data as shown below:

5. ORL direct, #data

    Assuming that RAM location 32H has the value 67H, find the contents of A after the following:

    ```
    ORL 32H,#44H  ;OR 44H with contents of RAM loc. 32H
    MOV A,32H      ;move content of RAM loc. 32H to A

    44H   0100 0100
    67H   0110 0111
    67H   0110 0111  Therefore, A will have 67H.
    ```

6. ORL direct, A

    Find the contents of B after the following:

    ```
    MOV B,#44H     ;B=44H
    MOV A,#67H     ;A=67H
    ORL 0F0H,A     ;OR A and B (B is at RAM F0H)
    ;After the operation B=67H.
    ```

Note: This cannot be used to modify data at input pins.

ORL   C, source-bit

Function: Logical OR for bit variables
Flags: CY

In this instruction, the carry flag bit is ORed with a source bit and the result is placed in the carry flag. Therefore, if the source bit is 1, CY is set; otherwise, the CY flag remains unchanged.

Set the carry flag if either P1.5 or ACC.2 is high.

```
MOV  C,P1.5      ;get P1.5 status
ORL  C,ACC.2
```

Write a program to clear A if P1.2 or P2.2 is high. Otherwise, make A = FFH.

```
        MOV  A,#FFH
        MOV  C,P1.2
        ORL  C,P2.2
        JNC  OVER
        CLR  A
OVER:
```

Another variation of this instruction involves ORing CY with the complement of the source bit. Its format is "ORL C,/bit". See the following example.

Clear A if P2.1 is high or P2.2 is low. Otherwise, make A = FFH.

```
        MOV  A,#0FFH
        MOV  C,P2.1      ;get a copy of P2.1 bit
        ORL  C,/P2.2     ;OR P2.1 with complement of P2.2
        JNC  OVER
        CLR  A
OVER:
```

POP   direct

Function: Pop from the stack
Flags: None

This copies the byte pointed to by stack pointer to the location whose direct address is indicated, and decrements SP by 1. Notice that this instruction supports only direct addressing mode. Therefore, instructions such as "POP A" or "POP R3" are illegal. Instead, we must write "POP 0E0H" where E0H is the RAM address belonging to register A and "POP 03" where 03 is the RAM address of R3 of bank 0.

PUSH direct

Function: Push onto the stack
Flags: None

This copies the indicated byte onto the stack and increments SP by 1. Notice that this instruction supports only direct addressing mode. Therefore, instructions such as "PUSH A" or "PUSH R3" are illegal. Instead, we must write "PUSH 0E0H" where E0H is the RAM address belonging to register A and "PUSH 03" where 03 is the RAM address of R3 of bank 0.

RET

Function: Return from subroutine
Flags: None

This instruction is used to return from a subroutine previously entered by instructions LCALL or ACALL. The top two bytes of the stack are popped into the program counter and program execution continues at this new address. After popping the top two bytes of the stack into the program counter, the stack pointer is decremented by 2.

RETI

Function: Return from interrupt
Flags: None

This is used at the end of an interrupt service routine (interrupt handler). The top two bytes of the stack are popped into the program counter and program execution continues at this new address. After popping the top two bytes of the stack into the program counter, the stack pointer is decremented by 2.

Notice that while the RET instruction is used at the end of a subroutine associated with the ACALL and LCALL instructions, IRET must be used for the interrupt service subroutines.

RL   A

Function: Rotate left the accumulator
Flags: None

This rotates the bits of A left. The bits rotated out of A are rotated back into A at the opposite end.

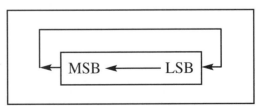

```
MOV A,#69H        ;A=01101001
RL  A             ;Now A=11010010
RL  A             ;Now A=10100101
```

RLC   A

Function: Rotate A left through carry
Flags: CY

This rotates the bits of the accumulator left. The bits rotated out of register A are rotated into CY, and the CY bit is rotated into the opposite end of the accumulator.

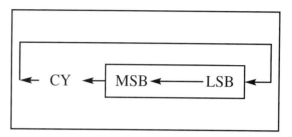

```
CLR C             ;CY=0
MOV A,#99H        ;A=10011001
RLC A             ;Now A=00110010 and CY=1
RLC A             ;Now A=01100101 and CY=0
```

RR   A

Function: Rotate A right
Flags: None

This rotates the bits of register A right. The bits rotated out of A are rotated back into A at the opposite end.

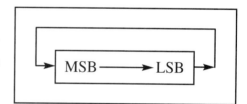

```
MOV A,#66H        ;A=01100110
RR  A             ;Now A=00110011
RR  A             ;Now A=10011001
```

RRC   A

Function: Rotate A right through carry
Flags: CY

This rotates the bits of the accumulator right. The bits rotated out of register A are rotated into CY and the CY bit is rotated into the opposite end of the accumulator.

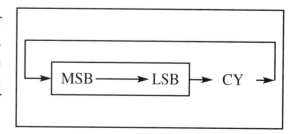

```
SETB  C              ;CY=1
MOV  A,#99H          ;A=10011001
RRC  A               ;Now A=11001100 and CY=1
SETB  C              ;CY=1
RRC  A               ;Now A=11100110 and CY=0
```

SETB bit

Function: Set bit

This sets high the indicated bit. The bit can be the carry or any directly addressable bit of a port, register, or RAM location.

```
SETB  P1.3           ;P1.3=1
SETB  P2.6           ;P2.6=1
SETB  ACC.6          ;ACC.6=1
SETB  05             ;set high D5 of RAM loc. 20H
SETB  C              ;Set Carry Flag CY=1
```

SJMP

See LJMP and SJMP.

SUBB A, source byte

Function: Subtract with borrow
Flags: OV, AC, CY

This subtracts the source byte and the carry flag from the accumulator and puts the result in the accumulator. The steps for subtraction performed by the internal hardware of the CPU are as follows:

1. Take the 2's complement of the source byte.
2. Add this to register A.
3. Invert the carry.

This instruction sets the carry flag according to the following:

	CY	
dest > source	0	the result is positive
dest = source	0	the result is 0
dest < source	1	the result is negative in 2's complement

Notice that there is no SUB instruction in the 8051. Therefore, we perform the SUB instruction by making CY = 0 and then using SUBB: A = (A − byte − CY).

```
        MOV  A,#45H
        CLR  C
        SUBB A,#23H     ;45H-23H-0=22H
```

Addressing modes

The following four addressing modes are supported for the SUBB.

1. Immediate: SUBB A, #data

```
            SUBB A,#25H     ;A=A-25H-CY
```

2. Register   SUBB A, Rn

```
            SUBB A,R3       ;A=A-R3-CY
```

3. Direct: SUBB A, direct

```
            SUBB A,30H      ;A - data at (30H) - CY
```

4. Register-indirect: SUBB A, @Rn

```
            SUBB A,@R0      ;A - data at (R0) - CY
```

SWAP A

        Function: Swap nibbles within the accumulator
        Flags: None

The SWAP instruction interchanges the lower nibble (D0–D3) with the upper nibble (D4–D7) inside register A.

```
        MOV A,#59H      ;A=59H (0101 1001 in binary)
        SWAP A          ;A=95H (1001 0101 in binary)
```

XCH A, byte

        Function: Exchange A with a byte variable
        Flags: None

This instruction swaps the contents of register A and the source byte. The source byte can be any register or RAM location.

```
        MOV A,#65H      ;A=65H
        MOV R2,#97H     ;R2=97H
        XCH A,R2        ;now A=97H and R2=65H
```

APPENDIX A: 8051 INSTRUCTIONS, TIMING, AND REGISTERS   571

For the "XCH A, byte" instruction, there are a total of three addressing modes. They are as follows:

1. Register: XCH A, Rn

       XCH A,R3

2. Direct: XCH A, direct

       XCH A,40H ;exchange A with data in RAM loc.40H

3. Register-indirect: XCH A, @Rn

       XCH A,@R0   ;XCH A with data pointed to by R0
       XCH A,@R1   ;XCH A with data pointed to by R1

XCHD A, @Ri

Function:	Exchange digits
Flags:	None

The XCHD instruction exchanges only the lower nibble of A with the lower nibble of the RAM location pointed to by Ri while leaving the upper nibbles in both places intact.

Assuming RAM location 40H has the value 97H, find its contents after the following instructions.

```
;40H= (97H)
MOV A,#12H      ;A=12H (0001 0010 binary)
MOV R1,#40H     ;R1=40H, load pointer
XCHD A,@R1      ;exchange the lower nibble of
                ;A and RAM location 40H
```

After execution of the XCHD instruction, we have A = 17H and RAM location 40H has 92H.

XRL   dest-byte, source-byte

Function:	Logical exclusive-OR for byte variables
Flags:	None

This performs a logical exclusive-OR on the operands, bit by bit, storing the result in the destination.

A	B	A XOR B
0	0	0
0	1	1
1	0	1
1	1	0

```
MOV     A,#39H   ;A=39H
XRL     A,#09H   ;A=39H ORed with 09

39H     0011 1001
09H     0000 1001
30      0011 0000
```

```
MOV    A,#32H    ;A=32H
MOV    R4,#50H   ;R4=50H
XRL    A,R4      ;(A=62H)


32H    0011 0010
50H    0101 0000
62H    0110 0010
```

For the XRL instruction, there are a total of six addressing modes. In four of them, the accumulator must be the destination. They are as follows:

1. Immediate: XRL A, #data

   ```
   XRL  A,#25H
   ```

2. Register: XRL A, Rn

   ```
   XRL  A,R3
   ```

3. Direct: XRL A, direct

   ```
   XRL A,30H  ;XRL A with data in RAM location 30H
   ```

4. Register-indirect: XRL A,@Rn

   ```
   XRL A,@R0 ;XRL A with data pointed to by R0
   ```

In the next two addressing modes, the destination is a direct address (a RAM location or one of the SFR registers), while the source is either A or immediate data as shown below:

5. XRL direct, #data
   Assume that RAM location 32H has the value 67H.
   Find the contents of A after execution of the following code.

   ```
   XRL 32H,#44H
   MOV A,32H ;move content of RAM loc. 32H to A


   44H   0100 0100
   67H   0110 0111
   23H   0010 0011 Therefore A will have 23H.
   ```

6. XRL direct, A

Find the contents of B after the following:

```
MOV B,#44H     ;B=44H
MOV A,#67H     ;A=67H
XRL 0F0H,A     ;OR register A and B
;(register B is located at RAM location F0H)
;after the operation B=23H
```

Note: We cannot use this instruction to exclusive-OR the data at the input port.

Table A-1. 8051 Instruction Set Summary

Mnemonic		Byte	Machine Cycle
Arithmetic Operations			
ADD	A,Rn	1	1
ADD	A,direct	2	1
ADD	A,@Ri	1	1
ADD	A,#data	2	1
ADDC	A,Rn	1	1
ADDC	A,direct	2	1
ADDC	A,@Ri	1	1
ADDC	A,#data	2	1
SUBB	A,Rn	1	1
SUBB	A,direct	2	1
SUBB	A,@Ri	1	1
SUBB	A,#data	2	1
INC	A	1	1
INC	Rn	1	1
INC	direct	2	1
INC	@Ri	1	1
DEC	A	1	1
DEC	Rn	1	1
DEC	direct	2	1
DEC	@Ri	1	1
INC	DPTR	1	2
MUL	AB	1	4
DIV	AB	1	4
DA	A	1	1
Logical Operations			
ANL	A,Rn	1	1
ANL	A,direct	2	1
ANL	A,@Ri	1	1
ANL	A,#data	2	1
ANL	direct,A	2	1
ANL	direct,#data	3	2
ORL	A,Rn	1	1
ORL	A,direct	2	1
ORL	A,@Ri	1	1
ORL	A,#data	2	1
ORL	direct,A	2	1
ORL	direct,#data	3	2
XRL	A,Rn	1	1
XRL	A,direct	2	1
XRL	A,@Ri	1	1
XRL	A,#data	2	1
XRL	direct,A	2	1
XRL	direct,#data	3	2
CLR	A	1	1
CPL	A	1	1
RL	A	1	1
RLC	A	1	1
RR	A	1	1
RRC	A	1	1
SWAP	A	1	1

Mnemonic		Byte	Machine Cycle
Data Transfer			
MOV	A,Rn	1	1
MOV	A,direct	2	1
MOV	A,@Ri	1	1
MOV	A,#data	2	1
MOV	Rn,A	1	1
MOV	Rn,direct	2	2
MOV	Rn,#data	2	1
MOV	direct,A	2	1
MOV	direct,Rn	2	2
MOV	direct,direct	3	2
MOV	direct,@Ri	2	2
MOV	direct,#data	3	2
MOV	@Ri,A	1	1
MOV	@Ri,direct	2	2
MOV	@Ri,#data	2	1
MOV	DPTR,#data16	3	2
MOVX	A,@Ri	1	2
MOVX	A,@DPTR	1	2
MOVX	@Ri,A	1	2
MOV	@DPTR,A	1	2
PUSH	direct	2	2
POP	direct	2	2
XCH	A,Rn	1	1
XCH	A,direct	2	1
XCH	A,@Ri	1	1
XCHD	A,@Ri	1	1
Boolean Variable Manipulation			
CLR	C	1	1
CLR	bit	2	1
SETB	C	1	1
SETB	bit	2	1
CPL	C	1	1
CPL	bit	2	1
ANL	C,bit	2	2
ANL	C,/bit	2	2
ORL	C,bit	2	2
ORL	C,/bit	2	2
MOV	C,bit	2	1
MOV	bit,C	2	2
JC	rel	2	2
JNC	rel	2	2
JB	bit,rel	3	2
JNB	bit,rel	3	2
JBC	bit,rel	3	2

(continued)

Mnemonic	Byte	Machine Cycle
Program Branching		
ACALL addr11	2	2
LCALL addr16	3	2
RET	1	2
RETI	1	2
AJMP addr11	2	2
LJMP addr16	3	2
SJMP rel	2	2
JMP @A+DPTR	1	2
JZ rel	2	2
(continued)		

Mnemonic	Byte	Machine Cycle
Program Branching *(continued)*		
JNZ rel	2	2
CJNE A,direct,rel	3	2
CJNE A,#data,rel	3	2
CJNE Rn,#data,rel	3	2
CJNE @Ri,#data,rel	3	2
DJNZ Rn,rel	2	2
DJNZ direct,rel	3	2
NOP	1	1

A.2: 8051 REGISTERS

Table A-2. Special Function Register (SFR) Addresses

Symbol	Name	Address
ACC*	Accumulator	0E0H
B*	B register	0F0H
PSW*	Program status word	0D0H
SP	Stack pointer	81H
DPTR	Data pointer 2 bytes	
DPL	Low byte	82H
DPH	High byte	83H
P0*	Port 0	80H
P1*	Port 1	90H
P2*	Port 2	0A0H
P3*	Port 3	0B0H
IP*	Interrupt priority control	0B8H
IE*	Interrupt enable control	0A8H
TMOD	Timer/counter mode control	89H
TCON*	Timer/counter control	88H
T2CON*	Timer/counter 2 control	0C8H
T2MOD	Timer/counter mode control	0C9H
TH0	Timer/counter 0 high byte	8CH
TL0	Timer/counter 0 low byte	8AH
TH1	Timer/counter 1 high byte	8DH
TL1	Timer/counter 1 low byte	8BH
TH2	Timer/counter 2 high byte	0CDH
TL2	Timer/counter 2 low byte	0CCH
RCAP2H	T/C 2 capture register high byte	0CBH
RCAP2L	T/C 2 capture register low byte	0CAH
SCON*	Serial control	98H
SBUF	Serial data buffer	99H
PCON	Power control	87H

* Bit-addressable

Byte address | Bit address

Byte address				Bit address					Register
FF									
F0	F7	F6	F5	F4	F3	F2	F1	F0	B
E0	E7	E6	E5	E4	E3	E2	E1	E0	ACC
D0	D7	D6	D5	D4	D3	D2	D1	D0	PSW
B8	--	--	--	BC	BB	BA	B9	B8	IP
B0	B7	B6	B5	B4	B3	B2	B1	B0	P3
A8	AF	--	--	AC	AB	AA	A9	A8	IE
A0	A7	A6	A5	A4	A3	A2	A1	A0	P2
99	Not bit-addressable								SBUF
98	9F	9E	9D	9C	9B	9A	99	98	SCON
90	97	96	95	94	93	92	91	90	P1
8D	Not bit-addressable								TH1
8C	Not bit-addressable								TH0
8B	Not bit-addressable								TL1
8A	Not bit-addressable								TL0
89	Not bit-addressable								TMOD
88	8F	8E	8D	8C	8B	8A	89	88	TCON
87	Not bit-addressable								PCON
83	Not bit-addressable								DPH
82	Not bit-addressable								DPL
81	Not bit-addressable								SP
80	87	86	85	84	83	82	81	80	P0

Special Function Registers

Figure A-1. SFR RAM Address (Byte and Bit)

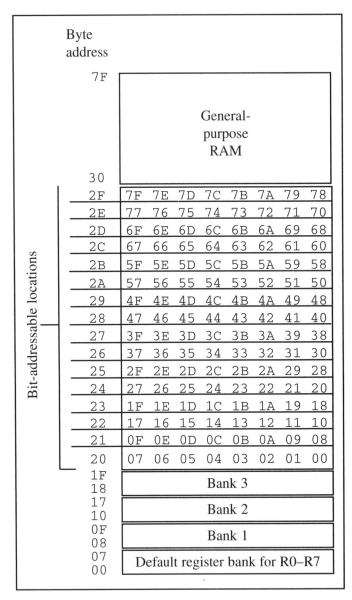

Figure A-2. 128 Bytes of Internal RAM

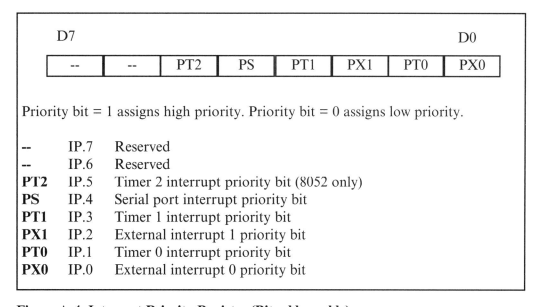

D7							D0
EA	--	ET2	ES	ET1	EX1	ET0	EX0

EA   IE.7   Disables all interrupts. If EA = 0, no interrupt is acknowledged. If EA = 1, each interrupt source is individually enabled or disabled by setting or clearing its enable bit.

--   IE.6   Not implemented, reserved for future use.*

ET2   IE.5   Enables or disables timer 2 overflow or capture interrupt (8952).

ES   IE.4   Enables or disables the serial port interrupt.

ET1   IE.3   Enables or disables timer 1 overflow interrupt.

EX1   IE.2   Enables or disables external interrupt 1.

ET0   IE.1   Enables or disables timer 0 overflow interrupt.

EX0   IE.0   Enables or disables external interrupt 0.

Figure A-3. IE (Interrupt Enable) Register
*User software should not write 1s to reserved bits. These bits may be used in future flash microprocessors to invoke new features.

D7							D0
--	--	PT2	PS	PT1	PX1	PT0	PX0

Priority bit = 1 assigns high priority. Priority bit = 0 assigns low priority.

--   IP.7   Reserved
--   IP.6   Reserved
PT2   IP.5   Timer 2 interrupt priority bit (8052 only)
PS   IP.4   Serial port interrupt priority bit
PT1   IP.3   Timer 1 interrupt priority bit
PX1   IP.2   External interrupt 1 priority bit
PT0   IP.1   Timer 0 interrupt priority bit
PX0   IP.0   External interrupt 0 priority bit

Figure A-4. Interrupt Priority Register (Bit-addressable)
Note: User software should never write 1s to unimplemented bits, since they may be used in future products.

SMOD	--	--	--	GF1	GF0	PD	IDL

Figure A-5. PCON Register (Not Bit-addressable)

Finding the TH_1 value for various baud rates:

SMOD = 0 (default on reset)

$$TH_1 = 256 - \frac{\text{Crystal frequency}}{384 \times \text{Baud rate}}$$

SMOD = 1

$$TH_1 = 256 - \frac{\text{Crystal frequency}}{192 \times \text{Baud rate}}$$

CY	AC	F0	RS1	RS0	OV	--	P

CY	PSW.7	Carry flag
AC	PSW.6	Auxiliary carry flag
F0	PSW.5	Available to the user for general purposes
RS1	PSW.4	Register bank selector bit 1
RS0	PSW.3	Register bank selector bit 0
OV	PSW.2	Overflow flag
--	PSW.1	User-definable bit
P	PSW.0	Parity flag. Set/cleared by hardware each instruction cycle to indicate an odd/even number of 1 bits in the accumulator

RS1	RS0	Register Bank	Address
0	0	0	00H–07H
0	1	1	08H–0FH
1	0	2	10H–17H
1	1	3	18H–1FH

Figure A-6. Bits of the PSW Register (Bit-addressable)

SM0	SM1	SM2	REN	TB8	RB8	TI	RI

SM0	SCON.7	Serial port mode specifier.
SM1	SCON.6	Serial port mode specifier.
SM2	SCON.5	Used for multiprocessor communication. (Make it 0.)
REN	SCON.4	Set/cleared by software to enable/disable reception.
TB8	SCON.3	Not widely used.
RB8	SCON.2	Not widely used.
TI	SCON.1	Transmit interrupt flag. Set by hardware at the beginning of the stop bit in mode 1. Must be cleared by software.
RI	SCON.0	Receive interrupt flag. Set by hardware halfway through the stop bit time in mode 1. Must be cleared by software.

Figure A-7. SCON Serial Port Control Register (Bit-addressable)
Note: Make SM2, TB8, and RB8 = 0.

Finding the TH_1 value for various baud rates:

SMOD = 0 (default on reset)

$$TH_1 = 256 - \frac{\text{Crystal frequency}}{384 \times \text{Baud rate}}$$

SMOD = 1

$$TH_1 = 256 - \frac{\text{Crystal frequency}}{192 \times \text{Baud rate}}$$

(MSB)   (LSB)

GATE	C/T	M1	M0	GATE	C/T	M1	M0
Timer 1				Timer 0			

GATE	Gating control when set. Timer/counter is enabled only when the INTx pin is high and the TRx control pin is set. When cleared, the timer is enabled whenever the TRx control bit is set.
C/T	Timer or counter selected cleared for timer operation (input from internal system clock). Set for counter operation (input from Tx input pin).
M1	Mode bit 1
M0	Mode bit 0

M1	**M0**	**Mode**	**Operating Mode**
0	0	0	13-bit timer mode
			8-bit timer/counter THx with TLx as 5-bit prescaler
0	1	1	16-bit timer mode
			16-bit timer/counters THx and TLx are cascaded; there is no prescaler.
1	0	2	8-bit auto-reload
			8-bit auto-reload timer/counter; THx holds a value that is to be reloaded into TLx each time it overflows.
1	1	3	Split timer mode

Figure A-8. TMOD Register (Not Bit-addressable)

D7							D0
TF1	TR1	TF0	TR0	IE1	IT1	IE0	IT0

TF1   TCON.7   Timer 1 overflow flag. Set by hardware when timer/ counter 1 overflows. Cleared by hardware as the processor vectors to the interrupt service routine.

TR1   TCON.6   Timer 1 run control bit. Set/cleared by software to turn timer/counter 1 on/off.

TF0   TCON.5   Timer 0 overflow flag. Set by hardware when timer/ counter 0 overflows. Cleared by hardware as the processor vectors to the service routine.

TR0   TCON.4   Timer 0 run control bit. Set/cleared by software to turn timer/counter 0 on/off.

IE1   TCON.3   External interrupt 1 edge flag. Set by CPU when the external interrupt edge (H-to-L transition) is detected. Cleared by CPU when the interrupt is processed. *Note:* This flag does not latch low-level triggered interrupts.

IT1   TCON.2   Interrupt 1 type control bit. Set/cleared by software to specify falling edge/low-level triggered external interrupt.

IE0   TCON.1   External interrupt 0 edge flag. Set by CPU when external interrupt (H-to-L transition) edge is detected. Cleared by CPU when interrupt is processed. *Note:* This flag does not latch low-level triggered interrupts.

IT0   TCON.0   Interrupt 0 type control bit. Set/cleared by software to specify falling edge/low-level triggered external interrupt.

Figure A-9. TCON (Timer/Counter) Register (Bit-addressable)

APPENDIX B

BASICS OF WIRE WRAPPING*

OVERVIEW

This appendix shows the basics of wire wrapping.

*Thanks to Shannon Looper and Greg Boyle for their assistance on this appendix.

Note: For this tutorial appendix, you will need the following:
Wire-wrapping tool (Radio Shack part number 276-1570)
30-gauge (30-AWG) wire for wire wrapping

The following describes the basics of wire wrapping.

1. There are several different types of wire-wrap tools available. The best one is available from Radio Shack for less than $10. The part number for Radio Shack is 276-1570. This tool combines the wrap and unwrap functions in the same end of the tool and includes a separate stripper. We found this to be much easier to use than the tools that combined all these features on one two-ended shaft. There are also wire-wrap guns, which are, of course, more expensive.

2. Wire-wrapping wire is available prestripped in various lengths or in bulk on a spool. The prestripped wire is usually more expensive and you are restricted to the different wire lengths you can afford to buy. Bulk wire can be cut to any length you wish, which allows each wire to be custom fit.

3. Several different types of wire-wrap boards are available. These are usually called perfboards or wire-wrap boards. These types of boards are sold at many electronics stores (such as Radio Shack). The best type of board has plating around the holes on the bottom of the board. These boards are better because the sockets and pins can be soldered to the board, which makes the circuit more mechanically stable.

4. Choose a board that is large enough to accommodate all the parts in your design with room to spare so that the wiring does not become too cluttered. If you wish to expand your project in the future, you should be sure to include enough room on the original board for the complete circuit. Also, if possible, the layout of the IC on the board needs to be done such that signals go from left to right just like the schematics.

5. To make the wiring easier and to keep pressure off the pins, install one standoff on each corner of the board. You may also wish to put standoffs on the top of the board to add stability when the board is on its back.

6. For power hook-up, use some type of standard binding post. Solder a few single wire-wrap pins to each power post to make circuit connections (to at least one pin for each IC in the circuit).

7. To further reduce problems with power, each IC must have its own connection to the main power of the board. If your perfboard does not have built-in power buses, run a separate power and ground wire from each IC to the main power. In other words, *do not* daisy chain (chip-to-chip connection is called daisy chain) power connections, as each connection

down the line will have more wire and more resistance to get power through. However, daisy chaining is acceptable for other connections such as data, address, and control buses.

8. You must use wire-wrap sockets. These sockets have long square pins whose edges will cut into the wire as it is wrapped around the pin.

9. Wire wrapping will not work on round legs. If you need to wrap to components, such as capacitors, that have round legs, you must also solder these connections. The best way to connect single components is to install individual wire-wrap pins into the board and then solder the components to the pins. An alternate method is to use an empty IC socket to hold small components such as resistors and wrap them to the socket.

10. The wire should be stripped about 1 inch. This will allow 7 to 10 turns for each connection. The first turn or turn-and-a-half should be insulated. This prevents stripped wire from coming in contact with other pins. This can be accomplished by inserting the wire as far as it will go into the tool before making the connection.

11. Try to keep wire lengths to a minimum. This prevents the circuit from looking like a bird nest. Be neat and use color coding as much as possible. Use only red wires for V_{cc} and black wires for ground connections. Also use different colors for data, address, and control signal connections. These suggestions will make troubleshooting much easier.

12. It is standard practice to connect all power lines first and check them for continuity. This will eliminate trouble later on.

13. It's also a good idea to mark the pin orientation on the bottom of the board. Plastic templates are available with pin numbers preprinted on them specifically for this purpose or you can make your own from paper. Forgetting to reverse pin order when looking at the bottom of the board is a very common mistake when wire wrapping circuits.

14. To prevent damage to your circuit, place a diode (such as IN5338) in reverse bias across the power supply. If the power gets hooked up backwards, the diode will be forward biased and will act as a short, keeping the reversed voltage from your circuit.

15. In digital circuits, there can be a problem with current demand on the power supply. To filter the noise on the power supply, a 100 µF electrolytic capacitor and a 0.1 µF monolithic capacitor are connected from V_{cc} to ground, in parallel with each other, at the entry point of the power supply to the board. These two together will filter both the high- and the low-frequency noises. Instead of using two capacitors in parallel, you can use a single 20–100 µF tantalum capacitor. Remember that the long lead is the positive one.

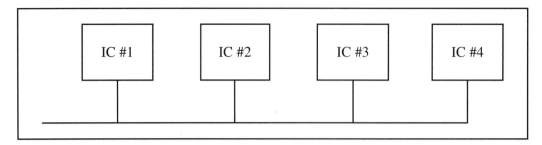

Figure B-1. Daisy Chain Connection (Not Recommended for Power Lines)

16. To filter the transient current, use a 0.1 μF monolithic capacitor for each IC. Place the 0.1 μF monolithic capacitor between V_{cc} and ground of each IC. Make sure the leads are as short as possible.

APPENDIX C

IC TECHNOLOGY AND SYSTEM DESIGN ISSUES

OVERVIEW

This appendix provides an overview of IC technology and 8051 interfacing. In addition, we look at the microprocessor-based system as a whole and examine some general issues in system design.

First, in Section C.1, we provide an overview of IC technology. Then, in Section C.2, the internal details of 8051 I/O ports and interfacing are discussed. Section C.3 examines system design issues.

C.1: OVERVIEW OF IC TECHNOLOGY

In this section, we examine IC technology, and discuss some major developments in advanced logic families. Since this is an overview, it is assumed that the reader is familiar with logic families on the level presented in basic digital electronics books.

Transistors

The transistor was invented in 1947 by three scientists at Bell Laboratory. In the 1950s, transistors replaced vacuum tubes in many electronics systems, including computers. It was not until 1959 that the first integrated circuit was successfully fabricated and tested by Jack Kilby of Texas Instruments. Prior to the invention of the IC, the use of transistors, along with other discrete components such as capacitors and resistors, was common in computer design. Early transistors were made of germanium, which was later abandoned in favor of silicon. This was due to the fact that the slightest rise in temperature resulted in massive current flows in germanium-based transistors. In semiconductor terms, it is because the band gap of germanium is much smaller than that of silicon, resulting in a massive flow of electrons from the valence band to the conduction band when the temperature rises even slightly. By the late 1960s and early 1970s, the use of the silicon-based IC was widespread in mainframes and minicomputers. Transistors and ICs at first were based on P-type materials. Later on, due to the fact that the speed of electrons is much higher (about two and a half times) than the speed of holes, N-type devices replaced P-type devices. By the mid-1970s, NPN and NMOS transistors had replaced the slower PNP and PMOS transistors in every sector of the electronics industry, including the design of microprocessors and computers. Since the early 1980s, CMOS (complementary MOS) has become the dominant technology of IC design. Next, we provide an overview of differences between MOS and bipolar transistors. See Figure C-1.

MOS versus bipolar transistors

There are two types of transistors: bipolar and MOS (metal-oxide semiconductor). Both have three leads. In bipolar transistors, the three leads are

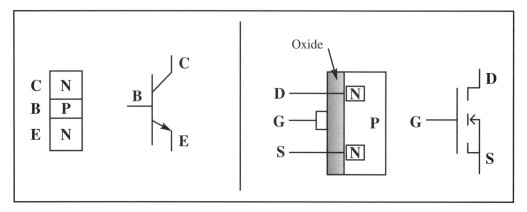

Figure C-1. Bipolar versus MOS Transistors

referred to as the *emitter*, *base*, and *collector*, while in MOS transistors they are named *source*, *gate*, and *drain*. In bipolar transistors, the carrier flows from the emitter to the collector, and the base is used as a flow controller. In MOS transistors, the carrier flows from the source to the drain, and the gate is used as a flow controller. In NPN-type bipolar transistors, the electron carrier leaving the emitter must overcome two voltage barriers before it reaches the collector (see Figure C-1). One is the N-P junction of the emitter-base and the other is the P-N junction of the base-collector. The voltage barrier of the base-collector is the most difficult one for the electrons to overcome (since it is reverse-biased) and it causes the most power dissipation. This led to the design of the unipolar-type transistor called MOS. In N-channel MOS transistors, the electrons leave the source and reach the drain without going through any voltage barrier. The absence of any voltage barrier in the path of the carrier is one reason why MOS dissipates much less power than bipolar transistors. The low power dissipation of MOS allows millions of transistors to fit on a single IC chip. In today's technology, putting 10 million transistors into an IC is common, and it is all because of MOS technology. Without the MOS transistor, the advent of desktop personal computers would not have been possible, at least not so soon. The bipolar transistors in both the mainframes and mini-computers of the 1960s and 1970s were bulky and required expensive cooling systems and large rooms. MOS transistors do have one major drawback: They are slower than bipolar transistors. This is due partly to the gate capacitance of the MOS transistor. For a MOS to be turned on, the input capacitor of the gate takes time to charge up to the turn-on (threshold) voltage, leading to a longer propagation delay.

Overview of logic families

Logic families are judged according to (1) speed, (2) power dissipation, (3) noise immunity, (4) input/output interface compatibility, and (5) cost. Desirable qualities are high speed, low power dissipation, and high noise immunity (since it prevents the occurrence of false logic signals during switching transition). In interfacing logic families, the more inputs that can be driven by a single output, the better. This means that high-driving-capability outputs are desired. This, plus the fact that the input and output voltage levels of MOS and bipolar transistors are not compatible mean that one must be concerned with the ability of one logic family to drive the other one. In terms of the cost of a given logic family, it is high during the early years of its introduction but declines as its production and use rise.

The case of inverters

As an example of logic gates, we look at a simple inverter. In a one-transistor inverter, the transistor plays the role of a switch, and R is the pull-up resistor. See Figure C-2. However, for this inverter to work most effectively in digital circuits, the R value must be high when the transistor is "on" to limit the current flow from V_{cc} to ground in order to have low

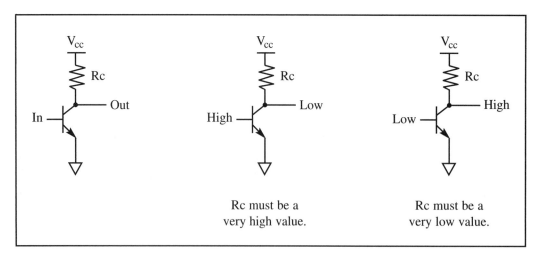

Figure C-2. One-Transistor Inverter with Pull-up Resistor

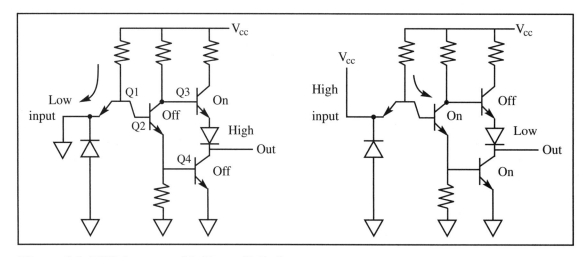

Figure C-3. TTL Inverter with Totem-Pole Output

power dissipation (P = VI, where V = 5 V). In other words, the lower the I, the lower the power dissipation. On the other hand, when the transistor is "off," R must be a small value to limit the voltage drop across R, thereby making sure that V_{OUT} is close to V_{cc}. This is a contradictory demand on R. This is one reason that logic gate designers use active components (transistors) instead of passive components (resistors) to implement the pull-up resistor R.

The case of a TTL inverter with totem-pole output is shown in Figure C-3. Here, Q3 plays the role of a pull-up resistor.

CMOS inverter

In the case of CMOS-based logic gates, PMOS and NMOS are used to construct a CMOS (complementary MOS) inverter, as shown in Figure C-4. In CMOS inverters, when the PMOS transistor is off, it provides a very high

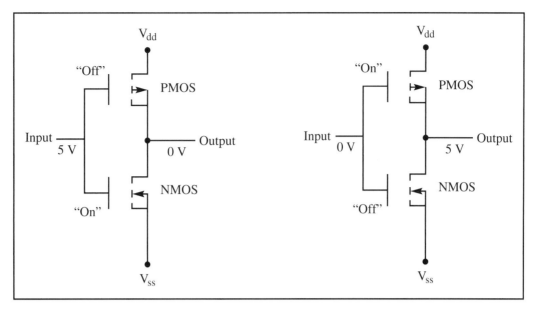

Figure C-4. CMOS Inverter

impedance path, making leakage current almost zero (about 10 nA); when the PMOS is on, it provides a low resistance on the path of V_{DD} to load. Since the speed of the hole is slower than that of the electron, the PMOS transistor is wider to compensate for this disparity; therefore, PMOS transistors take more space than NMOS transistors in the CMOS gates. At the end of this section, we will see an open-collector gate in which the pull-up resistor is provided externally, thereby allowing system designers to choose the value of the pull-up resistor.

Input/output characteristics of some logic families

In 1968, the first logic family made of bipolar transistors was marketed. It was commonly referred to as the standard TTL (transistor-transistor logic) family. The first MOS-based logic family, the CD4000/74C series, was marketed in 1970. The addition of the Schottky diode to the base-collector of bipolar transistors in the early 1970s gave rise to the S family. The Schottky diode shortens the propagation delay of the TTL family by preventing the collector from going into what is called deep saturation. Table C-1 lists major characteristics of some logic families. In Table C-1, note that as the CMOS circuit's operating frequency rises, the power dissipation also increases. This is not the case for bipolar-based TTL.

History of logic families

Early logic families and microprocessors required both positive and negative power voltages. In the mid-1970s, 5 V V_{cc} became standard. In the late 1970s, advances in IC technology allowed combining the speed and drive of the S family with the lower power of LS to form a new logic family called FAST

Table C-1. Characteristics of Some Logic Families

Characteristic	STD TTL	LSTTL	ALSTTL	HCMOS
V_{cc}	5 V	5 V	5 V	5 V
V_{IH}	2.0 V	2.0 V	2.0 V	3.15 V
V_{IL}	0.8 V	0.8 V	0.8 V	1.1 V
V_{OH}	2.4 V	2.7 V	2.7 V	3.7 V
V_{OL}	0.4 V	0.5 V	0.4 V	0.4 V
I_{IL}	–1.6 mA	–0.36 mA	–0.2 mA	–1 µA
I_{IH}	40 µA	20 µA	20 µA	1 µA
I_{OL}	16 mA	8 mA	4 mA	4 mA
I_{OH}	–400 µA	–400 µA	–400 µA	4 mA
Propagation delay	10 ns	9.5 ns	4 ns	9 ns
Static power dissipation (f = 0)	10 mW	2 mW	1 mW	0.0025 nW
Dynamic power dissipation at f = 100 kHz	10 mW	2 mW	1 mW	0.17 mW

(Fairchild Advanced Schottky TTL). In 1985, AC/ACT (Advanced CMOS Technology), a much higher speed version of HCMOS, was introduced. With the introduction of FCT (Fast CMOS Technology) in 1986, the speed gap between CMOS and TTL was at last closed. Since FCT is the CMOS version of FAST, it has the low power consumption of CMOS but the speed is comparable with TTL. Table C-2 provides an overview of logic families up to FCT.

Table C-2. Logic Family Overview

Product	Year Introduced	Speed (ns)	Static Supply Current (mA)	High/Low Family Drive (mA)
Std TTL	1968	40	30	–2/32
CD4K/74C	1970	70	0.3	–0.48/6.4
LS/S	1971	18	54	–15/24
HC/HCT	1977	25	0.08	–6/–6
FAST	1978	6.5	90	–15/64
AS	1980	6.2	90	–15/64
ALS	1980	10	27	–15/64
AC/ACT	1985	10	0.08	–24/24
FCT	1986	6.5	1.5	–15/64

Source: Reprinted by permission of Electronic Design Magazine, c. 1991.

Recent advances in logic families

As the speed of high-performance microprocessors reached 25 MHz, it shortened the CPU's cycle time, leaving less time for the path delay. Designers normally allocate no more than 25% of a CPU's cycle time budget to path delay. Following this rule means that there must be a corresponding decline in the propagation delay of logic families used in the address and data path as the system frequency is increased. In recent years, many semiconductor manufacturers have responded to this need by providing logic families that have high speed, low noise, and high drive I/O. Table C-3 provides the characteristics of high-performance logic families introduced in recent years. ACQ/ACTQ are the second-generation advanced CMOS (ACMOS) with much lower noise. While ACQ has the CMOS input level, ACTQ is equipped with TTL-level input. The FCTx and FCTx-T are second-generation FCT with much higher speed. The "x" in the FCTx and FCTx-T refers to various speed grades, such as A, B, and C, where A means low speed and C means high speed. For designers who are well versed in using the FAST logic family, FASTr is an ideal choice since it is faster than FAST, has higher driving capability (I_{OL}, I_{OH}), and produces much lower noise than FAST. At the time of this writing, next to ECL and gallium arsenide logic gates, FASTr was the fastest logic family in the market (with the 5 V V_{cc}), but the power consumption was high relative to other logic families, as shown in Table C-3. The combining of high-speed bipolar TTL and the low power consumption of CMOS has given birth to what is called BICMOS. Although BICMOS seems to be the future trend in IC design, at this time it is expensive due to extra steps required in BICMOS IC fabrication, but in some cases there is no other choice. (e.g., Intel's Pentium microprocessor, a BICMOS product, had to use high-speed bipolar transistors to speed up some of the internal functions.) Table C-3 provides advanced logic characteristics. The "x" is for different speeds designated as A, B, and C. A is the slowest one, while C is the fastest one. This data is for the 74244 buffer.

Table C-3. Advanced Logic General Characteristics

Family	Year	Number Suppliers	Tech Base	I/O Level	Speed (ns)	Static Current	I_{OH}/I_{OL}
ACQ	1989	2	CMOS	CMOS/CMOS	6.0	80 μA	−24/24 mA
ACTQ	1989	2	CMOS	TTL/CMOS	7.5	80 μA	−24/24 mA
FCTx	1987	3	CMOS	TTL/CMOS	4.1 - 4.8	1.5 mA	−15/64 mA
FCTxT	1990	2	CMOS	TTL/TTL	4.1 - 4.8	1.5 mA	−15/64 mA
FASTr	1990	1	Bipolar	TTL/TTL	3.9	50 mA	−15/64 mA
BCT	1987	2	BICMOS	TTL/TTL	5.5	10 mA	−15/64 mA

Source: Reprinted by permission of Electronic Design Magazine, c. 1991.

Since the late 1970s, the use of a +5 V power supply has become standard in all microprocessors and microprocessors. To reduce power consumption, 3.3 V V_{cc} is being embraced by many designers. The lowering of V_{cc} to 3.3 V has two major advantages: (1) it lowers the power consumption, prolonging the life of the battery in systems using a battery, and (2) it allows a further reduction of line size (design rule) to submicron dimensions. This reduction results in putting more transistors in a given die size. As fabrication processes improve, the decline in the line size is reaching submicron level and transistor densities are approaching 1 billion transistors.

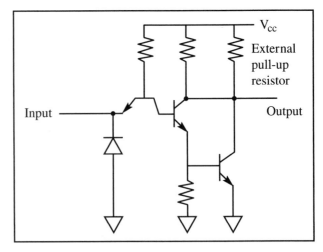

Figure C-5. Open Collector

Open-collector and open-drain gates

To allow multiple outputs to be connected together, we use open-collector logic gates. In such cases, an external resistor will serve as load. This is shown in Figures C-5 and C-6.

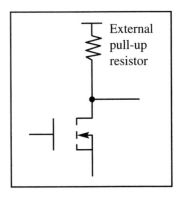

Figure C-6. Open Drain

C.2: 8051 I/O PORT STRUCTURE AND INTERFACING

In interfacing the 8051 microprocessor with other IC chips or devices, fan-out is the most important issue. To understand the 8051 fan-out, we must first understand the port structure of the 8051. This section provides a detailed discussion of the 8051 port structure and its fan-out. It is very critical that we understand the I/O port structure of the 8051 lest we damage it while trying to interface it with an external device.

IC fan-out

When connecting IC chips together, we need to find out how many input pins can be driven by a single output pin. This is a very important issue and involves the discussion of what is called IC fan-out. The IC fan-out must be addressed for both logic "0" and logic "1" outputs. Fan-out for logic low and logic high are defined as follows:

$$\text{fan-out (of low)} = \frac{I_{OL}}{I_{IL}} \qquad \qquad \text{fan-out (of high)} = \frac{I_{OH}}{I_{IH}}$$

Of the above two values, the lower number is used to ensure the proper noise margin. Figure C-7 shows the sinking and sourcing of current when ICs are connected together.

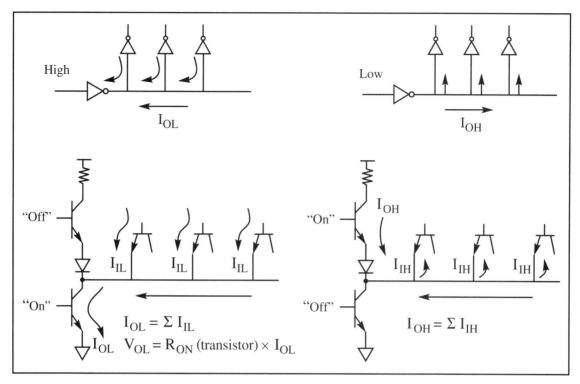

Figure C-7. Current Sinking and Sourcing in TTL

Notice that in Figure C-7, as the number of input pins connected to a single output increases, I_{OL} rises, which causes V_{OL} to rise. If this continues, the rise of V_{OL} makes the noise margin smaller, and this results in the occurrence of false logic due to the slightest noise. See Example C-1.

74LS244 and 74LS245 buffers/drivers

In cases where the receiver current requirements exceed the driver's capability, we must use buffers/drivers such as the 74LS245 and 74LS244.

Example C-1

Find how many unit loads (UL) can be driven by the output of the LS logic family.

Solution:

The unit load is defined as I_{IL} = 1.6 mA and I_{IH} = 40 µA. Table C-1 shows I_{OH} = 400 µA and I_{OL} = 8 mA for the LS family. Therefore, we have

$$\text{fan-out (low)} = \frac{I_{OL}}{I_{IL}} = \frac{8 \text{ mA}}{1.6 \text{ mA}} = 5$$

$$\text{fan-out (high)} = \frac{I_{OH}}{I_{IH}} = \frac{400 \text{ µA}}{40 \text{ µA}} = 10$$

This means that the fan-out is 5. In other words, the LS output must not be connected to more than 5 inputs with unit load characteristics.

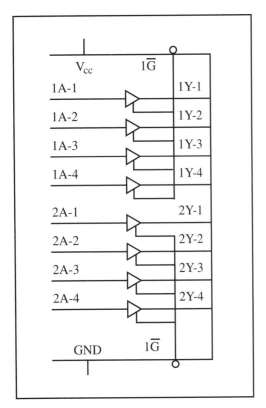

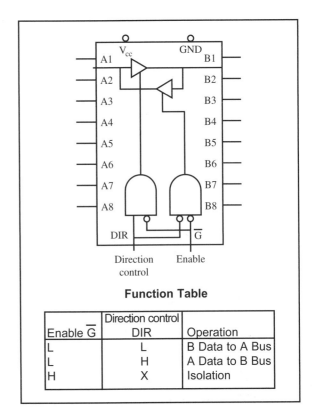

Function Table

Enable $\overline{G}$	Direction control DIR	Operation
L	L	B Data to A Bus
L	H	A Data to B Bus
H	X	Isolation

Figure C-8(a). 74LS244 Octal Buffer
Source: Reprinted by permission of Texas Instruments, Copyright Texas Instruments, 1988

Figure C-8(b). 74LS245 Bidirectional Buffer
Source: Reprinted by permission of Texas Instruments, Copyright Texas Instruments, 1988

Figure C-8 shows the internal gates for the 74LS244 and 74LS245. The 74LS245 is used for bidirectional data buses, and the 74LS244 is used for unidirectional address buses.

Tri-state buffer

Notice that the 74LS244 is simply eight tri-state buffers in a single chip. As shown in Figure C-9, a tri-state buffer has a single input, a single output, and the enable control input. By activating the enable, data at the input is transferred to the output. The enable can be an active low or an active high. Notice that the enable input for the 74LS244 is an active low whereas the enable input pin for Figure C-9 is active high.

74LS245 and 74LS244 fan-out

It must be noted that the output of the 74LS245 and 74LS244 can sink and source a much larger amount of

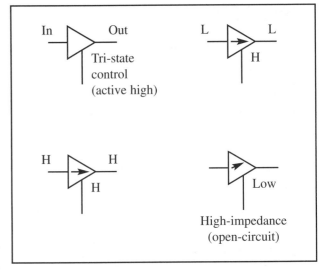

Figure C-9. Tri-State Buffer

Table C-4. Electrical Specifications for Buffers/Drivers

	I_{OH} (mA)	I_{OL} (mA)
74LS244	3	12
74LS245	3	12

current than that of other LS gates. See Table C-4. That is the reason we use these buffers for driver when a signal is travelling a long distance through a cable or it has to drive many inputs.

Next, we discuss the structure of 8051 ports. We first discuss the structure of P1–P3 since their structure is slightly different from the structure of P0.

P1–P3 structure and operation

Since all the ports of 8051 are bidirectional, they all have the following three components in their structure:

1. D latch
2. Output driver
3. Input buffer

Figure C-10 shows the structure of P1 and its three components. The other ports, P2 and P3, are basically the same except with extra circuitry to allow their dual functions (see Chapter 14). Notice in Figure C-10 that the L1 load is an internal load for P1, P2, and P3. As we will see at the end of this section, that is not the case for P0.

Also notice that in Figure C-10, the 8051 ports have both the latch and buffer. Now the question is, in reading the port, "Are we reading the status of the input pin or the status of the latch?" That is an extremely important question and its answer depends on which instruction we are using. Therefore, when reading the ports there are two possibilities: (1) reading the input pin

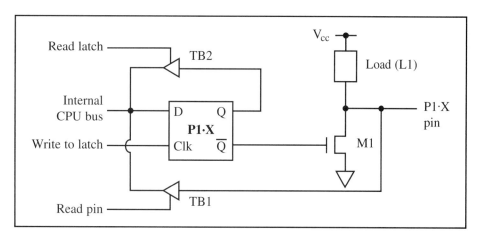

Figure C-10. 8051 Port 1 Structure

or (2) reading the latch. The above distinction is very important and must be understood lest you damage the 8051 port. Each is described next.

Reading the input pin

As we stated in Chapter 4, to make any bits of any port of 8051 an input port, we first must write a 1 (logic high) to that bit. Look at the following sequence of events to see why.

1. As can be seen from Figure C-11, a 1 written to the port bit is written to the latch and the D latch has "high" on its Q. Therefore, Q = 1 and $\overline{Q}$ = 0.

2. Since $\overline{Q}$ = 0 and is connected to the transistor M1 gate, the M1 transistor is off.

3. When the M1 transistor is off, it blocks any path to the ground for any signal connected to the input pin and the input signal is directed to the tri-state TB1.

4. When reading the input port in instructions such as "MOV A, P1", we are really reading the data present at the pin. In other words, it is bringing into the CPU the status of the external pin. This instruction activates the read pin of TB1 (tri-state buffer 1) and lets data at the pins flow into the CPU's internal bus. Figures C-11 and C-12 show high and low signals at the input, respectively.

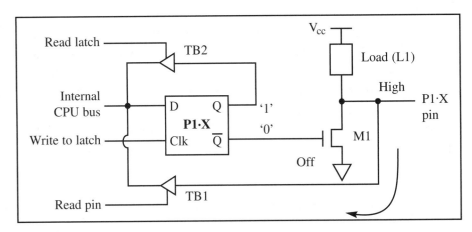

Figure C-11. Reading "High" at the Input Pin

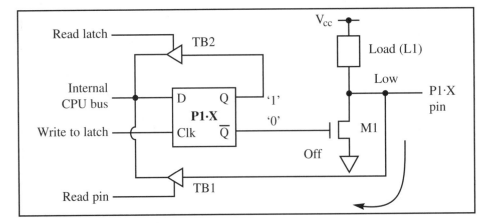

Figure C-12. Reading "Low" at the Input Pin

Writing "0" to the port

The above discussion showed why we must write a "high" to a port's bits in order to make it an input port. What happens if we write a "0" to a port that was configured as an input port? From Figure C-13, we see that if we write a 0 (low) to port bits, then Q = 0 and $\overline{Q}$ = 1. As a result of $\overline{Q}$ = 1, the M1 transistor is "on." If M1 is "on," it provides the path to ground for both L1 and the input pin. Therefore, any attempt to read the input pin will always get the "low" ground signal regardless of the status of the input pin. This can also damage the port, as explained next.

Avoid damaging the port

We must be very careful when connecting a switch to an input port of the 8051. This is due to the fact that the wrong kind of connection can damage the port. Look at Figure C-13. If a switch with V_{cc} and ground is connected directly to the pin and the M1 transistor is "on," it will sink current from both internal load L1 and external V_{cc}. This can be too much current for M1, which will blow the transistor and, as a result, can damage the port bit. There are several ways to avoid this problem. They are shown in Figures C-14–C-16.

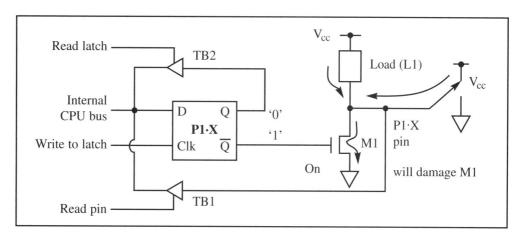

Figure C-13. Never Connect Direct V_{cc} to the 8051 Port Pin

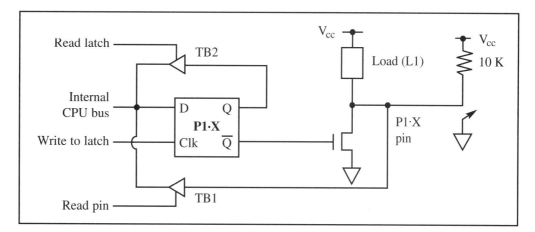

Figure C-14. Input Switch with Pull-Up Resistor

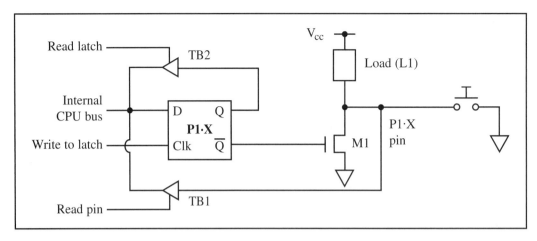

Figure C-15. Input Switch with No V$_{cc}$

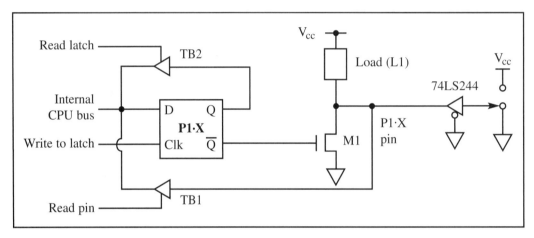

Figure C-16. Buffering Input Switch with Direct V$_{cc}$

1. One way is to have a 10K-ohm resistor on the V$_{cc}$ path to limit current flow through the M1 transistor. See Figure C-14.

2. The second method is to use a switch with a ground only, and no V$_{cc}$, as shown in Figure C-15. In this method, we read a low when the switch is pressed and a high when it is released.

3. Another way is to connect any input switch to a 74LS244 tri-state buffer before it is fed to the 8051 pin. This is shown in Figure C-16.

The above points are extremely important and must be emphasized since many people damage their ports and wonder how it happened. We must also use the right instruction when we want to read the status of an input pin. Table C-5 shows the list of instructions in which reading the port reads the status of the input pin.

Table C-5. Instructions for Reading the Status of Input Port

Mnemonics	Examples
MOV A,PX	MOV A,P1
JNB PX.Y,...	JNB P1.2,TARGET
JB PX.Y,...	JB P1.3,TARGET
MOV C,PX.Y	MOV C,P1.4
CJNE A,PX,...	CJNE A,P1,TARGET

Reading latch

Since, in reading the port, some instructions read the port and others read the latch, we next consider the case of reading the port where it reads the internal port latch. "ANL P1,A" is an example of an instruction that reads the latch instead of the input pin. Look at the sequence of actions taking place when an instruction such as "ANL P1,A" is executed.

1. The read latch activates the tri-state buffer of TB2 (see Figure C-17) and brings the data from the Q latch into the CPU.
2. This data is ANDed with the contents of register A.
3. The result is rewritten to the latch.

After rewriting the result to the latch, there are two possibilities: (1) If Q = 0, then $\overline{Q}$ = 1 and M1 is "on," and the output pin has "0," the same as the status of the Q latch. (2) If Q = 1, then $\overline{Q}$ = 0 and the M1 is "off," and the output pin has "1," the same as the status of the Q latch.

From the above discussion, we conclude that the instruction that reads the latch normally reads a value, performs an operation (possibly changing the value), and rewrites the value to the latch. This is often called "read–modify–write." Table C-6 provides a list of read–modify–write instructions. Notice from Table C-6 that all the read–modify–write instructions use the port as the destination operand.

P0 structure

A major difference between P0 and other ports is that P0 has no internal pull-up resistors. (The reason is to allow it to multiplex address and data. See Chapter 14 for a detailed discussion of address/data multiplexing.) Since P0 has no internal pull-up resistors, it is simply an open-drain, as shown in Figure C-18. (Open-drain in MOS is the same as open-collector in TTL). Now by writing a "1" to the bit latch, the M1 transistor is "off" and that causes the pin to float. That is the reason why when P0 is used for simple data I/O

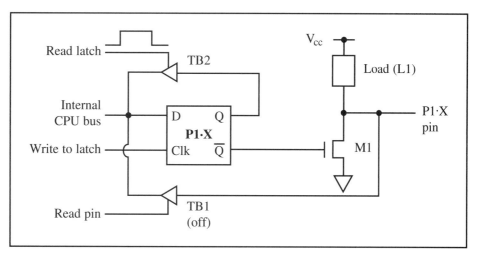

Figure C-17. Reading the Latch

we must connect it to external pull-up resistors. As can be seen from Figures C-18 and C-19, for a P0 bit to drive an input, there must be a pull-up resistor to source current.

Notice that when P0 is used for address/data multiplexing and it is connected to the 74LS373 to latch the address, there is no need for external pull-up resistors, as shown in detail in Chapter 14.

8051 fan-out

Now that we are familiar with the port structure of the 8051, we need to examine the fan-out for the 8051 microprocessor. While the early 8051 microprocessors were based on NMOS IC technology, today's 8051 microprocessors are all based on CMOS technology. However, note that while the core of the 8051 microprocessor is CMOS,

Table C-6. Read–Modify–Write Instructions

Mnemonics	Example
ANL	ANL P1,A
ORL	ORL P1,A
XRL	XRL P1,A
JBC	JBC P1.1,TARGET
CPL	CPL P1.2
INC	INC P1
DEC	DEC P1
DJNZ	DJNZ P1,TARGET
MOV PX.Y,C	MOV P1.2,C
CLR PX.Y	CLR P1.3
SETB PX.Y	SETB P1.4

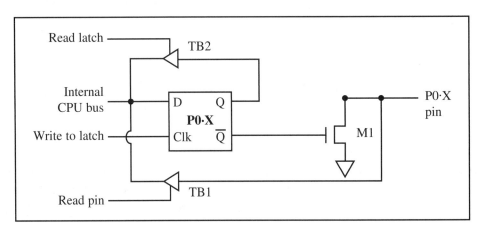

Figure C-18. P0 Structure (Open drain)

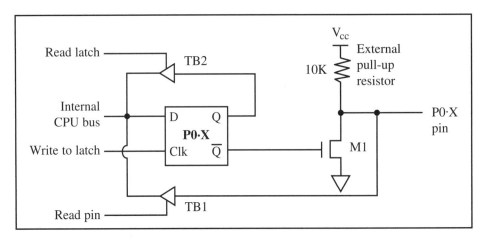

Figure C-19. P0 With External Pull-Up Resistor

Table C-7. 8051 Fan-out for P1, P2, and P3

Pin	Fan-out
IOL	1.6 mA
IOH	60 μA
IIL	50 μA
IIH	650 μA

Note: P1, P2, and P3 can drive up to 4 LS TTL inputs when connected to other IC chips.

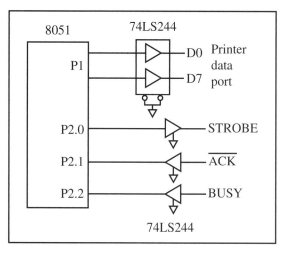

Figure C-20. 8051 Connection to Printer Signals

the circuitry driving its pins is all TTL-compatible. That is, the 8051 is a CMOS-based product with TTL-compatible pins.

P1, P2, and P3 fan-out

The three ports of P1, P2, and P3 have the same I/O structure, and therefore the same fan-out. Table C-7 provides the I/O characteristics of P1, P2, and P3.

Port 0 fan-out

P0 requires external pull-up resistors in order to drive an input since it is an open-drain I/O. The value of this resistor decides the fan-out. However, since I_{OL} = 3.2 mA for V_{OL} = 0.45 V, we must make sure that the pull-up resistor connected to each pin of the P0 is no less than 1422 ohms, since (5 V – 0.45 V) / 3.2 mA = 1422 ohms. In applications in which P0 is not connected to an external pull-up resistor, or is used in bus mode connected to a 74LS373 or other chip, it can drive up to 8 LS TTL inputs.

74LS244 driving an output pin

In many cases when an 8051 port is driving multiple inputs, or driving a single input via a long wire or cable (e.g., printer cable), we need to use the 74LS244 as a driver. When driving an off-board circuit, placing the 74LS244 buffer between your 8051 and the circuit is essential since the 8051 lacks sufficient current. See Figure C-20.

C.3: SYSTEM DESIGN ISSUES

In addition to fan-out, the other issues related to system design are power dissipation, ground bounce, V_{cc} bounce, crosstalk, and transmission lines. In this section, we provide an overview of these topics.

Power dissipation considerations

Power dissipation of a system is a major concern of system designers, especially for laptop and handheld systems in which batteries provide the power. Power dissipation is a function of frequency and voltage as shown below:

$$Q = CV$$

$$\frac{Q}{T} = \frac{CV}{T}$$

$$\text{since} \quad F = \frac{1}{T} \qquad \text{and} \quad I = \frac{Q}{T}$$

$$I = CVF$$

$$\text{now} \quad P = VI = CV^2F$$

In the above equations, the effects of frequency and V_{cc} voltage should be noted. While the power dissipation goes up linearly with frequency, the impact of the power supply voltage is much more pronounced (squared). See Example C-2.

Dynamic and static currents

Two major types of currents flow through an IC: dynamic and static. A dynamic current is $I = CVF$. It is a function of the frequency under which the component is working. This means that as the frequency goes up, the dynamic current and power dissipation go up. The static current, also called DC, is the current consumption of the component when it is inactive (not selected). The dynamic current dissipation is much higher than the static current consumption. To reduce power consumption, many microprocessors, including the 8051, have power-saving modes. In the 8051, the power saving modes are called *idle mode* and *power down mode*. Each one is described next.

Idle mode

In idle mode, which is also called *sleep mode*, the core CPU is put to sleep while all on-chip peripherals, such as the serial port, timers, and interrupts, remain active and continue to function. In this mode, the oscillator continues to provide clock to the serial port, interrupt, and timers, but no clock is provided to the CPU. Notice that during this mode all the contents of the registers and on-chip RAM remain unchanged.

Power down mode

In the power down mode, the on-chip oscillator is frozen, which cuts off frequency to the CPU and peripheral functions, such as serial ports, interrupts,

---

Example C-2

Compare the power consumption of two 8051 systems. One uses 5 V and the other uses 3 V for V_{cc}.

Solution:

Since $P = VI$, by substituting $I = V/R$ we have $P = V^2/R$. Assuming that $R = 1$, we have $P = 5^2 = 25$ W and $P = 3^2 = 9$ W. This results in using 16 W less power, which means power saving of 64%. $(16/25 \times 100)$ for systems using 3 V for power source.

---

and timers. Notice that while this mode brings power consumption down to an absolute minimum, the contents of RAM and the SFR registers are saved and remain unchanged.

Ground bounce

One of the major issues that designers of high-frequency systems must grapple with is ground bounce. Before we define ground bounce, we will discuss lead inductance of IC pins. There is a certain amount of capacitance, resistance, and inductance associated with each pin of the IC. The size of these elements varies depending on many factors such as length, area, and so on.

The inductance of the pins is commonly referred to as *self-inductance* since there is also what is called *mutual inductance*, as we will show below. Of the three components of capacitor, resistor, and inductor, the property of self-inductance is the one that causes the most problems in high-frequency system design since it can result in ground bounce. Ground bounce occurs when a massive amount of current flows through the ground pin caused by many outputs changing from high to low all at the same time. See Figure C-21. The voltage is related to the inductance of the ground lead as follows:

$$V = L \frac{di}{dt}$$

As we increase the system frequency, the rate of dynamic current, di/dt, is also increased, resulting in an increase in the inductance voltage L (di/dt) of the ground pin. Since the low state (ground) has a small noise margin, any extra voltage due to the inductance can cause a false signal. To reduce the effect of ground bounce, the following steps must be taken where possible.

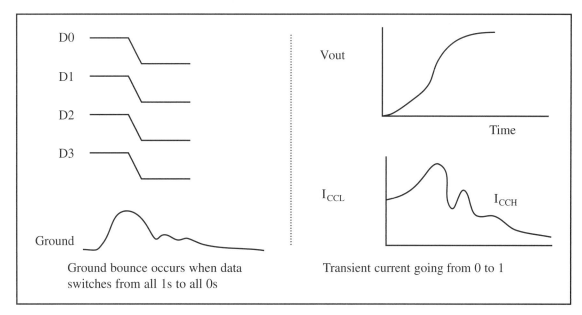

Figure C-21. Ground Bounce versus Transient Current

1. The V_{cc} and ground pins of the chip must be located in the middle rather than at opposite ends of the IC chip (the 14-pin TTL logic IC uses pins 14 and 7 for ground and V_{cc}). This is exactly what we see in high-performance logic gates such as Texas Instruments' advanced logic AC11000 and ACT11000 families. For example, the ACT11013 is a 14-pin DIP chip in which pin numbers 4 and 11 are used for the ground and V_{cc}, instead of 7 and 14 as in the traditional TTL family. We can also use the SOIC packages instead of DIP.

2. Another solution is to use as many pins for ground and V_{cc} as possible to reduce the lead length. This is exactly why all high-performance microprocessors and logic families use many pins for V_{cc} and ground instead of the traditional single pin for V_{cc} and single pin for GND. For example, in the case of Intel's Pentium processor there are over 50 pins for ground, and another 50 pins for V_{cc}.

The above discussion of ground bounce is also applicable to V_{cc} when a large number of outputs changes from the low to the high state; this is referred to as *V_{cc} bounce*. However, the effect of V_{cc} bounce is not as severe as ground bounce since the high ("1") state has a wider noise margin than the low ("0") state.

Filtering the transient currents using decoupling capacitors

In the TTL family, the change of the output from low to high can cause what is called *transient current*. In a totem-pole output in which the output is low, Q4 is on and saturated, whereas Q3 is off. By changing the output from the low to the high state, Q3 turns on and Q4 turns off. This means that there is a time when both transistors are on and drawing current from V_{cc}. The amount of current depends on the R_{ON} values of the two transistors, which in turn depend on the internal parameters of the transistors. However, the net effect of this is a large amount of current in the form of a spike for the output current, as shown in Figure C-21. To filter the transient current, a 0.01 μF or 0.1 μF ceramic disk capacitor can be placed between the V_{cc} and ground for each TTL IC. However, the lead for this capacitor should be as small as possible since a long lead results in a large self-inductance, and that results in a spike on the V_{cc} line [V = L (di/dt)]. This spike is called V_{cc} bounce. The ceramic capacitor for each IC is referred to as a *decoupling capacitor*. There is also a bulk decoupling capacitor, as described next.

Bulk decoupling capacitor

If many IC chips change state at the same time, the combined currents drawn from the board's V_{cc} power supply can be massive and may cause a fluctuation of V_{cc} on the board where all the ICs are mounted. To eliminate this, a relatively large decoupling tantalum capacitor is placed between the V_{cc}

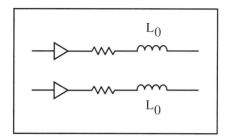

Figure C-22. Crosstalk (EMI)

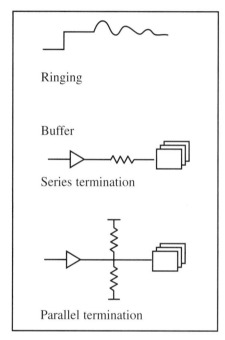

Figure C-23. Reducing Transmission Line Ringing

and ground lines. The size and location of this tantalum capacitor varies depending on the number of ICs on the board and the amount of current drawn by each IC, but it is common to have a single 22 μF to 47 μF capacitor for each of the 16 devices, placed between the V_{cc} and ground lines.

Crosstalk

Crosstalk is due to mutual inductance. See Figure C-22. Previously, we discussed self-inductance, which is inherent in a piece of conductor. *Mutual inductance* is caused by two electric lines running parallel to each other. The mutual inductance is a function of l, the length of two conductors running in parallel, d, the distance between them, and the medium material placed between them. The effect of crosstalk can be reduced by increasing the distance between the parallel or adjacent lines (in printed circuit boards, they will be traces). In many cases, such as printer and disk drive cables, there is a dedicated ground for each signal. Placing ground lines (traces) between signal lines reduces the effect of crosstalk. This method is used even in some ACT logic families where there are a V_{cc} and GND pin next to each other. Crosstalk is also called *EMI* (electromagnetic interference). This is in contrast to *ESI* (electrostatic interference), which is caused by capacitive coupling between two adjacent conductors.

Transmission line ringing

The square wave used in digital circuits is in reality made of a single fundamental pulse and many harmonics of various amplitudes. When this signal travels on the line, not all the harmonics respond in the same way to the capacitance, inductance, and resistance of the line. This causes what is called *ringing*, which depends on the thickness and the length of the line driver, among other factors. To reduce the effect of ringing, the line drivers are terminated by putting a resistor at the end of the line. See Figure C-23. There are three major methods of line driver termination: parallel, serial, and Thevenin.

In serial termination, resistors of 30–50 ohms are used to terminate the line. The parallel and Thevenin methods are used in cases where there is a need to match the impedance of the line with the load impedance. This requires a detailed analysis of the signal traces and load impedance, which is beyond the scope of this book. In high-frequency systems, wire traces on the printed circuit board (PCB) behave like transmission lines, causing ringing. The severity of this ringing depends on the speed and the logic family used. Table C-8 provides the length of the traces, beyond which the traces must be looked at as transmission lines.

Table C-8. Line Length Beyond Which Traces Behave Like Transmission Lines

Logic Family	Line Length (in.)
LS	25
S, AS	11
F, ACT	8
AS, ECL	6
FCT, FCTA	5

Source: Reprinted by permission of Integrated Device Technology, copyright. IDT 1991

APPENDIX D

FLOWCHARTS AND PSEUDOCODE

OVERVIEW

This appendix provides an introduction to writing flowcharts and pseudocode.

D.1: FLOWCHARTS

If you have taken any previous programming courses, you are probably familiar with flowcharting. Flowcharts use graphic symbols to represent different types of program operations. These symbols are connected together into a flowchart to show the flow of execution of a program. Figure D-1 shows some of the more commonly used symbols. Flowchart templates are available to help you draw the symbols quickly and neatly.

D.2: PSEUDOCODE

Flowcharting has been standard practice in industry for decades. However, some find limitations in using flowcharts, such as the fact that you can't write much in the little boxes, and it is hard to get the "big picture" of what the program does without getting bogged down in the details. An alternative to using flowcharts is pseudocode, which involves writing brief descriptions of the flow of the code. Figures D-2 through D-6 show flowcharts and pseudocode for commonly used control structures.

Structured programming uses three basic types of program control structures: sequence, control, and iteration. Sequence is simply executing instructions one after another. Figure D-2 shows how sequence can be represented in pseudocode and flowcharts.

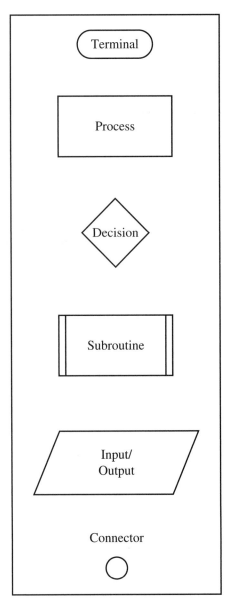

Figure D-1. Commonly Used Flowchart Symbols

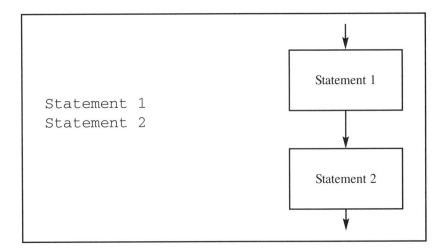

Figure D-2. SEQUENCE Pseudocode versus Flowchart

Figures D-3 and D-4 show two control programming structures: IF-THEN-ELSE and IF-THEN in both pseudocode and flowcharts.

Note in Figures D-2 through D-6 that "statement" can indicate one statement or a group of statements.

Figures D-5 and D-6 show two iteration control structures: REPEAT UNTIL and WHILE DO. Both structures execute a statement or group of statements repeatedly. The difference between them is that the REPEAT UNTIL structure always executes the statement(s) at least once and checks the condition after each iteration, whereas the WHILE DO may not execute the statement(s) at all since the condition is checked at the beginning of each iteration.

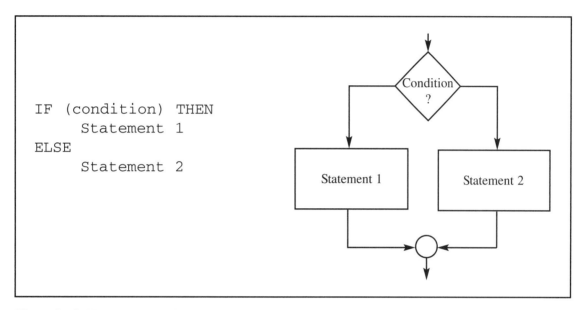

```
IF (condition) THEN
     Statement 1
ELSE
     Statement 2
```

Figure D-3. IF-THEN-ELSE-Pseudocode versus Flowchart

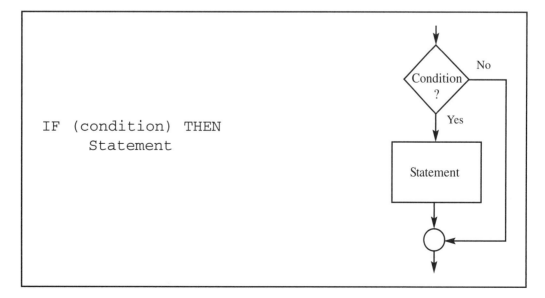

```
IF (condition) THEN
     Statement
```

Figure D-4. IF-THEN Pseudocode versus Flowchart

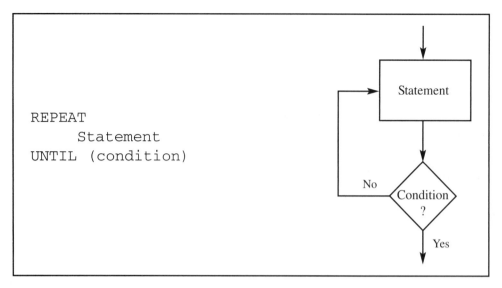

Figure D-5. REPEAT UNTIL Pseudocode versus Flowchart

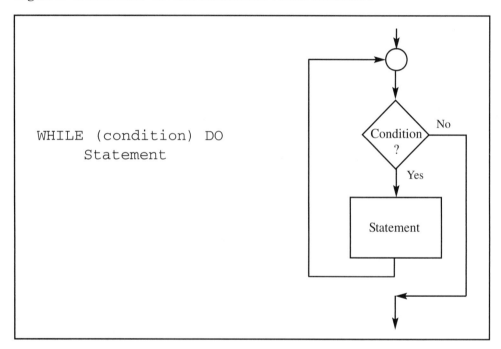

Figure D-6. WHILE DO Pseudocode versus Flowchart

Program D-1 finds the sum of a series of bytes. Compare the flowchart versus the pseudocode for Program D-1 (shown in Figure D-7). In this example, more program details are given than one usually finds. For example, this shows steps for initializing and decrementing counters. Another programmer may not include these steps in the flowchart or pseudocode. It is important to remember that the purpose of flowcharts or pseudocode is to show the flow of the program and what the program does, not the specific Assembly language instructions that accomplish the program's objectives. Notice also that the pseudocode gives the same information in a much more compact form than does the flowchart. It is important to note that sometimes pseudocode is written in layers, so that the outer level or layer shows the flow of the program and subsequent levels show more details of how the program accomplishes its assigned tasks.

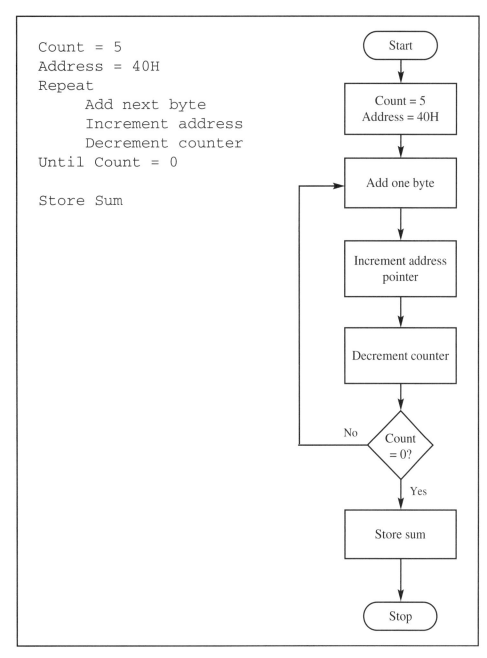

```
Count = 5
Address = 40H
Repeat
     Add next byte
     Increment address
     Decrement counter
Until Count = 0

Store Sum
```

Figure D-7. Pseudocode versus Flowchart for Program D-1

```
           CLR   A            ;A = 0
           MOV   R0,#40H      ;address
           MOV   R2,#5        ;counter
BACK:      ADD   A,@R0
           INC   R0
           DJNZ  R2,BACK
           MOV   B,A
```

Program D-1 for Figure D-7

APPENDIX E

8051 PRIMER FOR X86 PROGRAMMERS

	X86	**8051**
8-bit registers:	AL, AH, BL, BH, CL, CH, DL, DH	A, B, R0, R1, R2, R3, R4, R5, R6, R7
16-bit (data pointer):	BX, SI, DI	DPTR
Program counter:	IP (16-bit)	PC (16-bit)
Input:		
	`MOV    DX,port addr` `IN     AL,DX`	`MOV A,Pn ;(n = 0 - 3)`
Output:		
	`MOV    DX,port addr` `OUT    DX,AL`	`MOV Pn,A ;(n = 0 - 3)`
Loop:		
	`DEC CL` `JNZ TARGET`	`DJNZ R3,TARGET` `(Using R0-R7)`

Stack pointer:	SP (16-bit)	SP (8-bit)
	As we PUSH data onto the stack, it decrements the SP.	As we PUSH data onto the stack, it increments the SP.
	As we POP data from the stack, it increments the SP.	As we POP data from the stack, it decrements the SP.

Data movement:

From the code segment:

```
MOV AL,CS:[SI]                 MOVC A,@A+PC
```

From the data segment:

```
MOV AL,[SI]                    MOVX A,@DPTR
```

From RAM:

```
MOV AL,[SI]                    (Use SI, DI, or BX only.)
MOV A,@R0                      (Use R0 or R1 only.)
```

To RAM:

```
MOV [SI],AL                    MOV @R0,A
```

APPENDIX F

ASCII CODES

Ctrl	Dec	Hex	Ch	Code
^@	0	00		NUL
^A	1	01	☺	SOH
^B	2	02	☻	STX
^C	3	03	♥	ETX
^D	4	04	♦	EOT
^E	5	05	♣	ENQ
^F	6	06	♠	ACK
^G	7	07	•	BEL
^H	8	08	◘	BS
^I	9	09	○	HT
^J	10	0A	◙	LF
^K	11	0B	♂	VT
^L	12	0C	♀	FF
^M	13	0D	♪	CR
^N	14	0E	♫	SO
^O	15	0F	☼	SI
^P	16	10	►	DLE
^Q	17	11	◄	DC1
^R	18	12	↕	DC2
^S	19	13	‼	DC3
^T	20	14	¶	DC4
^U	21	15	§	NAK
^V	22	16	▬	SYN
^W	23	17	↨	ETB
^X	24	18	↑	CAN
^Y	25	19	↓	EM
^Z	26	1A	→	SUB
^[	27	1B	←	ESC
^\	28	1C	∟	FS
^]	29	1D	↔	GS
^^	30	1E	▲	RS
^_	31	1F	▼	US

Dec	Hex	Ch
32	20	
33	21	!
34	22	"
35	23	#
36	24	$
37	25	%
38	26	&
39	27	'
40	28	(
41	29	)
42	2A	*
43	2B	+
44	2C	,
45	2D	−
46	2E	.
47	2F	/
48	30	0
49	31	1
50	32	2
51	33	3
52	34	4
53	35	5
54	36	6
55	37	7
56	38	8
57	39	9
58	3A	:
59	3B	;
60	3C	<
61	3D	=
62	3E	>
63	3F	?

Dec	Hex	Ch
64	40	@
65	41	A
66	42	B
67	43	C
68	44	D
69	45	E
70	46	F
71	47	G
72	48	H
73	49	I
74	4A	J
75	4B	K
76	4C	L
77	4D	M
78	4E	N
79	4F	O
80	50	P
81	51	Q
82	52	R
83	53	S
84	54	T
85	55	U
86	56	V
87	57	W
88	58	X
89	59	Y
90	5A	Z
91	5B	[
92	5C	\
93	5D	]
94	5E	^
95	5F	_

Dec	Hex	Ch
96	60	`
97	61	a
98	62	b
99	63	c
100	64	d
101	65	e
102	66	f
103	67	g
104	68	h
105	69	i
106	6A	j
107	6B	k
108	6C	l
109	6D	m
110	6E	n
111	6F	o
112	70	p
113	71	q
114	72	r
115	73	s
116	74	t
117	75	u
118	76	v
119	77	w
120	78	x
121	79	y
122	7A	z
123	7B	{
124	7C		
125	7D	}
126	7E	~
127	7F	⌂

Dec	Hex	Ch
128	80	Ç
129	81	ü
130	82	é
131	83	â
132	84	ä
133	85	à
134	86	å
135	87	ç
136	88	ê
137	89	ë
138	8A	è
139	8B	ï
140	8C	î
141	8D	ì
142	8E	Ä
143	8F	Å
144	90	É
145	91	æ
146	92	Æ
147	93	ô
148	94	ö
149	95	ò
150	96	û
151	97	ù
152	98	ÿ
153	99	Ö
154	9A	Ü
155	9B	¢
156	9C	£
157	9D	¥
158	9E	Pts
159	9F	ƒ

Dec	Hex	Ch
160	A0	á
161	A1	í
162	A2	ó
163	A3	ú
164	A4	ñ
165	A5	Ñ
166	A6	ª
167	A7	º
168	A8	¿
169	A9	⌐
170	AA	¬
171	AB	½
172	AC	¼
173	AD	¡
174	AE	«
175	AF	»
176	B0	░
177	B1	▒
178	B2	▓
179	B3	│
180	B4	┤
181	B5	╡
182	B6	╢
183	B7	╖
184	B8	╕
185	B9	╣
186	BA	║
187	BB	╗
188	BC	╝
189	BD	╜
190	BE	╛
191	BF	┐

Dec	Hex	Ch
192	C0	└
193	C1	┴
194	C2	┬
195	C3	├
196	C4	─
197	C5	┼
198	C6	╞
199	C7	╟
200	C8	╚
201	C9	╔
202	CA	╩
203	CB	╦
204	CC	╠
205	CD	═
206	CE	╬
207	CF	╧
208	D0	╨
209	D1	╤
210	D2	╥
211	D3	╙
212	D4	╘
213	D5	╒
214	D6	╓
215	D7	╫
216	D8	╪
217	D9	┘
218	DA	┌
219	DB	█
220	DC	▄
221	DD	▌
222	DE	▐
223	DF	▀

Dec	Hex	Ch
224	E0	α
225	E1	β
226	E2	Γ
227	E3	π
228	E4	Σ
229	E5	σ
230	E6	µ
231	E7	τ
232	E8	Φ
233	E9	θ
234	EA	Ω
235	EB	δ
236	EC	∞
237	ED	ø
238	EE	ε
239	EF	∩
240	F0	≡
241	F1	±
242	F2	≥
243	F3	≤
244	F4	⌠
245	F5	⌡
246	F6	÷
247	F7	≈
248	F8	≈
249	F9	·
250	FA	·
251	FB	√
252	FC	ⁿ
253	FD	²
254	FE	∎
255	FF	

APPENDIX G

ASSEMBLERS, DEVELOPMENT RESOURCES, AND SUPPLIERS

OVERVIEW

This appendix provides various sources for 8051 assemblers and trainers. In addition, it lists some suppliers for chips and other hardware needs. While these are all established products from well-known companies, neither the authors nor the publisher assumes responsibility for any problem that may arise with any of them. You are neither encouraged nor discouraged from purchasing any of the products mentioned; you must make your own judgment in evaluating the products. This list is simply provided as a service to the reader. It also must be noted that the list of products is by no means complete or exhaustive. To suggest other products to be included in future editions of this book, please send your company's name, product name and description, and Internet address to the authors' e-mail in the Preface.

G.1: 8051 ASSEMBLERS

The 8051 assembler is provided by many companies. Some of them provide shareware versions of their products, which you can download from their Web sites. However, the size of code for these shareware versions is limited to 1K (or 2K). Figure G-1 lists some suppliers of assemblers.

G.2: 8051 TRAINERS

There are many companies that produce and market 8051 trainers. Figure G-2 provides a list of some of them.
The following is a Web site for FAQ (frequently asked questions) about the 8051: http://www.faqs.org/faqs/microprocessor-faq/8051/

G.3: PARTS SUPPLIERS

Figure G-3 provides a list of suppliers for many electronics parts.

---

www.MicroDigitalEd.com

Keil
www.keil.com

Franklin Software Proview32
The company is no longer in business. You can find the Proview32 on the Internet.

Figure G-1. Assembler Suppliers

---

www.MicroDigitalEd.com

RSR Electronics
www.elexp.com

www.digilentinc.com

www.futurlec.com

http://rigelcorp.com

www.silabs.com

Figure G-2. Trainer Suppliers

RSR Electronics
Electronix Express
365 Blair Road
Avenel, NJ 07001
Fax: (732) 381-1572
Mail Order: 1-800-972-2225
In New Jersey: (732) 381-8020
www.elexp.com

Digi-Key
1-800-344-4539 (1-800-DIGI-KEY)
FAX: (218) 681-3380
www.digikey.com

Radio Shack Mail order: 1-800-THE-SHACK

JDR Microdevices
1850 South 10th St.
San Jose, CA 95112-4108
Sales 1-800-538-5000
(408) 494-1400
Fax: 1-800-538-5005
Fax: (408) 494-1420
www.jdr.com

Mouser Electronics
958 N. Main St.
Mansfield, TX 76063
1-800-346-6873
www.mouser.com

Jameco Electronic
1355 Shoreway Road
Belmont, CA 94002-4100
1-800-831-4242
(415) 592-8097
Fax: 1-800-237-6948
Fax: (415) 592-2503
www.jameco.com

B. G. Micro
P. O. Box 280298
Dallas, TX 75228
1-800-276-2206 (orders only)
(972) 271-5546
Fax: (972) 271-2462
This is an excellent source of LCDs, ICs, keypads, etc.
www.bgmicro.com

Figure G-3. Electronics Suppliers

INDEX

Note: Locators following 'f' and 't' refer to figures and tables respectively.

Lab Manual

Basic Tutorial for Keil Software

Edited for uVision 4.22

Written by

www.MicroDigitalEd.com

Introduction

This tutorial will assist you in writing your first 8051 Assembly language program using the popular Keil Compiler. Keil offers an evaluation package that will allow the assembly and debugging of files 2K or less. This package is freely available at their web site. Keil's website address is www.keil.com.

The sample program included in the tutorial toggles Ports 1 and 2 on the 8051. The compiled program has been tested using the 8051 board from MicroDigitalEd.com. The program also works with other systems that have Port 1 and 2 available.

Basic Keil Tutorial

1. Open Keil from the Start menu.

2. The Figure below shows the basic names of the windows referred in this document.

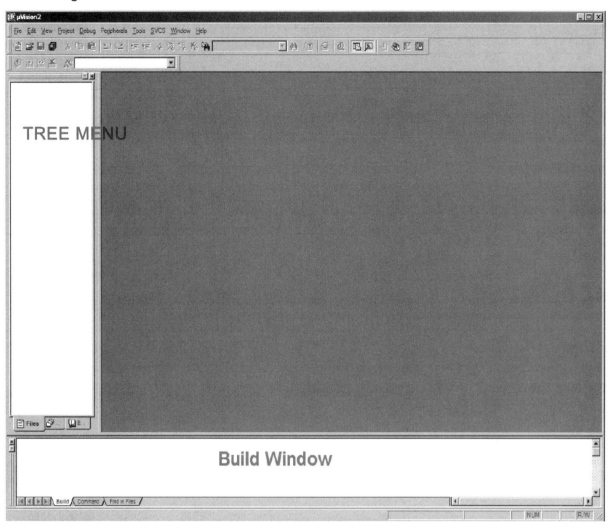

Starting a new Assembler Project

1. Select New Project from the Project Menu.

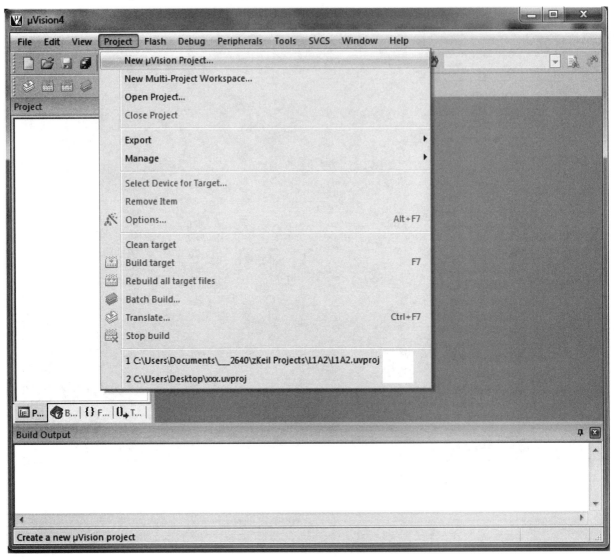

2. Name the project 'Toggle'. Navigate to a location to store your program, preferably your flash drive. Create a directory called Keil Demo.
3. Click on the Save Button.

4. The device window will be displayed.

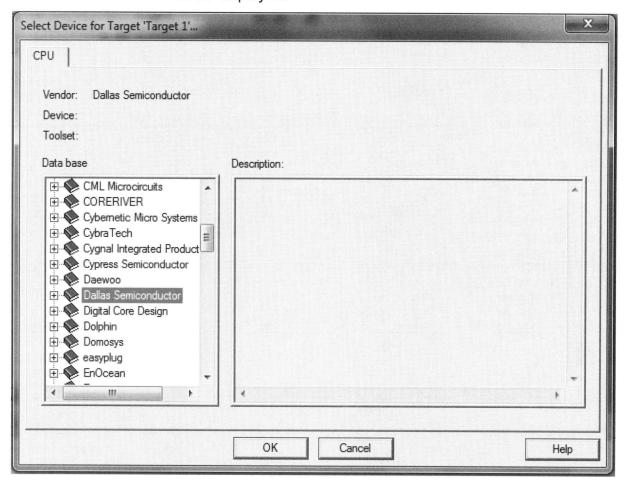

5. Scroll down and double Click on the Dallas Semiconductor.

6. Scroll down and select the DS89C450 Part.

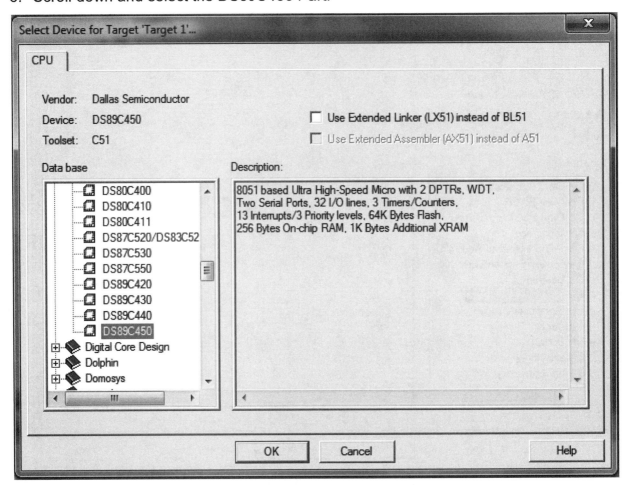

7. Click OK

8. Select No, do not copy the startup code into the project folder.

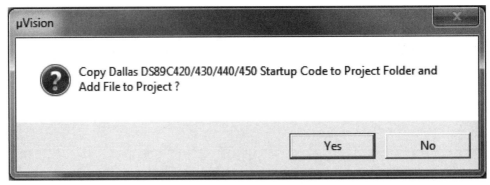

Creating Source File

1. Click File Menu and select New.

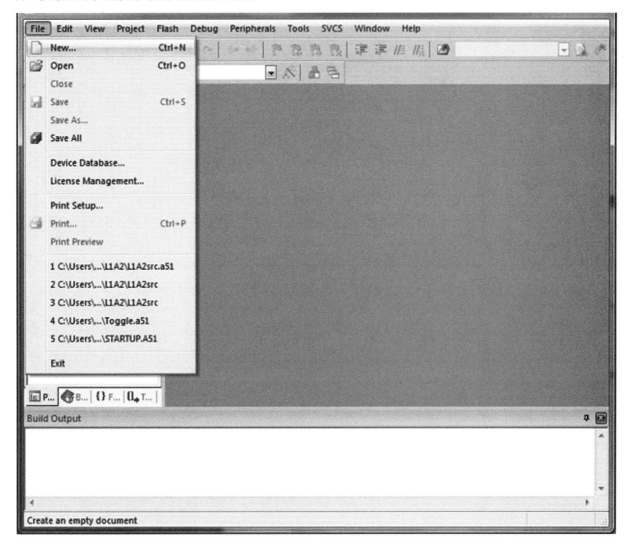

2. A new window will open up in the Keil IDE.

3. Click File Menu and select Save As…

4. Name as Toggle.a51 and click Save.

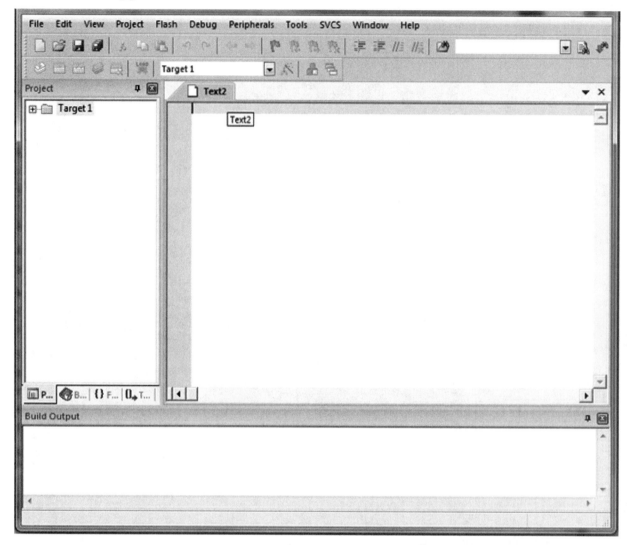

5. Copy the example code into the new window. This will toggle Ports 1 and 2.

```
ORG 0H
       MOV A, #55H
AGAIN:
       MOV P1, A
       MOV P2, A
       ACALL DELAY
       CPL A
       SJMP AGAIN
DELAY:
       MOV R3, #200
OUTER:
       MOV R2, #0255
INNER:
       DJNZ R2, INNER
       DJNZ R3, OUTER
       RET
END
```

6. Click on File menu and select Save All... You should see the following.

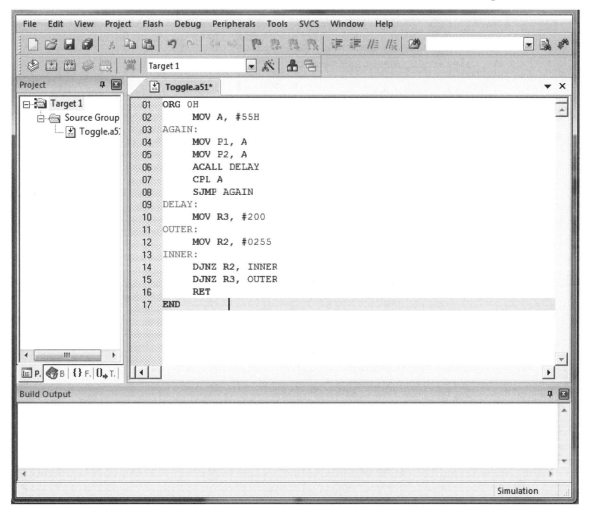

Adding File to the Project

1. Expand Target 1 in the Tree Menu and select and right click on Source Group 1.

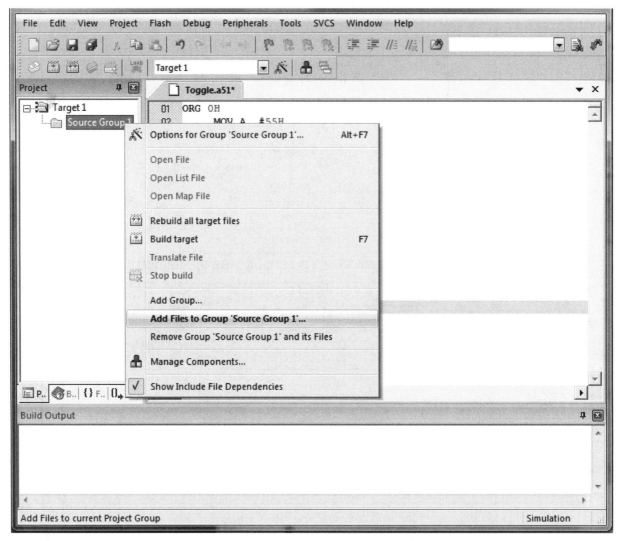

2. Select Add Files to Source Group 1

Change file type to Asm Source file(*.a*; *.src)

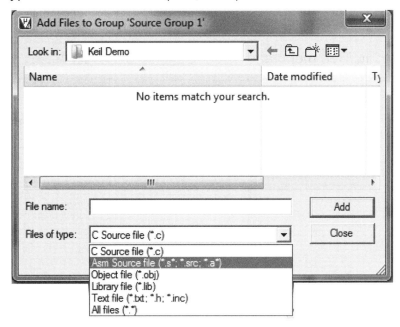

Click on toggle.a51

Click Add button

Click Close Button

Expand the Source Group 1 in the Tree menu to ensure that the file was added to the project

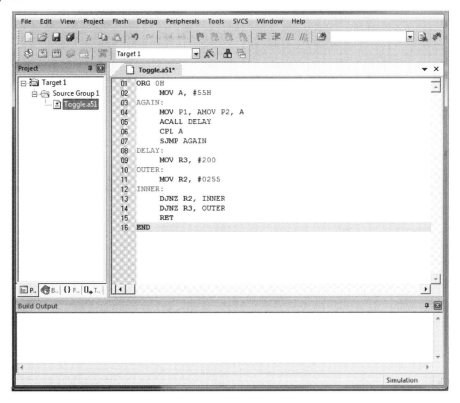

Creating HEX for the Part

1. Right click on Target 1 in Tree menu and select Options for Target 1.

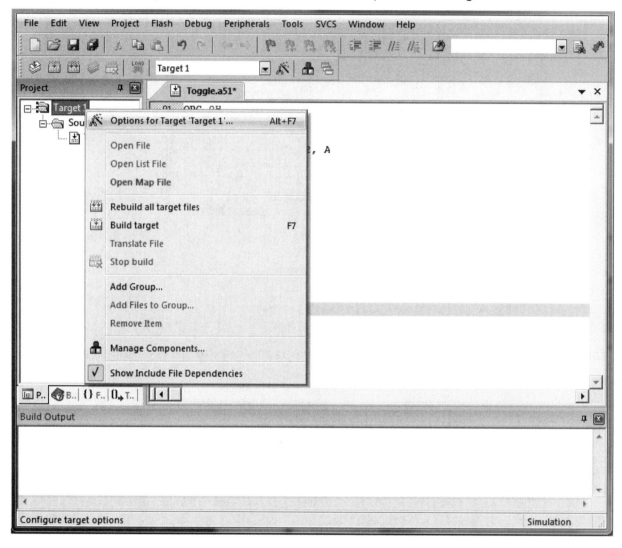

2. Select Target Tab

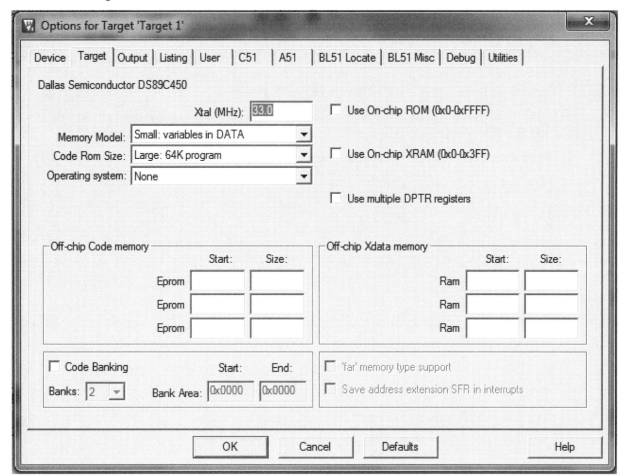

3. Change Xtal (Mhz) from 33.0 to 11.0592

4. Select Output Tab

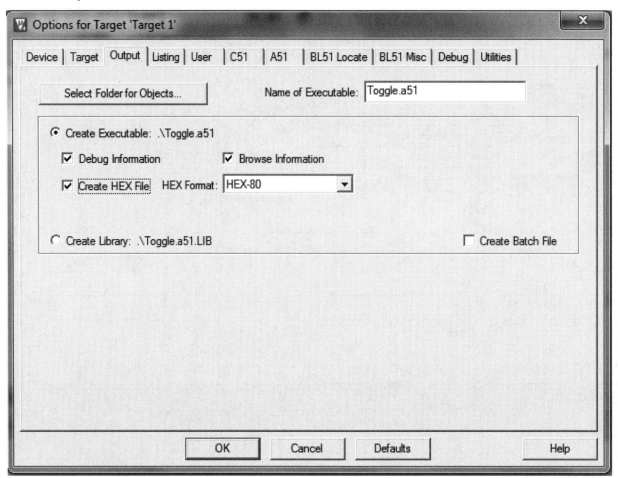

5. Click on Create Hex File check box
6. Click OK Button

7. Click on Project Menu and select Rebuild all Target Files

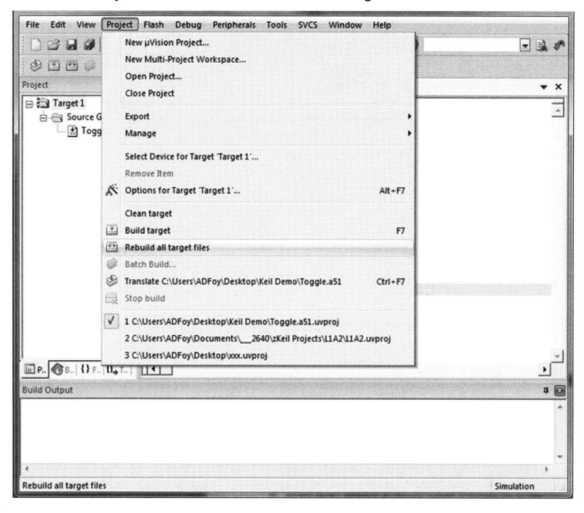

8. In the Build Window it should report '0 Errors (s), 0 Warnings'

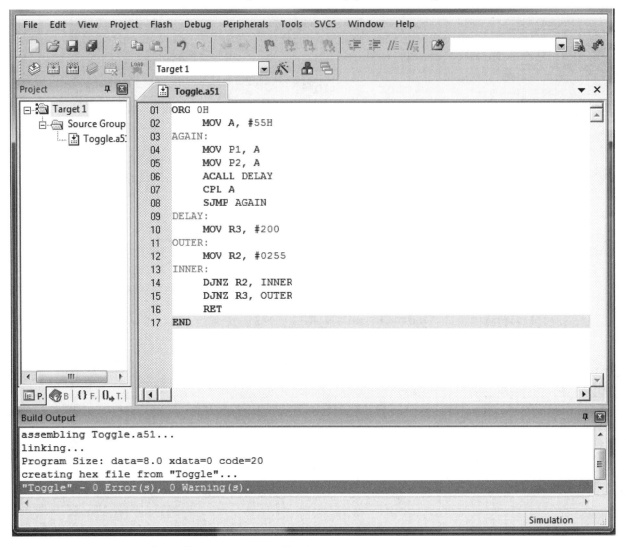

9. You are now ready to Program your Part

Testing Program in Debugger

1. Comment out line ACALL DELAY by placing a Semicolon at the beginning. This will allow you to see the port change immediately.

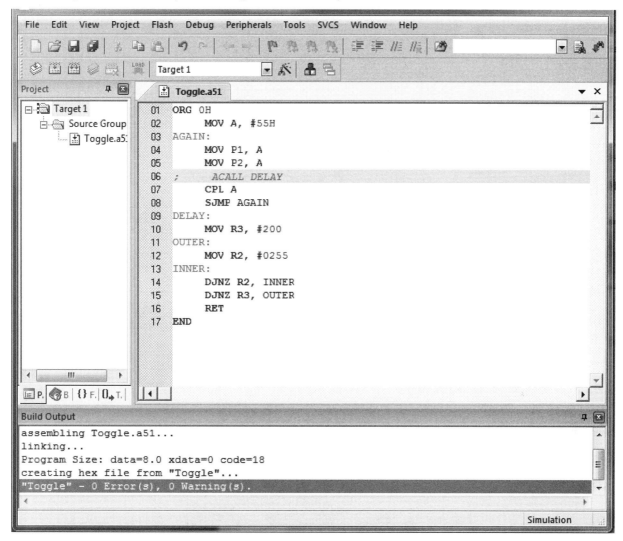

2. Click on the File Menu and select Save

3. Click on Project Menu and select Rebuild all Target Files

4. In the Build Window it should report '0 Errors (s), 0 Warnings'

5. Click on Debug Menu and Select Start/Stop Debug Session

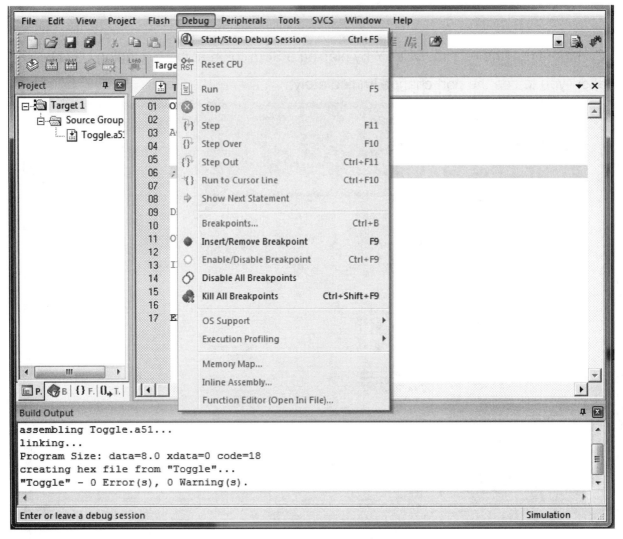

6. This dialog will pop up to inform you that the maximum code size is 2K for the evaluation version of Keil uVision. Select OK to continue.

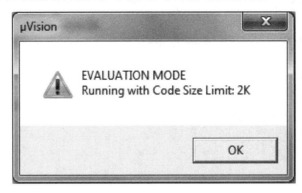

Running the Keil Debugger

1. The Keil Debugger should be now be Running. You should notice that new windows open that display Registers, Dissassembly, Command and Call Stack.

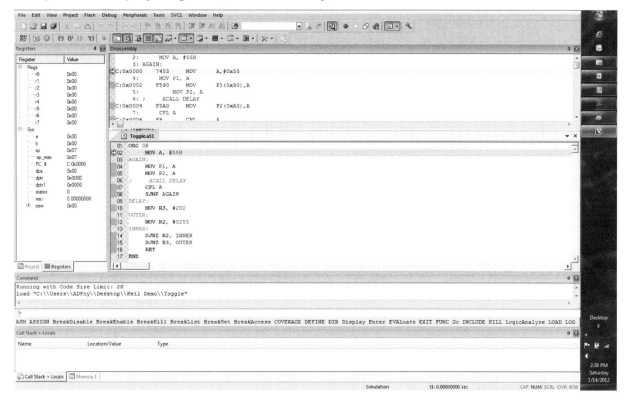

2. Click on Peripherals. Select I/O Ports, Select Port 1

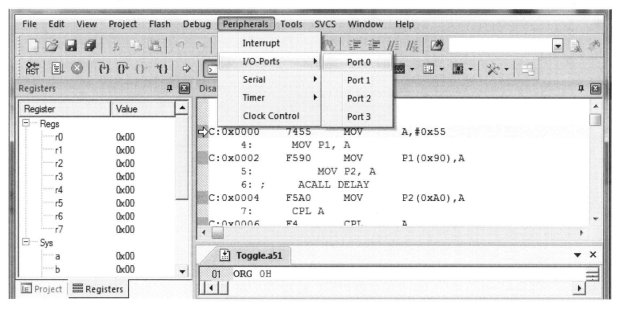

3. A new window should port will pop up. This represent the Port and Pins.

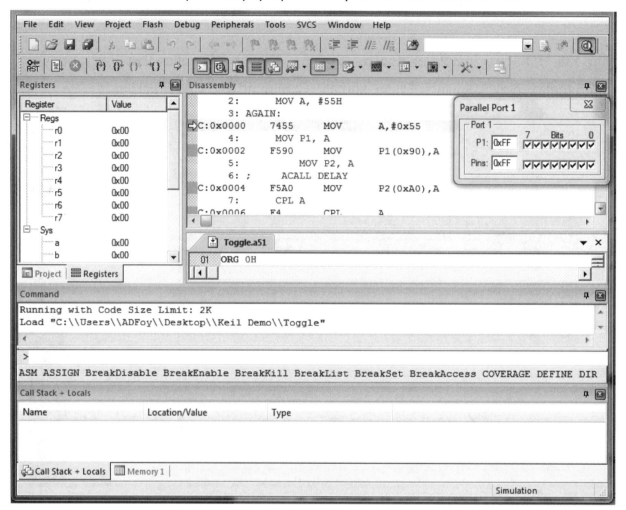

4. Step through the code by pressing F11 on the Keyboard. The Parallel Port 1 Box should change as you completely step through the code.
5. To exit out, Click on Debug Menu and Select Start/Stop Debug Session

Unit 1 Lab 1: The Keil 8051 Assembler and Simulator

Name: _____   Date: _____   Grade: _____

1. Indicate the size (8- or 16-bit) of each of the following registers.

   PC = _____   A = _____   B = _____

   R0 = _____   R1= _____   R2 = _____   R7 = _____

2. Indicate the largest value *in decimals* that each register can contain.

   PC = _____   A = _____   B = _____

   R0 = _____   R1 = _____   R2 = _____   R7 = _____

3. Indicate the largest value *in hex* that each register can contain.

   PC = _____   A = _____   B = _____

   R0 = _____   R1 = _____   R2 = _____   R7 = _____

4. What is the source of each of the following file types and what is each file type used for?

   .asm

   Generated by _____

   Used for   _____

   _____

   .lst

   Generated by _____

   Used for   _____

   _____

   .hex

   Generated by _____

   Used for   _____

   _____

Tutorial to use the Bray Terminal with the MDE 8051 Trainer

Introduction

This tutorial will assist you in linking the MDE 8051 trainer to the Bray Terminal. You will connect the trainer, configure the terminal, link the trainer to the system, download a hex file and run the downloaded program.

The Bray terminal is free and can be obtained at the following address:

https://sites.google.com/site/terminalbpp/

Determine the PC Com port used

Open the Windows Control Panel, open the Device Manager and determine which Com port that you will use to connect to the trainer. Your instructor will provide assistance if you cannot determine the correct com port.

Connect the 8051 Trainer to the Personal Computer

The 8051 Trainer comes with AC-to-DC power Adaptor (5V) and DB-9 connector cable in which one side is DB-9 female and the other side is DB-9 male.

Connect the Serial 0 connector of the 8051 Trainer to serial port of the PC using DB-9 cable, as shown below. If your PC does not have any serial port then you must use a USB to serial cable.

Connect power to the 8051 Trainer

Connect the power cable from a 5VDC, 1A regulated power adapter.

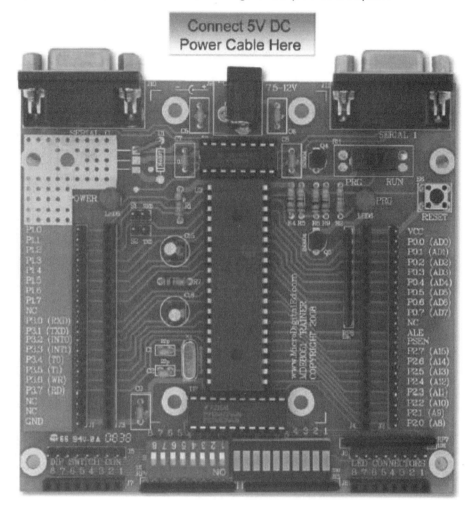

Start a Bray Terminal Session

On your personal computer, locate the Bray Terminal icon and start a terminal session.

Examine the Bray Terminal

The Bray terminal has seven sections:

- Configuration
- Settings
- Receive
- Communications Window
- Transmit
- Macros
- Command Input

Configuration- RS232 serial configuration

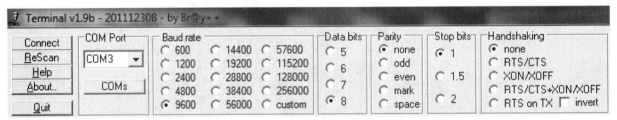

Settings- Bray terminal settings, note the ASCII table button. It provides a list of 128 ASCII values.

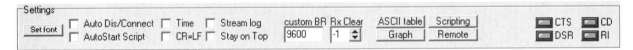

Receive- Bray terminal receive settings

Communications Window- display of communication activities to and from the device

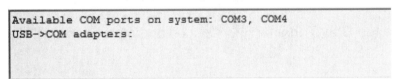

Transmit- Bray terminal transmit settings

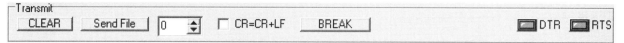

Macros- set up macros

Command Input- user command line input

Configure the Bray Terminal

1. Locate the serial configuration section of the Bray terminal at the top of the screen.

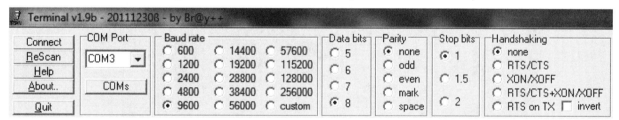

2. Select the correct COM port. If the correct COM port is not listed, click the rescan button to update the COM port list.

3. Configure as follows

Baud Rate	9600
Data Bits	8
Parity	none
Stop Bits	1
Handshaking	none

Link the Bray Terminal to the Trainer

1. Put the Switch on PRG, as Shown bellow. (The PRG LED should light).

2. Click on the Bray terminal Connect button.

3. Locate the Transmit section and check the CR=CR+LF box. This will allow the terminal to automatically send what you type to the MDE 8051 Trainer when you press the enter key.

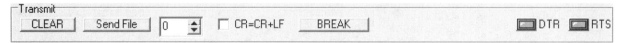

4. Locate the Command input section and check the +CR box. This will allow you to enter info into the command line box and click the -> Send key to send instructions to the MDE 80511 Trainer.

5. You have two options to communicate with the trainer.

   a. You can enter information into the Command Input box and click on the -> Send button.

   b. You can enter information into the gray area beneath the Command Input box and press return.

6. To link the Bray terminal to the MDE 8051 Trainer Loader, chose one of the two methods.

   a. Press enter two or three times.

   b. Locate the -> Send button at the bottom of the screen on the right side.

7. Click the +CR box and click -> Send two or three times. You will see when the Trainer board loader connects with the Bray terminal in the Communications Window.

```
Available COM ports on system: COM3, COM4
USB->COM adapters:
DS89C450 LOADER VERSION 2.1  COPYRIGHT (C) 2002 DALLAS SEMICONDUCTOR
>
```

Note: if you do not receive the message, the wrong COM port is selected or the configuration settings are wrong, or the cables are not connected properly or the trainer is not in PRG mode.

Download and Run Programs on 8051 Trainer

1. Clear (Erase) the MDE 8051 Trainer on board Flash by entering letter K and then click -> Send.

2. You should see the letter K show up in the Communications Window.

3. Ready to DownLoad the hex file to the MDE 8051 trainer on board flash by entering letter L and then click -> Send.

4. You should see the letter L show up in the Communications Window.

5. Locate the Transmit section and click on Send File.

665

6. The dialog box used to locate and select the file will appear. Locate the hex file for the program that you would like to download to the MDE 8051 trainer on board flash.

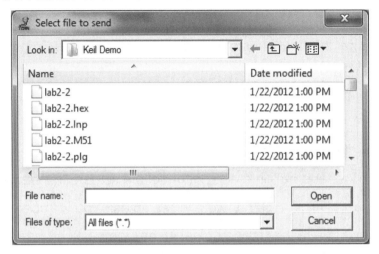

7. You should see a series of Gs appear on your screen if the download is successful. Otherwise repeat the process or ask your instructor for assistance.

```
Available COM ports on system: COM3, COM4
USB->COM adapters:
DS89C450 LOADER VERSION 2.1  COPYRIGHT (C) 2002 DALLAS SEMICONDUCTOR
> K

> L
GG
>

>
```

8. Locate the Receive section.

9. You can customize the output to the communications window by checking Dec, Hex and/or Bin. You can also have the output be in hexadecimal by selecting HEX.

10. If the Download is successful, you can move the Switch to Run position and press RESET button to execute the code.

11. The program will not run, pressing reset will restart the program.

Tutorial to use the Tera Terminal with the MDE 8051 Trainer

Introduction

This tutorial will assist you in linking the MDE 8051 trainer to the Tera Terminal. You will connect the trainer, configure the terminal, link the trainer to the system, download a hex file and run the downloaded program.

The Tera terminal is free and can be obtained at the following address:

http://ttssh2.sourceforge.jp

Determine the PC Com port used

Open the Windows Control Panel, open the Device Manager and determine which Com port that you will use to connect to the trainer. Your instructor will provide assistance if you cannot determine the correct com port.

Connect the 8051 Trainer to the Personal Computer

The 8051 Trainer comes with AC-to-DC power Adaptor (5V) and DB-9 connector cable in which one side is DB-9 female and the other side is DB-9 male.

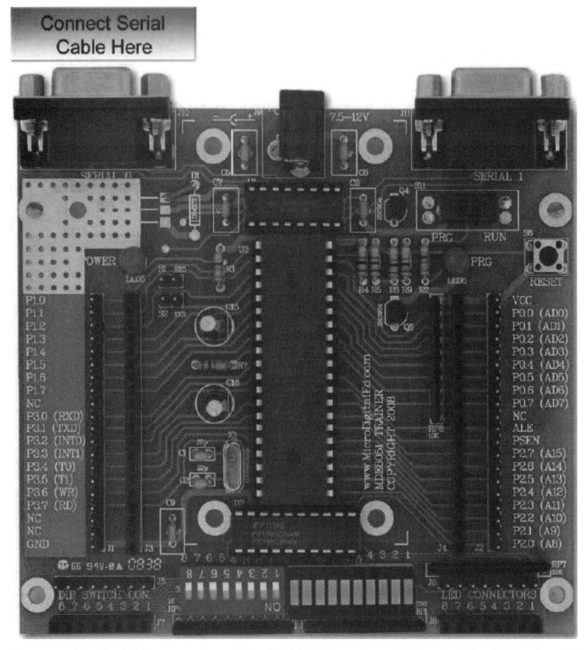

Connect the Serial 0 connector of the 8051 Trainer to serial port of the PC using DB-9 cable, as shown below. If your PC does not have any serial port then you must use a USB to serial cable.

Connect power to the 8051 Trainer

Connect the power cable from a 5VDC, 1A regulated power adapter.

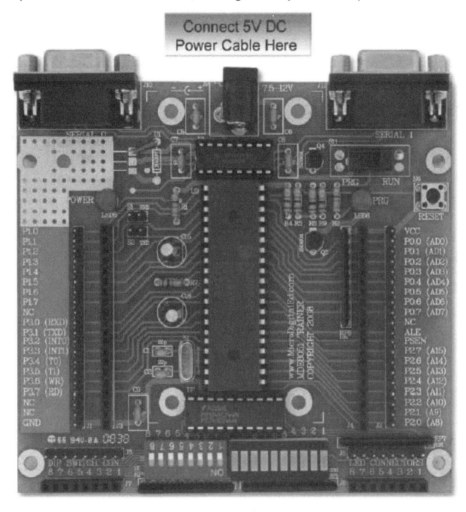

Start a Tera Terminal Session

On your personal computer, locate the Tera Terminal icon and start a terminal session.

Examine Tera Terminal New Connection

The Tera terminal will open with the following window.

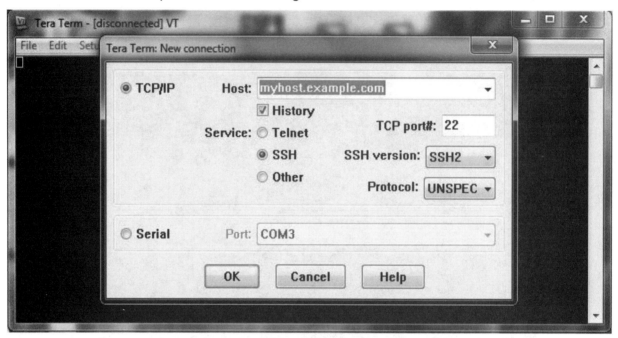

Select the Serial option and chose the correct COM port.

This is the main terminal window.

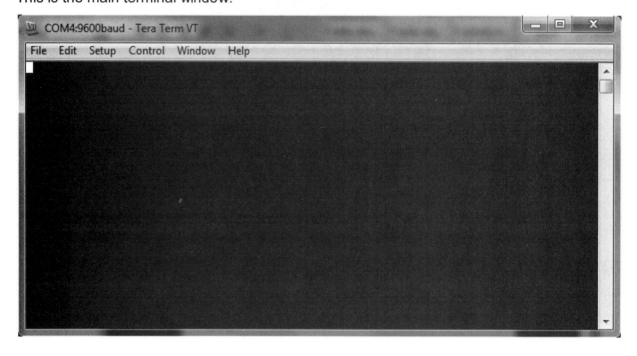

Take a moment and review the menu options.

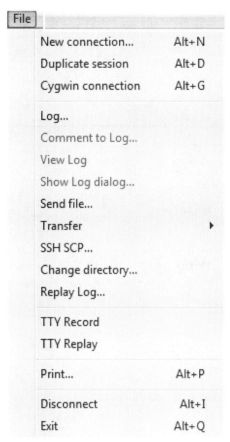

File		
New connection...	Alt+N
Duplicate session	Alt+D
Cygwin connection	Alt+G
Log...	
Comment to Log...	
View Log	
Show Log dialog...	
Send file...	
Transfer	▶
SSH SCP...	
Change directory...	
Replay Log...	
TTY Record	
TTY Replay	
Print...	Alt+P
Disconnect	Alt+I
Exit	Alt+Q

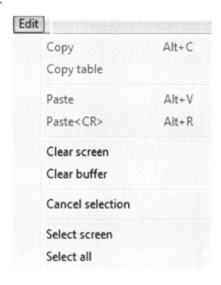

Edit		
Copy	Alt+C
Copy table	
Paste	Alt+V
Paste<CR>	Alt+R
Clear screen	
Clear buffer	
Cancel selection	
Select screen	
Select all	

Setup
Terminal...
Window...
Font...
Keyboard...
Serial port...
Proxy...
SSH...
SSH Authentication...
SSH Forwarding...
SSH KeyGenerator...
TCP/IP...
General...
Additional settings...
Save setup...
Restore setup...
Load key map...

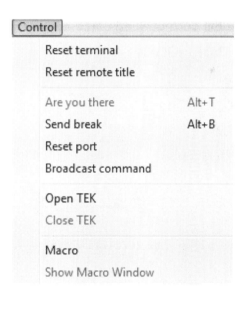

Control		
Reset terminal	
Reset remote title	
Are you there	Alt+T
Send break	Alt+B
Reset port	
Broadcast command	
Open TEK	
Close TEK	
Macro	
Show Macro Window	

Configure the Tera Terminal

1. Locate the Setup Serial port menu option in the Tera terminal.
2. Select the Serial port... option.

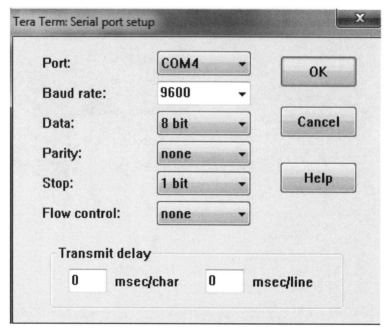

3. Configure as follows:

   Select the correct COM port.

Baud Rate	9600
Data Bits	8
Parity	none
Stop Bits	1
Handshaking	none

Link the Tera Terminal to the Trainer

1. Put the Switch on PRG, as Shown bellow. (The PRG LED should light).

2. From the Tera Terminal window, press enter once or twice.

3. You will see the following when the Trainer board loader connects with the Tera terminal in the Communications Window.

Note: if you do not receive the message, the wrong COM port is selected or the configuration settings are wrong, or the cables are not connected properly or the trainer is not in PRG mode.

Download and Run Programs on 8051 Trainer

1. Clear (Erase) the MDE 8051 Trainer on board Flash by entering letter K and pressing enter.

2. You should see the letter K show up in the Communications Window.

3. Ready to DownLoad the hex file to the MDE 8051 trainer on board flash by entering letter L and pressing enter.

4. You should see the letter L show up in the Communications Window.

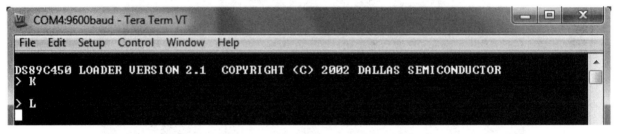

5. Locate the File Send file... option menu option in the Tera terminal.

6. The dialog box used to locate and select the file will appear. Locate and select the hex file for the program that you would like to download to the MDE 8051 trainer on board flash and click Open.

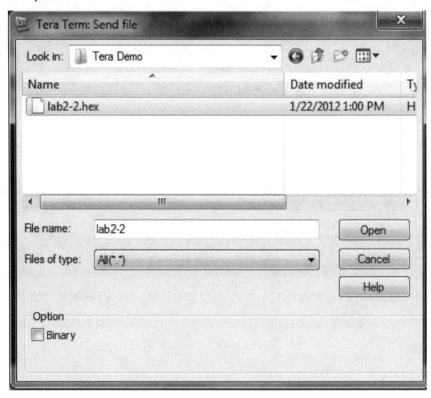

7. You should see a series of Gs appear on your screen if the download is successful. Otherwise repeat the process or ask your instructor for assistance.

8. If the Download is successful, you can move the Switch to Run position and press RESET button to execute the code.

9. The program will not run, pressing reset will restart the program.

Unit 2 Lab 1: 8051 Registers, Stack, Ports, Trainer, and Program Download

Name: _____   Date: _____   Grade: _____

1. Find the value of the CY flag after the execution of the following code.

   (a) MOV   A,#85H
       ADD   A,#92H   CY=_____

   (b) MOV   A,#15H
       ADD   A,#72H   CY=_____

   (c) MOV   A,#0F5H
       ADD   A,#52H   CY=_____

   (d) MOV A,#0FF
       INC A   CY=_____

2. Upon processor reset, what is the value in the SP register? _____

3. Upon pushing data onto the stack, the SP register is _____.
                                                      (decremented, incremented)

4. Upon popping data from the stack, the SP register is _____.
                                                      (decremented, incremented)

5. Can you change the value of the SP register other than using a push or pop instruction? If **yes**, explain why you would want to do that.

6. The stack uses the same area of RAM as bank _____.

7. List the names of all the 8051 I/O ports.

8. Which I/O ports were tested in this lab?

9. Name the pins of P3, I/O Port 3, that are alternatively used for TxD and RxD.

10. Which I/O ports of the 8051 have internal pull-up resistors?

11. Which of the 8051 I/O ports require the connection of external pull-up resistors in order to be used for I/O?

12. Upon reset, all of the 8051 I/O ports are configured as _____.
    (output, input)

Unit 3 Lab 1: Performing I/O Operations on 8051 Ports and Transferring Data in Memory

Name: _____   Date: _____   Grade:

1. Upon reset, all the ports of the 8051 are configured as _____.

   (input, output)

2. To configure all the bits of a port an input port, you must write ____ hex to it.

3. Which ports of the 8051 are bit-addressable?

4. On the 8051 Trainer, which port is closest to the DIP switches?

5. In this lab, which port of the 8051 Trainer was used for inputting data into 8051?

6. On the 8051 Trainer, which port is closest to the LED bar?

7. In this lab, which port of the 8051 Trainer was used for outputting?

8. For the 8051 Trainer, why is it necessary to write "1" to a port in order for it to be used for input?

9. What is the highest number (in decimal) that can be used on switches without clearing the carry bit?

10. Explain why you need to buffer all input switches in order to avoid damaging the 8051 port.

11. Identify the addressing mode of these lines of code:

    MOV P0, #0AAH

    MOV P1, A

    MOVE A, @R0

12. Explain the difference of operation between the following two instructions:

    MOVC A, @A+DPTR

    MOV A, @R0

13. Circle invalid instructions:

MOV A, @R1   MOV A, @R2

MOVC A, @R0+DPTR   MOV @R3, A

14. Explain the difference of operation between the following two instructions:

MOV A, 40H

MOV A, #40H

15. Give the RAM hexadecimal address for the following registers:

A= _____   B= _____   R0= _____   R2= _____

PSW= _____   SP= _____   DPL= _____   DPH= _____

Unit 4 Lab 1: Data Manipulation and Arithmetic Operations

Name: _____   Date: _____   Grade: [   ]

1. What is the maximum count value possible for register A?

2. In this lab, which port was used to display the count?

3. Which port was used to set the maximum count?

4. Can the same port be use for both inputting the maximum count and displaying the count?

5. In this lab, the CJNE instruction was used. Explain how it works.

6. Is there a CJE (Compare Jump Equal) instruction for the 8051?

7. Is the following a valid instruction?
   CJNE A, P2, OVER

8. Explain the difference between the ADD and ADDC instructions. Why not always use the ADDC instruction?

9. Show how to perform this subtraction in software:
   29H - 21H

10. Can we use the "DA   A" instruction to convert data, such as 9CH into BCD, without first performing an ADD instruction? Explain your answer.

11. In the 8051, when dividing a byte by a byte, what is the largest value that can be used for the numerator?

12. In the 8051, when dividing a byte by a byte, what is the largest value that can be used for the denominator? Give the value in both hex and decimal.

13. In the 8051, when multiplying two numbers, what is the largest value that can be used for each number?

14. Explain the role of the OV flag in division and multiplication instructions.

15. Find the value in A, the accumulator, after the following code is executed:
    MOV A, #45H
    RR   A
    RR   A
    RR   A

    A = _____ in hex

Unit 5 Lab 1: Hardware Connections, 8051 C Programming

Name: _____   Date: _____   Grade:

1. What is the frequency of the oscillator on your 8051 Trainer?

2. What data type (unsigned char, unsigned int) is required to create a loop of 10,000 iterations?

3. What data type (unsigned char, unsigned int) is required to create a loop of 200 iterations?

4. What setting of MSDelay causes a 1 second delay?

5. What setting of MSDelay allows the speaker to emit a 1kHz tone?

6. What is the opposite of 0x55?

7. What is the opposite of 0xAA?

8. True or false. For the Keil C language syntax we can use 0b01010101 for binary in place of 0x55 in hex.

9. In the toggle program reduce the size of the delay to the point in which the LEDs looks to be "on" all the time (no longer toggling). How many milliseconds is that?

10. What must be done before a port will be ready to accept another input?

Unit 6 Lab 1: Timer Programming

Name: _____ Date: _____ Grade: [   ]

1. What is the maximum frequency that can be generated using Mode 1 if the crystal frequency is W11.0592 MHz? Show your calculations.

2. What is the lowest frequency that can be generated using Mode 1 if the crystal frequency is 11.0592 MHz? Show your calculations.

3. What is the maximum frequency that can be generated using Mode 2 if the crystal frequency is 11.0592 MHz? Show your calculations.

4. What is the lowest frequency that can be generated using Mode 2 if the crystal frequency is 11.0592 MHz? Show your calculations.

5. In mode 1, what will cause the TFx flag to be set high?

6. In mode 2, will cause the TFx flag to be set high?

7. Describe the difference between the operation of mode 1 and mode 2.

8. What is the main difference between a timer and a counter?

Unit 7 Lab 1: Serial Communications Programming

Name: _____   Date: _____   Grade: [   ]

1. The 8051 TxD and RxD signals _____ (are, are not) TTL-compatible.

2. On the MDE8051 trainer, locate the MAX232. What is the role of the MAX233 (MAX232) chip?

3. With XTAL=11.0592 MHz, what is the maximum baud rate for the 8051?

4. Show how to configure the registers to achieve the maximum baud rate in Question 3.

5. What is the role of TI and RI?

6. For full duplex, what are the absolute minimum signals needed between the 8051 and the PC? Give their names.

7. Give the ASCII value (in hex and binary) used for a carriage return (CR).
   - hex: _____
   - binary: _____

8. Give the ASCII value (in hex and binary) used for a line feed (LF).
   - hex: _____
   - binary: _____

9. What is the role of the CR and LF when used with serial communications?

10. Is RS232 synchronous or asynchronous?

Unit 8 Lab 1: 8051 Interrupt Programming and Counters

Name: _____   Date: _____   Grade: [   ]

1. Explain the role of the C/T bit in the TMOD register.

2. If timer/counter 0 is used as an event counter, what is the maximum count for the following modes?

   - Mode 1: _____

   - Mode 2: _____

3. Indicate which pin is used to trigger a count for the two timer/counters.

   - Timer/counter 0: _____

   - Timer/counter 1: _____

4. If timer/counter 0 is used in Mode 1 to count an external event, explain when TF0 is set to high.

5. If timer/counter 1 is used in Mode 2 to count an external event, explain when TF0 is set to high.

6. Name all of the interrupts in the 8051 and their vector table addresses.

7. In timer Mode 1, indicate when TF0 causes the interrupt.

8. In timer Mode 2, indicate when TF0 causes the interrupt.

9. On reset, INT0 (and INT1) are _____ triggered. (edge, level)

10. On reset, which interrupt has the highest priority?

Unit 9 Lab 1: Interfacing and Programming LCDs with the 8051

Name: _____   Date: _____   Grade: _____

1. How does the LCD distinguish data from instruction codes when receiving information at its data pin?

2. To send the instruction command code 01 and to clear the display, RS = _____.

3. To send the letter "A" to be displayed on the LCD, RS = _____.

4. What is the purpose of the E signal line? Is it an input or an output as far as the LCD is concerned?

5. What condition of EN is required to latch data and instructions into the LCD?

6. Why delays are often needed when sending commands to the LCD?

7. Provide the command code to start on line 1, character 1.

8. Provide the command code to start on line 2, character 1.

9. Provide the command code to start on line 2, character 5.

10. What pin can be tested to determine whether the LCD module is ready to receive the next instruction or data?

HD162A SERIES

CHARACTERISTICS:

CHAR. DOTS: 5 x 8

DRIVING MODE: 1/16D

AVAILABLE TYPES:

    TN，STN(YELLOW GREEN、GREY、B/W)

    REFLECTIVE、WITH EL OR LED BACKLIGHT

    EL/100VAC，400HZ

    LED/4.2VDC

DISPLAY CONTENT：16 CHAR x 2ROW

PARAMETER（V_{DD}=5.0V±10%, V_{SS}=0V, T_a=25℃）

Parameter	Symbol	Testing Criteria	Standard Values			Unit
			Min.	Typ.	Max	
Supply voltage	V_{DD}-V_{SS}	-	4.5	5.0	5.5	V
Input high voltage	V_{IH}	-	2.2	-	V_{DD}	V
Input low voltage	V_{IL}	-	-0.3	-	0.6	V
Output high voltage	V_{OH}	-I_{OH}=02mA	2.4	-	-	V
Output low voltage	V_{OL}	I_{OL}=1.2mA	-	-	0.4	V
Operating voltage	I_{DD}	V_{DD}=5.0V	-	1.5	3.0	mA

APPLICATION CIRCUIT

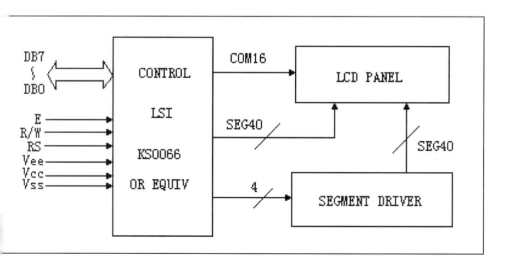

DIMENSIONS/DISPLAY CONTENT

695

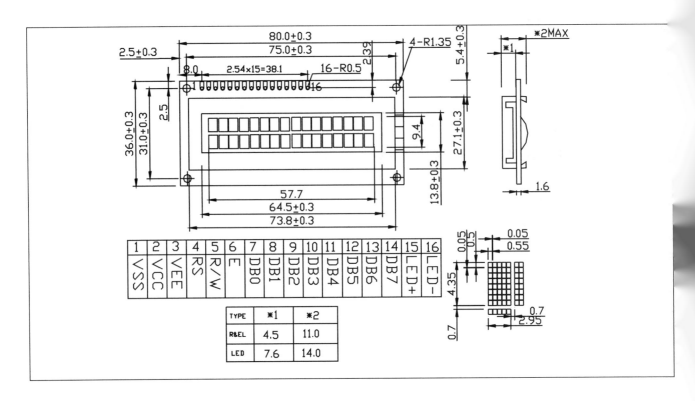

1	2	3	4	5	6	7	8	9	10	11	12	13	14	15	16
VSS	VCC	VEE	RS	R/W	E	DB0	DB1	DB2	DB3	DB4	DB5	DB6	DB7	LED+	LED-

■ **AC Characteristics Read Mode Timing Diagram**

le 12. AC Characteristics (V$_{DD}$ = 4.5V ~ 5.5V, Ta = -30 ~ +85°C)

Mode	Characteristic	Symbol	Min.	Typ.	Max.	Unit
Write Mode (Refer to Fig-6)	E Cycle Time	tc	500	-	-	ns
	E Rise / Fall Time	t_R, t_F	-	-	20	
	E Pulse Width (High, Low)	tw	230	-	-	
	R/W and RS Setup Time	tsu1	40	-	-	
	R/W and RS Hold Time	t_{H1}	10	-	-	
	Data Setup Time	tsu2	80	-	-	
	Data Hold Time	t_{H2}	10	-	-	
Read Mode (Refer to Fig-7)	E Cycle Time	tc	500	-	-	ns
	E Rise / Fall Time	t_R, t_F	-	-	20	
	E Pulse Width (High, Low)	tw	230	-	-	
	R/W and RS Setup Time	tsu	40	-	-	
	R/W and RS Hold Time	t_H	10	-	-	
	Data Output Delay Time	t_D	-	-	120	
	Data Hold Time	t_{DH}	5	-	-	

ble 13. AC Characteristics (V$_{DD}$ =2.7V ~ 4.5V, Ta = -30 ~ +85°C)

Mode	Characteristic	Symbol	Min.	Typ.	Max.	Unit
Write Mode (Refer to Fig-6)	E Cycle Time	tc	1000	-	-	ns
	E Rise / Fall Time	$t_R t_F$	-	-	25	
	E Pulse Width (High, Low)	tw	450	-	-	
	R/W and RS Setup Time	tsu1	60	-	-	
	R/W and RS Hold Time	t_{H1}	20	-	-	
	Data Setup Time	tsu2	195	-	-	
	Data Hold Time	t_{H2}	10	-	-	
Read Mode (Refer to Fig-7)	E Cycle Time	tc	1000	-	-	ns
	E Rise / Fall Time	t_R, t_F	-	-	25	
	E Pulse Width (High, Low)	tw	450	-	-	
	R/W and RS Setup Time	tsu	60	-	-	
	R/W and RS Hold Time	t_H	20	-	-	
	Data Output Delay Time	t_D	-	-	360	
	Data Hold Time	t_{DH}	5	-	-	

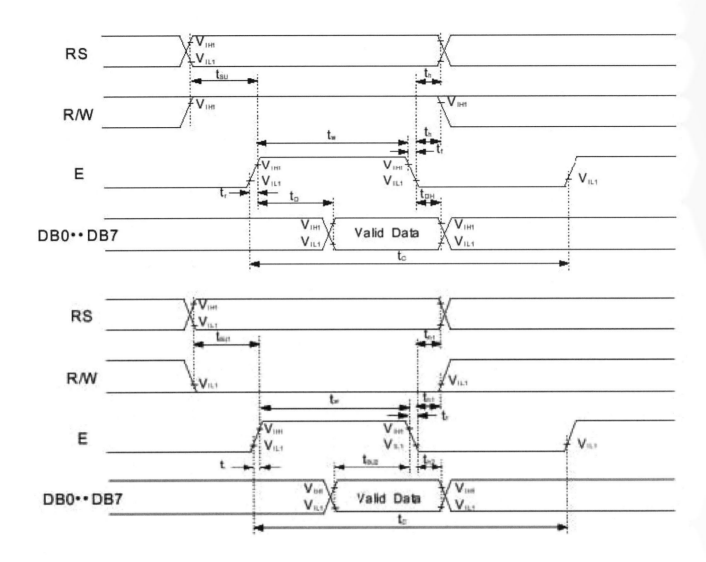

Write Mode Timing Diagram

Timing

1) Interface with 8-bit MPU
   When interfacing data length are 8-bit, transfer is performed at a time through 8 ports, from DB0 to DB7. Example of timing sequence is shown below.

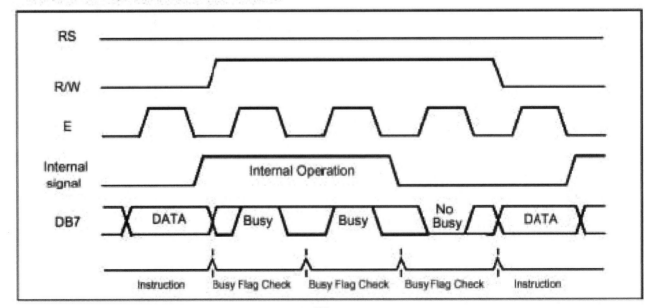

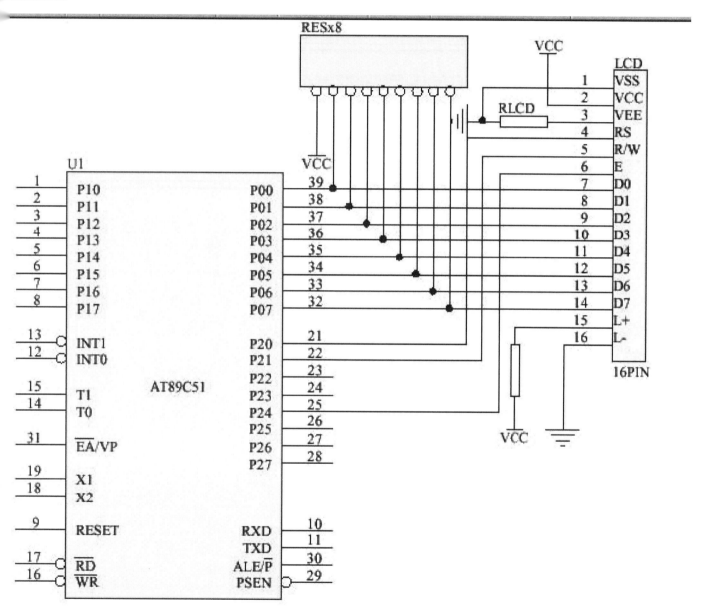

CGROM

Table 5. Relationship between Character Code (DDRAM) and Character Pattern (CGRAM)

Character Code (DDRAM data)								CGRAM Address						CGRAM Data								Pattern number
D7	D6	D5	D4	D3	D2	D1	D0	A5	A4	A3	A2	A1	A0	P7	P6	P5	P4	P3	P2	P1	P0	
0	0	0	0	×	0	0	0	0	0	0	0	0	0	×	×	×	0	1	1	1	0	pattern 1
											0	0	1				1	0	0	0	1	
											0	1	0				1	0	0	0	1	
											0	1	1				1	1	1	1	1	
											1	0	0				1	0	0	0	1	
											1	0	1				1	0	0	0	1	
											1	1	0				1	0	0	0	1	
											1	1	1				0	0	0	0	0	
0	0	0	0	×	1	1	1	0	0	0	0	0	0	×	×	×	1	0	0	0	1	pattern 8
											0	0	1				1	0	0	0	1	
											0	1	0				1	0	0	0	1	
											0	1	1				1	1	1	1	1	
											1	0	0				1	0	0	0	1	
											1	0	1				1	0	0	0	1	
											1	1	0				1	0	0	0	1	
											1	1	1				0	0	0	0	0	

Example

```c
#include <reg51.h>
#include <intrins.h>

sbit dc=0xa0;          /*P2.0 LCD 的 RS      21*/
sbit rw=0xa1;          /*P2.1 LCD 的R/W 22*/
sbit cs=0xa4;          /*P2.4 LCD 的 E      25*/
sfr  lcdbus=0x80;      /*p0LCD 数据 D0=P0.0*/
unsigned int sys10mscounter;
unsigned char syslimitcounter;
char path1[8]={0x00,0x1f,0x00,0x1f,0x00,0x1f,0x00,0x1f};/*自定义符号    横1*/
char path2[8]={0x1f,0x00,0x1f,0x00,0x1f,0x00,0x1f,0x00};/*自定义符号    横2*/
char pats1[8]={0x15,0x15,0x15,0x15,0x15,0x15,0x15,0x15};/*自定义符号    竖1*/
char pats2[8]={0x0a,0x0a,0x0a,0x0a,0x0a,0x0a,0x0a,0x0a};/*自定义符号    竖2*/

void soft_nop(){}
void soft_10ms()/***********12MHZ 提供10MS 软件延时***********/
{    register int i;
for(i=0;i<711;i++);
```

700

```c
}
void soft_20ms()/**********12MHZ 提供20MS 软件延时***********/
{    soft_10ms();
soft_10ms();
}
void hard_10ms(unsigned int delaytime) /*基于10MS 的硬件延时*/
{    sys10mscounter=delaytime;
while(sys10mscounter);
}
unsigned char data lcdcounter;
bit lcdusing1,lcdusing2;
bit lcd_checkbusy()/*检查LCD 忙*/
{    register lcdstate;
    dc=0;                /*dc=1为数据,=0 为命令.*/
    rw=1;                /*rw=1为读,=0 为写.*/
    cs=1;                /*cs=1选通.*/
soft_nop();
lcdstate=lcdbus;
cs=0;
return((bit)(lcdstate&0x80));
}
void lcd_wrcmd(unsigned char lcdcmd) /*写LCD 命令*/
{    lcdusing1=1;
while(lcd_checkbusy());
lcdbus=lcdcmd;
        dc=0;        /*dc=1为数据,=0 为命令.*/
        rw=0;        /*rw=1为读,=0 为写.*/
        cs=1;        /*cs=1选通.*/
soft_nop();

    cs=0;
    lcdbus=0xff;
    lcdusing1=0;

}
            void lcd_moveto(char position) /*移动光标到指定位.0-79*/
            {register cmd=0x80;

    lcdcounter=position;
        if (position > 59)
        position += 0x18;
        else
```

```
        {   if (position > 39)position -= 0x14;
            else
            {                    if (position > 19)position += 0x2c;
            }
        }

    cmd=cmd|position;
    lcd_wrcmd(cmd);} void lcd_wrdata(char lcddata) /*在当前显示位置显示数据*/ { char i;
    lcdusing2=1;
    while(lcd_checkbusy());
    if(lcdcounter==20){

        lcd_moveto(20);
        while(lcd_checkbusy());
        }

    if(lcdcounter==40){
        lcd_moveto(40);
        while(lcd_checkbusy());
        }

    if(lcdcounter==60){
        lcd_moveto(60);
        while(lcd_checkbusy());
        }

    if(lcdcounter==80){
        lcd_moveto(0);
        while(lcd_checkbusy());
        lcdcounter=0;
        } /*为通用而如此*/

    lcdcounter++;
    lcdbus=lcddata;
    dc=1; /*dc=1为数据,=0 为命令.*/
    rw=0; /*rw=1为读,=0 为写.*/
    cs=1; /*cs=1选通.*/
    soft_nop();
    cs=0;

    lcdbus=0xff;
    lcdusing2=0;} void lcd_string(char *strpoint) /*在当前显示位置显示LCD 字符串*/
{ register i=0;
    while(strpoint[i]!=0){
                                702
```

```c
                lcd_wrdata(strpoint[i]);
                i++;
                }

} void lcd_init()/*初始化*/

{   lcd_wrcmd(0x38);        /*设置8 位格式,2 行,5*7*/
    lcd_wrcmd(0x0c);        /*整体显示,关光标,不闪烁*/
    lcd_wrcmd(0x06);        /*设定输入方式,增量不移位*/
    lcd_wrcmd(0x01);        /*清除显示*/
    lcdcounter=0;
}

void lcd_cls()/*清除显示*/ { lcd_wrcmd(0x01);
    lcdcounter=0; } void timer0(void) interrupt 1 /*T0  中断*/ { TH0=0xd8; /*12M,10ms*/
    TL0=0xf6;
    TR0=1;
    if(sys10mscounter!=0)sys10mscounter--; /*定时器10ms*/
    if(syslimitcounter!=0)syslimitcounter--; /*定时器10ms*/

}
                main()
                {
                unsigned char j;
                IE=0;P0=0xff;P1=0xff;P2=0xff;P3=0xff; /*初始化T*/
                lcd_init();soft_20ms();
                TMOD=0x51;
                TH0=0xd8; /*12M,10ms*/
                TL0=0xf6;
                TR0=1;ET0=1;EA=1;

        while(1)
        {
        /*全黑横一横二竖一竖二U Q ABCD... */
        lcd_init(); /*全黑*/
        for(j=0;j<80;j++){lcd_wrdata(0xff);}
        hard_10ms(50);
        lcd_init(); /*横一可参考自行设计符号*/
        lcd_wrcmd(0x40);
        for(j=0;j<8;j++)lcd_wrdata(path1[j]);

        for(j=0;j<100;j++)lcd_wrdata(0);
        hard_10ms(50);
        lcd_init(); /*横二*/
```
703

```
lcd_wrcmd(0x40);
for(j=0;j<8;j++)lcd_wrdata(path2[j]);
for(j=0;j<100;j++)lcd_wrdata(0);
hard_10ms(50);
lcd_init(); /*竖一*/
lcd_wrcmd(0x40);
for(j=0;j<8;j++)lcd_wrdata(pats1[j]);
for(j=0;j<100;j++)lcd_wrdata(0);
hard_10ms(50);
lcd_init(); /*竖二*/
lcd_wrcmd(0x40);
for(j=0;j<8;j++)lcd_wrdata(pats2[j]);
for(j=0;j<100;j++)lcd_wrdata(0);
hard_10ms(50);
lcd_init();
lcd_string("UUUUUUUUUUUUUUUUUUUUUUUUUUUUUUUUUUUUUUUUUUUUUUUUUUUUUUUUUUUU
UUUUUUUUUUUUUUUUUUUUUUUUU

UUUUU"); hard_10ms(50); lcd_init();
lcd_string("QQQQQQQQQQQQQQQQQQQQQQQQQQQQQQQQQQQQQQQQQQQQQQQQQQQQQQQ
QQQQQQQQQQQQQQQQQQQQQQQQQQQ
QQQQQ"); hard_10ms(50); lcd_init();
lcd_string("ABCDEFGHIJKLMNOPQRSTUVWXYZ0123456789abcdefghijklmnopqrstuvwx
yz0123456789+-!
#$%&?"); hard_10ms(50); }
}
```

Unit 10 Lab 1: Interfacing with A/D and D/A Converters

Name: _____   Date: _____   Grade:

1. What is the direction of the ALE, SC, EOC, and OE signals from the ADC808/809 point of view (input or output)?

2. Give the steps for converting input voltage and obtaining the data from the ADC809. State the status of the SC and EOC pins in each step.

3. Describe the role of the ALE, A, B, and C signals in selecting the ADC channel.

4. In the ADC809, assume that V_{ref} is connected to 5 V. Determine the following:

    Step size is _____ (in volts).

    Maximum range for V_{in} is _____.

If V_{in} = 1.2 V, what are the D7-D0 values (binary value of conversion)? _____

If D7-D0 (binary value of conversion) = 11111111, V_{in} is _____.

V_{in}, if D7-D0 = 10011100, is _____.

5. The LM35 and LM34 produce a _____ mV output for every degree of change in temperature.

6. The LM35 is an example of a temperature transducer. What other types of transducers might be used in various systems, such as a car, coffee machine, or burglar alarm?

Final Presentation Grading Rubric

Rate Each from 1 to 5

Project Demonstration						
Grading Area	5 Pts	4 Pts	3 Pts	2 Pts	1 Pt	Points Given
Demonstration Participation	All members participated equally in the demo	All members participated equally but not all members were equally prepared	Some participants participated more than others in the demo	Only one participant participated in the demo	None of the participants put enough time into the demo	
Design Complexity	Original design showing all required features of the amplifier	Original design showing most of the required features of the amplifier	Original design showing some of the required features of the amplifier	Original design showing only a few required features of the amplifier	Unoriginal design	
Embedded System Performance	The embedded system performed perfectly with no errors	The embedded system performed well with few errors	The embedded system performed somewhat well with some errors	The embedded system had considerable difficulty during its performance	The embedded system did not function at all	
Demonstration TOTAL						

PowerPoint Presentation						
Grading Area	5 Pts	4 Pts	3 Pts	2 Pts	1 Pt	Points Giv
Presentation Participation	All members participated equally in the presentation	All members participated equally but not all members were equally prepared	Some participants participated more than others in the presentation	Only one participant participated in the presentation	None of the participants put enough time into the presentation	
PowerPoint Slide Quality	Excellent use of graphics and PowerPoint theme	Moderate use of graphics and PowerPoint theme	Average use of graphics and PowerPoint theme	Below average use of graphics and PowerPoint theme	Poor use of graphics and PowerPoint theme	
Effective Communication of Design	Clear description of design including all design features	Clear description of design including most design features	Clear description of design including some design features	Clear description of design including few design features	Unclear description of design	
Presentation TOTAL						

Project Presentation Grade Calculation

The scores from the demonstration and PowerPoint presentation combine for the total project presentation score. The maximum project presentation score is 30 points. The presentation is worth 5% of the total project grade, so divide the presentation score by 6 to get the presentation grade.

Example: A score of 26 will result in a grade of 4.3% of the possible 5%.

October 1999

ADC0808/ADC0809
8-Bit μP Compatible A/D Converters with 8-Channel Multiplexer

General Description

The ADC0808, ADC0809 data acquisition component is a monolithic CMOS device with an 8-bit analog-to-digital converter, 8-channel multiplexer and microprocessor compatible control logic. The 8-bit A/D converter uses successive approximation as the conversion technique. The converter features a high impedance chopper stabilized comparator, a 256R voltage divider with analog switch tree and a successive approximation register. The 8-channel multiplexer can directly access any of 8-single-ended analog signals.

The device eliminates the need for external zero and full-scale adjustments. Easy interfacing to microprocessors is provided by the latched and decoded multiplexer address inputs and latched TTL TRI-STATE® outputs.

The design of the ADC0808, ADC0809 has been optimized by incorporating the most desirable aspects of several A/D conversion techniques. The ADC0808, ADC0809 offers high speed, high accuracy, minimal temperature dependence, excellent long-term accuracy and repeatability, and consumes minimal power. These features make this device ideally suited to applications from process and machine control to consumer and automotive applications. For 16-channel multiplexer with common output (sample/hold port) see ADC0816 data sheet. (See AN-247 for more information.)

Features

- Easy interface to all microprocessors
- Operates ratiometrically or with 5 V_{DC} or analog span adjusted voltage reference
- No zero or full-scale adjust required
- 8-channel multiplexer with address logic
- 0V to 5V input range with single 5V power supply
- Outputs meet TTL voltage level specifications
- Standard hermetic or molded 28-pin DIP package
- 28-pin molded chip carrier package
- ADC0808 equivalent to MM74C949
- ADC0809 equivalent to MM74C949-1

Key Specifications

- Resolution   8 Bits
- Total Unadjusted Error   ±½ LSB and ±1 LSB
- Single Supply   5 V_{DC}
- Low Power   15 mW
- Conversion Time   100 μs

Block Diagram

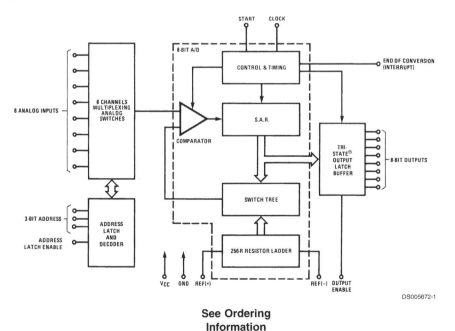

DS005672-1

See Ordering Information

Connection Diagrams

Dual-In-Line Package

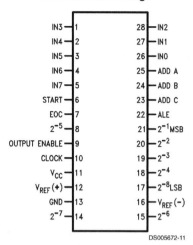

```
IN3 ──┤1        28├── IN2
IN4 ──┤2        27├── IN1
IN5 ──┤3        26├── IN0
IN6 ──┤4        25├── ADD A
IN7 ──┤5        24├── ADD B
START ┤6        23├── ADD C
EOC ──┤7        22├── ALE
2⁻⁵ ──┤8        21├── 2⁻¹MSB
OUTPUT ENABLE ┤9   20├── 2⁻²
CLOCK ┤10       19├── 2⁻³
V_CC ─┤11       18├── 2⁻⁴
V_REF(+) ┤12    17├── 2⁻⁸LSB
GND ──┤13       16├── V_REF(−)
2⁻⁷ ──┤14       15├── 2⁻⁶
```

DS005672-11

Order Number ADC0808CCN or ADC0809CCN
See NS Package J28A or N28A

Molded Chip Carrier Package

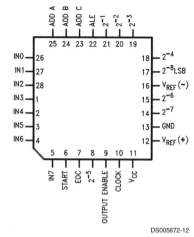

DS005672-12

Order Number ADC0808CCV or ADC0809CCV
See NS Package V28A

Ordering Information

TEMPERATURE RANGE		−40°C to +85°C			−55°C to +125°C
Error	±½ LSB Unadjusted	ADC0808CCN	ADC0808CCV	ADC0808CCJ	ADC0808CJ
	±1 LSB Unadjusted	ADC0809CCN	ADC0809CCV		
Package Outline		N28A Molded DIP	V28A Molded Chip Carrier	J28A Ceramic DIP	J28A Ceramic DIP

Absolute Maximum Ratings (Notes 2, 1)

If Military/Aerospace specified devices are required, please contact the National Semiconductor Sales Office/ Distributors for availability and specifications.

Supply Voltage (V_{CC}) (Note 3)	6.5V
Voltage at Any Pin	−0.3V to (V_{CC}+0.3V)
Except Control Inputs	
Voltage at Control Inputs	−0.3V to +15V
(START, OE, CLOCK, ALE, ADD A, ADD B, ADD C)	
Storage Temperature Range	−65˚C to +150˚C
Package Dissipation at T_A=25˚C	875 mW
Lead Temp. (Soldering, 10 seconds)	
Dual-In-Line Package (plastic)	260˚C

Dual-In-Line Package (ceramic)	300˚C
Molded Chip Carrier Package	
Vapor Phase (60 seconds)	215˚C
Infrared (15 seconds)	220˚C
ESD Susceptibility (Note 8)	400V

Operating Conditions (Notes 1, 2)

Temperature Range (Note 1)	$T_{MIN} \leq T_A \leq T_{MAX}$
ADC0808CCN,ADC0809CCN	−40˚C≤T_A≤+85˚C
ADC0808CCV, ADC0809CCV	−40˚C ≤ T_A ≤ +85˚C
Range of V_{CC} (Note 1)	4.5 V_{DC} to 6.0 V_{DC}

Electrical Characteristics

Converter Specifications: V_{CC}=5 V_{DC}=V_{REF+}, $V_{REF(-)}$=GND, $T_{MIN} \leq T_A \leq T_{MAX}$ and f_{CLK}=640 kHz unless otherwise stated.

Symbol	Parameter	Conditions	Min	Typ	Max	Units
	ADC0808					
	Total Unadjusted Error	25˚C			±½	LSB
	(Note 5)	T_{MIN} to T_{MAX}			±¾	LSB
	ADC0809					
	Total Unadjusted Error	0˚C to 70˚C			±1	LSB
	(Note 5)	T_{MIN} to T_{MAX}			±1¼	LSB
	Input Resistance	From Ref(+) to Ref(−)	1.0	2.5		kΩ
	Analog Input Voltage Range	(Note 4) V(+) or V(−)	GND−0.10		V_{CC}+0.10	V_{DC}
$V_{REF(+)}$	Voltage, Top of Ladder	Measured at Ref(+)		V_{CC}	V_{CC}+0.1	V
$\dfrac{V_{REF(+)} + V_{REF(-)}}{2}$	Voltage, Center of Ladder		V_{CC}/2-0.1	V_{CC}/2	V_{CC}/2+0.1	V
$V_{REF(-)}$	Voltage, Bottom of Ladder	Measured at Ref(−)	−0.1	0		V
I_{IN}	Comparator Input Current	f_c=640 kHz, (Note 6)	−2	±0.5	2	µA

Electrical Characteristics

Digital Levels and DC Specifications: ADC0808CCN, ADC0808CCV, ADC0809CCN and ADC0809CCV, 4.75≤V_{CC}≤5.25V, −40˚C≤T_A≤+85˚C unless otherwise noted

Symbol	Parameter	Conditions	Min	Typ	Max	Units
ANALOG MULTIPLEXER						
$I_{OFF(+)}$	OFF Channel Leakage Current	V_{CC}=5V, V_{IN}=5V,				
		T_A=25˚C		10	200	nA
		T_{MIN} to T_{MAX}			1.0	µA
$I_{OFF(-)}$	OFF Channel Leakage Current	V_{CC}=5V, V_{IN}=0,				
		T_A=25˚C	−200	−10		nA
		T_{MIN} to T_{MAX}	−1.0			µA
CONTROL INPUTS						
$V_{IN(1)}$	Logical "1" Input Voltage		V_{CC}−1.5			V
$V_{IN(0)}$	Logical "0" Input Voltage				1.5	V
$I_{IN(1)}$	Logical "1" Input Current	V_{IN}=15V			1.0	µA
	(The Control Inputs)					
$I_{IN(0)}$	Logical "0" Input Current	V_{IN}=0		−1.0		µA
	(The Control Inputs)					
I_{CC}	Supply Current	f_{CLK}=640 kHz		0.3	3.0	mA

Electrical Characteristics (Continued)

Digital Levels and DC Specifications: ADC0808CCN, ADC0808CCV, ADC0809CCN and ADC0809CCV, 4.75≤V$_{CC}$≤5.25V, −40°C≤T$_A$≤+85°C unless otherwise noted

Symbol	Parameter	Conditions	Min	Typ	Max	Units
DATA OUTPUTS AND EOC (INTERRUPT)						
V$_{OUT(1)}$	Logical "1" Output Voltage	V$_{CC}$ = 4.75V				
		I$_{OUT}$ = −360µA		**2.4**		V(min)
		I$_{OUT}$ = −10µA		**4.5**		V(min)
V$_{OUT(0)}$	Logical "0" Output Voltage	I$_O$=1.6 mA			0.45	V
V$_{OUT(0)}$	Logical "0" Output Voltage EOC	I$_O$=1.2 mA			0.45	V
I$_{OUT}$	TRI-STATE Output Current	V$_O$=5V			3	µA
		V$_O$=0	−3			µA

Electrical Characteristics

Timing Specifications V$_{CC}$=V$_{REF(+)}$=5V, V$_{REF(−)}$=GND, t$_r$=t$_f$=20 ns and T$_A$=25°C unless otherwise noted.

Symbol	Parameter	Conditions	Min	Typ	Max	Units
t$_{WS}$	Minimum Start Pulse Width	(*Figure 5*)		100	200	ns
t$_{WALE}$	Minimum ALE Pulse Width	(*Figure 5*)		100	200	ns
t$_s$	Minimum Address Set-Up Time	(*Figure 5*)		25	50	ns
t$_H$	Minimum Address Hold Time	(*Figure 5*)		25	50	ns
t$_D$	Analog MUX Delay Time From ALE	R$_S$=0Ω (*Figure 5*)		1	2.5	µs
t$_{H1}$, t$_{H0}$	OE Control to Q Logic State	C$_L$=50 pF, R$_L$=10k (*Figure 8*)		125	250	ns
t$_{1H}$, t$_{0H}$	OE Control to Hi-Z	C$_L$=10 pF, R$_L$=10k (*Figure 8*)		125	250	ns
t$_c$	Conversion Time	f$_c$=640 kHz, (*Figure 5*) (Note 7)	90	100	116	µs
f$_c$	Clock Frequency		10	640	1280	kHz
t$_{EOC}$	EOC Delay Time	(*Figure 5*)	0		8+2 µS	Clock Periods
C$_{IN}$	Input Capacitance	At Control Inputs		10	15	pF
C$_{OUT}$	TRI-STATE Output Capacitance	At TRI-STATE Outputs		10	15	pF

Note 1: Absolute Maximum Ratings indicate limits beyond which damage to the device may occur. DC and AC electrical specifications do not apply when operating the device beyond its specified operating conditions.

Note 2: All voltages are measured with respect to GND, unless othewise specified.

Note 3: A zener diode exists, internally, from V$_{CC}$ to GND and has a typical breakdown voltage of 7 V$_{DC}$.

Note 4: Two on-chip diodes are tied to each analog input which will forward conduct for analog input voltages one diode drop below ground or one diode drop greater than the V$_{CCn}$ supply. The spec allows 100 mV forward bias of either diode. This means that as long as the analog V$_{IN}$ does not exceed the supply voltage by more than 100 mV, the output code will be correct. To achieve an absolute 0V$_{DC}$ to 5V$_{DC}$ input voltage range will therefore require a minimum supply voltage of 4.900 V$_{DC}$ over temperature variations, initial tolerance and loading.

Note 5: Total unadjusted error includes offset, full-scale, linearity, and multiplexer errors. See *Figure 3*. None of these A/Ds requires a zero or full-scale adjust. However, if an all zero code is desired for an analog input other than 0.0V, or if a narrow full-scale span exists (for example: 0.5V to 4.5V full-scale) the reference voltages can be adjusted to achieve this. See *Figure 13*.

Note 6: Comparator input current is a bias current into or out of the chopper stabilized comparator. The bias current varies directly with clock frequency and has little temperature dependence (*Figure 6*). See paragraph 4.0.

Note 7: The outputs of the data register are updated one clock cycle before the rising edge of EOC.

Note 8: Human body model, 100 pF discharged through a 1.5 kΩ resistor.

Functional Description

Multiplexer. The device contains an 8-channel single-ended analog signal multiplexer. A particular input channel is selected by using the address decoder. *Table 1* shows the input states for the address lines to select any channel. The address is latched into the decoder on the low-to-high transition of the address latch enable signal.

TABLE 1.

SELECTED ANALOG CHANNEL	ADDRESS LINE		
	C	B	A
IN0	L	L	L
IN1	L	L	H
IN2	L	H	L
IN3	L	H	H
IN4	H	L	L
IN5	H	L	H
IN6	H	H	L
IN7	H	H	H

CONVERTER CHARACTERISTICS

The Converter

The heart of this single chip data acquisition system is its 8-bit analog-to-digital converter. The converter is designed to give fast, accurate, and repeatable conversions over a wide range of temperatures. The converter is partitioned into 3 major sections: the 256R ladder network, the successive approximation register, and the comparator. The converter's digital outputs are positive true.

The 256R ladder network approach (*Figure 1*) was chosen over the conventional R/2R ladder because of its inherent monotonicity, which guarantees no missing digital codes. Monotonicity is particularly important in closed loop feedback control systems. A non-monotonic relationship can cause oscillations that will be catastrophic for the system. Additionally, the 256R network does not cause load variations on the reference voltage.

The bottom resistor and the top resistor of the ladder network in *Figure 1* are not the same value as the remainder of the network. The difference in these resistors causes the output characteristic to be symmetrical with the zero and full-scale points of the transfer curve. The first output transition occurs when the analog signal has reached +½ LSB and succeeding output transitions occur every 1 LSB later up to full-scale.

The successive approximation register (SAR) performs 8 iterations to approximate the input voltage. For any SAR type converter, n-iterations are required for an n-bit converter. *Figure 2* shows a typical example of a 3-bit converter. In the ADC0808, ADC0809, the approximation technique is extended to 8 bits using the 256R network.

The A/D converter's successive approximation register (SAR) is reset on the positive edge of the start conversion (SC) pulse. The conversion is begun on the falling edge of the start conversion pulse. A conversion in process will be interrupted by receipt of a new start conversion pulse. Continuous conversion may be accomplished by tying the end-of-conversion (EOC) output to the SC input. If used in this mode, an external start conversion pulse should be applied after power up. End-of-conversion will go low between 0 and 8 clock pulses after the rising edge of start conversion.

The most important section of the A/D converter is the comparator. It is this section which is responsible for the ultimate accuracy of the entire converter. It is also the comparator drift which has the greatest influence on the repeatability of the device. A chopper-stabilized comparator provides the most effective method of satisfying all the converter requirements.

The chopper-stabilized comparator converts the DC input signal into an AC signal. This signal is then fed through a high gain AC amplifier and has the DC level restored. This technique limits the drift component of the amplifier since the drift is a DC component which is not passed by the AC amplifier. This makes the entire A/D converter extremely insensitive to temperature, long term drift and input offset errors.

Figure 4 shows a typical error curve for the ADC0808 as measured using the procedures outlined in AN-179.

Functional Description (Continued)

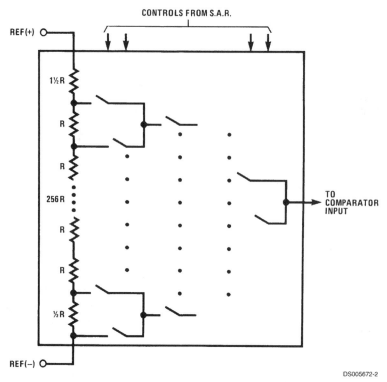

FIGURE 1. Resistor Ladder and Switch Tree

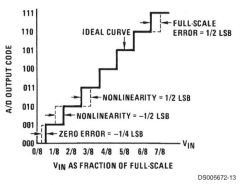

FIGURE 2. 3-Bit A/D Transfer Curve

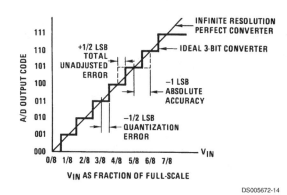

FIGURE 3. 3-Bit A/D Absolute Accuracy Curve

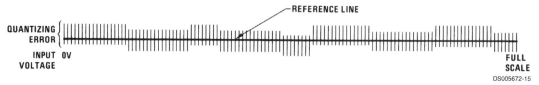

FIGURE 4. Typical Error Curve

Timing Diagram

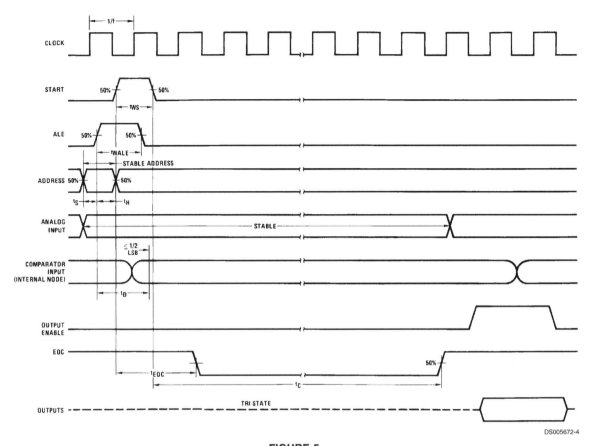

FIGURE 5.

DS005672-4

Typical Performance Characteristics

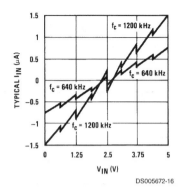

FIGURE 6. Comparator I_{IN} vs V_{IN}
($V_{CC}=V_{REF}=5V$)

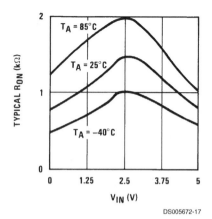

FIGURE 7. Multiplexer R_{ON} vs V_{IN}
($V_{CC}=V_{REF}=5V$)

TRI-STATE Test Circuits and Timing Diagrams

t_{1H}, t_{H1}

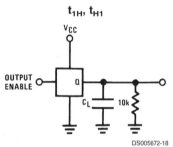

t_{1H}, C_L = 10 pF

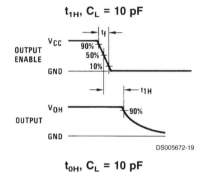

t_{H1}, C_L = 50 pF

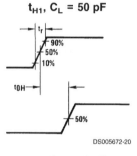

t_{OH}, t_{HO}

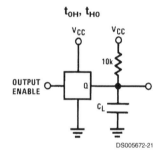

t_{OH}, C_L = 10 pF

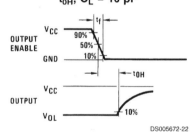

t_{HO}, C_L = 50 pF

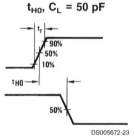

FIGURE 8.

Applications Information

OPERATION

1.0 RATIOMETRIC CONVERSION

The ADC0808, ADC0809 is designed as a complete Data Acquisition System (DAS) for ratiometric conversion systems. In ratiometric systems, the physical variable being measured is expressed as a percentage of full-scale which is not necessarily related to an absolute standard. The voltage input to the ADC0808 is expressed by the equation

$$\frac{V_{IN}}{V_{fs}-V_Z}=\frac{D_X}{D_{MAX}-D_{MIN}} \quad (1)$$

V_{IN}=Input voltage into the ADC0808
V_{fs}=Full-scale voltage
V_Z=Zero voltage

D_X=Data point being measured
D_{MAX}=Maximum data limit
D_{MIN}=Minimum data limit

A good example of a ratiometric transducer is a potentiometer used as a position sensor. The position of the wiper is directly proportional to the output voltage which is a ratio of the full-scale voltage across it. Since the data is represented as a proportion of full-scale, reference requirements are greatly reduced, eliminating a large source of error and cost for many applications. A major advantage of the ADC0808, ADC0809 is that the input voltage range is equal to the supply range so the transducers can be connected directly across the supply and their outputs connected directly into the multiplexer inputs, (*Figure 9*).

Ratiometric transducers such as potentiometers, strain gauges, thermistor bridges, pressure transducers, etc., are suitable for measuring proportional relationships; however, many types of measurements must be referred to an absolute standard such as voltage or current. This means a sys-

Applications Information (Continued)

tem reference must be used which relates the full-scale voltage to the standard volt. For example, if $V_{CC}=V_{REF}=5.12V$, then the full-scale range is divided into 256 standard steps. The smallest standard step is 1 LSB which is then 20 mV.

2.0 RESISTOR LADDER LIMITATIONS

The voltages from the resistor ladder are compared to the selected into 8 times in a conversion. These voltages are coupled to the comparator via an analog switch tree which is referenced to the supply. The voltages at the top, center and bottom of the ladder must be controlled to maintain proper operation.

The top of the ladder, Ref(+), should not be more positive than the supply, and the bottom of the ladder, Ref(−), should not be more negative than ground. The center of the ladder voltage must also be near the center of the supply because the analog switch tree changes from N-channel switches to P-channel switches. These limitations are automatically satisfied in ratiometric systems and can be easily met in ground referenced systems.

Figure 10 shows a ground referenced system with a separate supply and reference. In this system, the supply must be trimmed to match the reference voltage. For instance, if a 5.12V is used, the supply should be adjusted to the same voltage within 0.1V.

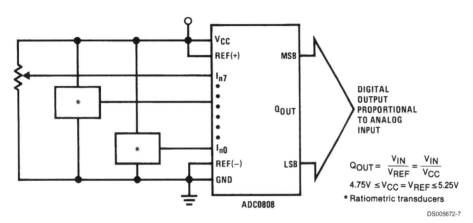

$$Q_{OUT} = \frac{V_{IN}}{V_{REF}} = \frac{V_{IN}}{V_{CC}}$$

$$4.75V \leq V_{CC} = V_{REF} \leq 5.25V$$

* Ratiometric transducers

DS005672-7

FIGURE 9. Ratiometric Conversion System

The ADC0808 needs less than a milliamp of supply current so developing the supply from the reference is readily accomplished. In *Figure 11* a ground referenced system is shown which generates the supply from the reference. The buffer shown can be an op amp of sufficient drive to supply the milliamp of supply current and the desired bus drive, or if a capacitive bus is driven by the outputs a large capacitor will supply the transient supply current as seen in *Figure 12*. The LM301 is overcompensated to insure stability when loaded by the 10 µF output capacitor.

The top and bottom ladder voltages cannot exceed V_{CC} and ground, respectively, but they can be symmetrically less than V_{CC} and greater than ground. The center of the ladder voltage should always be near the center of the supply. The sensitivity of the converter can be increased, (i.e., size of the LSB steps decreased) by using a symmetrical reference system. In *Figure 13*, a 2.5V reference is symmetrically centered about $V_{CC}/2$ since the same current flows in identical resistors. This system with a 2.5V reference allows the LSB bit to be half the size of a 5V reference system.

Applications Information (Continued)

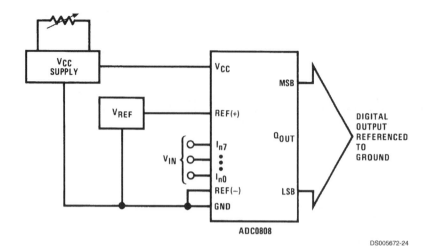

$$Q_{OUT} = \frac{V_{IN}}{V_{REF}}$$

$$4.75V \leq V_{CC} = V_{REF} \leq 5.25V$$

**FIGURE 10. Ground Referenced
Conversion System Using Trimmed Supply**

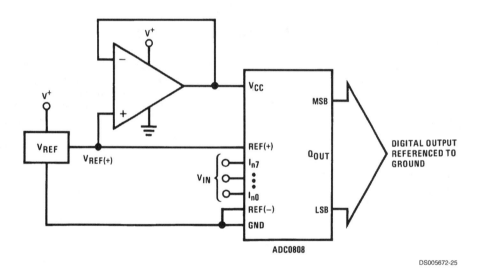

$$Q_{OUT} = \frac{V_{IN}}{V_{REF}}$$

$$4.75V \leq V_{CC} = V_{REF} \leq 5.25V$$

**FIGURE 11. Ground Referenced Conversion System with
Reference Generating V_{CC} Supply**

720

Applications Information (Continued)

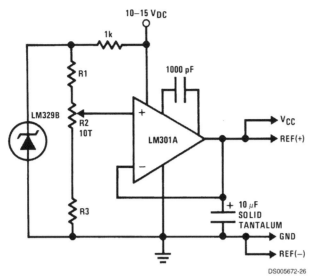

DS005672-26

FIGURE 12. Typical Reference and Supply Circuit

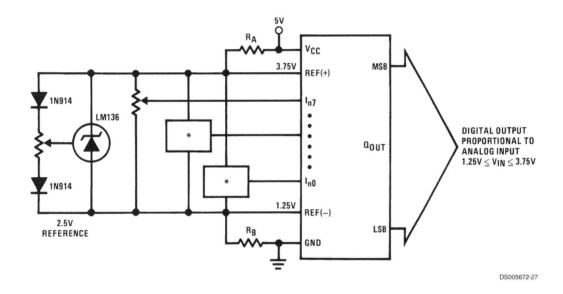

DS005672-27

$R_A = R_B$

*Ratiometric transducers

FIGURE 13. Symmetrically Centered Reference

3.0 CONVERTER EQUATIONS

The transition between adjacent codes N and N+1 is given by:

$$V_{IN} = \left\{ (V_{REF(+)} - V_{REF(-)}) \left[\frac{N}{256} + \frac{1}{512} \right] \pm V_{TUE} \right\} + V_{REF(-)} \tag{2}$$

The center of an output code N is given by:

$$V_{IN} \left\{ (V_{REF(+)} - V_{REF(-)}) \left[\frac{N}{256} \right] \pm V_{TUE} \right\} + V_{REF(-)} \tag{3}$$

The output code N for an arbitrary input are the integers within the range:

$$N = \frac{V_{IN} - V_{REF(-)}}{V_{REF(+)} - V_{REF(-)}} \times 256 \pm \text{Absolute Accuracy} \tag{4}$$

Where: V_{IN} = Voltage at comparator input

$V_{REF(+)}$ = Voltage at Ref(+)

$V_{REF(-)}$ = Voltage at Ref(−)

V_{TUE} = Total unadjusted error voltage (typically $V_{REF(+)} \div 512$)

Applications Information (Continued)

4.0 ANALOG COMPARATOR INPUTS

The dynamic comparator input current is caused by the periodic switching of on-chip stray capacitances. These are connected alternately to the output of the resistor ladder/switch tree network and to the comparator input as part of the operation of the chopper stabilized comparator.

The average value of the comparator input current varies directly with clock frequency and with V_{IN} as shown in Figure 6.

If no filter capacitors are used at the analog inputs and the signal source impedances are low, the comparator input current should not introduce converter errors, as the transient created by the capacitance discharge will die out before the comparator output is strobed.

If input filter capacitors are desired for noise reduction and signal conditioning they will tend to average out the dynamic comparator input current. It will then take on the characteristics of a DC bias current whose effect can be predicted conventionally.

Typical Application

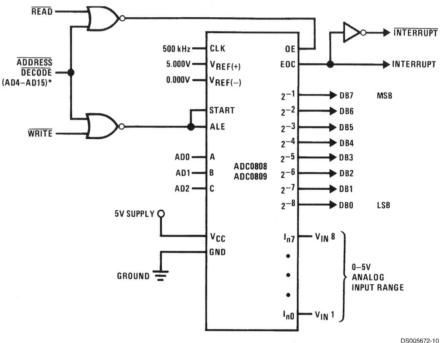

DS005672-10

*Address latches needed for 8085 and SC/MP interfacing the ADC0808 to a microprocessor

TABLE 2. Microprocessor Interface Table

PROCESSOR	READ	WRITE	INTERRUPT (COMMENT)
8080	$\overline{\text{MEMR}}$	$\overline{\text{MEMW}}$	INTR (Thru RST Circuit)
8085	$\overline{\text{RD}}$	$\overline{\text{WR}}$	INTR (Thru RST Circuit)
Z-80	$\overline{\text{RD}}$	$\overline{\text{WR}}$	$\overline{\text{INT}}$ (Thru RST Circuit, Mode 0)
SC/MP	NRDS	NWDS	SA (Thru Sense A)
6800	VMA•ϕ2•R/W	VMA•ϕ•$\overline{\text{R/W}}$	$\overline{\text{IRQA}}$ or $\overline{\text{IRQB}}$ (Thru PIA)

Physical Dimensions inches (millimeters) unless otherwise noted

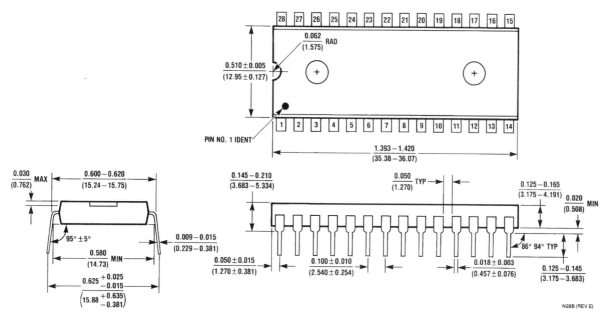

0.062
(1.575) RAD

0.510 ± 0.005
(12.95 ± 0.127)

PIN NO. 1 IDENT

1.393 − 1.420
(35.38 − 36.07)

0.030
(0.762) MAX

0.600 − 0.620
(15.24 − 15.75)

95° ± 5°

0.580 MIN
(14.73)

0.625 +0.025
      −0.015

(15.88 +0.635
       −0.381)

0.009 − 0.015
(0.229 − 0.381)

0.145 − 0.210
(3.683 − 5.334)

0.050 TYP
(1.270)

0.125 − 0.165
(3.175 − 4.191)

0.020 MIN
(0.508)

86° 94° TYP

0.050 ± 0.015
(1.270 ± 0.381)

0.100 ± 0.010
(2.540 ± 0.254)

0.018 ± 0.003
(0.457 ± 0.076)

0.125 − 0.145
(3.175 − 3.683)

N28B (REV E)

Molded Dual-In-Line Package (N)
Order Number ADC0808CCN or ADC0809CCN
NS Package Number N28B

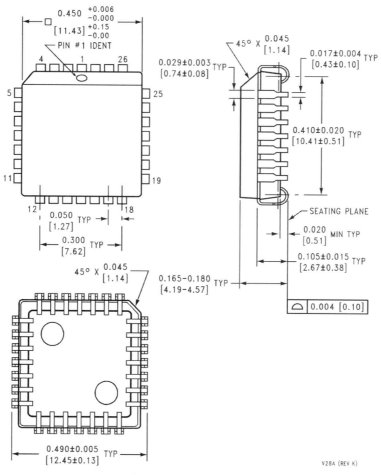

0.450 +0.006
      −0.000

[11.43] +0.15
        −0.00

PIN #1 IDENT

0.050 TYP
[1.27]

0.300 TYP
[7.62]

45° X 0.045
        [1.14]

0.490 ± 0.005 TYP
[12.45 ± 0.13]

45° X 0.045
       [1.14]

0.029 ± 0.003 TYP
[0.74 ± 0.08]

0.017 ± 0.004 TYP
[0.43 ± 0.10]

0.410 ± 0.020 TYP
[10.41 ± 0.51]

SEATING PLANE

0.020 MIN TYP
[0.51]

0.105 ± 0.015 TYP
[2.67 ± 0.38]

0.165 − 0.180 TYP
[4.19 − 4.57]

0.004 [0.10]

V28A (REV K)

Molded Chip Carrier (V)
Order Number ADC0808CCV or ADC0809CCV
NS Package Number V28A

Notes

 National Semiconductor Corporation
Americas
Tel: 1-800-272-9959
Fax: 1-800-737-7018
Email: support@nsc.com

www.national.com

National Semiconductor Europe
Fax: +49 (0) 1 80-530 85 86
Email: europe.support@nsc.com
Deutsch Tel: +49 (0) 1 80-530 85 85
English Tel: +49 (0) 1 80-532 78 32
Français Tel: +49 (0) 1 80-532 93 58
Italiano Tel: +49 (0) 1 80-534 16 80

National Semiconductor Asia Pacific Customer Response Group
Tel: 65-2544466
Fax: 65-2504466
Email: sea.support@nsc.com

National Semiconductor Japan Ltd.
Tel: 81-3-5639-7560
Fax: 81-3-5639-7507

LM35

LM35 Precision Centigrade Temperature Sensors

Literature Number: SNIS159B

National Semiconductor

LM35
Precision Centigrade Temperature Sensors

General Description

The LM35 series are precision integrated-circuit temperature sensors, whose output voltage is linearly proportional to the Celsius (Centigrade) temperature. The LM35 thus has an advantage over linear temperature sensors calibrated in ° Kelvin, as the user is not required to subtract a large constant voltage from its output to obtain convenient Centigrade scaling. The LM35 does not require any external calibration or trimming to provide typical accuracies of ±¼°C at room temperature and ±¾°C over a full −55 to +150°C temperature range. Low cost is assured by trimming and calibration at the wafer level. The LM35's low output impedance, linear output, and precise inherent calibration make interfacing to readout or control circuitry especially easy. It can be used with single power supplies, or with plus and minus supplies. As it draws only 60 µA from its supply, it has very low self-heating, less than 0.1°C in still air. The LM35 is rated to operate over a −55° to +150°C temperature range, while the LM35C is rated for a −40° to +110°C range (−10° with improved accuracy). The LM35 series is available pack-

aged in hermetic TO-46 transistor packages, while the LM35C, LM35CA, and LM35D are also available in the plastic TO-92 transistor package. The LM35D is also available in an 8-lead surface mount small outline package and a plastic TO-220 package.

Features

- Calibrated directly in ° Celsius (Centigrade)
- Linear + 10.0 mV/°C scale factor
- 0.5°C accuracy guaranteeable (at +25°C)
- Rated for full −55° to +150°C range
- Suitable for remote applications
- Low cost due to wafer-level trimming
- Operates from 4 to 30 volts
- Less than 60 µA current drain
- Low self-heating, 0.08°C in still air
- Nonlinearity only ±¼°C typical
- Low impedance output, 0.1 Ω for 1 mA load

Typical Applications

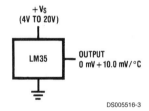

DS005516-3

FIGURE 1. Basic Centigrade Temperature Sensor
(+2°C to +150°C)

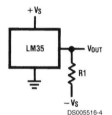

DS005516-4

Choose $R_1 = -V_S/50$ µA
$V_{OUT} = +1,500$ mV at +150°C
  $= +250$ mV at +25°C
  $= -550$ mV at −55°C

FIGURE 2. Full-Range Centigrade Temperature Sensor

Connection Diagrams

TO-46
Metal Can Package*

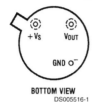

BOTTOM VIEW
DS005516-1

*Case is connected to negative pin (GND)

Order Number LM35H, LM35AH, LM35CH, LM35CAH or LM35DH
See NS Package Number H03H

TO-92
Plastic Package

BOTTOM VIEW
DS005516-2

Order Number LM35CZ, LM35CAZ or LM35DZ
See NS Package Number Z03A

SO-8
Small Outline Molded Package

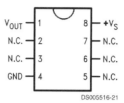

DS005516-21

N.C. = No Connection

Top View
Order Number LM35DM
See NS Package Number M08A

TO-220
Plastic Package*

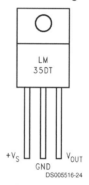

DS005516-24

*Tab is connected to the negative pin (GND).
Note: The LM35DT pinout is different than the discontinued LM35DP.

Order Number LM35DT
See NS Package Number TA03F

Absolute Maximum Ratings (Note 10)

If Military/Aerospace specified devices are required, please contact the National Semiconductor Sales Office/ Distributors for availability and specifications.

Supply Voltage	+35V to −0.2V
Output Voltage	+6V to −1.0V
Output Current	10 mA
Storage Temp.;	
TO-46 Package,	−60°C to +180°C
TO-92 Package,	−60°C to +150°C
SO-8 Package,	−65°C to +150°C
TO-220 Package,	−65°C to +150°C
Lead Temp.:	
TO-46 Package, (Soldering, 10 seconds)	300°C

TO-92 and TO-220 Package, (Soldering, 10 seconds)	260°C
SO Package (Note 12)	
Vapor Phase (60 seconds)	215°C
Infrared (15 seconds)	220°C
ESD Susceptibility (Note 11)	2500V
Specified Operating Temperature Range: T_{MIN} to T_{MAX} (Note 2)	
LM35, LM35A	−55°C to +150°C
LM35C, LM35CA	−40°C to +110°C
LM35D	0°C to +100°C

Electrical Characteristics

(Notes 1, 6)

Parameter	Conditions	LM35A			LM35CA			Units (Max.)
		Typical	Tested Limit (Note 4)	Design Limit (Note 5)	Typical	Tested Limit (Note 4)	Design Limit (Note 5)	
Accuracy	T_A=+25°C	±0.2	±0.5		±0.2	±0.5		°C
(Note 7)	T_A=−10°C	±0.3			±0.3		±1.0	°C
	T_A=T_{MAX}	±0.4	±1.0		±0.4	±1.0		°C
	T_A=T_{MIN}	±0.4	±1.0		±0.4		±1.5	°C
Nonlinearity (Note 8)	$T_{MIN}{\leq}T_A{\leq}T_{MAX}$	±0.18		±0.35	±0.15		±0.3	°C
Sensor Gain (Average Slope)	$T_{MIN}{\leq}T_A{\leq}T_{MAX}$	+10.0	+9.9, +10.1		+10.0		+9.9, +10.1	mV/°C
Load Regulation	T_A=+25°C	±0.4	±1.0		±0.4	±1.0		mV/mA
(Note 3) 0≤I_L≤1 mA	$T_{MIN}{\leq}T_A{\leq}T_{MAX}$	±0.5		±3.0	±0.5		±3.0	mV/mA
Line Regulation	T_A=+25°C	±0.01	±0.05		±0.01	±0.05		mV/V
(Note 3)	4V≤V_S≤30V	±0.02		±0.1	±0.02		±0.1	mV/V
Quiescent Current	V_S=+5V, +25°C	56	67		56	67		µA
(Note 9)	V_S=+5V	105		131	91		114	µA
	V_S=+30V, +25°C	56.2	68		56.2	68		µA
	V_S=+30V	105.5		133	91.5		116	µA
Change of	4V≤V_S≤30V, +25°C	0.2	1.0		0.2	1.0		µA
Quiescent Current (Note 3)	4V≤V_S≤30V	0.5		2.0	0.5		2.0	µA
Temperature Coefficient of Quiescent Current		+0.39		+0.5	+0.39		+0.5	µA/°C
Minimum Temperature for Rated Accuracy	In circuit of *Figure 1*, I_L=0	+1.5		+2.0	+1.5		+2.0	°C
Long Term Stability	T_J=T_{MAX}, for 1000 hours	±0.08			±0.08			°C

Electrical Characteristics

(Notes 1, 6)

Parameter	Conditions	LM35			LM35C, LM35D			Units (Max.)
		Typical	Tested Limit (Note 4)	Design Limit (Note 5)	Typical	Tested Limit (Note 4)	Design Limit (Note 5)	
Accuracy, LM35, LM35C (Note 7)	$T_A=+25°C$	±0.4	±1.0		±0.4	±1.0		°C
	$T_A=-10°C$	±0.5			±0.5		±1.5	°C
	$T_A=T_{MAX}$	±0.8	±1.5		±0.8		±1.5	°C
	$T_A=T_{MIN}$	±0.8		±1.5	±0.8		±2.0	°C
Accuracy, LM35D (Note 7)	$T_A=+25°C$				±0.6	±1.5		°C
	$T_A=T_{MAX}$				±0.9		±2.0	°C
	$T_A=T_{MIN}$				±0.9		±2.0	°C
Nonlinearity (Note 8)	$T_{MIN}≤T_A≤T_{MAX}$	±0.3		±0.5	±0.2		±0.5	°C
Sensor Gain (Average Slope)	$T_{MIN}≤T_A≤T_{MAX}$	+10.0	+9.8, +10.2		+10.0		+9.8, +10.2	mV/°C
Load Regulation (Note 3) 0≤I_L≤1 mA	$T_A=+25°C$	±0.4	±2.0		±0.4	±2.0		mV/mA
	$T_{MIN}≤T_A≤T_{MAX}$	±0.5		±5.0	±0.5		±5.0	mV/mA
Line Regulation (Note 3)	$T_A=+25°C$	±0.01	±0.1		±0.01	±0.1		mV/V
	4V≤V_S≤30V	±0.02		±0.2	±0.02		±0.2	mV/V
Quiescent Current (Note 9)	$V_S=+5V, +25°C$	56	80		56	80		µA
	$V_S=+5V$	105		158	91		138	µA
	$V_S=+30V, +25°C$	56.2	82		56.2	82		µA
	$V_S=+30V$	105.5		161	91.5		141	µA
Change of Quiescent Current (Note 3)	4V≤V_S≤30V, +25°C	0.2	2.0		0.2	2.0		µA
	4V≤V_S≤30V	0.5		3.0	0.5		3.0	µA
Temperature Coefficient of Quiescent Current		+0.39		+0.7	+0.39		+0.7	µA/°C
Minimum Temperature for Rated Accuracy	In circuit of Figure 1, $I_L=0$	+1.5		+2.0	+1.5		+2.0	°C
Long Term Stability	$T_J=T_{MAX}$, for 1000 hours	±0.08			±0.08			°C

Note 1: Unless otherwise noted, these specifications apply: $-55°C≤T_J≤+150°C$ for the LM35 and LM35A; $-40°≤T_J≤+110°C$ for the LM35C and LM35CA; and $0°≤T_J≤+100°C$ for the LM35D. $V_S=+5Vdc$ and $I_{LOAD}=50$ µA, in the circuit of Figure 2. These specifications also apply from $+2°C$ to T_{MAX} in the circuit of Figure 1. Specifications in **boldface** apply over the full rated temperature range.

Note 2: Thermal resistance of the TO-46 package is 400°C/W, junction to ambient, and 24°C/W junction to case. Thermal resistance of the TO-92 package is 180°C/W junction to ambient. Thermal resistance of the small outline molded package is 220°C/W junction to ambient. Thermal resistance of the TO-220 package is 90°C/W junction to ambient. For additional thermal resistance information see table in the Applications section.

Note 3: Regulation is measured at constant junction temperature, using pulse testing with a low duty cycle. Changes in output due to heating effects can be computed by multiplying the internal dissipation by the thermal resistance.

Note 4: Tested Limits are guaranteed and 100% tested in production.

Note 5: Design Limits are guaranteed (but not 100% production tested) over the indicated temperature and supply voltage ranges. These limits are not used to calculate outgoing quality levels.

Note 6: Specifications in **boldface** apply over the full rated temperature range.

Note 7: Accuracy is defined as the error between the output voltage and 10mv/°C times the device's case temperature, at specified conditions of voltage, current, and temperature (expressed in °C).

Note 8: Nonlinearity is defined as the deviation of the output-voltage-versus-temperature curve from the best-fit straight line, over the device's rated temperature range.

Note 9: Quiescent current is defined in the circuit of Figure 1.

Note 10: Absolute Maximum Ratings indicate limits beyond which damage to the device may occur. DC and AC electrical specifications do not apply when operating the device beyond its rated operating conditions. See Note 1.

Note 11: Human body model, 100 pF discharged through a 1.5 kΩ resistor.

Note 12: See AN-450 "Surface Mounting Methods and Their Effect on Product Reliability" or the section titled "Surface Mount" found in a current National Semiconductor Linear Data Book for other methods of soldering surface mount devices.

729

Typical Performance Characteristics

Thermal Resistance
Junction to Air

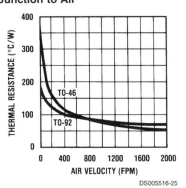

DS005516-25

Thermal Time Constant

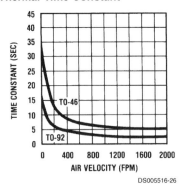

DS005516-26

Thermal Response
in Still Air

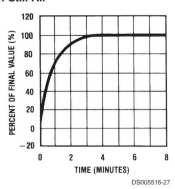

DS005516-27

Thermal Response in
Stirred Oil Bath

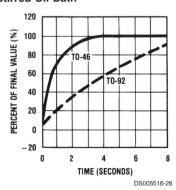

DS005516-28

Minimum Supply
Voltage vs. Temperature

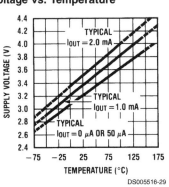

DS005516-29

Quiescent Current
vs. Temperature
(In Circuit of *Figure 1*.)

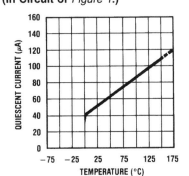

DS005516-30

Quiescent Current
vs. Temperature
(In Circuit of *Figure 2*.)

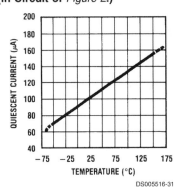

DS005516-31

Accuracy vs. Temperature
(Guaranteed)

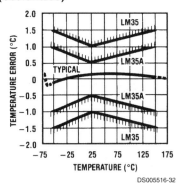

DS005516-32

Accuracy vs. Temperature
(Guaranteed)

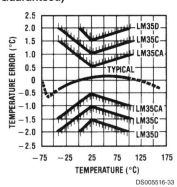

DS005516-33

730

Typical Performance Characteristics (Continued)

Noise Voltage

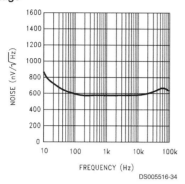

DS005516-34

Start-Up Response

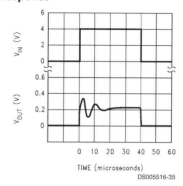

DS005516-35

Applications

The LM35 can be applied easily in the same way as other integrated-circuit temperature sensors. It can be glued or cemented to a surface and its temperature will be within about 0.01°C of the surface temperature.

This presumes that the ambient air temperature is almost the same as the surface temperature; if the air temperature were much higher or lower than the surface temperature, the actual temperature of the LM35 die would be at an intermediate temperature between the surface temperature and the air temperature. This is expecially true for the TO-92 plastic package, where the copper leads are the principal thermal path to carry heat into the device, so its temperature might be closer to the air temperature than to the surface temperature.

To minimize this problem, be sure that the wiring to the LM35, as it leaves the device, is held at the same temperature as the surface of interest. The easiest way to do this is to cover up these wires with a bead of epoxy which will insure that the leads and wires are all at the same temperature as the surface, and that the LM35 die's temperature will not be affected by the air temperature.

The TO-46 metal package can also be soldered to a metal surface or pipe without damage. Of course, in that case the V− terminal of the circuit will be grounded to that metal. Alternatively, the LM35 can be mounted inside a sealed-end metal tube, and can then be dipped into a bath or screwed into a threaded hole in a tank. As with any IC, the LM35 and accompanying wiring and circuits must be kept insulated and dry, to avoid leakage and corrosion. This is especially true if the circuit may operate at cold temperatures where condensation can occur. Printed-circuit coatings and varnishes such as Humiseal and epoxy paints or dips are often used to insure that moisture cannot corrode the LM35 or its connections.

These devices are sometimes soldered to a small light-weight heat fin, to decrease the thermal time constant and speed up the response in slowly-moving air. On the other hand, a small thermal mass may be added to the sensor, to give the steadiest reading despite small deviations in the air temperature.

Temperature Rise of LM35 Due To Self-heating (Thermal Resistance, θ_{JA})

	TO-46, no heat sink	TO-46*, small heat fin	TO-92, no heat sink	TO-92**, small heat fin	SO-8 no heat sink	SO-8** small heat fin	TO-220 no heat sink
Still air	400°C/W	100°C/W	180°C/W	140°C/W	220°C/W	110°C/W	90°C/W
Moving air	100°C/W	40°C/W	90°C/W	70°C/W	105°C/W	90°C/W	26°C/W
Still oil	100°C/W	40°C/W	90°C/W	70°C/W			
Stirred oil	50°C/W	30°C/W	45°C/W	40°C/W			
(Clamped to metal, Infinite heat sink)	(24°C/W)				(55°C/W)		

*Wakefield type 201, or 1" disc of 0.020" sheet brass, soldered to case, or similar.
**TO-92 and SO-8 packages glued and leads soldered to 1" square of 1/16" printed circuit board with 2 oz. foil or similar.

Typical Applications

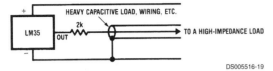

FIGURE 3. LM35 with Decoupling from Capacitive Load

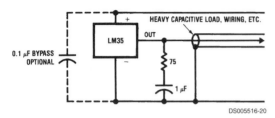

FIGURE 4. LM35 with R-C Damper

CAPACITIVE LOADS

Like most micropower circuits, the LM35 has a limited ability to drive heavy capacitive loads. The LM35 by itself is able to drive 50 pf without special precautions. If heavier loads are anticipated, it is easy to isolate or decouple the load with a resistor; see *Figure 3*. Or you can improve the tolerance of capacitance with a series R-C damper from output to ground; see *Figure 4*.

When the LM35 is applied with a 200Ω load resistor as shown in *Figure 5*, *Figure 6* or *Figure 8* it is relatively immune to wiring capacitance because the capacitance forms a by-pass from ground to input, not on the output. However, as with any linear circuit connected to wires in a hostile environment, its performance can be affected adversely by intense electromagnetic sources such as relays, radio transmitters, motors with arcing brushes, SCR transients, etc, as its wiring can act as a receiving antenna and its internal junctions can act as rectifiers. For best results in such cases, a bypass capacitor from V_{IN} to ground and a series R-C damper such as 75Ω in series with 0.2 or 1 μF from output to ground are often useful. These are shown in *Figure 13*, *Figure 14*, and *Figure 16*.

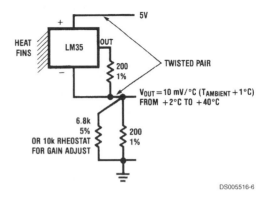

FIGURE 6. Two-Wire Remote Temperature Sensor
(Output Referred to Ground)

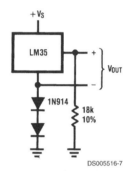

FIGURE 7. Temperature Sensor, Single Supply, –55° to +150°C

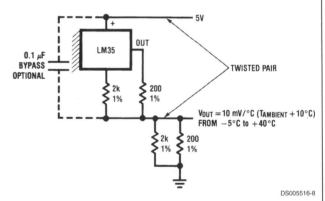

FIGURE 8. Two-Wire Remote Temperature Sensor
(Output Referred to Ground)

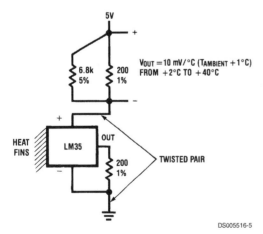

FIGURE 5. Two-Wire Remote Temperature Sensor
(Grounded Sensor)

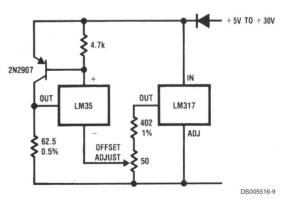

FIGURE 9. 4-To-20 mA Current Source (0°C to +100°C)

732

Typical Applications (Continued)

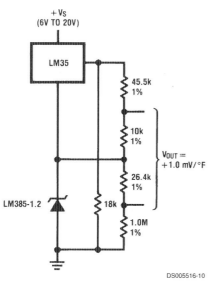

DS005516-10

FIGURE 10. Fahrenheit Thermometer

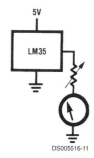

DS005516-11

FIGURE 11. Centigrade Thermometer (Analog Meter)

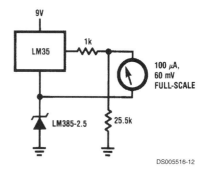

DS005516-12

**FIGURE 12. Fahrenheit ThermometerExpanded Scale Thermometer
(50° to 80° Fahrenheit, for Example Shown)**

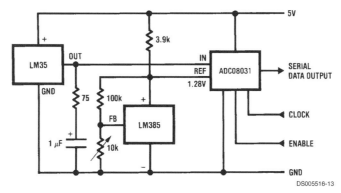

DS005516-13

FIGURE 13. Temperature To Digital Converter (Serial Output) (+128°C Full Scale)

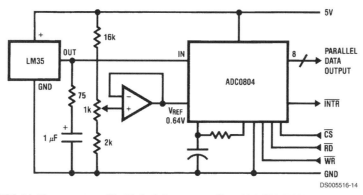

DS005516-14

**FIGURE 14. Temperature To Digital Converter (Parallel TRI-STATE™ Outputs for
Standard Data Bus to µP Interface) (128°C Full Scale)**

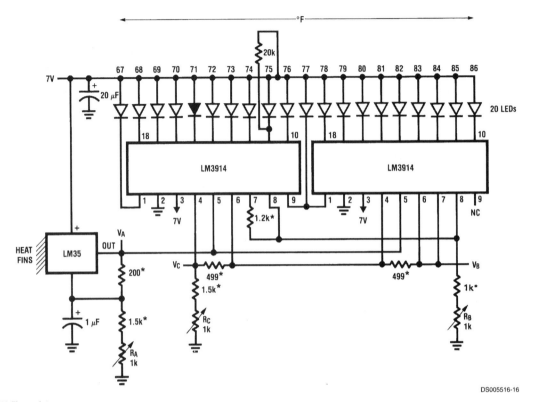

*=1% or 2% film resistor
Trim R_B for V_B=3.075V
Trim R_C for V_C=1.955V
Trim R_A for V_A=0.075V + 100mV/°C x $T_{ambient}$
Example, V_A=2.275V at 22°C

DS005516-16

FIGURE 15. Bar-Graph Temperature Display (Dot Mode)

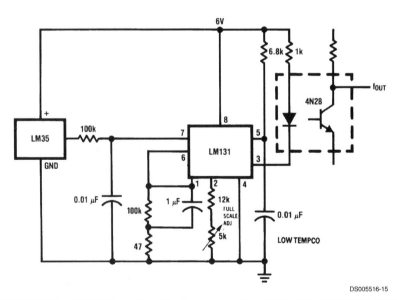

DS005516-15

FIGURE 16. LM35 With Voltage-To-Frequency Converter And Isolated Output
(2°C to +150°C; 20 Hz to 1500 Hz)

734

Block Diagram

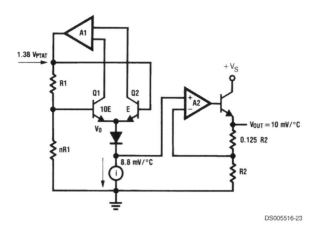

DS005516-23

Physical Dimensions inches (millimeters) unless otherwise noted

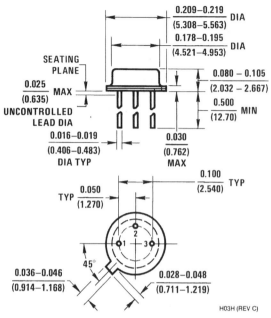

TO-46 Metal Can Package (H)
Order Number LM35H, LM35AH, LM35CH,
LM35CAH, or LM35DH
NS Package Number H03H

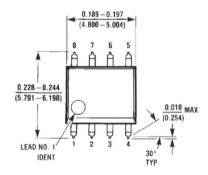

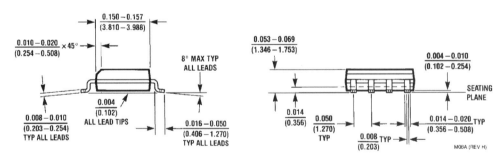

SO-8 Molded Small Outline Package (M)
Order Number LM35DM
NS Package Number M08A

736

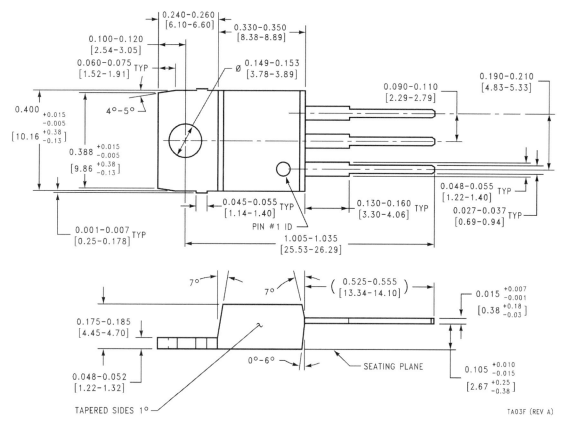

0.240−0.260
[6.10−6.60]

0.100−0.120
[2.54−3.05]

0.060−0.075
[1.52−1.91] TYP

0.330−0.350
[8.38−8.89]

Ø 0.149−0.153
[3.78−3.89]

0.090−0.110
[2.29−2.79]

0.190−0.210
[4.83−5.33]

0.400 $^{+0.015}_{-0.005}$
[10.16 $^{+0.38}_{-0.13}$]

4°−5°

0.388 $^{+0.015}_{-0.005}$
[9.86 $^{+0.38}_{-0.13}$]

0.048−0.055 TYP
[1.22−1.40]

0.045−0.055 TYP
[1.14−1.40]

0.130−0.160 TYP
[3.30−4.06]

0.027−0.037 TYP
[0.69−0.94]

0.001−0.007 TYP
[0.25−0.178]

PIN # 1 ID

1.005−1.035
[25.53−26.29]

7°

7°

(0.525−0.555
[13.34−14.10])

0.015 $^{+0.007}_{-0.001}$
[0.38 $^{+0.18}_{-0.03}$]

0.175−0.185
[4.45−4.70]

0.048−0.052
[1.22−1.32]

0°−6°

SEATING PLANE

0.105 $^{+0.010}_{-0.015}$
[2.67 $^{+0.25}_{-0.38}$]

TAPERED SIDES 1°

TA03F (REV A)

Power Package TO-220 (T)
Order Number LM35DT
NS Package Number TA03F

Physical Dimensions inches (millimeters) unless otherwise noted (Continued)

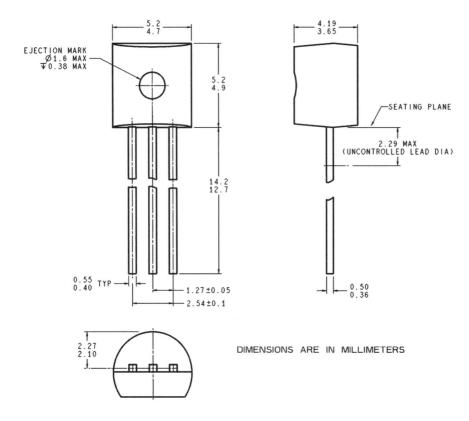

EJECTION MARK
⌀1.6 MAX
⩗0.38 MAX

5.2 / 4.7

5.2 / 4.9

4.19 / 3.65

SEATING PLANE

2.29 MAX
(UNCONTROLLED LEAD DIA)

14.2 / 12.7

0.55 / 0.40 TYP

1.27±0.05

2.54±0.1

0.50 / 0.36

2.27 / 2.10

DIMENSIONS ARE IN MILLIMETERS

Z03A (Rev G)

TO-92 Plastic Package (Z)
Order Number LM35CZ, LM35CAZ or LM35DZ
NS Package Number Z03A

LIFE SUPPORT POLICY

NATIONAL'S PRODUCTS ARE NOT AUTHORIZED FOR USE AS CRITICAL COMPONENTS IN LIFE SUPPORT DEVICES OR SYSTEMS WITHOUT THE EXPRESS WRITTEN APPROVAL OF THE PRESIDENT AND GENERAL COUNSEL OF NATIONAL SEMICONDUCTOR CORPORATION. As used herein:

1. Life support devices or systems are devices or systems which, (a) are intended for surgical implant into the body, or (b) support or sustain life, and whose failure to perform when properly used in accordance with instructions for use provided in the labeling, can be reasonably expected to result in a significant injury to the user.

2. A critical component is any component of a life support device or system whose failure to perform can be reasonably expected to cause the failure of the life support device or system, or to affect its safety or effectiveness.

 National Semiconductor Corporation
Americas
Tel: 1-800-272-9959
Fax: 1-800-737-7018
Email: support@nsc.com
www.national.com

National Semiconductor Europe
Fax: +49 (0) 180-530 85 86
Email: europe.support@nsc.com
Deutsch Tel: +49 (0) 69 9508 6208
English Tel: +44 (0) 870 24 0 2171
Français Tel: +33 (0) 1 41 91 8790

National Semiconductor Asia Pacific Customer Response Group
Tel: 65-2544466
Fax: 65-2504466
Email: ap.support@nsc.com

National Semiconductor Japan Ltd.
Tel: 81-3-5639-7560
Fax: 81-3-5639-7507

National does not assume any responsibility for use of any circuitry described, no circuit patent licenses are implied and National reserves the right at any time without notice to change said circuitry and specifications.

738

IMPORTANT NOTICE

Products		Applications	
Audio	www.ti.com/audio	Communications and Telecom	www.ti.com/communications
Amplifiers	amplifier.ti.com	Computers and Peripherals	www.ti.com/computers
Data Converters	dataconverter.ti.com	Consumer Electronics	www.ti.com/consumer-apps
DLP® Products	www.dlp.com	Energy and Lighting	www.ti.com/energy
DSP	dsp.ti.com	Industrial	www.ti.com/industrial
Clocks and Timers	www.ti.com/clocks	Medical	www.ti.com/medical
Interface	interface.ti.com	Security	www.ti.com/security
Logic	logic.ti.com	Space, Avionics and Defense	www.ti.com/space-avionics-defense
Power Mgmt	power.ti.com	Transportation and Automotive	www.ti.com/automotive
Microcontrollers	microcontroller.ti.com	Video and Imaging	www.ti.com/video
RFID	www.ti-rfid.com		
OMAP Mobile Processors	www.ti.com/omap		
Wireless Connectivity	www.ti.com/wirelessconnectivity		

TI E2E Community Home Page   e2e.ti.com